TRANSPORTATION

A GLOBAL SUPPLY CHAIN PERSPECTIVE

EIGHTH EDITION

TRANSPORTATION

A GLOBAL SUPPLY CHAIN PERSPECTIVE

John J. Coyle
The Pennsylvania State University

Robert A. Novack
The Pennsylvania State University

Brian J. Gibson
Auburn University

CENGAGE Learning®

Australia • Brazil • Mexico • Singapore • United Kingdom • United States

CENGAGE
Learning®

Transportation: A Global Supply Chain Perspective, Eighth Edition

John J. Coyle, Robert A. Novack, and Brian J. Gibson

Vice President, General Manager: Balraj Kalsi

Product Director: Joe Sabatino

Product Manager: Jason Guyler

Content Developer: Christopher Santos

Manufacturing Planner: Ron J. Montgomery

Marketing Communications Manager: Heather Mooney

Art and Cover Direction, Production Management, and Composition: Lumina Datamatics, Inc.

Cover Image: © viktor vector; © Digital Genetics/Shutterstock; © Maximus256/Shutterstock; © Toria/Shutterstock; © Evgeny Karandaev/Shutterstock

Intellectual Property

Analyst: Christina Ciaramella

Project Manager: Betsy Hathaway

Library of Congress Control Number: 2015932319

ISBN: 978-1-133-59296-9

Cengage Learning
20 Channel Center Street
Boston, MA 02210
USA

Cengage Learning is a leading provider of customized learning solutions with employees residing in nearly 40 different countries and sales in more than 125 countries around the world. Find your local representative at **www.cengage.com**

Cengage Learning products are represented in Canada by Nelson Education, Ltd.

To learn more about Cengage Learning Solutions, visit **www.cengage.com**

Purchase any of our products at your local college store or at our preferred online store **www.cengagebrain.com**

Printed in the United States of America
Print Number: 01 Print Year: 2015

A very special note of thanks and appreciation is due to our families. John Coyle would like to thank his wife Barbara, their children John and Susan, and their grandchildren Lauren, Matthew, Elizabeth Kate, Emily, Ben, Cathryn, and Zachary. Bob Novack would like to thank his wife Judith and their children Tom, Elizabeth, and Alex. Brian Gibson would like to recognize his wife Marcia, son Andy, and his longtime mentor, Dr. Bob Cook (1947–2014). Special mention should be made in reference to Dr. Edward J. Bardi to express our deep appreciation of his many contributions not only to the continuing development of this text but also to the supply chain management text.

Brief Contents

Contents

Part II

Part III

Preface

AST&L AMERICAN SOCIETY OF TRANSPORTATION AND LOGISTICS, INC.®

This textbook is required by the American Society of Transportation and Logistics® for the Transportation Economics Management module in the Certified in Transportation and Logistics (CTL) professional certification program. For details go to www.astl.org.

In this book *Transportation: A Global Supply Chain Perspective* while attention was paid to the global aspect of transportation in previous editions, especially the seventh edition, the authors realized that the global dimension required even more emphasis to reflect the increased challenges and requirements of 21st century supply chains. Transportation has become even more important for efficient and effective supply chains in today's complex and competitive global environment. It has become the critical link in successful supply chains and may be the most important industry for the economic advancement in the economies of the world. The authors are convinced much more attention and focus must be given to transportation infrastructure investment to meet the needs of the global economy.

The text follows the format of the previous edition with three sections and 14 chapters, but substantive additions and changes have been made to enhance the global discussions, improve the content and organization, and streamline and update relevant parts of text. Part I provides the foundation for the overall text. Chapter 1 explores global thrust of this edition examining key critical areas such as population trends and related issues for developing and developed economies. Chapter 2 provides the economic foundation and rationale for the role of transportation as well as its political and social importance. Chapter 3 explores the regulatory and public policy issues associated with transportation while Chapter 4 offers a discussion of transportation costing and pricing in a market-based economy.

Part II provides an overview of the major transportation alternatives available to individual and organizational users. Chapters 5 through 8 discuss and examine the key features and issues of the five basic modes of transportation, namely, motor (5), rail (6), airline (7), water, and pipeline (8). Each of the basic modes provide some inherent advantages for shippers of particular commodities or locations that need to be appreciated and understood to gain the economic benefits they offer. The competitive environment of market that exists in some economies provides a dynamic that promotes continual change and improvement in the services that can be offered by the basic modes.

The chapters in Part III were significantly changed in the previous edition, which enhanced the overall text. The six chapters in this section have been updated and revised to further improve their value to the readers. Chapter 9 discusses the topic of risk management that has become a critical focus for many organizations because of the increasing threats to the interruption of supply chain flows in the global economy. Strategies, methods, and outcomes for risk management are explored as well as overall security. Chapters 10 and 11 provide an important and in-depth discussion of the planning and execution for efficient and effective global transportation flows with emphasis on flexibility, documentation, intermodal options, and service providers. Chapters 12 and 13 add to the information provided in Part II with a detailed discussion of third-party service providers and private transportation respectively. Both are options that can improve efficiency, effectiveness, and execution for global supply chains, especially transportation and logistics services. Finally, Chapter 14 explores some of the major challenges and issues for transportation in the 21st century, namely, infrastructure, environmental sustainability, and technology. While all of these topics were discussed to some extent in previous chapters, the authors felt that they deserved more attention as we move ahead in our complex and competitive global environment.

Overall, we are convinced that transportation is a critical ingredient on many levels but is often taken for granted unless some crisis arises. As stated previously, it may be the most important industry for all economies regardless of their stage of development. Such recognition needs to be accorded to transportation in the future.

Features

1. Learning objectives in the beginning of each chapter provide students with an overall perspective of chapter material and also serve to establish a baseline for a working knowledge of the topics that follow.
2. Transportation Profile boxes are the opening vignettes at the beginning of each chapter that introduce students to the chapter's topics through familiar, real-world examples.
3. On the Line features are applied, concrete examples that provide students with hands-on managerial experience of the chapter topics.
4. Transportation Technology boxes help students relate technological developments to transportation management concepts.
5. Global Perspectives boxes highlight the activities and importance of transportation outside of the United States.
6. End-of-chapter Summaries and Study Questions reinforce material presented in each chapter.
7. Short cases at the end of each chapter build on what students have learned. Questions that follow the cases sharpen critical thinking skills.

Ancillaries

1. The *Instructor's Manual* includes chapter outlines, answers to end-of-chapter study questions, commentary on end-of-chapter short cases, and teaching tips.
2. A convenient *Test Bank* offers a variety of multiple-choice, short-answer, and essay questions for each chapter.
3. *PowerPoint slides* cover the main chapter topics and contain figures from the main text.
4. The book companion site (www.cengage.com/decisionsciences/coyle) provides additional resources for students and instructors. Appendix A, Selected Transportation Publications, and Appendix B, Transportation-Related Associations, can be found on the companion site. The Instructor's Manual and PowerPoint files are downloadable from the site for instructors.

Acknowledgements

The authors are indebted to many individuals at our respective academic institutions as well as other individuals with whom we have had contact in a variety of venues. Our university students and our executive program students have provided an important sounding board for the many concepts, techniques, metrics, and strategies presented in the book. Our faculty and corporate colleagues have provided invaluable insights and appropriate criticism of our ideas. Some individuals deserve special consideration: Nicholas F. Hood (Penn State), Ms. Tracie Shannon (Penn State), and Kusumal Ruamsook (Penn State). The authors would also like to thank the following fellow faculty members for their insightful contributions to several chapters in this text: John C. Spychalski, Professor Emeritus of Supply Chain Management (Penn State), and Joe Hanna, Associate Dean and Professor of Supply Chain Management (Auburn).

About the Authors

John J. Coyle is Director of Corporate Relations for the Center for Supply Chain Research (CSCR) and Professor Emeritus of Logistics and Supply Chain Management in the Smeal College of Business at Penn State University. He holds a B.S. and an M.S. from Penn State and earned his doctorate from Indiana University in Bloomington, Indiana, where he was a U.S. Steel Fellow. He joined the Penn State faculty in 1961 and attained the rank of Full Professor in 1967. In addition to his teaching responsibilities, he served in a number of administrative positions, including Chairman of the Department of Business Logistics, Faculty Director and Assistant Dean for Undergraduate Programs, Senior Associate Dean, and Executive Director of the CSCR. He also played a major role in the development of Smeal's Executive Education Programs. At the university level, he served as Chairman of the Faculty Senate, Special Assistant for Strategic Planning to two university presidents (Jordan and Thomas). He also served as Penn State's Faculty Representative to the NCAA for 30 years and to the Big Ten for ten years.

Dr. Coyle was the Editor of the Journal of Business Logistics from 1990 to 1996. He has authored or coauthored 23 books or monographs and 38 articles in reputable professional journals. He has received 14 awards at Penn State for teaching excellence and/or advising. Former students and friends have endowed a scholarship fund and two Smeal Professorships in his honor. He received the Council of Logistics Management's Distinguished Service Award in 1991; Penn State's Continuing/Distance Education Award for Academic Excellence in 1994; the Eccles Medal for his contributions to the U.S. Department of Defense and the Lion's Paw Medal from Penn State for Distinguished Service, both in 2004. Dr. Coyle currently serves on the board of three logistics and supply chain companies.

Robert A. Novack is currently an Associate Professor of Supply Chain Management and Associate Director in the Center for Supply Chain Research at Penn State. Dr. Novack worked in operations management and planning for the Yellow Freight Corporation and in planning and operations for the Drackett Company. He received his bachelor's and MBA degrees from Penn State and a Ph.D. from the University of Tennessee in Knoxville. Dr. Novack has numerous articles published in the *Journal of Business Logistics,* the *Transportation Journal,* and the *International Journal of Physical Distribution and Logistics Management.* He is also the coauthor of three textbooks: *Creating Logistics Value: Themes for the Future, Supply Chain Management: A Logistics Perspective* (8e), and *Transportation.* He is on the editorial review board for the *Journal of Business Logistics* and is an area editor for the *Journal of supply Chain Management.* Dr. Novack is very active in the Council for Supply Chain Management Professionals, having served as overall program chair for the annual conference, as a track chair, and as a session speaker. In addition, he has served on numerous committees with this organization. Dr. Novack holds the CTL designation from the American Society of Transportation and Logistics. His current research interest is on the development and use of metrics in managing supply chains. In 2009, he received the Atherton Teaching Award from Penn State, the highest award given for teaching at that university.

Brian J. Gibson is a professor of Supply Chain Management and Executive Director of the Supply Chain Resource Center at Auburn University. Previously, he served on the faculty of Georgia Southern University and as director of the Southern Center for Logistics and Intermodal Transportation. Dr. Gibson also has ten years of experience as a logistics manager for two major retailers. He is an accomplished faculty member who has received multiple awards for outstanding teaching, research, and outreach, most notably the Teaching Innovations Award from the Council of Supply Chain Management Professionals in 2009. Dr. Gibson has coauthored more than 50 refereed and invited articles in the *Journal of Business Logistics*, *Supply Chain Management Review*, *International Journal of Logistics Management*, *International Journal of Physical Distribution and Logistics Management*, and other leading publications. He is actively engaged in executive education, seminar development, and consulting with leading organizations. Dr. Gibson currently serves in leadership roles for the Council for Supply Chain Management Professionals, the National Shippers Strategic Transportation Council, and the Retail Industry Leaders Association. Dr. Gibson earned a B.S.B.A. from Central Michigan University, an MBA from Wayne State University, and a Ph.D. in logistics and transportation from the University of Tennessee.

PART I

The major driving forces of change for supply chains during the first two decades of the 21st century have been globalization and technology. That is not to say that there are not additional exogenous factors impacting supply chains and necessitating changes in managerial tactics and/or strategies because there have been. However, none have been of the magnitude of globalization and technology. Interestingly, they were major forces in the last two decades of the 20th century as was cited in previous editions of this text. The fact that they continue to have such an impact is certainly worth noting, but one must also appreciate the depth and scope of these two external forces not only on supply chains but also upon consumer and organizational behavior.

Transportation is an important part of supply chain management that has been described figuratively previously as the "glue" that holds the supply chain together and is a key enabler for important customer oriented strategies such as overnight or same-day delivery. Transportation is often the final phase or process to touch the customer and may have a lasting impact on the success of the transaction. This is the micro dimension, but on a macro level transportation can be viewed as the "life blood" of global supply chains, and it has been argued that efficient and effective transportation is the most important business for a country or region and the cornerstone of a modern economy.

Global transportation systems have been seriously challenged in the 21st century by escalating fuel costs along with volatility in fuel prices. In addition, the transportation infrastructure, namely seaports, airports, highways, and so on, is not sufficient to accommodate the flow of global commerce in many countries thus stymying the economic progress of the region. Many parts of the infrastructure require government or public funding because of the different users. The public coffers are frequently financially strained because of the many alternative demands for these somewhat limited resources. Transportation infrastructure has to "compete" for an allocation of public funds, and the benefits, while real, are more long run in terms of outcome and value. Consequently, such needed resources may not be allocated in a timely manner. This is the dilemma of the 21st century. Transportation and the related logistics systems are a necessary requirement for all economies, developed and underdeveloped, but the public investment in social capital necessary to not only improve but also to sustain the infrastructure has not been forthcoming in many countries. Hopefully, one of the outcomes of this text will be a better understanding and appreciation for the criticality of efficient and effective transportation systems for economic development and social welfare.

Part I will provide an overview and foundation for the role and importance of improved transportation from a micro and macro perspective in global supply chains. The discussion will cover economic and managerial dimensions of transportation in the global economy, including regulation and public policy issues. Part I is designed to provide the framework for the analysis and discussion in the following sections of the book.

Chapter 1 examines the nature, importance and critical issues in the global economy, which are important to understand for the current and future transportation systems, that will provide the needed service for the diverse requirements of the various regions and countries. This chapter will also discuss the special nature of transportation demand and how transportation adds value to products. There is also an overview of the concept of supply chain management and the important role of transportation in supply chains of various organizations.

Chapter 2 examines the role of transportation from a macro and micro perspective. The chapter adds to the discussion in Chapter 1 but explores more broadly the special significance of improved transportation systems. The analysis includes not only the economic impact but also the political and social impact of transportation. Current and historical perspectives are provided in the discussion to help the reader appreciate and better understand the contribution of improved transportation in an economy. The discussion also examines the impact of improved transportation upon land values and prices of products and services.

Chapter 3 provides an overview and examines the development and role government regulation and public policy directed at transportation services, particularly in the United States. Local, state, and federal regulation of private transportation companies has been in existence since the 19th century in the United States countries. These controls are on one level a recognition of the importance of transportation to the development and ongoing vitality of an economy. In many countries of the world, important parts of the transportation system are provided by the government. This is especially true of railroad and air carrier service. There have been major changes in the regulatory structure in the United States and elsewhere, but regulations, particularly in the area of safety, continue to play a role that needs to be understood.

Chapter 4 extends the discussion of costing and pricing introduced in Chapters 1 and 2. Given the importance of transportation on a micro and macro level to the cost and value of products and services, costing and pricing deserves a more detailed examination. There are unique dimensions to transportation services in general and between the basic modes that need to be understood by managers and public officials. Chapter 4 provides an analysis of the differences and unique dimensions of transportation services.

CHAPTER

1

GLOBAL SUPPLY CHAINS: THE ROLE AND IMPORTANCE OF TRANSPORTATION

Learning Objectives

After reading this chapter, you should be able to do the following:

- Appreciate why efficient transportation systems are so critical to advance the growth and development of regions and countries, and how they contribute to social and political systems as well as national defense
- Discuss the importance of transportation to globalization and how it contributes to the effective flow of commerce among close and distant regions
- Understand how global supply chains can contribute to the competitive position of countries and allow them to penetrate global markets
- Appreciate the dynamic nature of the global economy, which can impact and change the competitive position of a region or country in a relatively short period of time
- Explain the underlying economic basis for international exchange of goods and services for the overall benefit of two or more countries or regions and gain some perspective on the volume and overall importance of the more advanced countries of the world
- Discuss the size and age distribution of the population and the growth rate of the major countries of the world and understand how the size of the population can impact a country positively or negatively
- Understand the challenges and opportunities associated with the worldwide growth in urbanization and why there has been such a major shift from rural to urban areas

- Appreciate the importance and impact of land and resources to the economic advancement and development of the various countries of the world and how they can be exploited to their advantage
- Explain why technology has become such an important ingredient for the economic progress of companies and countries in today's global economy and understand the need for and types of technology
- Discuss the overall characteristics and importance of globalization and supply chains in the highly competitive world economies of the 21st century

TRANSPORTATION **PROFILE**

Critical Role of Transportation in Global Economy

Transportation is one of the most important tools or methods that developing societies or countries use to advance economically, politically, and socially. It impacts every phase and facet of our existence. Transportation is probably the most important industry in any country or in the global economy. Without it, we could not operate a grocery store or run a factory. The more complex or developed a country is, the more indispensable an efficient and effective transportation system is for continued survival and growth.

In advanced societies, transportation systems are so well developed that most citizens do not think about or realize the many benefits that accrue from good transportation systems. They use transportation everyday directly or indirectly. It provides the thoroughfare for commerce, the means of travel locally or for longer distances, and the assistance for many other important aspects of their lives. People seldom stop to think how restricted their lives would be without good transportation. However, if one travels to an underdeveloped country, it is obvious that the lack of good transportation is inhibiting their economic prosperity and personal convenience. The current physical decay of the highway infrastructure in the United States and the lack of investment for improvement is a critical concern to many private and public organizations because of its importance to continued economic growth and global expansion.

The development of the global economy has increased the criticality of transportation for economic, political, and national defense purposes. Globalization has brought many benefits to countries throughout the world, but we are much more interdependent and at risk when some calamity occurs in another part of the world that can interrupt supply of raw materials or finished products and/or shut down a market for domestic products. Efficient and effective transportation can help to mitigate the impact, for example, of a natural disaster such as a hurricane, typhoon, or flood by providing products and services from alternate sources and access to other markets quickly and efficiently.

The importance of transportation cannot be overemphasized. It is a necessary ingredient for the progress and well-being of all citizens. An appreciation and understanding of its historical and economic role and significance, as well its political and social significance, is a requisite for managers in any organization and other interested parties. An appreciation of this tenet will be an important part of the discussion in this text.

Introduction

In previous editions of this text, transportation was referred to as the "glue" that holds the supply chain together and an enabler of the underlying tactics and strategies that have catapulted supply chain management to the level of acceptance, which it now enjoys in many organizations, both private and public. For example, transportation management systems technology along with complimentary software is used by many organizations to improve logistics and supply chain efficiency, effectiveness, and execution. Transportation has moved from playing a reactive or supporting role to a role that is more proactive and enabling. In other words, transportation has become much more strategic for organizations in determining their ability to compete in the growing and complex global marketplace.

The global marketplace is also changing on a continuing basis, that is, it has become very dynamic, and is buffeted by economic, political, social, and natural forces, which can impact a country or region negatively or positively in the short or long run. For example, the rising cost of fuel has impacted the rates charged by transportation service providers, which in turn impacts the distance that it is economically feasible to transport goods. The cost of labor can change over time to the disadvantage of some geographic areas and benefit others. For example, the labor cost advantage that China enjoyed, along with low rates for ocean carrier movement, had a positive impact on their ability to sell products on a global basis. These advantages have diminished somewhat allowing other countries to develop an improved competitive position because of market proximity, labor costs, or other factors. These changes in turn impact global supply chains and their associated flow of goods.

In this chapter, the initial focus will be upon developing an overview of the flow of global commerce and trade overtime on a worldwide basis not only to understand the importance and magnitude of global supply chain flows but also to gain some perspective on important changes that have occurred. A variety of economic data will be used to illustrate the impact of the overall changes that have occurred. The next section will examine the underlying rationale and economics of global flows of goods and services. In other words, the "why" of global flows will be discussed to understand the advantages of international trade to countries and consumers in contrast to the "what" of the first section of this chapter. The third section will provide additional insights into the factors that can contribute to the economic advancement and development of countries. The final section of the chapter will provide an overview of the supply chain concept including its development, key characteristics, and major activities.

Global Supply Chain Flows

Early in the 21st century, frequent reference was made to acronyms such as the BRIC (Brazil, Russia, India, and China) or VISTA (Vietnam, Indonesia, South Africa, Turkey, and Argentina) countries. The former were identified as the top emerging economies and the latter as those developing at a fast pace. The development of the BRIC and VISTA countries was seen an indication of opportunities for "sourcing" of materials, products, and services and the identification of potential markets for the more developed economies such as the United States, the European Union (EU), and Japan. Also, they were a sign of a more economic balance in the world and continued growth. Consequently, one noted author[1] declared that the world was really flat because of the developing economies. Interestingly, there have been some economic shifts already with respect to these countries, and the future importance of some of the VISTA countries is not clear.

For example, South Africa has been added to the first group, BRICS, by some economic pundits. Nevertheless, all of this supports the observation made earlier about the dynamic and competitive nature of world markets. An important caveat is the potential for disruption caused by political instability, associated acts of terrorism, and military actions, which can cause a major disruption in global trade flows.

Figure 1-1 and Exhibit 1-1 indicate export trade flows of merchandise from various country or region origins. In Figure 1-1 the size of the circle indicates the importance and volume of exports on a worldwide basis. It is interesting to note the large number of exporting countries and the big differences in the volume. Exhibit 1-1 and the associated bar chart show the value of world exports in U.S. dollars. China is clearly number one for exports of merchandise and the United States is second, but what may be surprising is Germany being third. They are relatively close to the United States in terms of the value of their exports. If we added up the value of exports for all the EU countries, it would by far exceed the United States (about double). The EU also compares favorably to the Asian block of countries in terms of exports.

Figure 1-2 and Exhibit 1-2 show the import trade flows of merchandise into various countries and regions. Figure 1-2 is interesting because it is a visual representation of the magnitude of the value of imports and provides some perspective of the differences in the world markets. In terms of regions, Exhibit 1-2 indicates that Asia is the largest importing region and is followed by the EU. North America is third in terms of the value of imports. Among individual countries, the United States is the largest importer, followed by China and then Germany.

A comparison of relative shares of imports and exports provides some additional perspectives. China's share of global exports in terms of value is 11.8 percent and their share of imports is 10.3 percent making them a net exporter, whereas the United States by comparison is a net importer with 8.4 percent of merchandise exports and 12.4 percent of the global imports. Germany is also a net exporter with exports representing 7.7 percent of the global total with imports of 6.3 percent of the total. There are economic

FIGURE 1-1 Export-Trade Flows of Merchandise

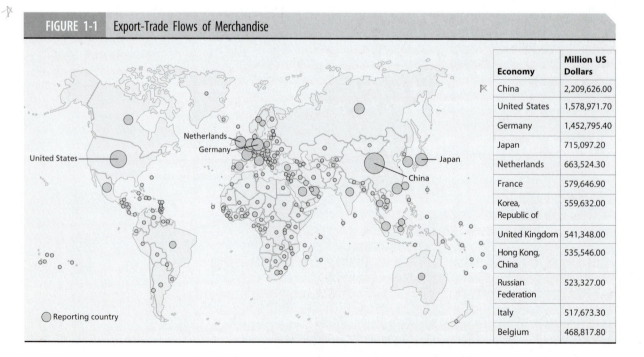

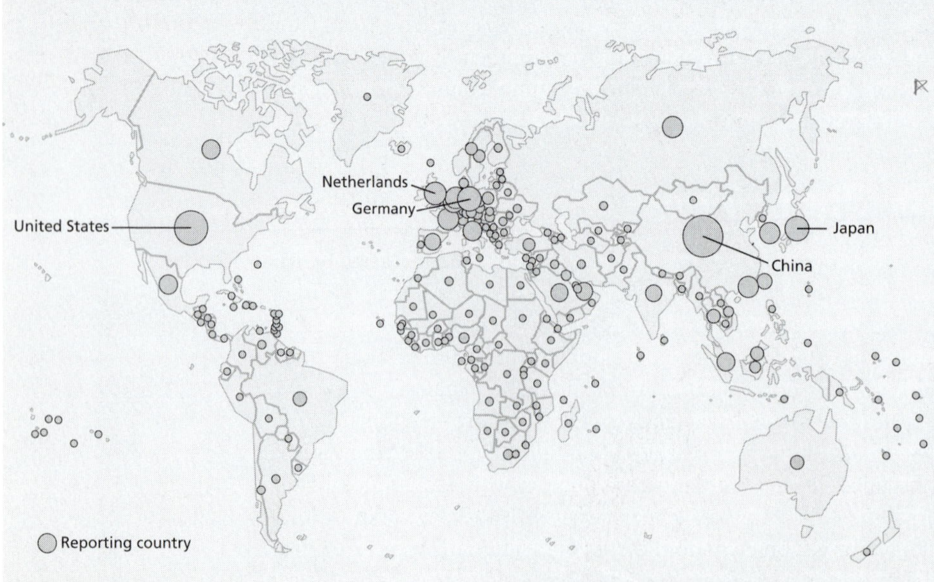

Economy	Million US Dollars
China	2,209,626.00
United States	1,578,971.70
Germany	1,452,795.40
Japan	715,097.20
Netherlands	663,524.30
France	579,646.90
Korea, Republic of	559,632.00
United Kingdom	541,348.00
Hong Kong, China	535,546.00
Russian Federation	523,327.00
Italy	517,673.30
Belgium	468,817.80

FIGURE 1-2 Import-Trade Flows of Merchandise

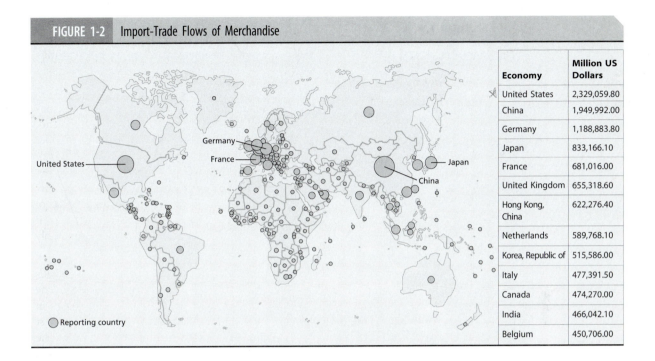

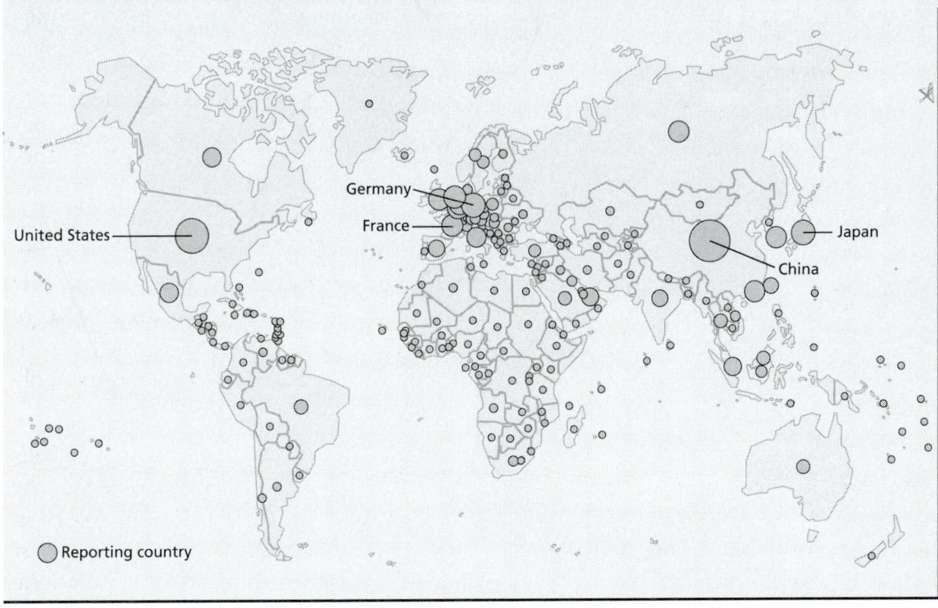

Economy	Million US Dollars
United States	2,329,059.80
China	1,949,992.00
Germany	1,188,883.80
Japan	833,166.10
France	681,016.00
United Kingdom	655,318.60
Hong Kong, China	622,276.40
Netherlands	589,768.10
Korea, Republic of	515,586.00
Italy	477,391.50
Canada	474,270.00
India	466,042.10
Belgium	450,706.00

implications associated with these differences, but the merchandise flows do not provide a complete economic picture because the value of services imported and exported are also important for the balance of payments of individual countries. However, the focus of this text is obviously upon merchandise flows.

The importance of the so-called developed countries/economies is evident from the information presented earlier, but additional insight can be gained by summarizing the impact of the top countries in each category (see Tables 1-1 and 1-2). In 2013, the top 30 exporting countries accounted for 81.7 percent of the world's exports, but the top three (China, United States, and Germany) accounted for about 30 percent of the total exports. The top 30 importing countries accounted for 82.1 percent of the total imports, but the top three (United States, China, and Germany) accounted for 30 percent of the total imports. The data presented in Tables 1-1 and 1-2 substantiate the observation about the important role of developed economies made earlier.

Additional insight can be gained by examining the growth in the volume of global trade over the course of the last 50 years (see Table 1-3). The 30-year growth from 1960 to 1990 was steady, but in recent years, especially the period from 2000 to the present, the growth has been spectacular. The total volume of trade more than doubled, led by China, Japan, the United States, and the EU. A number of factors came into play to explain the increased growth rate including trade agreements among countries along with a reduction in tariffs, which promoted global trade and its associated benefits. There was also greater acceptance of importing finished products that were manufactured in foreign countries.

Traditionally, many countries imported raw materials that were scarce or not available in the importing country, and they then produced finished products mostly for domestic consumption. The raw materials were much lower in value than the finished products that contributed to the imbalance of trade among developing and developed economies. However, that situation has changed, countries that previously imported materials for domestic production and consumption are exporting more finished

TABLE 1-1 Top 30 Exporters, 2013

RANK	EXPORTERS	VALUE	SHARE	ANNUAL % CHANGE
1	China	2210	11.8	8
2	United States	1579	8.4	2
3	Germany	1453	7.7	3
4	Japan	715	3.8	−10
5	Netherlands	664	3.5	1
6	France	580	3.1	2
7	Korea, Republic of	560	3.0	2
8	United Kingdom	541	2.9	15
9	Hong Kong, China	536	2.9	9
	- domestic exports	20	0.1	−11
	- re-exports	516	2.7	10
10	Russian Federation	523	2.8	−1
11	Italy	518	2.8	3
12	Belgium	469	2.5	5
13	Canada	458	2.4	1
14	Singapore	410	2.2	0
	- domestic exports	219	1.2	−4
	- re-exports	191	1.0	6
15	Mexico	380	2.0	3
16	Saudi Arabia, Kingdom of c	376	2.0	−3
17	United Arab Emirates c	365	1.9	4
18	Spain	316	1.7	7
19	India	312	1.7	5
20	Chinese Taipei	305	1.6	1
21	Australia	253	1.3	−1
22	Brazil	242	1.3	0
23	Switzerland	229	1.2	1
24	Thailand	229	1.2	0
25	Malaysia	228	1.2	0
26	Poland	202	1.1	9
27	Indonesia	184	1.0	−3
28	Austria	174	0.9	5
29	Sweden	167	0.9	−3
30	Czech Republic	161	0.9	3
	Total of above d	15339	81.7	–
	World d	18784	100.0	2

Source: World Trade Organization.

TABLE 1-2 Top 30 Importers, 2013

RANK	IMPORTERS	VALUE	SHARE	ANNUAL % CHANGE
1	United States	2331	12.4	0
2	China	1950	10.3	7
3	Germany	1187	6.3	2
4	Japan	833	4.4	−6
5	France	681	3.6	1
6	United Kingdom	654	3.5	−5
7	Hong Kong, China	622	3.3	12
	- retained imports	141	0.7	4
8	Netherlands	590	3.1	0
9	Korea, Republic of	516	2.7	−1
10	Italy	477	2.5	−2
11	Canada a	474	2.5	0
12	India	466	2.5	−5
13	Belgium	450	2.4	3
14	Mexico	391	2.1	3
15	Singapore	373	2.0	−2
	- retained imports b	182	1.0	−9
16	Russian Federation a	344	1.8	3
17	Spain	339	1.8	0
18	Chinese Taipei	270	1.4	0
19	Turkey	252	1.3	6
20	Thailand	251	1.3	0
21	Brazil	250	1.3	7
22	United Arab Emirates c	245	1.3	7
23	Australia	242	1.3	−7
24	Malaysia	206	1.1	5
25	Poland	204	1.1	2
26	Switzerland	200	1.1	1
27	Indonesia	187	1.0	−2
28	Austria	182	1.0	2
29	Saudi Arabia, Kingdom of	164	0.9	5
30	Sweden	158	0.8	−3
	Total of above d	15492	82.1	–
	World d	18874	100.0	1

Source: World Trade Organization.

products while so-called underdeveloped countries are participating more in manufacturing, especially of parts of a finished product. A very good example is the automobile industry. The typical automobile of today has over 10,000 parts, which can be manufactured in many different countries. Furthermore, the individual parts may be exported

TABLE 1-3 Volume of World Merchandise Exports and Gross Domestic Product, 1950–2010 (Annual Percentage Change)

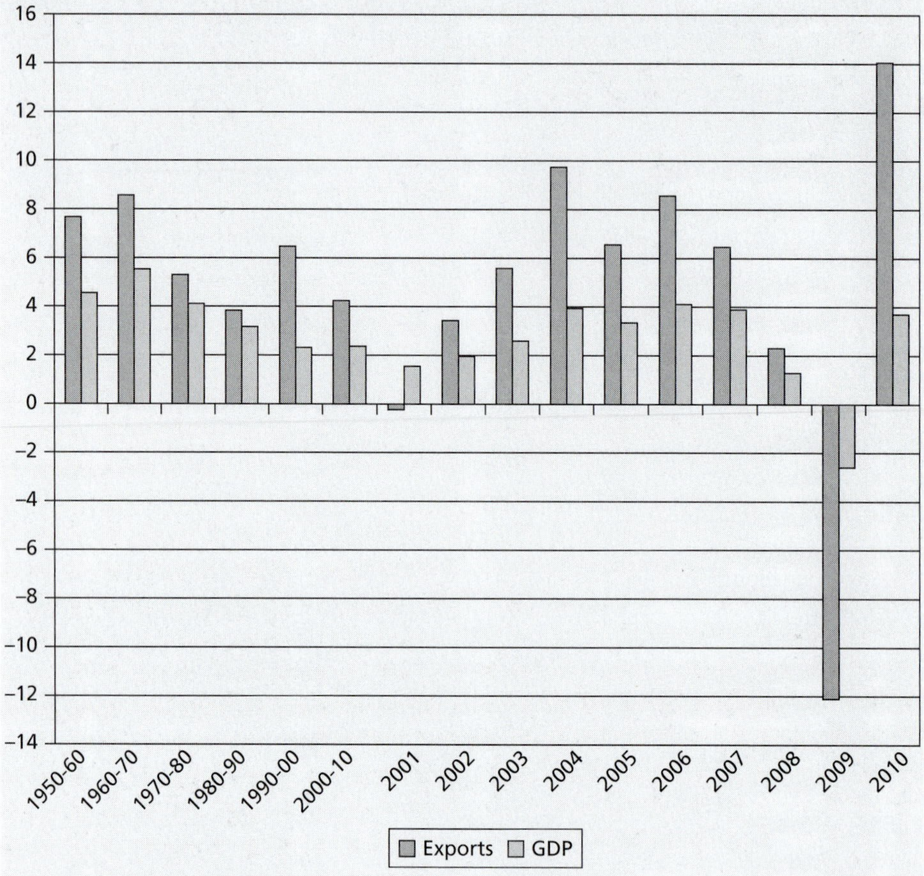

Source: World Trade Organization.

and put together into subassemblies that are frequently shipped to an assembly plant in another location. So a Ford assembled in Detroit may have less U.S.-made parts than a Toyota assembled in Mexico. The efficiency of the global supply chains and especially the transportation systems afford these more complex operations as compared to an earlier era when the auto parts were produced in locations, which were more contiguous to the assembly plants. This is also an excellent example of companies using logistics systems analysis to evaluate the trade-offs among production costs, transportation services, and inventory carrying costs to arrive at the overall best location for efficiency and effectiveness.

As indicated earlier, the global supply chains of today allow production of products with parts being produced in several countries before the final finished product is assembled. A major contributing factor to the global supply chains and the economics of production is the efficiency and effectiveness of global transportation and associated services. The improved global supply chains with faster transit times and lower rates help to promote global trade. Consumers received not only lower prices but in many instances better quality food and manufactured products. In the next section, we will examine the economic basis and complimentary logic for global trade.

The Economic Basis and Logic of Improved Global Trade

International trade is not a post–World War II phenomenon. During the Middle Ages, it was not uncommon for "traders" to cross regional and country borders by land or sea to buy, sell, or trade selected commodities. The Bible even references traders from other regions. The exploits of European explorers studied in high school and college history books were often rationalized upon finding high value or exotic products to bring back to their home country in exchange for their domestic products or valued items. The discovery of foreign lands for future settlement was also a motive but with the recognition of the potential trade opportunities. Obviously, the trading was inefficient and slow because of the bartering required and the transportation.

Absolute and Comparative Advantage

As the European countries advanced economically in the 18th century, there was a growing recognition of the value and potential of international trade. Adam Smith in his 1776 book, *The Wealth of Nations*,[2] not only provided a rational basis for a market economy based upon open or free competition, but he also advanced the so-called Theory of Absolute Advantage that provided an economic basis for "free trade" among countries. Essentially, he stated that if two regions or countries produced and consumed the same two products, for example, eggs and butter, but had different costs of production, trade could be beneficial. For example, if Country A had an advantage with producing eggs (50 cents versus $1 per dozen) and Country B had the advantage with butter (75 cents versus $1.25 per pound), Smith concluded that A should produce eggs and buy butter from B, while B should produce butter and buy eggs from A. Both would benefit by being able to buy more of each product at lower prices than if they each continued to produce both products. This example is somewhat simplistic because it does not consider transportation costs for delivery or other costs that could be incurred. If the additional costs were added to the production costs, the subsequent "landed cost" would have to be lower than the importing country's cost of production. In other words, in the example earlier, the eggs produced in A would have to have a landed cost in B (50 cents plus transportation costs) less than $1.00.

This same logic was used by Smith to advance the rationale for specialization or division of labor that supported the concept of mass or assembly line production, which will be discussed more fully in the next chapter. The important point is that global or regional trade could be based upon the lack of certain materials or products in an area, but also upon differences in the cost of producing two or more products in two or more different countries.

The Theory of Comparative Advantage was advanced about 40 years after the publication of Smith's *Wealth of Nations* by several economists.[3] They maintained that even if two countries produced and consumed the same two products and one country could produce both products at a lower cost (absolute advantage in both products) than the other country, it could possibly be beneficial for both countries to specialize and trade. It would require the country with the advantages to specialize in the product that it had the greatest comparative advantage over the other country. For example, if Country A could produce butter for 75 cents less than Country B and Country B could produce eggs for 25 cents more than Country A, A should produce butter while B should produce eggs. Again, transportation cost and other costs would have to be considered to develop a landed cost.

The concepts of absolute and comparative advantage are logical but relatively simple for the more complex economic environment of the 21st century. As one would expect, there have been economists who have enhanced or modified these earlier concepts. For example, one such enhancement is the so-called Factor Endowment Theory advanced by Heckscher and Ohlin that enhances Ricardo's Theory of Comparative Advantage.[4] Ricardo's theory was based upon a difference in efficiency associated with better technology, whereas the Factor Endowment Theory postulates that when a country has more of one of the four factors of production (land, labor, capital, or entrepreneurship), they can have a comparative advantage in producing one or more products. Therefore, a country with an abundance of capital and an educated workforce can produce high-tech products and import agriculture products from other countries.

In today's more complex, global economy, there are more variables than the traditional factors of production (land, labor, capital, and entrepreneurship) that can give advantages to countries and provide a basis for global trade flows. Some of these factors help to explain the development of the so-called BRIC and VISTA countries that were previously discussed. For example, two of the BRIC countries, India and China, have developed and prospered during the last 20 years because of factors such as improved global transportation, faster communication with lower costs, population growth, and technology advancement. China, for example, has taken advantage of their low labor costs, including skilled workers, ample raw materials, and capital to invest in production facilities. India's expanding population and growth in technology expertise contributed to their economic advancement. In a later section of this chapter, China and India's advancing economies and leadership positions in the world economy will be discussed in more detail.

Contributing Factors for Global Flows and Trade

Important factors that are frequently cited for greater economic development may include population growth and age distribution, urbanization, land and resources, economic integration, knowledge dissemination, labor mobility, financial flows, and investment in infrastructure by public and/or private agencies to promote improved transportation, faster communication systems, improved financial services, and increased flow of goods and services. These same factors also become the driving forces for overall globalization. At this juncture, it would be worthwhile to examine some of these factors in terms of the global economic growth and development of selected countries.[5]

Population Size and Distribution

Table 1-4 shows the population of the 10 largest countries and the total world population, which can be used as a basis for understanding current and future economic growth and development potential. The table includes totals for 2000, 2010, and 2012 and a projection for 2050. The top 10 countries account for about 58 percent of the total world population and China plus India account for over 36 percent of the total. Additionally, China has over a billion more people than the United States. By 2050, it is projected that both India and China will each have over a billion more people than the United States, and India will have a larger population than China unless there is some change in their respective birth rates. The sheer size of their respective populations is an important

TABLE 1-4 Top Ten Countries With the Highest Population

	COUNTRY	2000 POPULATION	2010 POPULATION	2014 POPULATION	2050 EXPECTED POPULATION
1	China	1,268,853,362	1,330,141,295	1,355,692,576	1,303,723,332
2	India	1,004,124,224	1,173,108,018	1,236,334,631	1,656,553,632
3	United States	282,338,631	310,232,863	318,892,103	439,010,253
4	Indonesia	213,829,469	242,968,342	253,609,643	313,020,847
5	Brazil	176,319,621	201,103,330	202,656,788	260,692,493
6	Pakistan	146,404,914	184,404,791	196,174,380	276,428,758
7	Nigeria	123,178,818	152,217,341	177,155,754	264,262,405
8	Bangladesh	130,406,594	156,118,464	166,280,712	233,587,279
9	Russia	146,709,971	139,390,205	142,470,272	109,187,353
10	Japan	126,729,223	126,804,433	127,103,388	93,673,826
	Top Ten	3,618,894,827	4,016,489,082	4,176,380,247	4,950,140,178
	Rest of the world	2,466,012,769	2,829,120,878	3,005,478,372	4,306,202,522
	Total	6,084,907,596	6,845,609,960	7,181,858,619	9,256,342,700

Source: Internet world stats, Usuge and Population Statistics Miniwatts Marketing Group.

advantage in terms of one of the previously noted factors of production, that is, labor. The size of their labor forces along with their education and skills will continue to be a strategic advantage, especially in light of the "aging" populations of other countries, which will be discussed later in this chapter.

Table 1-5 depicts the total world population and indicates a decrease in the birth rate. Interestingly, Russia and Japan show a decrease in their population between 2012 and 2050. Experts point out that the worldwide rate of population growth has already peaked and is now declining, which is important in terms of global resource base.[6] Additionally, the population growth rate is greatest in some areas that can probably least afford it. Unless there is some change in their economic development, the population explosion in certain underdeveloped economies could lead to dire levels of poverty and other health-related problems and potential political unrest.

While the total population of a country is an indicator of economic growth potential in terms of workforce and consumers, it has some limits. We need additional information about the population to draw meaningful conclusions such as age distribution and education levels. If we examine population age distribution on a macro level, the young-age balance is shifting throughout the world. In the more developed regions, the proportion of older people (over age 60) already exceeds that of children (under age 15), 19 percent versus 18 percent, but by 2050 the numbers are predicted to be 34 percent versus 16 percent, respectively. Europe will have the greatest disparity followed by North America. The longer life spans in developed countries is exacerbating the young-age disparity ratio and has important implications for the labor force in various countries and the needs of consumers for food, housing, and medical care. Figure 1-3 shows the number of persons aged 65 or older per 100 children under age 15 for 2000 and a projection for 2050. The difference between 2000 and 2050 is quite evident. Figure 1-4 shows the median ages for 1950 and 2000 and the projection for 2050—the total world, less developed, more

TABLE 1-5 Population by Major Age Group and Percentage Distribution by Age Group for the World and the Development Groups, 1950, 1975, 2005, 2025 and 2050

	POPULATION (MILLIONS)					PERCENTAGE				
AGE GROUP	1950	1975	2005	2025	2050	1950	1975	2005	2025	2050
					WORLD					
0-14	864	1 498	1 821	1 909	1 833	34.3	36.8	28.2	24.2	20.2
15-24	459	757	1 159	1 211	1 225	18.2	18.6	17.9	15.3	13.5
25-59	991	1 469	2 812	3 593	4 051	39.3	36.1	43.5	45.4	44.6
60-79	192	318	586	1032	1 574	7.6	7.8	9.1	13.1	17.3
80+	14	31	87	160	394	0.5	0.8	1.3	2.0	4.3
Total	2519	4 074	6 465	7 905	9 076	100.0	100.0	100.0	100.0	100.0
					MORE DEVELOPED REGIONS					
0-14	222	254	206	196	193	27.4	24.2	17.0	15.7	15.6
15-24	138	176	165	140	133	17.0	16.8	13.7	11.2	108
25-59	357	456	596	570	510	43.9	43.5	49.2	45.7	41.2
60-79	87	143	200	275	284	10.7	13.7	16.5	22.0	23.0
80+	9	13	44	68	116	1.0	1.8	3.7	5.4	9.4
Total	813	1 047	1 211	1 249	1 236	100.0	100.0	100.0	100.0	100.0
					LESS DEVELOPED REGIONS					
0-14	642	1 244	1 615	1 713	1 639	37.6	41.1	30.7	25.7	20.9
15-24	321	581	994	1 071	1 091	18.8	19.2	18.9	16.1	13.9
25-59	634	1 014	2 216	3 023	3 541	37.1	33.5	42.2	45.4	45.2
60-79	105	175	386	757	1 290	6.1	5.8	7.3	11.4	16.5
80+	5	13	42	92	278	0.3	0.4	0.8	1.4	3.6
Total	1 707	3 027	5 253	6 656	7 840	100.0	100.0	100.0	100.0	100.0

Source: *World Population Prospects: The 2004 Revision,* Datasets in Excel and PDF Formats. Extended Dataset, United Nations, 2005.

developed, and least developed regions. The median age has and will change for all four regions, but the differences among the regions are important, especially between the more developed and the least developed.

The private sector and the public sector will be challenged by these changes in terms of the size of the workforce, medical care, and even retirement benefits, but some opportunities are likely for certain types of businesses including health care, housing, transportation, food products, and so on. Much depends upon immigration policies, technology, retirement ages, and educational opportunities. Net, net there could be benefits but challenges also will persist. An interesting opportunity could occur with more mobile migration among countries. The European countries with their "graying" populations could probably benefit with a migration of younger individuals from less developed countries not only to help care for the older citizens but also to provide a younger workforce for the developed economies. Even in the United States this could be a possible benefit. Table 1-6 compares selected age groups in the United States for 2000 and 2010, and an interesting group is the 25–44-age bracket showing that in 2010 there was a decline of almost 3 million people in this group compared to 2000. Furthermore, it was the only

FIGURE 1-3 Number of Persons 65 or Over Per Hundred Children Under 15: World and Development Regions, 1950–2050

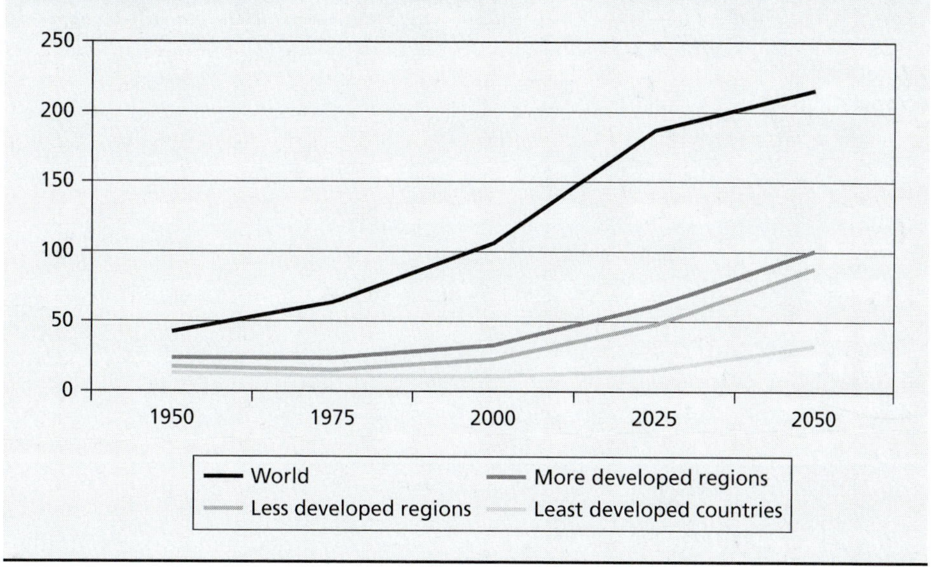

Source: United Nations, Department of Economic and Social Affairs, Population Division, World Ageing Population: 1950–2050, Chapter 3.

FIGURE 1-4 Median Age of the Population: World and Development Regions, 1950–2050

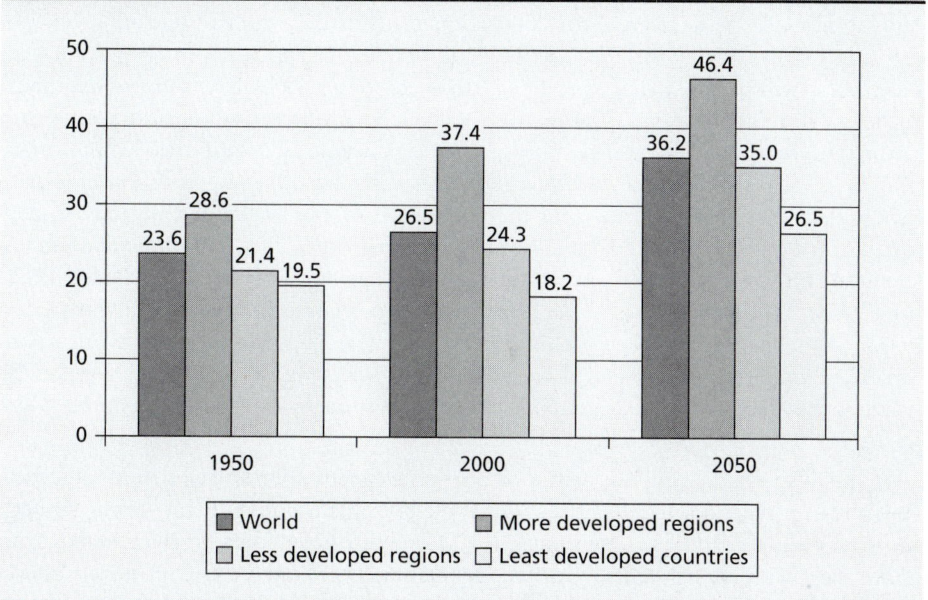

Source: United Nations, Department of Economic and Social Affairs, Population Division, World Ageing Population: 1950–2050, Chapter 3.

TABLE 1-6 Breakdown of the United States by Age, 2000–2010

	2000		2010		CHANGE	
	NUMBER	PERCENT	NUMBER	PERCENT	NUMBER	PERCENT
Total population	281,421,906	100	308,745,538	100	27,323,632	9.7
Sex						
Male	138,053,563	49.1	151,781,326	49.2	13,727,763	9.9
Female	143,368,343	50.9	156,964,212	50.8	13,595,869	9.5
Selected Age Groups						
<18 Years	72,293,812	25.7	74,181,467	24	1,887,655	2.6
18 to 24 Years	27,143,454	9.6	30,672,088	9.9	3,528,634	13
25 to 44 Years	85,040,251	30.2	82,134,554	26.6	−2,905,697	−3.4
45 to 64 Years	61,952,636	22	81,489,445	26.4	19,536,809	31.5
> = 65 Years	34,991,753	12.4	40,267,984	13	5,276,231	15.1

Sources: U.S. Census Bureau, Census 2000 Summary File 1 and 2010 Census Summary File 1.

age group where that was the case. The ripple effect in future years may turn out to be important for population growth and workforce productivity. We could join Japan and Russia with an overall decline in population at some point.

Urbanization

There has been a noticeable demographic shift in a number of countries with the migration from rural to urban areas. In 2000, 47 percent of the world's population lived in urban areas. By 2030, it is estimated that the number will increase to 60 percent, and the change will be most rapid in underdeveloped countries. This will cause additional challenges for those countries to provide the housing, infrastructure, health care, and security necessary for effective and prosperous expansion. The rural areas will also face challenges with smaller and likely older populations. There will be opportunities for business to help alleviate the burdens for the public sector and develop new business opportunities for domestic and global economic expansion. The challenges will be daunting in some cases. A relatively new term is the *megacity* (more than 10 million people). It has been estimated that Asia will have 18 megacities, the United States will have five, but there will be none in Europe.[7] This will be an interesting demographic change with important implications for global trade. The megacities in some countries especially Africa will be faced with inadequate infrastructure, especially transportation and utilities, to support the population growth.

One of the interesting megacities or a so-called metropolis is Lagos in West Africa, which is being referred to as Africa's Big Apple by some economists and demographers. Lagos has new tech hubs, a new wealthy class, and an exploding population but with many in poverty status. The estimated population based on U.N. data is 15 million although local officials claim a population of 18 million. In the 1970s, the population was estimated to be about 2 million. Lagos has developed into a powerful economic engine based upon an oil boom and a growing economy. The average Nigerian woman gives birth to more than five children in her lifetime, and the population of Lagos expands by about 600,000 a year. The growth has pluses and minuses and has many challenges with its limited infrastructure. However, there are those who maintain that

Lagos is Africa's future, which you can interpret in different ways, good or bad. One of the critical ingredients needed for improvement is local and inter-regional transportation systems. As pointed out previously, the lack of adequate transportation will hinder and restrain economic development.

Land and Resources

The availability of land and critical resources such as energy, food, and water are of paramount importance for economic viability and future development. Technology will play a critical role in mitigating the scarcity of key resources from desalinization of ocean water, to fracking for increased oil and gas production, to biotechnology for improving crop yield and food production. Fracking for oil and gas has already changed the global dynamics for energy with the United States likely to become a net exporter and the changes in transportation requirements, which will be discussed in later chapters. All three are keys to stable economic growth and development but the geographic disparity among areas of the world could be daunting and lead to political conflicts. The public and private sectors can both be instrumental in alleviating the challenges and potential crises. Our success in this area will be of immeasurable importance for peace and prosperity. Transportation can play an important role in resolving the disparity by moving these resources efficiently and effectively among regions and countries, but governments and businesses have to provide the stable and economic basis for this to happen. The expansion of oil and gas pipelines in recent years and improvements in rail tank cars and water vessels are based upon such growth.

Technology and Information

Technology has two important dimensions. It can be viewed as an internal change agent that can enhance the efficiency and effectiveness of an organization and its ability to compete in the global marketplace. However, technology can also be viewed as an external driver of change similar to globalization. In many organizations, the rapid development of new technology by technology companies whether it was hardware or software changed the "rules of engagement" and enabled new forms of competition or new business models. The new technology and new companies changed the nature of the competition, which meant that existing companies had to change or perish. There are many examples of established organizations that were blindsided by the technology. The Internet alone was the biggest "culprit" or agent of change because it made information available in real time to large segments of the population via their personal computers, telephones, or other devices.

The development and sharing of so much information is a major force for changing business models and for the obsolescence of some businesses. Travel agents, for example, became passé. Amazon without stores can compete with WalMart's store network, as can Zappos with more traditional shoe sales organizations. Technology and transportation services have been major factors supporting these changes. For example, companies have been able to outsource selected internal functions like customer service centers or personnel services. One of the most significant impacts has probably been more efficient and effective supply chains and related services such as high-tech warehousing and overnight delivery via Federal Express or UPS. From the specially designed supply chains of Amazon and Zappos to the realigned supply chains of companies like Macy's or Kimberly Clark, supply chains have become a critical ingredient for profitability and customer service. In other words, supply chains are a staple for the success of overall corporate strategy, and transportation is an integral part of these new supply chains.

While information technology has become an important dynamic for external and internal change, there is another important dimension of technology, especially for supply chains, and that is industrial robotics. They have been around for over 50 years and do not resemble R2D2, as depicted in the *Star Wars* film. The first generation of industrial robots was "one-armed" and installed in a permanent position to carry out simple and routine tasks usually on an assembly line. It has been estimated by the International Federation of Robotics that there are over 1.1 million working robots around the world.[8] The largest users are in the automotive industry, and they operate about 80 percent of the total. There is a new wave of less expensive and more flexible robots becoming available for a wider array of manufacturing and distribution tasks. In distribution, these robots will store, retrieve, and pack goods for efficient and effective delivery.

As businesses and other logistics organizations invest in robotic development, the robots will have a positive impact on global trade flows. The newer robots will be used in an environment where humans will be working with them side by side combining the skills of humans with the precision and efficiency of robots. This may allow for smaller scale operations not only for manufacturing but also for distribution, for example, warehouses and transportation terminals with logistics and supply chain networks being changed accordingly.[9]

Another technology with the potential of having a major impact upon supply chains, logistics, and transportation systems is digitization of manufacturing with facilities being run with smarter software using inputs from product development, historical production data, and advanced computational methods to model and change the entire manufacturing process for individual orders quickly and efficiently. This will also reduce the required scale of operations and allow faster responses to change in the short run as well as the long run.

A related technology is additive manufacturing or so-called 3-D printing, which has been creating a real buzz in business circles, and even, President Obama mentioned it in one of his speeches as being a potential force for positive change in the future to make the United States more competitive on a global basis. Essentially, a 3-D printer would allow organizations to make a physical 3-D copy of a product or a part. Despite the buzz, 3-D printing is a long way from producing a car or making assembly lines obsolete. Material costs are extremely high for a number of reasons including higher purity standards and the "middlemen" in the material supply chains. However, 3-D printing is already being used to produce some customized, smaller products such as the covers for iPhones and some specialized parts for automobiles. The latter use will probably continue to be the leader for 3-D printing in the short run, but the long-run development of more, smaller, and better machines will have a major impact on logistics and supply chains. For example, if repairmen who travel about in vans with inventory can have a 3-D printer in the van with one of each part, they could reduce inventory costs and never be out of stock. Many smaller-scale operations could also benefit with major implications as indicated earlier for supply chains including producers of products. It would probably be comparable to the impact that the improved printers for personal and business computers and related software have had upon commercial printing operations. Some organizations or parts of supply chains will become obsolete or redundant. Like globalization, to be discussed next, technology will continue to be a an agent for change up and down supply chains making them and the transportation system more efficient.[10]

Globalization

Globalization has become a very frequently used term or concept not only in business-related conversations but also in more casual settings. Individuals probably have many interpretations and use the word differently in different settings. However, in this particular context, globalization can be used synonymously with economic integration and development across country and regional borders. The integration will increase the flow of goods and services globally based upon the logic of comparative advantage discussed previously. Also the efforts to eliminate and/or reduce tariff and non-tariff barriers will promote greater interregional flows. However, military and terroristic interruption pose a real threat to increased global economic progress as demonstrated in the Middle East and the Gaza Strip in 2014.

The global interdependence can be good or bad news. On the good side, the lower prices, wider availability of goods and services, land and resource development, and new employment opportunities have benefited many countries and regions of the world, both developed and developing areas. However, the benefits and advantages have not been equal for all, that is, some have benefited more than others, but on a macro level, and one could argue that the wins have outnumbered the losses. The BRIC and VISTA countries mentioned previously are an indication of some positive outcomes of globalization. On the negative side, the interdependence can lead to global recessions as was the case in 2009 with serious repercussions felt throughout the world. The economic recovery has been very painful and has required government intervention. There are still lingering economic problems from this recession in some areas of the world. However, there have been strong recoveries in other regions such as North America and some countries in Europe.

On a micro level, the global interdependence has increased the level of complexity and competition with shorter product life cycles, new forms of competition, and new business models. Outsourcing, offshoring, and insourcing have become part of the lexicon of businesses. The information technology previously discussed has allowed supply chains to be reexamined and redesigned for more efficiency and effectiveness and even better execution. The fast or even real-time information flows globally have allowed companies to connect in sharing information and to collaborate much more expeditiously than in the past. This has placed a premium on flexibility of planning and operations to respond and adjust to changes in the competitive environment. Also, visibility of inventory and other assets has become an important dimension for efficiency and effectiveness. Successful and well-established business enterprises have felt the impact of the new competitive environment and changing consumer tastes and needs. Again, it is important to recognize the importance and need for good transportation for the success of global supply chains—their efficiency and effectiveness depend on good transportation.

Supply Chain Concept

References to supply chain management can be traced to the 1980s, but it was not until the 1990s that supply chains captured the attention of senior level management in many organizations. They began to recognize the potential of effective supply chain management to improve global competitiveness and to increase market share with consequent improvement in share-holder value.

Development of the Concept

Supply chain management is not a new concept. Rather, supply chain management represents the third phase of an evolution that started in the 1960s with the development of the physical distribution concept, which focused on finished goods or the outbound side of a firm's logistics system—in other words, the distribution-related activities that occurred after a product was produced. In the 1980s, the concept of business logistics or integrated logistics was developed and added the inbound side to the outbound side.

GLOBAL **PROFILE**

P&G May Jettison Half of Their Brands

The Procter and Gamble (P&G) company has been recognized for its expertise in the area of managing product brands to improve sales and profits. It is probable that many consumers may purchase Tide soap or Pampers without associating P&G with the products. It is the brand recognition, which is important to the sale. Their advertising, promotions, and sales administration have emphasized the brands.

It could be argued that the term, *brand management*, is associated most closely with P&G. Their success over the years has been legendary, and they have been a model for many other consumer product companies. While they have jettisoned some brands and product lines in the past for product and company profitability, they have more frequently expanded the number of their brands, especially under the leadership of CEO A.G. Lafley. The recently announced plans to jettison half or more of their brands represents a major change in their strategy. Some will likely be sold and others may be abandoned. Their lesser known brands will probably be attractive to private equity companies or companies in other countries. They intend to focus upon 70 to 80 brands and shed as many as 100 or more others. It should be noted that P&G probably gets about 90 percent of their sales revenue from their largest selling brands. Profits may increase but growth will probably be a challenge in the future unless they can expand the sales of the brands that they maintain. Global sales will be a critical part of their long-run growth. This is where their ability to respond more quickly to changes in the more competitive global market will be a critical aspect of their long-run success.

It would appear that P&G, like some other large consumer product companies, has become "bloated" and that the "extra baggage" has contributed to a slower response to shifts in the marketplace. P&G has recognized their need to be more nimble and speed up their response time and hence the decision to jettison a large number of brands. Globalization has impacted the competitive nature of the markets for consumer products. The failure to recognize the extent of these changes and develop an effective competitive response can quickly lead to failure. Pure size cannot insulate large companies and allow them to stumble along as they did sometimes in the past. Previous success sometimes creates a culture that resists change and hinders flexibility and responsiveness.

The changes that are being contemplated by P&G will require major changes in their supply chains and related transportation systems to serve those supply chains. The product decisions cannot be made without considering the related aspects of their total systems including the flow of materials and information, that is, a supply chain perspective. In other words, the product decisions cannot be made in isolation. There are interrelations among products and facilities that will need to be considered for the efficiency and effectiveness of their various global supply chains and related transportation services.

Logistics management was the second phase of development for the supply chain concept. As indicated previously, the supply chain management concept was developed primarily in the 1990s and represented the third phase of development.

The focus of **physical distribution management** was on system costs and analyzing trade-off scenarios to arrive at the best or lowest physical distribution system cost. The system relationships that exist among transportation, inventory levels, warehousing, protective packaging, materials handling, and customer service were analyzed and evaluated. For example, rail and motor carrier service impact inventory, warehousing, packaging, customer service, and materials handling costs, but motor carriers would have a different impact on the same cost centers. Rail service would usually have the lowest transportation rate, but there could be higher costs for inventory, warehousing, and packaging that would result in higher total costs than motor carrier service. The type of product, volume, distance, and other factors would influence which mode of transportation would have the lower total cost. Managers in certain industries, such as consumer package or grocery products, high-tech companies, and other consumer product companies, as well as some academicians, became very interested in physical distribution management. A national organization called the National Council of Physical Distribution Management (NCPDM) was organized to focus the leadership, education, research, and interest in the area of physical distribution management.

The 1980s were a decade of change with the deregulation of transportation, financial institutions, and the communication industry. The technology revolution was also underway. During the 1980s, the **business logistics** or **integrated logistics management** concept developed in a growing number of organizations (see Figures 1-5 and 1-6). The deregulation of transportation provided an opportunity to coordinate the inbound and outbound transportation movements of large shippers, which could impact a carrier's outbound costs by minimizing empty backhauls, and lead to lower rates for the shipper. Also, international or global sourcing of materials and supplies was growing in importance. As will be discussed subsequently in more detail, global transportation presents some special challenges for production and scheduling. Therefore, it became increasingly apparent that coordination between the outbound and the inbound sides of logistics

FIGURE 1-5 Typical Logistics Network—Physical Distribution

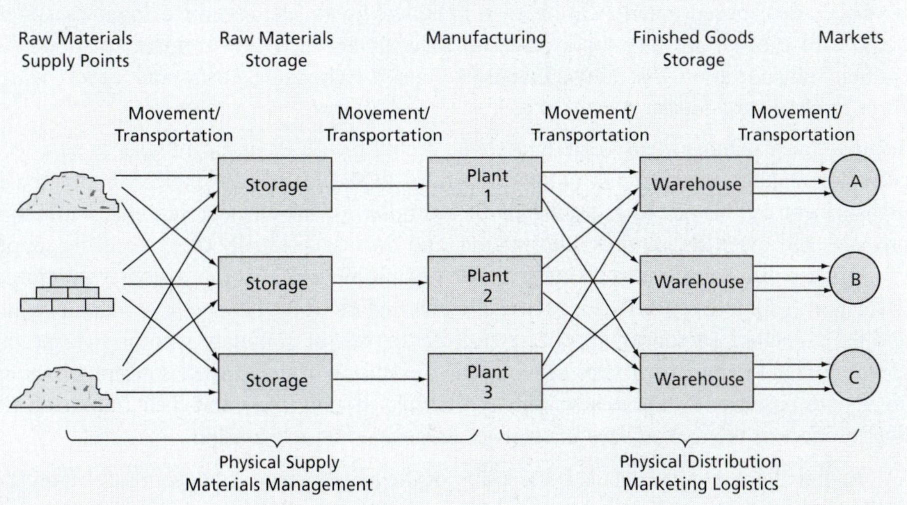

FIGURE 1-6 Typical Logistics Network—Materials Management

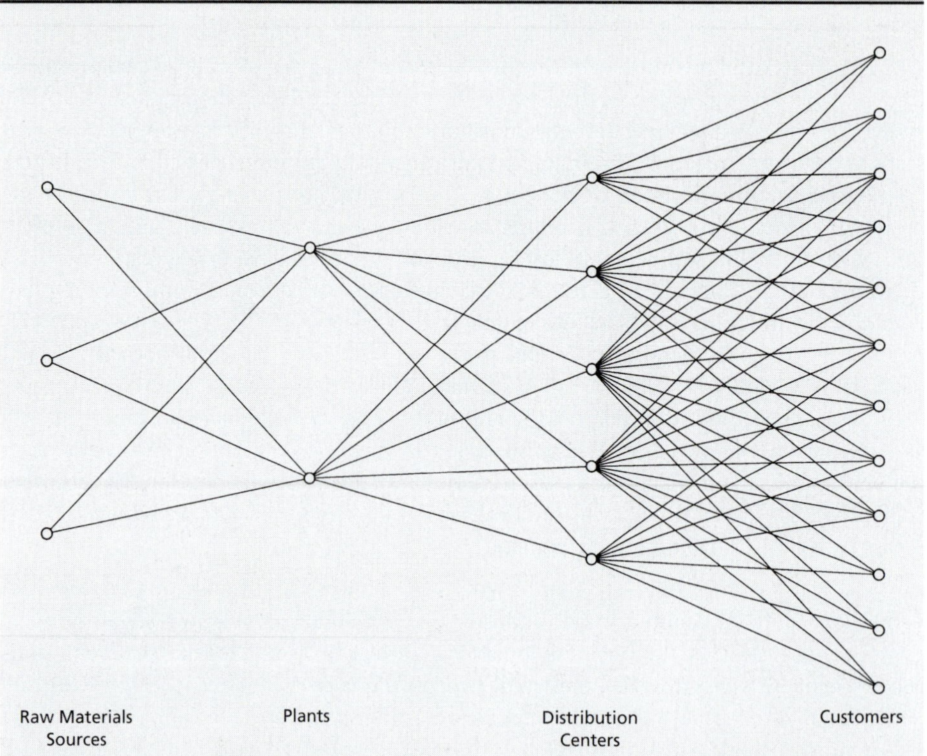

Source: Center for Supply Chain Research, Penn State University, 2004.

systems provided an opportunity for the increased efficiency and also better levels of customer service.

The underlying logic of the systems concept was also the rationale for the development of the logistics management concept, because in addition to analyzing trade-offs for total cost it could also include the value of demand aspects of customer service effectiveness. Also, procurement was usually included as an element in a logistics system because of the opportunity for a trade-off analysis between procurement quantity discounts, transportation discounts, inventory, and warehousing costs, and other related costs to obtain the lowest cost.

Supply chain management came into vogue during the 1990s and continues to be a focal point for making organizations more competitive in the global marketplace. Supply chain management can be viewed as a pipeline or a conduit for the efficient and effective flow of products and materials, services, information, and financials (usually cash) from the supplier's supplier through the various intermediate organizations out to the customer's customer (see Figure 1-7). In essence, it is a system of connected networks between the original vendor and the ultimate final consumer. The extended enterprise or boundary spanning perspective of supply chain management represents a logical extension of the logistics concept, providing an opportunity to view the total system of interrelated companies and their impact on the final product in the marketplace in terms of its price–value relationship.

At this point, a more detailed discussion of the supply chain is appropriate. Figure 1-7 presents a simplified, linear example of a hypothetical supply chain. A real-world

FIGURE 1-7 Integrated Supply Chain

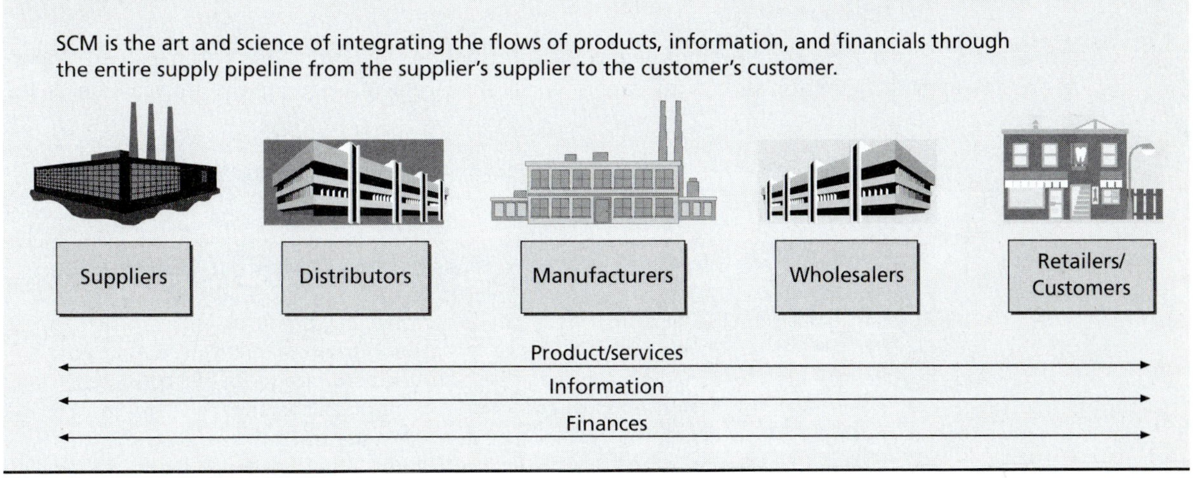
SCM is the art and science of integrating the flows of products, information, and financials through the entire supply pipeline from the supplier's supplier to the customer's customer.
Suppliers
Distributors
Manufacturers
Wholesalers
Retailers/ Customers
Product/services
Information
Finances

Source: Center for Supply Chain Research, Penn State University.

supply chain would usually be more complex than this example because supply chains are often nonlinear and have more supply chain participants. Also, Figure 1-7 does not adequately portray the importance of transportation in the supply chain. As indicated previously, transportation can be viewed as the glue that holds the supply chain together to allow the member organizations to operate efficiently and effectively as a system. It should be noted that some companies may be a part of several supply chains. For example, chemical companies may provide ingredients for manufacturers of different products that will be distributed by many different retail and wholesale establishments.

Figure 1-7 does illustrate the basic characteristics of a supply chain that are important to this discussion. The definition, which is a part of the illustration, indicates several important points. A supply chain is an **extended enterprise** that crosses the boundaries of the individual firms to span their related activities involved in the supply chain. This extended enterprise should attempt to execute a coordinated or integrated two-way flow of goods, information, and financials (especially cash). The three flows illustrated in the figure are very important to the competitive success of the organizations. Integration across the boundaries of the several organizations in the essence means that the supply chain needs to function like one organization in satisfying the ultimate customer by delivering an appropriate price–value relationship for products in the marketplace.

The top flow, products and related services, has traditionally been an important focus of logistics and transportation and is an important element in supply chain management. This particular flow is directly dependent upon effective transportation, which is the focus of this text. Customers expect their orders to be delivered in a timely, reliable, and damage-free manner, and transportation is critical to this outcome. Figure 1-7 also indicates that product flow is a two-way flow in the environment of the 21st century because a growing number of organizations are involved in **reverse logistics systems** for returning products that were unacceptable to the buyer for some reason—damage, maintenance, obsolescence, and so forth. Note also that networks for reverse systems usually have to be designed somewhat differently than for forward systems. The location, size, and layout of facilities are frequently different. The transportation carriers that need to be utilized may be different. Consequently, there are a growing number of logistics companies (including transportation companies) that specialize in managing reverse flow systems for retailers and manufacturers. They can provide a valuable service in appropriate situations.

The second flow indicated is the **information flow,** which has become a very important factor for success in supply chain management. Figuratively, information is the

ON THE LINE

Transportation's Impact on the Global Supply Chains

Many global supply chains are characterized by outsourcing production to low labor cost countries such as China and India. These global supply chains often evolved as a consequence of trade agreements and aggressive government incentives, along with cheap fuel prices, which gave rise to low cost development of collaborative relationships on a real-time basis across globally extended enterprise systems. Consequently, world trade has flourished between and among developed and underdeveloped economies. For example, U.S. imports have grown at an accelerated rate, increasing from 10 percent of its aggregate demand in the late 1980s to approximately 20 percent by 2008.

The transportation landscape, which is a key factor or link in the success of global supply chains, is facing some major challenges. The rapid growth that has occurred in global trade in the United States has placed much pressure on the ports, which are the gateways for about 80 percent by weight of the international freight moving in and out of the United States. Congestion has become a problem, especially on the West Coast during peak periods. This is mainly attributable to the tremendous growth in the trade between the United States and the Asia-Pacific countries. Congestion has also become a widely acknowledged problem on the highways and at major rail gateways, which increases the West Coast port congestion problem. A further challenge is the potential for a shortage of over-the-road drivers, especially in the long-haul sector. The average driver age is such that retirements by 2020 could cause a shortage of over 140,000 drivers.

A concern of major proportions is volatile energy costs. While fuel prices did decline toward the end of the first decade of the 21st century, the expectation is that they may increase again. Motor carriers and airlines are affected by these higher fuel prices because they are relatively inefficient in fuel consumption compared to the other three major modes of transportation—rail, water, and pipeline. When you consider the fact that about 75 to 80 percent of the freight shipments in the United States move via motor carrier for at least part of the distance, the higher fuel costs have major implications for the transportation system and the economy.

Sustainability is also an issue for the 21st century as individuals, organizations, and the government are showing a growing concern for the environment. **Green supply chains** have become a part of our vernacular. Organizations discuss their carbon footprint in the context of sustainability and evaluate methods to reduce their carbon footprint. Transportation is an area that receives much attention in such discussions because the modes of transportation vary in terms of their impact. As pointed out previously, rail, water, and pipelines are more fuel efficient than motor and air carriers. Fuel consumption relative to ton-miles moved is important to the size of the carbon footprint. Consequently, shippers will be placing more emphasis in this area in making modal choices and will place more emphasis on network efficiency, that is, on reducing trip miles, eliminating empty moves, and using cargo capacity. The implications for transportation are significant. There has been discussion over the last two decades of demand-driven supply chains. The supply chain of the future may be transport-driven.

trigger or signal for the logistics or supply chain system to respond to a customer order. Traditionally, we have viewed information as flowing back from the marketplace as customers purchased products and wholesalers and retailers replenished their inventory. The information was primarily demand or sales data, which triggered replenishment and was also the basis for forecasting future sales or orders. Note that in addition to the retailer or final seller, the other members of the supply chain traditionally reacted to replenishment orders. If there were long time intervals between orders, the members of the supply chain were faced with uncertainty about the level and the potential pattern of demand, which usually resulted in higher inventory (safety stock) or stock out costs. The uncertainty contributed to a phenomenon known as the **bull whip effect** in the supply chain. One of the objectives of supply chain management is to mitigate the bull whip effect by reducing the level of uncertainty. In traditional supply chains with independent organizations, the level or magnitude of uncertainty increased with the "distance" from the market or customer. Therefore, the level of safety stock increased to cover the degree of uncertainty as you moved back through the supply chain.

One of the realizable outcomes of supply chain management is the sharing of sales information on a more real-time basis to reduce uncertainty, which reduces the need for safety stock. In this sense, the supply chain is compressed through timely information flows from the marketplace. In other words, inventory can be reduced in the supply chain by timely, accurate information about demand. If point of sale (POS) data were available from the retail level on a real-time basis, it would help to mitigate the bull whip effect associated with supply chain inventories and would reduce costs. It should also be noted that transportation plays an important role in the level of supply chain inventory. One of the components of transportation service as discussed was reliability of delivery. It was noted that if service was unreliable, companies carried more inventory or safety stock, which would be true along the whole supply chain. It was also noted that transit time had an effect upon inventory, namely, longer transit times could contribute to higher inventory levels. Longer transit times combined with unreliable service exacerbate the need for safety stock in the supply chain. Consequently, transportation is an important cog in the whole supply chain in terms of efficiency and effectiveness.

Note the illustration also indicates a two-way flow of information. In a supply chain environment, information flowing forward in the supply chain has taken on increased significance and importance. Forward information can take many forms, such as **advanced shipment notices** (ASNs), order status information, and inventory availability information. The overall impact of good forward information has been to reduce uncertainty with respect to order replenishment. A related aspect of forward information flow has been the increased utilization of bar codes and radio frequency tags, which can increase inventory visibility and help reduce uncertainty in the safety stock. The improved visibility of pipeline inventory, including transportation equipment, also makes possible many opportunities for improved efficiency such as transportation consolidation and merging in transit strategies. These latter two have contributed to some shift in modal selection because of the opportunity for consolidation of larger shipments and the opportunity to use merging in transit strategies to eliminate warehousing. The combined two-way flow of timely, accurate information lowers supply chain–related costs (including transportation), which also improves effectiveness or customer service.

The third and final flow indicated is financials, or usually and more specifically, cash. Traditionally, financial flows have been viewed as one-directional—backward in the supply chain. In other words, this flow is payment for goods, services, and orders received. A major impact of supply chain compression and faster cycle times has been faster cash flow. Customers receive orders faster, they are billed sooner, and companies can collect sooner. The faster cash-to-cash or order-to-cash cycle has been very important for companies because it reduces the amount of working capital they need in their system. If cash flow is slow, a company needs more working capital to finance the processes until they collect from the customers. There are some companies that have negative working capital or what financial organizations refer to as **"free" cash flow.** They collect from their customers before they have to pay their vendors or suppliers. In such companies as Dell and Hewlett Packard, the period between collection and payment may be as much as 30 or more days. This cash can be used for financial investment purposes or another source of funding for product development or other improvements. Cash flow measures have become an important metric of the financial community to gauge the viability of companies. Slower cash flows increase the need for working capital and may require loans from time to time to pay suppliers, service providers, or even employees. Frequently, one will see in the financial analysis of an organization references to their cash flow situation. Supply chain management provides organizations with an opportunity to improve customer service and cash flow, and transportation service is an important part of this equation.

As indicated previously, it is important to be aware of the significant role that transportation provides in the supply chain framework. At the "end of the day," the customer expects to have the right product, delivered at the right place, at the right time, in the right quantity, in the right condition, and at the right cost. Transportation plays a critical role in these attributes for an efficient and effective logistics and supply chain system.

SUMMARY

- Transportation is one of the most critical and important ingredients for the economic and social advancement of geographic regions. From the corner grocery stores to large complex factories, efficient and effective transportation is the life blood of their ability to operate and compete. Globalization has made transportation even more important with the increased distances and the importance of reliability for today's organizations.
- Transportation was often viewed as the "glue" to hold complex global supply together to make good on the potential, competitive advantages that were frequently extolled for effective supply chain management. Globalization has elevated transportation to a more strategic role in many organizational supply chains.
- There have been some notable changes in the global economic landscape in the last 20 years or so. The emergence of the so-called BRIC (Brazil, Russia, India, and China) and VISTA (Vietnam, Indonesia, South Africa, Turkey, and Argentina) countries are examples of that change. The first group is the more advanced of the two groups, especially China and India who are challenging the more advanced economies. The second group are more appropriately labeled emerging economies, but some faster than others.
- The global flow between countries of imports and exports continues to expand, which is a clear indication of the theories of absolute and comparative advantage at work. While many countries participate in these flows, the more developed countries in Asia, the EU, and the United States dominate the volume. China, the United States, Germany, and Japan are the world leaders.
- An important contributing factor to the growth in trade flows among countries is the more sophisticated supply chains and transportation services, which permit the production and assembly of parts for finished products to be produced in several countries with appropriate sequencing. Overall growth of global trade more than doubled between 2000 and the present with help from trade agreements and increased acceptance of foreign products.
- Population growth, age distribution, and urbanization will play important roles in fostering economic development and associated global trade flows. The populations of China and India exceed a billion in each country and represent an important advantage for these two countries in terms of labor and potential consumers as their economies have grown and developed in the last 25 years.
- Land and resources are also important elements for increased economic development, especially energy, food, and water. Energy has provided the basis for improved economies in a number of countries in the Middle East and Africa, but even developed countries in Europe and the Unites States and Canada have added growth because of energy growth associated with new technology for recovering oil and natural gas. Advancements in crop production have helped to alleviate food shortages, but there is much more that can and should be done in this area.
- Technology has played a major role on a macro and micro level to influence the growth of global trade flows. Information technology and knowledge dissemination have promoted economic growth and development by allowing more countries to participate in the production of goods and services while separated by distance but connected through information technology.

- Technology is broader than information and consideration has to be given to the "hard side" of technology. Industrial robots are making inroads into the production and distribution phases of global supply chains making them more efficient as well as more effective. In some cases, technology is replacing humans while in other instances complementing human effort. Industrial robotics can play an increased and important role in the future.
- Increased globalization by crossing country borders through economic integration has the potential to improve the economies of many countries of the world with consequent economic advantage of their respective citizenry, but the political tensions and actual combat will thwart these efforts and protectionism may rear its "ugly head" again to the detriment of all.

STUDY QUESTIONS

1. Transportation has sometimes been described as the glue that holds global supply chains together. What is the meaning of this statement and do you agree? Why or why not?
2. During the last 20 to 30 years, there have been a number of countries whose economies have experienced important economic expansion and development. One group of countries has been labeled the BRIC and the other the VISTA. Identify each of the nine countries and provide some insights about their economies and economic importance.
3. The theories of absolute and comparative advantage have been offered as economic rationale for trade between and among regions and countries. Compare and contrast the two concepts. Which of the two do you think is more important for explaining the growth in global trade during the last 25 years? Why?
4. The overall growth of global trade has more than doubled since 2000. Why? What has been the most important factor prompting this growth. Is this rate of growth likely to continue in the future? Why or why not?
5. The size of a country's population and the associated age distribution can be causal factors for economic growth. Why is the size of the population important to economic development? Can size be a disadvantage? Why is age distribution important?
6. Energy, food, and water are frequently cited resources that are critical for economic development. Explain the importance of each one to economic development. What disparities exist among countries with respect to these three resources? How can these challenges be resolved?
7. Technology can impact economic development on both a macro and a micro level. What types of technology do we need to have such impacts on a macro basis? On a micro basis?
8. Robotics have attracted more attention in recent years. Why? How are robots being used in supply chains?
9. The economic integration associated with should globalization can provide an opportunity for more widely dispersed development. Why is this possible? What are the major stumbling blocks to such integration?
10. Supply chain management has enabled some companies to operate more efficiently and compete more effectively on a global basis. What inherent characteristics of supply chain management contribute to these outcomes?

NOTES

1. Thomas Friedman, *The World Is Flat: A Brief History of the Twenty-First Century*, New York: Farrar, Strauss, and Giroux, 2005.
2. Pierre David, *International Logistics: The Management of International Trade Operations*, 4th ed., 2013, Berea, OH: Cicero Books, pp. 21–22.
3. Ibid., pp. 26–27.
4. Fariborz Ghadar and Erik Peterson, *Global Tectonics*, University Park, PA: Center for Global Business Studies, Smeal College of Business, Penn State University, 2008, pp. 13–18.
5. Ibid.
6. Ibid.
7. Vienne Walt, "Africa's Big Apple," Fortune.com, June 30, 2014.
8. Kusumal Roansook, "Supply Chain Technology," Working Paper, Center for Supply Chain Research, Smeal College of Business, Penn State University, University Park, PA, 2014.
9. Ibid.
10. Ibid.

CASE 1-1

Clearfield Cheese Company Case: A Sequel

Background

The Clearfield Cheese Company was established by two brothers, Terry and Ted Edwards, in 1931, in Clearfield, Pennsylvania. This section of Central Pennsylvania's economy was based largely upon coal and agriculture at this point in time. The U.S. economy was in the throes of what is usually referred to as the Great Depression, and coal production and agriculture were both experiencing the effects of the slumping economy. The farms in the area were mostly small- to medium-size dairy operations. The farmers were under financial duress because they could not sell their milk in the local area for a price to cover their cost of production. There were better market opportunities in Pittsburgh and Harrisburg, Pennsylvania, but their transportation costs put their "landed cost" at a disadvantage with dairy farmers in Erie, Pennsylvania, and Eastern Ohio. The Edwards brothers were not farmers but rather entrepreneurs and owned several tanker trucks, which could be used for hauling milk. They decided that instead of using their equipment to haul milk to potential markets for very meager profits they would start a cheese processing operation in Clearfield. They had some savings and were able to borrow money from The First National Bank of Clearfield, which was still solvent. Their grandfather who had emigrated from Switzerland was knowledgeable about cheese production and processing helped them get started. They purchased milk from local farmers with lenient payment terms and started a successful venture. World War II presented some challenges in terms of labor supply and fuel rationing, but they survived and prospered by hiring more women and utilizing more rail service.

The next major hurdle was the government-subsidized cheese producers in Canada selling into the Pennsylvania market in the 1980s. Tom Powers, CEO of the Clearfield Cheese Company, with the assistance of two of his key executives, Andy Reisinger (CIO) and Sandy Knight (CSCO), developed a plan, which included improving their supply chain operation efficiency by lowering inventory levels with better forecasting and procurement practices. They expanded their product offerings by adding cottage cheese, sour cream, and yogurt. They also purchased a Canadian company in 1995 because they their Canadian sales were growing. This lowered their costs to serve the growing Canadian market and made them much more competitive in Canada. This was an important step to make them a global company.

Current Situation

Their board of directors in 2014 was delighted with their cash flow and profits. However, they were concerned about future growth because of changing diets of many consumers who had become more concerned about consuming milk-based products. The company had already added low-fat versions of the major products but the board members were concerned that this would not be sufficient to sustain their growth and profits. Some possibilities that were suggested for consideration included (1) setting up a new company to produce non-dairy-based products such as almond milk and other alternatives to cow milk. All the new products would have a healthy "spin" such as the White

Wave company; (2) market expansion of their existing product lines into Mexico and Central America; (3) expanding their current product offerings by adding ice cream, high-end cheeses made from goat and sheep milk, and high-end milk-based candy; and (4) a combination of one or more of these alternatives.

1. Evaluate all three alternatives offering pros and cons of each.
2. What would you recommend? Why?

CASE 1-2
KEMS LLP

Industry Overview

The chemical industry is diverse and complex, and its supply chains reflect this complexity and diversity, particularly when you consider the array of products produced from chemicals. Everything from food storage containers to paint, shampoo to lawn care products, and even food products are based upon chemicals. Almost every product found on the shelves of homes and offices start with chemicals. Chemical supply chains handle all of these products plus many, many more. Some of these products, especially the raw materials like corrosives and acids, need special handling and unique transportation services as well as special storage facilities to prevent combustion, contamination, and spoilage.

The high-risk nature of the logistics and supply chain services require high safety standards, flexibility, and adaptability. The supply chains are long and complex and require careful and sophisticated management as well as excellent information systems support and, therefore, often require special expertise as that offered by third-party logistics services companies, such as the so-called 3PLs. The chemical companies are effective and efficient in designing and producing chemicals and various chemical products but may need the special services and expertise of the logistics service providers for transporting, storing, and delivering their products to customer locations in a safe and timely manner. Consequently, it is not uncommon for chemical companies to outsource all or part of their logistics and supply chain needs to one or more of the available service providers.

Company Background

KEMS LLP is a chemical logistics services company located in Chester, Pennsylvania, a suburb of Philadelphia. The company was founded in 1995 by four former managers of a large and diverse, asset-based logistics service provider. The four founders saw an opportunity to specialize in offering service for chemical and related products without investing in transportation equipment or storage facilities. Essentially, they planned to operate as what is called a third-party logistics company (3PL) that would offer services to small- to medium-size companies in the chemical industry. The actual transportation and related services were purchased from asset-based service providers such as motor carriers and railroads. KEMS managed these services for their customers and provided them with efficient and effective deliveries. All four partners had solid but complimentary experience, which enabled them to get started quickly. In addition, they were able to purchase part of the business from their former owners with very favorable terms, which provided a solid basis for their growth.

The first 10 years were challenging as they tried to establish a foothold and an identity in the marketplace. They experimented with a portfolio of services offerings that included consulting, telemetrics to measure available stock levels in tanks on a remote basis, and selected educational services. They were very flexible and operated leanly that allowed them to adjust to the ups and downs of the very competitive marketplace. By 2005, they had established an identity and expanded their service offerings by leasing and purchasing rail tank cars to provide a more competitive service; partnered with a large computer and software company to offer Transportation Management Services (TMS) to coordinate shipments and lower transportation costs. They also purchased a small European company that offered similar services in the EU countries to provide a footprint there and to expand their global operations. KEMS has now successfully integrated the EU company and retained most their employees.

Future Expansion and Opportunities

The four partners are considering expanding their geographic reach either in North America (Canada and/or Mexico) or in South America. One of their advisory board members recommends considering other bulk liquid products that are less risky such as vegetable oil and other liquid agricultural products and stick to their current market area.

1. Based upon the information in this chapter and other sources at your disposal, evaluate potential global geographic opportunities for their consideration and make appropriate recommendations.
2. Would you support the recommendation of the advisory board member? Why or why not?

CHAPTER

2 TRANSPORTATION AND THE ECONOMY

Learning Objectives

After reading this chapter, you should be able to do the following:

- Understand the importance of transportation to the economic vitality of the United States and other countries and regions and why it is probably our most important industry.
- Appreciate the role and contributions of transportation systems to the economic development of countries or regions.
- Understand how transportation of goods and people impacts the social and political dimensions of an economy or region.
- Appreciate the historical role of transportation from an economic, social, and political perspective.
- Discuss the impact that improved transportation has upon land values and economic development.
- Understand how transportation affects the price of goods, services, and market areas.
- Appreciate the function and scope of transportation in advanced and developed economies.

Introduction

Transportation is a pervasive and extremely vital function in all industrialized economies. Transportation systems provide the necessary critical links between producers and consumers both domestically and globally. The citizens of industrialized countries are dependent upon transportation systems to move products from distant locations where they are produced to markets where they are needed and where they can be sold and consumed. An efficient and effective transportation system is essential for businesses to produce and sell products and services. It has long been recognized that one of the critical ingredients for underdeveloped countries to improve economically is the need to invest in transportation infrastructure. This investment is frequently referred to as social capital, that is, society as a whole is the beneficiary of such investment because of the economic benefits associated with new businesses, higher wages, more jobs, and social benefits associated with mobility, improved educational systems, and communication. Even developed countries like the United States need to continually evaluate the adequacy of their transportation infrastructure to insure that the system needs of the economy.

Transportation is one of the requirements of a developed economy because it can bring order out of chaos. It reaches and touches every phase and facet of our well-being. Viewed in totality from a historical, economic, social, and political perspective, it is the most important industry in the world. Without transportation, you could not operate a retail store or win a war. The more complex society becomes and the more developed the economy, the more indispensable is the transportation system.

Unfortunately, the transportation system is frequently taken for granted, and the benefits that accrue to the economy from the transportation system are not fully appreciated. Therefore, it would be appropriate at this point to discuss the many benefits of improved transportation. This chapter will investigate the historical, economic, environmental, social, and political impact of a well-designed and improved transportation system.

Up and Down with the Big Muddy

The Mississippi River has been an important avenue of commerce for several centuries in the United States. It has been referred to as the Big Muddy by many individuals because of the color of the water and the amount of soil that washes down the river from northern states, especially during the spring, and is deposited in the so-called deltas near the Gulf of Mexico. That dimension of the River may be important for agricultural and other important reasons, but from the perspective of the economy, it indicates a challenge to utilizing the River as a major transportation artery because flooding and droughts change the channel depths. "The Big Muddy" is an important component of our transportation system and especially for the Inland River System since the volume of traffic (672.5 million tons in 2011) is very significant.

Like many parts of the transportation system, there is a tendency to take the Mississippi River for granted and not recognize its impact on the economy until there is an obstacle to navigation on the River. Some potential obstacles are probably obvious to many people such as flooding or freezing, but one that is not as obvious to many is a long-term draught, which lowers the depth of the river. The newer, larger vessels to be discussed in Chapter 8 require deeper channels. In normal times, these larger vessels are an important dimension of the efficiency of river transportation, but when the river is low, they are stymied. Also, the solution is basically in the "hands of Mother Nature." Flooding is frequently a problem for a shorter duration, but a serious draught is usually more long term and requires seeking alternative means of transportation.

The recent major variation in weather patterns (flooding in 2011 and draught in 2012) have been a growing problem for shippers and the barge lines. Shippers of harvested agricultural products like corn and wheat do not want to be caught without service to bring their product to market. Low water levels will halt barge service and/or mandate reduction in the loads that the barges can carry. The higher costs by alternate types of carriers, rail or motor carrier, can reduce farm profits significantly. The lesson here is that efficient and reliable transportation service is a critical ingredient for all segments of our economy. Shippers that use the Mississippi River System regularly need to have alternative shipping plans in place to protect their businesses from the vagaries of the river.

Historical Significance

The importance of transportation becomes more apparent when one understands its historical role. The growth of civilizations is associated with the development of transportation systems. For example, the strengths of ancient Egypt demonstrated how one form of transportation, water, could become the foundation for a great society. The Nile River helped to integrate Egypt. It provided a means to transport Egyptian goods, a way to communicate, and a method for Egyptian soldiers to move to defend their country. The Nile River, like all transportation systems, also affected the society's political and cultural development as people traveled and communicated.

A transportation system can help create a social structure because people traveling or living within the bounds of a particular transportation network will tend to share ideas and experiences. Eventually a society develops, with somewhat unified political opinions, cultural ideals, and educational methods. However, methods of transportation also can disrupt societies. People may become alienated from a distant central government system. For example, America's succession from Great Britain is partly attributable to localized transportation systems developing in the 13 colonies. Transportation to and from Britain was slow and inefficient, and American families could lead better lives trading among themselves without having to pay duties (taxes) to the government of King George III. As the colonies developed into a separate economic system, political and cultural attitudes that were unique to America prevailed, which led to alienation with Great Britain and eventually to the Revolutionary War.

The United States continued to grow in tandem with its transportation networks in the 19th century. Few families thought to move west without first knowing that explorers had blazed trails and found rivers suitable for travel. The **Erie Canal**, steamboats, early turnpikes, and the early rail system were developed to meet the economic and social needs of the growing nation. Table 2-1 provides an overview of transport developments in the United States.[1]

Transportation also plays a major role in **national defense**, which has been recognized by governments. The Roman Empire built its great system of roads, primarily for military purposes, but they had an overall positive economic impact. Sir Winston Churchill pointed out that transport was the underlying basis for all that could be accomplished in effectively fighting a war. In other words, transportation was a critical ingredient for success on the battlefield. United States requirements for national defense have been a major reason for a number of important transportation projects. As indicated previously, under the Eisenhower Administration, enabling legislation was passed for a National System of Interstate and Defense Highways. This highway system was envisioned as being a system of superhighways connecting the states and their major centers within the states, which could enhance our ability to defend against enemy attack. The economic and social benefits of the Interstate Highway System have far

TABLE 2-1 U.S. Transport Developments

YEAR	DEVELOPMENT	YEAR	DEVELOPMENT
1774	Lancaster Turnpike: first toll road—Pennsylvania	1940	National Transportation Policy Statement
1804	Fulton's steamboat—Hudson River, New York	1961	Manned space flights begin
1825	Erie Canal: first canal—New York	1970	Amtrak established
1830	Baltimore and Ohio Railroad begins service	1976	Conrail established
1838	Steamship service—Atlantic Ocean	1978	Act to deregulate airlines passed
1865	First pipeline—Pennsylvania	1980	Act to deregulate motor carriers and Staggers Rail Act
1866	Completion of transcontinental rail link	1982	Double Stack Rail container service initiated
1869	Bicycles introduced—United States	1986	Conrail profitable and sold by government
1887	First daily rail service coast to coast	1990	Amended National Transportation Policy Statement
1887	Federal regulation of transportation begins	1995	ICC succeeded by Surface Transportation Board
1903	First successful airplane flight—Wright Brothers	1998	Internet applications widely used in transportation
1904	Panama Canal opens	1999	Norfolk Southern and CSX acquire Conrail
1919	Transcontinental airmail service by U.S. Post Office begins	2002	Protective action against Terrorist attacks after 9/11
1925	Kelly Act: airmail contract to private companies	2002	Airline industry enters decade of restructuring
1927	Lindbergh solo flight—New York to Paris	2014	Political disputes of infrastructure funding

exceeded the defense contribution. Generally, the expenditures on air transport infrastructure are based primarily on military and political consideration as opposed to economic benefits, but the economic benefits usually outweigh the political and military benefits over the longer run.[2]

In the 21st century, transportation systems will face significant challenges and problems because of global competition, government budget constraints, increasing demand from special interest groups such as senior citizens, infrastructure challenges, sustainability issues, and energy costs. The pattern of trade that helps to drive transportation requirements is changing more quickly and becoming more complex because of the dynamic global environment and the changing economic base in the United States.

Economics of Transportation

Transportation touches the lives of all U.S. citizens and citizens in other areas of the world. It affects their economic well-being, their safety, their access to other people and places, and the quality of their environment. When the transportation system does not function well, it is a source of great personal frustration and perhaps economic loss. But when the transportation system performs well it provides opportunity and rewards for everyone. Understanding the basic fundamentals of transportation economics will provide important insights into the role of transportation in the economic viability of a country, and also the businesses and other organizations that provide the output, revenue, and income that really drives an economy.

Demand for Transportation

The economic growth of the U.S. economy, as well as the economies of most industrialized countries, is attributable, in part, to the benefits derived from mass production and the associated division or specialization of labor, which enables mass production to occur. Specialization of labor and production can result in an oversupply of goods at one location and unmet demand for these goods in another area. For example, a large food processing plant in Hanover, Pennsylvania, can produce far more product than can be consumed in the immediate market area and will need to sell its output in distant markets to take advantage of the scale of their plant operations. Transportation plays an important role in helping to bridge the supply and demand gap inherent in the mass production oriented approach.

The interrelationship between transportation and mass production points out the dependency of our global economy upon transportation. As geographical areas begin to specialize in the production of particular goods and/or services, they are relying more upon the other regions to produce the additional goods and services that they need or desire. We depend upon transportation to move these goods and provide these services in an efficient and effective manner. Like the citizens of most industrialized countries, U.S. citizens, as individuals, are not self-sufficient. On a global scale, countries recognize their international interdependencies. United States supplies many countries with a variety of agricultural products, manufactured products, and other types of services. While other countries provide the United States with raw materials, other agricultural products and additional manufactured products. For example, the United States is dependent upon the Middle East, South America, and Canada for energy production. Even though the United States produces energy, the amount produced is not sufficient to provide what is needed. Other countries usually rely on the United States to provide a variety of manufactured goods such as aircraft, clothing, and computers to meet their needs. Again, transportation plays a key role in this international or global dependency by providing the ability to match supply and demand requirements on a global basis. The ability of countries to trade among themselves and to efficiently move goods is a key element in the success of global development.

Passenger Demand

Similarly, people move from areas where they are currently situated to areas where they desire to be on a daily, weekly, or permanent basis. Transportation also provides the bridging function between supply and demand for people to move from their current places of residence to new locations. As with freight people depend on transportation for mobility. The more developed a society, the more critical an efficient economical passenger system is to its citizens. With today's technology, an executive in Chicago can leave home early on a Monday morning and catch a flight to Los Angeles to attend an early afternoon meeting. At the end of the afternoon that same executive can board a flight to Australia with a continuation to London later in the week. This global work week is possible because of the speed and effectiveness of air transportation, and such travel has become more commonplace in the global economy.

The automobile has been a form of transportation that affects most people's lifestyle, particularly in the United States. The convenience, flexibility, and relatively low cost of automobile travel allow individuals to live in locations distant from where they work. The growth of suburban areas is usually attributable largely to the automobile and the appropriate roadway infrastructure. Although in some areas, efficient mass transportation or passenger transportation is also important. It is not unusual in some areas of the United States for people to travel 20 plus miles one way to go to work. The automobile also enables people to seek medical, dental, and recreational services at various locations throughout their region or even their country.

Rising costs of automobile and air travel occurring as a result of escalating energy, labor, and equipment costs is beginning to cause some change in lifestyles. Instead of traveling longer distances for vacation, some people may stay closer to home or not travel at all. Areas of a country that are highly dependent on tourists have experienced some economic difficulties and a need for changing their economic base. This same set of factors is impacting the movement of freight and causing companies to source or purchase for their supply chains in more contiguous locations. The combination of low labor costs in some global locations and relatively low transportation costs made some distant sources of supply more attractive, but this has been changing with the rising costs of energy and labor mentioned above. Consequently some companies are reevaluating their logistics and transportation networks to determine more optimum, usually closer, locations.

Transport Measurement Units

Transportation demand is essentially a request to move a given weight or amount of cargo a specific distance between two specific points. The demand for transportation is usually measured in weight-distance units for freight and passenger-distance units for people. For freight, the usual demand metric is the **ton-mile**, and for people, the unit is the **passenger-mile**. Both measurements are two dimensional, which can present some challenges for modal comparisons. The ton-mile, for example, is not homogeneous for comparison purposes. The demand for 200 ton-miles of freight transportation could be a movement of 200 tons for one mile, 100 tons for two miles, or 1 ton for 200 miles. In fact, any combination of weight and distance that equals 200 ton-miles would be regarded as the same or equal. In addition, the unique transportation requirements for transportation, equipment, and service may vary among customers for a 200 ton-mile movement. The same unit of demand could have different costs for producing it and different user requirements. However, measuring only the miles moved or the weight moved does not adequately reflect the components of freight transport demand for comparison purposes. The relative importance of transportation movements can best be measured using the ton-mile concept.

Similarly the passenger-mile is a heterogeneous unit. Five hundred passenger-miles could be one passenger moving 500 miles or 500 passengers moving 1 mile. The demand for 500 passenger-miles could be automobile, railroad, or airplane. The demand attributes of the passenger-mile vary from passenger to passenger. However, the passenger-mile is still the single best measure of the relative importance of transportation alternatives. While neither the ton-mile nor the passenger-mile is perfect, they are still the best metric available. As long as we recognize, the challenges inherent in the units when comparisons are made both are useful.

ON THE LINE

"It's a Bird, It's a Plane ... No, It's a Drone"

Remote controlled devices were developed during World War II for use in the military and later, as toys for children and/or as adult entertainment for racing small-scale cars on a table board. Later, remote controlled model airplanes and boats were developed for kids and adults for outdoor use. These remote controlled devices became much more sophisticated and expensive over time. In the last 20 years, other, more commercial, uses were envisioned for these pilotless aircraft, directed by remote control, in agriculture and safety and security including traffic control. The military continued their development of remote controlled land and air devices after World War II. The ability to attach powerful, small cameras greatly enhanced the commercial and military uses of remote controlled devices.

The use of the term *drone* became the most widely used descriptor for airborne devices and has become a part of our vernacular. The origin of the term is associated with the name of the male bee, which emits an engine sounding humming or buzzing. Also, male bees are effectively disposable after they accomplish their single "mission." The military drone was viewed as less costly to develop and to replace in case of loss and also to minimize human casualties.

When Amazon announced their intention in 2013 to experiment with the use of drones for the delivery of selected items in the San Francisco area, it attracted a lot of attention from doubters and proponents. The interest of Amazon in drone delivery should not be surprising to the reader at this point. As has been pointed out, transportation provides many economic and social benefits including accessibility and connectivity. The selective use of drones to improve effectiveness and/or efficiency for transportation service offers some interesting opportunities given their flexibility and lack of an elaborate infrastructure for support.

More recently DHL, a German parcel delivery company, which competes with UPS and FEDEX, announced that they were going initiate drone delivery of medication and drugs on a routine basis to a remote German Island (Juist) in the North Sea. Unlike Amazon and Google who have been stymied by regulatory challenges in the United States, DHL was able to get approval because of the cooperation of several government agencies to allow regular service. Amazon is testing a similar service to remote locations in Canada and Google in Australia. There is widespread interest in these new services for future development to other remote areas and to locations, which have similar or analogous challenges, for example, traffic challenges.

The demand for transportation can be examined at different levels of aggregation. Aggregate demand for transportation is the sum of the individual demands for freight or for passengers. In addition, aggregate demand is the sum of the demand for transportation via different modes or the aggregate demand for a particular mode. Table 2-2 shows the allocation of aggregate passenger-miles, and Table 2-3 shows the allocation of aggregate ton-miles via different modes of transportation. The dominance of the private auto for passengers is clearly demonstrated in Table 2-2, but note the decline in 2006, which is probably indicative of a downward trend as individuals react to higher fuel prices. Table 2-3 is interesting in light of the discussion above about the ton-mile measurement unit. Motor carriers account for 75 to 80 percent of the individual shipments, but their shorter hauls and lower shipment weights place them second to rail in terms of ton-miles. Surprisingly, pipelines are close in terms of ton-miles to the motor carrier even though they carry a very limited array of products. Again, the ton-mile unit

TABLE 2-2 Passenger Miles: 2007–2010 (millions)

	AIR	RAIL	BUS	LIGHT DUTY VEHICLES
2007	607,564	34989	307,753	4,341,984
2008	583,292	36142	314,278	4,248,783
2009	551,741	36044	305,014	3,625,598
2010	564,790	35774	292,319	3,645,368

Source: U.S. Department of Transportation, Bureau of Transportation Statistics, *Pocket Guide to Transportation*, 2013, Washington, D.C.

TABLE 2-3 U.S. Ton-Miles of Freight (millions)

YEAR	AIR	TRUCK	RAIL	WATER	PIPELINE
1990	9,064	1,707,373	1,064,408	833,544	1,041,044
2000	14,983	2,326,063	1,546,319	645,799	967,819
2005	15,745	2,453,347	1,733,324	591,277	865,700
2006	15,361	2,405,811	1,855,897	561,629	860,766
2007	15,141	2,495,786	1,819,626	553,151	855,831
2008	13,774	2,752,658	1,729,734	520,521	981,323
2009	12,027	2,449,509	1,582,092	477,122	947,252
2010	12,541	2,512,429	1,706,505	502,212	955,986
2011	12,134	2,643,567	1,725,634	499,748	1,018,082

Source: U.S. Department of Transportation, Bureau of Transportation Statistics, *National Transportation Statistics*, Table 1-50, July 2014.

enhances their importance in this comparison. Overall, the ton-mile and passenger-mile metrics are useful modal comparisons or modal splits.

Modal split is a useful analytical tool for the study of transportation because it divides the total transportation market for passenger and freight movements according to use or volume by the major modes of transportation. Highway transportation (public and private) dominates the movement of people in the United States and represents more than 77 percent of passenger-miles traveled in the United States. The proportion of highway travel decreased slightly over the past three decades due to growth in airline travel and higher fuel prices. Deregulation of airline service in the late 1970s brought about an increase in travel options and services for the traveling public. During this period, the relative level of airfares did not keep pace with the overall inflation level. As a result, air travel became more convenient and relatively cheaper for long-distance travel.

The freight intercity modal split is dominated by trucks, with about 45 percent of the ton-miles in 2011. Railroads declined in relative share after World War II but have increased in share since 1990 because of fuel prices and other factors. Motor carriers have also increased their relative share of the total ton-mile market after 1980, but their share has remained relatively stable since 2000. Railroads typically move bulk, low-value commodities such as grain, coal, ore, and chemicals for longer distances, which impacts their ton-miles share. In recent years, rail traffic by container, which transports relatively higher-value finished goods, has increased. The air mode, while more visible, still handles less than one percent of the total ton-miles in the United States. Each of these modes will be accorded more detailed analysis in subsequent chapters (Chapters 5 through 8).

In recent years, the economy has expanded at a faster rate than the demand for freight transportation. The increase in global trade is one of the reasons for this phenomenon. For example, in the past, a domestic steel firm usually purchased transportation service for inbound raw materials (ore, lime, coal) and the movement of the outbound finished goods to the customer domestically. At the very minimum, this involved four different movements. Today the steel may be imported, requiring one domestic movement between the port and the customer. Even if the steel is being used in the economy, fewer transportation moves are involved in making it available to the customer.

As stated previously, good transportation spurs economic development by giving mobility and lower **landed cost** to production factors, which permits scale economies and increased efficiency. Good transportation enlarges the area that consumers and industries can draw on for resources and products. Good transportation expands the area to which a given plant or warehouse can distribute its products economically, and the resulting specialization and scale economies provide a wider choice of products for consumers at a lower cost. The overall economic importance and significance of improved transportation systems need to be understood and appreciated.

Demand Elasticity

Demand elasticity refers to the sensitivity of customers to changes in price. If customers are sensitive to price, a price reduction should increase the demand for the item and the total revenue should also usually increase. An increase in price will have the opposite effect-less revenue and a reduction in sales. If customers are not sensitive to a change in price, we consider that demand to be inelastic because a price reduction will result in a small relative increase in the quantity demanded, and the total revenues will decrease. In mathematical terms, demand elasticity is the ratio of the percentage change in the quantity demanded to the percentage change in price or elasticity equals percentage change in quantity divided by percentage change in price. If demand is elastic, the quantity demanded changes more than the change in price, and the elasticity coefficient is greater than one. Conversely, a product or service said to be price inelastic or insensitive to price changes, if the quantity demanded changes less than the change in price or in other words, the coefficient is less than one.

$$\text{Elasticity} = \%\text{ change in quantity}/\%\text{ change in price}$$

In general, aggregate demand for transportation is **inelastic**. Freight rate reductions will not dramatically increase the demand for freight transportation because transportation costs generally represent, in the aggregate, less than 4 percent of a product's landed cost, and the demand is a derived demand (to be discussed subsequently). Substantial rate reductions would be required for a meaningful increase in the demand for the product and consequently, the demand for transportation of that product. On the other hand, if we consider specific modes of transportation or specific carriers, the demand is generally elastic or price sensitive. The modal share of the aggregate demand is, in part, determined by the rates charged. Reductions in rates charged by a particular mode will usually result in increases in the volume of freight by that mode, other things being equal. This assumes that the mode that reduced the rate is physically capable of transporting the freight.

For example, long-haul transportation of new automobiles was dominated by motor carriers in the 1960s and into the 1970s. The railroads developed a new railcar specifically designed to transport new automobiles. This new railcar enabled the railroads to improve efficiency and reduce the rates that they charged for hauling automobiles while also improving some of the service characteristics of the movements. The percentage of new automobiles hauled by railroads increased with the introduction of the new railcar and the lower rates, and the share of intercity ton-miles of new automobiles transported by motor carriers decreased. Today, motor carriers are usually used primarily to transport new automobiles shorter distances from rail yards to dealerships. Also, when plant locations are close to the points where new cars are needed or where dealers are located, motor transportation is frequently used.

For modal shipments or for a specific carrier within that mode, demand may also have service elasticity. Assuming no price changes, the mode or specific carrier demand is often sensitive to changes in service levels provided by competing carriers. For example, many air passengers monitor the on time service levels of the various air carriers and when possible will select the air carrier that provides the best on time transportation service. Transit time and service reliability have become much more important to freight movement during the last several decades, as shippers have become increasingly aware of the impact of carrier service on inventory levels and customer service. Consequently, higher cost service providers such as USP and Federal Express now move larger-sized shipments because of their superior direct service and some of the ancillary logistics services that they provide.

Freight Transportation Demand

The demand for freight transportation is usually dependent upon the demand for a product in another location. As indicated previously, specialization and mass production create a need for market expansion at more distance locations, which gives rise to increased demand for freight transportation. In this section, attention is given to the characteristics of freight transportation demand.

Derived Demand The demand to transport a product in a given location usually depends on the existence of demand to consume or use that product in the distant location. Freight is not usually transported to another location unless there is a need for the product. Thus, the demand for freight transportation is generally referred to as a **derived demand**. Sometimes it is also referred to as a secondary as opposed to a primary demand. Derived demand is not unique to transportation since the demand for many raw materials is dependent upon the demand for the finished products, which are produced from these raw materials. Figure 2-1 illustrates the derived demand nature of freight transportation. If a supply widget is available at the production site, City A, widgets will not be moved or transported to City C because there is no demand for widgets at City C. However, there is a demand for widgets at City B. Because of the demand for 100 widgets in City B, there is a demand for transportation of 100 widgets from City A to City B.

The derived demand characteristics implied that freight transportation would not be effected by transport carrier actions. As noted above, this assumption is true for the demand for transportation at the aggregate level. For example, if a freight carrier lowers the rate to zero for moving high-tech personal computers from the United States to a developing nation, this free transportation may not materially change the demand for personal computers in a developing nation since it is a derived demand. The demand for personal computers is dependent on the educational level of the citizens, electrical availability, and the price of the computer itself. However, at the disaggregate level

FIGURE 2-1 Derived Demand for Freight Transportation

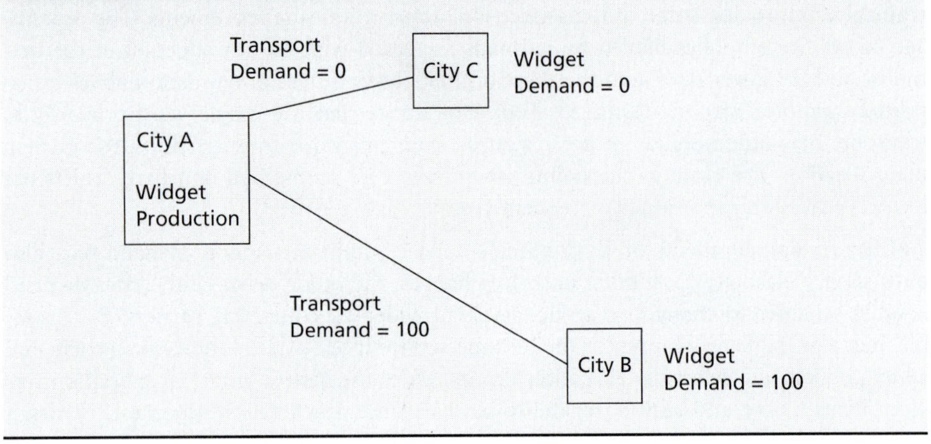

(modal carrier or specific traffic lane) the rates charged for the service level provided usually influence the demand for the product and the demand to transport the product. The impact on product demand considers the value of the service provided to the user of the product, which is discussed in the next section.

Value of Service **Value of service** considers the impact of transportation costs and service on the demand for the product. Lower transportation costs can cause a shift in demand for transportation among the modes and the specific carriers. It can also affect the demand to transport freight over a specific traffic lane where several carriers are competing for the traffic. The impact of transportation costs on the demand for a product at a given location usually focuses on what the landed cost of the product. The landed cost includes the cost of the product at the source, the cost to transport the product to its destination, plus any ancillary expenses such as insurance or loading costs. If the landed cost of the product is lower than that of other sources, there usually will be a demand for that product and also for the transportation of that product from its origin point.

For example, in Figure 2-2, a manufacturer of bicycle tires located in Chicago is competing in Boston with local producers. For the Chicago bicycle tire manufacturer to be competitive, the landed costs of the tire must be lower than the cost of the local manufacturer's tire prices. Assume that the Boston manufacturers have a cost of $4.00 per tire, whereas, the Chicago manufacturer can produce the same tire for $3.00 because of its inherent advantages in labor productivity. As long as the transportation costs per tire

FIGURE 2-2 Demand and Landed Cost

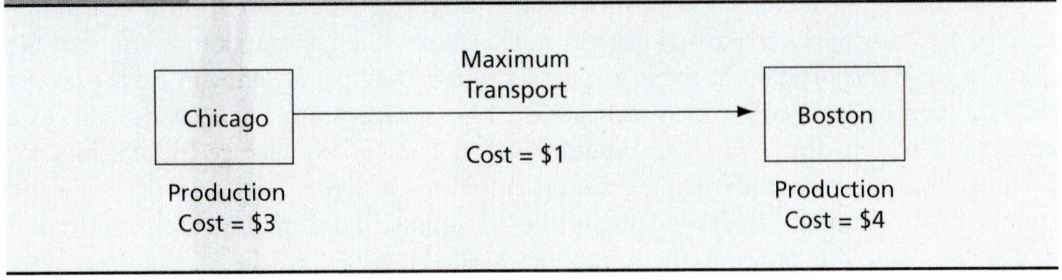

from Chicago to Boston are less than \$1, the Chicago tire maker will have a landed cost advantage and a demand for the Chicago tire will probably exist in Boston (assuming the quality is equal to that of the locally produced tires). Conversely, if transportation costs exceed a \$1 per tire, Boston consumers will not likely purchase tires from Chicago.

The **landed cost** also determines the extent of the market for business. The greater the distance the product is shipped, usually the higher the landed cost. At some distance from the product's source, the landed cost usually becomes prohibitive to the buyer, and there will be no demand for that product at that point. Also, the landed cost usually determines the extent of the market between two competing companies. To illustrate this concept, Figure 2-3 presents an example of two producers located 200 miles apart. Producer P has a production cost of \$50 per unit and transportation cost of \$.60 per unit per mile. Producer S also has a production cost of \$50 per unit but a transportation cost of \$.50 per unit per mile. The extent of the market between the two producers is the point at which their landed costs of P is equal to the landed cost of S:

FIGURE 2-3 Extent of Market Area

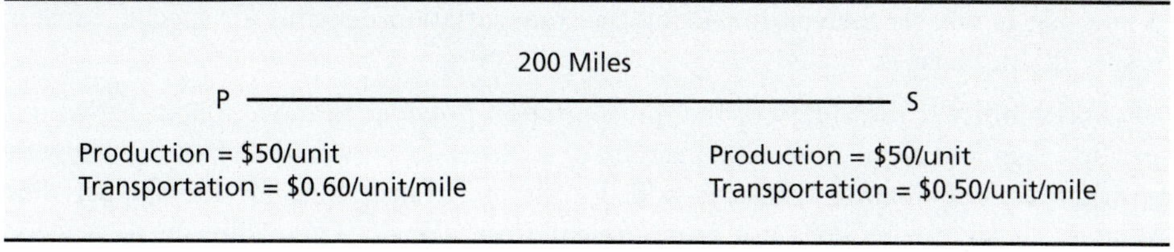

$$\text{LC (P)} = \text{LC (S)}$$
$$\text{Production Cost (P)} + \text{Transportation Cost (P)} = \text{Production Cost (S)} + \text{Transporation Cost (S)}$$
$$\$50 + \$0.60(x) = \$50 + \$0.50(200 - x)$$
$$\$0.60(x) + \$0.50(x) = \$50 + \$100 - \$50$$
$$\$1.10(x) = \$100$$
$$x = 90.9 \text{ miles from P}$$

Solving the equation for x, P's market area will extend 90.9 miles from its plant and x will have a market area that extends about 109 miles from its facility. Just examining the numbers, one would conclude that the company located at S with the transportation costs of \$.50 per unit would have an advantage, but this formula will allow a precise calculation of the distance of the market areas between the two companies.

Service Components of Freight Demand

Shippers of freight have varying service requirements for their transportation providers, as indicated previously. These service requirements range from specific pickup times to communication requirements. The service demands affect the cost of the service provided. The transportation service characteristics to be discussed include transit time, reliability, accessibility, capability, and security.

Service Characteristics of Freight Demand[3] **Transit time** can affect the level of inventory held by the shipper and the receiver as well as the associated carrying cost of holding that inventory. The longer the transit time, the higher the inventory levels required and the higher the carrying costs. Also, transit times impact the inventory costs in the overall supply chain. For example, the supply of clothing produced in the Pacific Rim might require 45 days transit time from manufacturer's shipping point to a specific retail store. While the clothes are in transit for 45 days, either a buyer or a seller incurs the cost of financing the inventory for the 45 days. If the transit time is reduced to 15 days by use of air transportation, the in-transit inventory financing costs will be reduced by two-thirds. Also, longer the transit time increases the potential cost for stock outs. Using the Pacific Rim example above, a stock out of clothing at the retail store could mean a maximum of 45 days without inventory with sales and the related profits lost during this period. Shorter transit times reduce the potential losses from stock outs.

Reliability refers to the consistency of transit times. Meeting pickup and delivery schedules enables shippers and receivers to optimize service levels and minimize stock out costs. Unreliable transit time requires the freight receiver to either increase inventory levels to guard against stock out conditions or incur stock out related costs. Reliable service directly affects the level of modal and specific carrier demand, that is, a shipper may shift from an unreliable carrier to one that is more reliable and service is more consistent. The customer may switch from a supplier who provides unreliable delivery service to one that is reliable thereby impacting the transportation demand for specific carriers or specific traffic lanes.

Accessibility is the ability of the transportation provider to move freight between a specific origin and destination. The inability of a carrier to provide direct service between an origin and destination results in added costs and transit time for the shipper. For example, an air carrier does not move freight from Toledo, Ohio, directly to Angers, France. First the freight is moved by motor carrier from Toledo to Detroit, Michigan, and then flown to Paris where it will be moved to Angers by either motor or rail. When a carrier cannot provide direct service between the shipping and receiving points, it usually requires additional transportation service by motor carrier, which adds to the transit time and the total cost. Motor carriers have a distinct advantage over other carriers in terms of accessibility in most countries.

The ability of the carrier to provide special service requirements is the essence of **capability**. Based on the physical and marketing characteristics of the freight, shippers might have unique demands for the transportation, facilities, and communication—for example, products requiring controlled temperature and necessitate the use of a refrigerated vehicle; time sensitive shipments that need state-of-the-art communications systems to monitor their exact location and arrival times; or even the cubic capacity for a large piece of equipment. Marketing considerations might dictate that the carriers provide freight consolidation and break-bulk facilities to lower freight costs and transit time. These are just a few of the many and varied demands placed on the transportation service providers. Their capability to provide these required services are often instrumental in getting the business.

Finally, **security** is concerned with the safety of the goods in transit. Shipments that are damaged or lost in transit can cause increased cost in the areas of inventory and/or stock outs. A damaged shipment will usually not be accepted and the buyer faces the possibility of losing a sale or stopping the production process. Increasing inventory levels to protect against stock out costs relating from a damaged shipment causes increased inventory carrying costs. Table 2-4 provides a summary to the transportation service components of freight demand. As indicated previously, the focus upon supply chain management has raised the awareness of shippers to the importance of carrier service characteristics to total cost and to customer service.

TABLE 2-4 Service Components of Freight Demand

SERVICE COMPONENT	USER IMPLICATION
Transit Time	Inventory, Stockout Costs
Reliability	Inventory, Stockout Costs
Accessibility	Transit Time, Transportation Cost
Capability	Meets Products' Unique Physical and Marketing Requirements
Security	Inventory, Stockout Costs

TRANSPORTATION **PROFILE**

"The Mailman May Ring Twice"

The U.S. Post Office has been plagued with operating deficits for over a decade. As a government organization that charges for its services, it is expected to break even. There are several factors that account for this situation including their expected contribution to the retirement fund for past and present employees. Their funding challenge is broader than the retirement issue since their revenues have been insufficient in spite of increases in postal rates. The underlying cause is the steady decline in the volume of first class mail over the last two decades. Historically, the revenue from first-class mail provided support for the other classes of mail and other services. Technology has been the root cause of the decline in mail volume and associated revenue flow. Interestingly, the start of this situation was the development of relatively inexpensive fax machines for use in offices and in the home. The transmission of the letter or document was almost instantaneous and there was a minimal cost. The fax machine was used primarily for business and other commercial documents. It also impacted Federal Express that was faster and more reliable than Post Office and their overnight delivery of letters and documents had initially been an important revenue source for them. The final blow was the development and use of the Internet by not only businesses but also the general public. The Internet provided a substitute for letter writing and even personal cards, and subsequently a variety of print media, which also has impacted mail volume.

The infrastructure of the U.S. Post Office is essentially ubiquitous since it touches almost every household and place of business in the United States. At the urging of many individuals over a long period, the Post Office has finally started to strategically analyze possible uses for its core function of delivery throughout the country much like FEDEX did 20 plus years ago when fax service became available. The Post Office is now exploring a cooperative venture with Amazon to deliver package groceries to individual homes and places of business in the San Francisco area much like they do with other items sold by Amazon. Their intention is to seek relationships with other retail chains to provide home delivery on a scalable, low cost basis. This is the latest step in a series of aggressive steps to compete more effectively with other delivery companies. These initiatives are designed to provide much needed revenue to stop their losses, and exploit their core, strategic competency of delivery. But not just mail.

Value of Goods

Transportation systems help determine the economic value of products. A simple model will serve to illustrate this point. Consider a certain commodity that is desired in one location, provided it is offered below a certain price. In Figure 2-4, this commodity is

FIGURE 2-4 Landed Cost with Old and New Transport Systems

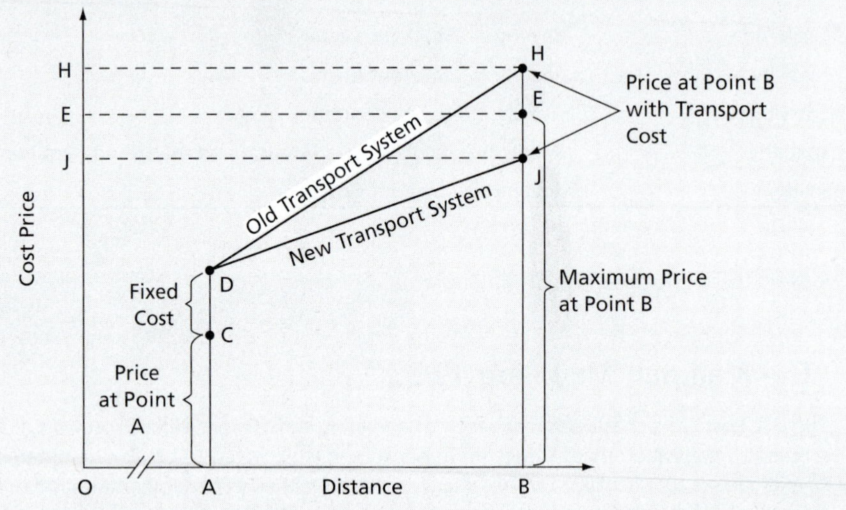

Source: Adapted from Morlok, Edward, *Introduction to Transportation, Engineering, and Planning*, New York: McGraw-Hill, 1978, p. 33.

produced at point A and costs OC at the point of production. The community that needs the commodity, located at point B, is the distance AB from A. The maximum price that people will pay for the commodity is shown on the vertical axis as OE, at community B.

If the original, inefficient transport system is used, moving the commodity from A to B will cost CH. The CD portion of the cost line is known as the fixed cost, and the DH portion of the line is the cost per mile (a variable cost) or slope of the line. With the inefficient system, the total cost at B is OH, a price greater than the maximum cost or price limit (OE) in community B.

Assume the transport system is improved, and the cost per mile or slope is reduced, and the transportation variable cost line becomes DJ. Now, the cost at community B becomes OJ, which is below the maximum cost or price limit of OE. The market for the commodity produced at A will be expanded to community B. The efficiency of the new system enables the producer located at Point A to expand their market area to include B, which is a value-added service.

Place Utility The reduction in transportation costs, illustrated above, between points A and B gives the commodity **place utility** or **place value**. In the less efficient system, the goods will have no value at B because they could not be sold at the market price. The more efficient method of transportation creates place utility; since the goods can now be sold at point B for a competitive price.

Reductions in transportation costs permit market areas to purchase products from more distant suppliers that might otherwise only be produced locally at a higher price. The reduction in transportation cost is actually greater for longer distances than for short ones because of the fixed charges. If a supplier can cover the transportation cost in their price range, an increase in the distance over which this given amount will cover the transport of goods will increase the market area of the product in an even greater ratio.

FIGURE 2-5 Lardner's Relevant Areas

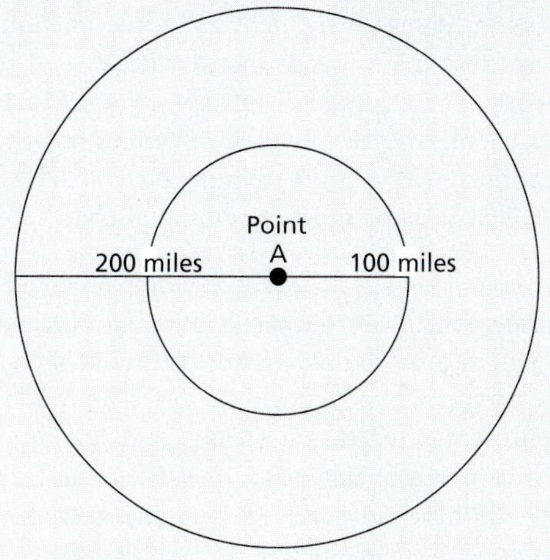

Dionysius Lardner, an early transportation economist, referred to this phenomenon as the **Law of Squares** in Transportation and Trade (also known as **Lardner's Law**). As shown in Figure 2-5, a producer at Point A can afford to transport a product 100 miles and meet competitive, laid landed costs. The boundary of the relevant market area is shown by the circumference of the smaller circle. If transportation cost is cut in half, the same sum will now transport the supplier goods for twice the distance, that is, 200 miles. Now the market boundary is shown by the circumference of the larger circle. The relevant market area increased four times in size when the radius doubled from 100 to 200 miles.

Time Utility The concept of **time utility** is closely aligned to that of place utility. The demand for a particular commodity may only exist during certain periods of time. If a product arrives in a market at a time when there is no demand for it, then it possesses no value. For example, the demand for Halloween costumes exists during a specific time of the year. After Halloween passes, these goods cannot be sold because they have little or no value in the market. Effective transportation can create time utility by ensuring that products arrive at the proper locations when needed. For example, raw materials for production, fruit, and Christmas toys all need to be at certain locations during specific times, or their value will be diminished. The increased emphasis upon just-in-time and scheduled deliveries as well as lean inventories has heightened the importance of time utility, especially for high value products and emergency shipments. Air freight shipments are an indication of the importance of time utility.

Lardner's Law can also be related to time utility. For example, the speed of transportation might be a governing factor for the transportation of certain perishable products that have a limited shelf life. Assume the small circle in Figure 2-5 represents the current market area based on a specific transportation speed. If the speed were doubled, the potential service area would quadruple.

Quantity Utility In addition, transportation provides **quantity utility** through the assurance that the goods demanded will arrive without damage in the right quantity. Quantity utility has increased in importance in recent years with the increased emphasis placed on minimizing safety stock inventories for both shippers and receivers. Shippers might alter the form of the product to ensure safe transportation or change carriers with repeated failures. Carriers can use special bracing, blocking, and/or strapping, along with temperature control, to help ensure damage-free delivery. Time and quantity utility generally increase in importance as the value of goods increase because of related inventory carrying cost and stock out costs. For example, if the sale of a product is dependent upon its delivery on Tuesday afternoon and it arrives on Wednesday, the potential buyer may reject delivery. If the product had a profit margin of $100.00, the late delivery would cost the seller $100.00 in lost sales or more if additional charges were incurred.

Large-Scale Production Geographic specialization is complemented by large-scale production or **economies of scale**, which are the result of more efficient operations. However, without the use of efficient transportation networks, the advantages of scale economies, production efficiencies, and specialization could be lost. The raw materials for production need to be transported to a manufacturing facility, and the finished products must be transported out of an area at reasonable costs to markets and consumers at acceptable prices. Otherwise, the goods have no value. Geographic specialization assumes that the large-scale production of goods is demanded at different locations. Therefore, an area cannot rely upon its comparative advantage and large-scale production without the use of efficient transportation systems. The more efficient the transportation, the larger the potential market area and the possibility of increased scale economies. Time value can also be important in these situations, especially with perishable and/or seasonal products.

Land Values Transportation improvements that enhance an area's economy also can increase the value of land that is adjacent to or served by the transport improvements because the land becomes more accessible and potentially more useful. Today, the suburban centers provide excellent examples of land areas that have increased in value due to the accessibility that results from efficient transportation systems or infrastructure. Suburbanites can take advantage of nearby city life for work and pleasure and then retire to rural areas via public transportation networks or highways to avoid crowded living conditions. Commuters from Greenwich, Connecticut, to New York City and from Cherry Hill, New Jersey, to Philadelphia all reap both city and suburban benefits as the result of reliable transportation systems. Consequently, the value of the land in the suburban areas has increased to reflect the advantageous lifestyles that the new or improved transportation systems have made possible. The land values within the city are obviously also enhanced by the economic development.

It is important to note that transportation may not always have a positive impact on land values. Noise and air pollution accompanying some networks can decrease adjacent land values. The homeowners who have to bear the burden of pollution can also suffer from overaccessibility. Like most system changes, there are always advantages and disadvantages when transportation improvements are made. Consequently, it is important that a thorough analysis be made of costs, including social costs, and potential benefits before an investment in transportation infrastructure is made. Such cost-benefit analysis is not an exact science, but careful analysis can help preclude a bad investment decision.

Gross Domestic Product (GDP)

Transportation plays a major role in the overall economy of the United States (see Table 2-5). On average, transportation accounts for about 10.2 percent of gross domestic product in the United States compared to housing (17.8%), health care (15.4%), food (9.7%), and education (6.1%). It is safe to say, that transportation is a major component

TABLE 2-5 U.S. Gross Domestic Product by Major Societal Function 2011

FUNCTION	PERCENT OF GDP
Housing	17.8%
Health Care	15.4%
Transportation-related	10.2%
Food	9.7%
Recreation	6.4%
Education	6.1%
Other	34.4%

Source: U.S. Department of Transportation, Bureau of Transportation Statistics, *Pocket Guide to Transportation-2013*, Washington, DC, p. 29.

TABLE 2-6 Average Household Expenditures, 2011

CATEGORY	PERCENT OF HOUSEHOLD EXPENDITURES
Housing	33.8%
Transportation	16.7%
Personal Insurance and pensions	10.9%
Food	13.0%
Health Care	6.7%
Apparel and Services	3.5%
Other	15.4%

Source: U.S. Department of Transportation, Bureau of Transportation Statistics, *Pocket Guide to Transportation-2013*, Washington, DC, p. 30.

of total expenditures in the U.S. economy. If we examine transportation as a component of household expenditures (Table 2-6), it accounts for 18% of household expenditures. Transportation expenditures are only exceeded by Housing (17.8%) and Health Care (15.4%). This is another indication of its importance not only in the economy but also to individual households.

Passenger transportation has been growing in relation to the GDP until recently. Much of this increase was due to the greater use of automobiles and the energy costs associated with operating them. Air travel also accounted for a major part of transportation expenditures in the economy. The U.S. Department of Transportation (DOT) reports that in 2006 airlines accounted for about 10.6% of the total passenger-miles. Travel for business, personal, and vacation purposes are an important activity in the economy. With fuel prices fluctuating but expected to spiral upward again, it is anticipated that private vehicle travel will decrease with a move to public transportation and increased joint ridership.

Environmental Significance

Although transportation provides the economy with numerous benefits, these positive aspects are not without some associated social costs. As indicated previously, transportation sometimes pollutes the environment and exploits natural resources, although many citizens feel that the overall benefits provided by transportation exceed these costs. The environmental challenge of the future will be to accurately assess the relationship between industrial and consumer benefits compared to their construction and external, societal costs associated with transportation improvements.

The Environment

There has been growing concern over the impact of transportation on the environment in recent years, with particular emphasis on air quality (pollution), noise, and water quality. The synergy between the transportation system and the environment is increasingly being investigated by both environmentalists and by transportation planners at all governmental levels. In fact, increasing pressure from the environmentalists has resulted in legal restrictions that help govern the balance between a sound and efficient transportation system and a safe and clean environment. The term, **sustainability**, has become a part of our vocabulary. Transportation is an important part of all supply chains and will receive increasing attention in environmental analyses and discussions. The major change that has occurred is the acceptance by businesses and other organizations that they have an important role to play in helping to make improvements in this area. Perhaps, even more important is a growing recognition that it does not have to be a "zero sum game." In other words, reductions in an organization's carbon foot print, for example, can be accomplished along with reductions in the cost of transportation operations with careful planning. Many companies are looking at their transportation operations from this "win-win" perspective.

There is already a growing challenge in the 21st century to ensure efficient transportation facilities and mobility by maintaining the present system and developing alternatives to meet the growing needs of individuals and organizations. There will probably be even more trade-offs between competing objectives. Highway and air planners will be particularly challenged to develop innovative design solutions because of the large number of federal statutes and executive orders governing the environment. From a user perspective, these constraints may be viewed as burdensome bureaucracy that slows down the completion of the project, but they are, for the most part, a necessary "filter" to screen and mitigate negative changes in our transportation infrastructure.

Maritime Water Quality The protection of the marine environment from the adverse effects of oil spills, garbage dumping from ships, hazardous material losses, and so on is a growing concern shared by many federal and state agencies. One of the largest oil spills occurred in 1989 near Valdez, Alaska, from a tanker ship carrying crude oil from Alaska for the Exxon Oil Company. Almost 11 million gallons of crude oil were spilled; this environmental disaster raised awareness for controls and better contingency preparedness to respond to such accidents. But there have been a continuing number of spills on various waterways and in the oceans. The increased size of vessels has heightened the concern and increased the potential for significant damage.

In recent years, there has been a growing concern about the damage that plastic items and other ship-generated garbage can cause to the marine environment. Birds, marine mammals, and sea turtles are susceptible to this type of refuse because they can ingest the materials and die as a result. It is estimated that more than one million birds die each year from ingesting these materials. It is very difficult to control and/or regulate this form of pollution.

Water quality, both for surface water and drinking water sources, is an area of risk and concern. Both surface water and drinking water sources are highly susceptible to many types of potential pollutants. Again, there will be continuing pressure to protect water quality by governmental controls and standards.

Noise Another type of pollution is noise, which can emit from many sources, including transportation. There is an annoyance factor, but also a health concern involved. Airplanes and motor vehicles are the major causes of noise. The U.S. DOT and the Federal Aviation Administration have been particularly active in this area, helping to guide land-use planning for compatibility with transportation facilities and conducting research to help solve the problem. Noise emissions are governed by the Noise Control Act of 1972, which allows the setting of operational standards for aircraft and trucks and even rail equipment operated by interstate carriers.

Safety

One of the more disturbing by-products of transportation is injury and loss of life. In 2006, a total of 44,912 persons lost their lives in the United States while engaged in transport. Approximately 95 percent of those fatalities occurred in highway vehicles. However, the number of deaths has remained relatively stable in relation to the ever-growing demand for transportation. This positive statistic is the result of increased licensing regulations and more reliable vehicle designs. Unfortunately, trends in the area of safety for freight transportation are not as promising. Train accidents, oil spills, and the threat of gaseous explosions while in transit have increased. With an increasing variety of products being shipped and an increasing volume of transportation, these problems require greater attention. We can hope that safety in freight transportation will soon parallel the progress made in passenger transportation; however, much work remains to be done.

Social Significance

A good transportation system also can enhance the health and welfare of a population. One of the major problems that has faced the famine relief efforts in the various regions of Africa is the lack of sufficient and effective transportation networks to move needed food and farm supplies from the ports inland to the population centers. Insufficient railroads, roads, vehicles, storage, and related distribution facilities hampered effective delivery of the needed food and supplies. In addition, one of the problems facing the region in normal times is insufficient transportation, which hinders inbound and outbound product flows.

A well-developed transportation also contributes improved health and education delivery systems and effective communications among regions of a country. Overall, transportation plays a major social role in our economy that is not always fully appreciated nor understood by the citizenry.

Political Significance

The origin and maintenance of transportation systems are dependent on the government. Government intervention is needed to design feasible routes, cover the expense of building public highways, and develop harbors and waterways. Adequate transportation is needed to create national unity; the transportation network permits the leaders of government to travel rapidly to and communicate with the people they govern.

Closely connected with transportation's political role is its function as a provider for national defense. Today our transportation system enhances our lifestyles and protects us from outsiders. The ability to transport troops acts as both a weapon and a deterrent in this age of energy shortages and global conflicts. The conflicts in Central America, Africa, and the Middle East place even greater emphasis on the importance of transportation in protecting our distant vital interests.

Although it is accurate to say that the American transportation system has been shaped by economic factors, political and military developments have also played important roles. Transportation policy incorporates more than economics—the expected benefits of the system extend beyond the economic realm.

SUMMARY

- Transportation is a pervasive and very important part of all developed economies and is a key ingredient for underdeveloped countries to progress to economic development and independence.
- The history of the United States is replete with evidence of the close correlation of advances in transportation technology with our advancing economic development from the Erie Canal to our modern highways and air systems.
- Transportation systems are the lifelines of cities and the surrounding suburbs. Tons of products are moved into cities every day to promote the health and welfare of its citizens. Also, products which are produced in the cities are moved out for shipment elsewhere.
- Transportation contributes to the value of goods by providing time and place utility. That is, effective and efficient transportation moves products to points where there is a demand for the product and at a time when it is needed.
- Geographic and labor specialization are important cornerstones of industrialized countries and transportation provides one of the necessary ingredients for this to occur.
- The more efficient the transportation system, the greater the possibility of scale economies and increased market areas.
- Improved transportation in an area will usually increase land values because of the improved accessibility to raw materials and markets.
- The flow and patterns for commerce influence transportation infrastructure patterns of developing countries.
- Transportation expenditures for freight and passengers are an important part of the gross domestic product in the United States.
- While transportation provides many benefits, it can also contribute to environmental problems including pollution, poor air quality, acid rain, and global climate changes.

STUDY QUESTIONS

1. There is much discussion on the local, state, and federal levels about the need to repair and improve the Interstate Highway System. Provide a rationale for this need.
2. "Transportation is the most important economic factor for economic development." Do you agree or disagree with this statement? Why or why not?
3. The opening of the Erie Canal and the building of the transcontinental railroads in the 19th century were described as significant milestones for the economic development in the United States. Explain their importance individually and collectively.
4. The highways and other transportation networks that serve major metropolitan areas are frequently described as the lifelines of the metropolitan area. Do you agree with this statement? Why or why not?
5. Compare and contrast time and place utility, and explain how they contribute to the value of products. What is the importance of time and place utility in our global economy?

6. Adam Smith stated that specialization of labor was limited by the extent of the market and that transportation helps to expand the market. Explain the meaning and importance of this statement.
7. Economists often point to the impact of improved transportation on land values and related economic development. What is the nature and significance of the transportation impact?
8. While improved transportation systems provide economic benefits, there may be some associated environmental costs. What are the major environmental costs associated with transportation and what are their potential negative impacts?
9. "Improved transportation systems can also have social and political significance." Why are these important considerations for evaluating existing and/or proposed additions to the transportation system
10. The service characteristics of freight movements are considered by some shippers to be as important as or more important than the freight rate. Discuss the various service characteristics for freight demand. Do you agree with the statement that they may be as important as or even more important than the freight rate? Why or why not?

NOTES

1. D. Philip Locklin, *Economics of Transportation*, 7th ed., Homewood, Illinois: Richard D. Irwin, Inc., 1972, pp. 28–33.
2. Ibid., pp. 34–37.
3. Ibid., pp. 38–40.

CASE 2-1

Highways Galore

Kelly Edwards, the recently appointed vice president of development for HOG, Inc., a highway construction company in central Pennsylvania, had just returned from meeting with the senior management team of the company. At the meeting, Harry O. Growbaker, president of HOG, Inc., had reported on his most recent meetings with the Pennsylvania Department of Transportation in Harrisburg. The focus of the presentation and discussion was a new state funding initiative that would support regional highway projects throughout the state. The highways, bridges, and overall infrastructure throughout the state needed improvements and expansion. The development of significant shale gas and oil drilling had strained the existing network but had provided additional tax funds for needed public projects. Harry O. Growbaker was convinced that HOG, Inc. was in a unique position to participate, but that they needed to be proactive to demonstrate the economic benefit and impact of such stimulus spending in central Pennsylvania. Harry asked Kelly to provide some discussion points for the next meeting of the senior management team.

Kelly decided to meet with two of her senior staff members, Shaun Knight and Barb Collins, to help with this assignment. During the course of their discussion, Kelly pointed out the lack of efficient and effective highway connections throughout the center of the state. Interstate 80 was a major east-west corridor for interstate traffic between the Midwest and major East Coast cities, but with limited impact overall in much of Central Pennsylvania, particularly for north-south flows. The potential economic growth in central Pennsylvania was creating a need for a more effective north-south links and also more efficient local roadways. Barb Collins felt that a proposed highway link would be attractive to the state and also the federal government.

Shaun, who had participated in many economic impact studies, pointed out the possible synergism with the University Park campus of Penn State and perhaps some of their satellite locations throughout the state. He noted the development of the research park at Penn State's University Park Campus and the new University President's interest in helping the state with economic development and playing a more active role in encouraging new companies based upon applied research at the University. Shaun felt that there was much opportunity to encourage and enhance such development with improved transportation.

Kelly Edwards became excited as she listened to this discussion and was convinced that they could develop a list of discussion points for the next senior management meeting that could then be developed into a white paper for the state and Federal Departments of Transportation.

You have recently been hired by HOG, Inc., and Ms. Edwards has asked you to develop an initial set of discussion points that would indicate the economic and, perhaps, social benefits from new highway links in central Pennsylvania.

CASE 2-2

The Sustainability Team

Yourway Subs, of Naperville, Illinois, like other quick serve restaurants, was an example of business organizations that had contributed to the growing environmental challenge of the 21st century. They had daily deliveries to their many relatively small and dispersed retail locations to ensure the freshness of their products. Their customers usually carried out their food purchases in plastic type containers and bags. They purchased their food-related products from large producers and distributors who were often located relatively long distances from the retail stores of Yourway Subs. Their store distribution network was based upon assured supply at the stores, that is, "never stock out of an item."

Carl Weber, CEO of Yourway Subs, had recognized the growing emphasis from the federal and local government, the general public and especially their younger customers to be more socially responsible and concerned about the environment. This was particularly true for city operations where environmental pollution was a great concern. The former president of the company had initiated a successful pilot program in the Midwest. She had appointed what she called her "Green Team" to initiate and develop the pilot. The Green Team had decided to set a sustainability standard for the organization and not just pay lip service to their Action Program. They identified a number of key initiatives to get the ball rolling:

- Procure produce locally
- Bake bread on-site
- Reduce the miles that inbound products were shipped
- Collaborate with suppliers to reduce packaging and transport miles

The Pilot Program had been deemed successful in reducing waste and their "carbon footprint" with the four initiatives listed above, but now Mr. Weber wanted to take the program to a new level of effectiveness with a goal of "zero waste" and further reduction of their "carbon footprint." You have been designated to help initiate this effort by researching the efforts of similar companies and developing a short working paper for internal discussion to help identify additional viable changes for improvement.

CHAPTER

3 TRANSPORTATION REGULATION AND PUBLIC POLICY

Learning Objectives

After reading this chapter, you should be able to do the following:

- Understand the bases for the regulation of transportation in the United States
- Appreciate the roles of regulatory agencies and the courts in regulating transportation
- Obtain a knowledge of previous and current regulations affecting transportation
- Understand the need for a national transportation policy
- Identify and assess the need and roles of public promotion in transportation
- Appreciate the role of user charges
- Obtain a knowledge of transportation safety and security regulations in the United States

TRANSPORTATION **PROFILE**

Congestion Ahead: Merging Disparate Transportation Bills into a Well-Funded Solution

Washington has a problem. It needs to produce a fully funded, multiyear surface transportation bill and find a way to pay for it in an election year before the end of September.

Even senators involved in the sausage-making exercise known as "lawmaking" are skeptical of being able to produce such legislation on a tight deadline.

According to Sen. Roy Blunt (R-Mo.), a member of the Senate Commerce Committee's Surface Transportation and Merchant Marine Infrastructure, Safety, and Security subcommittee, "In the Senate today, I am hesitant to use the words 'produce legislation.'"

Blunt spoke at an "Infrastructure Week" event coordinated by the American Trucking Associations (ATA) at its Capitol Hill office last month. However, other senators were slightly more optimistic during the event.

Sen. Tom Carper (D-Del.), chairman of the Senate Environment and Public Works Committee's Transportation and Infrastructure subcommittee, said that there were "all kinds of ideas" floating around Capitol Hill on infrastructure. "There is no silver bullet, but maybe there are some silver BBs," Carper said. "Maybe we could put together a tapestry of ideas."

So far that tapestry of ideas to replace the current two-year, $109 billion "MAP-21" that expires September 30 includes President Obama's four-year, $302 billion proposal of interstate tolling or a mileage-based revenue system to replace or supplement the federal fuel tax, and the Senate Environment and Public Works (EPW) Committee's six-year proposal that keeps funding at the current levels—but with no specific way to pay for it.

Indeed, paying for the bill is a necessity. The Highway Trust Fund (HTF) is on track to be exhausted by August, when Congress will be on its six-week summer vacation. However, this wouldn't be the first time this has happened. Since 2008, the General Fund of the U.S. Treasury has bailed out the HTF to the tune of about $54 billion, and it's likely to do the same late this summer.

Some 87 percent of the HTF comes from the federal tax on fuel—18.4 cents on gasoline, 24.4 cents on diesel. These amounts have remained unchanged since 1993. Truckers have been openly pleading with Congress to raise the fuel tax, partially because it's commonly called an "Ex-Lax" tax by truckers—because it's easily passed on to shippers.

Sen. Carper is proposing to restore the buying power of the federal fuel tax to where it was 21 years ago and then indexing it to inflation. He's calling for a 3- to 4-cent increase annually for four years to restore the tax's effective buying power. That's considered a long shot in an election year, but remains unbowed.

"We have to figure out the right thing to do, not the most expedient thing," Carper said, adding that even some Republicans like his idea. "If I had said that six months ago they would have thrown me out of the room. I mentioned it a few weeks ago, and they didn't."

Then there's the idea of tolling. Putting tolls on the existing free lanes of 50,000 miles of the interstate system could provide more than $50 billion annually; however, that proposal faces stiff headwinds.

Trucking interests much prefer the tax hike to increased tolling. Phil Byrd, president and CEO of Bulldog Hiway Express and ATA chairman, said truckers are against tolls on existing interstates for three reasons: Those highways already have been built and paid for; it's effectively double taxation; and tolls are inefficient, with overhead consuming as much as 25 percent of overall revenue.

In one of the few instances where big trucking companies and independent owner-operators agree, the Owner-Operator Independent Drivers Association (OOIDA) blasted the Obama administration's tolling proposal. OOIDA called it a "negative provision" that would create a "patchwork" of state-controlled toll roads in place of a unified interstate system.

"Any proposal that moves away from a user-fee funded transportation system is not going to be acceptable to the American trucking industry—period," ATA president and CEO Bill Graves said.

Source: John Schultz, *Logistics Management*, June 2014, pp. 13–14. Reprinted with permission of Peerless Media, LLC.

Introduction

Transportation has long been a critical component of every world economy. From the development of the Egyptian empire because of the Nile River to the establishment of colonies on the east and west coasts of the United States because of ocean transportation, transportation has allowed civilizations to expand through trade with other countries. Because of its impact on a nation's economy, many countries have developed policies and regulations for transportation to assure a safe, reliable, and fair transportation network for their citizens.

When the United States was an agricultural society, it relied on wagons and railroads to move products from points of surplus to points of demand. As the United States evolved into a manufacturing economy, it utilized railroads, motor carriers, water carriers, pipelines, and air carriers to create time and place utilities. Today, while the United States is mainly an Internet-based society, it still relies on transportation to add value to products not only for domestic movements but also for global movements. All through this history, the United States has attempted to set policies and establish regulations, at both the state and federal levels, to govern its transportation network so it is fair and equitable to transportation providers, shippers, and citizens. However, because of the boundary-spanning nature of transportation and its multiple constituents, developing a fair and equitable transportation network for all parties has been and continues to be a challenge for U.S. government agencies.

This chapter will examine the basis of this regulation, along with the roles of the regulatory commissions and the courts. A discussion of the development of transportation regulation from its inception at the federal level in 1887 to its role today will be presented, along with the national transportation policies directing and promoting transportation and national security.

Regulation of Transportation

Nature of Regulation

In the United States, the government influences the activities of industries in many different ways. The amount of influence in industry activity varies from providing the legal foundation and framework in which industries operate to government ownership and control of firms in some industries. The degree of government regulation in some industries has sometimes met with stiff opposition from firms in those industries. However, because of the impact some industries have on the economy of the United States, some level of government intervention is necessary.

The amount of government control and regulation has increased as the United States has grown and prospered. If the amount of government controls in existence 150 years ago was compared to that in place today, the former would seem insignificant. The expansion of government influence, however, has been necessitated by the increase in the scope of activity, complexity, and size of individual firms.

In the United States, our economic activity is usually viewed as one of private enterprise. Competition is a necessary requirement for a free-market economy. A competitive market can decide the allocation of scarce resources. Economists have soundly developed the concepts of competition and free markets for years.

The definitions of *pure competition* and *free market* involve several conditions that might not exist in reality. Products are justified only by the market's willingness to buy them. A product should not be sold at a price below the marginal cost of making the last unit. The free-market theory also assumes that producers and consumers are able to assess whether or not a given economic act will provide them with a positive return.

Although pure competition provides a marketplace that is desirable to consumers, a **monopoly** does not. In a monopoly, only one seller exists and can control the price of each individual unit of output. Consumers have no opportunity to switch suppliers. If all market structures took the form of either pure competition or monopoly, the solution would be simple. Most individuals would not disagree with government regulation of a monopoly, and a valid case could be made for no government intervention in an economy characterized by pure competition. However, the prevailing situation is not that simple. Market structures usually take some form between the extremes of pure competition and monopoly.

The imperfections in the marketplace in a free-enterprise economy provide the rationale for government controls. The controls exercised by the government can take one of several forms. One form is that of maintaining or enforcing competition—for example, the antitrust laws set forth by the government. Second, the government can substitute economic regulation for competition, as it has done in the transportation industry. Third, the government can assume ownership and direct control, as it has done with the U.S. Post Office.

The basic challenge of regulation in our society is that of establishing or maintaining the conditions necessary for the economical use of resources under a system of private enterprise. Regulation should seek to maintain a competitive framework and rely on competitive forces whenever possible. The institutional framework for regulating transportation is provided by federal statute. A perspective on the overall legal basis for regulation is important to the student of transportation and will be examined in the next section.

Common Law

The legal system in the United States is based upon **common law** and civil or statutory law. The former is a system basic to most English-speaking countries because it was developed in England. Common law relies on judicial precedent or principles of law developed from former court decisions. When a court decision establishes a rule for a situation, then that rule becomes part of the law. As conditions change, the law sometimes needs further interpretation. Therefore, an important feature of the common law system is that it changes and evolves as society changes. There are many examples of such change in the interpretation of the areas of federal and state control or responsibility for regulation of transportation.[1]

The common law approach fits well with a free-market economy because the individual is the focus of attention and can engage in any business that is not prohibited. Each individual is regarded as possessing equal power and responsibility before the law.[2] The early regulation of transportation developed under common law. The obvious connection is with the concept of *common carriage*, in which transportation providers were required to serve all shippers and charge reasonable rates without discrimination.

Statutory law or civil law is based upon the Roman legal system and is characteristic of continental Europe and the parts of the world colonized by European countries. Statutory law is enacted by legislative bodies, but it is a specific enactment. A large part of the laws pertaining to business in general and to transportation are based upon statutory law. However, two points are important to note in this regard. First, common law rules are still very important in the transportation industry because many statutes were, in effect, copied from common law principles. Second, statutes are usually general in nature and need to be interpreted by the courts. Thus, in the United States, there is a very close relationship between common law and statutory law.

The regulation of transportation in the United States began at the state level under the common law system when a number of important regulations, as well as the basic issue of whether a business could even be regulated at all, were developed. In the latter regard, a concept of "business affected with the public interest" was developed under common law. **State regulation** also included the use of charters for some of the early turnpike companies and canal operations. The development of the railroad industry necessitated a move to statutory regulation, which was in effect by 1870 with the passage of **granger laws** in several states. Granger laws were the product of the granger movement, which began about 1867 in states such as Illinois, Iowa, Minnesota, and Wisconsin. Granges were organizations formed by farmers in various states and functioned as political action groups where farmers could discuss problems. Farmers joined the granger movement because of their dissatisfaction with railroad rates and service. The development of state laws, and later federal laws, also gave rise to independent regulatory commissions, which are the topic of the next section.

Role of the Independent Regulatory Commissions

The U.S. federal government is subject to a system of checks and balances in three separate branches—executive, judicial, and legislative. An independent regulatory commission is an administrative body created by legislative authority operating within the framework of the U.S. Constitution. The members of these commissions are appointed by the president and approved by the Senate for a fixed term in office.

The **Interstate Commerce Commission** (ICC) was the first federal independent regulatory commission established in the United States under the Act to Regulate Commerce of 1887. This Act gave the ICC the power to regulate the U.S. railroad industry. Originally, the ICC had limited powers, partially because of the inexperience of the U.S. government in regulating an entire industry. However, over several years many additional pieces of legislation were passed to strengthen the powers of the ICC over the railroad industry. The Motor Carrier Act of 1935, the Transportation Act of 1940, and the Freight Forwarder Act of 1942 gave similar powers to the ICC over the motor carrier, domestic water carrier, and freight forwarding industries, respectively.

The ICC served as an expert body, providing continuity to regulation that neither the courts nor the legislature could provide. The ICC exercised legislative, judicial, and executive powers. As a result, it was often labeled a quasi-legislative, quasi-judicial, and quasi-executive body. Regulatory agencies can be regarded as a fourth branch of the government. When the ICC enforced statutes, it served in its executive capacity. When it ruled upon the reasonableness of a rate, it served in its judicial capacity. When it expanded legislation by promulgating rules or prescribing rules or rates, it exercised its legislative powers.

On December 31, 1995, the ICC was abolished. The ICC Termination Act of 1995 (ICCTA) ended the 108-year-old ICC and replaced it with the **Surface Transportation Board** (STB), which today is focused only on the railroad industry. The STB is housed in the **U.S. Department of Transportation** (DOT), but it is still considered to be an independent regulatory agency. The president appoints members of the STB with the approval of the Senate.

The role of the STB in the economic operations of the railroads has been greatly reduced from that of the ICC. Congress intended for the marketplace, not the STB, to be the primary control mechanism for rates and service. (See "Current Economic Regulations," later in this chapter, for more details on the ICCTA regulations.)

In addition to the ICC and STB, other independent regulatory commissions were established for transportation. In 1938, the **Civil Aeronautics Board** (CAB) was established to administer the economic regulations imposed upon airlines. The CAB was abolished in 1985 by the Civil Aeronautics Board Sunset Act and the remaining regulatory jurisdictions (safety issues) were transferred to the DOT.

The **Federal Maritime Commission** (FMC) was created in 1961 to administer the regulations imposed on international water carriers. The FMC exercises control over the rates, practices, agreements, and services of common carriers operating in international trade and domestic trade to points beyond the continental United States. The Ocean Shipping Reform Act of 1998 relaxed some of the economic powers of the FMC by allowing shippers and ocean carriers to enter into confidential contracts. This will be discussed more in Chapter 8.

The **Federal Energy Regulatory Commission** (FERC) was created to administer the regulations governing rates and practices of oil and natural gas pipelines. However, the FERC is not an independent regulatory commission that reports to Congress, as is the STB or FMC. Rather, it is a semi-independent regulatory commission that reports to the Department of Energy.

Our regulatory laws are often stated in vague terms, such as *reasonable rates, inherent advantages,* and *unjust discrimination.* The roles of the regulatory commissions are to interpret the meaning of these terms as they are stated in the law and to develop regulations that define their intent. These regulations, then, are codified and serve as the basis for decisions made by the regulatory commissions. However, these decisions are still subject to the intent of the law and to decisions made by the courts.

Role of the Courts

Even though the regulatory commissions play a powerful role in regulating transportation, they are still subject to judicial review. The courts are the sole determinants of the intent of the law, and only court decisions can serve as legal precedent under common law. The courts make the final ruling on the constitutionality of regulatory statutes and the interpretation of the regulation. The review of the courts act as a check on arbitrary or capricious actions, on actions that do not conform to statutory standards or authority, or on actions that are not in accordance with fair procedure or substantial evidence.

The parties involved in a commission decision have the right, therefore, to appeal the decision to the courts.

Over the years, the courts had come to recognize the ICC as an expert body on policy and the authority on matters of fact. This recognition has now been given to the STB. The courts limited their restrictions on ICC and STB authority. The courts would not substitute their judgment for that of the ICC or STB on matters such as what constitutes a reasonable rate or whether discrimination is unjust because such judgments would usurp the administrative function of the commission.

Safety Regulations

Various federal agencies administer transportation safety regulations. Some of these regulations are enacted into law by Congress, whereas others are promulgated by the respective agencies. A thorough discussion of the specific regulations pertaining to each type of transportation is beyond the scope of this book, but a general description of safety regulations is warranted.

Safety regulations have been established to control operations, personnel qualifications, vehicles, equipment, hours of service for vehicle operators, and so forth. The **Federal Aviation Administration** (FAA) enforces and promulgates safety regulations governing the operations of air carriers and airports. The **Federal Motor Carrier Safety Administration** (FMCSA) administers motor carrier safety regulations, and the **National Highway Traffic Safety Administration** (NHTSA) has jurisdiction over safety features and the performance of motor vehicles and motor vehicle equipment. The **Federal Railroad Administration** (FRA) has authority over railroad safety regulations while the **Coast Guard** is responsible for marine safety standards for vessels and ports. The newly created **Pipeline and Hazardous Material Safety Administration** (PHMSA) contains a Pipeline Safety Office that is responsible for hazardous materials standards for oil and natural gas pipelines and a Hazardous Materials Safety Office that manages hazardous materials regulations for all other modes of transportation. The **National Transportation Safety Board** (NTSB) is charged with investigating and reporting the causes, facts, and circumstances relating to transportation accidents.

In addition, the states, through the **police powers** contained in the Constitution, exercise various controls over the safe operation of vehicles. These safety regulations set standards for speed, vehicle size, operating practices, operator licensing, and so forth. The purpose of the state safety regulations is to protect the health and welfare of the citizens of that state.

Often, federal and state safety regulations conflict. For example, the federal government restricted the automobile speed limit to 55 miles per hour on the highway system during the energy crisis of the 1970s. Some states did not agree with the mandate but followed the requirement to qualify for federal money to construct and maintain the highway system. In 1982, the Surface Transportation Act established federal standards for vehicle weight and length of tractor-trailers operating on the interstate highway system. The states complied with the standards for the interstate highways but many maintained different standards for state highways.

After the September 11, 2001 terrorist attack on the United States, transportation security has taken on a new dimension. Securing the nation's transportation system from terrorism became a major governmental focus because of the massive geographic expanse of the U.S. border and the millions of tons of freight and millions of passengers entering and leaving the United States. The Aviation and Transportation Security Act, enacted in November of 2001, created the Transportation Security Agency (TSA), which is responsible for securing the safety of the U.S. air transportation network. In 2002, Congress passed the Maritime Transportation Security Act, which governs the security of U.S. ports. Also, the Homeland Security Act of 2002 was passed to provide a central coordinating mechanism, along with the DOT, for all security issues dealing with transportation of passengers and freight within the United States and flowing into and out of the United States.

State Regulations

The states establish various transportation safety regulations to protect the health and welfare of their citizens. In addition, the states exercise limited economic regulations over the transportation of commodities and passengers wholly within the state. These powers were given to the states by the Commerce Clause of the U.S. Constitution. The states' powers were greatly limited under various federal laws. States generally cannot impose stricter regulation than imposed on a given mode at the federal level. States can still regulate safety, provided these regulations do not impose an undue burden on interstate commerce. This type of transportation is known as **intrastate commerce**, and most states had a regulatory commission that was charged with enforcing these intrastate controls. These agencies might still exist to regulate utilities, such as telephone or electric companies.

Intrastate economic regulations vary from state to state, but they are generally patterned after federal economic regulations. In 1994, the federal government eliminated the intrastate economic regulation of motor carriers with the passage of the FAA Authorization Act. The law, which applies to all motor carriers of property except household goods carriers, prohibits the states from requiring operating authority or regulating intrastate motor carrier rates, routes, and services. The states have the option to regulate the uniform business practices, cargo liability, and credit rules of intrastate motor carriers.

The determination as to what constitutes commerce subject to state economic regulations is generally based on whether the shipment crosses a state boundary. If the shipment has an origin in one state and a destination in another state, it is an interstate shipment and is subject to federal regulations, if any exist. However, for shipments that are moved into a distribution center from a point outside the state and then moved from the distribution center to a destination in the same state, the distinction is not that clear. The move within the state from the distribution center to the final destination can be considered interstate commerce and subject to federal regulations.

Development of Regulation

As has been seen in this chapter, transportation does not operate in a completely free-market environment. Government has controlled the economic operations of transportation since the 1860s. The driving force behind this regulation was the recognition in the 1800s of the importance of the railroad industry to the development of our country and its inherently monopolistic nature. The role of economic regulation by the government is to transform a monopolistic industry into a competitive one. Under economic regulation, the government can (1) determine if a firm can enter an industry; (2) determine which market(s) a firm can serve in that industry; and (3) determine the prices that firm can charge customers in the markets it serves. By enforcing these three regulatory practices, the government can provide the basis for competition in a monopolistic industry.

Table 3-1 provides a chronology of transportation regulation. The regulatory history is broken down into four eras. First, the Initiation Era from 1887 to 1920 saw the establishment of federal transportation regulation and the ICC. Second, the Era of Positive Regulation from 1920 to 1935 was oriented toward promoting transportation. Third, the Intermodal Era from 1935 to 1976 witnessed the expansion of regulation to motor carriers, air carriers, water carriers, and freight forwarders. Finally, the New Economic Era from 1976 to the present was the period of gradual lessening and eventual elimination of economic regulation, culminating in the elimination of the ICC. This era also saw the development and strengthening of transportation safety and security regulations.

TABLE 3-1 Chronology of Major Transportation Regulation

DATE	ACT	NATURE OF REGULATION
Initiation Era		
1887	Act to Regulate Commerce	Regulated railroads and established ICC; required rates to be reasonable; discrimination prohibited
1903	Elkins Act	Prohibited rebates and filed rate doctrine
1096	Hepburn Act	Established maximum and joint rate controls
1910	Mann-Elkins Act	Gave shipper right to route shipment
1912	Panama Canal Act	Prohibited railroads from owning water carriers
Positive Era		
1920	Transportation Act of 1920	Established a rule of rate-making; pooling and joint use of terminals permitted; began recapture clause
1933	Emergency Transportation Act	Granted financial assistance to railroads
Intermodal Era		
1935	Motor Carrier Act	Federal regulation of trucking, similar to rail
1938	Civil Aeronautics Act	Federal regulation of air carriers; established Civil Aeronautics Board (CAB)
1940	Transportation Act	Provided for federal regulation of water carriers; declaration of national transportation policy
1942	Freight Forwarder Act	Federal Reregulation of surface freight forwarders
1948	Reed-Bulwinkle Act	Established antitrust immunity for joint rate making
1958	Transportation Act	Eliminated umbrella (protective) rate making and provided financial aid to railroads
1966	Department of Transportation Act	Established the U.S. Department of Transportation
1970	Rail Passenger Service Act	Established Amtrak
1973	Regional Rail Reorganization Act	Established Consolidation Rail Corporation (Conrail)
New Economic Era		
1976	Railroad Revitalization and Regulatory Reform Act	Granted rate freedom; allowed ICC to exempt rail operations; began abandonment and merger controls
1977	Airline Deregulation Act	Deregulated air transportation, sunset CAB (1985)

(continued)

TABLE 3-1 Continued

DATE	ACT	NATURE OF REGULATION
1980	Motor Carrier Act	Eased entry restrictions and permitted rate negotiation
1980	Rail Staggers Act	Permitted railroads to negotiate contracts, allowed rate flexibility, and defined maximum rates
1993	Negotiated Rate Act	Provided for settlement options for motor carrier undercharges
1994	Trucking Industry Regulatory Reform Act	Eliminated motor carrier filing of individual tariffs; ICC given power to deregulate categories of traffic
1994	FAA Reauthorization Act	Prohibited states from regulating (economic) intrastate trucking
1995	ICC Termination Act	Abolished ICC; established STB; eliminated most truck economic regulation
1996	Maritime Security Act	Authorized a program to assist an active, privately owned U.S.-flagged and U.S.-crewed merchant shipping fleet
1998	Transportation Equity Act for the 21st Century	Allocated $216+ billion for the maintenance and safety of surface transportation
2001	Aviation and Transportation Security Act	Established the Transportation Security Administration
2002	Homeland Security Act	Moved Coast Guard and TSA into Department of Homeland Security
2010	Compliance, Safety, And Accountability Act	Created scoring system for motor carrier companies and drivers to help promote safer operations
2013	Hours of Service	Places stricter rules on a driver's restart options: maintains 11-hour daily driving limit and 14-hour workday

The next section will provide a summary of current regulations as they pertain to railroads and motor carriers.

Current Economic Regulations

As previously stated, the air carrier industry is free from economic regulation. Cargo and passenger rates are not controlled by the government and domestic air carriers are permitted to serve any market as long as the carrier meets safety regulation and landing slots are available.

The majority of the economic regulation of pipelines has been transferred to the Federal Energy Regulatory Commission. Because most water carrier operations are exempt from economic regulation, domestic water carrier economic regulation is a moot issue.

Effective January 1, 1996, the ICC Termination Act of 1995 abolished the Interstate Commerce Commission, further deregulated transportation, and transferred the remaining ICC functions to the STB located within the DOT. The STB now administers the remaining economic regulations exercised over railroads, motor carriers, freight forwarders, freight brokers, water carriers, and pipelines. However, the majority of the remaining economic regulations pertain to railroad transportation. The key provisions of the ICCTA are summarized below:

Railroad Regulations

- Rail economic regulation is basically unchanged by the ICCTA.
- The STB has jurisdiction over rates, classifications, rules, practices, routes, services, facilities, acquisitions, and abandonments.

- Railroads continue to be subject to the common carrier obligations (to serve, not discriminate, charge reasonable rates, and deliver).
- Rail tariff filing is eliminated; railroads must provide 20 days advance notice before changing a rate.
- Rail contract filing is eliminated except for agricultural products.

Motor Carriers

- All tariff filing and rate regulation is eliminated, except for household goods and noncontiguous trade (trade between the continental United States and Hawaii, for example).
- Motor carriers are required to provide tariffs to shippers upon request.
- Motor carriers are held liable for damage according to the conditions of the Carmack Amendment (that is, the full value of the product at destination). However, motor carriers can use released value rates that set limits on liability.
- The Negotiated Rates Act undercharge resolution procedures are retained and the unreasonable practices defense is extended indefinitely for pending undercharge cases.
- Undercharge/overcharge claims must be filed within 180 days from receipt of the freight bill.
- The STB has broad powers to exempt operations from economic regulation with the existing exemptions remaining.
- Antitrust immunity for collective rate making (publishing the national motor freight classification, for example) is retained.
- The motor carrier is required to disclose to the person directly paying the freight bill whether and to whom discounts or allowances are given.
- The concepts of common and contract authorities are eliminated; all regulated carriers can contract with shippers.

Freight Forwarders and Brokers

- Both are required to register with the STB.
- The freight forwarder is regulated as a carrier and is liable for freight damage.
- The broker is not a carrier and is not held liable for freight damage.
- The STB can impose insurance requirements for both.

The Surface Transportation Board Reauthorization Act of 1999 removed most of the remaining economic regulations imposed by the STB on motor carriers. The STB would no longer consider competitive issues and would eliminate references to federal regulatory approval requirements for collective motor carrier activities submitted to it for approval. The STB would no longer be able to grant antitrust immunity for motor carriers for collective activities such as rate bureaus and national freight classification. The motor carrier industry would be subject to competitive regulations as in other industries.

In summary, the ICCTA brought the economic regulation of transportation back to its beginning in 1887 by retaining regulatory powers over the railroads, while allowing the other modes to operate in a free-market economy. While all of the modes, except rail, operate in this environment, they are subject to antitrust and other regulations that govern all other industries. Because of the decreasing cost nature of the railroad industry and its tendency towards monopoly, the STB maintains comprehensive guidelines to assure that railroads operate without discrimination or undue or unjust prejudice towards shippers.

Current Motor Carrier Safety Regulations

While there has been no activity in the development of economic regulation, new legislation continues to evolve that strengthens current safety regulations as they pertain to motor carriers. In 2010, the federal government initiated the **Compliance, Safety, and Accountability Act of 2010 (CSA 2010)** with the goal of reducing accidents by identifying and addressing areas of concern. CSA 2010 is under the management of the FMCSA. This legislation applies to any carriers with one or more vehicles over 10,000 pounds that participates in interstate commerce and/or vehicles that transport hazardous materials in intrastate commerce. CSA 2010 has three main areas of focus:

- Measurement: CSA uses inspections and crash results to measure safety performance;
- Evaluation: CSA addresses these behaviors using the Safety Measurement System (SMS), which helps identify safety performance issues and to monitor compliance issues over time; and
- Intervention: CSA specifies how data is collected, analyzed, and stored.

CSA weights safety violations based on their statistical likelihood to cause accidents and it groups violations into categories called BASICs (Behavior Analysis and Safety Improvement Categories). The categories in BASICs are:

- Unsafe driving;
- Fatigued driving (hours of service);
- Driver fitness;
- Controlled substances and alcohol;
- Vehicle maintenance;
- Cargo-related; and
- Crash history.

Ratings in each category range from 1 to 10, with the least serious violations rated a "1" and most serious rated a "10." CSA rates carriers in percentiles from 0 to 100 by comparing their measurements with their peers. The lower the percentile, the better the overall safety performance of the carrier. To calculate scores for carriers, CSA uses the last 24 months of data; for drivers, CSA uses the last 36 months of data.[3]

The other significant piece of legislation enacted that has significant impacts on motor carriers operations was the new **Hours of Service (HOS)** regulations effective July 1, 2013. While there have been several pieces of legislation passed over the last several years regarding HOS, the new requirements place stricter rules on a driver's restart options with the intent to improve safety. The main provisions of this new legislation include:

- Limiting the maximum average workweek for drivers to 70 hours—a decrease from the current maximum of 82 hours;
- Allowing drivers who reach the maximum 70 hours of driving within a week to resume if they rest for 34 consecutive hours, including at least two nights from 1 a.m. to 5 a.m.;

- Requiring drivers to take a 30-minute break during the first 8 hours of a shift;
- Retaining the current 11-hour daily driving limit and 14-hour workday; and
- Prescribing that drivers may not drive after 60/70 hours on duty in 7/8 consecutive days—may restart 7/8 days after 34 or more consecutive hours off-duty.[4]

These new requirements will require a more strict adherence by motor carriers and drivers to maintain accurate and timely driver logs to monitor hours. Violations of the new HOS rules will fall under the regulations contained in CSA 2010.

Antitrust Laws in Transportation

The deregulatory movement has exposed many practices to be in violation of antitrust laws. Antitrust regulations were first established in 1890 with passage of the **Sherman Antitrust Act**. The key points of this Act are as follows:

> *Section 1: Trusts, etc., in restraint of trade illegal; penalty.*
>
> *Every contract, combination in the form of trust or otherwise, or conspiracy, in restraint of trade or commerce among the several States, or with foreign nations, is declared to be illegal. Every person who shall make any contract or engage in any combination or conspiracy declared by Section 1 to 7 of this title to be illegal shall be deemed guilty of a felony, and, on conviction thereof, shall be punished by fine not exceeding one million dollars if a corporation, or if any other person, one hundred thousand dollars, or by imprisonment not exceeding three years, or both said punishments, in the discretion of the court.*
>
> *Section 2: Monopolizing trade a felony; penalty.*
>
> *Every person who shall monopolize, or attempt to monopolize, or combine or conspire with any other person or persons, to monopolize any part of the trade or commerce among the several States, or with foreign nations, shall be deemed guilty of a felony....*[5]

The thrust of the Sherman Act was intended to outlaw price fixing among competing firms, eliminate business practices that tended toward monopolization, and prevent any firm or combination of firms from refusing to sell or deal with certain firms or avoiding geographic market allocations.

The law was strengthened in 1914 by the **Clayton Act**. This Act specifically described some other practices that would be interpreted as attempts to monopolize, or as actual monopolization. These practices include exclusive dealing arrangements whereby a buyer and/or seller agree to deal only with the other party for a period of time. Another prohibited practice is a tying contract. This is where a seller agrees to sell goods to a buyer only if the buyer also buys another product from the seller.

Also in 1914 legislation was passed that created the **Federal Trade Commission** (FTC). This agency was the primary overseer and enforcement agency in antitrust situations.

Collective rate making by transportation carriers was made exempt from antitrust laws by the passage of the **Reed-Bulwinkle Act of 1948**, which empowered the ICC to oversee carrier rate making. As such, it limited traditional jurisdiction by the FTC and the Department of Justice in this area. The **Motor Carrier Act of 1980** and the **Staggers Act of 1980** eliminated many of the exemptions from antitrust laws for motor carriers and railroads, respectively. The **ICC Termination Act of 1995** confirmed the role of antitrust laws in transportation and further limited exemptions from these laws.

Another major law that might apply to the deregulation of transportation is the **Robinson-Patman Act of 1936**. This law prohibits sellers from practicing price discrimination among buyers unless the difference in price can be justified by true differences in the costs of servicing these buyers (this will be discussed further in Chapter 4, "Costing and Pricing for Transportation"). Defenses against such a practice are (1) differences in cost, (2) the need to meet competition, and (3) changing market conditions. Although this law was created for application to the buying and selling of goods, it may be applicable to contracts for transportation services. Whether this law applies in carrier pricing is only determined by the courts as suspected violations occur.

In the selling and purchase of transportation services, two types of antitrust violations can occur. The first is called a **per se violation**. This type of violation is illegal regardless of whether any economic harm is done to competitors or other parties. Types of per se violations include price fixing, division of markets, boycotts, and tying agreements. If economic harm has been caused to any party because of this violation, the damages are tripled as compensation to the harmed parties.

The second type of antitrust violation is called **rule of reason**. In this type of violation, economic harm must be shown to have been caused to competitors or other parties because these activities can be undertaken by firms with no antitrust implications. Rule of reason violations include exclusive deals, requirements contracts, joint bargaining, and joint action among affiliates.

Carriers, in the selling of transportation services, are normally thought to be the party to which antitrust regulations apply. However, in buying these services, shippers are also subject to the same laws and are at an equal risk of committing an antitrust violation. Because transportation has been subject to antitrust laws for a short period of time, these laws as they pertain to transportation have not yet been fully tested in the courts.

Transportation Policy

The federal government has played an important role in molding the transportation system that exists in the United States today. The federal government's role has been defined through various laws, rules, and funding programs directed toward protecting and promoting the different modes of transportation. The federal government's policy toward transportation is a composite of these federal laws, rules, funding programs, and regulatory agencies. However, there is no unified federal transportation policy statement or goal that guides the federal government's actions.

In addition to the Congress and the president, more than 60 federal agencies and 30 congressional committees are involved in setting transportation policy. Independent regulatory agencies interpret transportation law, establish operating rules, and set policy. Lastly, the Justice Department interprets statutes involving transportation and reconciles differences between the carriers and the public.

The purpose of this section is to examine the national transportation policy, both explicit and implicit, that has molded the current U.S. transportation system. Although the national transportation policy is constantly evolving, there are some major underpinnings upon which the policy is built. These basic policy issues will be examined, as well as the declared statement of national transportation policy contained in the ICC Termination Act of 1995.

Why Do We Need a Transportation Policy?

A good starting point for examining the nature of our national transportation policy is the consideration of our need for such a policy. The answer to the question of need lies in the significance of transportation to the very life of the country. Transportation permeates every aspect of a community and touches the life of every member. The transportation system ties together the various communities of a country, making possible the movement of people, goods, and services. The physical connection that transportation gives to spatially separated communities permits a sense of unity to exist.

In addition, transportation is fundamental to the economic activity of a country. Transportation furthers economic activity—the exchange of goods that are mass-produced in one location to locations deficient in these goods. The secondary benefits of economic activity—jobs, improved goods and services, and so on—would not be enjoyed by a country's citizens without a good transportation system.

An efficient transportation system is also fundamental to national defense. In times of emergencies, people and materials must be deployed quickly to various trouble spots within the United States or throughout the world to protect American interests. Without an efficient transportation system, more resources would have to be dedicated to defense purposes in many more locations. Thus, an efficient transportation system reduces the amount of resources consumed for national defense.

Many of our transportation facilities could not be developed by private enterprise. For example, the capital required to build a transcontinental highway would very likely be beyond the resources of the private sector. Efficient rail and highway routes require government assistance in securing land from private owners; if the government did not assert its power of eminent domain, routes would be quite circuitous and inefficient. Furthermore, public ownership and the operation of certain transportation facilities, such as highways or waterways, are necessary to ensure access to all who desire to use the facilities.

The purpose of transportation policy is to provide direction for determining the amount of national resources that will be dedicated to transportation and for determining the quality of service that is essential for economic activity and national defense. National policy provides guidelines to the many agencies that exercise transportation decision-making powers and to Congress, the president, and the courts that make and interpret the laws affecting transportation. Thus, transportation policy provides the framework for the allocation of resources to the transportation modes.

The federal government has been a major factor in the development of transportation facilities—highways, waterways, ports, and airports. It also has assumed the responsibility to:

- Ensure the safety of travelers;
- Protect the public from the abuse of monopoly power;
- Promote fair competition;
- Develop or continue vital transportation services; balance environmental, energy, and social requirements in transportation; and
- Plan and make decisions.[6]

The statement of the federal government's transportation responsibility indicates the diversity of public need that transportation policy must serve. The conflicts inherent in such a diverse set of responsibilities will be discussed in a later section.

Declaration of National Transportation Policy

The ICC Termination Act of 1995 included statements of national transportation policy. Congress made these statements to provide direction to the STB in administering transportation regulation over railroads, motor carriers, water carriers, and pipelines.

The declaration of national transportation policy is stated in Public Law 104-88.

In regulating the railroad industry, it is the policy of the U.S. government:

1. to allow, to the maximum extent possible, competition and the demand for services to establish reasonable rates for transportation by rail;
2. to minimize the need for Federal regulatory control over the rail transportation system and to require fair and expeditious regulatory decisions when regulation is required;
3. to promote a safe and efficient rail transportation system by allowing rail carriers to earn adequate revenues, as determined by the Board;
4. to ensure the development and continuation of a sound rail transportation system with effective competition among rail carriers and with other modes, to meet the needs of the public and the national defense;
5. to foster sound economic conditions in transportation and to ensure effective competition and coordination between rail carriers and other modes;
6. to maintain reasonable rates where there is an absence of effective competition and where rail rates provide revenues which exceed the amount necessary to maintain the rail system and to attract capital;
7. to reduce regulatory barriers to entry into and exit from the industry;
8. to operate transportation facilities and equipment without detriment to the public health and safety;
9. to encourage honest and efficient management of railroads;
10. to require rail carriers, to the maximum extent practicable, to rely on individual rate increases, and to limit the use of increases of general applicability;
11. to encourage fair wages and safe and suitable working conditions in the railroad industry;
12. to prohibit predatory pricing and practices, to avoid undue concentrations of market power, and to prohibit unlawful discrimination;
13. to ensure the availability of accurate cost information in regulatory proceedings, while minimizing the burden on the rail carriers of developing and maintaining the capability of providing such information;
14. to encourage and promote energy conservation; and
15. to provide for the expeditious handling and resolution of all proceedings required or permitted to be brought to this part.

The declaration of national transportation policy for motor carriers, water carriers, brokers, and freight forwarders is stated in the same document:

In General. To ensure the development, coordination, and preservation of a transportation system that meets the transportation needs of the United States Postal

Service and national defense, it is the policy of the U.S. government to oversee the modes of transportation and:

1. in overseeing these modes:
   A. to recognize and preserve the inherent advantage of each mode of transportation;
   B. to promote safe, adequate, economical, and efficient transportation;
   C. to encourage sound economic conditions in transportation, including sound economic conditions among carriers;
   D. to encourage the establishment and maintenance of reasonable rates for transportation, without unreasonable discrimination or unfair or destructive competitive practices;
   E. to cooperate with each State and the officials of each State on transportation matters; and
   F. to encourage fair wages and working conditions in the transportation industry;
2. in overseeing transportation by motor carrier, to promote competitive and efficient transportation in order to:
   A. encourage fair competition, and reasonable rates for transportation by motor carriers of property;
   B. promote efficiency in the motor carrier transportation system and to require fair and expeditious decisions when required;
   C. meet the needs of shippers, receivers, passengers, and consumers;
   D. allow a variety of quality and price options to meet changing market demands and the diverse requirements of the shipping and traveling public;
   E. allow the most productive use of equipment and energy resources;
   F. enable efficient and well-managed carriers to earn adequate profits, attract capital and maintain fair wages and working conditions;
   G. provide and maintain service to small communities and small shippers and intrastate bus services;
   H. provide and maintain commuter bus operations;
   I. improve and maintain a sound, safe, and competitive privately owned motor carrier system;
   J. promote greater participation by minorities in the motor carrier system;
   K. promote intermodal transportation;
3. in overseeing transportation by motor carriers of passengers:
   A. to cooperate with the States on transportation matters for the purpose of encouraging the States to exercise intrastate regulatory jurisdiction in accordance with the objectives of this part;
   B. to provide Federal procedures which ensure the intrastate regulation is exercised in accordance with this part; and
   C. to ensure that Federal reform initiatives enacted by section 31138 and the Bus Regulatory Reform Act of 1982 are not nullified by State regulatory actions; and
4. in overseeing transportation by water carrier, to encourage and promote service and price competition in the noncontiguous domestic trade.

The declaration of pipeline national transportation policy is as follows:

In General. To ensure the development, coordination, and preservation of a transportation system that meets the transportation needs of the United States, including the national defense, it is the policy of the United States Government to oversee the modes of transportation and in overseeing these modes:

1. to recognize and preserve the inherent advantage of each mode of transportation;
2. to promote safe, adequate, economical, and efficient transportation;
3. to encourage sound economic conditions in transportation; including sound economic conditions among carriers;
4. to encourage the establishment and maintenance of reasonable rates for transportation without unreasonable discrimination or unfair or destructive competitive practices;
5. to cooperate with each State and the officials of each State on transportation matters; and
6. to encourage fair wages and working conditions in the transportation industry.

GLOBAL **PERSPECTIVES**

TTI Releases NAFTA 20 Years After

When the Texas A&M Transportation Institute (TTI) released a meta-analysis of research on the North American Free Trade Agreement (NAFTA) last month, it confirmed that the long-term outlook for North American competitiveness is "promising." But that doesn't mean trade policy can't be improved.

"Findings from the meta-analysis show that all three North American economies have benefitted enormously from NAFTA over the last 20 years," says Juan Carlos Villa, trade expert and Latin America Regional Manager at TTI. "Efficient border-crossing processes, improved cross-border trucking, updated infrastructure with increased use of technology, and information exchange are some of the key elements that require continued work."

The TTI research team reviewed numerous research reports published over the past 10 years to identify points of consensus among researchers on the outcomes of NAFTA implementation and on recommendations for improvement.

Chief among the successes are harmonization of climate change policies and efficient tri-lateral energy production supply chains. These developments have contributed to U.S.-Canada surface trade doubling and U.S.-Mexico trade quadrupling in the 20 years since the implementation of NAFTA. The study also provides an overview of broadly agreed upon barriers holding back further economic success.

"*NAFTA 20 Years After* identifies expert agreement on unresolved issues stalling the advancement of economic integration that would make the entire North American trade bloc more competitive," says Dr. Stephen Blank, co-chair of the North American Transportation Competitiveness Research Council. "Policy and process modernization is lagging behind the pace of growth."

Source: *Logistics Management*, June 2014, p. 42. Reprinted with permission of Peerless Media, LLC.

Policy Interpretations

Although the declarations of national transportation policy are general and somewhat vague, they do provide a guide to the factors that should be considered in transportation decision making. However, the statements contain numerous conflicting provisions. This section analyzes the incompatibility of the various provisions.

Provisions The declarations are statements of policy for those modes regulated by the STB. Therefore, only railroads, oil pipelines, motor carriers, and water carriers are considered. **Air carriers** are excluded from consideration.

The requirement of "fair and impartial regulation" also overlooks **exempt carriers** in motor and water transportation. The exempt carriers are eliminated from the economic controls administered by the STB and therefore are not included in the stated policy provisions.

Congress requested the STB to administer transportation regulation in such a manner as to recognize and preserve the inherent advantage of each mode. An inherent advantage is the innate superiority one mode possesses in the form of cost or service characteristics when compared to the other modes. Such modal characteristics change over time as technology and infrastructure change.

It has been recognized that railroads have an inherent advantage of lower cost in transporting freight long distances and that motor carriers have the advantage for moving freight short distances—less than 800 miles. If the preservation of inherent advantage were the only concern, the STB would not permit motor carriers to haul freight long distances (more than 800 miles) nor railroads to haul freight short distances. However, shippers demand long-distance moves from motor carriers and short-distance moves from railroads, and the STB permits these services to be provided.

Safe, adequate, economical, and efficient service is not totally attainable. An emphasis on safety might mean an uneconomical or inefficient service. Added safety features on equipment and added safety procedures for employees will increase total costs and cost per unit of output and might reduce the productivity of employees. However, when lives are involved, safety takes precedence over economical and efficient service.

Providing adequate service has been construed to mean meeting normal demand. If carriers were forced to have capacity that is sufficient to meet peak demand, considerable excess capacity would exist, resulting in uneconomical and inefficient operations. Fostering sound economic conditions among the carriers does not mean ensuring an acceptable profit for all carriers. Nor does it imply that the STB should guarantee the survival of all carriers. The STB must consider the economic condition of carriers in rate rulings so as to foster stability of transportation supply.

The policy statement regarding reasonable charges, unjust discrimination, undue preference, and unfair competitive practices is merely a reiteration of the **common carrier** obligations. Congress made no attempt to define these concepts. The STB was given the task of interpreting them as it hears and decides individual cases.

A number of laws provide some degree of definition for these common carrier policy statements. For example, the Staggers Rail Act of 1980 defined a reasonable rail rate as one that is not more than 160 percent of variable costs. The Motor Carrier Act of 1980 defined a zone of rate freedom in which a rate change of 10 percent either up or down in one year is presumed to be reasonable. Both acts defined the normal business entertainment of shippers as acceptable practice and not an instance of undue preference.

The cooperative efforts between the federal and state governments have not always been amicable. The very foundation for federal regulation of transportation was the judicial decision that only the federal government could regulate interstate transportation. Through police powers, the states have the right to establish laws regarding transportation safety. Thus, for example, states have enacted laws governing the height, length, weight, and speed of motor carrier vehicles. However, the federal government has standardized weight and speed laws on interstate highways. One approach the federal government has taken has been to threaten to withhold federal highway money from states that do not comply with federal regulations.

Finally, the STB was charged with the responsibility of encouraging fair wages and working conditions in transportation. No attempt was made to interpret the terms **fair wage** and **working conditions**. A wage that is deemed fair by an employee might be unfair to an employer. This might also conflict with the policy statement regarding the promotion of economical and efficient service.

The stated goals of the national transportation policy are to provide a system of transportation that meets the needs of commerce, the U.S. Postal Service, *and* national defense. A possibility exists that a system that meets the needs of commerce might be insufficient to meet the needs of national defense during an emergency situation. In addition, a system that has the capacity to meet national defense needs will have excess capacity for commerce and postal service needs during peace times. For example, the United States maintains a merchant marine fleet that can be called into service to transport defense material during a national defense emergency. However, this fleet might be twice the size of that needed for commerce. Many government critics claim a fleet with such excess capacity is a waste of resources. Defense advocates argue that national defense needs dictate that such a fleet be operated to preclude dependency on a foreign country for water transportation during defense emergencies. From these two viewpoints it is easy to see how conflicts can occur in the national transportation goals.

The ICCTA provides specific direction to the STB regarding the railroads and motor carriers. For the railroads, the STB is directed to minimize the need for federal regulatory control, reduce regulatory barriers to entry and exit, prohibit predatory pricing, and promote energy conservation. For motor carriers, the STB is to allow pricing variety, to promote greater participation by minorities, and to promote transportation.

Who Establishes Policy?

National transportation policies are developed at various levels of government and by many different agencies. The specifics of a particular policy might reflect the persuasion of a group of individuals (for example, a consumer group) or of a single individual (for example, an elected official). The purpose of this section is to examine the basic institutional framework that aids in the development of national transportation policy.

Executive Branch[7] Many departments within the executive branch of government influence (establish) transportation policy. Leading these departments is the office of the president. The president has authority over international air transportation and foreign air carriers operating in the United States. The president also appoints individuals to lead the various agencies that influence transportation and to lead the two regulatory agencies—the STB and the FMC.

The Department of State is directly involved in developing policy regarding international transportation by air and water. The policies and programs designed to encourage foreign visitors to the United States are implemented by the U.S. Travel Service. The Maritime Administration is involved with ocean (international) transportation policy.

It determines ship requirements, service, and routes essential to foreign commerce. In addition, international transportation policies and programs are shaped by the Military Sealift Command, Military Airlift Command, and Military Traffic Management Command—agencies responsible for the movement of military goods and personnel.

On the domestic level, the Department of Energy develops policies regarding energy availability and distribution (fuel and rationing). The U.S. Postal Service contracts for transportation of the mail; such contracts have been used to promote air transportation as well as motor and rail transportation. The Department of Housing and Urban Development (HUD) consults with the DOT regarding the compatibility of urban transportation systems within the HUD-administered housing and community development programs. The Army Corps of Engineers is responsible for constructing and maintaining rivers, harbors, locks, and dams for the protection of navigable waterways.

The DOT, however, is the most pervasive influence of transportation policy at the domestic level. The Secretary of Transportation is responsible for assisting the president in all transportation matters, including public investment, safety, and research. (See Appendix 3A at the end of this chapter for a list of agencies within the DOT.)

Congressional Committees The laws formulated by Congress are the formal method by which Congress influences national transportation. The congressional committee structure is the forum in which Congress develops policies, programs, and funding for transportation.

Within the Senate, the two committees that influence transportation are the Committee on Commerce, Science, and Transportation and the Committee on Environment and Public Works. Within the Committee on Commerce, Science, and Transportation is the Subcommittee on Surface Transportation and Merchant Marine Infrastructure, Safety, and Security. This subcommittee is concerned with bus safety, supply chain security, motor carrier driver hours of service, the STB, railroad safety, hazardous material transportation by motor carriers, the Maritime Administration, and the Coast Guard. Another subcommittee is concerned with Aviation Operations, Safety, and Security. This subcommittee focuses on air traffic congestion, aviation safety, the FAA, and the NTSB. The Environment and Public Works Committee deals with internal waterway and harbor projects, highway construction and maintenance projects, and air and water pollution regulations.

The House of Representatives has restructured its committees regarding transportation. The two main House committees on transportation are the Transportation and Infrastructure Committee and the Energy and Commerce Committee. The Transportation and Infrastructure Committee is concerned with the FAA, rail infrastructure projects, the STB, pipeline safety, hazardous material transportation, the NTSB, and the Coast Guard. The other House committee is the Energy and Commerce Committee. Its basic responsibility is interstate and foreign commerce.

In addition to the above committees, numerous other congressional committees have an impact on transportation. Federal funding can be decided in the Appropriations Committee, Senate Banking Committee, Housing and Urban Affairs Committee, House Ways and Means Committee, or the Senate Finance Committee.

Regulatory Agencies The STB and FMC are independent agencies charged with implementing the laws regulating transportation. The agencies have quasi-judicial, quasi-executive, and quasi-legislative powers. They can establish policy when they interpret law, can decide on cases (such as the reasonableness of rates), and can enforce their decisions with the help of the court system.

Judicial System The courts have been called upon to interpret laws or reconcile conflicts. In doing so, the courts have an impact on transportation policies. Carriers, shippers, and the general public can call upon the courts to change existing policy through interpretation of statutes. As the regulatory agencies exercise quasi-legislative, quasi-judicial, and quasi-executive powers, the affected parties seek recourse to the courts to determine the legality of the decisions. The role of the courts is basically to interpret the meaning of policy as stated in laws, regulations, and executive orders.

Industry Associations One facet of national policy development that is often overlooked in the study of transportation is the role of industry associations in shaping national, state, and local promotion, regulation, and policy. These associations exist in most industries and their focus is to lobby Congress and other influential groups in the government to pass laws that will help their members.

These associations are nonprofit entities that derive their powers and resources from member firms. They act on the charges given to them by their members. In transportation, the railroads in the Association of American railroads (AAR) and the motor carriers in the American Trucking Associations (ATA) often meet to resolve matters of equipment uniformity and loss and damage prevention. On the policy side, these associations develop legislative and administrative ruling concepts that favor the collective membership, or they serve as a united front against proposals that are perceived to be harmful to the group.

The major industry associations in the transportation industry have evolved from specific modes. The AAR represents the large railroads in the United States; it was instrumental in the passage of the Staggers Rail Act of 1980. The ATA is divided into sub-conferences including agriculture and food transporters, automobile carriers, and intermodal motor carriers. The Air Transport Association represents the airline industry in the United States. The American Waterways Operators (AWO) consists of barge operators on the inland waterway network. The American Bus Association represents common and charter bus firms.

Two major associations exist for the interests of large shippers. One is the National Industrial Transportation League (NITL), and the other is the National Shippers Strategic Transportation Council (NASSTRAC). Both are active before congressional bodies, regulatory agencies, and carrier groups.

The Transportation Association of America (TAA), which ceased operation in 1982, had as its concern the health and vitality of the entire U.S. transportation system. It became involved in policy issues relating to two or more modes, or between modes and shippers, as well as investors. The TAA was largely instrumental in the passage of the Act that created the DOT, as well as the passage of the Uniform Time Standards Act, which caused all areas of the United States electing to recognize daylight savings time to do so at the same time in April. Previously, each state did so on different dates, which caused major confusion in railroad and airline scheduling systems and timetable publication. At one point, United Airlines had to publish 27 different timetables during the spring as various states recognized daylight savings time on different dates. Since it was enacted in 1967, the Uniform Time Standards Act has simplified these facets of transportation management.

Other groups and associations are involved in transportation policy, including non-transportation special interest groups such as the grange and labor unions. Various government agencies such as the Department of Agriculture and the Department of Defense influence existing and proposed transportation legislation on their behalf, or on the behalf of groups within them.

One of the most important government policy issues has been the public promotion of transportation. All of the above groups and associations have been involved over the years in this important area. The topic is of such importance as a policy issue that it is considered in detail in the next section.

ON THE **LINE**

Bill That Would Jack Up Insurance Minimum by 400 Percent Seen as a Long Shot

The way the trucking industry and several major shipper groups see it, the candidate for the author of the most ridiculous bill in Congress is Rep. Matt Cartwright (D-Pa.), a rookie congressman who wants to jack up the minimum injury and property damage insurance level for trucking companies by over 400 percent.

Rep. Cartwright, a personal injury attorney before winning his congressional seat last year, says that the current truck insurance minimum has not been changed since the Motor Carrier Act of 1980 deregulated the trucking industry.

Cartwright said he wants it increased from its current $750,000 to $4.4 million under the bill, which is considered a long shot to pass the Republican controlled House of Representatives. Still, Cartwright seems passionate about its merits.

"This legislation is essential to protecting our nation's highways and ensuring victims receive the proper amount of compensation for their losses," Cartwright said in a statement.

The ATA and at least one leading industry chief executive strongly disagreed with the freshman congressman, saying current insurance minimums are adequate.

"I think it would be a big industry issue because of the number of small companies that might have to exit the industry because of this," said James Welch, chief executive office of YRC Worldwide. "I don't see it passing, and I don't think we need to go that high. Most of the reputable carriers carry sufficient levels of insurance. It would be a big thing if it were to pass, but I don't think it has much of a chance of passing."

Industry officials say that the marketplace for trucking insurance is working adequately without Congressional interference. They say unsafe carriers generally have to pay higher insurance premiums while the larger, better-capitalized fleets tend to better emphasize safety and have better safety records, and generally pay lower premiums.

For example, the five operating companies that comprise YRC Worldwide currently have in excess of 2,300 drivers who currently have streaks in excess of 1 million accident free miles. Hundreds of those drivers have more than 2 million accident free miles, with dozens exceeding the 3 million mile mark.

John Cutler, general counsel for NASSTRAC and the Health and Personal Care Distribution Conference, called Rep. Cartwright's proposal a solution in search of a problem.

"I have had several inquiries on this from shipper clients and my advice to them has been: Hardly anything is going anywhere in Congress these days, but let's keep an eye on it," said Cutler, who added that NASSTRAC and the health care conference have yet to take a formal position on the bill.

"We would probably oppose it," Cutler said. "When you think about it, what the guy is saying is that we have this fee that it hasn't been raised or indexed for inflation and times have changed. Well, you can say that about thousands of user fees. How about the fuel tax? That hasn't been raised since 1993. The idea of singling out the trucking industry alone doesn't make any sense to us."

Source: John D. Schultz, *Logistics Management*, September 2013, pp. 14–15. Reprinted with permission of Peerless Media, LLC.

Public Promotion

This section presents an overview of the major transportation planning and promotion activities conducted in the U.S. public sector. Promotion connotes encouragement or provision of aid or assistance so transportation can grow or survive. *Planning* and *promotion* are general terms used to refer to programs, policies, and actual planning. Programs involve actual public cash investments into or funding for transportation activities both privately and publicly owned. Agencies make policies to encourage beneficial actions or impacts for transportation. Planning determines future transportation needs and then establishes policies or programs to bring about certain goals through the public or private sector. All three activities promote transportation and cause it to grow or survive in instances in which pure market forces could not have done so.

Transportation Planning and the Public Sector

Transportation project planning is the process whereby federal, state, or local groups review the movement needs or demands of a region or population segment, develop transportation alternatives, and usually propose and implement an alternative. This process enables the development of new movement processes or allows existing ones to continue in an environment of change.

Transportation project planning is a public activity; purely financial returns and other concerns are not the overriding benefits sought. It is a major part of the public activity in the U.S. economy for several reasons. First, public transportation processes can facilitate trade or movement where private actions have not or would not have been enticed to do so for financial gain alone. Second, various cultural and political benefits often come from projects and programs provided publicly. Third, transportation planning also lowers the cost of living or reduces the social costs of delay or congestion. Finally, transportation planning provides services that are not remunerative but are deemed socially necessary or desirable.

Transportation planning has been a critical factor in the beginning of the 21st century. There are many areas of transportation investment from which private firms have withdrawn. Many forms of transportation today are no longer economically profitable or compensatory. Urban bus systems, commuter railroads, rail and urban research and development, and many rail services are examples of transportation forms that would not exist without public sector involvement.

Many forms of transportation require large capital investments that would normally discourage or basically prohibit private investment. Port dredging and development, as well as airport and highway construction, are examples of capital items that are not affordable by the carriers using them. Instead, the ability of a public authority to attract capital enables the asset to be built; cost is recovered through user charges.

Public planning of transportation is generally found in situations where environmental or social needs override financial ones. A major argument used in modern subway construction is that, although the system might not recover its full costs from passenger fares, the city as a whole will benefit by increased access to already existing downtown facilities, including buildings, offices, stores, and water utility systems. Constructing other facilities in developing suburban areas will not be necessary. Also, commuters save money because the subway eliminates the need for a second family auto, long driving times, excess fuel consumption, costly parking in downtown areas, and so on. Public planning of transportation involves a different viewpoint and set of objectives than does capital investment analysis in private firms.

An Approach to Public Project Planning Analysis

While a private firm seeks a financial return to the firm itself, public planning agencies compare the initial costs of a project to the financial, environmental, and measurable social benefits to everyone affected by the project. Thus, it compares total societal cost to total societal benefits, whether they be monetary or nonmonetary in nature.

The specific analytical tool typically used in public planning is the **benefit/cost ratio** (BCR). In essence, the BCR is a measure of total measurable benefits to society divided by the initial capital cost. The formula in its basic form is as follows:

$$\text{BCR} = \frac{\text{Sum of yearly benefits to society}}{\text{Sum of costs to agencies and those in society initially impacted}}$$

$$= \frac{\text{Sum of benefits}}{\text{Sum of initial costs}} = \frac{\text{Year 1 benefit} + \text{Year 2 benefit} + \ldots}{\text{Sum of all initial costs}}$$

If the resulting answer is greater than one, the project is said to produce a "profit" for society. A BCR of one indicates the break-even point; less than one indicates that the agency will spend more on the project than society will reap in long-term benefits.

The major costs of a project include those expenses typically involved in private projects. Planning, engineering, construction, and financing costs are critical to the decision. Other costs include delay or congestion measured in terms of dollars per hour and in terms of everyone in society who will be inconvenienced during the construction phase of a transportation project. Project costs can also include a cost of lost sales to businesses; for example, stores are more difficult to access during several years of subway construction. The costs of bond financing incurred to construct the system are also pertinent. All costs are measured or translated into monetary terms and listed according to the year in which they will occur. Typically, the major expenses arise in the initial years of construction; financing is a major cost carried through the project's life.

The benefits of a project include any measurable benefit to the agency, other agencies, and the public. Benefits include increased employment, decreased prices for products, lowered costs of commuting or freight transport, reduced maintenance, improved health due to lessened pollution, and so on. Many benefits are easily quantified, though others pose analytical difficulties in the form of forecasting volumes and cost relationships in future periods.

The timing and **time value of funds** are important parts of any capital project analysis. Political controversy exists about the choice of the specific discount rate and its application. Several analytical points can be examined that will shed light on this task. First, the discount rate should reflect the interest cost and impact to the public agency that borrows the initial funds. Second, the rate should become higher in later years to reflect increasing risk, inflation, uncertainty, and forecasting difficulties. This is a conservative practice of private project financial managers, and the logic of it can be applied soundly in a public setting. Third, the counting of benefits should cease in some future period, even though the project might last longer. This is another practice that is an implicit way of conservatively considering only those benefits within the intermediate term, unless a logical case can be made for an extended period of time. These points are made as to ensure that benefit overcounting is minimized.

An example of a benefit/cost ratio application to a proposed subway line will show how public planning processes are employed. Costs include those of organization development, design, engineering, initial financing, land purchases, relocation, and disruption to the public. Costs projected into the future include operations, lost property taxes, interest costs, and any other costs directly tied to the project. Benefits to the agencies include lowered operational costs of city buses; alternative application of funds released from the bus operation (reduced street and highway requirements); decreased need to expand highways or downtown parking; increased property, sales, and wage taxes from higher economic activity downtown; avoidance of federal penalties for not reducing city-wide auto emissions; and many others. Benefits to society include the income multiplier effect from the initial project investment in the form of employment and flow of dollars from the construction itself. The system will improve society in the form of saved time, lower pollution levels, and reduced commuting stress. The subway will generally cause the downtown to become more fully utilized resulting in a steady or increasing tax base.

From the earlier discussion it can be concluded that public planning involves many of the basic concepts inherent in private planning, but the application is different. The public agency is concerned about costs and benefits to all parties affected by the project. Thus, costs, benefits, and "profits" are measured for society as a whole in tangible and intangible ways. The following discussion presents those forms of modal promotion found in the United States.

Air

The domestic air system receives the benefits of several government programs. Foremost is the FAA **air traffic control system**. This system provides navigation and safety for every aircraft in flight within the United States. The system assesses no direct fee to the airlines for its use and captures its operating expenses from airlines and passengers through user charges.

Another direct airline benefit is the subsidy program. These subsidies generally apply to short and medium non-jet flights to cities that are unable to support high traffic volumes. The subsidy has been a significant support mechanism for regional airlines. In recent years, the growth of commuter airlines has enabled regional airlines to discontinue service to small cities. The Air Deregulation Act of 1978 accelerated this trend, which resulted in a lessened need for regional airline subsidies.

The U.S. Postal Service also provides substantial support to airlines. The prime source of income for airlines during their early years came from this subsidy program. In recent years, mail income has not been as significant, but this subsidy is a major revenue source for the industry.

State and local agencies help promote the airline industry through air terminal development and construction. Terminals represent substantial capital investments and would be difficult for the industry to finance and construct. State and local agencies are able to raise the necessary construction funds at reasonable municipal bond interest rates, often backed by the taxing power of the community. The airlines then rent terminal and hangar facilities and pay landing fees for each flight.

Many aircraft safety matters are handled by the federal government. The FAA provides aircraft construction and safety rules as well as pilot certification. In another capacity, the NTSB investigates accidents so that others might be avoided or reduced through aircraft specifications or flight procedures.

Another indirect form of promotion to the airline industry comes from the military. Defense contracts for military aircraft development often provide direct benefits to commercial aviation in the form of mechanical or navigational aircraft improvements. Without military-related research and development activity, advancements in this area would take place at a slower pace and at a higher cost to the private sector.

A last form of airline promotion, which is not found in the U.S. system, is direct government ownership, operation, or subsidy of air service. This is common with foreign airlines that serve the United States. In these instances, African, Asian, Latin American, and many European airlines are subsidized so the countries can operate their airlines for purposes of national defense, have some degree of control over traffic to and from their nations, and gain balance-of-payment benefits and hard currencies through ticket revenues.

A related form of such **home-flag airline** promotion exists in the United States and in most foreign nations. In the United States, there is a requirement that only United States flag carriers with domestically owned aircraft and domestic crews may originate and terminate domestic passengers and freight. Many foreign lines serve both New York and Los Angeles, for example, with a flight originating abroad, but these flights are limited to international passengers. The only way in which a foreign line can originate and terminate a passenger in two U.S. cities is when that passenger is exercising stopover privileges as part of a tour or through movement. This home-flag requirement serves to protect U.S. airlines.

Several forms of **user charges** are designed, in whole or part, to have the modes pay for many of the public benefits they receive. As mentioned before, landing fees are charged to repay investments or generate revenue for specific airports. A major user charge is levied against passenger movements through ticket taxes. An international per-head tax is also part of this user tax, as are some aircraft registration fees. Many of these funds go into the **Airport and Airway Trust Fund**, which is used for airport facility projects on a shared basis with local agencies.

Motor and Highway

With regard to public promotion, the highway system and motor carrier firms have a joint relationship. There is no direct promotion to the motor carriers themselves, but indirect benefit comes to the industry through **highway development** because most highway projects are completed with government funds.

The Federal Highway Administration (FHWA) branch of the DOT is responsible for federal highway construction and safety. A predecessor agency, the Bureau of Public Roads, carried out the mandate to build the Interstate Highway System, which was paid for on a 90 percent/10 percent federal/state sharing basis. Today the FHWA is largely devoted to highway research, development, and safety. It also is charged with certain repair projects on critical parts of the federal and interstate highway system. Motor carriers benefit from the increased access, speed, and safety of this system because without it they would have to travel more congested routes, presenting safety hazards.

The National Highway Traffic Safety Administration (NHTSA) is responsible for highway and auto safety. It also conducts major research into vehicle safety, accidents, and highway design related to safety. This agency provides administrative regulations for certain minimum automobile safety features.

The FMCSA is a non-economic regulatory body whose main purpose is motor carrier vehicle safety. Though this agency imposes strict standards on motor carrier vehicle safety, the long-term benefit is increased safety for everyone on the highways.

Highway development also comes from states and various regional planning commissions. One example is the Appalachian Regional Commission, which is charged with improving the infrastructure and economy of that region. Many highway and improvement projects are funded by this agency.

User charges are present in the highway systems in several forms. A major form is the fuel tax. States look to this per-gallon tax as a major revenue source for highway construction and maintenance. The federal government's fuel taxes go to the **Federal Highway Trust Fund**, which is the financing source for the Interstate Highway System. Some states have switched from a per-gallon to a percent of sales price method of fuel-based taxation because, in recent years, the number of gallons of fuel sold has decreased, leaving state agencies with less revenue in times that demand greater highway maintenance. The percent of sales price approach can avoid much of this decline. Another public revenue source is the federal excise tax on vehicle tires. States also obtain revenues through vehicle registration fees. These mostly are assessed on a vehicle weight basis so as to recoup, somewhat, a proportionate share of construction costs related to heavier versus lighter vehicles. Further, some states (such as Oregon) assess a ton-mile tax. Finally, tolls are a form of user taxes on turnpikes and many bridges.

Two major controversies are taking place with regard to highway user charges. One concerns the Federal Highway Trust Fund. The tax money that goes into this fund is collected primarily for interstate highway construction. Approximately 96 percent of the interstate system has been built, but doubt exists over whether the remaining portions, mostly very costly urban sections, will ever be built. Meanwhile, the fuel tax continues to be collected and accumulated in the fund.

A second problem with user taxes is on the state level. Most states collecting vehicle fees and vehicle taxes only return a portion of them for highway purposes. Some states have earmarked some of these funds for education and other uses. In addition, industry groups continue to seek a greater share of these funds for highway development and improvement.

Rail

The railroads currently can avail themselves of direct assistance from the Regional Railroad Reorganization Act of 1973, the Railroad Revitalization and Regulatory Reform Act of 1976, and the Staggers Rail Act of 1980. Most of the assistance is in the form of track repair and motive power acquisition financing. These provisions are attempts to overcome the problem of poor equipment and facilities, which lead to ineffective service and severe financial conditions.

Another form of funding has been available as a subsidy to lines that are abandoned by railroads but that states and other groups continue to operate. This assistance was designed to make rail line abandonment easier for railroads while still allowing service to continue.

The Consolidated Rail Corporation (Conrail) had been the subject of special federal funding and promotion. It had received special appropriations for operations capital improvements, mainly through provisions of the Regional Railroad Reorganization Act of 1973. Recently, after a successful transformation, Conrail was purchased by the Norfolk Southern and CSX Railroads. Conrail's routes were integrated into these two companies.

Research and development in this mode essentially disappeared in the late 1950s. Financial problems in most railroads caused reductions in the research and development area, thereby stagnating the technology. In response to this situation, the FRA was created as part of the DOT in 1966. The FRA has become a major source of gains in railroad technology as well as in safety. A test facility located near Pueblo, Colorado, originally owned by the FRA, is used to test improvements in existing motive power and rolling equipment and to develop advanced high-speed rail technologies for the future. This facility, now known as the Transportation Technology Center, has been privatized and is managed by the AAR.

Another form of assistance to the railroad industry is **Amtrak**. In 1969, the industry's intercity passenger deficit reached more than $500 million. Because the ICC, the DOT, and the public deemed many of these services essential to the public need, the railroads could only discontinue them slowly after major procedural steps were taken. Amtrak was created to relieve this burden from the railroads, while at the same time providing some of the needed services to the public. Thus, much of the passenger train deficit was shifted from the railroads and their customers and stockholders to the federal taxpayer.

Domestic Waterway Operations

The inland barge industry receives two major forms of federal promotion. The first is from the **Army Corps of Engineers**, which is responsible for river and port channel dredging and clearances, as well as lock and dam construction. Operation and maintenance of these facilities rest with the Corps as well. The second is provided by the **U.S. Coast Guard**, which is responsible for navigation aids and systems on the inland waterway system.

Historically, the barge industry paid no user charges except what could be interpreted as a very indirect form through general income taxes. A major controversy over a critical lock and dam on the upper Mississippi River in Alton, Illinois, brought the free-use issue to a decision. The competing railroad industry lobbied to prevent this lock from being improved and enlarged. The resulting legislation and appropriation provided for improvement of that lock and initiated a fuel tax user charge for the barge industry.

International Water Carriage

The American flag overseas steamship industry receives major assistance from the federal government through the Maritime Administration (**MARAD**). The Merchant Marine Act of 1936 was designed to prevent economic decline of the U.S. steamship industry. One major portion of this Act is construction differential subsidies (CDS). These are paid by MARAD to U.S. steamship yards that are constructing subsidized lines' ships. A ship that might only cost $20 million to build in Asia might cost $30 million to build in a U.S. yard. A CDS of $10 million is given to the U.S. shipyard so it can charge the U.S. steamship company $20 million, rather than $30 million, to build its ship. Without CDS, U.S. lines would build their ships abroad and American ship-building capacity would cease to exist. The survival of the U.S. shipyard is also viewed as essential to U.S. military capability. The Merchant Marine Act of 1936 also provides for operating differential subsidies (ODS), which cover the higher cost increment resulting from having higher-paid American crews on ships, rather than less costly foreign labor.

Several **indirect** forms of **promotion** exist in this industry as well. The U.S. cabotage laws state that freight or passengers originating or terminating in two U.S. points can only be transported in ships constructed in the United States and owned and managed by U.S. citizens. The United States also has a **cargo preference** law that assists the U.S.

fleet. Enacted in 1954, it stipulates that at least 50 percent of the gross tonnage of certain U.S. government-owned and -sponsored cargoes must be carried by U.S. flag ships. This law extends to Department of Defense military goods, foreign aid by the State Department, surplus food movements by the Department of Agriculture, and products whose financing is sponsored by the Export-Import Bank. To be granted a U.S. flag registry, all of a ship's officers and pilots, as well as 75 percent of its other on-board personnel, must be U.S. citizens or residents. The ship must also be owned by U.S. citizens and constructed in a U.S. shipyard.

Several planning and facilitating promotional efforts also assist the American flag ocean fleet. MARAD continually studies and develops plans for port improvements and ways in which export-import movements can be made more efficient. The Department of Commerce has a subagency (the International Trade Administration) whose prime purpose is to stimulate export sales that also benefit the U.S. fleet.

Two points should be mentioned with regard to the major funding and support roles played by MARAD. One deals with the control MARAD has over the lines it subsidizes. The agency exercises decision powers over the design and construction of each ship. It also plays a major role in the routes taken by each one. In this manner, the agency makes certain decisions that are normally within the discretion of carrier managements. This form of control is unique to the transportation industry in the United States.

The other point relates to the rationale for such extensive assistance to this one industry. A strong U.S. shipping fleet is a vital part of national defense sealift capacity in the event of war. Also, existence of the fleet tends to exert some influence on services and rates on various trade routes to the benefit of the United States and its interests.

The **Shipping Act of 1984** (now replaced with the Foreign Shipping Practices Act of 1998) is a further example of the U.S. policy toward supporting a strong U.S. ocean fleet. The Act was designed to reduce the regulation on foreign ocean shipping with the following goals:

- Establishing a nondiscriminatory regulatory process for common ocean carriers with a minimum of government intervention and regulatory costs;
- Providing an efficient and economic transportation system in the ocean commerce of the United States that is in harmony and responsive to international shipping practices; and
- Encouraging the development of an economically sound and efficient U.S. flag fleet capable of meeting national security needs.

The St. Lawrence Seaway Development Corporation within the DOT functions as the U.S. financing and operating arm of the joint United States/Canada venture to upgrade the Great Lakes waterway and lock system to accommodate oceangoing ships. This waterway opened a fourth seacoast for the United States, enabling oceangoing ships to call at Buffalo, Cleveland, Toledo, Chicago, Duluth, and other inland ports.

A final, and major, positive role in the water carrier industry is played by various port authorities. These agencies provide financing, major construction, and leasing of facilities in much the same way that the airport authorities provides facilities to the air industry.

Pipeline

The pipeline industry receives no public financial support, but it has benefited in a legal sense from the right of eminent domain permitted to oil, gas, and petroleum product lines. Typically, a pipeline will negotiate for land acquisition or rental. If the landowner will not negotiate at all or in good faith, the law of eminent domain will uphold the use of the land for a pipeline right-of-way in a court of law.

Miscellaneous Forms of Promotion

Various other activities directly or indirectly benefit the transportation industry. The DOT conducts planning and research activities in several ways. First, the Office of Assistant Secretary for Policy and International Affairs is involved with improving international goods flow and conducting studies about the transportation system and data coordination. Second, other research and development studies of benefit to transportation are conducted by the Transportation Research Board and the National Science Foundation. Third, a small but effective group within the Department of Agriculture is concerned with improving loading, unloading, packaging, and carriage methods of food products on all modes of transportation. Many of these efforts result in equipment design changes that make transportation equipment more efficient for food movements. Finally, the Department of Defense continually examines methods to improve shipping, and many improvements carry over to the commercial sector.

Transportation Promotion in Perspective

Two major concepts override the entire topic of transportation promotion: user charges and nationalization. User charges often are created and assessed to pay for some or all of the services used by the carrier or mode. Nationalization represents an extreme form of public assistance or provision of transportation.

User Charges

User charges are assessments or fees charged by public bodies against carriers. They are created for a variety of reasons. One is to compensate the public for assistance during modal conception and encouragement. Some user charges are assessed to finance construction. The federal fuel tax on gasoline and diesel is an example, as is the barge fuel tax. Coverage of operating costs is often a reason for the origin of user charges. Examples here are airport landing fees, road tolls, and state fuel tax when it is applied to road maintenance. In addition, a user charge can also serve to equalize intermodal competitive conditions. The barge fuel tax, while paying for some lock construction, also makes barge operators bear some of the full cost of providing their service. This lessens, to a degree, some of the advantage that existed when right-of-way costs were borne by the public and not by the barge firm.

Forms User charges are present in three basic forms. The first is an **existence charge**, a charge related to the existence of some tangible item. This is similar to driver's license and auto registration fees. A charge is made against the person or unit regardless of the extent of use made of the services.

A second user charge is a **unit charge**. This is a fee assessed for use of a facility or resource. This fee is variable according to use, but it does not distinguish between passengers or freight within each unit. Tolls and fuel mileage taxes are examples. Thus, a bus with two passengers pays the same as does a bus with 40 passengers. An empty tractor-trailer or one that is full is charged the same. This form of fee assessment does not take into account the economic value of the service being performed.

A third user fee is based upon **relative use**. This form assesses fees according to the investment of cost incurred by the agency to provide the service. An increased vehicle registration fee for heavier tractor-trailers is an example. Deeper road bases are required for heavier vehicles. Road and bridge wear and damage are believed to be experienced on the basis of vehicle weight. Another example of relative use charge is a commuter route bridge toll. In the San Francisco area, bridge tolls are assessed for each vehicle. However, cars and vans having more than four passengers can cross the bridge toll-free. In this instance, the user charge becomes a behavior inducement. A form of *non-user fee* has arisen in recent years. Atlanta and San Francisco and area counties are partially paying for their shares of rapid transit development through a one-cent additional sales tax on all retail transactions within those areas. Here, many persons do not, or might not, ever use the rapid transit system, but they do bear some of its costs. A major rationale behind this non-user charge is that all persons in a community benefit at least indirectly from the improved infrastructure provided by the system.

Nationalization

Nationalization is an extreme form of public promotion. It basically consists of public ownership, financing, and operation of a business entity. No true forms of nationalization exist in the U.S. transportation system except the Alaska Railroad, which was owned by the DOT and is now owned by the state of Alaska. Nationalization is a method of providing transportation service where financing, ownership, or operations are not possible by private sources. Railroads and airlines in foreign countries are examples of nationalization, but many countries, such as Mexico, New Zealand, and Great Britain, are privatizing their railroads. Transportation service in many lands probably would not exist in a desirable form, or at all, without such government intervention. Advantages of nationalization that are often cited are that services can be provided that would not exist under private ownership, and that capital can be attracted at favorable rates. But nationalized organizations have been criticized as being slow to innovate, unresponsive to the general public, dependent on large management staffs, and subject to political influence.

Transportation Safety

As noted earlier, the federal government has assumed the responsibility of ensuring the safety of travelers. It has promulgated numerous safety regulations for all modes and has centralized safety enforcement in the DOT. Protection of the traveler and the general public is an increasing government concern in light of the reduced economic regulation of transportation and the resultant concerns that carriers will sacrifice safety matters for profitability or economic viability.

Since **economic deregulation**, greater attention has been given to the establishment and enforcement of safety regulation to ensure that the transportation providers do not defer required vehicle and operating safety requirements in lieu of competition. Critics of economic deregulation cite the market pressures on carriers to increase productivity and improve efficiency at the expense of safety. The deregulation experience in the airline and motor carrier industries has resulted in economic pressures on the carriers and a deleterious effect on safety, whereas the opposite is true for the railroads, which have been able to increase profitability and safety.[8]

Federal safety regulations cover all aspects of transportation operations from labor qualifications and operating procedures to equipment specifications. The primary objective of the safety regulations is to establish a **minimum level of safety** for transportation providers to maintain. Many transportation companies establish higher safety levels than those required by law, and these companies have their own enforcement personnel to ensure compliance.

Labor safety regulations have established minimum qualifications for operating personnel, including such factors as age, health, training, licensing, and experience. Minimum age requirements were established for driving a tractor-trailer in interstate commerce, and a nationwide commercial driver-licensing program was initiated in 1988. Airline pilots are required to pass a physical exam, to have training and experience on specific types of aircraft, and to be certified for various types of flying conditions. Similar regulations govern rail engineers and ship captains.

The policy of safe transportation has been extended to the specification of **standards** for transportation vehicles. These standards range from design specifications for aircraft to required safety equipment for automobiles. The vehicle manufacturer is obligated to adhere to the safety specifications, and the vehicle operator is required to maintain the vehicle and equipment in good operating condition and to use the safety equipment. For example, the automobile manufacturer must equip each vehicle with seat belts, a minimum number of headlights and taillights, a horn, and so forth. The auto owner then is required by state law to use the seat belts and to ensure proper functioning of the lights, horn, and other features.

Of all the commodities moved within the boundaries of the United States, **hazardous materials** pose the greatest threat to public safety. Consequently, the movement of hazardous materials and hazardous wastes has been subjected to considerable regulations. A hazardous material is a substance that poses more than a reasonable risk to the health and safety of individuals and includes products such as explosives, flammables, corrosives, oxidizers, and radioactive materials. Regulations regarding the transportation of hazardous materials can be found in the Code of Federal Regulations, Title 49. The safety regulations govern the movement of hazardous wastes as well, and can be found in the Code of Federal Regulations, Title 40. Technical requirements for transporting hazardous materials internationally by air and sea are managed by the International Civil Aviation Organization (ICAO) and the International Maritime Dangerous Goods Code. Many hazardous material and hazardous waste safety regulations have been imposed upon their transportation. The regulations govern loading and unloading practices, packaging, routing, commodity identification, and documentation. Transportation personnel must be trained to properly handle hazardous cargoes and to respond to emergencies.

These regulations overlap somewhat because of the overlapping jurisdiction of the regulatory agencies originating and enforcing the rules. For example, the DOT promulgates and enforces hazardous materials regulation, while the Environmental Protection Agency regulates the movement of hazardous wastes. In addition, the various states and municipalities within the states establish laws affecting the movement of hazardous commodities through their jurisdiction.

As indicated earlier, the states are involved in regulating the safe operation of transportation vehicles. The police powers of the Constitution grant the states the right to protect the health and welfare of their citizens. The states have used this power to establish safety regulations governing the safe operations of trains through a state, and to limit the maximum speed, height, length, and weight of tractor-trailers. These regulations are not standard from state to state because of the differing political, economic, sociological, and geographic conditions. However, the common denominator in state safety regulations is that all states regulate transportation safety matters.

Transportation safety matters have been extended to include environmental safety. Auto emission standards are designed to protect air quality; flight take-off procedures and patterns are designed to reduce noise levels for the citizens living near airports; and tanker loading and unloading procedures for petroleum products are designed to protect animals, sea life, and the landscape from the devastating effects from an oil spill.

One effect of the myriad safety regulations is an increase in the cost of transporting people and goods. The safety controls exercised by government usually add a direct cost to a transportation operation, making its service more costly to consumers. However, when the indirect social costs are considered, society feels that the benefits of safety regulations, including fewer deaths and injuries and a cleaner environment, more than offset the direct cost. In the future, the number and scope of safety regulations will increase as government expands its safety regulating authority into additional transportation areas.

TRANSPORTATION **TECHNOLOGY**

ATA, Shippers Applaud FMCSA Proposal for ELDs in Trucks

Large trucking companies and shippers are welcoming a government proposal that requires electronic logging devices (ELDs) in heavy trucks as a way to bolster trucking safety.

However, representatives of nearly 1 million owner-operators say that they have concerns over costs, privacy, how the data will be stored, and whether it could be used to harass drivers.

The March 13 proposal by the Federal Motor Carrier Safety Administration (FMCSA) is expected to cost the industry $1.6 billion. However, the mandated use of ELDs in commercial trucks is being hailed by the administration as a potential improvement for highway safety.

Trucking-related crash fatalities are on the rise, despite a decades-long crackdown on unsafe drivers through the greater use of accident data, mandatory drug and alcohol testing, and other measures. In 2012, the last full year for government statistics on the issue, 3,921 people died in trucking accidents—a 3.7 percent rise from the 3,781 fatalities in 2011. That was the third straight year of increases in trucking-related fatalities.

"ATA supports FMCSA's efforts to mandate these devices in commercial vehicles as a way to improve safety and compliance in the trucking industry and to level the playing field. Thousands of fleets have already voluntarily moved to this technology," said Bill Graves, president and CEO of the American Trucking Associations (ATA).

ATA Chairman Phil Byrd, president of Bulldog Hiway Express, added: "It's past time to replace pencil and paper with 21st century technology."

Shippers also seemed pleased with the new rule. Jeff Brady, director of transportation and logistics for Harry & David, a multi-channel specialty retailer and producer of branded premium gift-quality fruit and gifts, said that while this was another layer of regulation for the trucking industry, it was a worthwhile trade-off because of its potential for greater highway safety.

"By working to implement ELDs across the industry, I expect to see the government's assumptions of reduced costs associated to paperwork and improved accuracy being largely true," said Brady.

Still, there could be economic trade-offs. The mandated use of ELDs could reduce the effective number of miles a driver could log, further tightening trucking industry capacity at a time of limited truck driver supply, rising pay, and higher overall costs for fleets.

"In the interest of public safety, I support these efforts as it will reduce subpar carriers from the industry, which is a good thing," Brady explained. "However, it adds to further shrinkage within the industry in terms of available capacity. It also adds expense, as carriers will look to recoup the costs associated with the acquiring and implementing of the technology."

Brady describes the proposal as a classic trade-off of "safety versus costs" that may have unintended consequences in driver supply and productivity for fleets. "This is another example of where the industry will be further regulated—for seemingly the right reasons," Brady added. "However, the true economic impact of the ripple effect is not well thought out."

The FMCSA estimates that the mandate will prevent between 1,400 and 1,700 crashes and save more than 20 lives per year. That would lead to a net benefit to the country of $394.8 million annually, according to the FMCSA.

The Owner-Operator Independent Driver Association (OOIDA) has long opposed electronic logging devices on privacy grounds—and likely will be counted on for a court challenge on this latest proposal. FMCSA will have a 60-day comment period on the proposal before issuing the final rule.

Tilden Curl, an OOIDA member and independent driver from Olympia, Washington, told an FMCSA "listening session" at a recent event that highway safety cannot be enhanced without fundamentally addressing the root problems in the industry. According to Curl, those would include driver and "regulatory fatigue," and a system that he says is "penalty driven, rather than reward driven."

OOIDA's concerns over ELDs are that the data collected may not be private and could be used by carrier dispatchers into harassing drivers or forcing them to operate while fatigued. However, FMCSA has said that ELDs would not go beyond recording actual hours-of-service compliance and could not be utilized to harass drivers.

Source: *Logistics Management*, April 2014, pp. 13–14. Reprinted with permission of Peerless Media, LLC.

Transportation Security

After the September 11, 2001, terrorist attack on the United States, the Department of Homeland Security (DHS) was established with the goal of mobilizing and organizing the nation to secure the homeland from terrorist attacks. Its mission is to lead a unified national effort to secure America; to prevent and deter terrorist attacks and protect against and respond to threats and hazards to the nation; and to ensure and secure borders, welcome lawful immigrants and visitors, and promote the free flow of commerce.

DHS is charged with protecting the security of the transportation system, encompassing approximately 826 million air passengers (domestic and international), 10 million imported containers, and 96 million personal vehicle crossings into the United States, from Canada and Mexico in 2013.[9] The DHS transportation security programs and regulations are administered through the Coast Guard (CG), Customs Service (CS), and Transportation Security Administration (TSA).

The CG patrols the U.S. coastline and internal navigable waterways implementing the various security measures set forth by the DHS. The CG can stop a vessel from entering a U.S. port, board the vessel, and prevent any undesirable freight from being off-loaded from a vessel.

The TSA administers the air passenger security-screening process at U.S. airports. TSA hires and manages the airport screeners and sets forth items that are prohibited from being carried on board commercial passenger aircraft. TSA is testing various security devices and procedures to ensure the safety of passengers as well as reduce delays resulting from the security-screening process.

TSA has conducted a transit and rail inspection program with the goal of implementing rail passenger and luggage screening similar to that in the air passenger industry. In conjunction with Amtrak and the DOT, TSA is implementing Phase III of a first-time rail security technology study to evaluate the use of emerging technologies to screen checked and unclaimed baggage as well as temporarily stored personal items and cargo for explosives. TSA has also outlines guidelines for freight railroads on the handling of Toxic Inhalation Hazard (TIH) materials when they are being transported near heavily populated areas.

The U.S. Customs and Border Protection Agency (CBP) has been focusing on implementing security measures for cargo entering the United States. CBP has established the 24-hour rule that requires shippers to electronically transmit a description of the cargo to CBP 24 hours before loading. CBP can block any prohibited cargo items from being unloaded at any U.S. port or airport. CBP is working in partnership with shippers to streamline the security paperwork in an attempt to reduce the negative consequences on global commerce entering the United States.

Transportation security has been increased to protect the public against future terrorist attacks. President Bush signed into law the Implementing Recommendations of the 9/11 Commission Act of 2007 (public law 110-53). This law has four major sections: (1) transportation security planning and information sharing; (2) transportation security enhancements; (3) public transportation security; and (4) surface transportation security. As the security measures increase, the impact on the transportation system and transportation users is increased transit time and cost. The transportation security agencies are aware of the commercial impact and are taking steps to reduce the shipping and traveling delays while at the same time maintaining the needed level of security.

SUMMARY

- Imperfections in the marketplace in a free-enterprise economy provide the rationale for government intervention in business operations.
- Potential monopolistic abuses in transportation motivated the federal government to create the Interstate Commerce Commission (ICC) to regulate the transportation industry. The Surface Transportation Board (STB) replaced the ICC.
- The U.S. court system, through decisions under a common law system, also influences transportation regulation.
- All modes are subject to safety regulations administered by both federal and state agencies.
- The Department of Transportation (DOT) is the federal agency responsible for developing and implementing the overall transportation policy for the United States.
- Transportation regulation has progressed through four phases: Initiation Era, Positive Era, Intermodal Era, and the New Economic Era.
- In today's transportation environment, the federal government is a proponent of less economic regulation, preferring to allow market forces to regulate carrier prices and availability of supply.
- Increasing regulations for safety and security are placing a higher burden on carriers but lessening the risk to the public at large.

STUDY QUESTIONS

1. Discuss the rationale for the economic regulation of transportation.
2. How has common law provided a basis for the government's regulation of transportation in the United States?
3. Discuss the role of antitrust laws in transportation during the regulated versus deregulated eras.
4. How do the police powers of the Constitution affect transportation?
5. Why does the United States need a national transportation policy? What purpose does it serve?
6. Analyze the major issues addressed by the ICC Termination Act national transportation policy statements.
7. Unlike may industrialized nations, the United States has fostered private ownership of transportation companies. What is the rationale for private ownership?
8. What is the rationale for the public promotion of transportation?
9. What are transportation user charges? What is the purpose of such charges?
10. Discuss the advantages and disadvantages of increasing regulations relating to transportation safety and security. Be sure to include both transportation providers and transportation users in your discussion.

NOTES

1. Dudley F. Pegrum, *Public Regulation of Business*, Homewood, IL: Richard D. Irwin, 1959, pp. 21–24.
2. Ibid.

3. Federal Motor Carrier Safety Administration, FMCSA, 2014.
4. Ibid.
5. Sherman Antitrust Act of 1890, Sections 1 and 2.
6. U.S. Department of Transportation, *A Statement of National Transportation Policy*, Washington, DC, 1975, p. 1.
7. The material in this section is adapted from Transportation Policy Associates, *Transportation in America*, 4th ed., Washington, DC, 1986, pp. 28–31.
8. Paul Stephen Dempsey, "The Empirical Results of Deregulation: A Decade Later, and the Band Played On," *Transportation Law Journal*, Vol. 17, 1988, pp. 69–81.
9. http://www.bts.gov.

CASE 3-1

Who Pays the Price?

Over the last 10 years the federal government has dramatically increased the number of regulations pertaining to transportation security and the effects of transportation on the environment. After the terrorist attack on the United States on September 11, 2001, the Department of Homeland Security (DHS) was established. Within the DHS is the Transportation Security Administration, which is responsible for implementing regulations to protect the safety of passengers using the U.S. airline industry. These regulations require passengers to be screened for illegal items before they enplane, limit the size and nature of items in carry-on luggage, and provide guidelines for more intense scrutiny of randomly selected passengers. Critics of these policies complain that these policies delay passengers, increase time through airports, cause delays, and increase costs for the airlines. Proponents of these policies argue that the safety of air passengers is more important that these delays and increased costs.

The federal government passed legislation requiring all motor carrier tractors purchased after 2007 to meet more stringent EPA guidelines for engine emissions of particulate matter. These new guidelines require new engine technology that has increased the cost of these engines by over $10,000. Motor carriers are critical of these guidelines, arguing that the increased engine cost and resulting increase in maintenance costs are prohibitive and are difficult to pass on to customers in the form of higher prices. Proponents of these guidelines argue that cleaner engine exhaust is better for the environment and, therefore, a benefit to the general public.

Legislation is being considered to dramatically increase the number of inspections on containers entering U.S. ports from foreign origins. The purpose of the inspection is to reduce the likelihood of terrorist activity that could occur by using a container to hold weapons or explosives that are meant to harm U.S. citizens. The inspection would require physically unloading the container at the port and inspecting its contents. The rationale behind increasing the number of containers inspected is the resulting reduction in the probability of a terrorist attack on U.S. soil. Critics of this legislation argue that with the thousands of containers entering U.S. ports every, increased inspection activity would increase congestion at the ports, slow down the movement of goods into the United States, and add costs to carriers and shippers.

CASE QUESTIONS

1. In each of the three scenarios presented in the case, opponents and proponents have divergent views of government regulations. One view is on the public benefit, the other is on the cost to private industry. How can you decide which view to accept?
2. In each of the scenarios earlier, identify the benefits versus the costs for both viewpoints.
3. Should the government intervene in setting regulations to increase security and help the environment? Or should private industry take on this role? Discuss.

CASE 3-2

Federal Highway Infrastructure Funding

The Federal Highway Trust Fund was designed and passed by Congress to set tax rates per gallon of gasoline and diesel consumed by vehicles using the federal interstate system. The fund is then used to maintain the thousands of miles of interstate highway in the United States. This program has worked successfully up until the last several years when stricter EPA rules on fuel consumption have been implemented along with the introduction of hybrid and electric vehicles. Total miles driven and fuel consumed have decreased and, as such, have resulted in a decrease in taxes coming into the fund. The per-gallon tax rates have not changed since 1993, and the fund is expected to run out of money by the end of this year.

With the U.S. interstate highway system in need of major repairs, the federal government is attempting to put together a multi-billion dollar, multi-year funding bill that will address these maintenance needs. However, what is not yet agreed upon is where the additional funding will come from. Three main ideas have surfaced to generate these funds: (1) a gradual increase in the per-gallon fuel taxes over several years; (2) indexing the fuel tax to inflation; and (3) tolling major portions of the interstate system. There has been much debate in Congress about these approaches and many interest groups have voiced their opinions. As of yet, no decision has been made about the funding level and its sources of fees.

CASE QUESTIONS

1. Which of the three approaches make the best economic sense? Which one makes the best political sense?
2. What are the pros and cons of each approach? Be sure to include in your discussion the views of personal vehicles versus commercial vehicles.
3. Is there another alternative not yet introduced? What would it be and how would it be implemented?

APPENDIX 3A

Department of Transportation

The United States Department of Transportation (DOT) was established in 1966 to coordinate the administration of government transportation programs and to establish overall transportation policy that enables the provision of fast, safe, efficient, and convenient transportation at the lowest cost. As indicated in Figure 3A-1, the DOT consists of 12 different agencies with the Secretary of Transportation having the responsibility of coordinating the activities of these agencies as each administers the programs under its respective jurisdiction. The centralization of federal transportation activities under the auspices of one department in the executive branch focuses attention on the critical nature of transportation in the economy.

The operating programs of most of the individual agencies are basically organized by mode. The secretary and deputy secretary are responsible for the overall planning, direction, and control of departmental activities but do not exercise direct operating control over the agencies. Rather, the secretary's office is concerned with policy development, resource allocation, program evaluation, agency coordination, and intermodal matters.

The secretary is the principal advisor to the president on matters relating to federal transportation. The responsibility for domestic and international transportation policy development and review is delegated to the assistant secretary for policy and international affairs. On the domestic level, this policy formulation is directed toward assessing the economic impact of government regulations and programs on the industry and the economy. Such policy issues as public trust funds, user charges, energy and environmental concerns, subsidy levels for subsidized carriers, international mail rates, aviation and maritime concerns in multilateral and bilateral negotiations, and coordination of efforts to combat transportation-related terrorist acts and drug smuggling are representative of the wide range of policy responsibilities of the Secretary of Transportation.

FIGURE 3A-1 Agencies of the U.S. Department of Transportation

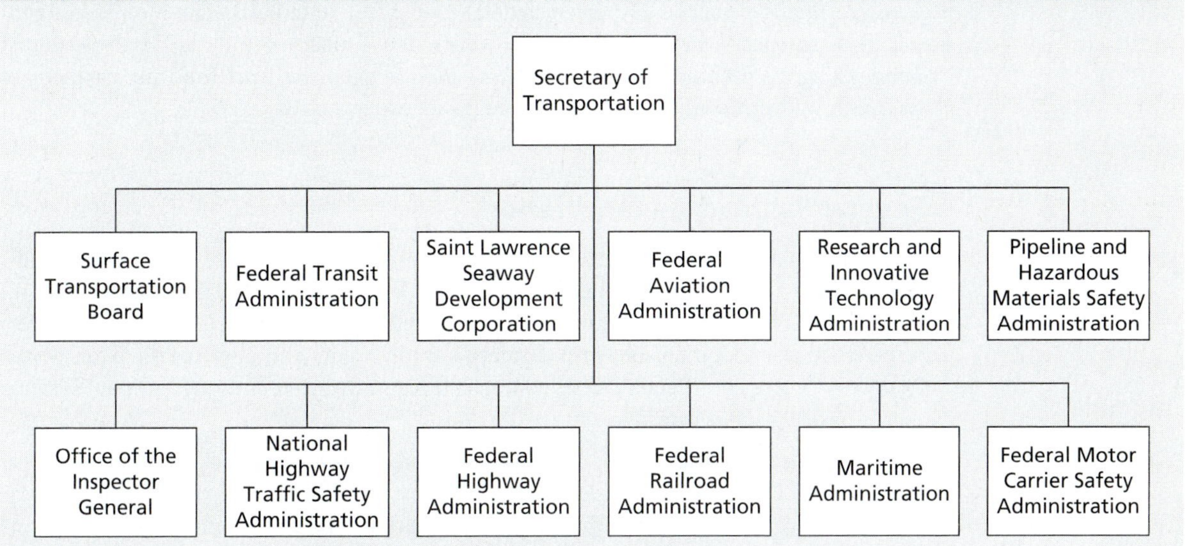

Through its various agencies and departments, the DOT has responsibility and control over transportation safety, promotion, and research. The individual agency programs provide insight into the overall role of government in transportation matters other than economic regulation. A brief description of some of the activities included in the DOT can be found on the following pages.

Federal Aviation Administration

The Federal Aviation Administration (FAA) is responsible for regulating air safety, promoting development of air commerce, and controlling navigable air space in the interest of safety and efficiency. The FAA is most noted for its air safety regulations governing the manufacture, operation, and maintenance of aircraft, the certification pilots and navigators, and the operation of air traffic control facilities. It conducts research and development of procedures, systems, and facilities to achieve safe and efficient air navigation and air traffic control.

The FAA administers a grant program for planning and developing public airports and provides technical guidance on airport planning, design, and safety operations. The agency maintains registration and records of aircraft, aircraft engines, propellers, and parts. It promotes international aviation safety by exchanging aeronautical information with foreign authorities, certifying foreign repair facilities and mechanics, and providing technical assistance in aviation safety training.

Federal Highway Administration

The Federal Highway Administration (FHWA) is concerned with the overall operation and environment of the highway system, including the coordination of research and development activities aimed at improving the quality and durability of highways. In this capacity, the FHWA administers the federal-aid highway program, which provides financial assistance to the states for the construction and improvement of highways and traffic operations. For example, the interstate system is a 47,714 mile network financed on a 90 percent federal/10 percent state basis. Improvements for other federal-aid highways are financed on the 75 percent federal/25 percent state basis. The monies are generated from special highway use taxes, which are deposited into the Highway Trust Fund. Congress authorizes disbursement of money from the trust fund for payment of the federal government's portion of the highway expenditures.

Federal Railroad Administration

The promulgation and enforcement of railroad safety regulations are major responsibilities of the Federal Railroad Administration (FRA). The safety regulations cover maintenance, inspection, and equipment standards and operating practices. It administers research and development of railroad safety improvements and operates the Transportation Test Center near Pueblo, Colorado, which tests advanced and conventional systems that improve ground transportation.

The FRA administers the federal assistance program for national, regional, and local rail services. The assistance is designed to support continuation of rail freight and passenger service and state rail planning. In addition, the FRA administers programs designed to improve rail transportation in the northeast corridor of the United States.

National Highway Traffic Safety Administration

Motor vehicle safety performance is the major jurisdiction of the National Highway Traffic Safety Administration (NHTSA). In this capacity, the NHTSA issues prescribed safety features and safety-related performance standards for vehicles and motor vehicle equipment. The agency reports to Congress and to the public the damage susceptibility, crashworthiness, ease of repair, and theft prevention of motor vehicles. It is charged with the mandate of reducing the number of deaths, injuries, and economic losses resulting from traffic accidents. Finally, the NHTSA establishes fuel economy standards for automobiles and light trucks.

Federal Transit Administration

The Federal Transit Administration (FTA) is charged with improving mass transportation facilities, equipment, techniques, and methods; encouraging the planning and establishment of urban mass transportation systems; and providing financial assistance to state and local governments in operating mass transportation companies. Capital grants or loans of up to 75 percent of the project cost are made available to communities to purchase equipment and facilities. Formula grants are available in amounts of up to 80 percent of the project cost for capital and planning activities and 50 percent for operating subsidies. In addition, the FTA makes funding available for research and training programs.

Maritime Administration

The Maritime Administration (MARAD) oversees programs designed to develop, promote, and operate the U.S. Merchant Marine fleet and to organize and direct emergency merchant ship operations. MARAD maintains a national defense reserve fleet of government-owned ships that are to be operated in times of national defense emergencies. It also operates the U.S. Merchant Marine Academy, which operates training for future Merchant Marine officers.

MARAD administers maritime subsidy programs through the Maritime Subsidy Board. The operating subsidy program provides U.S. flag ships with an operating subsidy that represents the difference between the costs of operating a U.S. flag ship and a foreign competitive flag ship. A construction subsidy program provides funds for the difference between the costs of constructing ships in U.S. shipyards and in foreign shipyards. It also provides financing guarantees for construction or reconditioning of ships.

St. Lawrence Seaway Development Corporation

The St. Lawrence Seaway Development Corporation (SLSDC) is a government-owned operation that is responsible for the development, maintenance, and operation of the U.S. portion of the St. Lawrence Seaway. The SLSDC charges tolls to ship operators who use the seaway. These tolls are negotiated with the St. Lawrence Seaway Authority of Canada. The U.S. and Canadian seaway agencies coordinate activities involving seaway operations, traffic control, navigation aids, safety, and length of shipping season.

Research and Innovative Technology Administration

Established in 2005 through the Norman Y. Mineta Research and Special Programs Improvement Act, the Research and Innovative Technology Administration (RITA) coordinates the DOT's research programs and is charged with advancing the deployment of cross-cutting technologies to improve our nation's transportation system. RITA is charged with (1) coordinating, facilitating, and reviewing the DOT's research and development programs and activities; (2) advancing innovative technologies, including intelligent transportation systems; (3) performing comprehensive transportation statistical research, analysis, and reporting; and (4) providing education and training in transportation and transportation-related fields.

The specific agencies that report to RITA are (1) the Bureau of Transportation Statistics; (2) the Transportation Safety Institute; (3) Intelligent Transportation Systems; (4) the National Transportation Library; (5) Research, Development, and Technology; (6) the University Transportation Centers; (7) Positioning, Navigation, and Timing; and (8) the Volpe National Transportation System Centers.

Pipeline and Hazardous Materials Safety Administration

The Pipeline and Hazardous Materials Safety Administration (PHMSA) was also established through the Norman Y. Mineta Research and Special Programs and Improvement Act of 2005. It replaced the Research and Special Programs Administration. The mission of the PHMSA is to protect people and the environment from the risks inherent in transportation of hazardous materials by pipeline and other modes of transportation. It regulates the safe, reliable, and environmentally sound operation of the nation's 2.6 million miles of pipeline and nearly 1 million daily shipments of hazardous materials by land, sea, and air.

PHMSA has four goals. First, PHMSA is charged to reduce the risk of harm to people due to the transportation of hazardous materials by pipelines and other modes. Second, it needs to reduce the risk of harm to the environment due to the transportation of oil and hazardous materials by pipeline and other modes. Third, it strives to harmonize and standardize the requirements for pipeline and hazardous materials internationally and to facilitate the efficient and safe transportation through ports of entry and through the supply chain. Finally, PHMSA is charged to reduce the consequences (harm to people, environment, and economy) after a pipeline or hazardous material failure has occurred.

Federal Motor Carrier Safety Administration

The Federal Motor Carrier Safety Administration (FMCSA) was established as a separate administration within the DOT on January 1, 2000, pursuant to the Motor Carrier Safety Improvement Act of 1999. The primary mission is to reduce crashes, injuries, and fatalities involving large tractor-trailers and buses. In carrying out its safety mandate, FMCSA:

- Develops and enforces data-driven regulations that balance motor carrier (motor carrier and bus companies) safety with industry efficiency;
- Harnesses safety information systems to focus on higher-risk carriers in enforcing the safety regulations;
- Targets educational messages to carriers, commercial drivers, and the public; and
- Partners with stakeholders including federal, state, and local enforcement agencies, the motor carrier industry, safety groups, and organized labor on efforts to reduce bus and motor carrier-related crashes.

FMCSA develops, maintains, and enforces Federal Motor Carrier Safety Regulations (FMCSRs), Hazardous Materials Regulations (HMRs), and the Commercial Driver's License (CDL) Program, among others.

Office of the Inspector General

The Office of the Inspector General (OIG) is committed to fulfilling its statutory mission and assisting members of Congress, the secretary, and senior department officials in achieving a safe, efficient, and effective transportation system that meets vital national interests and enhances the quality of life of the American people, today and into the future.

The OIG works within the DOT to promote effectiveness and to stop waste, fraud, and abuse in departmental programs. This is accomplished through audits and investigations. OIG also consults with Congress about programs in progress and proposed new laws and regulations.

Surface Transportation Board

The Surface Transportation Board (STB) was created by the Interstate Commerce Commission Termination Act of 1995 and is the successor agency to the Interstate Commerce Commission. The STB is an economic regulatory agency that Congress charged with the fundamental missions of resolving railroad rate and service disputes and reviewing proposed railroad mergers. The STB is an independent agency, although it is administratively affiliated with the DOT.

The STB serves as both an adjudicatory and a regulatory body. The agency has jurisdiction over railroad rate and service issues and rail restructuring transactions (mergers, line sales, line construction, and line abandonments). Although the STB does have regulatory authority over a few matters regarding other modes, its primary focus is on the railroad industry.

SUMMARY

- The agencies that make up the DOT administer federal programs covering all modes of transportation.
- DOT establishes national transportation policy, enforces safety regulations, provides funding for transportation programs, and coordinates transportation research efforts.
- The Secretary of Transportation is the principal advisor to the president on transportation matters.

CHAPTER

4 COSTING AND PRICING FOR TRANSPORTATION

Learning Objectives

After reading this chapter, you should be able to do the following:

- Understand the relationship between a rate and a price
- Be familiar with the various types of market structures found in the transportation industry
- Gain knowledge of the impact of transportation prices on the relevant market area for a product
- Be able to explain the differences between cost-of-service and value-of-service pricing
- Understand the different forms of rates used in transportation
- Appreciate how transportation rates have changed under deregulation
- Determine the strategic role of pricing for transportation firms
- Calculate the costs of both truckload and less-than-truckload freight moves

TRANSPORTATION **PROFILE**

Some LTL Carriers Shun Annual GRIs in Favor of "Customer-Centric" Approach

General rate increases (GRIs) in the less-than-truckload (LTL) sector of the trucking industry are an annual event, but is anyone paying attention anymore? And more importantly, is anyone actually paying these announced GRIs this year ranging anywhere from 3.9 to 5.4 percent range? Increasingly, the answer appears to be "no."

GRIs used to be announced in the dead of winter, designed to take effect around January 1, the way parcel giants UPS and FedEx still do it. Then, a few years ago, the LTL carriers shifted to earlier announcements designed to take effect in late summer during the peak shipping season when presumably shippers are more worried about capacity.

Today they've been moved up to take effect in spring, at the very start of the peak season. This year, FedEx Freight, UPS Freight, YRC Freight, ABF, Conway, and Saia have all announced GRIs. Significantly, market leader Old Dominion Freight Line has not, as of press time, made their announcement, leaving the others with no choice but to significantly discount away some of those announced rate hikes.

It's important to keep in mind that GRIs don't have much effect on contract freight rates. Contract freight is estimated to comprise as much as 80 percent of all LTL traffic, according to estimates by trucking analyst firm SJ Consulting.

GRIs are a vestige of government regulation of trucking rates, which ceased in 1980 when the industry was economically deregulated. While they might still have some significance in providing a ceiling from which all contract freight is discounted, GRIs long ago ceased to have significant impact.

In fact, some leading LTL carriers have significantly moved away from annual GRIs in favor of a more tailored approach to pricing, taking into consideration a more precise analysis of exactly what that customer's freight mix means to a carrier's efficient operation—and therefore what rate that shipper pays.

Pittsburgh-based Pitt Ohio, the nation's 17th largest LTL carrier with $362 million in revenue last year, is just such a carrier. It began eschewing GRIs about 10 years ago in favor of what it calls a more "customer-centric" approach to pricing. And technology has played a huge role in that.

"Access to actionable information has changed the price and service discussion for most carriers and shippers," said Geoff Muessig, Pitt Ohio's executive vice president.

In recent years, carriers have developed sophisticated lane-based costing models and shippers have gained access to low-cost transportation management systems, Muessig adds. Today, carriers and shippers can easily exchange information and discuss which lanes allow a carrier to meet the market price, provide good service, and generate an adequate margin.

"General rate increases were needed back in the day when carriers and shippers didn't have easy access to this type of information," Muessig says. "One-size-fits-all, across the board rate increases remain easy for a carrier to implement. However, over time, a carrier will find that its pricing programs have become distorted to the point where some customers are charged too much and others are not charged enough."

In fact, the effects of GRIs can be somewhat misleading, noted Stifel Nicolaus analyst David Ross.

Ross says that the tradition of GRIs is driven by the "legacy union operating environment" where the leading cost input, labor, rose contractually every year. Even though the LTL industry is now predominantly nonunion, and union workers at YRC and ABF have actually taken wage concessions recently, this practice continues.

"The increases are not, however, indicative of the overall pricing environment, in our view," Ross says.

If there is overcapacity in the LTL industry, most, if not all, of the announced increase ends up getting discounted away, Ross says. When supply and demand are tight, rates increase more, no matter what the GRIs indicate. Ross adds that LTL pricing is pretty solid currently, with most carriers getting net pricing increases north of 3 percent this year.

Ironically, Ross adds that it's small shippers—the most profitable accounts for the LTL carrier—who are actually most vulnerable to effects of GRIs, compared with the large national accounts, which enjoy negotiating leverage due to their volumes.

Source: *Logistics Management*, May 2014, pp. 13–14. Reprinted with permission of Peerless Media, LLC.

Introduction

Federal regulation of transportation business practices was initiated in the United States in 1887 when Congress passed the Act to Regulate Commerce (later named the Interstate Commerce Act). This legislation established a framework of control over interstate rail transportation and created the Interstate Commerce Commission (ICC) to administer it. Between 1906 and 1940, oil pipelines, motor carriers, and domestic water carriers were also subjected to ICC control. Air transportation came under federal economic regulation in 1938, with the passage of the Civil Aeronautics Act.

Reduction of federal economic regulation of the various modes began with partial curtailment of rail regulation in 1976 (Railroad Revitalization and Regulatory Reform Act), air cargo in 1977, and air passenger transportation in 1978 (Airline Deregulation Act). Two years later, interstate motor carriage was almost completely deregulated (Motor Carrier Act of 1980), and extensive additional reductions in railroad regulation were enacted (Staggers Rail Act of 1980). In the 1980s, legislative moves to further curtail transportation regulation continued. Intercity bus service was deregulated in 1982, followed by surface domestic freight forwarders in 1986.

A federal political climate favorable to deregulation continued in the 1990s. Passage of the Trucking Industry Regulatory Reform Act of 1992 removed the power of the states to regulate intrastate motor freight transportation. Three years later, passage of the ICC Termination Act of 1995 (ICCTA) eliminated almost all remaining elements of motor carrier regulation, further reduced rail regulation, and replaced the 108-year-old ICC with the Surface Transportation Board (STB). The STB holds responsibility for administering the remnants of economic rail regulation that remain law within the ICCTA.

A prime objective of deregulation was market-driven pricing of transportation services free from regulatory intervention. Thus, motor carriers are free to charge whatever rates they can to generate revenue. Deregulation also freed motor carriers to operate wherever they choose, geographically. Rail carriers are also free to charge rates based exclusively on market conditions, except in situations where the STB might find a rail firm's market power strong enough to subject rail customers to economic abuse or injury.

Before deregulation, all interstate rail freight traffic and much motor freight traffic was moved on published (tariff) rates. Both motor and rail carriers still offer tariff rates. However, under freedom from economic regulation, the use of rates set in confidential contracts between carriers and shippers has become prominent, particularly for traffic tendered by large-volume shippers.

The use of contracts, if managed well, ensures that both the carrier and the shipper have a clear understanding of each other's requirements (for instance, profitability of service rendered for the carrier and value derived from freight movement for the shipper) when they enter into a binding agreement. However, if a shipper or carrier negotiates terms that are unwise, no federal agency will be available to offer a remedy.

Individuals studying transportation should understand the theoretical underpinnings of the rates and prices of transportation agencies. A key point to master at the outset is the idea that a difference exists between the terms *rate* and *price*.

In the past, when transportation regulation was at its peak, it was more appropriate to use the term *rate* than *price*. A rate is an amount that can be found in a rate tariff book, as payment to a carrier for performing a given transportation service. This rate is the *lawful* charge that a carrier can impose on a given commodity movement; therefore, a rate has the full force of the law behind it for its timely payment. A rate is determined primarily by considering a carrier's costs only and not by assessing the overall market situation at that moment in time and how these market forces influence supply and demand. A discussion of cost concepts can be found in Appendix 4A.

A price, however, involves a much clearer notion of how post-deregulation transportation firms determine and impose charges for their services. A price implies a value or level that is determined based on prevailing market forces. Clearly, the notion of *price* implies a dynamic economic environment, one that is receptive to changes in customer demand and carrier supply.

Although the transportation industry is not completely unique compared to other industries, there are enough differences to justify a thorough discussion of transportation pricing. The first part of this chapter on transport prices will explore the market structure of the transportation industry. The section on market structure will be followed by an analysis of cost-of-service pricing. This analysis will provide the basis for a discussion on value-of-service pricing. The final part of the chapter will address rate systems and pricing in transportation.

Market Considerations

Before discussing the characteristics of the transportation market, a brief review of basic market structure models is appropriate. Such a discussion will provide some insights into the unique nature of transportation market situations.

Market Structure Models

The necessary conditions for **pure competition** are generally stated as follows:

- There are a large number of sellers.
- All sellers and buyers are of such a small size that no one can influence prices or supply.
- There is a homogeneous product or service.
- There is unrestricted entry.

The demand curve facing the individual firm is one of perfect elasticity, which means the producer can sell all output at the one market price, but none above that price. Although pure competition is not a predominant market structure, it is frequently used as a standard to judge optimal allocation of resources.

If pure competition is one type of market structure, the other extreme is a perfectly **monopolistic** market with only one seller of a product or service for which there is no close competitor or substitute. In such a situation, the single seller is able to set the price for the service offered and should adjust the price to its advantage, given the demand curve. To remain in this situation, the single seller must be able to restrict entry. The single seller maximizes profits by equating marginal cost and marginal revenue and might make excess profit.

A third type of market structure is **oligopoly**. Oligopoly can be defined as competition between a few large sellers of a relatively homogeneous product that has enough cross-elasticity of demand (substitutability) that each seller must take into account competitors' reactions in making pricing decisions. In other words, oligopoly is characterized by mutual interdependence among the various sellers. The individual seller is aware that in changing price, output, sales promotion activities, or the quality of the product, the reactions of competitors must be taken into account. All modes encounter some form of oligopolistic competition.

The fourth type of market structure is **monopolistic competition**. In this type of market structure there are many small sellers but there is some differentiation of products. The number of sellers is great enough and the largest seller small enough that no one controls a significant portion of the market. No recognized interdependence of the related sellers' prices or price policies is usually present. Therefore, any seller can lower price to increase sales volume without necessarily eliciting a retaliatory reaction from competitors.

This brief description of the four basic market models is by no means complete. The interested student can obtain additional perspectives from any standard microeconomics text. For our purposes, the earlier discussion provides enough background to focus more closely on transportation markets.

Theory of Contestable Markets[1]

The relevant market structure faced by each mode of transportation provided the basis for arguments made by proponents of deregulation. This was especially the case with airline deregulation. For deregulation to work for a mode, its market structure must closely resemble pure competition. On the surface, it appeared that the passenger airline industry was oligopolistic and therefore would prevent the free entry of competitors. However, there was some consensus that the airline industry could perform in a competitive manner. This rationale resulted in what can be called the *theory of contestable markets*, which substitutes potential competition for the active participation of many sellers.[2]

For this theory to work, several conditions had to be met. First, barriers to entry could not exist. Such barriers could include physical barriers, informational barriers, and capital barriers.[3] Second, economies of scale could not be present. In the airline industry, this meant that operating many aircraft could not have a cost advantage over operating a single aircraft. Third, consumers had to be willing and able to switch quickly among carriers.[4] Finally, existing carriers had to be prevented from responding to new entrants' lower prices, assuming that the entrant possessed a lower cost structure than the incumbent.[5]

Although the theory of contestable markets proved to be correct in the early days of deregulation, incumbent airlines have been able to remove the potential threat of new entrants in today's operating environment, thus weakening the theory's application.[6] This conclusion points to the importance of understanding the market structures of the modes and how they will behave in a deregulated environment. It also leads to the conclusion that the passenger airline industry is indeed an oligopoly, and thus is subject to the potential abuses of this type of market.

Relevant Market Areas

A general statement classifying the market structure of the entire transportation industry cannot be made because it is necessary to view structures in particular market areas. In the railroad industry, for example, there exists a variety of different services, involving the transportation of thousands of different commodities between tens of thousands of different stations or geographic points, via a multiplicity of different routes and under various conditions of carriage.[7] The market structure in transportation must describe the situation at any one point, and even then the situation will differ between commodities. Therefore, to determine pricing in transportation, we must describe the situation between two points, for one commodity, in one shipment size, moving in one direction.[8]

For example, a particular railroad that provides service between Pittsburgh and Cincinnati might find that the movement of ordinary steel approximates what we have described as monopolistic competition. There is likely to be a large number of other carriers, especially motor carriers, that provide essentially the same service.

However, for the movement of a very large, sophisticated generator, the railroad might face an oligopolistic market on the move between Pittsburgh and Cincinnati because none of the motor carriers might be able to haul such a large piece of equipment and the railroad might be competing with only a few water carriers. It is possible to find some commodity where the railroad would be operating in a monopolistic position because of restrictions on operating authorities. Finally, there might even be a product for which the situation approaches pure competition. In fact, this might be true for certain steel products, given the availability of rail, motor, water, and private carrier. In summary, the relevant market situation for transportation consists of one commodity, moving between two points, in one shipment size, in one direction.

The market structure for a particular mode of transportation in one market could be described in more detail. This is especially true with respect to the railroad industry, the water carrier industry, and the pipeline industry. A typical situation in each of these industries could be described and made to fit one of the economic models previously mentioned. For example, it could be stated that between two particular cities the water carriers are faced with oligopolistic conditions. From this, the general pricing behavior of the industry could be discussed.[9] However, there is intermodal competition present in transportation, and it is necessary to take this fact into consideration to adequately describe market situations. Also, as has been stated, the situation varies by commodity.

The complexity of the situation does not eliminate the validity of the economic models described earlier. It only means that in order to make use of these models knowledge of the situation that exists in a particular market must be obtained. Although this might seem to be too much to expect at first, it can be accomplished. The elaborate classification system for rates (discussed later in this chapter) distorts the situation somewhat, but in our economy commodity rates are the most important in terms of total intercity ton-miles. Commodity rates are competitive on commodities between specific points. In setting prices, a carrier must have knowledge of the relevant market area. With this knowledge, it is possible to use one of the economic models described.

Although there will be instances when carriers might find it expedient to generalize in adjusting prices, a much narrower focus is customary in the day-to-day negotiation and analysis of these prices.

The deregulation that has occurred in transportation between 1978 and 1996 has made these conclusions even more appropriate. Although it is true that there has been a general increase in competition, the competition has been uneven among market areas, commodities, and shipment sizes. The new competitive environment has made carriers and shippers more sensitive to the importance of the relevant market area concept. More prices are being negotiated by shippers and carriers and are taking into account the particular demand-and-supply situations for the movements affected.

The important point about this analysis is that, although transportation competition has indeed become more intense in the last three or four decades, the intensity is uneven. Therefore, all four types of markets can be found in transportation industries. This makes pricing very challenging. In addition, the derived nature of transportation demand further complicates the pricing situation.

Cost-of-Service Pricing[10]

There are two alternative concepts for **cost-of-service pricing**: basing prices on marginal cost or basing prices on average cost. To give adequate treatment to each alternative, some simplifying assumptions will be made and exhibited using Figure 4-1. The assumptions are that (1) the firm's product or service (such as transportation) is homogeneous, (2) only one group of customers is involved, (3) this group of customers is responsible for all costs, and (4) the firm possesses some degree of monopoly power, as indicated by a downward sloping demand curve as seen in Figure 4-1.

If the firm desires to maximize its profits (see Figure 4-1), it will produce quantity Q_m and charge price P_m. By doing so, the firm would be making excess profits in the economic sense (that is, earning a rate of return on its invested assets in excess of that needed

FIGURE 4-1 Cost-of-Service Pricing

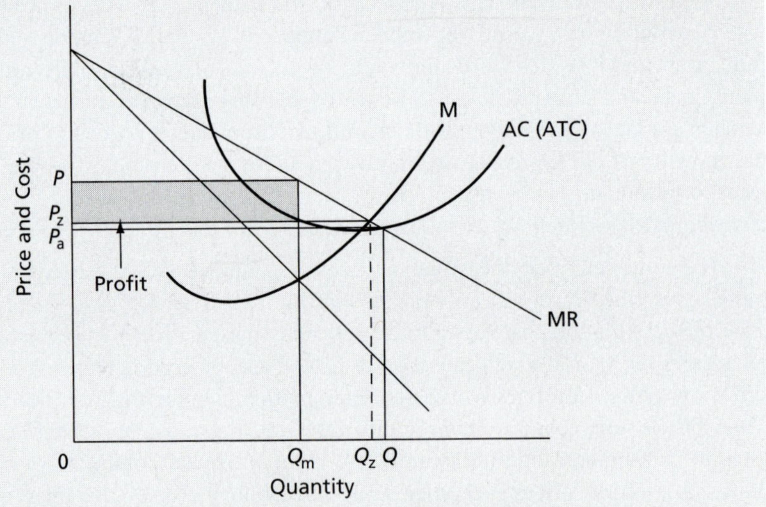

to attract and retain financial capital from investors). This result is good for the firm's investors (shareholders). However, it is not good from the standpoint of optimal allocation of resources for the economy at large, because the price is above **average cost** and the firm is not producing and selling as much as it would (Q_a) if its selling price was set equal to the average cost (P_a). This is a basic result of the firm's exercise of monopoly power.

This result might induce government regulation of the firm's pricing. If regulation is imposed, the regulatory agency has two alternatives for attempting to improve economic efficiency in the economy at large and to increase the economic well-being of existing and prospective buyers of the firm's output. By ordering the firm to set its price at P_z, the firm's output and sales would increase from Q_m to Q_z, the firm's **marginal cost** would equal its average cost of production, and the firm would neither earn excess profit nor incur a loss on any of the additional (marginal) units of output that it sells. Conceptually, this is identical to the outcome that would result under pure competition, where the forces of the market would cause a firm to sell its output at the going market price and where (assuming the firm is in a state of perfect equilibrium) the market price would be equal to both the firm's marginal cost and average cost.

It should be noted here that some advocates of regulation have argued that ordering a firm to set price equal to average cost is more socially desirable, because the firm's customers would be obtaining more output (Q_a) at an even lower price (P_a). However, critics of this approach point out that the units of output between Q_z and Q_a are being sold at a price (P_a) that is less than the marginal cost of producing them and hence that buyers of these units are receiving a subsidy from investors in the firm.

In Adam Smith's terminology, the value in use is not as great as the cost of producing the additional output. Therefore, there are alternate uses in which the resources used to produce this additional output are valued more highly by consumers. When stated in this manner, the argument is based upon logic usually advanced under a label of "welfare economics."[11] Under the marginal-cost solution presented in Figure 4-1, there would be excess profits because price is above the average cost. However, this need not be a problem because the excess profits can be used to pay taxes.

One of the arguments frequently raised against a strict marginal-cost approach to pricing is that, under decreasing cost conditions, if the firm equates marginal cost with demand, then it will necessitate the firm's operating at a loss (see Figure 4-2). However, the advocates of a strict marginal-cost approach would still present the argument that individuals are willing to pay the marginal cost of the additional output between Q_m and Q_r and therefore it should be produced. There is one obvious solution and that is to allow the government to make up the deficit through a subsidy.[12] These subsidies could be offset by the taxes collected in the previous example. These are also additional ways to offset governmental subsidies.

Thus far in this discussion, no attempt has been made to substantiate one approach or the other. The arguments advanced by advocates of each approach have been presented. Before any critique can be presented of these alternate approaches, the assumptions that were made at the outset should be examined.

The assumption that only one group of customers is served is not the typical situation, except in very special cases among transportation companies. Likewise, costs are not usually separable according to the classes of customers receiving the same type of service, but rather, common costs are quite typical, particularly with respect to railroads. Already mentioned is that output is not homogeneous in many instances; rather, what exists are heterogeneous or multiple services. Transportation firms are not peculiar in this respect because so many firms have common costs.

FIGURE 4-2 Decreasing Cost Situation

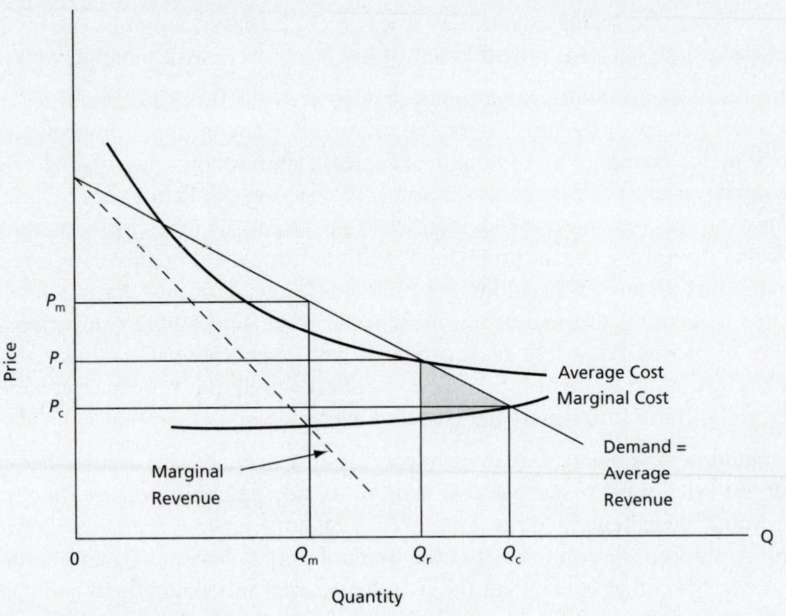

The presence of **common costs** raises some problems for cost-of-service pricing, particularly the average-cost approach. If rates are based upon average or fully allocated costs, it becomes necessary to apportion these costs by some arbitrary means. Average cost pricing with fixed or common costs or both makes these costs price–determining when they should be price-determined. In other words, fixed costs per unit depend on the volume of traffic, and the volume of traffic depends on the rate charged. To some extent then, cost is a function of the prices; the prices are not a function of the cost.[13] In fact, it could be argued that not only do costs determine prices, but also that prices determine cost; in other words, the situation is analogous to the chicken and the egg argument.

The presence of common costs does not raise the same theoretical problem for marginal-cost pricing because no arbitrary allocation of these costs is technically necessary. However, problems might be encountered because marginal cost can only be determined with large blocks of output such as a trainload or even a truckload. The output unit to be priced can be smaller with LTL shipments. There are some additional problems of a more practical nature, however, with respect to strict marginal-cost pricing. For example, in transportation, marginal costs could fluctuate widely, depending on the volume of traffic offered. The requirement of published rates would necessitate the averaging of these marginal costs to stabilize them, which would make them unequal with theoretical marginal costs.

Some theoretical and practical problems with cost-of-service pricing have been raised. An obvious question is whether cost-of-service pricing has any relevance for establishing prices. Prices charged by transportation companies are actually one of the criteria that guide intelligent shippers in selecting the mode of transportation or carrier that is most appropriate for their shipment. When the modal choice or carrier decision is made properly, the shipper will balance the carrier's price against the carrier's service characteristics such as transit time, reliability, and loss and damage record.

For the transportation decision to be properly made, the price charged should reflect the cost of providing the service to ensure carrier and economic system efficiency. The price(s) of carriers should be related to cost, but not to some arbitrary allocation of cost.

Railroads and pipelines require large, indivisible capital inputs because of their rights-of-way, terminals, and so on. The associated high fixed costs that are common costs to most of the traffic, if averaged over the units of traffic, will have to be allocated on an arbitrary basis, which will in turn lead to unwise and uneconomical pricing decisions. Adherence to an average cost or fully allocated cost approach does not make any sense in such situations.

Cost-oriented prices should be related to what we have defined as marginal cost or variable cost. Such costs, measured as precisely as possible, should serve as the conceptual floor for individual prices. Some traffic will move if prices are above marginal or variable cost, whereas other traffic will move at prices close to marginal cost, particularly under competitive circumstances. In other words, differential pricing seems to make sense in most instances, but the rationale needs further explanation.

In the presentation of cost-of-service pricing, mention was made of **decreasing cost industries**. Some transportation firms fall into this category. If prices are based on strict marginal cost, the firm experiences a loss. A subsidy could be paid, but this is not likely to be done. Therefore, the firm has to recover its fixed costs. To accomplish this on the basis of an average-cost approach is not acceptable. However, it can be accomplished by using marginal cost as a floor for prices and using the value of service, or demand, to establish how far above this minimum the rate or price should be set.

Value-of-service pricing is sometimes defined as **charging what the traffic will bear**. In actuality, this phrase can assume two meanings. First, it can be used to mean that prices are set so that on each unit the maximum revenue is obtained regardless of the particular costs involved. That is, no service should be charged a lower price when it could bear a higher price. The second meaning, which can be more conveniently expressed in a negative form and which is germane to this discussion, is that no service should be charged a price that it will not bear when, at a lower price, the service could be purchased. This lower price will always cover the marginal cost incurred by the company in providing the service.

The differences in the elasticities of demand for the different services will determine the actual level of the prices. The presence of indivisibilities in the cost structure necessitates the dissimilar pricing. Therefore, the greater the amount of the indivisibilities in the cost structure, the greater the need for dissimilar pricing and the consequent practice of segregating services according to demand elasticity.

One final point should be discussed, and that is the desirability of dissimilar pricing. Dissimilar pricing allows common and fixed costs to be spread out over large volumes of traffic. In other words, dissimilar pricing might render economical benefits because prices might be lower than they otherwise would be. It is not unusual to hear statements in the railroad industry that the prices on captive traffic subsidize competitive traffic; coal, for example, will not move unless the rates are relatively low. It could be argued that, as long as the coal rates cover more than the marginal cost of the movement, they allow the railroad to charge lower rates on other traffic.

As previously mentioned, the variable or marginal cost of providing the service should serve as the floor for carriers when setting prices. This relies entirely on how

FIGURE 4-3 Cost of Service As Price Floor—Generic Example

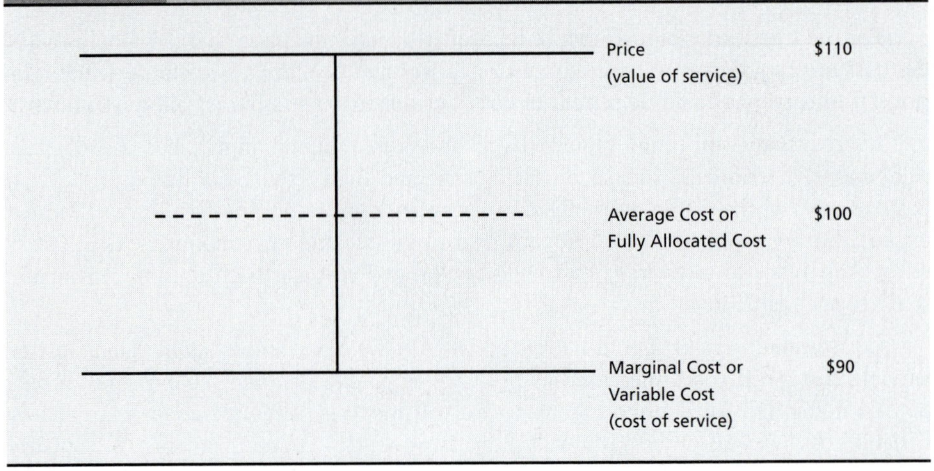

marginal or variable cost is defined, as we will see in this discussion. With this mentality, a carrier will be able to recover related costs of providing a service, at least in the short run. This relationship can be seen in Figure 4-3. In this example, a carrier's variable cost for a particular move is $90, its average cost (also called *fully allocated cost*) is $100, and its potential price is $110 (which could result in a $10 profit). This example assumes that (1) the carrier knows its costs and (2) it is able to charge a price that will result in a profit. This second assumption can be called *value-of-service pricing,* which will be discussed in the next section.

It can be said that dissimilar pricing is the logical approach for pricing in regulated industries. Cost indivisibilities necessitate the practice of discriminatory pricing, but this was approached within what might be called a cost framework. Marginal cost sets the minimum basis for prices, whereas fixed or common costs are, in effect, allocated on the basis of demand elasticity.

Value-of-Service Pricing

Value-of-service pricing is a frequently mentioned and often criticized approach to pricing that has generally been associated with the railroad industry. Part of the problem associated with value-of-service pricing is that a number of different definitions of it are offered by various sources. Therefore, a workable definition of the term will be developed.

One rather common definition of value-of-service pricing in transportation is pricing according to the value of the product; for example, high-valued products are assessed high prices for their movement, and low-valued commodities are assessed low prices. Evidence can be found to substantiate this definition by examining the class rate structure of railroads.

Several points are in order here. First, even if a cost-based approach is taken to setting prices, high-valued commodities would usually be charged higher prices because they are typically more expensive to transport. There is generally more risk involved in moving high-valued commodities and more expensive equipment is necessary. Second, the value of the commodity is a legitimate indicator of elasticity of demand; for example, high-valued commodities can usually bear higher prices because transportation cost is such a small percentage of the final selling price.

This concept can be seen in Figure 4-4. The demand curves of two different types of commodities for transportation services are shown. The high-value item has a steeply sloping demand curve implying price inelasticity. On the other hand, the low-value item has a gradual slope, implying price elasticity. To see how these elasticities relate to how a transportation firm can set prices based on product value, consider a price increase from price P_1 to price P_2. When the price of the transportation service increases for the high-value product, a small quantity-demanded decrease is observed from quantity Q_1 to quantity Q_2. For the same price increase, the low-value product cannot absorb the increased price. This inability to support the added price of the service is seen as a drop in the quantity demanded from Q_1 to Q_2. Clearly the decrease in quantity demanded for the low-value product is of a larger magnitude than the decrease for the higher-value product for the same price increase.

In a situation where a carrier has a complete monopoly, to consider value-of-service pricing only in terms of the commodity's value would not lead to serious traffic losses. It would be analogous to the idea behind progressive income taxes; that is, setting prices upon the ability or willingness to pay.[14] But where alternatives are present at a lower price, shippers are not willing to pay higher prices based upon the value of the product alone. This is one of the reasons why the motor carriers were able to make serious inroads in rail traffic during their early development. They undercut the prices on high-valued commodities when the railroads were the most susceptible to competition. In essence, the value of the commodity gives some indication of demand or the ability to bear a charge, but competition also will affect the demand for the service, that is, the height and slope of the demand curve.

Value-of-service pricing also has been defined as **third-degree price discrimination** or a situation in which a seller sets two or more different market prices for two or more separate groups of buyers of essentially the same commodity or service.[15] Three necessary conditions must exist before a seller can practice third-degree price discrimination. First, the seller must be able to separate buyers into groups or submarkets according to their different elasticities of demand; this separation enables the seller to charge different

FIGURE 4-4 Differential Pricing Based on Place Route

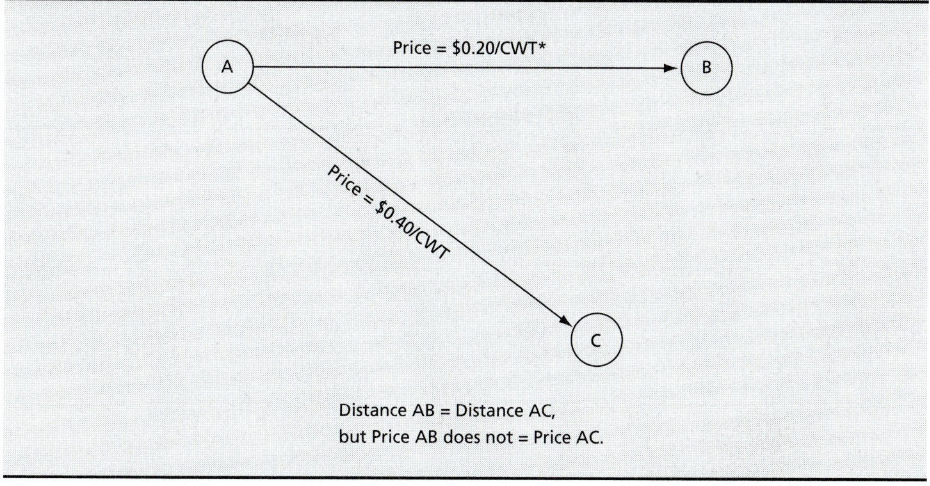

*CWT "hundred weight:" 100-pound increments.

prices in the various markets. The second condition is that the seller must be able to prevent the transfer of sales between the submarkets. That is, the buyer must not buy in the lower-priced market and sell in the higher-priced markets. Third, the seller must possess some degree of monopoly power.

Another name given to value-of-service pricing is **differential** pricing. Differential pricing can be done based on several methods of segregating the buyers into distinct groups. It can be done by commodity (such as coal versus computers), by time (seasonal discounts or premium rates), by place (as Figure 4-5 demonstrates), or by individual person. It should be noted, however, that discrimination based on an individual person is illegal per se on traffic that remains economically regulated by the STB.[16]

These conditions for third-degree price discrimination can be fulfilled in the transportation industry, as well as in other regulated industries. For example, in transportation shippers are separated according to commodities transported and between points of movement. The previous discussion of the relevant market area in transportation implied that there were different or separable customer-related markets—for example, one commodity between each pair of shipping points, each with a separate elasticity.

Another relevant point is the nature of "essentially the same commodity or service."[17] Actually, many transportation companies sell multiple or heterogeneous services that are technically similar. For example, rail movements of television sets or glassware are very different in terms of time, equipment, terminal facilities, and so on.

Value-of-service or differential pricing makes sense from the perspective of the railroads, considering their high level of fixed costs and need to attract traffic. Remember that railroads will experience declining average costs with increases in volume. If shipments are priced properly, this could mean increased revenues from higher volumes with more profit.

The key to success lies in being able to determine the appropriate costs and to estimate demand elasticity in the various markets. This essentially means determining what

FIGURE 4-5 Influence of Value and Demand Elasticity on Price

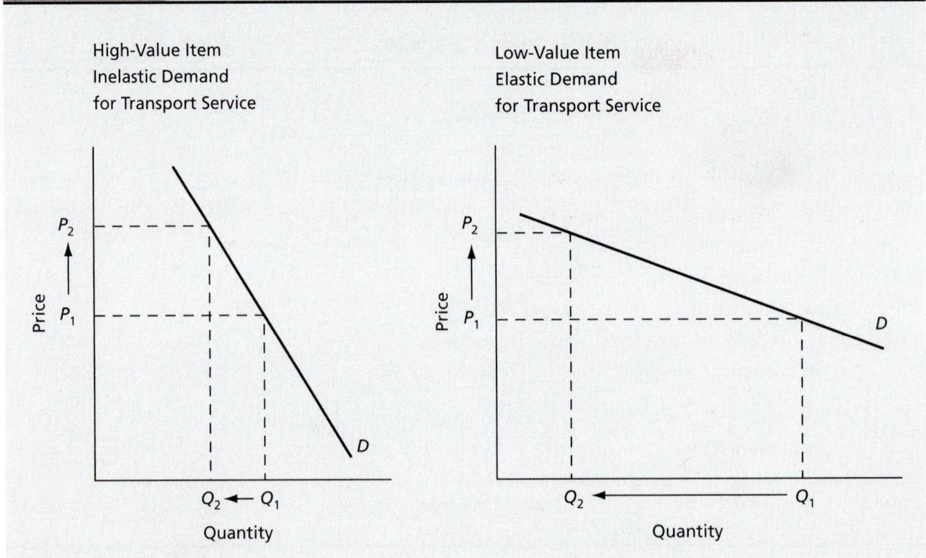

the shipper is willing to pay for the service given the competition in the market from other carriers, the demand for the product itself, and any other factors affecting demand.

Assume that a particular railroad is establishing prices on three different commodities.[18] One of the commodities is large computer systems, which have a very high value and for which there is limited substitutability. The second commodity is color television sets, which are of medium value and have some substitutes. The third commodity is coal, which is low in value and has substitutes.

Assume further that the value of a particular computer system is $200,000 and that it weighs one ton. If the rate charged for movement was $1,000 per ton, it would still only be one-half percent (0.005) of the value of the product. The color television might have a value of $10,000 per ton. Therefore, a rate of $1,000 between the same points would represent 10 percent of the value. Finally, the coal might be worth $50 per ton. A rate of $1,000 would represent 2,000 percent of its value. Therefore, charging a common price would discourage some shippers, particularly of low-value products.

This example is obviously simplified. However, it does point out some of the underlying logic behind value-of-service or differential pricing. In all three instances, each particular commodity is paying more than its variable cost and making a contribution to average cost, which also might be a concept of fully allocated cost.

An argument can be made that the coal shippers are not paying their full share and the computer shippers are paying too much. However, another argument that is frequently advanced in such instances is that, if the coal did not move (remember it is paying more than the associated variable cost), then the other traffic (computers and televisions) would have to pay an even higher price to help cover the costs of running the railroad. The same analogy applies to the supersaver fares charged by airlines. Full-fare passengers complain sometimes that they are subsidizing discount-fare passengers. Actually, full fares might be higher if the special fares were not offered.

The essential ingredient in the value-of-service analysis is the notion that each commodity movement has its own unique demand characteristics. If the railroad placed the same price on all commodities shipped, it would discourage some shippers from moving their goods at that price. Consider what would happen if the meat counter at the local supermarket priced all the various cuts and types of meats at the same level. Obviously, it would sell the T-bone steaks quickly and have only chopped steak left.

Several points about this example need to be emphasized. First, the example is simplified. The determination of cost is a difficult task. Second, most railroads and many other carriers would be considering more than three commodities between two points. Third, the example applies to the railroad industry because it is more attractive in situations with high fixed costs, yet other carriers, even motor carriers, might find differential pricing attractive. Fourth, some difference would exist in rates among commodities because of cost differences; for instance, televisions cost more to handle than coal. Finally, the elasticity of demand for a particular commodity might change with competition or because of some other factors. Therefore, high rates on higher-valued commodities have to be continually evaluated.

The three commodity examples presented here are extensions of the example presented for cost-of-service pricing as shown in Figure 4-3. Conceptually, if cost-of-service pricing serves as the floor for carrier pricing, then value-of-service pricing can serve as the ceiling. This can be especially seen in the color television and computer examples. However, if we accept the notion that value-of-service pricing is pricing based on what the traffic will bear, then an argument can be made that value-of-service pricing is also the floor for carrier prices, rather than the marginal cost of providing the service. This will depend on how marginal cost is defined in the context of the move.

An example might best represent this hypothesis. Assume that a truckload carrier moves a shipment from point A to point B with a variable cost of $90, an average cost of $100, and a price of $110. This relationship can be seen in Figure 4-6. This is called the carrier's **headhaul** because it is this demand that initiated the original movement of the carrier's equipment and the shipper's goods. As such, the carrier might be able to use value-of-service pricing, charging $110 (profit maximization) because of commodity and competitive circumstances. With the carrier's equipment at point B, it is necessary to bring the equipment and driver back to point A. This is called a **backhaul** because it is the result of the original move (headhaul). The carrier now faces a totally different market in this backhaul lane. Assume that marginal cost in this backhaul lane is defined as the variable cost of fuel and driver wages, or $90. If the carrier decides to price based on its marginal cost of $90 (cost-of-service pricing), it is very possible that the market from point B to point A will not bear this price and the carrier will be forced to return empty. This will result in a loss to the carrier of $90. Now suppose that the carrier prices this backhaul in accordance with market demands at a level of $80. Although this results in a price below marginal cost, the carrier has minimized its losses by losing only $10 on the move instead of $90. Pricing in this manner can be called *loss minimization.* So it can be argued that value-of-service pricing can be used as the price ceiling (profit maximization) and as the price floor (loss minimization). Both situations can be seen in Figure 4-6, and both assume that the carrier knows its costs and the market environment.

Now assume that the marginal cost in this backhaul lane is defined as those costs that would be avoided if the carrier, in fact, returned empty; that is, because the vehicle and driver are going to return anyway, the $90 for fuel and wages now becomes the fixed cost, which will now be included in the average-cost figure. Marginal cost now becomes the added cost of loading the shipment and the reduced fuel efficiency, which will be

FIGURE 4-6 Value of Service as Price Floor and Price Ceiling

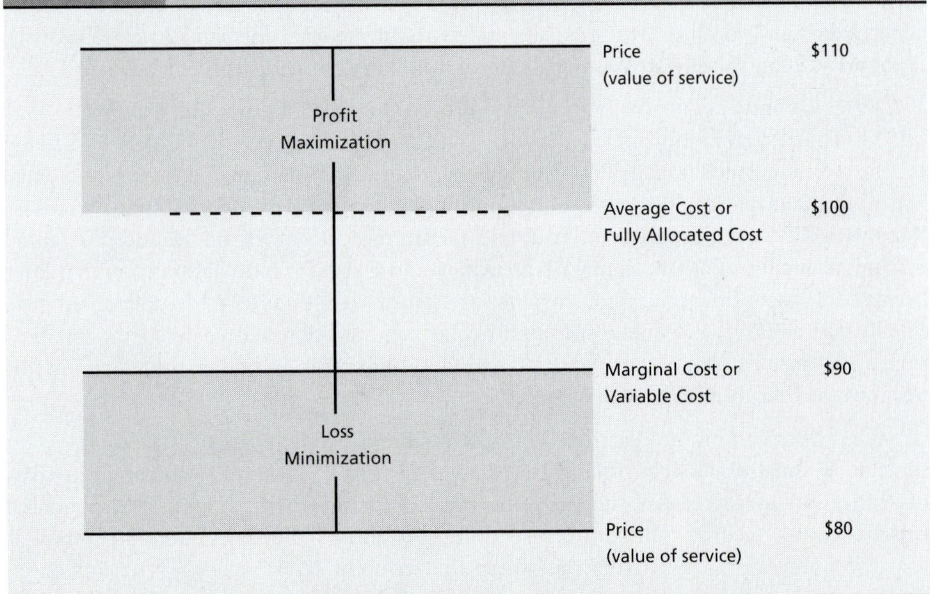

assumed to be $20. Figure 4-7 shows these relationships. On the headhaul, the price of $110 covers both the average cost of $100 and the marginal cost of $90. On the backhaul, the $90 is allocated as a fixed cost over the units of output to result in an average cost of $50. Now the $80 price charged covers both the average cost and marginal cost and results in a profit, just as the price produced a profit in the headhaul example. In this example, value of service provided the price ceiling and cost of service provided the price floor, as shown in Figure 4-3. The point of showing how different price floors can be justified is that prices will be set depending on how costs are defined. In Figure 4-6, backhaul variable costs were defined from an accounting perspective, that is, those costs directly related to the return move. In Figure 4-7, backhaul variable costs were defined from an economic perspective, that is, those costs that would be avoided if the carrier, in

FIGURE 4-7 Cost of Service as Price, Floor, and Value of Service as Price Ceiling—Headhaul/Backhaul Example

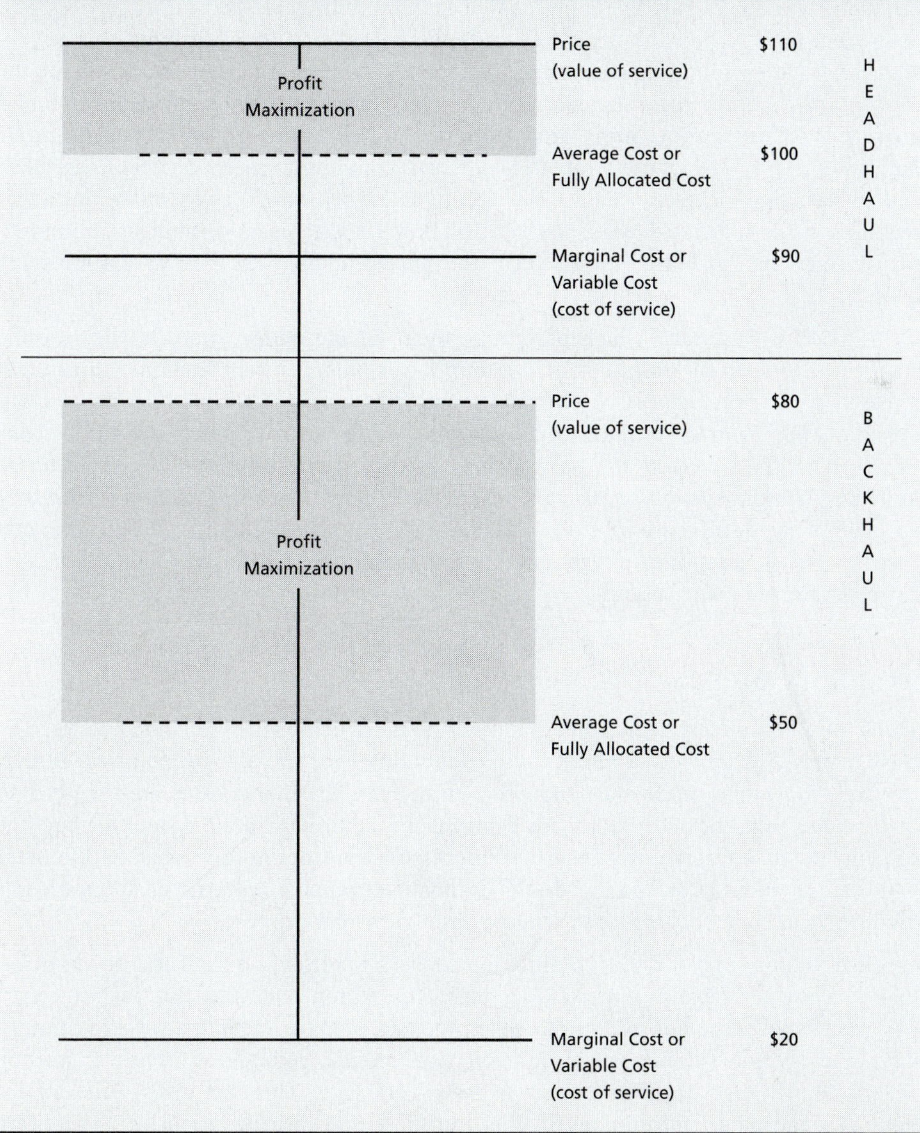

fact, returned empty. These two definitions result in two distinct perspectives on the profitability of the move for the carrier and would probably affect pricing and operations decisions of the carrier. Thus, when using costs as a basis for price, care must be taken to identify the proper role and definition of those costs in the pricing decision.

Rate Making in Practice

A complete understanding of carrier cost economics and behavior is a necessary prerequisite to effective management of carrier pricing. This section presents an overview of the general forms of pricing that are employed by carriers of all types. The form of each rate is discussed and analyzed, along with the primary inducements for the carrier and its users.

The overall carrier pricing function revolves around costing, rates, and tariffs. Carriers employ costing personnel who are responsible for determining the overall cost and productivity of the carrier operations as well as the specific routes, customer services, and equipment needs. The work of cost analysts should serve as a pricing input to rate personnel who are responsible for establishing specific rates and general rate levels for the carrier. Tariffs are the actual publications in which most rates are printed or are found on carrier websites. Some firms print their own tariffs, which are often referred to as *individual tariffs*, or they use a rate bureau that is common to many carriers to establish and publish rates. These tariffs are referred to as *bureau tariffs*. Carriers are no longer required to file individual tariffs with the STB. With the repeal of antitrust immunity for collective rate making, carriers today are more cautious with their efforts involving bureau tariffs.

Carriers today move a high percent of their volume under contracts with specific shippers. The form the rates take (for example, per mile, per container) in the contract is based on the preferences of the carrier and the shipper. So, the concepts of class, exception, and commodity rates would not apply under these contracts but will be contained in tariffs. However, the methodology used to determine these three rate forms underlies the construction of all rates, regardless of how they are quoted or where they are published. All rates are based on distance, weight, and commodity. As such, the discussion of class, exception, and commodity rates is still relevant today. These will be discussed in the following sections.

General Rates

These are the class, exception, and commodity rate structures in the United States. The **class rate** system provides a rate for any commodity between any two points. It is constructed from uniform distance and product systems. **Exception rates** are designed so that carriers in particular regions can depart from the product scale system for any one of many possible reasons, which will be discussed later. **Commodity rates**, on the other hand, are employed for specific origin–destination shipping patterns of specific commodities. Each one of these three systems has a particular purpose.

It would be simple if all transportation services were sold on the basis of ton-miles; that is, we would have to pay x dollars to move one ton one mile. But, in fact, transportation services are not sold in ton-miles; they are sold for moving a specific commodity in a specific shipment size between two specific points—for example, moving 10,000 pounds of glass from Toledo to New York City. This fact gives some insight into the enormous magnitude of the transportation pricing problem. There are thousands of important shipping and receiving points in the United States. Theoretically, the number of different possible routes would be all the permutations of these points. The result is in the trillions and trillions of possible rates. In addition, it is necessary to consider the thousands and thousands of different commodities and products that might be shipped over any of these routes. There are also the different modes to consider and different companies within each mode. It also might be necessary to consider the specific supply–demand situation for each commodity over each route.

Class Rates Because it is obviously impossible to quote trillions and trillions of rates, the transportation industry has taken three major steps toward simplification. Figure 4-8 summarizes this class rate simplification.

The first step consolidated the thousands of shipping points into groups by dividing the nation into geographic squares. The most important shipping point for all other shipping points (based on tonnage) in each square serves as the **rate base point** for all other shipping points in the square. These grouped points are found in a groupings tariff. This reduces the potential number of distance variations for rate-making purposes. The distance from each base point to each other base point was determined by the railroads and placed on file with the ICC (now the STB) and published in the National Rate Basis Tariff. The distance between any two base points is referred to as the **rate basis number**. The first simplifying step reduced the number of possible origins and destinations for pricing purposes. (See Tables 4-1 and 4-2 for examples of grouping and rate basis number tariffs.)

The second step deals with the thousands and thousands of different items that might be shipped between any two base points. The railroads have established a national scale of rates that has been placed on file with the ICC (now the STB) and gives a rate in dollars per hundredweight (cwt), which is dollars per cwt for each rate basis number. (The motor carriers established a similar rate structure.) The actual rate to move a commodity considered the commodity's transportation characteristic by means of the classification, the third simplification step.

FIGURE 4-8 Class Rate Simplification

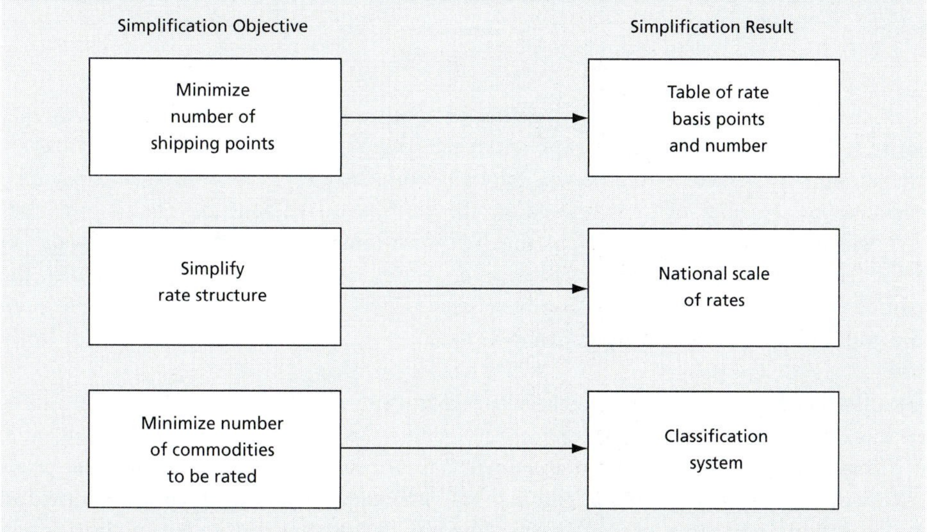

TABLE 4-1 Groupings Tariff Example[a]

STATE	POINT	APPLY RATES FROM OR TO
Michigan	Climax	Battle Creek
	Coleman	Clare
	Comstock	Kalamazoo
	Columbiaville	Flint
	Cross Village	Cheboygan
Ohio	Clay Center	Toledo
	Clifford	Chillicothe
	Clement	Dayton
	Cleves	Cincinnati
	Climax	Marion

[a]Alphabetical listing of points by states from and to which rates apply.

Source: Tariff ICC CMB 575-C.

TABLE 4-2 Rate Basis Numbers Tariff Example

And Points Taking the Following Basing Points	Between Points Taking the Following Basing Points: Chilicothe OH	Cincinnati OH	Columbus OH	Dayton OH
	Rate Basis Numbers			
Cheboygan, MI	550	570	490	510
Clare, MI	400	420	360	380
Flint, MI	275	300	227	214

Source: Tariff ICC CMB 575-C.

The third step simply groups together products with similar transportation characteristics so that one rating can be applied to the whole group. Now one rate is quoted for the group into which a number of different commodities have been placed, thereby reducing the number of rates quoted by the carriers. Items that are placed into class 125 will be charged 125 percent of the first-class rate found in the uniform scales of rates. This percentage number is called a *class rating*, and it is the group into which the commodity is placed for rate-making purposes. Table 4-3 is a classification example from the National Motor Freight Classification.

Classification Factors The factors that are used to determine the rating of a specific commodity are the product characteristics that impact the carrier's costs. In particular, the ICC has ruled and the STB has maintained that four factors are to be considered: product density, storability, handling, and liability. Although no specific formulas are used to assign a commodity to a particular class, the four factors are considered in conjunction

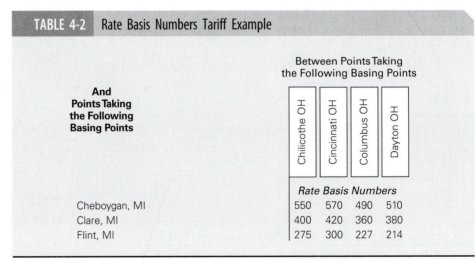

TABLE 4-3 National Motor Freight Classification

ITEM	ARTICLES	CLASSES LTL	TL	MW
156300	PLASTIC MATERIALS, OTHER THAN EXPANDED, GROUP: subject to Item 156100 Sheet or Plate, NOI. Self-supporting (rigid), see Note, Item 156302, other than in rolls or coils, in boxes, crates or Packages 248, 384, 930, 1029, 2187, 2207 or 2310			
Sub 1	Exceeding 9 feet, 6 inches in two dimensions or 20 feet in one dimension	85	45	30
Sub 2	Not exceeding 9 feet, 6 inches in more than one dimension nor 20 feet in one dimension	60	35	30
156500	PLASTIC OR RUBBER ARTICLES, OTHER THAN EXPANDED, GROUP: Articles consist of Plastic or Rubber Articles, other than foam, cellular, expanded or sponge articles, see Item 110, Sec. 15 and Note, Item 156502, as described in items subject to this grouping			
156600	Articles, NOI, in barrels, boxes or crates, see Note, Item 156602, also in Packages 870, 1078, 1170, 1241, 1273, 1409, 1456, 2195, 2212, 2213 or 2230			
Sub 1	LTL, having a density of, subject to Item 170			
Sub 2	Less than one pound per cubic foot, see Note, Item 156608	400		
Sub 3	One pound per cubic foot, but less than two pounds, see Note, Item 156608	300		
Sub 4	Two pounds per cubic foot, but less than four pounds, see Note, Item 156608	250		
Sub 5	Four pounds per cubic foot, but less than five pounds, see Note, Item 156608	150		
Sub 6	Six pounds per cubic foot, but less than 12 pounds, see Note, Item 156608	100		
Sub 7	12 pounds per cubic foot, but less than 15 pounds, see Note, Item 156608	85		
Sub 8	15 pounds or greater per cubic foot	70		
Sub 9	TL		100 70 60 45	10 16 21 30
155000	Personal effects, other than household effects or furnishings, of commissioned or enlisted personnel of the U.S. Army, Air Force, Navy, or Marine Corps, or deceased veterans, moving on government bills of lading, see Note, Item 155024, in bags, traveling bags, boxes, or army trunk lockers or navy cruise boxes or foot lockers securely locked or sealed			
Sub 1	Each article in value in accordance with the following, see Note, Item 155022			
Sub 2	Released value not exceeding 10 cents per pounds	100	70	16
Sub 3	Released to value exceeding 10 cents per pounds, but not exceeding 20 cents per pounds	125	77½	16
Sub 4	Released to value exceeding 20 cents per pounds, but not exceeding 50 cents per pound	150	85	16
Sub 5	Released to value exceeding 50 cents per pounds, but not exceeding $2.00 per pound	200	110	16
Sub 6	Released to value exceeding $2.00 per pound, but not exceeding $5.00 per pound	300	150	16

Source: National Motor Freight Classification 100-H.

by a carrier classification committee. This committee resides in the National Motor Freight Traffic Association and determines the characteristics of each of the 18 product classes. An individual carrier can establish a commodity classification that differs from the national classification; this individual carrier classification is termed an exception and takes precedence over the national classification.

Product density directly impacts the use of the carrier's vehicle and the cost per hundredweight. The higher the product density, the greater the amount of weight that can be hauled and the lower the cost per hundredweight. Conversely, the lower the product density, the lower the amount of weight that can be hauled and the higher the cost per hundredweight hauled.

As shown in Table 4-4, only 6,000 pounds of a product that has a density of 2 pounds per cubic foot can be loaded into the trailer, which means the cost per hundredweight shipped is $6.67. However, 48,000 pounds of a product with a density of 16 pounds per cubic foot can be hauled at a cost of $0.83 per hundredweight. Therefore, the higher the product density, the lower the carrier's cost per weight unit and the lower the classification rating assigned to the product.

Stowability and handling reflect the cost the carrier will incur in securing and handling the product in the vehicle. Product characteristics such as excessive weight, length, and height result in higher stowage costs for the carrier and a corresponding higher classification rating. Likewise, products that require manual handling or special handling equipment increase the carrier's costs and are given a higher rating.

The final classification factor, **liability**, considers the value of the product. When a product is damaged in transit, the common carrier is liable for the value of the product. Because higher-valued products pose a greater liability risk (potential cost), higher-valued products are classified higher than lower-valued products. In addition, products that are more susceptible to damage or are likely to damage other freight increase the potential liability cost and are placed into a higher classification rating.

In Table 4-3, the stowability and handling factors are evidenced in the classification of Item 156300. Plastic sheets or plates that exceed 9 feet, 6 inches (Sub 1) have a higher rating than the same product that does not exceed 9 feet, 6 inches (Sub 2). The density factor is embodied in the classification of Item 156600, Subs 1 through 8; the higher the density, the lower the rating. Finally, product liability is a primary factor in the classification of Item 155000, personal effects of military personnel; the higher the declared value of the shipment, the higher the rating.

Determining a Class Rate The procedure for determining a class rate for moving a specific commodity between two points is outlined in Figure 4-9. The first step is to

TABLE 4-4 Product Density and Carrier Cost per Hundredweight (cwt) Hauled

	PRODUCT DENSITY		
	16 LB/FT^3	10 LB/FT^3	2 LB/FT^3
Shipment weight (lb)[1]	48,000	30,000	6,000
Carrier cost[2]	$400.00	$400.00	$400.00
Cost/cwt[3]	$0.83	$1.33	$6.67

[1]Shipment weight = product density × 3,000 ft^3 assumed capacity of 48-ft trailer.

[2]Carrier cost assumed for a given distance to be the same for each shipment weight.

[3]Carrier cost/shipment weight/100.

FIGURE 4-9 Procedure for Determining a Class Rate

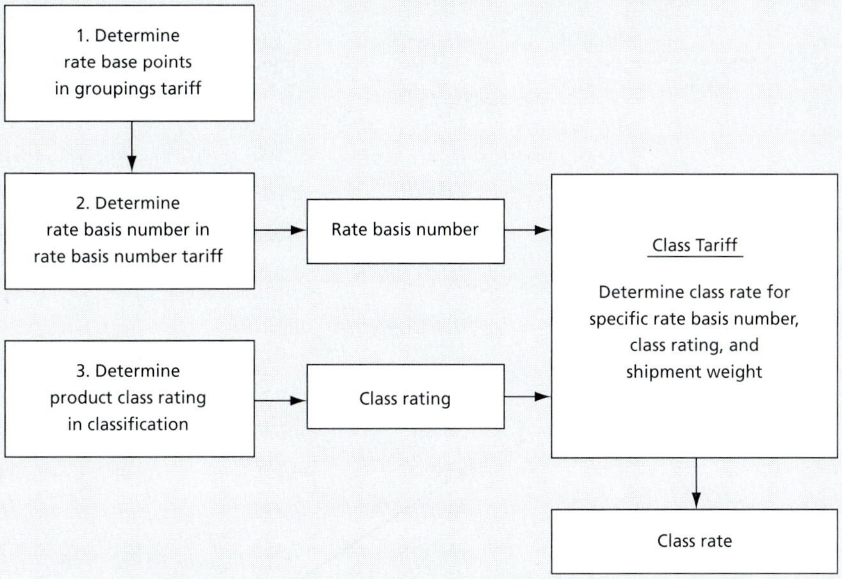

determine the rate base points for the specific origin and destination from the groupings tariff. Next, from the rate basis number tariff, determine the rate basis number for the relevant rate basis points. The class rating for the particular commodity being shipped is found in the classification. Finally, the rate is found in the class rate tariff for the appropriate rate basis number and class rating. The shipping charge for moving a product between a specific origin and destination is determined by multiplying the class rate, which is in cents per hundredweight, by the total shipment weight in hundredweight.

As an example, the total shipping charges for moving 11,000 pounds of plastic sheets, exceeding 9 feet, 6 inches, from Cross Village, Michigan, to Clifford, Ohio, will be determined. From the groupings tariff (Table 4-1), it can be seen that the rate basis point for Cross Village is Cheboygan, Michigan, and that for Clifford it is Chillicothe, Ohio. Next, the rate basis numbers tariff (Table 4-2) indicates that the rate basis number for rate basis points Cheboygan and Chillicothe is 550. From the classification (Table 4-3), it can be seen that the class rating for plastic sheets (Item 156300, Sub 1) is 85. Consulting the class tariff (Table 4-5) for a rate basis number of 550 and a class rating of 85, the resulting class rate is 846 cents per hundredweight for the weight group M10M (minimum of 10,000 pounds).

The computation of total shipping charges is as follows:

$$\text{Shipment weight in cwt} = 11{,}000/100 \text{ cwt}$$
$$\text{Shipping charges at class rate} = \$8.46/\text{cwt} \times 110 \text{ cwt} = \$93.06$$

The term *tariff* is commonly used to mean almost any publication put out by a carrier or publishing agency that concerns itself with the pricing of services performed by the carrier. All the information needed to determine the cost of a move is in one or more tariffs.

TABLE 4-5 Sample Class Rate Tariff

RATE BASIS NUMBER	MINIMUM CHARGE	WEIGHT GROUP	CLASSES (CENTS/100 LB) 200	100	85
201 to 250		L5C	3,850	1,860	1,650
	4,500	M5C	3,105	1,500	1,325
		M1M	2,231	1,078	957
		M2M	1,825	882	781
		M5M	1,370	662	582
		M10M	1,264	611	540
		M20M	813	393	319
		M30M	650	314	255
		M40M	586	283	229
501 to 550		L5C	4,556	2,201	1,957
		M5C	3,775	1,824	1,633
	4,500	M1M	2,900	1,401	1,264
		M2M	2,488	1,202	1,092
		M5M	2,035	983	888
		M10M	1,933	934	846
		M20M	1,459	705	640
		M30M	1,292	624	572
		M40M	1,223	591	547

Exception Rates An exception rate is a modification (change in rating, minimum weight, density group, and so on) to the national classification instituted by an individual carrier. Exception ratings are published when the transportation characteristics of an item in a particular area differ from those of the same article in other areas. For example, large-volume movements or intensive competition in one area might require the publication of a lower exception rating; in this case the exception rating applies, rather than the classification rating. The same procedures described above apply to determining the exception rate, except now the exception rating (class) is used instead of the classification rating. There does not have to be an exception rate for every class rate.

Commodity Rates A commodity rate can be constructed on a variety of bases, but the most common is a specific rate published on a specific commodity or group of related commodities between specific points and generally via specific routes in specific directions. Commodity rates are complete in themselves and are not part of the classification system. If the commodity being shipped is not specifically stated, or if the origin-destination is not specifically spelled out in the commodity rate, then the commodity rate for the particular movement is not applicable.

When the commodity rate is published, it takes precedence over the class rate or exception rate on the same article between the specific points. A sample is shown in Table 4-6. The commodity rate in the table applies only to reclaimed, dispersed, liquid, or paste rubber. In addition, the commodity is direction-specific and applies from

TABLE 4-6 Example of Commodity Rate

ITEM	COMMODITY	FROM	TO	RATE (CENTS PER 100 LB)	MINIMUM WEIGHT (LB)
2315	Rubber (reclaimed, dispersed, liquid, or paste)	Akron, OH Barberton, OH Ravenna, OH Cleveland, OH	Warren, MI	726 518 496	2,000 5,000 10,000

Akron, Barberton, Ravenna, and Cleveland, Ohio, to Warren, Michigan. This commodity rate is not applicable from Warren to Akron, for example.

This type of rate is offered for those commodities that are moved regularly in large quantities. Such a pricing system, however, completely undermines the attempts to simplify transportation pricing through the class rate structure. It has caused transportation pricing to revert to the publication of a multiplicity of rates and adds to the complexity of the pricing system.

Rate Systems Under Deregulation

General rate structures were the basis of tariffs published by rate bureaus. These rate-making bodies consisted of carriers that collectively met, established rates, published them in tariff form, and sold them on a subscription basis. Deregulation changes in both rail and motor modes have prohibited rate bureaus from discussing or voting on rates that involve only a single carrier. Similarly, joint rate making is limited to only those carriers involved in a movement and not all carriers in the bureau.

The diminished role of the rate bureau in carrier rate making has resulted in a plethora of individual carrier tariffs. In addition, the greater reliance upon the marketplace to control carrier rates has enabled the shippers to greatly increase negotiations, resulting in rate reductions, discounts, and contract rates. Although deregulation has somewhat diminished the use and application of the class, exception, and commodity tariff systems, various features of these tariff systems are widely used today for the pricing of small LTL freight.

The product classification feature of the former class rate system will no doubt survive for some time to come. This system of describing and classifying products simplifies the entire product description processes for all carriers. Carriers that are not even a part of the classification process often refer to these groupings to simplify their rate-making processes.

The class rate system also serves as a benchmark against which specific carrier rates and contract rates are created. Discount plans for specific shippers often are published as a percentage from the published class or exceptions-based rate.

Commodity rates published by individual carriers are similar in form to those published by the former rate bureaus. Most individual carriers publish commodity rates in a form similar to the one shown in Table 4-6.

Many innovative carriers have simplified their own class and commodity rate structures further. One way of accomplishing this is by providing shippers with small tariffs for moves from one or a few shipper points to any points within three-digit zip codes throughout the country. Thus, instead of describing the thousands of points in the United States, as in the rate base-point system, a maximum of 1,000 groupings is used. For a five-state region, one carrier has 85 three-digit groupings.

Many large motor carriers have computerized and/or web-based zip code tariffs. The shipper enters into the computer the three-digit zip code for the origin, destination, and class rating of the commodity being shipped. The computer program searches for the appropriate rate and determines the freight charges with any applicable discounts. These computerized zip code tariffs are simply a variation of the class rate structure, relying on the classification rating and zip codes to delineate the product being shipped and the origin and destination (rate basis points) of the shipment.

Another variation on the commodity tariff system is the **mileage rate**. The mileage rate is quoted in cents per mile and not in cents per hundredweight. For example, the shipper pays $1.25 per mile times the number of miles the shipment moves, regardless of the shipment weight, which is limited by the physical or legal operating constraints.

In summary, the innovative rate structures being used in today's deregulated environment are variations of the class and commodity rate structures. The next section discusses the special rates used by carriers.

Special Rates

A myriad of special rate forms have evolved over the years either as a result of special cost factors or to induce certain shipment patterns. In their basic form, these special rates appear as class, exception, or commodity rates.

Character-of-Shipment Rates

One set of special rates relates to the size or character of the shipment. Carriers generally have certain fixed costs for each shipment. Many rate forms have been developed that take advantage of the fact that additional units or weight in each shipment do not incur additional amounts of these fixed costs.

LTL/TL Rates Less-than-truckload (LTL) shipments require several handlings. Each one of these handlings requires dock personnel, materials-handling equipment, terminal investment, and additional communications and tracking effort. A truckload (TL) shipment, on the other hand, is generally loaded by the shipper and moved intact to the destination, where the consignee unloads it. No intermediate handlings are required, nor does it have to be loaded or unloaded by carrier personnel. The direct movement also avoids intermediate terminals. As a result of these factors, larger TL shipments have lower rates than LTL shipments.

Multiple-Car Rates Railroads offer volume discounts for moves of more than one carload that are shipped as a single string of cars from one point to another. The cost of moving several cars in a single shipment is proportionally less than the cost of each car moved singly. For example, the multiple-car movement of 10 cars can be handled by the same effort (empty car drop-off, pickup, intermediate and delivery efforts, and documentation) as a single-car shipment. The only basic difference is the additional weight moved in the larger string of cars. Because of this economy of movement, railroads offer such rates in coal, grain, fertilizer, chemical, oil, and many other basic commodity moves.

Incentive Rates The term **incentive rates** generally applies to a rate designed to induce the shipper to load existing movements and equipment more fully. These special rates usually apply only to weight or units loaded over and above the normally shipped quantities. For example, suppose an appliance manufacturer typically ships in carload quantities that only fill a car to 80 percent of its actual capacity. That is, the carload rate minimum is 40,000 pounds and the car is typically loaded to 48,000 pounds, but 60,000 pounds of appliances can be physically loaded into it. The carrier would prefer to have this car more fully loaded. In an incentive rate situation, the carrier would offer a rate lower than the carload rate that would only apply to the weight above the 48,000-pound norm in this example. It is more economical for the carrier to handle more weight in existing moves than to handle additional moves. By inducing the shipper to load each car more fully, fewer cars and moves would be required over the course of a year, and the same actual volume would be shipped.

Unit-Train Rates Unit trains are integrated movements between an origin and destination. These trains usually avoid terminals and do not require intermediate switching or handling of individual cars. In many situations, the shipper or consignee provides the car investment. The railroad experiences economies through high car utilization and reduced costs of movement because the rates are low in comparison to individual moves. Again, it is more economical to handle larger single movements than many individual moves. Rail carriers many times use this type of rate for trailer on flatcar (TOFC) or container on flatcar (COFC) movements.

Per-Car and Per-Truckload Rates Per-car or per-truckload rates are single-charge rates for specific origin–destination moves regardless of shipment commodity or weight. These rates also apply to container movements where the carriers' costs of movement are dominated by moving the equipment and not specifically by the weight of the shipment.

Any-Quantity Rates Any-quantity (AQ) rates provide no discount or rate break for larger movements. That is, there exists an LTL rate but no TL rate for large shipments. The AQ rates apply to any weight in a shipment. They are usually found with large, bulky commodities such as boats, suitcases, and cages where no economies are realized by the carrier for larger shipments.

Density Rates Some rates are published according to density and shipment weight, rather than by commodity or weight alone. These rates are common in air container shipments. For example, a density rate is published as, say, $10 per hundredweight for shipments up to 10 pounds per cubic foot, $9 per hundredweight for 11 to 20 pounds per cubic foot, and $8 per hundredweight for 21 pounds per cubic foot and up. These are applied when the carrier assesses rates on the basis of weight but does not experience lower costs for lighter-weight containers. Here, in fact, the carrier would experience a loss of revenue (due to a low weight) when moving a given amount of cubic footage.

A motor carrier variation on the density rate is the linear foot rule. The generalized linear foot rule applies on shipments that weigh more than 2,000 pounds and occupy more than one linear foot of space for every 350 pounds. If the shipment meets these criteria, the carrier reconstructs the weight of the shipment based on 350 pounds times the number of linear feet of space occupied and eliminates any discounts the shipper has negotiated. Air carriers use a similar approach to handling low-density articles. All rates except household goods are exempt.

ON THE LINE

Big Rate Changes Ahead for FedEx Ground

Effective January 1, 2015, FedEx Ground, a unit of FedEx, will apply dimensional weight pricing to all shipments moved via FedEx Ground, as opposed to its current method of applying dimensional weight pricing to packages that measure 3 cubic feet or more. FedEx defines dimensional weight pricing as "a common industry practice that sets the transportation price based on package volume—the amount of space a package occupies in relation to its actual weight." Jerry Hempstead, president of Orlando, Florida-based parcel consultancy Hempstead Consulting, told *Logistics Management* that this is not a pricing change for the better for shippers. "Say you put 5 pounds in a box that is 3 cubic feet," he said. "Today you get charged for 5 pounds, and January 1 you get charged for 32 pounds. Based on the new rule, a one-cubic-foot box, or a box of 1,728 cubic inches, will be charged the greater of the actual weight or the dimensional weight, which in this case is 11 pounds."

Source: *Logistics Management*, June 2014, pp. 2–3. Reprinted with permission of Peerless Media, LLC.

Area, Location, or Route Rates

A number of rates relate to area, location, or route. These special rates deserve consideration and discussion.

Local Rates Local rates apply to any rate between two points served by the same carrier. These rates include full-cost factors for pickup, documentation, rating, billing, and delivery.

Joint Rates Joint rates are single rates published from a point on one carrier's route to another carrier's destination. They are usually lower in total charges than the combination of the local rates because of through-movement economy.

Proportional Rates Many carriers experience a competitive disadvantage when their line is part of a through line that competes with another, more direct line. If a combination of local rates were charged, the through-movement cost might still be higher than the charges over the direct route. In this situation, the carrier might publish a proportional rate (lower than the regular local rate) that applies only to through moves to certain destination points beyond its line.

Differential Rates The term *differential rates* generally applies to a rate published by a carrier that faces a service time disadvantage compared to a faster carrier or mode. For example, water carriers often publish differential rates that are below those of railroads. In this way, the lower rate somewhat overcomes the longer transit time disadvantage inherent to the water carriers. The term *differential* is also found in situations where an extra charge is assessed for high-cost services such as branch lines. With all the recent mergers, this type of rate making has fallen from widespread use.

Per-Mile Rates Some rail, motor, and air carriers provide rates that are based purely upon the mileage involved. This is a common practice in bulk chemical truck moves and air charter movements. Railroads also use these rates in special train movements (high, wide, and heavy). Similarly, special moves, such as the movement of circus trains and some postal moves, are based on these rates.

Terminal-to-Terminal Rates Terminal-to-terminal rates, often referred to as *ramp-to-ramp rates*, apply between terminal points on the carrier's lines. These rates require the shipper and consignee to perform the traditional pickup and delivery functions. Many air freight rates and some piggyback rates are found in this form.

Blanket or Group Rates These rates apply to or from whole regions, rather than points. For example, all shippers of lumber from an area in Oregon and Washington are generally treated as having the same origin. Destinations eastward are grouped into zones in which all receivers in an entire state pay the same rates regardless of the special origin point in the Pacific Northwest. Blanket systems are found in food shipments from California and Florida. These rates equalize shippers and consignees because plant location is not a factor in determining the rate charged.

Time/Service Rate Structures

The Staggers Rail Act of 1980 specifically sanctioned rail contract rates, many of which can be classified as time/service rate structures. These rates are generally dependent on the transit time performance of the railroad in a particular service. One such contract provides for a standard rate for a transit time service norm. The shipper pays a higher rate for faster service and a lower rate for slower service. Another contract calls for additional shipper payments to the carrier for the fast return of empty backhaul shipper-leased cars. These rate forms either place incentives or penalties in areas where they tend to create desired results, or they reduce undesirable performance.

Contract Rates Contract services are commonplace in motor carriage and rail moves, as well as in water and some air moves. These services are governed by contracts negotiated between the shipper and carrier, not by generally published tariffs. Some specific contract service features that are typically found are described here.

One basic contract service feature calls for a reduced rate in exchange for a guarantee of a certain minimum tonnage to be shipped over a specified period. Another contract service feature calls for a reduced rate in exchange for the shipper tendering a certain percentage of all tonnage over to the contracting carrier. In both these instances, a penalty clause requires the shipper to pay up to the regular rate if the minimum tonnage is not shipped.

Another type of rail contract service feature calls for the rate to be higher or lower depending on the specific type of car supplied for loading and shipment, called a **car-supply charge**. The higher rates apply on cars whose contents have not been braced or blocked by the shipper; the higher charge is used to compensate the carrier for a potentially higher level of damage to the contents and ultimately to the higher liability level of the carrier. These are also the same cars that represent higher capital investment or per diem expense for the railroads.

A few contract service features require the shipper to pay a monthly charge to the railroad that supplies certain special equipment for the shipper's exclusive use. This charge tends to increase the shipper's use of the cars; the shipper no longer views them as free capital goods that can be used for temporary storage or loosely routed and controlled. Here the shipper firm has the incentive to use these cars in a way that benefits the firm and the carrier.

Many different rate and service configurations are found in motor carriage. These contract rates call for such services as scheduled service, special equipment movements, storage service in addition to movement, services beyond the vehicle (such as retail store shelf stocking by the driver), small package pickup and movement, bulk commodity movement, or hauling a shipper-owned trailer.

A great degree of flexibility surrounds the contracts of both rail and motor carriage. Carriers and shippers are relatively free to specifically tailor contract services to particular movements, equipment, and time-related services. The key in any contract service is to identify the service and cost factors important to each party and to construct inducements and penalties for each.

Deferred Delivery The deferred delivery rate is common in air transportation. In general, the carrier charges a lower rate in return for the privilege of deferring the arrival time of the shipment. For example, air express companies offer a discount of 25 percent or more for second-or third-day delivery, as opposed to the standard next-day delivery. The deferred delivery rate gives the carrier operating flexibility to achieve greater vehicle utilization and lower costs.

Other Rate Structures

Several other rate forms serve particular cost or service purposes.

Corporate Volume Rates A rate form called the *corporate volume rate* came into existence in 1981. It is a discounted rate for each LTL shipment that is related to the total volume of LTL shipments that a firm ships via a specific carrier from all shipping points. Generally, the more volume a shipper tenders to a particular carrier, the greater the discount.

The corporate volume rate is not widely used today, but the principle of gaining lower rates for shipping larger volumes via a carrier is the basis of many negotiated rates. The corporate volume concept brings the full market power of the shipper (total dollars spent on moving all inbound and outbound company freight) to bear on negotiations. Also, the practice of placing blocks of freight up for bid, such as all the freight moving into and out of the southeastern United States, uses the corporate volume approach to gain special rates from the accepted bidder.

Discounts In the motor carrier industry, a discount is a common pricing practice for LTL shipments moving under class rates. The typical discount ranges from 25 to 50 percent, with some discounts as high as 60 to 65 percent, off the published class rate. The discounts might apply to specific classes of LTL traffic moving between given origins and destinations, or all LTL commodities moving between any origin and destination. For the smaller shipper that does not have the corporate volume to effectively negotiate lower rates, the discount is a viable alternative to achieving reduced rates.

Loading Allowances A loading (unloading) allowance is a reduced rate or discount granted to the shipper that loads LTL shipments into the carrier's vehicle. Motor carriers are required to load and unload LTL shipments and their LTL rate structures include this loading and unloading cost. The shipper/receiver that performs this function is incurring a cost that would have been incurred by the carrier. Thus, the carrier agrees to reimburse the shipper for this expense in the form of a lower rate.

Aggregate Tender Rates A reduced rate or discount is given to the shipper that tenders two or more class-rated shipments to the carrier at one time. Usually, the aggregate shipment weight must equal 5,000 pounds or some other minimum established by the carrier. By tendering two or more shipments to the carrier at one time, the shipper reduces the carrier's pickup costs by reducing the number of times the carrier goes to the shipper's facility to pick up freight. With the aggregate tender rate, the shipper reaps part of the cost-reduction benefit that the carrier realizes from the multiple shipment pickup.

FAK Rates **FAK rates**, also known as *all-commodity rates* or *freight-all-kinds rates*, are rates expressed in cents per hundredweight or total cost per shipment. The specific commodity being shipped is not important, which means the carrier is basing the rate on the cost of service, not the value of service. The FAK rate is most valuable to shippers that ship mixed commodity shipments to a single destination, such as a grocery distributor shipping a wide variety of canned goods, paper products, and so on, to a local warehouse.

Released Value Rates Released value rates are lower than the regular full-value rates that provide for up-to-total-value carrier compensation in the event of loss or damage. Instead, released rates only provide for carrier obligation up to certain limited dollar amounts per pound shipped. They traditionally are found in air freight, household goods, and a small number of motor-and rail-hauled commodities. The 1980 and 1995 regulatory changes allowed flexible use of this rate form in most types of service and commodities.

Empty-Haul Rates An empty-haul rate is a charge for moving empty rail or motor equipment that is owned or leased by, or assigned to, a particular shipper. The existence of this type of rate tends to induce the shipper to fully load all miles of the equipment movements.

Two-Way or Three-Way Rates The terms *two-way rates* and *three-way rates* apply to rates that are constructed and charged when backhaul or triangular moves can be made. The intent here is to tie a headhaul move with what would have been another firm's backhaul move. In this way, neither firm incurs the penalty for empty backhauls. Some bulk chemical motor carriers offer these rates. They reduce total transportation charges for the shippers, and the carrier's equipment is more fully utilized than it would be otherwise.

Spot-Market Rates "Spot-market" rates can be used to facilitate the movement of the equipment or product. For example, if an excess supply of empty trailers begins to accumulate in a geographic region, spot-market rates can be quoted to allow the trailers to begin moving full back to their origin. These are similar to those types of prices used in the buying and selling of commodities on the "spot market." This is also common in air freight. Today, carriers and shippers can use Internet-based auctions to fill empty vehicles or move freight with spot-market rates.

Menu Pricing Carriers are beginning to provide more and more value-added services for shippers, such as loading/unloading, packaging, merge-in-transit, and sorting, along with traditional transportation services. Menu pricing allows the shipper to pick and choose those services the carrier should perform, and the shipper is charged accordingly. This concept is the same as that used in a la carte menus in restaurants. This type of pricing also requires the carrier to understand and know its costs in providing these services.

The regulatory standards legislated in 1980 and 1995, as well as altered administrative STB policies, have created a realm of flexibility and creativity in rate forms. Carriers

GLOBAL **PERSPECTIVES**

Ocean Carriers Hike Rates

Trans-Pacific container lines continue to experience a surge in the eastbound bookings that began in January, an upswing that's expected to continue into the second half of 2014, with vessel utilization in the mid-90 percent range via the West Coast ports and in the upper 90 percent range heading to East and Gulf Coasts ports. To cover contingencies in the event of an earlier than usual peak season, member lines in the Transpacific Stabilization Agreement (TSA) have adopted a $400-per-40-foot container (FEU) peak season surcharge (PSS) for all shipments, effective June 15, 2014. Prior to the PSS, TSA carriers have recommended a guideline general rate increase of $300 per FEU to the West Coast and $400 per FEU to all other U.S. destinations to further help offset rate erosion seen in recent months.

Source: *Logistics Management*, June 2014, p. 1. Reprinted with permission of Peerless Media, LLC.

are relatively free to develop rate systems to benefit them and shippers in ways that were neither common in the past, nor even existent. Any pricing system, however, should induce the buyer to buy in ways beneficial to the seller, be simple to understand and apply, and maximize the financial resources of the seller.

Many carriers have published their rate forms and structure in computerized form or on websites. Computerization of the former rate structures in the 1960s and 1970s was frustrated by the multitude of product classifications, locations, and footnote items that applied to specific movements. Tariffs of today are often greatly simplified, and computers are capable of greater memories and computational processes.

Pricing in Transportation Management

For many years, carriers relied on tariffs as their price lists for their services. Under traditional economic regulation, little incentive was present for carriers to differentiate themselves through either service enhancements or pricing strategies. Today, however, both of these differentiating tactics are critical to carriers in all modes, regardless of market structure. Unfortunately, however, many carriers still rely on the tariff mentality when setting prices as a competitive weapon. This way of thinking normally uses cost as a base and pays little or no attention to price as a part of the marketing mix. Many carriers will admit that they know their costs but do not know how to price.

This section will present a basic discussion on pricing for transportation management. Its intent is to introduce some common pricing strategies and techniques that are commonly used in such industries as retailing. Further in-depth discussions on these topics can be found in any basic marketing textbook.[19]

Factors Affecting Pricing Decisions

Many carrier pricing decisions are based on some reaction to a stimulus from the business environment. In transportation, the environment comprises many constituencies, four of which include customers (market), government, other channel members, and competition.

The discussion presented on value-of-service pricing in this chapter focused on the role of the market to determine prices. Obviously, a profit-maximization–oriented carrier will not set a price in the long run that prohibits the movement of freight or passengers. The carrier's price will be set at the level that maximizes its return. This, however, is dependent on what the market perceives to be a reasonable price and/or what the market is forced to pay (in monopolistic situations). The concept of price elasticity also plays an important role in the market's impact on carrier prices. For example, business travelers might be willing to absorb increases in air fares in exchange for the convenience of short-notice reservations, whereas leisure travelers might not. Customers then have a formidable impact on carrier prices.

Transportation was economically regulated by the federal government for well over 100 years because of potentially monopolistic abuses. Part of this regulation dealt with carrier prices in the forms of how they are constructed and how they are quoted. All of the economic transportation regulation falls under the responsibility of the STB. After the deregulatory efforts of the late 1970s through the 1990s, however, the Justice Department also entered the carrier pricing arena to monitor for antitrust violations. In some respects, these government agencies help mitigate the imperfections in the marketplace to control carrier pricing. As such, governmental controls affect how carriers price their services. (Government impact on carrier pricing is discussed at length in Chapter 3, "Transportation Regulation and Public Policy.")

In the case of carriers, other **channel members** can include other carriers in the same mode and in different modes. For example, interline movements between different carriers that involve revenue splits will certainly impact how each carrier prices its services. If one carrier decides to raise its price, the other carrier either has to reduce its price or risk losing business, given that the market has a high price elasticity. This can be especially true in airline movements using two different trunk line carriers or using trunk line/commuter combinations. Another case involves interline agreements between railroads for track usage. Because there is no single transcontinental railroad, it is quite likely that a shipment will have to use the tracks of more than one railroad in a cross-country move. If costs increase, rail carriers might have to increase their prices to customers, reduce their operating margins, or risk losing tonnage on that move.

Finally, competitors will impact carrier pricing strategies. History has shown that even in transportation oligopolies (such as airlines and LTL motor carriers), price leaders that offer discounts to customers will find that competitors will match those discounts, even at the risk of reducing industry profits. This could be a symptom of the continual pressure on carrier customers to reduce transportation costs in their firms. Across-the-board price increases are also usually matched by all the major competitors in a particular mode. However, occasions do occur when competitors do not follow price leader actions. An attempt by one airline to simplify its pricing structure by reducing the number of special fares was not matched by its competitors. Because of this, that airline was forced to abandon its original simplification strategy and return to normal airline pricing tactics.

Carriers then must respond to changes and directions from their operating environment. Sometimes these changes might not favor the carriers, such as when government regulations force carriers to make a change that reduces efficiency. However, these environmental forces do exert pressure on carrier pricing strategies and price levels.

Major Pricing Decisions

Every firm involved in delivering either a product or service faces major pricing decisions. These decisions can range from the very simple to the extremely complex. However, pricing decisions can be grouped into three categories. First, a carrier faces a decision when setting prices on a new service. For example, Federal Express had no precedent when setting prices on its first overnight delivery service. Today, same-day delivery is gaining in popularity with many Internet companies. Setting prices for these services could be difficult because it is based on little knowledge concerning the elasticity of the market to prices and the actual cost of providing the service. Also, if the price is set high enough to generate substantial profits, competitors will be enticed to enter the market at perhaps a lower price. On the other hand, if the price is set too low, although significant traffic might be generated, the carrier will not be maximizing its profits.

Second, a carrier must make decisions to modify prices over time. Market changes, operating changes, and service changes will require prices to be changed.

An important aspect of this decision is how and when to announce the changes to the market. For example, a major price increase by a carrier after announcing record company profits might get negative reactions in the market. In a manufacturing or retailing environment, price increases are sometimes announced in advance so customers can increase purchases to help offset the higher price. However, in transportation, services cannot be inventoried, so prior notification of a price increase does not accomplish the same objective, yet prior notification does allow for customers to seek alternative sources of supply.

Finally, carriers will make decisions initiating and responding to price changes. The concept of a *price leader* within an industry is not new. If a carrier is the price leader, then that carrier initiates the change; if not, then the carrier responds to the change. In transportation, where many of the markets are oligopolistic, downward price changes can be dangerous because of their potential to decrease industry revenues. Upward price changes can make a carrier the sole high-price service provider if competition does not follow the change, so how this decision is made can have a substantial impact on market share and profits.

Although there might be other types of price decisions, these represent the major ones that carriers will make. These can be considered strategic decisions because of the importance they have on carrier market position within the industry. For example, People's Express once offered a low-price, no-frills airline service and did not expect other carriers to match the low fares. However, some of the major trunk lines actually offered fares below People's, even though it meant a loss. With a high debt and stiff competition, People's Express eventually went out of business. Pricing, then, is a major marketing decision for every carrier.

Establishing the Pricing Objective

Pricing objectives for a carrier should reflect overall company objectives and reflect, in many ways, how the carrier will compete in its markets. Pricing objectives might also change for a particular service offering as it progresses through its product life cycle. Carriers with multiple markets might also establish various pricing objectives for these markets. For example, passenger airlines have separate pricing objectives for first-class and coach markets as well as for business and leisure travelers. This section will present several different pricing objectives that can be utilized in the transportation industry.

Especially in the case of ailing passenger airlines, **survival-based pricing** is aimed at increasing cash flow through the use of low prices. With this price level, the carrier attempts to increase volume and also encourage the higher utilization of equipment. Because an empty airline seat cannot be inventoried and is lost at takeoff, the marginal cost of filling that seat is small. Survival pricing then tries to take advantage of the marginal-cost concept. Closely related is a **unit volume pricing** objective. This attempts to utilize a carrier's existing capacity to the fullest, so the price is set to encourage the market to fill that capacity. Multiple pickup allowances in the LTL industry, space-available prices in the freight airline industry, and multiple-car prices in the railroad industry are examples of this type of pricing objective.

Another price objective is called **profit maximization**, which can occur in the short run or in the long run. Carriers using this type of pricing usually are concerned with measures such as return on investment. This type of objective also can utilize what is called a **skimming price**. A skimming price is a high price intended to attract a market that is more concerned with quality, uniqueness, or status and is insensitive to price.[20] For example, although a high-cost move, pricing for the maiden flight of the Concorde was certainly aimed at those who would be willing to pay a high price because of the limited number of seats. This strategy works if competition can be kept out of a market through high investment costs or firm loyalty.

Many times a skimming price strategy is followed by a **penetration price** strategy. This can lead to a sales-based pricing objective, which can be an effective strategy because (1) a high price can be charged until competition starts to enter; (2) a higher price can help offset initial outlays for advertising and development; (3) a high price portrays a high-quality service; (4) if price changes need to be made, it is more favorable to reduce a price than to raise it; and (5) after market saturation is achieved, a lower price can appeal to a mass market with the objective of increasing sales.[21] A sales-based pricing objective also follows the life cycle approach of using skimming during the introduction and growth stages and penetration during the maturation stage. The recent reintroduction of luxury passenger railroad service might be a good example of this type of strategy. In transportation, this strategy would more likely be successful with passenger movements because of the reliance it places on the price–value relationship.

A **market share pricing** objective can be used in an industry whose revenues are stagnant or declining. This objective tries to take market share from competitors through the use of lower prices. This strategy is used frequently in passenger airlines and the LTL motor carrier industries. In some cases, this strategy assumes that competitors' offerings are substitutes and that competitors are not in a position to match the lower prices; if the services were not substitutes, a lower price would not provide a competitive advantage. For example, an airline that lowers its fares for business travelers to gain more of this market but does not offer the same number of departures and arrivals as a competitor might not succeed at gaining any market share.

Finally, a **social responsibility pricing** objective forgoes sales and profits and puts the welfare of society and customers first.[22] For example, after the tragic incident in New York City on September 11, 2001, many carriers offered to carry such items as food, clothing, building supplies, and medical supplies into the devastated area at greatly reduced prices or for free.

Because carriers in the various transportation industries service multiple markets, it is quite possible for them to employ several pricing objectives at one time. A carrier must be careful when setting an overall company pricing strategy to assure that these multiple pricing objectives are complementary, not conflicting.

Estimating Demand

Probably one of the most difficult tasks associated with pricing is estimating demand. In a perfectly competitive market, unit demand will decrease as price increases. This is reflected in the traditional demand-and-supply curve offered in basic economic theory.

However, transportation carriers do not function in perfectly competitive markets. Demand estimation can become very tedious and difficult. However, certain concepts and procedures can be used in this process. One of these is the concept of *price elasticity*. Price elasticity refers to the change in demand because of a change in price. In an established market for a carrier, this relationship should be well developed to the point where demand implications from a price change should be easy to estimate. The example of business versus leisure travelers in the airline industry can be used to explain this concept. Business travelers are relatively price inelastic because demand for business travel by air does not fluctuate widely with increases in price. However, leisure travelers are very price elastic and might tend to delay travel or seek travel by an alternative mode if there is an increase in air fares. In a new market, estimations of price elasticity can be made by comparing the new market with a similar existing market.

A direct attitude survey might also be used in determining demand under a new pricing structure. For example, asking customers and/or potential customers how much business they would provide at certain price levels might produce some feel of how sensitive demand is to price. Caution has to be used in this method in how this question is asked because customers will usually tend to favor the lowest price.

Finally, a market test is a possible way to determine potential demand when market testing is feasible. This might involve a carrier introducing a new service at a high price in one area and at a higher price in another area to see how sensitive demand is to price. Important in this method is choosing test market areas that resemble the entire market for which the service is applicable.

Although not a science, demand estimation is a critical part of pricing strategy. Demand estimation results in potential revenue estimation. (Some of the theory behind demand estimation was presented earlier in this chapter, under the topic "Value-of-Service Pricing.") With revenue estimated, costs should next be established.

Estimating Costs

A significant portion of this chapter is devoted to the concepts of costs and cost-of-service pricing, so a detailed explanation of either is not necessary here. However, a decision must be made as to which costs should be included in the total cost analysis. In the example given under value-of-service pricing, the fuel expense and driver wages generated on a backhaul can be considered a fixed cost and, as such, need not be included in the backhaul pricing decision.

Another cost relationship that must be examined is how costs behave at different levels of output or capacity. The existence or nonexistence of scale economies in transportation, for example, will affect how costs behave at different capacity levels. This information can be used to determine such factors as break-even points. Regardless of the methods used, the cost of providing a service must be calculated to determine the attractiveness of a market for a carrier.

Price Levels and Price Adjustments

With demand and cost estimates generated, it is possible to set the actual price. Many methods for doing this exist, including demand-based methods, cost-based methods, profit-based methods, and competition-based methods. Lengthy discussions of these can be found in any basic marketing-text chapter on pricing.[23] However, a discussion of price adjustments is warranted because of the federal government regulations on such concepts as rebates.

Discounts are a reduction from a published price that rewards a buyer for doing something that is beneficial for the supplier.[24] In transportation, LTL versus TL prices reflect carrier savings from larger shipments, a portion of which is passed on to the customer in the form of a lower price. This could be called a quantity discount. Airlines use a form of seasonal discounts to encourage vacation passengers to travel during carrier off-peak periods. Cash discounts, relatively new to the transportation industry, reward customers who pay their bills within a stated period of time. A common form of a cash discount is "2/10, net 30," which means that the customer can take a 2 percent discount if the bill is paid within 10 days, or else pay the full amount within 30 days. This helps speed the cash flow for carriers, which is important for their financial stability.

Geographic adjustments are common in the transportation industry. Although not directly used by carriers, geographic adjustments are used by shippers and receivers to compensate for transportation costs in the final price to the customer. One common type of geographic price is FOB origin or FOB destination pricing. In FOB origin pricing, the buyer is responsible for transportation costs; in destination pricing, the shipper is responsible (see Figure 4-10).

Uniform-delivered pricing, a form of FOB destination pricing, offers a final price to customers for a product that includes all transportation costs. Related to this is **zone pricing**, in which every customer within a certain zone pays exactly the same price for a product based on average transportation costs within the zone.

When using discounts and allowances in the transportation industry, an important rule to remember is that a discount or allowance passed on to a customer must be the result of a reduction in carrier costs because of an action by the customer. Also, the discount or allowance given to the customer may not exceed the cost savings to the carrier. Violating either of these rules of thumb exposes the carrier to the jurisdiction of the STB (rebates) and the Justice Department (antitrust and rebates).

Most Common Mistakes in Pricing

As previously mentioned, carriers have not had many years of experience in setting and managing prices on a strategic level. However, just like firms in any other industry, they are prone to certain mistakes. The first common mistake is to make pricing too reliant on costs. Although it is important to know the costs of providing a service, many other factors play a role in setting the appropriate price for a market. Competitive factors, customer preferences and values, and government regulations will affect the level at which the price will be most beneficial to the carrier.

The second common mistake is that prices are not revised frequently enough to capitalize on market changes. Under the previous regulatory environment, it was difficult for carriers to change prices because of the requirement of public notice and the burden of proof on the carrier. However, today's environment has allowed tremendous freedom and the flexibility for carriers to change prices. Unfortunately, for some carriers, the traditional mentality remains and can prevent a carrier from entering a market or, in some cases, creating a new market.

Setting the price independently of the marketing mix is a third common mistake. The **marketing mix**, also known as the "4 Ps," consists of product, price, promotion, and place. A carrier's product or output is transportation; its promotion is how it creates demand or advertises itself to customers; price is what it charges for its product or output; place is how it delivers its service to customers. All of these interact within a carrier's organization to provide access to and, it is hoped, success in current and potential

FIGURE 4-10 The Variety of Fob Pricing Arrangements

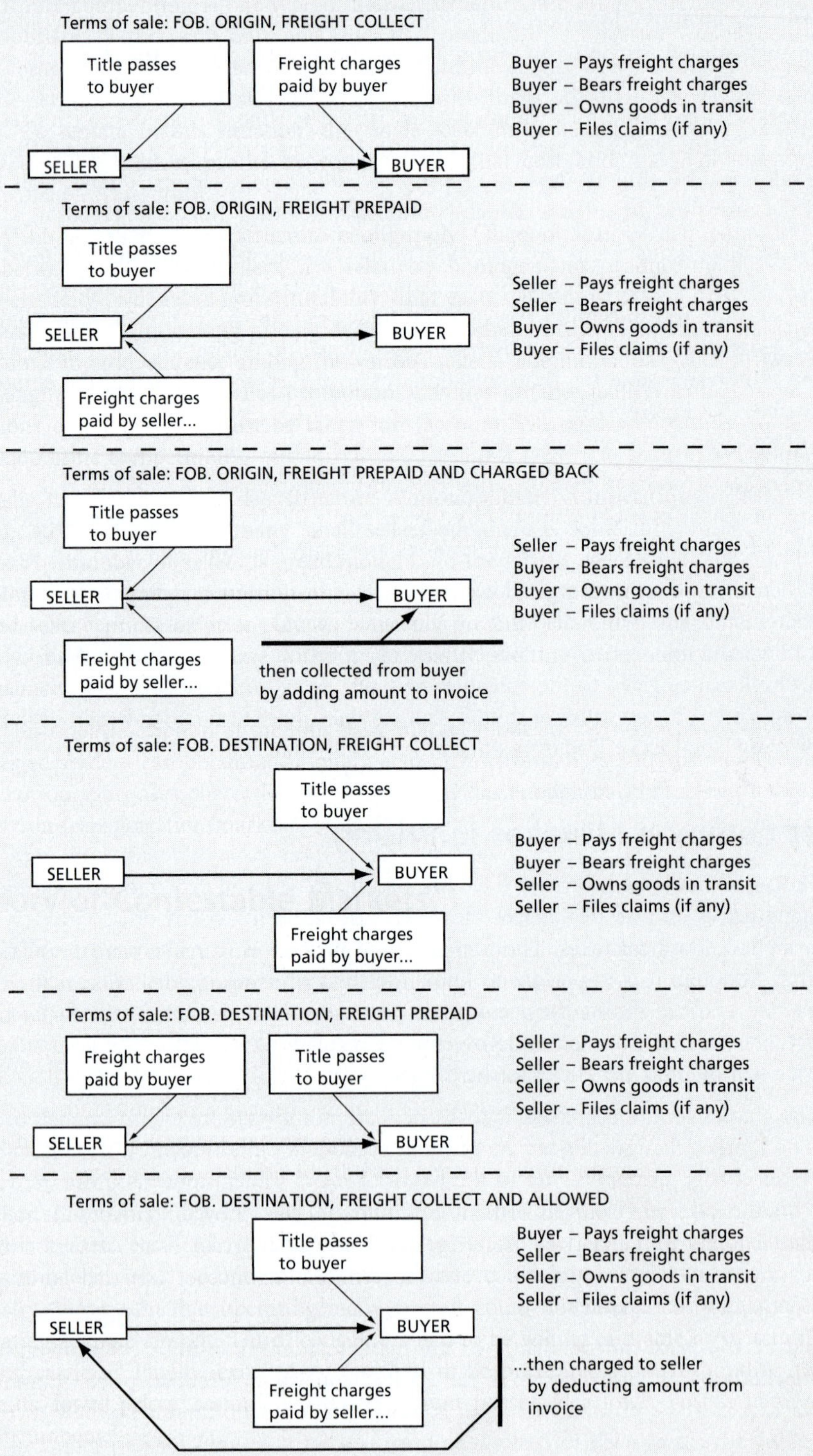

Source: Bruce J. Riggs, "The Traffic Manager in Physical Distribution Management," *Transportation & Distribution Management*, June 1968, p. 45. Penton Media Inc.

markets. Managing one of these areas independently of the others will result in a suboptimization of the carrier's resources and its profits.

Finally, price is sometimes not varied enough for different service offerings and market segments. A "one price for all" mentality does not work in the transportation industry. As previously stated, carriers service multiple markets with differing service/price requirements. Airlines use a concept called *yield management pricing*, a form of value-of-service pricing, which relates price to the availability of capacity and the willingness of passengers to pay, or to address this situation.[25] Charging one price for all services is not going to maximize the profits for the carrier.

Pricing is a complex and challenging process that applies to all business entities. Pricing is also critical to a business's competitive advantage, position within its markets, and overall profitability. It must be managed within the context of the carrier's overall strategic plan, not independently of it.

SUMMARY

- The market structure for a carrier will be related to its cost structure; having a knowledge of this cost structure is necessary for the development of carrier prices.
- Cost-of-service pricing relies on the marginal cost of providing a service.
- Value-of-service pricing relies on the average cost of providing the service or on what the market will bear.
- Because of the high number of possible freight rates for commodities, tariffs were constructed to simplify them into class, exception, or commodity rates.
- Various types of special rates exist that allow carriers and shippers the flexibility to tailor rate structures to meet market needs.
- Pricing in transportation can be a strategic advantage if managed within the context of corporate strategy.
- Setting and managing prices in transportation are affected by actions of government, customers, competition, and other channel members.

STUDY QUESTIONS

1. Compare and contrast pure competition with monopoly from a pricing perspective. If you were a shipper, which would you prefer? Which would a carrier prefer?
2. Describe an oligopolistic market structure. What alternatives to price competition exist in such markets? Why would these alternatives be important to shippers?
3. What is value-of-service pricing? Is this approach to pricing valid today?
4. What is cost-of-service pricing? What is the relationship between value-of-service pricing and cost-of-service pricing?
5. What is a released value rate and how does its use affect a shipper's transportation costs?
6. What are the major forces that affect carrier pricing strategies?
7. How might pricing strategies differ among carriers in competitive markets, oligopolistic markets, and monopolistic markets?
8. What are the various factors used in classifying commodities for tariff purposes?
9. What are the differences among class, exception, and commodity rates?
10. Why were tariffs created? Are they still useful in today's transportation environment?

NOTES

1. For a more thorough discussion of contestable market theory, see W. J. Baumol, J. C. Panzar, and R. D. Willig, *Contestable Markets and the Theory of Industry Structure*, New York: Harcourt, Brace, Jovanovich, 1982.
2. Stanley E. Fawcett and Martin T. Farris, "Contestable Markets and Airline Adaptability Under Deregulation," *Transportation Journal*, Vol. 29, No. 1, 1989, pp. 12–24.
3. Ibid., p. 17.
4. Ibid., p. 14.
5. Ibid.
6. For a more detailed discussion of this conclusion, see ibid.

7. Winthrop M. Daniels, *The Price of Transportation Service,* New York: Harper and Brothers, 1942, p. 1.

8. John R. Meyer et al., *The Economics of Competition in the Transportation Industries,* Cambridge, MA: Harvard University Press, 1959, p. 205.

9. For an excellent analysis of industry pricing behavior, see ibid., pp. 203–211.

10. This section is based on the discussion in J. J. Coyle, "Cost-of-Service Pricing in Transportation," *Quarterly Review of Economics and Business,* Vol. 57, 1964, pp. 69–74.

11. Harold Hotelling, "The General Welfare in Relation to Problems of Taxation and of Railway and Utility Rates," *Econometrics,* Vol. 6, No. 3, 1938, p. 242.

12. R. W. Harbeson, "The Cost Concept and Economic Control," *Harvard Business Review,* Vol. 17, 1939, pp. 257–263.

13. Ibid.

14. George W. Wilson, "Freight Rates and Transportation Costs," *The Business Quarterly,* Summer 1960, pp. 161–162.

15. John J. Coyle, "A Reconsideration of Value of Service Pricing," *Land Economics,* Winter 1964, pp. 193–199.

16. George W. Wilson, *Theory of Transportation Pricing,* Bloomington, IN: Indiana University, 1985, p. 160.

17. For an extended discussion, see Coyle, "A Reconsideration of Value of Service Pricing," pp. 195–198.

18. This example is adapted from George W. Wilson and George W. Smerk, "Rate Theory," in *Physical Distribution Management,* Bloomington, IN: Indiana University, 1963, pp. 7–10.

19. See, for example, Eric N. Berkowitz, Roger A. Kerin, Steven W. Hartley, and William Rudelius, *Marketing,* 3rd ed., Homewood, IL: Richard D. Irwin, 1992.

20. Joel R. Evans and Barry Berman, *Marketing,* New York: Macmillan, 1982, p. 532.

21. Ibid.

22. Berkowitz et al., *Marketing,* p. 321.

23. Ibid., pp. 339–352.

24. Ibid., p. 354.

25. For a discussion of yield management pricing, see Sheryl Kimes, "The Basics of Yield Management," *The Cornell H.R.A. Quarterly,* November 1989, pp. 14–19; Walter J. Relihan III, "The Yield Management Approach to Hotel Room Pricing," *The Cornell H.R.A. Quarterly,* May 1989, pp. 40–45; Peter P. Belobaba, "Application of a Probabilistic Decision Model to Airline Seat Inventory Control," *Operations Research,* Vol. 37, No. 2, 1989.

CASE 4-1

Hardee Transportation (A)

Jim O'Brien has realized for quite some time that some of Hardee's customers are more profitable than others. This is also quite true for certain freight lanes. However, Hardee has traditionally structured its prices around discounts off their published tariff rates. Most of the discounts have been based on freight volume only. Jim knows that his drivers and dock people do more for certain customers than move volume; they count freight during loading, sort and segregate freight on the dock, weigh shipments, and do some labeling.

Jim foresees some of the new service demands from his customers being very difficult to cost and price because they won't necessarily be based on freight volume. Some of these new demands will include merge-in-transit, event management, continuous shipment tracking RFID capability, and dedicated customer service personnel. Traditionally, Hardee has used average-cost pricing for its major customers. Some of his pricing managers have urged Jim to consider marginal-cost pricing. However, Jim has developed a keen interest in value-of-service pricing methods versus the traditional cost-of-service pricing.

The problem with both approaches for Hardee is that they have no form of activity-based costing or any other methodology that will allow them to really get a handle on where their costs are hidden. Jim knows what Hardee pays its drivers, knows the costs of equipment and fuel, and knows the overall costs of dispatch and dock operations. Hardee's average length of haul is 950 miles, and its loaded mile metric is 67 percent.

CASE QUESTIONS

1. What would be the advantages/disadvantages of using cost-of-service versus value-of-service pricing for Hardee's customers? When discussing cost-of-service pricing, what type of cost (average versus marginal) would make more sense for Hardee?
2. How would you develop a methodology for Hardee to price its existing services? Its evolving services? Would you use the same or different strategies for each?

CASE 4-2

Hardee Transportation (B)

One of Jim O'Brien's customers has presented him with an opportunity for a significant amount of freight moving into a new market for Hardee. Hardee is a truckload carrier primarily moving freight in the East/West market in the United States. Although it has some movements in and out of Canada and Mexico, Hardee has focused on moving freight in eastward and westward directions. Hardee has dispatch centers located throughout the United States, which have some dock capacity.

The new move would be between Pittsburgh and Miami. Hardee has avoided this market because of the lack of backhaul opportunities that exist outbound from Florida. However, this new move offers a significant increase in volume for Hardee. A complicating factor in this move is the request that Hardee perform sorting and segregation at its dispatch centers. Each shipment will consist of straight (one product) pallet loads of various types of consumer goods freight destined for a retailer's distribution center in Miami. Sorting and segregation at Hardee's locations would consist of breaking the pallets and sorting the freight by the retailer's store locations, then repalletizing into rainbow (mixed products) pallets for each store.

Hardee has never experienced this type of request before. Jim knows that he needs to put some type of costs to this move to make sure that the moves are profitable. Because of the large volume involved, not covering Hardee's costs in pricing could result in large losses for Hardee. The relevant information for costing this move is as follows:

Equipment Cost Data

Equipment Purchase Price

1. Line-haul tractors = $120,000
2. Line-haul trailers = $40,000

Depreciation

1. Tractors = 5-year straight line
2. Trailers = 8-year straight line

Interest

1. Tractors = 6 percent APR for 5 years
2. Trailers = 6 percent APR for 8 years

Fuel

1. $3.83 per gallon for diesel
2. Line-haul tractors = 6.0 miles per gallon

Labor

1. Line-haul drivers = $0.45 per mile
2. Pickup and delivery (PUD) drivers = $30 (fully loaded) per hour
3. Dock workers = $25 (fully loaded) per hour

Miscellaneous

1. Insurance cost = $0.067 per mile
2. Maintenance cost = $0.152 per mile
3. Billing cost = $1.95 per freight bill
4. Tractors and trailers are available for use 24 hours per day, 365 days per year
5. Administrative/overhead cost = 10 percent of total cost of move
6. Dock facility cost = $15 per hour
7. Line-haul vehicle averages 45 mph between origin and destination

Route and Time of Move

The shipment (45,000 pounds) originates at a customer location in Pittsburgh, located 20 miles from Hardee's dispatch center. A PUD driver is dispatched from the Hardee location at 8:30 a.m. on January 12, 2015, and arrives at destination at 9:00 a.m. the same day. The shipment is loaded from 9:00 a.m. to 12:00 p.m. The PUD driver departs the customer location at 12:00 p.m. and arrives back at the Hardee dispatch center at 12:30 p.m.

The sort process starts at 12:30 p.m. and ends at 8:30 p.m. on January 12. It requires unloading the trailer, sorting, and repalletizing the load. This operation requires two dock workers, each working the same trailer for 8 hours in the dispatch center.

The line-haul portion begins with the vehicle being dispatched from the Pittsburgh location at 8:30 p.m. on January 12 and traveling to Charlotte, North Carolina, a distance of 481 miles, and arriving at Charlotte at 7:12 a.m. on January 13. The driver rests from 7:12 a.m. until 3:12 p.m. The trip continues with the vehicle departing Charlotte at 3:12 p.m. on January 13 and traveling to Jacksonville, Florida, a distance of 399 miles, arriving at Jacksonville at 12:06 a.m. on January 14. The driver rests from 12:06 a.m. until 10:06 a.m. The line-haul portion concludes with the vehicle departing Jacksonville at 10:06 a.m. and traveling to the customer's location in Miami, a distance of 369 miles, and arriving at the distribution center at 6:18 p.m. on January 14.

The line-haul driver stays with the vehicle while it is being unloaded (2 hours unload time). The driver then deadheads at 8:18 p.m. from the customer's distribution center and arrives at a Hardee dispatch center located in Miami at 8:48 p.m., a distance of 15 miles from the distribution center.

CASE QUESTIONS

1. What are the pickup, sort, line-haul, and delivery costs to Hardee for this move?
2. What is the total cost of this move? Cost per cwt? Cost per revenue mile?
3. If Hardee would put two drivers in the tractor for the line-haul move, there would be no rest required for drivers during the line-haul move. What would happen to total costs?
4. Assume that Hardee has no loaded backhaul to return the vehicle and driver to Pittsburgh. How would you account for the empty backhaul costs associated with this move? Would you include those in the headhaul move? How would this impact your pricing strategy?

APPENDIX 4A

Cost Concepts

Accounting Cost

The simplest concept or measure of cost is what has sometimes been labeled accounting cost, or even more simply as money cost. These are the so-called bookkeeping costs of a company and include all cash outlays of the firm. This particular concept of cost is not difficult to grasp. The most difficult problem with accounting costs is their allocation among the various products or services of a company.

If the owner of a motor carrier, for example, was interested in determining the cost associated with moving a particular truckload of traffic, all the cost of fuel, oil, and the driver's wages associated with the movement could be quickly determined. It might also be possible to determine how much wear and tear would occur on the vehicle during the trip. However, the portion of the president's salary, the terminal expenses, and the advertising expense should be included in the price. These costs should be included in part, but how much should be included is frequently a perplexing question. The computation becomes even more complex when a small shipment is combined with other small shipments in one truckload.

Some allocation would then be necessary for the fuel expense and the driver's wages.

Economic Cost

A second concept of cost is economic cost, which is different from accounting cost. The economic definition of cost is associated with the alternative cost doctrine or the opportunity cost doctrine. Costs of production, as defined by economists, are futuristic and are the values of the alternative products that could have been produced with the resources used in production.

Therefore, the costs of resources are their values in their best alternative uses. To secure the service or use of resources, such as labor or capital, a company must pay an amount at least equal to what the resource could obtain in its best alternative use. Implicit in this definition of cost is the principle that if a resource has no alternative use, then its cost in economic terms is zero.

The futuristic aspect of economic costs has special relevance in transportation because, once investment has been made, one should not be concerned with recovering what are sometimes referred to as **sunk costs**.[1] Resources in some industries are so durable that they can be regarded as virtually everlasting. Therefore, if no replacement is anticipated, and there is no alternative use, then the use of the resource is costless in an economic sense. This is of special importance in the railroad industry.

Railroads have long been regarded as having durable and therefore costless resources. That is, some of the resources of railroads, such as concrete ties, some signaling equipment, and even some rolling stock, are so durable and so highly specialized that they have no alternative production or use potential. So the use of such resources, apart from maintenance, is costless in an economic sense. Consequently, in a competitive pricing situation, such resources could be excluded from the calculation of fixed costs. Also, such specialized resources can be eliminated in comparing cost structures.[2]

Although the economic logic of the earlier argument on the use of durable, specialized resources is impeccable, it is frequently disregarded by pricing analysts and regulators. In a sense, the elimination of such costs from pricing calculations defies common sense. From the money or accounting cost perspective, these costs usually should be included.

The conclusion that must be drawn is that economic costs differ from money or accounting costs. Money costs are by their very nature a measure of past costs. This does not mean that money costs do not have any relevance in the economic sense. Past costs do perform a very important function because they provide a guide to future cost estimates. However, complete reliance should not be put upon historical costs for pricing in the transportation industry.

Social Cost

A third category of costs—social costs—might also be considered. Some businesses might not concern themselves with social costs unless required to do so by law. These costs take into consideration the cost to society of some particular operation and, in fact, might outweigh money cost. For example, what is the cost to society when a company releases its waste materials into a stream? Today many regulations and controls are administered by various regulatory agencies to protect society from such costs. These agencies make the business organizations responsible for social costs. (For example, strip-mine operators are customarily required to backfill and plant.) In spite of such controls, however, there are still instances when chemicals or other hazardous materials are discharged or leak out, and society has to bear the cost of the cleanup operations as well as the health hazards.

This discussion is not trying to castigate business organizations or suggest that all investment decisions result in negative social costs because, in fact, there can be social benefits from business investments. However, to ensure that the discussion is complete, social costs must be considered.

Analysis of Cost Structures

There are two general approaches to an analysis of a particular cost structure. Under one approach, costs can be classified as those that are directly assignable to particular segments of the business (such as products or services) and those that are incurred for the business as a whole. These two types of cost are generally designated as separable and common costs, respectively. Usually, common costs are further classified as joint common costs or conjoint common costs. **Separable costs** refer to a situation in which products are necessarily produced in fixed proportions. The classic example is that of hides and beef. Stated simply, the production or generation of one product or service necessarily entails the production or generation of another product. In terms of transportation, joint costs occur when two or more services are *necessarily* produced together in fixed proportions. One of these services is said to be a by-product of the other. The most obvious illustration is that of the backhaul situation; the return capacity is the by-product of the loaded trip to the destination.[3]

It is a generally accepted fact that large transportation companies, especially railroads, have a significant element of common costs because they have roadbed, terminals, freight yards, and so on, the cost of which is common to all traffic. However, the only evidence of true jointness appears to be the backhaul.[4] Nonjoint common costs are those

FIGURE 4A-1 Directly Assignable Cost Approach

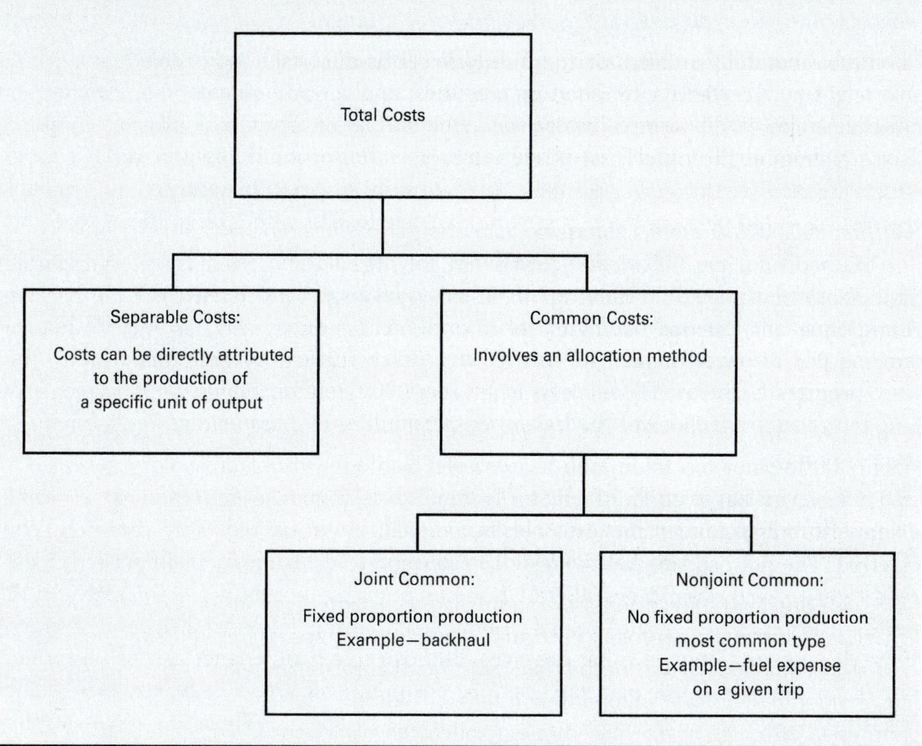
Total Costs
Separable Costs:
Costs can be directly attributed to the production of a specific unit of output
Common Costs:
Involves an allocation method
Joint Common:
Fixed proportion production
Example—backhaul
Nonjoint Common:
No fixed proportion production
most common type
Example—fuel expense on a given trip

that do not require the production of fixed proportions of products or services. Nonjoint common costs are more customary in transportation. For example, on a typical train journey on which hundreds of items are carried, the expenses of the crew and fuel are common costs incurred for all the items hauled (see Figure 4A-1).

A technique for allocating costs directly to activity centers has been implemented in both the carrier and shipper communities. **Activity-based costing (ABC)** identifies costs specifically generated by performing a service or producing a product. ABC does not allocate direct and indirect costs based on volume alone; it determines which activities are responsible for these costs and burdens these activities with their respective portion of overhead costs.

One application for ABC today by both carriers and shippers is the calculation of customer profitability.[5]

Under the other basic approach to analyzing a particular cost structure, costs are divided into those that do not fluctuate with the volume of business in the short term and those that do. The time period here is assumed to be that in which the plant or physical capacity of the business remains unchanged, or the short run. The two types of costs described are usually referred to as *fixed* and *variable* costs, respectively.

In the first approach, the distinction between common and separable costs is made with the idea that costs can be traced to specific accounts or products of the business.

In the second approach, the distinction between fixed and variable is made to study variations in business as a whole over a period of time and the effect of these variations upon expenses. In other words, with fixed and variable costs the focus is on the fact that some costs increase and decrease with expansion and contraction of business volume, whereas other costs do not vary as business levels change.

Because of the two different approaches to studying costs, it is possible that a certain cost might be classified as common on one hand and variable on the other, or common under one approach and fixed under the other, and so on, for all the possible combinations. Therefore, the only costs directly traceable or separable are the variable costs, which are also separable. For example, fuel expense is generally regarded as a variable cost, but it would be a common cost with a vehicle loaded with LTL traffic.

The second approach of cost analysis—namely, fixed and variable costs—is important and should be discussed further. As indicated previously, **total fixed costs** are constant regardless of the enterprise's volume of business. These fixed costs can include maintenance expenses on equipment or right-of-way (track) caused by time and weather (not use), property taxes, certain management salaries, interest on bonds, and payments on long-term leases. **Fixed costs per unit** of output decline as more volume is allocated to a fixed-cost asset.

A business has a commitment to its fixed costs even with a zero level of output. Fixed costs might, in certain instances, be delayed, or to use the more common term, deferred. The railroads frequently delay or defer costs. For example, maintenance of railroad rights-of-way should probably be done each spring or summer, particularly in the northern states. Freezing and thawing, along with spring rains, wash away gravel and stone (ballast) and may do other damage. Although this maintenance can be postponed, just as, for example, house painting might be postponed for a year or two, sooner or later it has to be done if the business wants to continue to operate. There is a fixed commitment or necessity that requires the corrective action and associated expense.[6] The important point is that total fixed expenses occur independently of the volume of business experienced by the organization.

Variable costs, on the other hand, are closely related to the volume of business. In other words, firms do not experience any variable costs unless they are operating. The fuel expense for trains or tractor–trailers is an excellent example of a variable cost. If a locomotive or vehicle does not make a run or trip, there is no fuel cost. Additional examples of variable costs include the wear and tear on tractor–trailers and the cost for tires and engine parts. Thus, variable cost per unit remains constant regardless of the level of output, while total variable costs are directly related to the level of output.

Another related point is that railroads and pipelines, like many public utility companies, are frequently labeled as decreasing cost industries. The relevance of this phenomenon to pricing was discussed earlier in this chapter, but it also deserves some additional explanation now. Railroads and pipelines have a high proportion of fixed costs in their cost structures. There is some debate about the percentage, but the estimates range from 20 to 50 percent. Contrast this with motor carriers whose average is 10 percent. As railroads produce more units, the proportion of fixed costs on each item will be lower. More importantly, this decline will occur over a long range of output because of the large-scale capacity of most railroads.

An example of the earlier situation is useful here. Assume that a particular railroad incurs $5 million of fixed costs on an annual basis. In addition, assume that the railroad is analyzing costs for pricing purposes between Bellefonte, Pennsylvania, and Chicago. In its examination of cost, the railroad determines that the variable cost on a carload is $250 between Bellefonte and Chicago.

Although it might be unrealistic, assume that the railroad only moves 10 cars per year. The cost would be as follows:

Fixed cost $5,000,000

Variable cost $2,500 (10 cars × $250)

Total cost $5,002,500

Average cost $500,250 per car

If it moves 1,000 cars, the cost would be:

Fixed cost $5,000,000

Variable cost $250,000 (1,000 cars × $250)

Total cost $5,250,000

Average cost $5,250 per car

If it moves 100,000 cars, the cost would be:

Fixed cost $5,000,000

Variable cost $25,000,000 (100,000 × $250)

Total cost $30,000,000

Average cost $300 per car

The relationship is easy to see. If the number of cars increased in our example, the average cost would continue to decline. Theoretically, average cost would have to level out and eventually increase due to decreasing returns, but the important point is that the high proportion of fixed costs and the large capacity cause the average cost to decline over a great range of output (see Figure 4A-2). There would be a point, however, at which additional cars would require another investment in fixed cost, thus shifting the average-cost curve.

The significance of the declining cost phenomenon to a railroad is that volume is a very important determinant of cost and efficiency. Furthermore, pricing the service to attract traffic is a critical factor in determining profitability, particularly where there is competition from alternate modes of transportation.

Another cost concept that is of major importance in this analysis is marginal cost, because of its key role in understanding pricing decisions. Marginal cost can be defined as the change in total cost resulting from a one-unit change in output, or as additions to aggregate cost for given additions to output. This latter definition probably makes more

FIGURE 4A-2 Average Cost and Output

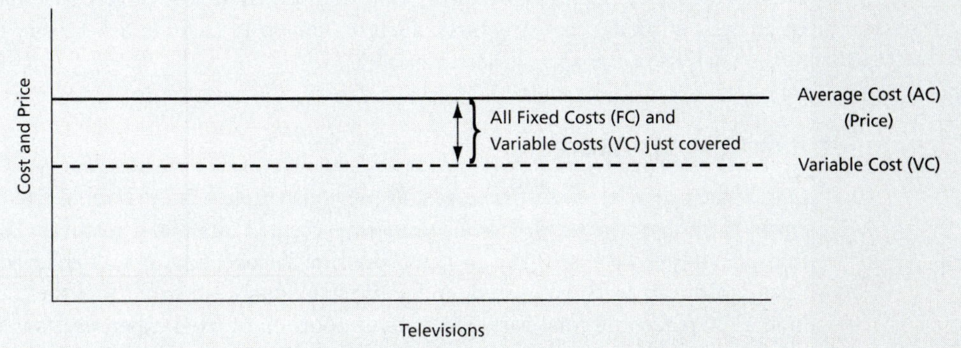

sense in transportation because of the difficulties of defining the output unit. Marginal cost also can be defined as the change in total variable cost resulting from a one-unit change in output, because a change in output changes total variable cost and total cost by exactly the same amounts. Marginal cost is sometimes referred to as *incremental cost*, especially in the transportation industry.

There is one other type of cost that should be mentioned because of its importance in price decision—**out-of-pocket costs**. Out-of-pocket costs are usually defined as those costs that are directly assignable to a particular unit of traffic and that would not have been incurred if the service or movement had not been performed. Within the framework of this definition, out-of-pocket costs could also be either separable costs or variable costs. Although the earlier definition states that out-of-pocket costs are specifically assignable to a certain movement, which implies separable costs, they can definitely be considered as variable costs because they would not have occurred if a particular shipment had not been moved. The definition also encompasses marginal cost because marginal cost can be associated with a unit increase in cost.

The vagueness of the out-of-pocket costs definition has left the door open to the types of cost included as a part of the total cost calculation. The difficulty lies in the fact that from a narrow viewpoint, out-of-pocket costs could be classified as only those expenses incurred because a particular unit was moved. For example, the loading and unloading expense attributable to moving a particular shipment, plus the extra fuel and wear and tear on equipment (relatively low for railroads) could be classified as out-of-pocket costs. On the other hand, a broad approach might be used in defining out-of-pocket costs in regard to a particular shipment, thereby including a share of all of the common variable expenses attributable to a particular movement between two points.

The confusion surrounding the concept of out-of-pocket costs would seem to justify elimination of its use. However, the continued use of the term would be acceptable if its definition was made synonymous with the definition of one of the particular economic costs that its definition implies—marginal costs—because this term is important in price and output decisions and evaluations of pricing economics. Typically, out-of-pocket costs are most important to the firm's accounting system because they are payments that must be made almost immediately as an operating expense. The out-of-pocket cost concept is useful in that it is used as a way to estimate the amount of liquid funds that a transportation firm must keep on hand for daily operations.[7]

Figure 4A-3 gives a good breakdown of the methods of cost analysis. It illustrates the close relationship between the three cost concepts of variable, marginal, and out-of-pocket costs.

Although attention is devoted to cost structure in the separate chapters dealing with each of the modes of transportation, some consideration will be given in this section to an analysis of modal cost structures. Such discussion is useful and necessary background to the analysis of the approaches to pricing.

Rail Cost Structure

One of the characteristics of railroads, as previously noted, is the level of fixed costs present in their cost structures. It is a commonly accepted fact that a relatively large proportion of railway costs are fixed in the short run. At one time it was believed that more than half of rail costs were fixed, and some individuals estimated that these costs ran as high as 70 percent of total cost. The exact proportion of fixed expenses is subject to some debate; however, it is generally accepted that fixed expenses constitute a significant

FIGURE 4A-3 Short-Run Cost/Volume Output Approach

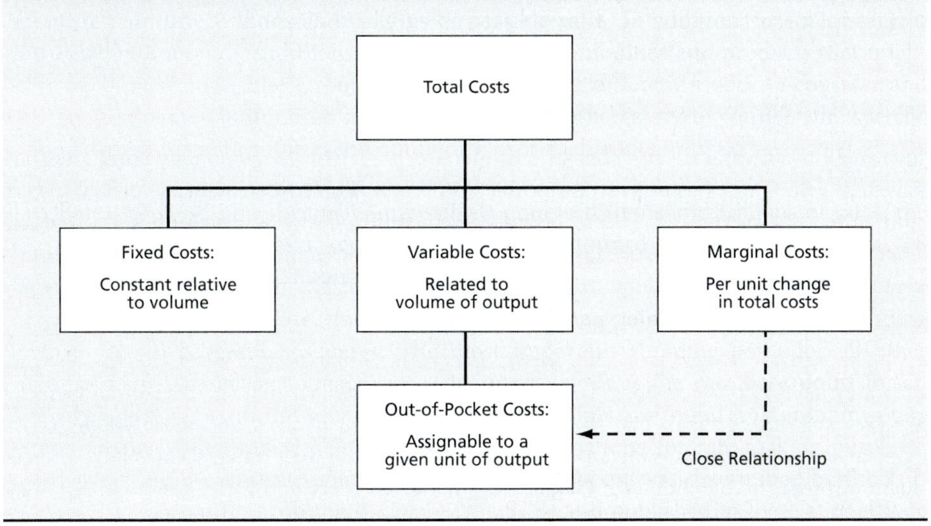

portion of railroad total costs. The high proportion of fixed costs can be explained by railroad investment (in such things as track, terminals, and freight yards), which is much larger than the investment of motor carriers, for example. For this reason, railroads are generally regarded as having increasing returns, or decreasing costs per unit of output.[8]

As has been indicated, a significant amount of railroad costs also include common expenses because replacement costs of a stretch of track are shared by all traffic moving over it. This is also true with respect to other items of cost, including officers' salaries. Some of these common costs are also fixed costs, while others are variable costs (refer to Chapter 6, "Railroads").

Motor Carrier Cost Structure

The motor carrier industry is exemplified by a high proportion of variable costs. It has been estimated that variable costs in the motor carrier industry are 90 percent or more of total costs.[9] This is typical in the truckload sector while the less-than-truckload sector will usually have lower variable cost and higher fixed cost percentages because of their terminal network. But both sectors of the motor carrier industry are dominated by variable costs. This high degree of variability is explained to a large extent by the fact that motor carriers do not have to provide their own right-of-way because roads are publicly provided. It is true that motor carriers do pay fuel taxes and other taxes to defray the cost of providing the highways, but these expenses are variable because they depend on the use made of the highway.

The economic concept of the "long run" is a shorter period in the motor carrier industry than in the railroad industry. The operating unit, the motor carrier vehicle, has a shorter life span than the rail operating unit. It is smaller and therefore more adaptable to fluctuating business conditions. The capital investment required is smaller too, and fleets can be expanded and contracted more easily.

The motor carrier situation varies greatly with respect to common costs. Companies that specialize in LTL traffic will have a significant proportion of common cost, whereas contract carriers with only two or three customers who move only TL traffic will have a high proportion of separable costs. Other companies that carry a mixture of TL and LTL traffic will be in the middle of the two extremes (refer to Chapter 5, "Motor Carriers").

Other Carriers' Cost Structures

Information on water carrier cost structure is less prevalent because many companies are privately owned or exempt from economic regulation. The cost structure is probably very similar to that of motor carriers because their right-of-way is also publicly provided. There are some differences, however, because the investment per unit of output is greater, and a large volume of traffic is necessary to realize mass movement potentialities.[10] (See Chapter 8, "Water Carriers and Pipelines.")

The pipeline companies have a cost structure similar to that of railroads. The fact that they have to provide their own right-of-way and the fact that their terminal facilities are very specialized mean that they have a large element of fixed and usually sunk costs. They also usually have significant common costs because they move a variety of oil products through the pipeline (see Chapter 8, "Water Carriers and Pipelines").

The airline companies have a cost structure similar to that of water carriers and motor carriers because of the public provision of their right-of-way. Also, terminal facilities are publicly provided to a large extent, and the airlines pay landing fees based upon use. Airlines tend to have a significant element of common cost because of small freight shipments and the individual nature of passenger movements; for example, airlines very seldom sell a planeload to one customer (see Chapter 7, "Airlines").

The differences in the cost structures of the modes of transportation and their differing service characteristics make pricing of their services very important. If motor carrier service is better than rail service, motor carrier prices can exceed rail prices. The cost structure of the motor carrier might dictate that their prices can exceed rail prices. The cost structure of the motor carrier might dictate that their prices have to be higher than the rail prices. The critical question is what the relationship between demand and cost (supply) is in such cases.

NOTES

1. William J. Baumol et al., "The Role of Cost in the Minimum Pricing of Railroad Services," *Journal of Business*, Vol. 35, October 1962, pp. 5–6. This article succinctly presents the essence of sunk versus prospective costs.
2. A. M. Milne, *The Economics of Inland Transport*, London: Pitman and Sons, 1955, p. 146.
3. Robert C. Lieb, *Transportation, the Domestic System*, 2nd ed., Reston, VA: Reston Publishing, p. 138.
4. This problem was argued in the economic journals at an early date by two notable economists. See F. W. Taussig, "Railway Rates and Joint Cost Once More," *Quarterly Journal of Economics*, Vol. 27, May 1913, p. 378; F. W. Taussig and A. C. Pigou, "Railway Rates and Joint Costs," *Quarterly Journal of Economics*, Vol. 27, August 1913, pp. 535, 687; A. C. Pigou, *The Economics of Welfare*, 4th ed., London: Macmillan, 1950, Chapters 17 and 18. An excellent discussion of this debate is contained in D. P. Locklin, "A Review of the Literature on Railway Rate Theory," *Quarterly Journal of Economics*, Vol. 47, 1933, p. 174.
5. For a more thorough discussion of this topic, see Terrance L. Pohlen and Bernard J. LaLonde, "Implementing Activity-Based Costing (ABC) in Logistics," *Journal of Business Logistics*, Vol. 15, No. 2, 1994, pp. 1–23.

6. For an excellent discussion, see George W. Wilson and George W. Smerk, "Rate Theory," in *Physical Distribution Management*, Bloomington, IN: Indiana University, 1963, pp. 2–4.
7. Wayne K. Talley, *Introduction to Transportation*, Cincinnati, OH: Southwestern, 1983, p. 27.
8. George W. Wilson, *Essays on Some Unsettled Questions in the Economics of Transportation*, Bloomington, IN: Foundation for Economic and Business Studies, 1962, pp. 32–33.
9. Interstate Commerce Commission, Bureau of Accounts and Cost Finding, *Explanation of Rail Cost Finding Principles and Procedures*, Washington, DC: Government Printing Office, 1948, p. 88.
10. John R. Meyer et al., *The Economics of Competition in the Transportation Industries*, Cambridge, MA: Harvard University Press, pp. 112–113.

APPENDIX 4B

LTL and TL Costing Models

As mentioned in this chapter, understanding costs for costing purposes is critical to a carrier's ability to price in order to maximize profits. Costing and pricing can be extremely complex exercises, depending on the amount and complexity of inputs. However, examining LTL and TL operations, it might be evident that defining their activities for costing purposes can be relatively simple. The purpose of this appendix is to offer basic and simplistic costing models for LTL and TL that can be used to get a feel for the costs associated with a particular move. Obviously, these are not complex models and would need to be adjusted for actual costing purposes.

Operational Activities

The examination of LTL and TL operations might result in the conclusion that they are significantly different in how they operate. Actually, they are very similar. The major difference between the two is in the dock rehandling that is associated with the LTL operations, not the TL. However, to move a shipment, both operations provide a pickup service, a line-haul service, and a delivery service. These three activities, along with dock rehandling for LTL, can be used to begin to break out the appropriate costs associated with a move.

Cost/Service Elements

Within each operational activity, those cost/service elements that will actually be responsible for shipment costs need to be identified. These cost/service elements can be defined as time, distance, and support. The time it takes a carrier to pick up, cross-dock, line-haul, and deliver a shipment will impact its fixed costs, such as depreciation and interest, because these costs are allocated and determined by units of time. The distance a carrier has to move a shipment during these operational activities will affect its variable costs, such as fuel and wages. Support costs, such as equipment insurance and maintenance, are considered semi-fixed and semi-variable because they will exist if no activity takes place but will increase as activity increases. Finally, shipment billing can be considered a fixed cost because normally the cost to generate a freight bill is not related to shipment size or distance.

Having identified four operational activities (pickup, cross-dock, line-haul, and delivery) and three cost/service elements (time, distance, and support), it is possible to develop a costing methodology that will allow the approximation of costs that a carrier could incur for moving a shipment.

TL Costing

This section will present a simplified TL costing model that can be used to approximate the costs of moving a shipment between two points. This model can be used for calculating headhaul costs but does not include an adjustment for a possible empty return trip. However, as will be seen, headhaul costs could be adjusted to compensate for variable costs of an empty backhaul.

The following scenario is used.

Shipment and Equipment Characteristics The shipment consists of 400 cartons at 110 pounds each with each carton measuring 5 cubic feet. Carriers' trailers have a weight capacity of 45,000 pounds and 3,500 cubic feet. The shipment weighs 44,000 pounds (98 percent of weight capacity) and occupies 2,000 cubic feet (almost 57 percent of trailer cubic capacity).

Equipment Cost Data

Equipment Purchase Price

1. Line-haul tractors = $120,000
2. Trailers = $40,000 (53-foot dry van)

Depreciation

1. Tractors = 5-year straight line
2. Trailers = 8-year straight line

Interest

1. Tractors = 6 percent APR for 5 years
2. Trailers = 6 percent APR for 8 years

Fuel

1. $3.83 per gallon for diesel
2. Line-haul tractors = 6.0 miles per gallon

Labor Cost

1. Line-haul drivers = $0.45 per mile
2. PUD operation drivers = $22.00 per hour

Miscellaneous

1. Insurance cost = $0.067 per mile
2. Maintenance cost = $0.152 per mile
3. Billing cost = $1.95 per freight bill
4. Tractors and trailers are available for use 365 days, 24 hours per day
5. Administrative/overhead cost = 10 percent of total cost of move

Route and Time of Move The shipment originates on June 2, 2014, from The Pennsylvania State University (located 35 miles from the carrier's dispatch/maintenance facility). A line-haul tractor and trailer are dispatched from the terminal at 7:30 a.m. (all times are Eastern Standard Time) and arrive at the shipper's dock at 8:30 a.m. The shipment is loaded from 8:30 a.m. to 12:00 p.m. Driver and tractor remain at Penn State during loading to visit the famous Nittany Lion statue. Driver and vehicle return to the carrier's terminal at 1:00 p.m. to pick up paperwork.

Total time for pickup = 5.5 hours

Total distance for pickup = 70 miles

The vehicle and the driver depart from the terminal at 1:00 p.m. on the same day for Dallas, Texas. The driver operates from 1:00 p.m. to 11:00 p.m. and travels 450 miles. The driver rests from 11:00 p.m. to 7:00 a.m. (on June 3) in Knoxville, Tennessee, and then operates another 8 hours (7:00 a.m. to 3:00 p.m.) and 375 miles.

The driver rests again from 3:00 p.m. to 11:00 p.m. in Memphis, Tennessee. The driver concludes the trip by traveling 450 miles from 11:00 p.m. to 9:00 a.m. (June 4) to the consignee in Dallas, the Dallas Cowboys' training facility.

Total time for line-haul = 44 hours or 1.83 days

Total distance for line-haul = 1,275 miles

The trailer is unloaded from 9:00 a.m. to 12:00 p.m. with the driver and tractor remaining at the home to tour the museum dedicated to former Dallas Cowboys. The driver and vehicle then go to the carrier's Dallas terminal, located 45 miles from the Cowboys' facility, arriving at 1:00 p.m. to wait for further dispatch instructions.

Total time for delivery = 4 hours

Total distance for delivery = 45 miles

Cost Analysis Using the equipment cost data and the distance traveled and time elapsed for the shipment, an approximate cost for this move can be calculated. This analysis can be seen in Table 4B-1. In a real costing situation, certain changes might need to be made to the cost data included in this example. Tractor fuel economy, for example, might need to be increased or maintenance cost per mile might need to be decreased. The cost analyst would need to determine the appropriate levels for each cost element, depending on the type of equipment and nature of the move.

Pickup As can be seen in Table 4B-1, the pickup operation generated seven types of costs. *Depreciation expense* per hour is calculated by:

equipment cost/years depreciation/365/24

This formula gives the hourly cost for depreciation for both the tractor and the trailer. *Interest expense (includes both principal plus interest)* per hour can be calculated using any interest payment calculator. The appropriate formulas can be found in tables in any introductory finance text.

Fuel cost per gallon and tractor fuel economy determine *fuel cost per mile.* This formula is:

fuel cost per gallon/miles per gallon

Labor, maintenance, insurance, and billing costs are given and are relatively easy to calculate. *Total pickup costs for this move are $223.24.*

Line-haul Notice that the line-haul costs categories for this move are the same as for the pickup operation, except for the billing expense. This is simply because only one freight bill needs to be generated for this move. This will also be seen by the absence of a billing cost in the delivery section.

Also, during the pickup operation, the driver was paid by the hour because waiting time was involved. In the line-haul section, the driver was paid by the mile. Obviously, pay scales for drivers will be determined by company or union policies. *Costs in the line-haul section are calculated in the same manner as they were in the pickup section.* Obviously, however, the time and distance generated by the line-haul activity are used. *Total line-haul costs for this move are $1,990.18.*

Delivery The delivery activity generates the same type of costs as did the pickup activity, except for billing. Again, the time and distance associated with delivery need to be

TABLE 4B-1 TL Costing Example

I. Pickup			
1. Depreciation	tractor	5.5 hr @ $2.74/hr =	$15.07
	trailer	5.5 hr @ $0.57/hr =	$3.14
2. Interest	tractor	5.5 hr @ $3.25/hr =	$17.88
	trailer	5.5 hr @ $0.74/hr =	$4.07
3. Fuel		70 miles @ $0.64/mile =	$44.80
4. Labor		5.5 hr @ $22/hr =	$121.00
5. Maintenance		70 miles @ $0.152/mile =	$10.64
6. Insurance		70 miles @ $0.067/mile =	$4.69
7. Billing			$1.95
		TOTAL PICKUP COST	$223.24
II. Line-haul			
1. Depreciation	tractor	44 hr @ $2.74/hr =	$120.56
	trailer	44 hr @ $0.57/hr =	$25.08
2. Interest	tractor	44 hr @ $3.25/hr =	$143.00
	trailer	44 hr @ $0.74/hr =	$32.56
3. Fuel		1,275 miles @ $0.64/mile =	$816.00
4. Labor		1,275 miles @ $0.45/mile =	$573.75
5. Maintenance		1,275 miles @ $0.152/mile =	$193.80
6. Insurance		1,275 miles @ $0.067/mile =	$85.43
		TOTAL LINE-HAUL COST	$1,990.18
III. Delivery			
1. Depreciation	tractor	4 hr @ $2.74/hr =	$10.96
	trailer	4 hr @ $0.57/hr =	$2.28
2. Interest	tractor	4 hr @ $3.25/hr =	$13.00
	trailer	4 hr @ $0.74/hr =	$2.96
3. Fuel		45 miles @ $0.64/mile =	$28.80
4. Labor		4 hr @ $22/hr =	$88.00
5. Maintenance		45 miles @ $0.152/mile =	$6.84
6. Insurance		45 miles @ $.067/mile =	$3.02
		TOTAL DELIVERY COST	$155.86
IV. Total Cost			
1. Pickup, line-haul, delivery			$2369.28
2. Administrative/overhead (10%)			$236.93
		TOTAL TL COST	$2,606.21
V. Revenue Needs			
1. Per cwt ($2,606.21/440) = $5.92			
2. Per revenue mile ($2,606.21/1,310 miles) = $1.99 miles)			

used in calculating costs. *Costs for delivery are calculated in the same manner as they were in the pickup section. Total costs for delivery for this move are $155.86.*

Total Cost Adding the costs associated with pickup, line-haul, and delivery generates the total cost for this move of $2,369.28. Remember, however, that a 10 percent additional cost is added to make a contribution to the carrier's administration and overhead, so the *total cost for this move is $2,606.21.*

Revenue Needs Carriers quote prices in many forms. Two of the more common methods are price per hundredweight (cwt) and price per revenue, or loaded, mile. In this example, although profit has not yet been added, to recover the fully allocated or average cost for this move, the carrier would quote a *price per cwt of $5.92 ($2606.21/440 cwt)* or a *price per revenue mile of $1.99 ($2606.21/1310 miles).*

Once again, this model is a simplified version of those used by carriers. Certain adjustments and additions would need to be made to this model to make it more reflective of an actual move. However, it does give the analyst some idea of the approximate costs associated with a shipment.

LTL Costing

This section will present a simplified version of an LTL costing model. LTL costing is more difficult than TL costing because it requires arbitrary allocations of common and fixed costs to individual shipments. Although this does not make costing an LTL shipment impossible, it does require that the individual using the costs understand that averages and allocations were used. Thus, the resulting costs might not be as accurate as would be desired. However, this model will produce ballpark estimates for the cost of moving an individual shipment. *All* of the formulas for calculating depreciation costs, interest costs, and fuel costs are the same as those used in the TL costing example.

Shipment and Equipment Characteristics The shipment to be costed consists of 15 cartons, each weighing 40 pounds and measuring 16 cubic feet. The carrier's pickup and delivery trailers have a weight capacity of 40,000 pounds and 2,972 cubic feet and the line-haul (LH) trailers have a weight capacity of 45,000 pounds and a cubic capacity of 3,500 cubic feet. This shipment then occupies 1.3 percent of the trailer's weight capacity and 6.85 percent of its cubic capacity. Because the cubic feet requirement is greater, it will be used to allocate costs in the line-haul move.

Equipment Cost Data

Equipment Purchase Price

1. PUD tractor = $65,000
2. LH tractor = $95,000
3. PUD trailer = $30,000 (45-foot)
4. LH trailer = $40,000 (53-foot)

Depreciation

1. Tractors = 5-year straight line
2. Trailers = 8-year straight line

Interest

1. Tractors = 6 percent APR for 5 years
2. Trailers = 6 percent APR for 8 years

Fuel

1. $3.83 per gallon for diesel
2. PUD tractors = 6.5 miles per gallon
3. LH tractors = 6.0 miles per gallon

Labor Cost

1. PUD drivers = $22.00 per hour
2. Dock handlers = $20.00 per hour
3. LH drivers = $22.00 per hour

Miscellaneous

1. Terminal variable cost per shipment at both origin and destination = $1.00
2. Terminal fixed cost per shipment at both origin and destination = $1.50
3. PUD equipment maintenance cost = $0.152 per mile
4. LH equipment maintenance cost = $0.152 per mile
5. PUD equipment insurance cost = $0.067 per mile
6. LH equipment insurance cost = $0.067 per mile
7. Billing cost = $1.95 per bill
8. Equipment is available 365 days, 24 hours per day
9. Administrative/overhead cost = 10 percent of total cost of move

Route and Time of Movement The shipment is picked up by the carrier's driver in a PUD city tractor/trailer unit on June 2, 2014, as one of 23 stops made by the driver that day from 7:30 a.m. to 6:30 p.m. The stops covered a total of 60 miles within the Altoona, Pennsylvania, satellite terminal service area. The shipment was one of four handled by the carrier at this particular shipper's location. Once the pickup vehicle returns to the Altoona terminal, it takes 15 minutes to move the shipment from the city unit across the dock to the line-haul trailer.

Total time for pickup = 11 hours

Total distance for pickup = 60 miles

Total dock time = 15 minutes

The line-haul tractor/trailer departs from the Altoona terminal at 11:00 p.m. on June 2 and arrives at the Cleveland break-bulk terminal, which is approximately 200 miles from the Altoona satellite, at 4:00 a.m. on June 3. The shipment moves from the line-haul trailer across the dock to a PUD city tractor/trailer unit in 15 minutes.

Total time of line-haul = 5 hours

Total distance for line-haul = 200 miles

Total dock time = 15 minutes

The shipment is delivered to the Cleveland consignee by the PUD driver in a PUD city tractor/trailer unit on June 2 as one of 16 stops made by the driver over the period from 7:30 a.m. to 6:00 p.m. The stops covered a total of 45 miles in the Cleveland area. This shipment is one of three delivered to this particular consignee by the driver.

Total time for delivery = 10.5 hours

Total distance for delivery = 45 miles

Cost Analysis With the equipment cost data and route and time of movement, an individual LTL shipment can be costed. This analysis can be seen in Table 4B-2. Once again, *the calculations for depreciation, interest, and fuel costs are the same as they were in the TL example.*

TABLE 4B-2 LTL Costing Example

I. Pickup				
A. Route Costs				
1. Depreciation	PUD tractor	1 day @ $35.62/day =	$35.62	
	PUD trailer	1 day @ $10.27/day =	$10.27	
2. Interest	PUD tractor	1 day @ $42.28/day =	$42.28	
	PUD trailer	1 day @ $13.24/day =	$13.24	
3. Fuel		60 miles @ $0.59/mile =	$35.40	
4. Labor		11 hr @ $22/hr =	$242.00	
5. Maintenance		60 miles @ $0.152/mile =	$9.12	
6. Insurance		60 miles @ $0.067/mile =	$4.02	
	SUBTOTAL		$391.95	
	# Stops		23	
	COST PER STOP		$17.04	
	# Shipments at stop		4	
	ROUTE COST PER SHIPMENT			$4.26
B. Shipment Costs				
1. Billing			$1.95	
2. Terminal variable cost			$1.00	
3. Terminal fixed cost			$1.50	
4. Dock		0.25 hr @ $20/hr =	$5.00	
	INDIVIDUAL SHIPMENT COST		$9.45	
C. Total Pickup Cost per Shipment				$13.71
II. Line-haul				
1. Depreciation	LH tractor	5 hr @ $2.74/hr =	$13.70	
	LH trailer	5 hr @ $0.57/hr =	$2.85	
2. Interest	LH tractor	5 hr @ $3.25/hr =	$16.25	
	LH trailer	5 hr @ $0.74/hr =	$3.70	
3. Fuel		200 miles @ $0.32/mile =	$128.00	
4. Labor		5 hr @ $22/hr =	$110.00	
5. Maintenance		200 miles @ $0.15/mile =	$30.40	
6. Insurance		200 miles @ $0.03/mile =	$13.40	
	TOTAL LINE-HAUL FULL TRAILER		$318.30	

(continued)

TABLE 4B-2 Continued

	% capacity occupied by shipment		6.85%
	SHIPMENT LINE-HAUL COST		$21.80
III. Delivery			
A. Route Costs			
1. Depreciation	PUD tractor	1 day @ $35.62/day =	$35.62
	PUD trailer	1 day @ $10.27/day =	$10.27
2. Interest	PUD tractor	1 day @ $42.28/day =	$42.28
	PUD trailer	1 day @ $13.24/day =	$13.24
3. Fuel		45 miles @ $0.28/mile =	$26.65
4. Labor		10.5 hr @ $22/hr =	$231.00
5. Maintenance		45 miles @ $0.15/mile =	$6.84
6. Insurance		45 miles @ $0.03/mile =	$3.02
	SUBTOTAL		$368.82
	# Stops		16
	COST PER STOP		$23.05
	# Shipments at stop		3
	ROUTE COST PER SHIPMENT		$7.68
B. Shipment Costs			
1. Terminal variable cost			$1.00
2. Terminal fixed cost			$1.50
3. Dock		0.25 hr @ $20/hr =	$5.00
	INDIVIDUAL SHIPMENT COST		$7.50
C. Total Delivery Cost per Shipment			$15.18
IV. Total Cost per Shipment			
1. Pickup, dock, line-haul, delivery			$50.69
2. Administrative/overhead (10 percent)			$5.07
	TOTAL COST PER SHIPMENT		$55.76
V. Revenue Needs			
1. Per cwt ($55.76/6)			$9.29

Pickup In this example, a PUD tractor and trailer were used in the pickup operation. This is specialized equipment that really has no alternative uses in the line-haul operation. As such, when this equipment is done with the PUD operation during the day, it will normally sit idle at the satellite terminal. This explains why a full day's depreciation and interest are charged to both the PUD tractor and PUD trailer, even though they were only utilized for 11 hours during this particular day. Some arguments might exist that this places an excessive cost burden on these shipments through fixed-cost allocation. This might be true. However, the cost analyst must make the decision as to where fixed costs will be recovered. If not through this allocation, then fixed costs must be covered by some other method so debt can be serviced and plans for equipment replacement can be implemented.

The fuel, labor, maintenance, and insurance cost calculations are relatively straightforward. *Total route costs for this move are $391.95.* Remember, however, that this cost is for all shipments picked up and delivered by the driver during the day. This calculation is for the cost of only one shipment. To do this, first divide the total route cost by the number of stops made by the driver. *This results in a route cost per stop of $17.04.* Second, divide the per stop cost by the number of shipments at the shipper's location that had the individual shipment. *This results in a route cost per shipment of $4.26.* Both the stop cost and the shipment cost are averages that assume that each stop is basically the same and each shipment is the same. Adjustments could be made to these figures to more accurately reflect the time and distance actually used for the individual shipment. Remember, however, the per-shipment-route costs used in this example are averages.

Shipment costs are those assigned to each individual shipment that are not generated by the PUD operation. Billing, terminal variable cost, and terminal fixed cost are not dependent on shipment size but are allocated to each shipment. The shipment took 15 minutes for its cross-dock operation resulting in the dock charge of $5.00.

> *Total shipment cost for this move is $9.45. Combining the route cost per shipment and the shipment cost results in a total pickup cost per shipment of $13.71.*

Line-haul Depreciation and interest for the line-haul equipment is charged only for the actual time the shipment is on this equipment. This is the same as in the TL example. Unlike the PUD equipment, this assumes that the line-haul equipment has alternative uses and is 100 percent utilized. Again, actual utilization rates can be used to adjust the allocation of depreciation and interest charges.

As previously mentioned, the shipment occupied 6.85 percent of the cubic capacity of the line-haul trailer. This is the basis used for allocating line-haul costs in a *line-haul cost per shipment of $21.80.* This allocation method assumes that all shipments in the line-haul trailer have approximately the same pounds per cubic foot requirement and that the trailer would probably be cubed out. The analyst might want to make adjustments for this based on the known average weight and cube per shipment in the carrier's system.

Delivery The calculations for delivery cost are the same as those used for pickup costs. For route shipment cost, 16 stops and 3 stops per shipment are used to determine the *average route cost per shipment of $6.99.* Shipment costs are also the same, except that billing cost is not included, resulting in a *shipment cost of $7.50 and a total delivery cost per shipment of $15.18.*

Total Shipment Cost Combining the pickup cost of $13.71, the line-haul cost of $21.80, and the delivery cost of $15.18 results in a total cost per shipment of $50.69. Remember, like the TL example, a 10 percent cost is added to cover administrative and other overhead expenses, resulting in a *total cost for the shipment of $55.76.*

Revenue Needs Although prices are quoted in many different forms in the LTL industry, one popular form is in price per cwt. Taking the total shipment charge of $55.76 and dividing it by 6 cwt results in a *price per cwt of $9.29.* Remember this price does not yet include an allowance for profit for the carrier.

Conclusion

Determining the cost for a particular shipment can be a very complex and time-consuming task.

Detailed data requirements and knowledge of a carrier's operations are necessary inputs to developing accurate costs. However, a simplified approach can be taken to shipment costing that does not need these complex requirements and results in approximate shipment costs. Thus, the advantage of these costing models is their simplicity and ease of calculation. Their disadvantage is that they use general data, allocations, and averages to determine shipment costs. The analyst must trade off these characteristics to determine the level of complexity needed for costing and whether these models will provide a sufficient level of cost detail.

Suggested Readings

Chapter 1 Global Supply Chains: The Role and Importance of Transportation

Bonney, Joseph, and William B. Cassidy, "Pain in the Dray," *Journal of Commerce* (March 31, 2014): 10–15.

Berman, Jeff, "UPS Expands Global Offerings with New China-Europe Rail Service," *Logistics Management* (July 2014): website.

Holdman, Jessica, "New N.D. Plan Looks to Identify Transport Bottlenecks," *Transport Topics* (July 14, 2014): 23.

O'Reilly, Joseph, "U.S. Welcomes European Invasion," *Inbound Logistics* (May 2014): 23–27.

Lapide, Larry, "Global Supply Chains: When Uncertainty Is a Certain Factor," *Supply Chain Management Review* (March/April 2014): 40–44.

Chapter 2 Transportation and the Economy

Pocket Guide to Transportation, *Bureau of Transportation Statistics* (2014).

Watson, Rip, "Broad-Based Growth Lifts All Trucking Sectors," *Transport Topics* (June 23, 2014): 1.

Krizner, Ken, "The Midwest Works," *World Trade* (May 2012): 39–41.

Fuetsch, Michele, "DOT to Slow Payments If Congress Doesn't Act," *Transport Topics* (July 7, 2014): 1.

McMahon, Jim, "Smart Robotics Meet E-Commerce," *World Trade 100* (July 2014): website.

Chapter 3 Transportation Regulation and Public Policy

Cassidy, William B., "Safety First," *Journal of Commerce* (March 31, 2014): 16–18.

Fuetsch, Michele, "States Slow Highway Projects as U.S. Funding Crisis Looms," *Transport Topics* (June 23, 2014): 1.

O'Reilly, Joseph, "U.S. Creates a 'Single-Window' for Import/Export Data Transmission," *Inbound Logistics* (April 2014): 25–28.

Terry, Lisa, "Protecting High-Value Cargo: A Sense of Security," *Inbound Logistics* (April 2014): 89–93.

Chapter 4 Costing and Pricing for Transportation

Watson, Rip, "UPS Prepares to Use Dimensional Pricing for Ground Shipment rates," *Transport Topics* (June 23, 2014): 31.

Moore, Peter, "Moore on Pricing: Your 2014 Pricing Checklist," *Logistics Management* (January 2014): 18.

Everett, Brian, "Successful Shippers Focus on Long-Term Partnerships," *World Trade* (May 2012): 12.

John D. Schultz, "25th Annual State of Logistics: It's Complicated," *Logistics Management* (July 2014): 28–31.

PART II

The first four chapters of this text provided a background of the environment faced by the transportation industry. Chapters 1 and 2 discussed the role of transportation in the economy and in the firm, respectively. Chapter 3 discussed the nature of transportation and public policy and how they affect the transportation industry. Chapter 4 provided a basic discussion of the economics of costs and pricing for transportation providers.

Part II of this text focuses on each of the five modes of transportation. Each modal chapter contains an industry overview, operating and service characteristics, cost structure, and current challenges and issues.

Chapter 5 focuses on the motor carrier industry and differentiates between both truckload (TL) and less-than-truckload (LTL) carrier operations. Capacity issues in the motor carrier is highlighted in the Transportation Profile. A detailed discussion of LTL network structures and network decisions is also offered in this chapter. Finally, the new Federal Highway Trust Fund Tax rates on motor carriers are discussed as well as some new safety legislation.

Chapter 6 examines the railroad industry and its current operations. Special attention is given to recent attempts by the federal government to reregulate the railroad industry. A detailed discussion of new service innovations, including TOFC and COFC, is given focusing on the growth of intermodal carloadings in the railroad industry. Because volatile fuel prices have substantial impacts on all transportation modes, a comparison is made in this chapter between railroad fuel efficiency and the other modes of transportation.

The airline industry is the topic of **Chapter 7**. As with the other modal chapters, a discussion of the impact of volatile fuel prices on the airline industry is offered. Along with this cost impact, labor costs in the airline industry are also discussed. This chapter offers a comprehensive view of aircraft operating characteristics as well as a listing of the top airlines in the United States. Because safety is critical in passenger air travel, a comparison of passenger fatalities between airlines and other passenger modes is offered.

Finally, **Chapter 8** presents a discussion of bulk carriers (water and pipeline). The historical development and significance of these modes are presented along with a discussion of the current status of each mode. The cost structures of each mode are presented along with their impacts on carrier operations and competitive advantage. Special attention has been given to the growing infrastructure issues faced by both water and pipeline carriers. Finally, the basics of intramodal and intermodal competition for each mode are examined.

CHAPTER

5

MOTOR CARRIERS

Learning Objectives

After reading this chapter, you should be able to do the following:

- Understand the development of motor carriers and their contributions to the U.S. economy
- Be familiar with the different types of firms in the motor carrier industry
- Appreciate the market forces shaping the motor carrier industry
- Gain knowledge of the service characteristics of motor carriers
- Identify the different types of vehicles and terminals used in the motor carrier industry
- Understand the impact of fuel and labor on the motor carrier cost structure
- Be aware of current issues facing the motor carrier industry

TRANSPORTATION **PROFILE**

Tight Capacity Outlook Will Likely Remain Intact for a While, Say Industry Stakeholders

Even with the most difficult winter weather conditions in years now in the rearview mirror, there's one issue in the trucking sector that remains unchanged: tight capacity.

Aside from the weather, capacity is tight for a few other reasons, including the ongoing driver shortage, which doesn't look to be improving anytime soon, as well as the impact of federal regulations, most notably CSA and the tweaks to the hours of service (HOS) rules that took effect in July 2013.

Richard Mikes, a partner at Transport Capital Partners, explained that carriers are of the mind-set that current conditions "look really good," but with the caveat that drivers and driver availability are the current controllers of capacity in the trucking sector.

And with the increased pressure coming from government regulations, carriers really have no choice but to increase driver compensation, which will serve as a major catalyst for rate increases, added Mikes.

"With the new HOS rules having been intact for a relatively short time, shippers have been receiving calls from carriers that previously were able to make on-time deliveries, but are now either getting delayed or being forced to turn down the load altogether," said Mikes.

Data from freight transportation forecasting consultancy FTR echoed similar sentiments. FTR said last month that shippers should work to acquire sufficient capacity through the spring seasonal shipping peak, as 2014 could be a "very volatile year." Jonathan Starks, FTR's director of transportation analysis, said that while the drag of tight capacity was highlighted during the winter, shippers now need to closely monitor signs of an economic uptick.

"If the economy stays stuck in the slow-growth mode and the weather finally behaves, we can expect the extremely tight capacity to normalize by mid-summer," Starks said. "If, however, we can finally get some additional economic activity, especially in the vital manufacturing sector, the tight truck environment will persist and could significantly worsen. For shippers, now is the time for careful planning for the fall shipping season."

In the meantime, shippers are being forced to adapt and change on the fly as a result of current capacity availability. "We're seeing a tightening this year in terms of capacity much earlier than normal," explained Jeff Brady, director of transportation and logistics at Harry & David, a multichannel specialty retailer. "As a highly seasonal shipper, it's usually available this time of year, but it's very tight this year, even ahead of produce season on the West Coast."

Brady said he believes that the current environment is the result of a conflux of HOS, a shrinking carrier base, and a true contraction in long-haul trucking. "I don't necessarily buy the so-called the economic recovery aspect; but regardless, we've got serious challenges in our industry that need to be addressed," he said.

According to Doug Waggoner, CEO of Echo Global Logistics, HOS took a little capacity out of the system for a lot of carriers, adding that this was contingent on how carriers ran their respective networks.

"The economic recovery looks to be above and beyond what we've seen for the last number of quarters, and industry capacity was mostly in balance but close to the edge of it," said Waggoner. "Things were also made more difficult by the inability of carriers to add capacity due to the driver shortage. These factors together, coupled with a tough first quarter, are, in effect, an anomaly as January and February are typically two of the slowest months of the year. In short we're going to see rates go up and capacity is going to stay tight."

Source: Jeff Berman, *Logistics Management*, May 2014, pp. 14–15.

Introduction

The motor carrier industry played an important role in the development of the U.S. economy during the 20th century, and it continues this role in the 21st century. The growth of this industry is noteworthy considering it did not get started until World War I, when converted automobiles were utilized for pickup and delivery in local areas. The railroad industry, which traditionally had difficulty with small shipments that had to be moved short distances, encouraged the early motor carrier entrepreneurs. It was not until after World War II that the railroad industry began to seriously attempt to compete with the motor carrier industry, and by that time it was too late.

The United States has spent more than $128.9 billion to construct its interstate highway system and in the process has become increasingly dependent on this system for the movement of freight. The major portion of this network evolved as the result of a bill signed into law in 1956 by President Dwight D. Eisenhower to establish the National System of Interstate and Defense Highways, which was to be funded 90 percent by the federal government through fuel taxes.

As the interstate system of highways developed from the 1950s to 1991, motor carriers steadily replaced railroads as the mode of choice for transporting finished and unfinished manufactured products. In 1980 railroads moved 1.6 billion tons, compared to more than 200 billion tons by motor carriers. By 2012 motor carriers were handling 9.4 billion tons.[1]

Industry Overview

Significance

In 2012 the United States paid over $642.1 billion for highway transportation, approximately 80.7 percent of the total nation's Freight Bill.[2] Motor carriers transported 9.4 billion tons in 2012, or 68.5 percent of the total domestic transported by all modes.[3] Figure 5-1 shows that, since the recession of 2009, motor carrier tonnage is increasing.

FIGURE 5-1 For-Hire Truck Tonnage Index

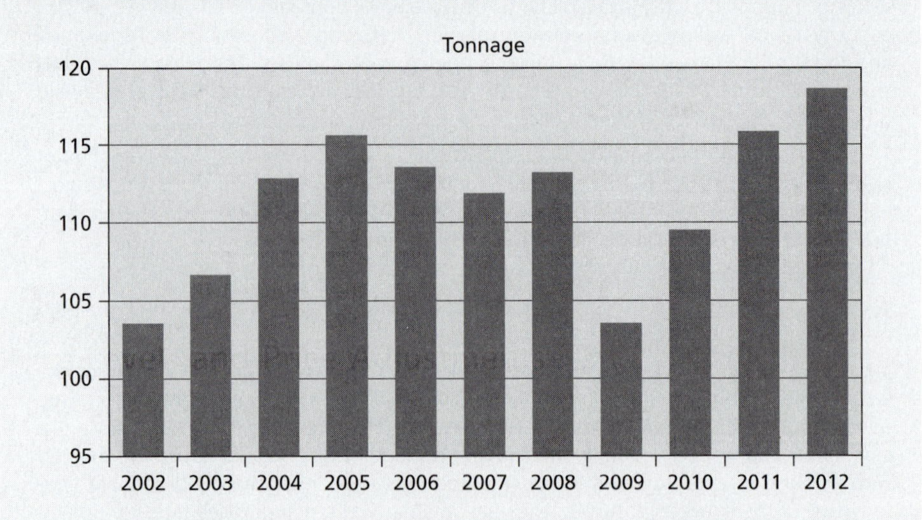

Source: *American Trucking Trends 2013*, American Trucking Association (Alexandria, VA: ATA, 2013).

FIGURE 5-2 For-Hire Trucking Revenue Index

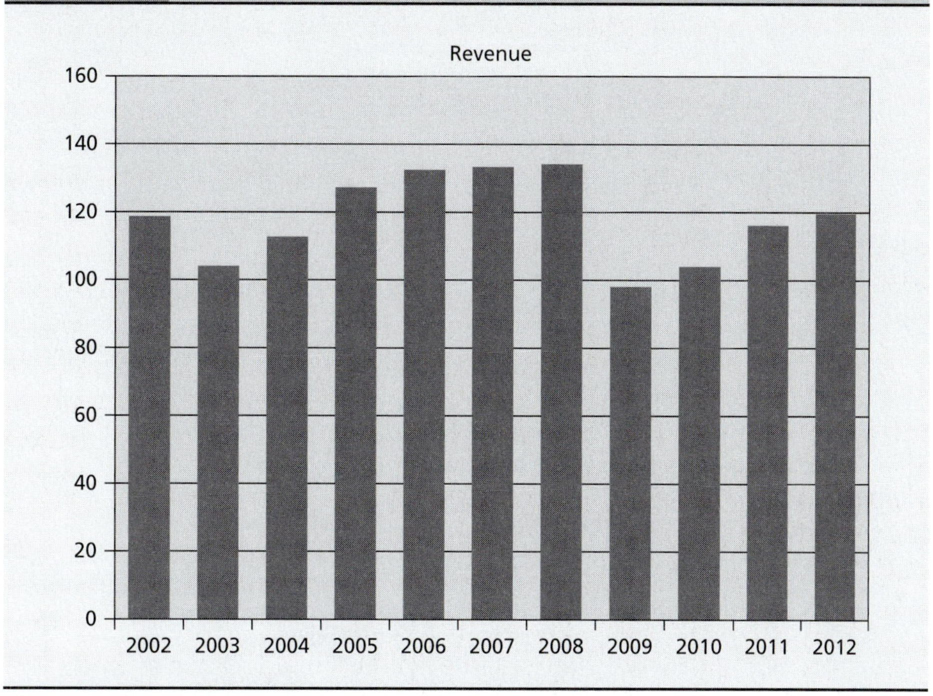

Source: *American Trucking Trends 2013*, American Trucking Association (Alexandria, VA: ATA, 2013).

During 2011, approximately 6.9 million people were employed in the motor carrier industry.[4] Figure 5-2 indicates that industry revenues have been increasing since 2009 but have not yet reached the record set in 2008. Finally, motor carriers travelled 397.8 billion miles used for business purposes in 2010 (excluding the government and farm sectors).[5] These figures clearly demonstrate the significant role that motor carriers play in our society and the dependence of U.S. companies on motor carrier service.

Types of Carriers

Figure 5-3 shows the structure of the motor carrier industry today. The first major division of motor carriers is between for-hire and private carriers. The **for-hire** carrier provides services to the public and charges a fee for the service. The **private** carrier provides a service to the industry or company that owns or leases the vehicles, and thus does not charge a fee, but obviously the service provider incurs cost. Private carriers might transport commodities for-hire, but when operating in such a capacity, the private carrier is really an exempt for-hire carrier.

For-hire carriers can be either local or intercity operators, or both. The local carriers pick up and deliver freight within the commercial zone of a city. The intercity carriers operate between specifically defined commercial zones to include the corporate limits of a municipality plus adjacent areas beyond the corporate limits determined by the municipal population. Local carriers frequently work in conjunction with intercity carriers to pick up or deliver freight in the commercial zone.

The for-hire carriers may be common and/or contract operators. The common carriers are required to serve the general public upon demand, at reasonable rates, and

FIGURE 5-3 Overview of the Motor Carrier Industry

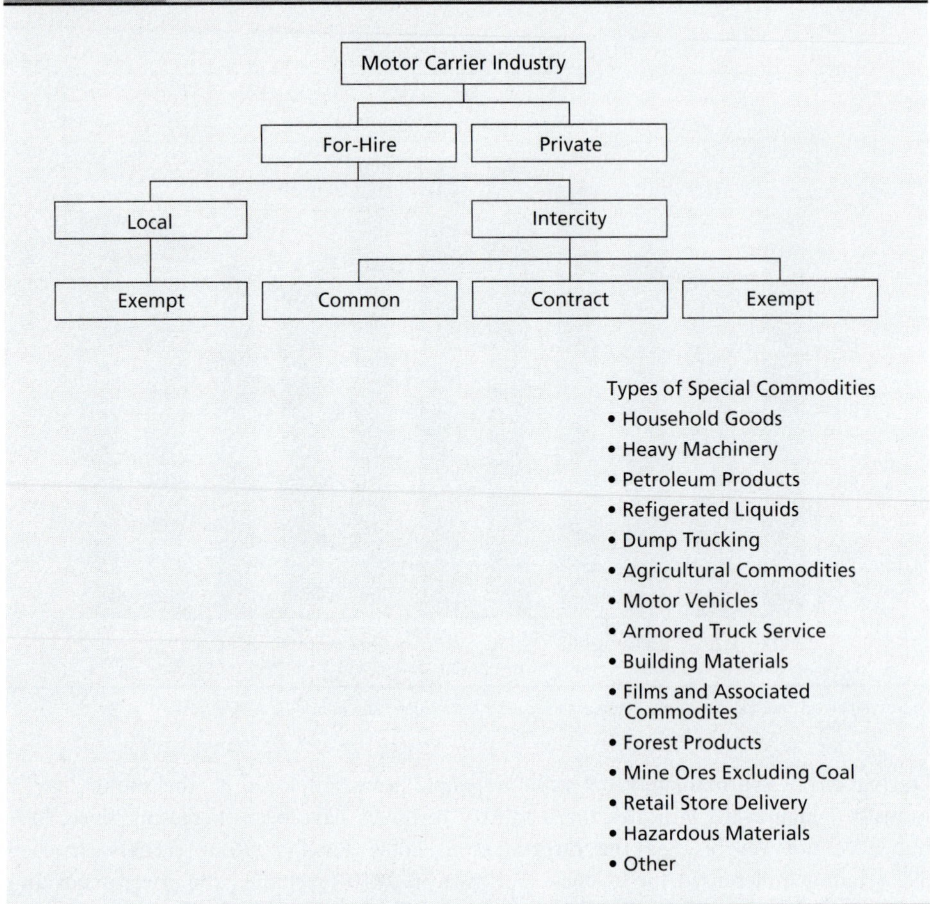

Source: Federal Motor Carrier Safety Administration, U.S. Department of Transportation, 2013.

without discrimination. The contract carriers serve specific shippers with whom the carriers have a continuing contract; thus, the contract carrier is not available for general public use. Contract carriers also typically adapt their equipment and service to meet shipper needs. Shippers must choose to use a commercial carrier or to operate their own private fleet. The decision is based on what is best for their business. Trade-offs exist for both options, but the decision will ultimately be determined by the needs of the shipper.

Another important distinction is between the truckload (**TL**) and less-than-truckload (**LTL**) carriers. The truckload carriers provide service to shippers who tender sufficient volume to meet the minimum weights required for a truckload shipment and truckload rate or who will pay the difference. Less-than-truckload carriers provide service to shippers who tender shipments lower than the minimum truckload quantities, such as 50 to 10,000 pounds. Consequently, the LTL carrier must consolidate the numerous smaller shipments into truckload quantities for the line-haul (intercity) movement and disaggregate the full truckloads at the destination city for delivery in smaller quantities. In contrast, the TL carrier picks up a truckload and delivers the same truckload at the destination.

A hybrid type of carrier that has developed can best be characterized as a "heavy LTL" motor carrier. Shipment sizes carried by this type of carrier are in the upper end of what can be considered LTL shipments (that is, 12,000 to 25,000 pounds). This carrier utilizes consolidation terminals (like LTL carriers) to fully load trailers but does not utilize break-bulk facilities for deliveries. Rather, it delivers from the trailer, much like a "pool" carrier, charging line-haul rates plus a charge for each stop-off (like TL carriers). This type of carrier specializes in shipment sizes less than the TL carriers haul and more than LTL carriers haul. It has some fixed costs (because of the consolidation terminals) but not as much as in the LTL industry.

Finally, interstate common carriers might be classified by the type of commodity they are authorized to haul. Historically, motor carriers were required to have operating authority issued by either federal or state authorities. Since 1996, with the repeal of the Interstate Commerce Act and the elimination of the Interstate Commerce Commission (ICC), such authority is no longer required. The ICC Termination Act of 1995 removed virtually all motor carrier regulation and preempted the states from exercising any economic control over the motor carrier industry. Carriers are now only required to register with the Federal Motor Carrier Safety Administration and provide proof of insurance. They can then transport any commodity they wish, with only household goods and related items being subject to any economic oversight.

ON THE **LINE**

Dedicated: One Bright Spot in the TL Picture

Whatever the vagaries of the general truckload (TL) market, carrier executives and analysts say that one area that has remained in constant vogue with shippers is the dedicated truckload market. As much as $40 billion of the roughly $300-billion TL market is moving under dedicated contract carriage, analysts say.

Dedicated carriage, which is contract freight movements secured with long-term contracts over "dedicated" regular routes, is a "win-win-win" for carriers, shippers, and their customers, according to Con-way Truckload president Saul Gonzalez.

Carriers stand to gain due to the assurance that a certain portion of their fleet is used on a regular basis, typically with the same drivers over the same routes, creating a familiarity that nearly guarantees topflight service.

Shippers gain because dedicated rates are typically 10 to 15 percent below what normal contract carriage sells for, depending on lane and freight characteristics, of course.

And finally, shippers say their customers win as well. That's because drivers become very familiar with the specific needs of certain customers—inside deliveries, time of day, set up, and removal of old merchandise—that makes dedicated carriage a customer-specific type of trucking service that other modes find impossible to match.

"My general sense is that it's paid off for shippers to go to dedicated," says Eric Starks, president of freight data research company FTR Associate. "They weren't paying significantly higher rates for that capacity, which you might have assumed to be the case. I would expect dedicated will stay on the forefront of a lot of shippers minds for the next year or two."

The only thing that would cause a drop in demand for dedicated truck carriage would be a significant economic slowdown, Starks says. "But I don't see that happening yet."

Source: John D. Schultz, *Logistics Management*, January 2014, p. 30. Reprinted with permission of Peerless Media, LLC.

Number of Carriers

The motor carrier industry consists of a large number of small carriers, particularly in the TL (truckload) segment of the industry. As illustrated in Figure 5-4, as of 2013 a total of 442,338 interstate motor carriers were on file with the Department of Transportation. Of these carriers, 90.5 percent operate with six or fewer vehicles.[6] This figure supports the small firm composition of the for-hire carrier industry. Keep in mind that many businesses do use their own private fleet.

A further explanation of the large number of small carriers is the limited capital needed to enter the TL industry. A motor carrier can be formed with as little as $5,000 to $10,000 equity, and the balance can be financed with the vehicle serving as collateral for the loan. However, LTL carriers have terminals that increase the capital requirements and thus add a constraint to entry.

There is a significant difference between TL and LTL carriers, both in terms of number and start-up costs. The great growth that occurred in the 1980s, when regulated carriers more than doubled, happened primarily in small TL carriers because of the low start-up costs indicated earlier.

The LTL segment of the motor carrier industry requires a network of terminals to consolidate and distribute freight, called a "hub-and-spoke" system. The large LTL carriers moved to expand their geographic coverage after 1980, and many of them eliminated their TL service. Because of this relatively high level of fixed costs, the LTL industry has continued to consolidate. In August 2003, Yellow Corporation announced

FIGURE 5-4 U.S. Distribution of Motor Carriers 2012

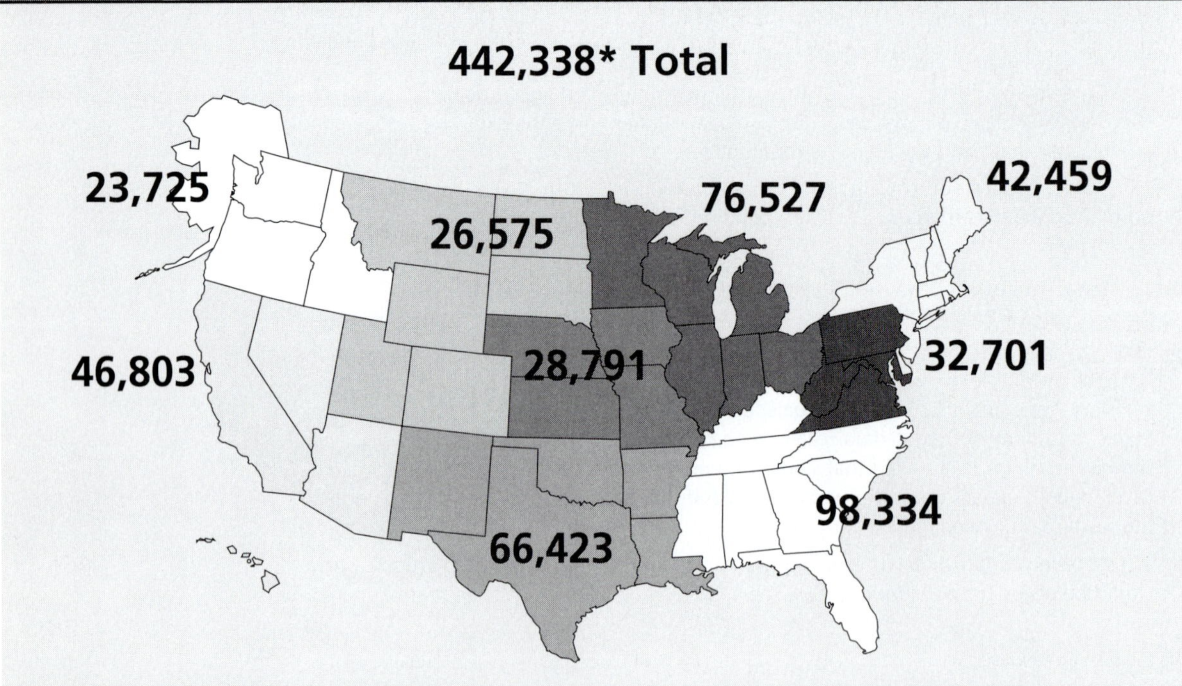

Source: Federal Motor Carrier Safety Administration, U.S. Department of Transportation, 2013.

that it would buy Roadway Corporation for $1.1 billion. After it was approved by the appropriate government agencies, this consolidation created a company that controls approximately 29 percent of the national LTL carrier market.[7]

Perhaps a brief description of an LTL operation would be helpful here. Shippers who have small shipping requirements use LTL carriers (for example, the cubic capacity of a 53-foot trailer is not needed for the shipment). Also, the LTL shipper typically has shipments headed for more than one destination. The LTL carrier collects the shipments at the shipper's dock with a **pickup and delivery (PUD)** vehicle. This vehicle, as its name implies, does the collection and delivery of all shipments. After a PUD vehicle has finished collecting and delivering shipments, it returns to a consolidation or break-bulk facility. Once at the consolidation facility, the packages collected are sorted by their final destination. The next part of the trip is called the **line-haul** segment. For this portion of the trip, the shipments are loaded into 28-foot, 48-foot, or 53-foot trailers. If 28-foot trailers are used, they are hooked together in combinations of twos and threes, depending on the state's trailer configuration permitted over the route of travel. The 28-foot trailer is used in this situation because it is easier to unload two 28-foot trailers at separate bays than to unload one 48-foot or 53-foot trailer at one bay. Another reason for using the 28-foot trailer is because LTL carriers find that it is easier to utilize the capacity of a 28-foot trailer. After the line-haul portion of the trip, the trailers are unloaded at another break-bulk facility and are then sorted and reloaded into a PUD vehicle to be delivered to the receiver.

The TL segment of the industry has been experiencing some limited concentration. Carriers such as Swift and Schneider National have become increasingly larger. The ability of the larger TL carriers to compete effectively with small TL companies with their value-added services might change the structure of the TL segment.

With the repeal of the Interstate Commerce Act, combined with changes in distribution patterns, a climate was created in which new TL carriers could easily enter the business. The "trucking recession" of 1994 and 1995, during which capacity greatly exceeded demand, removed many of the weaker firms through either bankruptcy or merger. However, low start-up costs in this sector still enabled new entrants to attempt success in this area.

Market Structure

When discussing the motor carrier industry, consideration must be given to the commodities hauled. Motor carrier vehicles, both for-hire and private, primarily transport manufactured, high-value products. These vehicles carry more than a majority of the various manufactured commodity categories. The commodity list includes food and manufactured products, consumer goods, and industrial goods. In addition, these vehicles transport almost all of the sheep, lambs, cattle, calves, and hogs moving to stockyards.[8]

Motor carriers transport less of commodities such as grain, primary nonferrous metal products, motor vehicles and equipment, and paper and allied products. Because such commodities generally must move long distances and in large volumes, shipping them by rail and water is usually less expensive.

From a market structure perspective, the TL market can be considered as monopolistic competition. With the low entrance to market requirements (that is, capital), individuals can easily obtain equipment and begin operation within a specific geographic region. The LTL market, on the other hand, is oligopolistic in nature. This is the result of the significant investment needed by these carriers in break-bulk and other facilities. As such, barriers to entry exist in the LTL industry.

Competition

Motor carriers compete vigorously with one another for freight. With the large number of for-hire motor carriers, rivalry between firms can be intense. However, the most severe competition for for-hire carriers often comes from the private carrier.

As indicated earlier, the TL motor carrier industry offers few capital constraints to entry. With a relatively small investment, an individual can start a motor carrier business and compete with an existing carrier. Thus, freedom of entry, discounting, and lack of regulatory constraints appear to dominate the industry and suggest that competition between firms can control the industry. Such a conclusion has been the basis for greater reliance on the marketplace and less reliance on regulation. Even though the LTL segment is more concentrated, there is still intense competition between the top carriers. Other competitors include United Parcel Service, FedEx, and FedEx Ground.

Certain segments of motor carriers have higher capital requirements than others, as indicated, and therefore have some degree of capital constraint for entry. The major segment that has extensive capital requirements for entry is the LTL carrier. The LTL carrier must invest in terminals and freight-handling equipment that are simply not needed by the TL carrier. Special equipment carriers—carriers of liquefied gases or frozen products—usually have larger investments in equipment and terminals than those involved with general freight. The large TL carriers like Swift and Schneider National also have significant capital investment.

On the whole, the motor carrier industry, especially for contract carriers, has been market oriented. Meeting customer requirements has been a common trait of motor carriers. The small size of the majority of for-hire carriers allows them to give individualized attention to customers. As carriers have grown in size, this close carrier–customer relationship has been strained. However, the responsiveness to customer demands for service still dominates all motor carrier organizations, and shippers expect carriers to respond to their needs.

Operating and Service Characteristics

General Service Characteristics

The growth and widespread use of motor carrier transportation can be traced to the inherent service characteristics of this mode. In particular, the motor carrier possesses a distinct advantage over other modes in the area of accessibility. The motor carrier can provide service to virtually any location as operating authority of the for-hire carrier no longer places restrictions on the areas served and commodities transported. Motor carrier access is not constrained by waterways, rail tracks, or airport locations. The U.S. system of highways is so pervasive that virtually every shipping and receiving location is accessible via highways. Therefore, motor carriers have potential access to almost every origin and destination.

The accessibility advantage of motor carriers is evident in the pickup or delivery of freight in an urban area. It is very rare to find urban areas not served by a pickup–delivery network. In fact, motor carriers provide the bridge between the pickup and delivery point and the facilities of other modes; that is, the motor carrier is referred to as the universal coordinator.

Another service advantage of the motor carrier is speed. For shipments going under 800 miles, the motor carrier vehicle can usually deliver the goods in less time than other modes. Although the airplane travels at a higher speed, the problem of getting freight to and from the airport via motor carrier adds to the air carrier's total transit time. In fact, the limited, fixed schedules of the air carriers might make motor carriers the faster method even for longer distances. For example, a delivery to a destination 800 miles away might take 17.8 hours by motor carrier (800 miles at 45 mph). Although the flying time between airports is 1.5 hours, 3 hours might be needed for pickup and 3 hours for delivery, plus time for moving the freight from one vehicle to another. If the airline has scheduled only one flight per day, the shipment could wait up to 24 hours before being dispatched. The motor carrier, however, proceeds directly from the shipper's door to the consignee's door. This service advantage became evident in the wake of September 11, 2001, when U.S. air traffic was shut down. The U.S. Post Office issued a statement alerting customers of delays for any package or letter traveling more than 800 miles because any Post Office shipment moving over 800 miles travels by air and under 800 miles travels by motor carrier.

When compared to the railcar and barge, the smaller **carrying capacity** of the motor carrier vehicle enables the shipper to use the TL rate, or volume discount, with a lower volume. Many TL minimum weights are established at 20,000 to 30,000 pounds. Rail carload minimum weights are often set at 40,000 to 60,000 pounds, and barge minimums are set in terms of hundreds of tons. The smaller shipping size of the motor carrier provides the buyer and seller with the benefits of lower inventory levels, lower inventory-carrying costs, and more frequent services.

Another positive service characteristic is the smoothness of transport. Given the suspension system and the pneumatic tires used on their vehicles, the motor carrier ride is smoother than rail and water transport and less likely to result in damage to the cargo (although there can still be some cargo damage with motor carrier transportation). This relatively damage-free service reduces the packaging requirements and thus packaging costs.

Lastly, the for-hire segment of the motor carrier industry is customer or market oriented. The small size of most carriers has enabled or even forced the carriers to respond to customer equipment and service needs.

Equipment

Many of the motor carrier service advantages emanate from the technical features of the transportation vehicle. The high degree of flexibility, the relatively smooth ride, and the small carrying capacity of the vehicle are the unique characteristics that result in greater accessibility, capability, frequency of delivery and pickup, cargo safety, and lower transit time.

The motor carrier vehicle can also be loaded quickly. A railroad operation needs to collect a number of freight cars to be pulled by one power unit; the motor carrier has just one or two. The ability to operate one cargo unit eliminates the time needed to collect several cargo units.

The other dimension of motor carrier equipment flexibility is the lack of highway constraint. Unlike the railroad and water carriers, the motor carrier is not constrained to providing service over a fixed railway or waterway. The motor carrier can travel over the highway, paved or unpaved, servicing virtually every conceivable consignee in the United States.[9] There are, however, gross vehicle weight and axle weight restrictions on vehicles while traveling the highway system.

In most cases, equipment represents the largest operating asset that a carrier maintains. With all of the different types and locations of equipment, positioning becomes critical to successful operations. Seasonal influences such as holidays or harvest times must also be considered, as they can drastically alter demand.

TL and LTL carriers need to make two types of equipment decisions: type of tractor (power) and type of trailer. In a TL operation, equipment positioning at terminals is not as important as in an LTL operation. However, power must be specified to be able to handle the size and length of the load, along with the terrain over which it travels. Many different specifications for tractors can be used, including single axle and twin axle, with different engine and drive train combinations. Decisions regarding trailers include length (28 feet, 45 feet, 48 feet, 53 feet, and so on) and trailer type (dry van, refrigerated, ragtop, container, flatbed, and so forth). These decisions will be made in light of market demands and the type of carrier operation.

LTL carriers must make the same types of equipment decisions as TL carriers along with deciding where to deploy this equipment. Similar to an airline equipment decision, LTL carriers need to position certain types of equipment at certain terminals. For example, city delivery vehicles and tractor–trailer combinations (either 28-foot or 40-foot trailers) will be positioned at PUD terminals, whereas line-haul trailers (usually 45, 48, or 53 feet) and line-haul tractors (single or twin axle) will be assigned to break-bulks. Compounding the LTL decision is the inclusion of 28-foot trailers (also called *pups*, *twins*, or *double bottoms*) in the equipment decision. Having the right mix of power and trailers at a particular terminal location determines the ability to efficiently serve customers.

Types of Vehicles

Motor carrier vehicles are either line-haul or city vehicles. Line-haul vehicles are used to haul freight long distances between cities. City straight trucks are used within a city to provide pickup and delivery service. On occasion, line-haul vehicles also will operate within a city, but the line-haul vehicle is normally not very efficient when operated this way.

Line-Haul Vehicles The line-haul vehicle is usually a tractor–trailer combination of three or more axles (see Figure 5-5). The cargo-carrying capacity of these vehicles depends on the size (length) and the federal/state maximum weight limits. A tractor–trailer combination with five axles (tandem-axle tractor and trailer) is permitted on the interstate system to haul a maximum of 80,000 pounds gross weight. States can have different maximum weights on their highway systems. For example, Michigan allows a maximum gross vehicle weight of 110,000 pounds on their state highways. For a vehicle to run with more than five axles, a permit is required. If the empty vehicle weighs 30,000 pounds, the maximum net payload is 50,000 pounds or 25 tons.

The net carrying capacity of line-haul vehicles is also affected by the density of the freight. A 53-foot × 102-inch × 110-inch trailer has 3,500 cubic feet of space. If the commodity has a density of 10 pounds per cubic foot, then the maximum payload for the vehicle is 35,000 ($3{,}500\ ft^3 \times 10\ lb/ft^3$). Shippers of low-density freight (below $16\ lb/ft^3$) advocate increased payload capacity of motor carrier vehicles.

FIGURE 5-5 Equipment Types

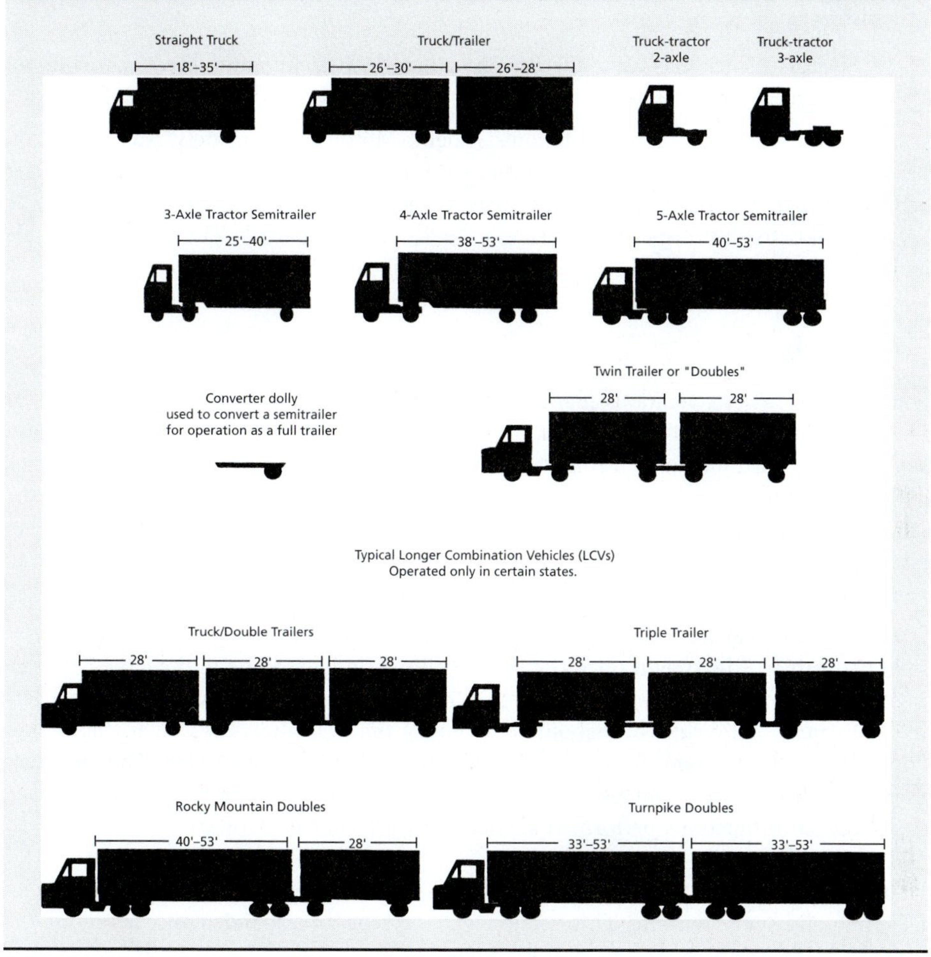

Source: *American Trucking Trends* 2003, American Trucking Associations (Alexandria, VA: ATA, 2003) p. 60.

City Straight Trucks City vehicles, or "straight trucks," are normally smaller than line-haul vehicles and are single units (see Figure 5-5). The city truck has the cargo and power unit combined in one vehicle. The typical city truck is approximately 20 to 25 feet long with a cargo unit 15 to 20 feet long. However, there is growing use of small trailers (28 feet) to pick up and deliver freight in the city. These trailers can also be used for line-haul, which increases efficiency. Shipments can be "loaded to ride," meaning they will not require handling at the origin terminal.

Special Vehicles In addition to the line-haul and city vehicle classifications, the following special vehicles are designed to meet special shipper needs:

- Dry van: Standard trailer or straight truck with all sides enclosed
- Open top: Trailer top is open to permit loading of odd-sized freight through the top
- Flatbed: Trailer has no top or sides; used extensively to haul steel
- Tank trailer: Used to haul liquids such as petroleum products

- Refrigerated vehicles: Cargo unit has controlled temperature
- High cube: Cargo unit has drop-frame design or is higher than normal to increase cubic capacity
- Special: Vehicle has a unique design to haul a special commodity, such as liquefied gas or automobiles

The Department of Transportation's Federal Motor Carrier Safety Administration has established many rules and regulations governing the specifications of motor carrier vehicles. These regulations cover such areas as the number of lights on the vehicle, the type of brakes used, tire specifications, and other operating parts.[10] The overall allowable length, weight, and height of the vehicle are prescribed in the various states.[11]

Terminals

Some motor carrier operations, namely TL operations, might not require terminals for the movement of freight. The carrier uses the shipper's plant for loading and the consignee's plant for unloading. Typically, TL terminals normally provide dispatching, fuel, and maintenance services. Some carriers, such as Schneider National, are expanding the services offered by their terminal facilities to include restaurant and hotel offerings to give their drivers alternatives to truck stops. These terminals are designed primarily to accommodate drivers and equipment, but not freight.

Heavy LTL carriers use terminals for loading, or consolidation, only. However, as indicated earlier, LTL freight operations do require terminals. Some of the large LTL carriers, such as Yellow/Roadway, have more than 500 terminals. A driver will leave a terminal to make deliveries throughout the country but will always return to his or her domicile. A driver's domicile is the terminal that the driver originally left. The terminals used by motor carriers can be classified as pickup or delivery, break-bulk, and relay. A discussion of functions performed at each type of terminal follows.

Pickup and Delivery Terminals (PUD) The terminal is a key facility in the operation of an LTL hub-and-spoke system. This section will present an expanded discussion of the types and roles of the terminals in this system.

The most common type of terminal found in the LTL system is the PUD terminal. These are also called *satellite* or **end-of-the-line (EOL)** terminals. The PUD terminal serves a local area and provides direct contact with both shippers and receivers. The basic transportation service provided at this terminal is the pickup and/or delivery of freight on peddle runs. A **peddle run** is a route that is driven daily out of the PUD terminal for the purpose of collecting freight for outbound moves or delivering freight from inbound moves. A PUD terminal will have several peddle runs in its customer operating area. Figure 5-6 gives an example of how a peddle run is designed. The PUD terminal is located in Altoona, Pennsylvania. Attached to it are four peddle runs, one each to Tyrone, State College, Lewistown, and Huntington. Every Monday through Friday morning, a driver will depart the Altoona terminal and deliver freight to customers located on that driver's assigned peddle. During and after the deliveries, freight will be picked up from customers and returned with the driver to the Altoona terminal at the end of the day. When all the drivers return at the end of their shifts, the Altoona terminal will have freight to be consolidated and moved outbound from customers in Tyrone, State College, Lewistown, and Huntington to customers in other areas of the country.

Note that there are two elements of a peddle run, one called **stem time** and the other called *peddle time*. Stem time is the time that elapses from when the driver leaves

FIGURE 5-6 Terminal Peddle Run

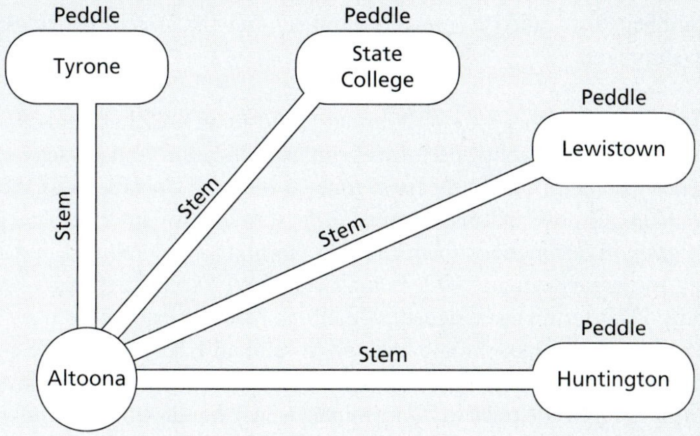

the terminal until the driver makes the first pickup or delivery; it is also the time that elapses from when the driver makes the last pickup or delivery until returning to the terminal. This is nonrevenue-producing time because no shipments are handled. A carrier would want to locate PUD terminals in such a way that this nonrevenue-producing travel time is minimized. (This aspect of LTL service will be discussed later in this chapter.) The other type of time is peddle time. This is the time during which the driver is actively involved in the pickup and delivery of freight. This is revenue-producing time because it occurs when shipments are handled. Obviously, carriers would want to maximize the amount of time a driver spent performing these activities.

The basic terminal services performed at these facilities are consolidation and dispersion. For example, freight moving inbound to Altoona from other terminals (passing through a break-bulk) will be broken into individual deliveries by peddle run to be handled by the driver during that particular shift. Freight that is brought back by the peddle drivers for movement outbound from Altoona will be consolidated into line-haul trailers for subsequent movement to the appropriate break-bulk. This is a basic cross-dock type of operation with a direction of freight flow across the dock that changes depending on whether the move is inbound or outbound.

The dispatch operation provided at the PUD terminal is critical to the operating efficiency of the peddle runs. Freight can be picked up on peddle runs in one of two ways. First, a customer on a peddle run might have a standing order for a pickup every day at 10 a.m. The PUD driver is aware of this, so the customer has no need to notify the carrier in advance for the pickup. Second, a customer might call or e-mail the local PUD terminal to order service for a pickup. This is where the local dispatcher becomes involved. The dispatcher records the nature of the shipment and required time of pickup and assigns that shipment to the driver on the appropriate peddle run. The PUD driver will periodically call in to or receive a satellite message from the dispatcher to determine the order and frequencies of new pickup requests. Obviously, the dispatcher needs to be familiar with the geography of the peddle runs and the capacity of the PUD drivers and trailers to efficiently route freight with the appropriate vehicle.

Other services that are provided at the PUD terminal might include tracing, rating and billing, sales, and claims. However, some carriers are beginning to centralize these functions at break-bulks or other locations by taking advantage of telecommunications technology. For example, some LTL carriers use the Internet for tracing purposes. When the customer accesses the carrier's website, the shipper keys in the pro number or waybill number (also called a tracking number) and the system provides the current status of the shipment.

Break-Bulk Terminals Another type of terminal found in an LTL hub-and-spoke system is called a **break-bulk**. This facility performs both consolidation and dispersion (or break-bulk) services. Customers will rarely have contact with the operations at the break-bulk facility. The main purpose of this terminal is to provide an intermediate point where freight with common destinations from the PUD terminals is combined in a single trailer for movement to the delivering PUD terminal. This can be seen in Figure 5-7. Break-bulks will have many PUD terminals assigned to them as primary loading points. For example, assume that a shipper in Toledo, Ohio, wanted to send an LTL shipment to a customer in Pottstown, Pennsylvania. The Toledo PUD terminal is attached to the Cleveland, Ohio, break-bulk, and the Philadelphia PUD terminal, which handles the Pottstown peddle, is attached to the Lancaster, Pennsylvania, break-bulk. At the completion of the peddle run, the Toledo driver brings the shipment back to the Toledo PUD terminal. There it is sorted and combined with other shipments going to the Lancaster break-bulk service area. (This could include all PUD terminals covering significant portions of Pennsylvania, New York, New Jersey, and parts of Maryland.) These shipments are consolidated into one trailer that will be dispatched to the Lancaster break-bulk.

Once the trailer arrives in Lancaster, it will be unloaded, and all of the freight destined to Philadelphia and its peddle runs will be loaded into an outbound trailer. This trailer will be dispatched from the break-bulk and will arrive at the Philadelphia terminal to be unloaded in the early morning so the freight can be segregated into peddle delivery vehicles for an early morning delivery schedule. So, just as with the airline hub-and-spoke system, the LTL system utilizes the full capacity of its vehicles in the line-haul operation.

Break-bulk facilities also serve as driver domiciles. City drivers located at a PUD terminal will always remain in their local area during their shift and will be able to return home when it is over. Line-haul drivers, however, might or might not be able to return home after a trip, depending on the length of haul they are assigned. For example, a *turn* means that a line-haul driver is assigned a load to be taken from the break-bulk (domicile) to a PUD terminal that is no more than 5.5 hours away. Because of DOT-mandated driving limits, that line-haul driver can make the trip, drop the trailer, and pick up another shipment destined back to the break-bulk within the hours of service driving limit. However, a movement that requires more than 5.5 hours driving time in one

FIGURE 5-7 Break-Bulk Terminal

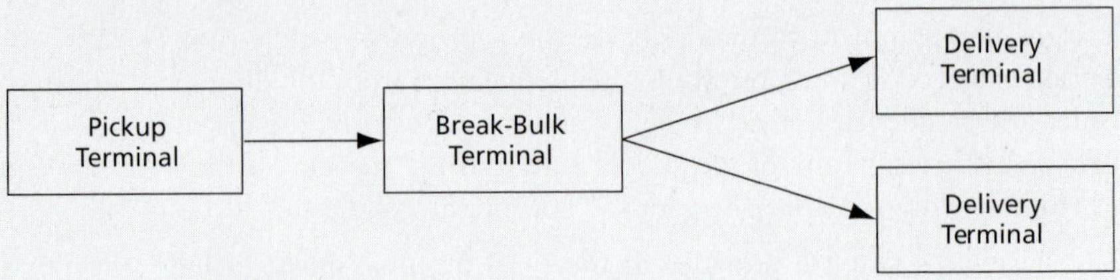

direction will require a layover; that is, when the driver reaches the destination, a 10-hour rest period is required before that driver will be able to take a return load back to the break-bulk and return to the domicile. Therefore, at the maximum, a driver facing an 11-hour run with an 10-hour layover and an 11-hour return trip will return to the domicile within 32 hours of the original departure. Sometimes, however, a return load is not immediately available, which will delay the driver's return.

Relay Terminals **Relay terminals** are different from the PUD and break-bulk terminals in that freight is never touched. The relay terminal is necessitated by the maximum hours of service regulation that is imposed on drivers. Under DOT enforcement, drivers were permitted to drive a maximum of 11 hours after 10 consecutive hours off duty. At the relay terminal, one driver substitutes for another who has accumulated the maximum hours of service. (The term **slip seat** also has been used to describe the relay terminal operation.)

As indicated in Figure 5-8, the location of the relay terminal is a maximum driving time of 11 hours from an origin. If the relay terminal is located 5.5 hours from an origin, the driver can drive to the relay terminal and return within the maximum 11 hours. (This is also called a *turn*.)

Using the example given in Figure 5-8, assume that the driving time is 15 hours between origin and destination. Without the relay terminal, the transit time is 26 hours. After 11 hours of driving, the driver goes off duty for 10 consecutive hours. Upon resuming duty, the driver drives 5 hours to the destination. The total elapsed time is 26 hours (11+10+5). The driver drives 11 hours to the relay terminal, and another driver takes over and drives the vehicle to the destination. In this instance, the relay terminal reduces the transit time by 10 hours, the mandated driver off-duty time. Under the new driver hours of service rules, relays still play an important role in LTL motor carrier operations. However, some carriers might have to rethink their relay structure because of the new, extended driver hours.

An alternative to the relay terminal is the use of a sleeper team—two drivers. While one driver accumulates the off-duty time in the sleeper berth of the tractor, the other driver is driving. The sleeper team has been most successful for long trips with many destinations.

Terminal Management Decisions

Many types of operating decisions need to be made when utilizing terminals in a carrier's network. Along with making these decisions, carrier management must also consider their strategic implications. This section will address a few of these types of decisions.

Number of Terminals In many modes, this is a relatively simple decision. For example, passenger airline terminals will be located close to major population centers. This decision, however, usually does not belong to the carrier but to some local government agency. Railroads must also make this decision but are limited by geography and track

FIGURE 5-8 Relay Terminal

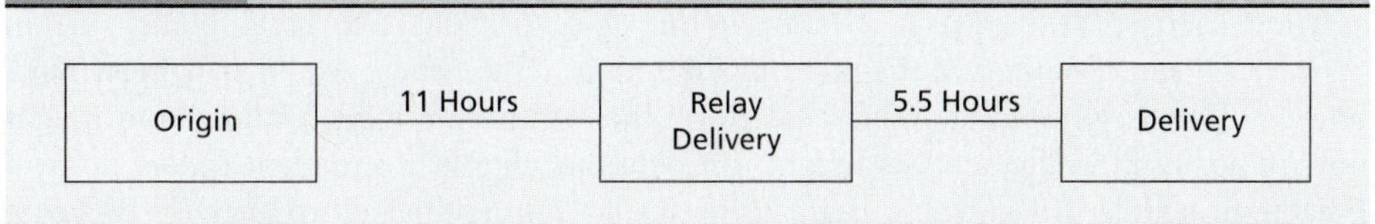

locations for terminal sites. Railroads will not normally have many terminals in their networks. The mode with probably the most difficult decision in this area is LTL motor carriage, primarily because of the vast numbers of terminals in these systems and the relatively small investment needed to develop a terminal site.

The obvious question for an LTL motor carrier is, "How many terminals should we have?" The obvious answer is, "It depends." First, the degree of market penetration and customer service desired by the carrier will help determine the number of terminals to establish. In theory, the more terminals closer to the customer, the better the service. This also has proven to be true in practice. Realistically, at some point additional terminals will result in no incremental increase in service and might even detract from service.

Second, the dilemma of small terminal versus long peddle must be addressed. Figure 5-9 represents this situation. In Example 1, assume that a carrier's market is the state of Pennsylvania, with one terminal located in Harrisburg with peddle runs to Erie, Scranton, Pittsburgh, and Philadelphia. This network utilizes only one terminal but has extremely long and expensive stem times for its peddle runs. The terminal must also be large to accommodate the volume of freight that will come from these four peddles. Example 2 shows a network that utilizes two terminals, each having two peddle runs with significantly shorter stem times. Each terminal in this scenario is smaller than the one terminal in Example 1. Thus, Example 2 has doubled the number of terminals but decreased stem times for customer PUD. The small-terminal-versus-long-peddle decision would be made based on the service implications of establishing terminals closer to customers versus the cost of adding another terminal.

Many times when shippers are making distribution system decisions, they assume that manufacturing facilities are fixed and that warehouse decisions must be made based on this fixed network. This assumption is also part of the terminal decision process for LTL motor carriers, except their "manufacturing facilities" are break-bulk terminals. Whether or not another terminal can be added to a break-bulk's operating region might simply be a question of available capacity at that break-bulk. Normally, each PUD terminal is assigned at least one door at a break-bulk. To add another PUD terminal means eliminating an existing terminal, physically adding another door to the break-bulk, or improving the productivity at the break-bulk to turn trailers in doors more than once per shift.

Locations of Terminals Closely related to the decision of how many terminals to establish is the decision of where to establish them. As previously mentioned, for airlines and railroads, this decision can be relatively simple because of geographic, government, and demand variables. LTL carriers, however, must consider some other variables. First, the DOT limits the amount of time a driver can continuously operate a vehicle before a rest period is required. Currently, this limit is 11 hours, so optimally PUD terminals should be located no more than 11 hours away from a break-bulk. This would allow a driver to complete the run in one trip. Second, PUD terminals should be located to minimize the distance that freight would need to be backhauled to the break-bulk. The assumption here is that freight flows from east to west and north to south in the United States. When a shipment is picked up, the idea is to send that freight in one of these directions as soon as possible. For example, given that a carrier has two break-bulks, one in Lancaster, Pennsylvania, and the other in Columbus, Ohio, where would a PUD terminal based in Pittsburgh send its freight? Based on the assumption made earlier about freight flows, Pittsburgh would send its freight to Columbus; that is, a shipment picked up by a Pittsburgh peddle driver would begin its east–west journey more productively by being

FIGURE 5-9 Small Terminal Versus Long Peddle

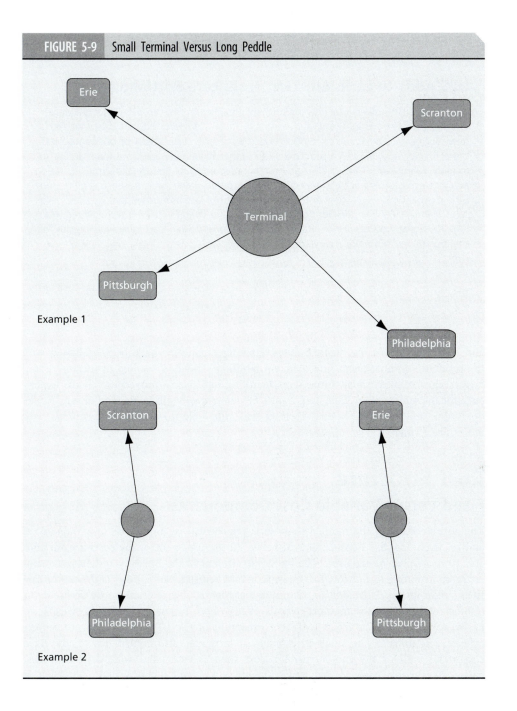

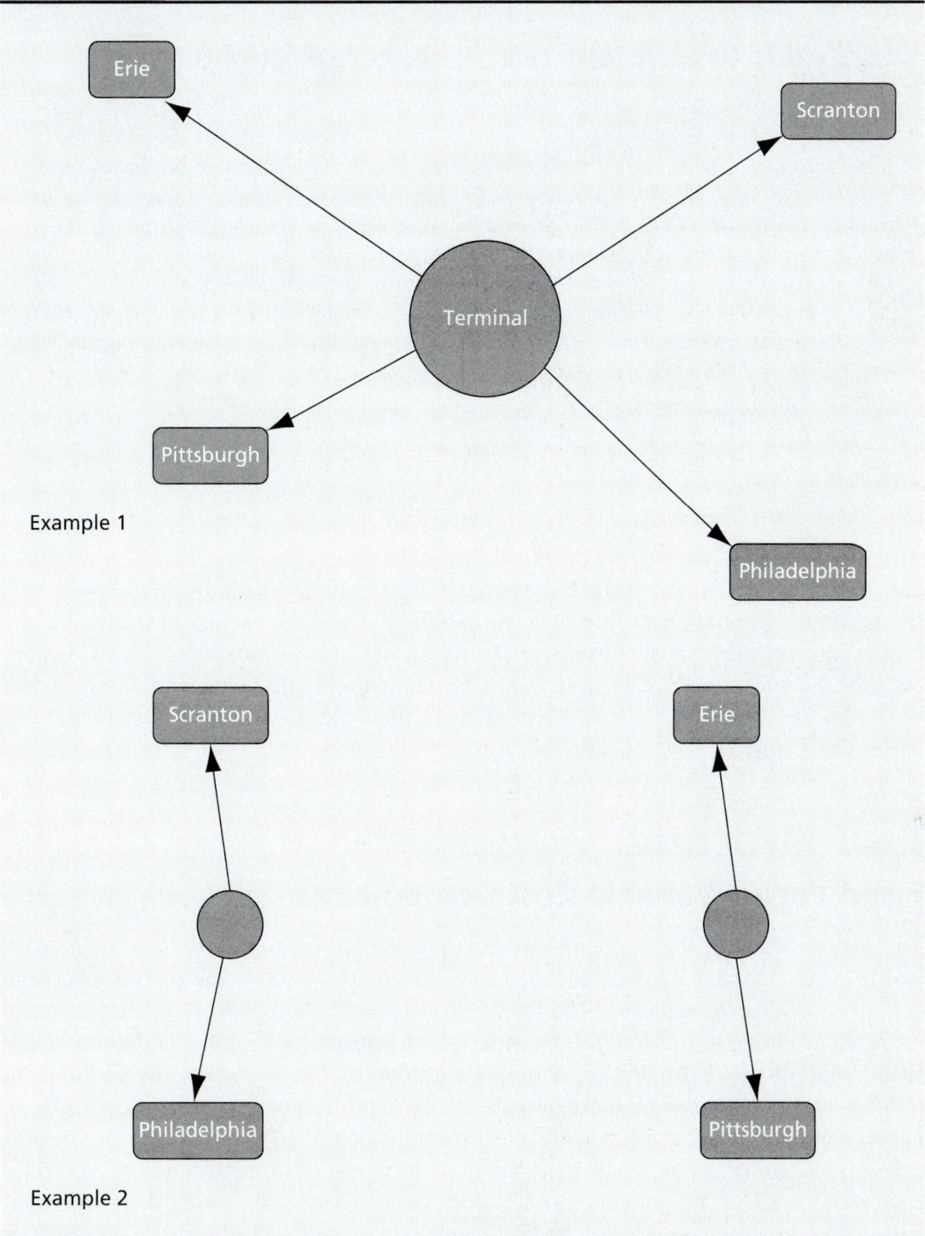

sent to Columbus because if it were sent to Lancaster, it would conceptually duplicate this distance when it began its journey from Lancaster to the west (actually passing right by Columbus). Finally, market penetration and potential will help determine terminal location. As mentioned in the decision process for determining the number of terminals, getting closer to the customer can many times improve the level of service given to that customer.

Recent trends in the LTL sector have seen significant reductions in the number of terminals as these carriers strive to provide overnight and second-day delivery to more

GLOBAL **PERSPECTIVES**

UPS Adds to Latin America Healthcare Portfolio

Last month, UPS rolled out new multi-client healthcare dedicated facilities in Mexico City, Mexico; San Paulo, Brazil; and Santiago, Chile. Company officials said that these new facilities are designed to support the storage and distribution of pharmaceutical, biotech, and medical device products, adding that these new additions have access to roughly 70 percent of the healthcare and manufacturing market in Latin America. "UPS healthcare customers are experiencing rapid growth in the Latin America region, and UPS is expanding its existing distribution footprint to accommodate that growth," said John Menna, UPS vice president of global healthcare strategy. "UPS provides integrated regional transportation and logistics solutions that will now reach a greater portion of the region's growing healthcare consumption market."

Source: *Logistics Management*, May 2014, p. 1. Reprinted with permission of Peerless Media, LLC.

and more customers. To do this, many inter-terminal runs have been realigned with the resultant elimination of intermediate handling. This has resulted in increased load factors and reduced transit times. Less handling has also improved the claims experience for the LTL carriers. The long-haul LTL carriers will still favor the hub-and-spoke operation, whereas the regional carriers will still look toward fewer terminals with more direct runs.

Cost Structure

Fixed Versus Variable Cost Components

The cost structure of the motor carrier industry consists of high levels of variable costs and relatively low fixed costs. Approximately 70 to 90 percent of the costs are variable, and 10 to 30 percent are fixed. The public investment in the highway system is a major factor contributing to this low fixed-cost structure because the highway is the motor carrier's "right-of-way." In addition, the motor carrier is able to increase or decrease the number of vehicles used in short periods of time and in small increments of capacity. Lastly, the carriers as a group (with the exception of the LTL carrier) do not require expensive terminals. The small investment in terminals also contributes to low fixed costs. The bulk of the motor carrier's cost then is associated with daily operating costs—the variable costs of fuel, wages, maintenance, and highway user fees (such as fuel tax and vehicle registration).

The discussion of motor carrier cost will begin with the vehicle operating costs of long-distance fleets transporting products in tractor–trailers. These data can be compared only to similar operations; that is, comparisons cannot be made to local motor carrier operations (PUD). Table 5-1 indicates that in 2012 the total variable cost to operate a tractor–trailer was 163.0 cents per mile. As indicated, approximately 80 percent of the cost to operate an intercity tractor–trailer is variable. The remaining 20 percent is associated with the fixed costs: vehicle interest; depreciation and interest on terminals, garages, and offices; management; and overhead (such as utilities). For carriers handling LTL freight, the fixed cost is higher; that is, additional

TABLE 5-1 Average Carrier Costs per Mile, 2012

MOTOR CARRIER COSTS	2012
Vehicle-based	
Fuel Costs	$0.641
Truck/Trailer Lease or Purchase Payments	$0.174
Repair & Maintenance	$0.138
Truck Insurance Premiums	$0.063
Permits and Licenses	$0.022
Tires	$0.044
Tolls	$0.019
Driver Based	
Driver Wages	$0.417
Driver Benefits	$0.116
Total	$1.633

Source: "An Analysis of the Operational Cost of Trucking: 2013 Update," *American Transportation Research Institute*, September 2013.

terminals, management, and overhead expenses are required to handle small-sized shipments.

The two categories with the largest share of the variable costs are labor and fuel. A discussion of each of these two variable costs will follow.

Labor The cost of drivers accounts for 25.6 percent of the total variable costs per vehicle mile, as shown in Table 5-1. Labor costs (wages plus fringe benefits) usually absorb about 32.7 percent of a carrier's revenue dollar. That is, 32.7 cents out of every dollar in revenue goes to labor.

The over-the-road (intercity) driver is typically paid on a mileage basis, such as 42.0 cents per mile; local drivers are paid by the hour. Over-the-road drivers are normally paid an hourly rate for operating delays resulting from loading/unloading, accidents, weather, and the like.

The DOT enforces maximum hours of service regulation. As of July 1, 2013, the DOT's **driving time regulations** permit drivers to drive a maximum of 11 hours after being off duty for 10 consecutive hours. A driver is permitted to be on duty a maximum of 14 hours after 10 consecutive hours off duty. In addition, no driver can drive after accumulating 60 hours on-duty in 7 consecutive days, or 70 hours in 8 consecutive days. For a more thorough discussion of the new HOS regulations, see Chapter 3.

The most pressing labor issue facing motor carriers, particularly TL carriers, is the shortage of qualified drivers. Part of the problem is that the federal government, as part of an overall safety program, imposed stringent driver licensing requirements. Since April 1992, all operators of vehicles over 26,000 pounds gross vehicle weight must hold a commercial driver's license (CDL). Although CDLs are issued by the driver's home state, the requirements are mandated by the federal DOT. Along with the new licensing requirements, the DOT also imposed stringent rules dealing with drug and alcohol abuse. Poor driving records and inability to pass the CDL test eliminated many marginal drivers.

The hardships imposed by the very nature of long-haul motor carrier operations have also impacted the availability of drivers. Drivers are frequently away from home for long periods and often have to assist with the loading and unloading of trailers. This lifestyle is not as attractive as other career choices, so the available pool from which drivers might be drawn has declined. The motor carrier industry has undertaken several initiatives to counteract the problem of driver retention and recruitment. They have raised the per-mile and per-hour pay rates, scheduled drivers home more frequently, and worked with shippers and consignees to make freight more "driver-friendly" (that is, easier to load/unload, tarp, brace, and so on).

Fuel Since 1974 the higher price of fuel has resulted in a rise in the relative proportion of fuel cost to total cost. For example, in 1976 fuel cost was 11.6 cents per mile or 19.8 percent of the total cost per mile, but in 1985 fuel cost was 24.6 cents per mile or 21.1 percent of total cost. In 2012 fuel cost was higher at 64.1 cents per mile or about 39.3 percent of total variable costs (see Table 5-1). Carriers have experienced a 251 percent increase in diesel fuel prices from 1994 to 2014—approximately $1.106 per gallon in 1994 to about $3.882 per gallon in 2014.

Included in the price of the diesel fuel is a highway user tax imposed by both the federal and state governments. The fuel tax plus other taxes for highway use are payments made by the carrier to the government for the construction, maintenance, and control of the highways. In 2011 the motor carrier industry paid $36.5 billion in federal and state highway user taxes.[12] The federal fuel tax is 24.4 cents per gallon of diesel fuel plus a state average of 30.0 cents per gallon.[13]

Economies of Scale

There do not appear to be major economies of scale for large-scale motor carrier operations. Economies of scale are realized through more extensive use of large-sized plants or indivisible inputs. However, the extensive use of indivisible inputs is not characteristic of all motor carrier operations. In addition, the large number of small firms, especially in the TL segment, suggests that small-sized operations are competitive. The concentration of the LTL business is indicative of economies of operation in this segment.

In the short run, certain economies exist in the greater use of indivisible inputs such as terminals, management specialists, and information systems. The average cost of such inputs will decrease as output (greater use) increases. Such economies of use justify the rather large-sized firms that operate transcontinentally, especially in the LTL segment. Carriers that operate over wide geographic areas require more terminals, more elaborate information systems, and more management specialists than those carriers that operate over narrow geographic areas.

For TL operations, very limited investment is required for terminals, but information systems are becoming increasingly important to efficient operations. Computers in tractors, direct satellite communication to drivers, and bar coding with optical scanners are a few examples of the sophisticated information systems and technology that now exist in the motor carrier industry. Many of the TL carrier inputs (vehicle, labor, fuel) can be increased one vehicle at a time in response to the small increases in demand.

Operational cost trade-offs exist between large and small carriers. A large-scale operation affords savings in purchase economies of equipment and in such inputs as fuel, parts, and interest in loans. (The small carrier might enjoy some of these purchase economies from larger retailers of motor carrier vehicle suppliers, such as truck stops.) On the other hand, large LTL motor carriers might be unionized and thus pay higher labor rates, but the motor carrier industry is less unionized today than it was in 1980.

Overall, long-term economies of scale appear not to be significant in TL motor carrier transportation and are present to some degree in the LTL segment. This degree of scale economies has implications for competition and the market's capability to control such competition.

Operating Ratio A measure of operating efficiency used by motor carriers is the **operating ratio**. The operating ratio measures the percent of operating expenses to operating revenue.

$$\textit{Operating Ratio} = (\textit{Operating expenses}/\textit{Operating revenue}) \times 100$$

Operating expenses are those expenses directly associated with the transportation of freight, excluding nontransportation expenses and interest costs. Operating revenues are the total revenues generated from freight transportation services; nontransportation services are excluded. Motor carriers might use the operating ratio to support a rate increase request. The closer the operating ratio is to 100, the more indicative of the possible need to raise rates to increase total revenues. In today's market, however, a rate increase might not be a feasible solution. Carriers are more likely to seek supply chain solutions with shippers and receivers to reduce operating expenses, thus increasing operating margin.

An operating ratio of 94 indicates that 94 cents of every operating revenue dollar is consumed by operating expenses, leaving 6 cents of every operating dollar to cover interest costs and a return to the owners. LTL motor carrier operating ratios usually range between 93 and 96, whereas the TL segment could see ratios in the low to mid 80s. The operating ratio is also a benchmark or barometer of financial viability. Obviously, if the operating ratio is equal to or greater than 100, there is no revenue available to cover fixed or overhead costs or to return a profit to owners or stockholders. Increasing revenues and/or reducing costs are viable approaches to resolving the problem of a high operating ratio.

Since the founding of the United States, the federal government has felt that it has the responsibility to provide highways to meet the national defense and commerce needs of the country. At first, the federal government was the sole financier of highways, but over the years, state and local governments have assumed a greater role. Today, the state and local governments assume the responsibility for maintaining the highways, while the federal government provides up to 90 percent of the construction cost of new highways with the designated network. The Federal Highway Administration (FHWA), part of the DOT, oversees the National Highway System (NHS). The NHS was defined in 1995 and consists of the 47,714-mile interstate highway system and 230,000 miles of existing state and federal non-interstate highways as a result of the MAP-21 Project. Although the NHS includes slightly over 4 percent of the total road mileage, this network sees the transportation of more than 75 percent of intercity freight traffic.

The Intermodal Surface Transportation Efficiency Act (ISTEA) has been replaced by the Transporation Equity Act for the Twenty-first Century (TEA21), which has continued the role of FHWA in this area. Additional funds were added under TEA21, which remained in place until 2004. More than $73 billion was expected to be spent on roads and related projects during this period. On June 29, 2012, the Moving Ahead for Progress in the 21st Century Act (MAP-21) was passed and allocated $105 billion to be spent on the nation's highways for the following two years.

Funding Highway users—motor carrier vehicle and automobile operators—pay for the construction, maintenance, and policing of highways through highway user taxes. The total amount of taxes paid depends on the use of the highway. The motor carrier incurs a cost for the use of the highway that is related to its amount of use. This situation contributes to the high variable cost structure of the motor carrier.

Federal and state governments assess highway user taxes. The federal highway user taxes are paid into the Federal Highway Trust Fund. From the Federal Highway Trust Fund, the federal government pays 90 percent of the construction costs for the interstate system and 50 percent of the construction costs for all other federal-aid roads. Table 5-2 indicates items taxed and the rate assessed by the Federal Highway Trust Fund.

The state also assesses highway user taxes to defray the cost of construction, maintenance, and policing of highways. The state taxes include fuel taxes, vehicle registration fees, ton-mile taxes, and special-use permits.

Implied in the highway user tax concept is the philosophy that the highway predominantly confers benefits on specific groups and individuals. Although the general public benefits from increased mobility and the availability of a wide variety of goods and services, the motor vehicle user is presumed to be the major benefactor and therefore is expected to pay a larger share of the costs. An analogy that illustrates this concept is the property owner who pays property taxes that include an assessment for streets (access to the property). Much debate exists as to whether motor carrier vehicles pay a fair share of the total cost of highways. In 2011 motor carriers paid $36.5 billion in federal and state highway user taxes.[14] The central issue is whether motor carriers should pay for the added construction and maintenance costs caused by their heavier weight.

TABLE 5-2 Federal Highway Trust Fund Tax Rates

COMMODITY	TAX
Gasoline	18.4 cents/gallon
Diesel fuel	24.4 cents/gallon
Special fuels	
General rate	18.4 cents/gallon
Liquefied petroleum gas	18.3 cents/gallon
Liquefied natural gas	24.3 cents/gallon
M85 (from natural gas)	18.4 cents/gallon
Compressed natural gas	18.4 cents/gallon
Tires	0 to 3,500 lb—no tax
	Over 3,500 lb—9.45 cents for each 10 lb in excess of 3,500
New truck and trailer sales	12% of manufacturer's sales price on trucks weighing more than 33,000 lb and trailers exceeding 26,000 lb
Highway vehicle use tax	For trucks weighing 55,000 lb or more, $100 + $22 for each additional 1,000 lb up to a maximum of $550

Source: MAP-21 Division D; Internal Revenue Code (26 U.S.C.), 2014.

Because each state must pay for the maintenance, policing, and construction of the highways within its boundaries, each state attempts to ensure receipt of taxes for using its highways. For a motor carrier operation over many states, this means buying vehicle registrations in many states and maintaining records of miles driven in a particular state so that the state will receive a fuel tax or ton-mile tax. Such record-keeping adds a cost to the carrier's operation.

Current Issues

Safety

Some members of the motor carrier industry have come to realize that improved safety can mean improved profitability. After the regulatory reform that took place in the early 1980s, motor carriers found themselves with more direct control of their economic and operating policies. Deficiencies in safety can translate into decreased profitability because of expensive claims for lost or damaged goods, increased insurance premiums, accidents, fines, and so on. These consequences are not unique to the motor carrier industry; in fact, they apply to the entire transportation industry.

The FMCSA enacted CSA 2010 to provide safety ratings for motor carrier drivers and companies with the intent of analyzing safety violations to prevent them from occurring in the future. This legislation replaced the SafeStat Program. See Chapter 3 for a more thorough discussion of CSA 2010.

Many shippers seek safety fitness information as part of their selection process, so there is considerable pressure on carriers to operate safely. Many transportation contracts contain clauses that permit the shipper to cancel the contract if the carrier's safety rating is Unsatisfactory.

A major related concern is that of alcohol and drug abuse. It has been estimated that American industry pays $50 to $100 billion for the effects and results of substance abuse in the workplace every year, for either the cost of accidents or losses in productivity. In response to this problem, the motor carrier industry has begun to move toward drug screening for its employees. Drug and alcohol testing are required in the following circumstances:

- As a requirement for employment
- As a part of a regular physical exam required of current employees
- For cause, required after any accident
- On a random selection basis

Drug and alcohol rules require motor carriers to have an anti-drug program, as well as drug testing that includes random and post-accident testing. All fleets, regardless of size, are required to have a complete program, including random and post-accident testing in place. These rules apply to the owner/operator as well. Many states have drug-testing programs of their own as well with which the carrier must comply.

When proper care is taken to implement a substance abuse program, most drivers support the program because it makes their job safer. Proper care in implementing a substance abuse program involves relating substance abuse to health problems, while leaving moral judgments to the individual. Such care also includes setting consistent policies that are enforceable and apply to every employee, making policies for violations known, and providing counseling and rehabilitation services for those employees who have substance abuse problems. Support for employees with problems is critical for any substance abuse program to be successful.

Other areas of safety concerns are drivers' hours of service and fatigue issues. Before January 3, 2004, the hours of service rules dated from before World War II and did not reflect modern realities. Under a complex formula of allowed driving and required rest periods, a driver can be on duty for no more than 60 hours in 7 days or 70 hours in 8 days. As previously discussed, these rules have been altered to address today's changing environment.

Another safety issue receiving attention deals with vehicle size and weight. As shown earlier, there are a number of different sizes of vehicles, and each has its own weight-carrying regulations. Recent studies have analyzed increasing total gross vehicle weight to 94,000 pounds with the addition of a third axle to the trailer. The studies have also addressed increased use of triples. All these issues include safety concerns and will require federal legislation before any changes can be made. In addition to safety, there are significant economic issues for the motor carrier industry because these larger vehicles will improve productivity and lower cost.

Technology

The use of satellite technology has a major impact on the motor carrier industry. Using global positioning technology (GPS), satellites are being used to track vehicles throughout their movement from origin to destination. The use of satellites allows the carriers to pinpoint the location of the vehicle and relay this information to the customer. The interaction between the driver, using an on-board computer, and a home-base computer allows route or arrival adjustment for poor weather or road conditions, and these adjustments can be communicated to the customers.

One area where satellite communication has had a very positive effect is in the movement of hazardous materials. For example, phosphorous pentasulfide (P_2S_5), a very dangerous chemical if not handled properly, is shipped by Bee Line Trucking for the Monsanto Company, a corporation in the food, medicine, and health industries. The two companies have teamed up to provide safe transportation for this dangerous chemical. The satellites used in the transport allow communication between the driver and a terminal in San Diego, which forwards the information on location and status to both Bee Line and Monsanto. This tracking allows for quick reaction to any accidents or spills, and the computers can give the name of the authority in the area to call in case any emergency action needs to be taken. Satellite communication will continue to play a role in improved safety and customer service for motor carriers into the future.

The use of electronic on-board recorders (EOBRs) is becoming more prevalent today in Class 8 tractors. Although efforts by the FMCSA to make them mandatory for companies with poor safety ratings have failed so far, motor carriers are installing the devices to improve both safety and productivity. EOBRs replace the traditional log book for drivers and monitor time on duty and off duty. EOBRs also measure idle time, speed limit, fuel consumption, and a host of other vehicle operating data that allow carriers to be more productive and save fuel.

LTL Rates

Since the early 1980s, the LTL segment of the motor carrier industry has used discounts from published tariffs as a means of pricing segments to attract traffic of large shippers. The ICC was eliminated under the ICC Termination Act of 1995 (ICCTA 1995) and with it most of the last vestiges of motor carrier rate regulation. Although certain portions of rate oversight were transferred to the then newly created Surface Transportation

TRANSPORTATION TECHNOLOGY

Filling the Gaps with TMS

For more that 80 years, Harrison, Ohio-based Wayne Water Systems has provided homeowners with durable, reliable, worry-free water handling solutions. But up until 2012, the manufacturer's transportation management system was stuck on "autopilot" and in need of an overhaul.

To help fill that gap, Jamie Graf, manufacturing operations manager, says that the firm went in search of a strategic partnership with a third-party logistics provider (3PL) that could go the extra mile to learn the ins and outs of the company's supply chain.

"We knew if we looked deeper into our supply chain, there was room for improvement," says Graf. "We needed a TMS that could drive efficiencies." After shopping around, the company partnered with Transportation Insight and began using the firm's Insight TMS. Graf says that the selection was made based on the low upfront and ongoing costs—and the fact that Wayne Water Systems would retain control over its logistics decisions.

"We can customize the TMS to meet our specific needs and match what we're trying to do," says Graf. For Wayne Water, the solution provides a customer-specific routing guide that factors in routing rules for the firm's big box retail customers—most of whom require approved carriers versus "lowest cost" carriers. Integrated with Wayne Water Systems' ERP, the TMS handles shipment creation to delivery and all steps in between.

"When our team receives an order via EDI, routing instructions are applied, with few exceptions," says Graf. "In one system, we can rate shop, auto-tender loads, generate shipping documents, and acquire tracking information." Rate shop, for example, is a TMS function that gives the manufacturer visibility over its entire carrier base and allows it to make selections based on cost and/or service needs.

Graf, who says that Wayne Water Systems has gained efficiencies and saved money using its new TMS, advises other shippers to select technology vendors or 3PLs that can grow and adapt to changing business needs without much additional investment in capital and time.

And don't overlook the need for a solid support team, Graf adds. "It's important to have a TMS that fits your business," he says, "but the support team behind the TMS is equally, if not more, important than the application itself."

Source: Bridget McCrea, *Logistics Management*, February 2014, p. 40. Reprinted with permission of Peerless Media, LLC.

Board, for all practical purposes LTL rates are subject to the free-market environment. In addition, the common carrier obligation to serve was preserved, but absent was an enforcement mechanism, which the marketplace will control as well. As it currently stands, the shipper has more choices for LTL today than existed during the height of regulation.

A limited amount of antitrust immunity was also preserved, but only for classifications, mileage guides rules, and general rate adjustments. Individual carrier rates are subject to antitrust action but cannot be challenged on the basis that the rate is unreasonably high. This is a direct reversal of the situation that existed under the old ICC.

There is no longer any requirement to file tariffs, and contracts can be used instead. Although carriers are still required to maintain rates, rules, and classifications, they only need be furnished to the shipper upon request. In a departure from previous regulation, rates need not be in writing to be enforceable. Shippers, however, must exercise due caution because federal oversight and enforcement is greatly diminished.

This law also reduced the time for recovery of disputed freight charges from 3 years to 18 months. If either the carrier or the shipper feels that the charges are incorrect, they must file suit no longer than 18 months from the date of the shipment. The lack of tariffs might make this more difficult unless the shippers have obtained the carrier's prices and rules in writing before tendering the shipment to the carrier.

Financial Stability

Another major concern in the motor carrier industry is financial stability. The operating ratios of many motor carriers have been in excess of 95 percent, and some companies have operating ratios of over 100. The high operating ratios are a clear indicator of the financial plight of many motor carriers and an indication of the low competitive rates.

Immediately after the initial lessening of economic regulation in 1980, a large number of motor carriers failed as the competitive environment became severe. Of the top 100 motor carriers in 1980, fewer than 10 were still in business in 1990. Only one new LTL was formed in this period that survived to the 1990s. The failures after 1990 were fewer but usually involved larger firms that could not continue to compete. In some cases, the unionized carriers were victims of labor unrest or shipper concerns about stability. In other cases, mergers and buyouts reduced the number of Class I carriers. Recent consolidations have also occurred in the TL sector as the larger carriers have taken over smaller firms to achieve market share. In 2012 a total of 495 motor carrier firms failed, mostly those having at least five trucks.[15]

Overcapacity has periodically been a severe problem for the motor carrier industry most recently during the recession of 2008 and 2009. Given that there is a finite amount of freight to be transported at any one time and there is little, if anything, that carriers can do to influence this, market share changes generally occur at the expense of one carrier over another. These periods of overcapacity also lead to severe pricing pressure, which can cause weaker carriers to exit the market. Shippers often exploit these factors and the spot market can drive prices below costs as carriers seek to move empty equipment.

Shippers have become increasingly cognizant of the failure rate among motor carriers, and many have introduced a financial evaluation of carriers into their overall decision framework for selecting carriers. When a carrier goes out of business, the interruption of service could have serious consequences.

SUMMARY

- Table 5-3 offers a summary of motor carrier industry characteristics.

TABLE 5-3 Summary of Motor Carrier Industry Characteristics

• General service characteristics	• Low investments/equipment
• Investments/Capital outlays	• 90% variable costs, 10% fixed
• Cost structure	• Pure competition
• Ease of entry	• Compete on price/service
• Market structure	• High-valued products
• How they compete	• Large number of small carriers (with few exceptions)
• Types of commodities	• Long-distance/metropolitan destinations
• Number of carriers	
• Markets in which they compete	
• Accessibility, speed, reliability, frequency, and lower loss and damage rates	

- Motor carriers have developed rapidly during the 20th century and now represent one of the most important modes of transportation for freight movement in the 21st century. U.S. business and most individuals depend in whole or in part upon motor carriers for the movement of goods.
- The public provision (federal, state, and local government units) of highways has played a major role in the development of the motor carrier industry because of the ubiquitous level of accessibility provided by the comprehensive U.S. highway system.
- The private carrier is a very important part of the motor carrier industry and a viable option to large and small companies requiring special services, such as grocery or food deliveries. The need of U.S. industry for dependable and controlled service has also contributed to the development.
- For-hire motor carriers can be classified in a number of useful ways, including local versus intercity, common versus contract, regulated versus exempt, general versus specialized, and TL versus LTL.
- One of the manifestations of deregulation has been the tremendous growth in the TL segment of the motor carrier business, especially among the small truckload carriers, which has significantly escalated the degree of intramodal competition.
- The LTL segment of the motor carrier industry has experienced increased concentration; that is, the larger carriers have generated a larger share of the total tonnage, as they have aggressively expanded and marketed their services.
- The motor carrier industry plays a major role in the movement of manufactured and food products (that is, higher-valued, time-sensitive traffic) because of its generally higher quality of service compared to other modes of transportation.
- The general service characteristics of motor carriers, including accessibility, speed, reliability, frequency, and lower loss and damage rates, have given motor carriers an advantage over other modes.

- Motor carriers offer a variety of equipment for use by shippers that reflect the distance of service and customer requirements.
- The cost structure of motor carriers is dominated by variable costs largely due to the carriers' ability to utilize a publicly provided right-of-way (highways) where payment is based upon user charges such as fuel taxes and licenses.
- Labor costs are an important element of the motor carrier industry, which tends to be much more labor intensive than other modes. Increased equipment size and more nonunion drivers have lessened the impact of wage costs during the 2000s.
- In contrast to railroads, motor carriers are regarded as having limited economies of scale; that is, small-scale operations are viable and competitive. The major exception would be the LTL carriers with their required investment in terminals. There is increasing evidence that there are some economies of scale among large LTL carriers.
- Public funding of highways and the level of user charges paid by motor carriers continue to be arguable issues because it is frequently maintained that motor carriers do not pay their fair share.
- A number of current issues face motor carriers, including safety, substance abuse, technology, undercharge claims, and state regulation.

STUDY QUESTIONS

1. The motor carrier industry is probably the most visible segment of the transportation system in the United States, but in many ways the motor carrier is also the most significant element of the freight transport industry. What factors account for the motor carrier's visibility and significance?
2. The railroad industry played a significant role in the development and growth of many cities and geographic regions during the 19th century. What role, if any, have motor carriers played during the 21st century in terms of economic development?
3. Private carriage is more important in the motor carrier segment of our transportation industry than any of the other four major modal segments. What factors have contributed to private carriage becoming so prevalent in the motor carrier area?
4. The so-called local carrier is also almost unique to the motor carrier industry. Why?
5. Compare and contrast the TL segment of the motor carrier industry with the LTL segment in terms of infrastructure, cost structure, market structure, and operating characteristics.
6. What is the nature of intramodal and intermodal competition in the motor carrier industry? How have the motor carriers fared in terms of intermodal competition since 1980?
7. Describe the general service characteristics of motor carriers and explain how these service characteristics have contributed to the growth of the motor carrier industry.
8. The cost structure of the motor carrier industry is affected by its infrastructure (such as highways and terminals). Discuss the cost structure of motor carriers and how it is affected by the infrastructure. Should there be changes made in public policy with respect to the motor carriers' use of public highways?
9. Describe how fuel and labor have impacted motor carrier cost structures and how they have altered motor carrier operations.
10. What are the major issues facing motor carriers in the 21st century? How should these issues be addressed?

NOTES

1. American Trucking Associations, Inc., *American Trucking Trends, 2013*, Washington, DC: American Trucking Associations, 2013.
2. Ibid.
3. Ibid.
4. Ibid.
5. Ibid.
6. Ibid.
7. "Yellow and Roadway Get It Together," *Logistics Management*, August 2003, p. 19.
8. Bureau of Transportation Statistics, *2007 Commodity Flow Survey*, Washington, DC, April 2010.
9. There are no notable exceptions to this ability to serve. Shippers located on an island are served by water or air transportation. Other unique examples exist where the motor carrier is physically unable to provide the transportation.
10. For a complete listing of federal equipment specifications, see the U.S. Department of Transportation, Federal Highway Administration, Bureau of Motor Carrier Safety, *Federal Motor Carrier Safety Regulations*, Washington, DC: U.S. Government Printing Office, 2008.
11. Through police powers contained in the U.S. constitution, each state has the right to establish regulations to protect the health and welfare of its citizens. Vehicle length and height laws are within these police powers, as are vehicle speed and weight laws.
12. American Trucking Associations, 2013.
13. Ibid.
14. Ibid.
15. Ibid.

CASE 5-1
Hardee Transportation

Hardee is a medium-sized, regional LTL carrier servicing the chemical industry. Because many of the shipments hauled by Hardee are hazardous in nature, its drivers need specialized training and must maintain high safety levels.

Jim O'Brien, Hardee's safety and compliance manager, takes great pride in his company's safety record as well as compliance with all local, state, and federal regulations. Being a relatively small carrier, Hardee has not yet invested in electronic on-board recorders (EOBRs) because the capital investment would put a financial strain on the company. Along with that, the average age of Hardee's drivers is 50 years, and many of these drivers are reluctant to give up their manual log books in favor of EOBRs.

Jim is concerned that if Hardee adopts the new technology, he will lose drivers. Compounding this is the driver's pool to replace these lost drivers and the new safety scoring system implemented by the passage of CSA 2010. Jim fears that even if he can find replacement drivers, their CSA scores will be too low for Hardee's standards as well as government standards for driving hazardous materials.

Although EOBRs and CSA 2010 are separate issues, they are related because both affect Hardee's drivers. Jim knows that Hardee will be required in the future to adopt EOBRs and that CSA 2010 is already in force.

CASE QUESTIONS

1. How would you advise Jim on adopting EOBRs? What would be your tactics to retain the current driver pool using the new technology?
2. If Hardee needs to replace drivers, what advice would you give Jim to make sure the drivers meet minimum CSA 2010 safety ratings and meet hazardous material driving requirements?

CASE 5-2

Squire Transportation

Squire Transportation (Squire) is a large national truckload (TL) carrier in the United States covering routes going both east-west and north-south. Squire's average length of haul is 1,200 miles with approximately 10 percent empty miles. Squire runs predominantly single driver tractors hauling 53-foot trailers. For years, Squire has relied on relatively inexpensive diesel fuel and nonunion drivers to keep its operating costs low. The location of its major customers requires either bobtailing tractors (repositioning without pulling trailers) or dead-heading equipment (running tractor-trailers empty) to pick up loads for delivery. These practices worked well when diesel prices were at the $1-per-gallon level.

However, the recent volatility of diesel prices has put a strain on Squire's operating costs. Drivers must refuel at truck stops where diesel prices are averaging $3 to $4 per gallon. Repositioning equipment is becoming cost prohibitive, but customers demand on-time pickups for on-time deliveries. Although these increasing diesel prices can be passed on to Squire's customers in the form of fuel surcharges, many customers are beginning to revolt against these rising surcharges. Squire's management can either accept these higher operating costs, thus reducing their profits, or begin to examine the implementation of regional TL operations.

CASE QUESTIONS

1. If you were advising Squire's management team on their impending decision, what would you tell them?
2. Is there an alternative to reduce the impacts of high diesel prices other than to develop regional operations?
3. If not, how would you advise Squire to develop a regional operation?

CHAPTER 6

RAILROADS

Learning Objectives

After reading this chapter, you should be able to do the following:

- Appreciate the contributions of the railroad industry to the development of the U.S. economy
- Gain an understanding of the size and types of firms in the railroad industry
- Discuss the relevance of intermodal and intramodal competition in the railroad industry
- Know the major types of commodities hauled by the railroads
- Recognize the different types of equipment used in the railroad industry
- Discuss the nature of costs in the railroad industry and how they impact pricing decisions
- Understand the importance of intermodal carloadings on the growth of the railroad industry
- Be aware of the current issues facing the railroad industry today

TRANSPORTATION **PROFILE**

Riding High

While there are currently more good signs than bad regarding the economy, it's safe to say that we may need to "curb our enthusiasm," as comedian Larry David may observe, until we see more sustained signs of growth and improvement. That is, of course, unless you follow the railroad and intermodal sectors.

It comes as little surprise to learn that both sectors are doing very well amid what has become the new normal—fits and starts in terms of economic growth.

A look at year-to-date numbers on the rails brings this into perspective. Domestic carload volumes are up 3.1 percent through the end of May, while intermodal volumes, which have returned to prerecession levels, are up 5.8 percent for the same period.

What's more, the weekly carload average for the month of May, at 296,759, stands as the highest weekly average for any month, according to the Association of American railroads (AAR). To top it off, the intermodal weekly average for May is the third-best ever recorded. These are better than good growth numbers for this time of year and are even more impressive when you consider what carriers went through in the first quarter as they endured one of the worst winters in years.

"Rail demand is real and is there," said Tony Hatch, rail analyst and principal of ABH Consulting. "And shippers anticipate enough rail capacity to handle it. There is plenty of evidence out there supporting volume growth, service improvement, and improving relationships between carriers and shippers."

One prescient reason for this is the ability of the railroads to truly leverage its strengths in terms of ever-improving service quality. Due to these improvements, more shippers have jumped on board. In turn, the carriers have leveraged these excellent returns and have reinvested into their networks and infrastructure to expand, upgrade, and enhance the U.S. rail freight.

Earlier this year, the AAR said that the seven North American-based Class I railroads plan to invest roughly $26 billion in 2014, adding that since 1980 freight railroads have anted up about $550 billion into their rail networks—with roughly $115 billion over the last five years.

"This year's projected record investments continue a decades-long trend of private railroad dollars that sustain America's freight rail network so taxpayers don't have to," said Edward Hamberger, AAR's president and CEO. "This massive private financial commitment is a demonstration of the industry's resolve to never stop improving."

The ability to make these investments comes with a caveat for shippers in the form of increased rates at an annual average clip of about 5 percent per year. This has resulted in what has ostensibly become an age-old dilemma between carriers and shippers, with carriers making the case that hikes are needed in order to make significant capital investments—while rail shippers want more for their money.

In recent years, there's been shipper momentum to reregulate the industry in various forms, whether it be to address the lack of railroad antitrust, fuel surcharges applied by the rails, and reciprocal switching. But given the tenuous culture in Congress, they've not made meaningful forward progress.

Despite the disconnect between rail shippers and carriers at times, industry experts are quick to point out that even with current growth levels, railroads are not revenue adequate, even if it seems that way to shippers.

Source: Jeff Berman, *Logistics Management*, July, 2014, pp. 36–38. Reprinted with permission of Peerless Media, LLC.

Introduction

The offering of scheduled common carrier freight and passenger service to the public began in the United States in 1830, with the start of operations on 13 miles of road between Baltimore and Ellicott's Mills, Maryland. At the start of the U.S. Civil War in 1860, 30,626 miles of road were in service. By then, rail transportation had proven overwhelmingly superior in both price and service quality to animal-powered road transportation, and superior in service quality to water transportation on lakes, rivers, and canals, and on the ocean between different ports within the United States.

During the first 30 years of its existence, the railroad industry evolved from a population of unconnected carriers focused on short-haul traffic to the completion of longer-distance lines located largely between the Atlantic seaboard on the east, the Mississippi River on the west, the St. Lawrence River and Great Lakes on the north, and the Potomac and Ohio Rivers on the south. The Civil War slowed but did not stop rail construction during the 1860s. Most notable was the completion in 1869 of the first rail link between the Midwest and the Pacific Coast. Total road mileage reached 52,922 in 1870. That year marked the beginning of the greatest boom in growth of railroad mileage. By 1900, total mileage stood at 196,346, accessing all parts of the country and providing shippers and travelers with a national network of carriers that connected with one another. Movement of traffic between connecting railroads was facilitated by the industry's almost universal adoption of standard track gauge (track gauge is the distance between the inside edge of the running rails of a rail track) of 4 feet 8 1/2 in (1435 mm.) and adherence to rolling stock design standards that permitted freight and passenger cars owned by one railroad to be run on the lines of another.

By 1900, the economic superiority of rail transportation had supplanted water transportation, on canals in particular but also on rivers, for many products and for almost all passenger traffic. Transportation of freight and passengers in horse-drawn vehicles continued, but only as short-distance feeders of traffic to and from rail terminals and from ocean, lake, and river ports. Rail transportation's cost and service quality advantages made possible the settlement and economic development, both agricultural and industrial, of landlocked areas in all parts of the United States. Many cities and towns were either founded or experienced significant growth because they stood at key points in the rail network.

The post-1870 boom in railroad network expansion was financed largely by private capital. In some locations, particularly in the East and Midwest, this led to overbuilding of the network. Some promoters of rail projects did not have profit from operation of a completed railroad as their objective. Instead, they sought profit from construction of a railroad and/or from its sale after completion to an already-existing parallel railroad that wanted to prevent erosion of its revenue base by rate competition from the new entrant. Much of this overbuilt capacity remained in operation until the 1970s and 1980s, when it was rationalized in the wake of financial failure of its owners.

Rail transportation remained the dominant, largely unchallenged, mode of intercity freight and passenger movement through the first two decades of the 20th century. However, erosion of its dominance began during the 1920s with the beginning of large-scale government-funded construction of hard-surface roads and superior service and/or cost characteristics of motor carriers and automobiles. Additional competition came from a revival of inland water transportation, which was aided by government-financed navigation improvements on rivers and by privately financed construction of oil pipelines. Air transportation emerged as a serious contender for rail passenger and mail traffic during the 1930s. Overall, the railroad industry suffered significant decline in relative importance after 1920. However, its role in freight transportation remains important in the 21st century.

The railroad industry has stabilized in relative importance during the first part of the 21st century. This trend has been well documented and can be attributed in part to the following factors: alternate transport modes with superior services and/or cost characteristics (primarily motor carriers and pipelines); a resurgence in water transportation; and the changing needs of the U.S. economy. In 2009 railroads transported only 39.9 percent of the total intercity ton-miles transported by all modes.[1] It is important to note that, on an actual basis, rail ton-miles have continued to increase, and railroads are still the largest carrier in terms of intercity ton-miles, but not in terms of tonnage or revenues.

Starting in 1984, the railroad industry adopted a new depreciation accounting system, and **return on investment (ROI)** shot up to 5.7 percent. In 2012 ROI again showed an increase to 12.49 percent.[2] Consequently, some rail stocks have become more attractive investments.

The railroads are still vital to our transportation system and play an important role in our economy. For example, in 2013 rail revenues accounted for approximately 8.7 percent of the nation's freight expenditures.[3] Railroads in 2012 employed 234,000 people.[4] Investment is another indication of importance. In 2012, rail investment in new plant and equipment was over $147 billion. In 2012, for example, rail locomotive and freight car acquisition increased sharply over 2010, increasing more than 123 percent.[5] These indicators have been hailed as further evidence of the success of the Staggers Rail Act of 1980.

As mentioned earlier, in 2009 the railroads shipped about 39.9 percent of all ton-miles moved by all transport modes in the United States. This percentage of total ton-miles has been declining since its peak of 75 percent in 1929. However, actual ton-miles have, for the most part, been steadily increasing. In 1980 a total of 932 billion ton-miles of domestic intercity freight were moved. The figure dropped to 810 billion ton-miles in 1982 due mostly to the recession of 1982 to 1983. In 2009 the ton-miles moved were 1,582 billion, representing 39.9 percent of transportation's total 3,961 billion.[6]

These figures highlight the fact that, even though railroads continue to move record amounts of goods, they are capturing less of the total transportation market because other modes have been growing even faster. However, there are indications that railroads may experience a resurgence on a relative basis because of more aggressive marketing and growth in intermodal traffic. Between 2005 and 2012, intermodal traffic increased from a little over 11.7 million loadings to just over 12 million, an increase of 4.9 percent.[7] Intermodal shipments have become more attractive as fuel prices escalate and highway congestion increases.

Industry Overview

Number of Carriers

The U.S. freight railroad industry consisted of 574 different railroads in 2012. Of them, seven were designated by the Surface Transportation Board (STB) as Class I companies (see Table 6-1), meaning that they each generated revenue of $452.7 million or more annually. The balance of 567 non-Class I rail carriers are identified by the AAR as either "regional" or "local" lines. Regional status applies to line-haul railroads operating at least

TABLE 6-1 Railroads in 2012

RAILROAD	NUMBER	MILES	EMPLOYEES	REVENUE ($ BILLION)
Class I	7	95,264	163,464	67.6
Regional	21	10,355	5,507	1.4
Local	546	32,858	12,293	2.6
Total	574	138,477	181,264	71.6

Source: Association of American Railroads, *Railroad Facts*, Washington, DC, 2013, p. 3.

350 route miles and/or earning annual revenue of at least $20 million but less than the Class I revenue threshold. Local status applies to line-haul railroads below the regional criteria (commonly referred to as short lines) plus railroads that provide only switching and terminal service. Some regional, short line, and switching and terminal railroads are stand-alone companies. Others are subsidiaries of holding companies such as Genesee & Wyoming, Inc. Genesee & Wyoming became one of the largest when it purchased Rail-America in 2012. In 2014, Genesee & Wyoming owned 112 subsidiary railroads operating across 11 regions over track totaling more than 15,000 miles.

Road mileage declined during the same 50-year period (see Table 6-2). Road mileage expanded rapidly during the initial construction period of 1830 to 1910 and reached a peak of 254,251 miles in 1916.[8] By 1929 road mileage was down to 229,530, and in 2012 it had been reduced to about 95,391 road miles.[9] This reduction is traceable largely to the abandonment of duplicate trackage that was built during the boom periods of the industry's developmental years that was no longer needed because of technology advances, market shifts, the rail merger movement, and intermodal competition.

TABLE 6-2 U.S. Railroad Miles and Trackage (Class I)

YEAR	MILES OF ROAD*	MILES OF TRACK**
2000	99,250	168,535
2001	97,817	167,275
2002	100,125	170,048
2003	99,126	169,069
2004	97,662	167,312
2005	95,830	164,291
2006	94,942	162,056
2007	94,440	161,114
2008	94,209	160,734
2009	94,048	160,781
2010	95,700	161,926
2011	95,514	162,393
2012	95,391	162,306

*This represents the aggregate length of roadway of all line-haul railroads exclusive of yard tracks, sidings, and parallel lines.

**This includes the total miles of railroad track owned by U.S. railroads.

Source: Association of American Railroads, *Railroad Facts*, Washington, DC, 2013, p. 45.

Competition

The competitive position of the railroad industry has changed dramatically after the first two decades of the 20th century. Today, the industry is faced with intense intermodal competition, particularly from the motor carrier industry, and selective intramodal competition. Consolidations within the industry have created a situation in which only seven Class I railroads generate 94.4 percent of railroad revenue.

The industry's economic structure has developed into a fine example of differentiated oligopoly. In other words, there are a small number of very large railroads, and they serve somewhat different market areas. Their major source of competition is intermodal in nature.

Intramodal Today, only a few railroads serve a particular geographic region. This situation gives rise to an oligopolistic market structure because there are a small number of interdependent large sellers. Barriers to entry exist because of the large capital outlays and fixed costs required, and, consequently, pricing of commodity movements not easily diverted to motor carriers and water carriers can be controlled by the existing railroad firms. For this reason, economic regulations enacted by Congress and administered by the ICC before 1980 brought the geographic coverage and the rate-making procedures of the railroads under federal scrutiny and control.

With the merger trend discussed earlier, the intramodal competition has been reduced. Many cities now have only one railroad serving them. Even major rail centers such as Chicago or Kansas City have seen the number of carriers serving those areas significantly reduced. Shippers are concerned that there will not be enough effective intramodal competition to preserve railroad-to-railroad competition.

Intermodal As noted earlier, the relative market share of railroad intercity ton-miles has been steadily declining because of increased intermodal competition. Inroads into the lucrative commodity markets have been facilitated by governmental expenditures on infrastructure that have benefited competing modes. For example, the government has provided an extensive local and national highway system, especially the interstate network, for motor carrier use.

Customers look for consistent on-time performance. Railroads need to provide this level of service to stay competitive. Railroad companies usually cannot deliver freight early because the customer then has to find a place to store it.

In addition, through improvements and maintenance of the inland waterway system by the U.S. Army Corps of Engineers, the government has also provided the right-of-way for water carriers. Because of the governmental programs and the response of the railroad industry to change, railways in 2009 accounted for 39.9 percent of total revenue freight ton-miles (see Table 6-3).

Overall, the railroads have been rate-competitive. Government expenditure programs aimed at promoting other modes, together with intermodal competition, forced the railways into making a determined effort to forestall industry decline by becoming more competitive. The Staggers Rail Act, which removed significant economic regulation, has allowed railroads to be much more price-competitive through contract rates and more tailored response to customers' service requirements.

Mergers Historically, many mergers have taken place in the railroad industry, and the size of the remaining carriers has correspondingly increased. Early rail mergers grew out of efforts to expand capacity to benefit from large-volume traffic efficiencies and

TABLE 6-3 Railroad Intercity Ton-Miles and Tonnage (billions)

YEAR	REVENUE TON-MILES	PERCENT OF TOTAL
2001	1,599	39.8
2002	1,606	39.5
2003	1,604	39.3
2004	1,684	40.1
2005	1,733	40.9
2006	1,856	43.1
2007	1,820	41.8
2008	1,730	40.2
2009	1,582	39.9

Source: Association of American Railroads, *Railroad Facts*, Washington, DC, 2013, p. 32.

economies. Later, **side-by-side** combinations were made to strengthen the financial positions of many of the railroads and eliminate duplication. More recently though, **end-to-end mergers** were created to provide more effective intermodal and intramodal competition.[10] Customer service and reliability can be improved by these mergers because the many types of operating costs, such as car switching, clerical costs, and record-keeping, can be reduced. However, such improvements, in some instances, have been slow to develop.

Previously we noted that the number of railroads (see Table 6-1) and the number of miles of track (see Table 6-2) have declined. One of the major reasons for this decline in both the number of companies and the miles of track has been the significant number of mergers or unifications that have occurred in the railroad industry during the past 30 years. A total of 28 mergers have taken place during the past 30 years, and 50 unifications overall. The latter included not only mergers but also consolidations and outright purchases for control. The decade of the 1970s was very active, but the tempo of rail consolidations in the 1980s was hyperactive.

In 1920 there were 186 Class 1 railroads; by 2013 the number had declined to seven. One reason for this drop was the way in which railroads are classified by revenue; as it was adjusted for inflation, fewer roads qualified. The primary reason, however, was the accelerating trend of mergers. After the Staggers Act was passed in 1980, there was a significant increase in mergers and acquisitions so that as of 2014 the seven Class I rail lines are BNSF, CSX Transportation, Grand Trunk Corporation, Kansas City Southern Railway, Norfolk Southern, Soo Line Corporation, and the Union Pacific Railroad.

Abandonments Recall that in 1916, at its peak, the railroad industry owned 254,037 miles of road. Today, more than half of that is gone, enough to circle the Earth three times. The early overexpansion left extensive amounts of excess trackage in many areas, and the railroads had to abandon significant portions of rail trackage to remain competitive. Parallel and overlapping routes, therefore, have been eliminated wherever possible.

Many factors led to the abandonment of track around the country. In the late 1950s, the government began the construction of the Interstate Highway System. This allowed motor carrier service to decrease transit time, which caused shippers to use these carriers. To effectively compete with motor carriers for time-sensitive traffic, railroads had to

GLOBAL PERSPECTIVES

Intermodal Volumes Finish 2013 Strong Reports IANA

According to the recent release of the Intermodal Market Trends & Statistics report from the Intermodal Association of North America (IANA), intermodal transportation continued to gain traction in 2013.

Total 2013 intermodal volume was up 4.6 percent compared to 2012. Domestic containers were up 9.4 percent, and international containers were up 1.2 percent. All domestic equipment was up 7.1 percent, but trailers fell 0.7 percent.

IANA officials noted that the strong performance in the domestic container segment has doubled in the last 10 years and again led all intermodal groups it tracks. They added that international and trailers both finished the year strong, showing their best performance in years.

While the growth rates are impressive, industry experts maintain that these strong domestic container intermodal volumes are due in large part to freight coming out of intermodal trailers into trailers, or from one box to another—coupled with the fact that the gross number of intermodal loadings were higher in 2006 that in 2013 as was gross GDP and industrial production.

IANA President and CEO Joni Casey told *Logistics Management* that there were various drivers for the late year surge in intermodal volume and performance, including continuing tight highway capacity, bad weather, the continued push of freight to rail, a compressed holiday season, and higher e-commerce related sales that required additional capacity.

And with domestic intermodal continuing to be the lead intermodal growth driver, Casey said that it's reasonable to expect more of the same. "It certainly looks like it was based on trends of the last three years," she said. "Domestic intermodal volumes have outgrown international at a more than 2:1 ratio over that time."

Casey observed that international volumes, which were solid in the fourth quarter, have increased in five of the last six months, while levels of monthly increases have fluctuated by as much as 5.5 percent.

"The encouraging sign is that international intermodal shipments are showing growth during the last half of the year versus losses. The rate of growth in 2014 remains to be seen."

Source: Jeff Berman, *Logistics Management*, March 2014, pp. 16–17. Reprinted with permission of Peerless Media, LLC.

focus on efficient routes. In the 1970s and 1980s, bankruptcies forced the abandonment of portions of railroad systems such as the Rock Island, Penn Central, and Milwaukee Road. In 1980, partial deregulation gave rail companies greater freedom to buy, sell, or abandon unprofitable track. Once the railroad companies abandoned the tracks, they sold the rails and ties to scrap dealers.

The land used for rights-of-way, abandoned by the railroads, could also be used unless the original deed required the return when the property was no longer being utilized for railroad purposes.

In some cases, all or part of the right-of-way was turned into hiking trails with some bridges left in place. The program, Rail to Trails Conservancy, has been highly successful in adding over 10,000 miles of trails to the country's recreational facilities. In other cases, the land and sometimes even the track was left in place as part of a program known as "rail-banking." The theory behind this is should the line be needed in the future, it would be much easier to restore it. In one case, a major railroad company reopened a major line after it was closed for over 10 years.

Even though the railroad industry reduced its road mileage by more than half, the lines remaining still carried a major share of the existing freight. The abandonments included both rural branches and mainlines made duplicate by mergers of parallel carriers. The ICC, and later the STB, still regulate abandonments, but changes in the law made it much easier for railroad companies to shed unprofitable lines. Not all the lines were scrapped, as discussed above, and regional and short-line operators took over some of this property.

New developments, such as unit trains carrying one commodity like coal or grain from one shipper to one consignee, helped the railroads operate more profitably. As more and more traffic was concentrated on fewer and fewer routes, overhead costs were spread over more businesses. Each time a railroad interchanged a car to another line, there was the chance for delay. As mergers reduced the number of railroads, fewer interchanges were needed.

Operating and Service Characteristics

General Service Characteristics

Commodities Hauled In the 19th century, when the railroads were the primary source of transportation, they moved almost every available type of product or raw material. Today, the railroad system has evolved into a system that primarily transports large quantities of heavyweight, low-value commodities (or bulk products).[11] However, intermodal containers and trailers, carrying high-value finished products, make up a significant portion of many railroads' movements. Motor carriers concentrate on the handling of small-volume, high-value finished goods, whereas water and pipelines carry the larger volumes of the lowest-value types of bulk commodities. The railroads therefore find themselves engaged in intense competition with these other modes for the opportunity to ship many product categories. Although railroads still handle a wide variety of commodities, more than 74 percent of total rail carloadings in 2012 involved the movement of bulk materials. Table 6-4 lists the products with almost 21.2 million carloadings carried by the railroads in 2012. Of the seven commodities shown in the table, only two, motor vehicles and equipment and miscellaneous and mixed shipments (intermodal), are not bulk commodities.

Coal Railroads are the primary haulers of coal, accounting for 41 percent of the total tonnage transported in 2012.[12] Table 6-4 indicates that 6.204 million carloadings moved in 2012, down by more than 851,000 from 2011 levels. Coal is an alternative energy source that will probably continue to be an important commodity shipped by the railroads, and this tonnage may increase if there are political challenges in the Middle East that limit the supply of petroleum and related products.

Farm Products When considered together, farm and food products constitute the fourth largest commodity group hauled by railroads. Total movement by rail amounted to about 1.528 million carloads in 2012.[13] The growth in domestic markets and the increase of exports to foreign customers have been steady for many years. For example, the exportation of grain and its related products accounted for more than 50 percent of the total grain market. Because of this growth, distribution patterns might change, but

TABLE 6-4 Carloads Originated by Commodity

COMMODITY GROUP	CARLOADS (THOUSANDS)		CHANGE	
	2012	2011	CARS	PERCENT
Miscellaneous Mixed Shipments*	7,509	7,858	−349	−4.4
Coal	6,204	7,055	−851	−12.1
Chemicals and Allied Products	2,066	2,279	−213	−9.3
Farm Products	1,528	1,719	−191	−11.1
Motor Vehicles and Equipment	1,048	1,245	−197	−15.8
Food and Kindred Products	1,559	1,585	−26	−1.6
Nonmetallic Minerals	1,279	1,263	16	1.3

*The miscellaneous mixed shipments category (STCC 46) is mostly intermodal traffic.

Source: Association of American Railroads, Washington, DC, 2013, p. 25.

the transportation of farm products will continue to be an important rail commodity movement.

Chemicals Chemicals and allied products, a great number of which are classified as hazardous by the U.S. Department of Transportation (DOT), are transported in specially designed tank cars. A total of 2.066 million carloads of this highly rated traffic traveled by rail in 2012.[14] Railroads can safely transport chemicals in comparison with highway movements, and this safety has been steadily increasing for years. This type of long-haul bulk material is ideally suited for rail movement. Interestingly, motor carriers move more chemicals, and they compete vigorously for this traffic.

Transportation Equipment Transportation equipment carloadings, which are linked to the relative health of the domestic automobile industry, have increased to more than 3.7 percent of total carloadings, but decreased by over 197,000 carloads from 2011 to 2012.

Although the commodities shipped by the railroad industry have changed over the years, with the emphasis placed on the movement of low-value, high-volume bulk materials, the railroads are still a possible mode of transport for many different types of goods, including both high-value merchandise and raw materials alike.

Traffic Shifts As indicated previously, the demand for freight transportation is a derived demand; that is, transportation demand is based upon the demand for products to be moved. Consequently, economic conditions have an impact upon the demand for transportation service. This is especially true for railroads because they primarily move basic raw materials and supplies (such as coal, chemicals, and so on).

There was almost universal agreement that the U.S. economy was recovering during the last three-quarters of 2003. In spite of the economic upturn, standard rail carload shipments during this period did not reflect the economic good news of 2003. However, intermodal movements by rail increased by 6.9 percent during this period. This trend toward intermodal moves could prove to be very beneficial to the railroad industry and allow them to be more competitive with the motor carriers.

Constraints

Railroads are constrained by fixed rights-of-way and therefore provide differing degrees of service completeness. For example, if both the shipper and receiver possess rail sidings, then door-to-door service can be provided. However, if no sidings are available, the movement of goods must be completed by some other mode.

The railroad system, although composed of individual companies, provides a truly nationwide network of service. Each railroad serves a specific geographic region, and freight and equipment are exchanged at interchange points. For example, a shipment between Philadelphia, Pennsylvania, and Portland, Oregon, might be handled by two or three railroads, depending on the route chosen. The through service is unique, but multiple handlings can create rate-division problems and delays in delivery.

Although on-time delivery performance and the frequency of service had deteriorated in the past, improvements have been made in recent years. The current position of the industry has been restored to competitive levels on selected movements (particularly over long distances). Railroads dominate the market for hauling 30,000 pounds or more over distances exceeding 300 miles. The industry hopes to expand its service to certain short-haul markets and selected lanes for manufactured products. Reliability and transit time, along with equipment availability, have improved to make railroads competitive in these markets.

Strengths

The large carrying capacity of rail freight cars and the economies of scale in freight train operations enable the railroads to handle large-volume movements of low-value commodities over long distances. Motor carriers, on the other hand, are constrained by volume and weight to the smaller truckload (TL) and less-than-truckload (LTL) markets. Furthermore, although pipelines compete directly with the railroads, they are restricted largely to the movements of liquid and gas (and then only in one direction).

This kind of carload capacity, along with a variety of car types, permits the railroads to handle almost any type of commodity. For the most part, the industry is not constrained to weight and volume restrictions, and customer service is available throughout the United States. In addition, railroads are able to use a variety of car types to provide a flexible service because the rolling stock consists of boxcars, tankers, gondolas, hoppers, covered hoppers, flatcars, and other special types of cars (see Table 6-5).

Another important service is that the **liability** for loss and damage is usually assumed by the railroads. Railroads, however, have had a comparatively high percentage of goods damaged in transit. In 2012 the total pay-out of freight claims for U.S. and Canadian railroads increased slightly to $79 million from $78 million in 2011.[15] Such damage occurs because rail freight often goes through a rough trip due to vibrations and shocks from steel wheels riding on steel rails. In addition, the incidence of loss is usually higher than on other modes because of the high degree of multiple handlings. Excessive loss and damage claims have tended to erode shipper confidence in the railroad's ability to provide adequate service.

TABLE 6-5 Types and Number of Freight Cars in Service in 2012

TYPE	TOTAL	CLASS 1 RAILROAD	OTHER RAILROADS	CAR COMPANIES AND SHIPPERS
Boxcars	90,739	51,696	29,818	9,225
Plain Box	11,377	1,072	3,263	7,042
Equipped Box	79,362	50,624	26,555	2,183
Covered Hoppers	418,126	94,008	15,962	308,156
Flatcars	160,765	83,857	20,817	56,091
Refrigerator Cars	14,252	10,784	731	2,737
Gondolas	200,578	89,124	15,720	95,734
Hoppers	141,768	50,039	8,913	82,816
Tank Cars	286,695	928	8	285,759
Others	3,262	205	773	2,284
Total	1,316,185	380,641	92,742	842,802

Source: Association of American Railroads, *Railroad Facts*, Washington, DC, 2013, p. 52.

To regain traffic lost to other modes and gain new traffic share, the railroads have placed an increasing amount of attention on equipment and technology. For example, to decrease damage to freight, improved suspension systems and end-of-car cushioning devices have been applied to freight cars assigned to the movement of shock-sensitive products.

Also, the AAR has developed a quality certification program (M-1003) to ensure freight car quality and technical specifications. Finally, equipping cars with instrumentation packages to measure forces that might cause damage reduces the damage potential. One area that has received much attention has been the intermodal area, namely, trailer-on-flatcar (**TOFC**) and container-on-flatcar (**COFC**) service. Of special importance in the COFC market is the use of double-stacks, which significantly improve railroad productivity. The railroads realized the necessity of improving the TOFC and COFC services to compete effectively with motor carriers. The developments include terminal facilities for loading and unloading, as well as changes in the railcars, trailers, and containers. However, the changes have not stopped here. The railroads have invested a significant amount of money recently in improving right-of-way and structures to enhance service by preventing delays.

Microprocessors have found use in the railroad industry, particularly in communications and signaling. Computer chips are also being used in vital safety-related circuits. Fiber optics are used to improve communications, which will in turn improve service and revenues. The railroad industry hopes that these service-related improvements will increase its traffic.

Equipment

The **carload** is the basic unit of measurement of freight handling used by the railroads. A carload can vary in size and capacity depending on the type of car being used. Historically, the number of carloadings has declined since the turn of the century;

there was a total of almost 37 million carloads in 1929. In 2012, the total railroad carloads equaled 28.4 million.[16] This decline has occurred primarily because of the introduction of larger cars and the increase in productivity per car type. Absolute tonnage has increased (see Table 6-3).

The increases in average carrying capacity of railroad freight cars over the past 50 years have been dramatic. In 2012 the average carrying capacity per car stood at 102.7 tons, compared to 46.3 tons in 1929.[17] Most of today's new cars have more than twice the capacity of the typical boxcar used 50 years ago. However, the carrying capacity of a new or rebuilt car could easily exceed 100 tons, and the trend of increasing average capacity will continue in the near future. A car with a 100-ton capacity probably represents the most efficient size with the present support facilities. Today's standard car gross vehicle weight is 263,000 pounds, with efforts being made to increase this to 286,000. However, bridge and track structures must be able to handle these weights.

The railroads own and maintain their own rolling stock. The characteristics of these cars have changed considerably to suit customer requirements; for example, the conventional boxcar had been de-emphasized but has seen resurgence in the past few years. Today's car fleet is highly specialized and is designed to meet the needs of the individual shipper. Following is a list of eight generalized car types:

- Boxcar (plain): Standardized roofed freight car with sliding doors on the side used for general commodities
- Boxcar (equipped): Specially modified boxcar used for specialized merchandise, such as automobile parts
- Hopper car: A freight car with the floor sloping to one or more hinged doors used for discharging bulk materials
- Covered hopper: A hopper car with a roof designed to transport bulk commodities that need protection from the elements
- Flatcar: A freight car with no top or sides used primarily for TOFC service machinery and building materials
- Refrigerator car: A freight car to which refrigeration equipment has been added for controlled temperature
- Gondola: A freight car with no top, a flat bottom, and fixed sides used primarily for hauling bulk commodities
- Tank car: Specialized car used for the transport of liquids and gases

The total number and percentage of freight cars in service in 2012 are shown in Table 6-5 and Figure 6-1. The boxcar has been surpassed in use by the covered hopper car, which is followed closely in number by the tank car. In addition, the largest increase in total new cars was in covered hopper cars. The composition of the railroad fleet has shifted from the accommodation of manufactured commodities to the movement of bulk goods. In 2012 almost 80 percent of the total fleet was designed for the transport of bulk and raw materials.

Class I railroads own 28.9 percent of the rolling stock in use, other railroads and private companies hold title to the remainder (see Table 6-5).[18] Car companies and shippers are becoming increasingly more important in the ownership of railroad cars. In 1991 they owned almost all of the specially designed tank cars in use, and in the past several years they have purchased a substantial number of covered hopper cars, more than 30,000.

FIGURE 6-1 Types of Freight Equipment, 2012

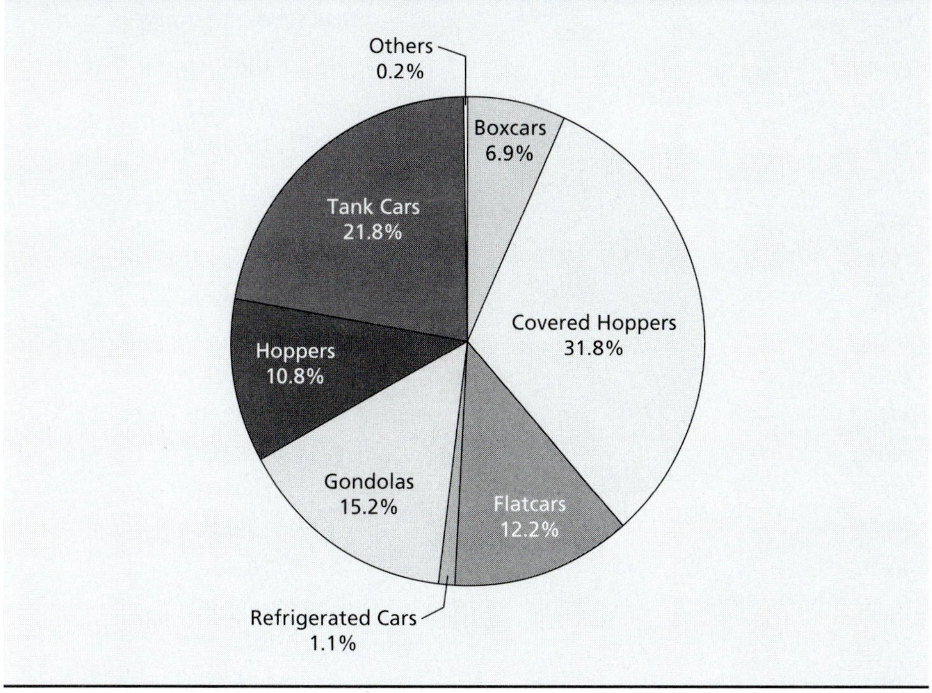

Source: Association of American Railroads, *Railroad Facts*, Washington, DC, 2013, p. 52.

To remain competitive with the other modes of transportation, the railroads have increased their capacity. The average freight train load also has increased; in 2012 more than 3,458 tons per load were carried as compared to 804 tons per load in 1929.[19] This increase in capacity is necessary if more bulk commodities are to be shipped longer distances in the future.

Service Innovations

The railroad cost structure makes it necessary to attract large and regular volumes of traffic to take advantage of scale economies and to operate efficiently. In recent years, rail management has developed or re-emphasized a number of service innovations to increase traffic volume.

The concept of piggyback service was designed by railroad management to increase service levels to intermodal customers. Piggyback traffic, which includes both TOFC and COFC services, accounted for 15.2 percent of total loadings in 1986, occupying a little less than 3 million cars and ranking second behind coal in total rail carloadings. In 2012 more than 12 million trailers and containers were loaded.[20] As can be seen in Table 6-6, intermodal carloadings increased until 2000, when there was a modest decline of 2.7 percent. When discussing piggyback service, consideration must be given to the individual concepts of TOFC and COFC movements.

TOFC service transports highway trailers on railroad flatcars. It combines the line-haul efficiencies of the railroads with the flexibility of local motor carrier pickup and delivery service. On-time deliveries, regularly scheduled departures, and fuel efficiency are the major reasons for the present growth and future potential of TOFC service.

TABLE 6-6 Intermodal Carloadings

YEAR	TRAILER AND CONTAINERS
1970	2,363,200
1975	2,238,117
1980	3,059,402
1985	4,590,952
1990	6,206,782
1995	7,936,172
2000	9,176,890
2001	8,935,444
2002	9,312,360
2003	9,955,605
2004	10,993,662
2005	11,693,512
2006	12,282,221
2007	12,026,631
2008	11,499,978
2009	9,875,967
2010	11,283,151
2011	11,892,418
2012	12,267,416

Source: Association of American Railroads, *Railroad Facts*, Washington, DC, 2013, p. 26.

For example, a 100-car train (which places two trailers on each flatcar) is more economical to run than 200 tractor-trailers over the road. Fuel is saved and railroad economies of scale are realized. Traffic congestion, road damage, and maintenance and repair costs are all reduced because of the reduction of number of tractor-trailers out on the highways.

Table 6-6 shows that the intermodal movement of trailers and containers grew rapidly during the 1980s and 1990s. This growth was stimulated by the advent of double-stack containers used in international trade. Also, the railroads have placed new emphasis on their intermodal business after a number of years of doubting its profitability. In recent years, the railroads have largely segregated their intermodal traffic from regular freight, with most of the intermodal trains operating on a priority schedule.

One result of the new schedules has been more reliable service for shippers, which has led to increased growth in loadings. The railroads have also simplified their billing procedures and made their computers accessible to customers for service innovations.

The growing use of TOFC by motor carrier companies has also contributed to the recent growth. United Parcel Service (UPS) has been a supporter of rail intermodal service for some time and is the largest single customer of some railroads. The LTL carriers began using intermodal service during the 1980s to handle their

FIGURE 6-2 Intermodal Traffic Flows

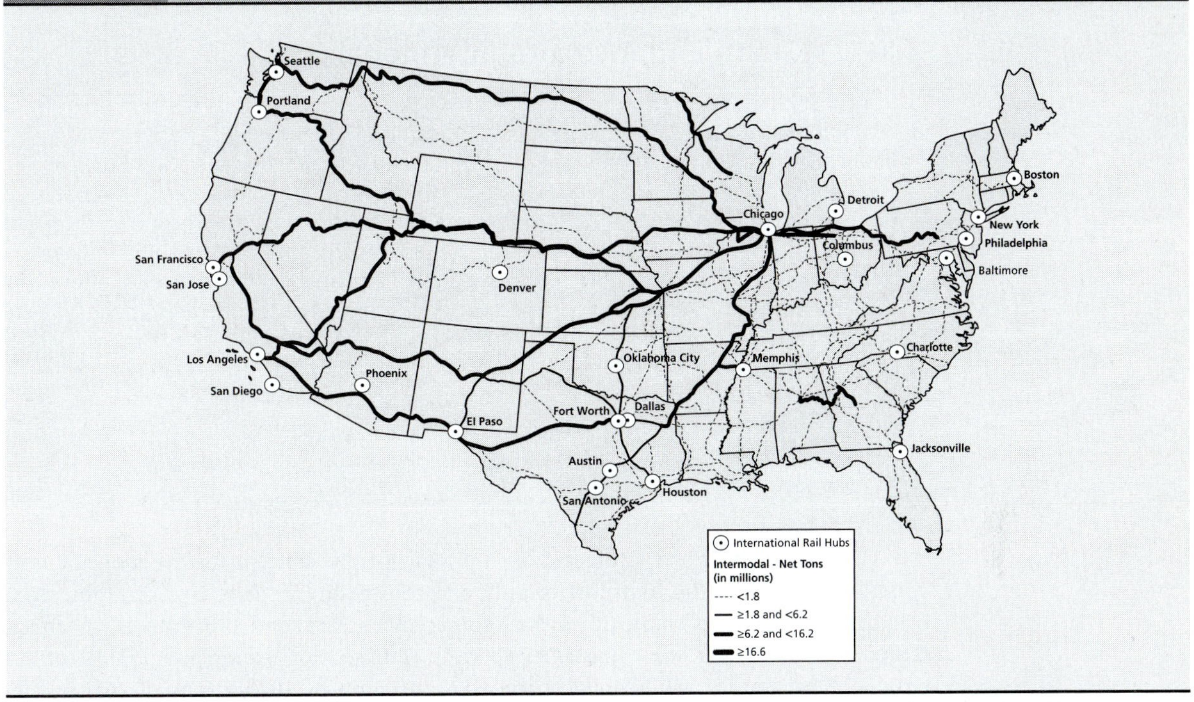

Source: Double Stack Container Systems: Implications for U.S. Railroads and Ports, Washington, DC: U.S. Department of Transportation, 1990.

Note: Line thickness corresponds to intermodal volume.

surges of traffic, and as rail service has become more reliable, they are using the rail service on a continuing basis. New labor agreements allow union motor carriers to substitute rail for over-the-road up to a certain percent of the total traffic. The biggest change came when two of the largest truckload carriers, Schneider National and J. B. Hunt, purchased equipment to use rail intermodal service on an extensive basis. This commitment by these two large carriers has had a significant influence on the growth of rail intermodal service. Figure 6-2 shows the flows of traffic in the United States.

COFC is the form of transportation for shipping containers and is equivalent to domestic TOFC for trailer movements. A container does not have wheels and must therefore be placed on a flatbed trailer for ramp-to-door delivery. The amount of handling is reduced because the container can be loaded and sealed at the origin and shipped directly to the consignee. Economies are realized because putting finished goods in containers means not only lower packaging and warehousing costs but also faster transit times because time and effort are saved in the loading, unloading, and delivery of goods. In addition, the TOFC piggyback plans can apply to COFC shipments with the substitution of the container for the trailer in the movement. Furthermore, land-bridge traffic, which substitutes railroads for ocean vessels for part of the journey, has become more widely used in international commerce because it facilitates the handling of export–import commodities.[21] The double stacking of the containers on traffic to and from West Coast ports has improved the productivity of the rail COFC service dramatically.

ON THE LINE

XPO's Grand Entrance into Intermodal

Non asset-based third-party logistics provider (3PL) XPO Logistics said last month that it has entered into a definitive agreement to acquire Dublin, Ohio-based Pacer International, a freight transportation and logistics services provider and the third largest provider of intermodal services in North America. The total purchase price of the acquisition, which XPO said is expected to close in the second quarter, is $335 million. XPO Chairman and CEO Brad Jacobs told *LM* that there were multiple reasons to bring Pacer into the fold. "The intermodal sector is one of the fastest growing areas of transportation, and Pacer is the third largest provider of intermodal services in North America," said Jacobs. "Pacer is the largest provider of intermodal cross-border services into Mexico, which is growing fast due to near-shoring manufacturing in Mexico, with more than one-third of its business focused on cross-border Mexico operations."

Source: *Logistics Management*, February 2014, p. 1. Reprinted with permission of Peerless Media, LLC.

The **unit train**, which evolved from the rent-a-train concept for the movement of goods, specializes in the transport of only one commodity, usually coal or grain, from origin to destination. Many times the shipper owns cars, and the train is, in effect, rented to the shipper for a particular period of time. For example, a typical utility coal unit train move would involve the transportation of 10,000 tons of coal in 100 hopper or gondola cars, each with a 100-ton capacity. The movement would be directly from the mine to an electric power-generating station with no stops in transit, and loading and unloading would be accomplished while the train was moving. Because of the single commodity nature of the concept and the need to maintain regularly scheduled movements, empty backhauls occur. However, this drawback is offset by the high revenue-producing capabilities of the unit train resulting from the improved overall car utilization.

Rail management has responded by increasing the use of computers and communications to help improve discipline and maintain control over rail operations. Elaborate information and communication systems have been developed so that a railroad's progress, status, and reliability can be monitored on an online basis. Car ordering and billing is simplified, while cars are traced and located, and orders are expedited at a faster rate. Computers are not a panacea, but they do help bring about increased efficiencies without any loss in service quality.

Cost Structure

Fixed Costs

The railroad industry's cost structure in the short run (a period when both plant and capacity remain constant) consists of a large proportion of indirect fixed costs rather than variable costs.[22] This situation exists because the railroads, along with the pipelines, are the only modes that own and maintain their own network and terminals.

In addition, railroads, like other modes, operate their own rolling stock. In the past, it has been estimated by some managers that up to two-thirds of the industry's cost did not vary with volume.[23] Today it is believed that this figure is closer to 30 percent.

The investment in long-lived assets has had a major impact on the cost characteristics of the industry. Cost structures were presented in Chapter 4.

The major cost element borne by the railroad industry, and not found in the cost structure of other modes (excluding pipelines), is the operation, maintenance, and ownership of rights-of-way. **Rights-of-way** describe what a carrier's equipment uses to provide movement. For example, the railroads operate trains on tracks they own and maintain, while the motor carriers use highways. Initially, a large capital investment is required and annual maintenance costs become a substantial drain on earnings. Capital expenditures in 2012 alone amounted to $13.5 billion.[24]

Another major component of the railroad industry's high fixed costs is the extensive investment in private terminal facilities. These terminal facilities include freight yards, where trains are sorted and assembled, and terminal areas and sidings, where shippers and connecting railroads are serviced. Because of the ownership of fixed assets, the railroads as a group are not as responsive as other modes to the volume of traffic carried. Motor and water carriers, as well as the airline industry, are able to shift resources more quickly in response to changes in customer demand because of their use of "free" rights-of-way. Motor carriers, for instance, pay for their costs through user charges, tolls, and various taxes (such as fuel taxes). These charges are related and vary directly with the volume handled, thereby creating a variable rather than a fixed cost for the user. Circumstances place the railroads at a disadvantage.

The investment for equipment in rail transport, principally for locomotives and various types of rolling stock, has been enormous. In 2012 more than $9.1 billion was spent on equipment.[25] The Class I railroads operated 24,707 locomotives and some 473,383 freight cars in 2012.[26] Other railroads, car companies, and shippers owned or leased about 842,802 cars.[27] The costs associated with equipment are both fixed and variable depending on which costs are used and what time period is being considered.

It is apparent that the railroads have a high proportion of expenses that are fixed and constant in the short run. However, they also have costs that vary substantially with volume.

Semivariable Costs

Semivariable costs, which include maintenance of rights-of-way, structures, and equipment, have accounted for more than 40 percent of railroad outlays in recent years and have amounted to more than $10 billion per year. These figures, however, are deceptive because some railroads that were in poor financial health in the 1960s and 1970s had allowed their physical plants and equipment to deteriorate at alarming rates. The Federal Railroad Administration estimated that the industry has deferred more than $4 billion in maintenance expenses in some years.[28] Railway management in financially weak railroads found it necessary to forego maintenance to pay expenses, such as increased fuel and labor. Recently, maintenance schedules have been implemented on a regular basis so that service would not further deteriorate, and additional business would not be lost.

Variable Costs

Variable costs are one of the immediate concerns of railroad management, accounting for a large proportion of every revenue dollar spent by the railways. Labor cost is the largest single element of variable costs for railroads. Fuel and power costs are the next largest group of variable costs. Together these two categories account for a major portion of variable costs.

Labor In 2012 the cost of labor was $16.2 billion or $0.231 cents of every revenue dollar.[29] The average hourly gross earning for all employees was $31.83, with an average annual earning of $78,085. Train and engine employees received an annual earning of $80,553, whereas maintenance workers received about $71,568. Together, these groups accounted for 62.5 percent of all the wages paid by the railroads.[30]

Railroad labor is represented by many different unions as opposed to the motor carrier industry, the vast majority of whose unionized employees are members of one union, the Teamsters. There are three major classifications of labor unions: operating, nonoperating craft, and nonoperating industrial. Each represents a different category of employee. The large number of unions has created difficulties for railroad management because each union guards its rights. Recently, some unions have merged and have shown much more flexibility in allowing innovation.

Railroad management believes that some of the work rules for the operating unions are either out of date or inefficient. The railroad industry has been reducing the size of the standard train crew wherever possible. Many positions, such as that of fireman, a carryover from the steam engine era, are no longer needed. Changes in how crews are paid have allowed railroads to gain operating efficiencies. Furthermore, "seniority districts," or the establishment of artificial boundaries beyond which an employee is not authorized to work, is a barrier to operating efficiency. Progress has been made with these issues, but they have not been completely resolved.

The railroad industry has been addressing work rules and staffing requirements in a very aggressive manner in the past several years. Several railroads have negotiated new crew agreements that have reduced the number of personnel required for trains. Conrail started a program in 1981 to buy off unnecessary brakemen and firemen; this program eliminated more than 1,900 positions, yielding a savings of $85 million.[31]

Starting in 1982, rail management took steps to remove cabooses from freight trains. It has been estimated that the elimination of cabooses saved as much as $400 million per year. The rail unions agreed that railroads could drop cabooses by local agreement, if possible, and by arbitration, if necessary.[32] Two-person crews are now the standard, with both riding on the locomotive.

Railroad managers feel that continuing changes in modifying or eliminating work rules for rail employees must be implemented in the near future if the industry is to survive in its present form. Mutual trust and cooperation should replace impediments between labor and management that restrict productivity gains, labor-savings methods, and technological advances. Progress in other industries has indicated the productivity gains that are possible.

Fuel Fuel costs make up the second largest percentage of the revenue dollar. Fortunately, railroads have very efficient propulsion units, and productivity and fuel efficiency have increased dramatically since 1929. In the past 50 years, the railroads have more than doubled the revenue of ton-miles while reducing the locomotive units to less than one-half the 1929 level. Thus, the industry has been able to partially offset the increase in fuel costs by making locomotives more efficient. In 2012, $11.5 billion was spent on fuel, showing an increase of $8.2 billion from the 1980s level of $3.3 billion. This is a result of using more fuel-efficient engines and other train devices, such as wind-resistance designs.[33] The railroad's efficiency in the use of fuel is an important factor in making intermodal movements more attractive for motor carriers.

Economies of Scale

As previously indicated, railroads have a high level of fixed costs as contrasted with variable costs. Fixed costs, such as property taxes, are incurred regardless of traffic volume. Variable costs, on the other hand, vary or change with the volume of traffic moved; that is, they rise with increases and fall with decreases in traffic levels.

The development of any railroad requires a very large capital investment because of the cost incurred in buying land, laying tracks, building bridges, providing terminals, and providing right-of-way facilities. In addition, equipment investment is significant. Maintenance of right-of-way structures also results in fixed costs because it is usually the weather rather than use that necessitates such expenditures. The same is also true to some extent of equipment maintenance because the equipment spends so much time in freight yards and on sidings.

All costs are generally regarded as being variable in the long run because, as traffic increases, capacity is reached and new investment is needed in plants and equipment. However, because railroads are so large and facilities are durable, the short run can be a long period of time.

The focus here is primarily on the short run. Consequently, special note should be made of the impact of the high level of fixed costs in the railroad industry. When fixed costs are present, a business will operate under conditions of increasing returns until capacity is reached. In other words, an increase in output (traffic) will not be accompanied by a proportionate increase in total costs because only the variable costs will increase. This will mean a decline in the per-unit costs because the fixed costs will be spread out over an increased number of units with subsequent unit-cost declines.

Consider several examples that illustrate the impact of fixed costs and economies of scale. Suppose that C. B. N. Railroad carries 200 million tons of freight at an average charge of $0.035 per ton. It has fixed costs of $3.5 million and variable costs of $2.5 million:

Fixed Costs	$3.5 million
Variable Costs	+$2.5 million
Total Costs	*$6.0 million*
Revenue	$7.0 million
Profit	$1.0 million
Cost Per Ton	*$0.03*

Assume a 20-percent increase in traffic at the same average charge of $.035 per ton and no need to increase plant size:

Fixed Costs	$3.5 million
Variable Costs	$3.0 million
Total Costs	*$6.5 million*
Revenue	$8.4 million
Profit	$1.9 million
Cost Per Ton	*$0.0271*

It is obvious from the above example that, if average revenue stays the same, the economies of scale not only lower costs per unit but also increase profit.

Financial Plight

As noted previously, the railroad industry once enjoyed a virtual monopoly on the efficient and dependable transportation of passengers and freight. Railroads played a very important role in achieving various national objectives during the 19th century. Because of this, the government promoted the growth of the industry until a distinct change in public attitudes toward railroads became apparent.

The establishment in 1887 of the Interstate Commerce Commission (ICC), which was created to regulate maximum rates and to prevent discrimination to protect the rail shipper, marked the beginning of this change. In later years, the ICC's objective was to promote competition between modes of transportation while ensuring the financial health of the regulated carriers. However, this objective was never completely accomplished. Competition tended to be restrained under the regulatory environment prior to 1975.

Over the decades, competition from other modes of transportation increased dramatically. By the 1950s, more people selected buses and planes for transportation, rather than using rail transportation. The rail industry's share of the intercity freight market also declined to less than 50 percent during this time. Although competition from other modes became progressively more intense, the railroads were subject to strict regulations that frequently treated them as if they were still the dominant form of freight transportation. Government funds were used to provide rail competitors with their rights-of-way without fully charging them the cost of constructing or maintaining them as with the rail industry. Between 1946 and 1975, the federal government spent more than $81 billion on highways, $24 billion on airports and supervision of airways, $10 billion on inland waterways, and only $1.3 billion on railroads.[34]

The financial position of the railroads grew increasingly worse after World War II. During the 1970s, the railroad industry's return on investment remained near 2 percent and never exceeded 3 percent. The railroads were plagued by decreasing market shares, poor future prospects, and high debt ratios. At least 20 percent of the industry was bankrupt by 1970. These poor conditions were evident in delayed or poor maintenance, increasing claims for damages, and accidents that cost the industry many of its much-needed customers. The railroads' share of intercity freight revenues had fallen from 72 percent in 1929 to less than 18 percent in the mid-1970s.[35]

It became obvious that the railroad industry could not continue to survive under these conditions and that the main obstacle that needed to be cleared from the railroads' path to survival was probably excessive regulation that restricted their ability to compete. Poor earnings made it difficult for the railroads to earn or borrow sufficient funds to make improvements in track and rail facilities.[36]

Legislation Reform

The Rail Passenger Act of 1970 created the government-sponsored National Railroad Passenger Corporation (**Amtrak**), which relieved the railroads of their requirement to provide passenger operations that were not profitable but considered necessary for fulfillment of public benefit needs.[37]

The **Regional Rail Reorganization Act of 1973 (3R Act)** attempted to maintain rail freight service in the Northeast by creating the Consolidated Rail Corporation

(Conrail), which was formed from six bankrupt northeastern railroads. The act also created the United States Railroad Association (USRA) as the government agency responsible for planning and financing the restructuring. By 1980, the federal government had granted Conrail more than $3.3 billion in federal subsidies to cover its operating expenses.[38]

Conrail proved to be very successful and was "spun off" by the sale of its stock to the investing public in 1987. Conrail's management was able to rationalize the excess track while preserving and improving service. In 1996, CSX and Conrail announced their intention to merge. This raised opposition from the Norfolk Southern (NS). This triggered a bidding war for Conrail stock between CSX and NS. Ultimately, the bidding war was settled by agreement between CSX and NS to split Conrail.

The **Railroad Revitalization and Regulatory Reform Act of 1976 (4R Act)** had two primary purposes. The first was to provide authorization for federal funding for the startup of Conrail. The second was to provide greater commercial freedom to all railroads in the United States by reducing some aspects of economic regulation that had constrained railroads to compete for freight traffic as effectively as they otherwise could have.[39]

The **Staggers Rail Act of 1980** made major reductions in the comprehensive framework of economic regulation of the railroad industry that had evolved over the years since 1887. Among the more significant changes was legalization of contract rate-making. This enabled rail carriers to attract business with the use of confidential contracts tailored to conditions that were specific to shippers' needs. This gave railroads freedom identical to what had prevailed for many years in the motor carrier and water industries.[40] The freedoms provided by the Staggers Act aided in driving improvement of the railroad industry's financial performance and condition during the decades that have followed its enactment.

The **ICC Termination Act of 1995** eliminated the ICC and transferred economic rail regulation to the Surface Transportation Board (STB), which is part of the DOT. Some critics contend that the STB has been too lenient in administering the remaining modest controls over railroad rates and services it is empowered to administer. Shippers of some types of commodities contend that railroad competition for the movement of their products is insufficient to prevent them from obtaining rates and service levels that would be attainable if railroad market power were constrained by more regulation by the STB.

Improved Service to Customers

As shown in Table 6-6, intermodal traffic has expanded by 319 percent during the period of 1980 to 2012, while productivity measures also have shown an increase.[41] An important indicator of improved performance is the railroads' continued good safety record. Train accidents per million train-miles declined by over 79 percent from 1980 to 2012.[42] Consequently, injuries and fatalities also have fallen.

Many signs indicate that deregulation has brought improvement to the railroads (improved financial status) and to their customers. The industry has changed dramatically in many ways, including providing more tailored service and equipment and negotiating contract rates for volume movements. The railroads have worked hard to improve their operating performance times and reliability. Table 6-7 provides a comprehensive summary of railroad characteristics for review.

TABLE 6-7 Summary: Railroad Industry Characteristics

• General service characteristics	• In competition with motor carriers; shippers of bulk products
• Investments/capital outlays	• High investments/equipment, track
• Cost structure	• High fixed costs, low variable costs
• Ease of entry	• Low
• Market structure	• Oligopoly/monopoly
• Ways in which they compete	• Price (intramodal) and service (intermodal)
• Types of commodities	• Low-value, high-volume bulk commodities
• Number of carriers	• Small number of large carriers
• Markets in which they compete	• High-value chemicals, long-haul but large commodities

Current Issues

Alcohol and Drug Abuse

Alcohol and drug abuse has affected almost every workplace in the United States. Many industries, including the rail industry, are taking a close look at the problem and at possible methods of dealing with it.

The problem of substance abuse can be brought on by the very nature of railroad work. Long hours, low supervision, and nights away from home can lead to loneliness and boredom, which can then lead to substance abuse. Because of this situation, the railroads have been dealing with the problem of substance abuse for a century. Rule G, which was established in 1897, prohibits the use of narcotics and alcohol on company property. Rail employees violating this rule could be subject to dismissal; however, the severity of this punishment led to the silence of many rail workers who did not want to jeopardize the jobs of their coworkers.

To deal with this problem, the railroad industry has attempted to identify and help employees with substance abuse problems. The industry has established **employee assistance programs** (EAPs) that enable these troubled employees to be rehabilitated.

Employees can voluntarily refer themselves to EAPs before a supervisor detects the problem and disciplinary actions become necessary. However, a Rule G violation—substance abuse while on the job—usually necessitates removal of the employee from the workplace to ensure his or her safety and the safety of coworkers. Employees who are removed can still use EAPs for rehabilitation and can apply for reinstatement after they have overcome their problem.

Railroad EAPs have proven to be very effective. A recent Federal Railroad Administration report found that the rate of successful rehabilitation has risen by 70 percent. The success of these programs depends largely on support from rail workers as well as all levels of management.[43]

Energy

The energy shortages of the 1970s made the United States increasingly aware of the need to conserve natural resources. The U.S. government, for example, decided to reduce the quantity of fuels and petroleum products that are imported into the country. Americans want to preserve and, wherever possible, clean up the environment. The railroads today

TABLE 6-8 Relative Fuel Efficiency of Transportation Modes

	TRILLION BTU*		PERCENT OF TOTAL BASED ON BTU'S	
MODE	2011	2012	2011	2012
Trucks	5800.5	5775.5	21.8%	22.0%
Air	2157.2	2091.9	8.1%	8.0%
Water	1392.3	1187.4	5.2%	4.5%
Pipe	953.4	997.0	3.6%	3.8%
Rail	609.1	597.8	2.3%	2.3%

*BTU = British thermal units.

Source: *Transportation Energy Data Book*, Oak Ridge National Laboratories, Department of Energy, Washington, DC, 2014, Table 2.6.

are in a favorable position, especially when compared to motor carriers, because they are efficient energy consumers. For instance, a train locomotive uses less fuel than a tractor–trailer in pulling the same amount of weight. Revenue ton-miles per gallon of fuel consumed by the railroads increased by almost 103 percent from 1980 to 2012.[44] Table 6-8 shows the relative energy consumption for the various modes of transportation.

A study by the U.S. DOT concluded that railroads are more energy-efficient than motor carriers, even when measured in terms of consumption per ton-mile.[45] In addition to being more energy-efficient, railroads cause less damage to the environment than do trucks. In 1980, railroad emissions (0.9 grams per net ton-mile) were 75 percent less than truck emissions.[46] Railroads, in comparison to trucks—a major competitor—are able to move large amounts of freight with less energy and less harm to the environment.

The railroads economically shipped 787.6 million tons of energy-yielding products in 2012; 91.6 percent of these loadings were coal movements.[47] Because coal, which can be converted into electricity, is an abundant substitute for oil, electric utility companies can convert their present processes to coal whenever economically possible. Because the railroads already transport approximately three-quarters of all the coal moved, they would be able to increase service to the utilities and capture more of the market by using high-volume unit coal trains.

Hence, the railroads can be an important factor in the development of the nation's energy policy.

Technology

To become more efficient and consequently more competitive, the railroad industry is becoming a high-tech industry. Computers are playing a large role in every mode of transportation, and the railroads are no exception. A line of "smart" locomotives is being equipped with onboard computers that can identify mechanical problems, and the legendary red caboose was phased out by a small device weighing 30 pounds that attaches to the last car of the train. This electric device transmits important information to engineers and dispatchers alike, including information about the braking system. Other applications of computer technology are as follows:

- Advanced Train Control Systems (ATCS): A joint venture between the United States and Canada that will use computers to efficiently track the flow of trains through the entire rail system

- Rail yard control: Computer control of freight yards that is used to sort and classify as many as 2,500 railcars a day
- Communications and signaling: Provides quick and efficient communications between dispatchers, yard workers, field workers, and train crews
- Customer service: By calling a toll-free number, customers can receive information on the status of their shipments, correct billing errors, and plan new service schedules
- Radio Frequency Identification (RFID): Tags to track equipment and shipments and improve visibility

The role of high technology and computers will continue to expand and increase the ability of the railroads to provide progressively higher levels of customer service.[48]

TRANSPORTATION **TECHNOLOGY**

GAO Report Calls on Congress to Extend Positive Train Control Deadline

With most U.S.-based railroads signaling that they will miss the 2015 deadline for installing Positive Train Control (PTC), the Government Accountability Office (GAO) said in a report that it's asking that Congress consider amending the Railroad Safety Improvement ACT (RSIA) and grant the Federal Railroad Administration (FRA) the authority to extend the deadline for certain rail lines on a case-by-case basis.

The GAO added that Congress should grant provisional certification of PTC systems and approve the use of alternative safety technologies in lieu of PTC to improve safety.

The objective of PTC systems is to prevent train-to-train collisions, overspeed derailments, and incursions into roadway work limits. PTC sends and receives a continuous stream of data transmitted by wireless signals about the location, speed, and direction of trains, according to the FRA.

PTC systems, added the FRA, utilize advanced technologies including digital radio links, global positioning systems and wayside computer control systems that aid dispatchers and train crews in safely managing train movements.

A mandate for PTC systems was included in House and Senate legislation—H.R. 2095/S. 1889, The Rail Safety and Improvement Act of 2008. The legislation was passed shortly after a September 12, 2008, collision between a freight train and a commuter train in Los Angeles. It calls for passenger and certain hazmat rail lines to take effect by 2015 and authorizes $250 million in Federal grants.

The GAO report echoes the Association of American railroads (AAR) and FRA's statements indicating they will miss the December 31, 2015, implementation deadline, coupled with most railroads saying they will as well.

Of the four major freight railroads cited in the report, GAO said just one—BNSF Railway—expects to meet the deadline, with the other three indicating that they expect to meet it by 2017 or later. The report said BNSF is on schedule to meet the deadline because of its "extensive experience working on PTC prior to RSIA, its iterative build and test approach, and the concurrent development of its PTC dispatching and back office systems."

As per the RSIA requirements, railroads are developing more than 20 major components that are in various stages of development, integrating them and installing them across the rail network, according to GAO. The AAR stated that, by the end of 2012, railroads had invested $2.8 billion on PTC and will ultimately spend $8 billion on it.

"The railroads have done everything possible to make PTC happen as quickly as possible," said Bill Rennicke, director of Oliver Wyman, a management consultancy. "The problem is that it's a hugely complex technology. In the RSIA, Congress required interoperability for all locomotives, meaning that if UP is operating on a CSX line, the traffic information needs to be built into a common technology that feeds that UP locomotive pulling trains across CSX territory with information on that train's characteristics—and that technology does not exist."

Another reason Congress should extend the deadline, said Rennicke, is that PTC is essentially an untested system, noting that PTC systems in Europe were tested for 10 years before going live.

What's more, Rennicke said that the current deadline is so tight that it does not allow for a test period, meaning that 100 percent operation is needed from the start with no system failures, which he described as unlikely.

"The railroad industry and ultimately shippers will have to pay for all of this in the form of hundreds of millions or more if Congress does not come up with a more reasonable schedule," Rennicke added.

Source: Jeff Berman, *Logistics Management*, October 2013, pp. 15–16.

Future Role of Smaller Railroads

As noted, the deregulation of the railroad industry in 1980 led to a number of important changes. The consolidation among so-called Class I railroads has been noted in this chapter. The obvious outcome was a reduction in the number of carriers in this category, but interestingly, it led to an increase in the number of regional and small rail carriers. These small and regional rail carriers typically took over part of the infrastructure abandoned by the large railroads that spun off parts of their system that had low traffic levels and/or were deemed not to be needed for market success.

The small and regional carriers often have to operate at a cost disadvantage compared to the large rail system carriers who have the advantage economies of scale. However, the smaller rail companies have some advantages given that they are more flexible and adaptable in meeting the needs of their customers (shippers). They are usually not unionized, which also helps to make them more flexible. Another possible advantage is local ownership of the rail companies and the related willingness to accept lower returns and/or pay closer attention to customer needs to promote regional economic development.

It should also be noted that some local and state governments have provided financial assistance, primarily for infrastructure improvements, for the formation of short lines that have come into being in recent years. This community support is usually based upon a need to continue the rail service for the economic benefit of existing and potential new businesses. Although motor carrier transportation has often filled the need of smaller communities for transportation service, rail service may be viewed by some communities as a necessary ingredient for the economic viability of the area. Consequently, many communities have had the advantage of continuing rail service that would not have been possible otherwise.

The large Class I railroads have been frequent targets for criticism about the service they provide to their customers. The smaller lines are usually viewed in a more favorable light because of their responsiveness at the local level. However, the small and regional rail carriers are usually more vulnerable if a large shipper decides to close its operations. The future role of some of those carriers is somewhat uncertain because of these factors.

Customer Service

As suggested in this chapter, the large Class I railroads are perceived by some shippers as not being customer focused. This criticism has grown in intercity transport during the 1990s as mergers continued to occur. The new, larger companies appeared insensitive to shipper needs and concerns about equipment and service. Some of the service and equipment issues are attributable to the challenges inherent in combining relatively large organizations with unique systems and procedures, and problems always occur in spite of serious up-front planning.

The extent to which those equipment and service problems have persisted during the last several years is indicative of the legitimacy of shipper complaints. There are differences among the "majors" or Class I railroads in terms of their customer service focus, but unfortunately some shippers are inclined to lump them altogether as being unsatisfactory. Consequently, this is a major issue for railroads, and improvements need to be made to increase rail market shares of freight traffic.

Drayage for Intermodal Service

As indicated previously in this chapter, one of the constraints on rail service is the fixed nature of the rail routes and the high cost of adding rail segments to provide direct service. Consequently, the beginning and/or the end of a rail movement may depend upon motor carrier service. This is, obviously, especially true for intermodal service using trailers or containers. The pickup and delivery of trailers and containers in conjunction with a line-haul rail movement is usually referred to as *local drayage*.

When the railroads are carrying the trailers or containers of a motor carrier as a substitute for the motor carrier providing the line-haul service, local drayage is not an issue because the motor carrier will provide these links. However, when the railroad is the land carrier, it will have to arrange for local drayage for pickup and delivery. Motor carriers that are willing and able to provide this service for the railroads are becoming scarce and charging relatively high rates for the service. In some instances, the pickup and delivery time adds significantly to the total transit time. This is another area that needs attention to improve rail service.

SUMMARY

- The railroads played a significant role in the economic and social development of the United States for about 100 years (1850–1950) and continue to be the leading mode of transportation in terms of intercity ton-miles, but they no longer dominate the freight market.
- The railroad segment of the transportation industry is led by a decreasing number of large Class I carriers, but the number of small Class III carriers has been increasing in number since the deregulation of railroads in 1980.
- Intermodal competition for railroads has increased dramatically since World War II, but the level of intramodal competition has decreased as the number of Class I railroads has decreased. The increased intermodal competition has led to more rate competition.
- Mergers have been occurring among railroads for many years, but the pace has accelerated during the past 30 years, leading to rapid decrease in the number of Class I railroads.
- In recent years, the railroads have become more specialized in terms of the traffic they carry, with the emphasis being on low-value, high-density bulk products; however, there is some evidence of a resurgence of selected manufactured products such as transportation equipment.
- In recent years, railroads have been emphasizing new technologies and specialized equipment to improve their service performance and satisfy customers.
- Intermodal service (TOFC/COFC) has received renewed interest since 1980, and there has been a dramatic growth in the movement of such traffic by railroads.
- Long-distance truckload carriers and other motor carrier companies such as UPS have also begun to use rail intermodal service.
- The railroads have a high proportion of fixed costs because they provide their own right-of-way and terminal facilities. Because the large railroads are multistate operators, the amount of fixed expenditures is significant.
- The cost of labor is the single most important component of variable costs for railroads, but the railroad industry has been striving to reduce labor costs on a relative basis by eliminating work rules that were a carryover from another era.
- The high level of fixed costs helps give rise to economies of scale in the railroad industry, which can have a dramatic impact upon profits when the volume of traffic increases.
- The financial plight of the railroads has improved since deregulation in 1980 as railroads have been able to respond more quickly and aggressively to market pressures from other modes, particularly motor carriers.
- A number of important issues are facing railroads at present, including substance abuse, energy, technology, small railroads, and local drayage.

STUDY QUESTIONS

1. Railroads no longer dominate the freight transportation market, but they still lead the market in terms of freight ton-miles. What factors contribute to their leadership in this area? Why is their share of the total expenditures for freight movement so small if they lead in freight ton-miles?
2. Since the passage of the Staggers Rail Act of 1980, there has been an increase in the number of small railroads (Class III). Why has this number increased while the number of Class I railroads has decreased?

3. Explain the difference between intramodal and intermodal competition in the railroad industry. Which form of competition is most beneficial to shippers? Why?
4. One of the significant factors in rail development has been the number of mergers that have occurred, but there have been different types of mergers that have occurred over time. Discuss the major types of mergers and explain why they occurred. Will mergers continue to occur in the rail industry? Why or why not?
5. What factors have contributed to the decline in the volume of higher-value freight by the railroads? What changes, if any, could the railroads make to attract back more higher-value freight from motor carriers?
6. Railroads have abandoned a significant number of miles of track (over 260,000 miles) since 1916. Why has this trend developed? Will it continue into the future? Why or why not?
7. The railroad industry has developed a number of new types of equipment to replace the standard boxcar. What is the rationale supporting the diversification of equipment?
8. The railroad industry's cost structure is different than that of the motor carrier industry. What factors contribute to this difference? What impact do these differences have for the railroads in terms of pricing, competitiveness, and investment?
9. Discuss the major current issues facing the railroad industry. Select one of these major issues and present appropriate recommendations for resolving the issue.
10. What factors have contributed to the success of intermodal rail service? What barriers exist to future expansion?

NOTES

1. Association of American Railroads, *Railroad Facts*, Washington, DC, 2013, p. 32.
2. Ibid., p. 18.
3. *25th Annual State of Logistics Report*, Council of Supply Chain Management Professionals, 2014.
4. Association of American Railroads, *Railroad Facts*, p. 56.
5. Ibid., p. 44.
6. Ibid., p. 32.
7. Ibid., p. 28.
8. U.S. Department of Commerce, Bureau of the Census, *Historical Statistics of the United States: Colonial Times to 1975*, Washington, DC: U.S. Government Printing Office, 1960, p. 429.
9. Association of American Railroads, *Railroad Facts*, p. 45.
10. Task Force on Railroad Productivity, *Improving Railroad Productivity*, p. 161. Presented to the National Commission of Productivity, November 1973.
11. The commodity groups included here are metals and metal products; food and kindred products; stone, clay, and glass products; and grainmill products.
12. Association of American Railroads, *Railroad Facts*, p. 29.
13. Ibid., p. 25.
14. Ibid., p. 25.
15. Ibid., p. 62.
16. Ibid., p. 24.

17. Ibid., p. 53.
18. Ibid., p. 52.
19. Ibid., p. 37.
20. Ibid., p. 26.
21. Association of American Railroads, press release, Washington, DC, 1979, p. 342.
22. Fixed costs remain the same over a period of time or a range of output (such as labor costs). Semi-variable costs contain some fixed variable elements (such as setup costs on a production line).
23. R. J. Sampson and M. I. Farris, *Domestic Transportation: Practice, Theory, and Policy*, 4th ed., Boston: Houghton Mifflin, 1979, p. 59.
24. Association of American Railroads, *Railroad Facts*, p. 44.
25. Ibid., p. 15.
26. Ibid., pp. 49, 51.
27. Ibid., p. 51.
28. U.S. Department of Transportation, *A Prospectus for Change in the Freight Railroad Industry*, Washington, DC: U.S. Government Printing Office, 1978, p. 65.
29. Association of American Railroads, *Railroad Facts*, p. 11.
30. Ibid., pp. 56, 57.
31. Frank Wilner, *Railroads and the Marketplace*, Washington, DC: Association of American Railroads, 1988, p. 7.
32. Ibid., p. 2.
33. Association of American Railroads, *Railroad Facts*, p. 61.
34. Wilner, *Railroads and the Marketplace*, p. 7.
35. Ibid., p. 9.
36. Ibid., pp. 8–12.
37. Ibid., p. 2.
38. Consolidated Rail Corporation, *Summary of Business Plan*, Philadelphia: Consolidated Rail Corporation, 1979, p. 5.
39. Wilner, *Railroads and the Marketplace*, p. 15.
40. Ibid.
41. Association of American Railroads, *Railroad Facts*, p. 26.
42. Ibid., p. 64.
43. Association of American Railroads, *What Are the Railroads Doing About Drug Abuse?* Washington, DC, 1986, pp. 1–4.
44. Association of American Railroads, *Railroad Facts*, p. 40.
45. Wilner, *Railroads and the Marketplace*, p. 15.
46. Ibid.
47. Association of American Railroads, *Railroad Facts*, p. 29.
48. Association of American Railroads, *High Technology Rides the Rails*, Washington, DC, 1988, pp. 1–3.

CASE 6-1

CBN Railway Company

CEO John Spychalski is concerned about a problem that has existed at CBN railroad for almost 20 years now. The continuous problem has been that the locomotives used by the company are not very reliable. Even with prior decisions to resolve the problem, there still has not been a change in the reliability of these locomotives. Between 2013 and 2014, 155 new locomotives were purchased and one of CBN's repair shops was renovated. The renovated shop has been very inefficient. Spychalski estimated that the shop would complete 300 overhauls on a yearly basis, but instead it has only managed to complete an average of 160 overhauls per year.

The company has also been doing a poor job servicing customers (that is, providing equipment). CBN has averaged only 87 to 88 percent equipment availability, compared to other railroads with availability figures greater than 90 percent. Increased business in the rail industry has been a reason for trying to reduce the time used for repairing the locomotives. CBN's mean time between failure rate is low—45 days—compared to other railroads whose mean time between failure rates is higher than 75 days. This factor, Spychalski feels, has contributed to CBN's poor service record.

CBN is considering a new approach to the equipment problem: Spychalski is examining the possibility of leasing 135 locomotives from several sources. The leases would run between 90 days to 5 years. In addition, the equipment sources would maintain the repairs on 469 locomotives currently in CBN's fleet, but CBN's employees would do the actual labor on the locomotives. The lease arrangements, known as "power-by-the-mile" arrangements, call for the manufacturers doing the repair work to charge only for maintenance on the actual number of miles that a particular unit operates. The company expects the agreements to last an average of 15 years. John Thomchick, the executive vice president, estimates that CBN would save about $5 million annually because the company will not have to pay for certain parts and materials. Problems with the locomotives exist throughout CBN's whole system, and delays to customers have been known to last up to five days. Spychalski and Thomchick feel that the leasing arrangement will solve CBN's problems.

CASE QUESTIONS

1. What are potential advantages and disadvantages of entering into these "power-by-the-mile" arrangements?
2. What should be done if the problem with the locomotives continues even with the agreements?
3. Do you think that the decision to lease the locomotives was the best decision for CBN? Explain your answer.

CASE 6-2

Railroad Reregulation?

Freight railroads were first economically regulated in the United States with the passage of the Act to Regulate Commerce of 1887. This legislation was in response to desires by several states to prevent the railroads from employing monopolistic practices. Railroads are considered natural monopolies because of their large fixed costs and natural barriers to entry into the industry. Monopolistic practices usually take the form of excessive prices and poor service to captive shippers. The 1887 Act was designed to prevent these practices and created the Interstate Commerce Commission to monitor railroad pricing and service activities.

In 1980, the Staggers Act was passed in an attempt to give more pricing freedom and market exit/entry freedom to the railroads. Part of the rationale of this Act was to allow railroads to operate in a more market-oriented environment and to take advantage of value-of-service pricing to increase industry profitability. In 1995, the ICC Termination Act was passed to provide even more freedom in pricing, exit/entry, and service to railroads. This Act also abolished the ICC and created the Surface Transportation Board (STB) to monitor railroad competitive practices.

Between 1996 and 2014, the railroads have enjoyed a resurgence in profitability. Their ability to freely price and to be exempt from antitrust laws allowed railroads to manage capacity more efficiently and expand their markets and products. During this time, railroads dramatically increased their volumes of TOFC and COFC business, becoming a significant business partner to the motor carrier industry in the United States.

However, there had been a push by Congress and a group known as Consumers United for Rail Equity (CURE) to pass legislation to once again economically reregulate the railroad industry and reduce the powers of the STB over rail competitive practices. The major argument for this legislation is that the railroads are once again employing monopolistic practices for shippers of bulk commodities such as grain, coal, and chemicals. The assertion is that railroads are charging excessively high prices to shippers of commodities of low value, thus making these commodities less price-competitive in the market. This is coupled with the assertion that many of these bulk shippers are "captive" and don't have access to multiple railroads to ship their products. This initiative has subsided over the last several years since Congress is hesitant to get into economic regulation again.

However, the federal government has stepped up its regulation of railroad safety as a result of the rapid growth of rail movements of Bakken crude oil across the United States and several derailments of trains carrying Bakken crude. The Rail Safety Improvement Act of 2008 required all railroads in the United States to have Positive Train Control (PTC) installed in all of their locomotives by the end of 2015. Only the BNSF will meet this deadline with the other Class I railroads stating their implementation won't be complete until the end of 2017. The Association of American Railroads estimates that this implementation will cost the rail industry $8 billion.

In May of 2014, the Department of Transportation issued an emergency order requiring that railroads notify State Emergency Response Commissions of any train carrying 1 million gallons or more (approximately 35 tank cars or more) through their states. Along with this, the Federal Railroad Commission and the Pipeline and

Hazardous Material Safety Commission have issued orders concerning the specifications of tank cars carrying Bakken crude. While rail safety should be monitored and regulated by the government, the railroads argue that the scope and timeline for implementing these regulations are placing significant investment requirements on them and will require them to pass on these cost increases to shippers in the form of higher prices, which is what CURE was fighting against with their proposal to economically reregulate the railroads.

CASE QUESTIONS

1. Is there a "mid-point" between safety regulation and the cost to the railroads and ultimately, to shippers? Should the railroad industry have input to the nature and cost of safety regulation imposed on them?
2. Does the probable price increases on the movement of Bakken crude justify economically reregulating the railroads? If so, to what extent?

CHAPTER

7

AIRLINES

Learning Objectives

After reading this chapter, you should be able to do the following:

- Appreciate the importance of air transportation in the U.S. economy
- Gain knowledge of the types and number of carriers in the U.S. airline industry
- Understand the level of competition in the U.S. airline industry
- Become aware of the operating and service characteristics of airline transportation
- Be familiar with the different types of equipment used by airlines
- Appreciate the impacts of fuel and labor costs on airlines cost structures
- Understand the concepts of economies of scale and density in the airline industry
- Be aware of current issues facing airlines today

TRANSPORTATION **PROFILE**

Slight Improvement Despite Headwinds

As noted in the *25th Annual State of Logistics Report*, the airfreight industry has been facing chronic overcapacity and deteriorating yields. New details surfacing in similar new research reports mirrors these findings.

Even though the overall airfreight logistics index has improved 4.4 points from June 2013, the June 2014 data contained in the *Stifel Logistics Confidence Index* suggests that the airfreight market still remains fragile, declining 1.9 points to 53.8. The present situation remained the same in May, with Europe to the U.S. the only lane to decline, down 2.0 points to 49.7.

The latest figures from the International Air Transport Association (IATA) for April indicate that while the freight market improved 3.2 percent above previous year levels, demand has not. Traffic levels in April were slightly below those of January and 1.1 percent lower than what was recorded in March.

IATA indicated that European airlines saw demand for air cargo fall by 0.7 percent compared to April 2013, marking a slower start for carriers as they entered second quarter—particularly as GDP growth in the Eurozone was just 0.2 percent in the first quarter.

However, a slightly different and more encouraging story for airfreight seems to be playing out in Asia, where preliminary traffic figures for the month of April showed some growth in international air cargo markets.

According to the Association of Asia Pacific Airlines (AAPA), international air cargo demand in freight ton kilometers (FTK) increased for regional carriers by 4.7 percent in April, on the back of sustained demand for Asian exports. However, freight load factors remained under pressure due to capacity expansion.

With offered freight capacity expanding by 5.3 percent, the international freight load factor averaged 64.3 percent in April, 0.4 percentage points lower than the same month last year.

"International passenger traffic demand continued to grow, with the region's carriers registering a 5.2 percent increase in international passenger numbers during the first four months of the year," says Andrew Herdman, AAPA director general. "This was on the back of an improvement in business and consumer sentiment in most economies worldwide. During the same period, air cargo demand for the region's carriers grew by 4.2 percent, thanks to an improvement in global trade conditions."

Analyst Rosalyn Wilson makes a similar observation in her report, noting that passenger jets are carrying growing volumes of cargo in their bellies, taking market share from cargo freighters.

All cargo airlines carry more than 79 percent of revenue ton-miles of freight and commercial passenger carriers account for the rest. The amount being carried by passenger jets has been increasing especially because there's more room in the bellies of these aircraft with the proliferation of baggage charges. According to Wilson, belly cargo in passenger planes is very profitable, estimated at close to 65 percent, so passenger airlines have been pursuing it more aggressively.

Source: Patrick Burnson, *Logistics Management*, July 2014, pp. 38–39. Reprinted with permission of Peerless Media, LLC.

Introduction

From the first flight, which lasted less than 1 minute, to space shuttles orbiting the earth, air transportation has come a long way in a short period of time. Wilbur and Orville Wright made their first flight in 1903 at Kitty Hawk and sold their invention to the federal government. In 1908 the development of air transportation began with the **U.S. Post Office** examining the feasibility of providing air mail service. Although airplanes were used in World War I, the use of airplanes for mail transport can be considered the beginning of the modern airline industry. Passenger transportation services developed as a by-product of the mail business and began to flourish in selected markets. Since that time, airplanes have become faster, bigger, and relatively more fuel-efficient. Although the level and degree of technological improvement have slowed in the airline industry, there is still opportunity for further innovation.

Airline travel is a common form of transportation for long-distance passenger and freight travel and the only reasonable alternative when time is of the essence. The tremendous speed of the airplane, coupled with more competitive pricing, has led to the growth of air transportation, particularly in the movement of passengers.

Industry Overview and Significance

In 2013 for-hire air carriers had total operating revenues of $199.7 billion, of which $120.6 billion (60.4 percent) came from passenger fares.[1] Between June 2013 and May 2014, air carriers transported 93.1 billion revenue ton-miles.[2] Employment in the air carrier industry totaled 589,151 people in June 2014.[3]

The airline industry is very dependent on **passenger revenues** to maintain its financial viability. However, to characterize airlines simply as movers of people presents too simplistic a view of their role in our transportation system. The airlines are a unique and important group of carriers that meet some particular needs in our society. Although their share of the freight movement on a ton-mile basis is small, the type of traffic that they carry (high-value, perishable, or emergency) makes them an important part of our total transportation system. Emphasis upon total logistics cost in a quick-response lead-time environment will continue to contribute to their growth in freight movements.

Types of Carriers

Private Carriers

Air carriers can be segmented into for-hire carriers and private carriers. A **private air carrier** is a firm that transports company personnel or freight in planes to support its primary business. The preponderance of private air transportation is used to transport company personnel, although emergency freight is sometimes carried on private airplanes as well. Rarely, however, is a private air carrier established to routinely carry freight. The private air carrier is subject to the federal safety regulations administered by the Federal Aviation Administration (FAA) of the U.S. Department of Transportation.

For-Hire Carriers

The for-hire carriers are no longer regulated on an economic basis by the federal government and cannot be easily categorized into specific types because carriers provide many types of services. For our purposes, the for-hire carriers will be discussed according to type of service offered (all-cargo, air taxi, commuter, charter, and international) and annual revenue (majors, nationals, and regionals).

A classification frequently used by U.S. air carriers is one based on annual operating revenues. The categories used to classify air carriers in terms of revenue are as follows:

- Majors—annual revenues of more than $1 billion
- Nationals—annual revenues of $100 million to $1 billion
- Regionals—annual revenues of less than $100 million

U.S. **major carriers** have $1 billion or more in annual revenues and provide service between major population areas within the United States such as New York, Chicago, and Los Angeles. The routes served by these carriers are usually high-density corridors, and the carriers use high-capacity planes. The U.S. majors also serve medium-sized population centers such as Harrisburg, Pennsylvania. Examples of major U.S. carriers are American/U.S. Airways, United/Continental, Delta/Northwest, and Southwest.

U.S. **national carriers** have revenues of $100 million to $1 billion and operate between less-populated areas and major population centers. These carriers operate scheduled service over relatively short routes with smaller planes. They "feed" passengers from outlying areas into airports served by the U.S. majors. Today, many of the U.S. national carriers operate over relatively large regional areas and are stiff competition for the U.S. majors on many routes. Examples of U.S. nationals include Frontier Airlines, jetBlue, and Midwest Express.

Regional carriers have annual revenues of less than $100 million and have operations similar to the nationals. The carriers operate within a particular region of the country, such as New England or the Midwest, and connect less-populated areas with larger population centers. Included in the regional category are carriers such as American Eagle Airlines, Atlantic Coast Airlines, and SkyWest Airlines.

The **all-cargo carrier**, as the name implies, primarily transports cargo. The transportation of air cargo was deregulated in 1977, permitting the all-cargo carriers to freely set rates, enter and exit markets, and use any size aircraft dictated by the market. Examples of all-cargo carriers include FedEx and UPS Airlines.

Commuter air carriers are technically regional carriers. The commuter publishes timetables on specific routes that connect less-populated routes with major cities. As certified carriers abandon routes, usually low-density routes, the commuter enters into a working relationship with the certified carrier to continue service to the community. The commuter then connects small communities that have reduced or no air service with larger communities that have better scheduled service. The commuter's schedule is closely aligned with connecting flight schedules at a larger airport. Many commuter firms use turboprop aircraft to feed the major hubs of the major airlines. Today, however, some commuters are adding regional jets that not only continue to feed these hubs but also offer direct service to larger metropolitan areas. Many commuter operators are franchised by the majors, such as US Airways Express.

The **charter carriers**, also known as air taxis, use small- to medium-size aircraft to transport people or freight. The supplemental carrier has no time schedule or designated route. The carrier charters the entire plane to transport a group of people or cargo between specified origins and destinations. Many travel tour groups use charter carriers. However, a big customer for charters is the Department of Defense; it uses charter carriers to transport personnel and supplies. For example, Operation Iraqi Freedom (OIF) relied upon charters for some of their moves of personnel and supplies. The rates charged and schedules followed are negotiated in the contract.

Many U.S. carriers are also international carriers and operate between the continental United States and foreign countries, and between the United States and its territories (such as Puerto Rico). Because service to other countries has an effect on U.S. international trade and relations, the president of the United States is involved in awarding the international routes. Examples of international carriers include United and American. Many foreign carriers, such as British Air and Air France, provide services between the United States and their country.

Market Structure

Number of Carriers

A small number of major airlines account for a majority of passenger and freight activity in the United States. Table 7-1 shows that the top 10 carriers account for approximately 86 percent of total operating revenue and approximately 90 percent of revenue passenger miles in 2010.

TABLE 7-1 Top 10 Airlines by Various Rankings—2013

PASSENGERS (MILLIONS)		REVENUE PASSENGER MILES (MILLIONS)	
1 Delta	118,934	1 United	176,388
2 Southwest	115,323	2 Delta	168,720
3 United	89,278	3 American	128,300
4 American	86,821	4 Southwest	90,178
5 US Airways	57,005	5 US Airways	66,119
6 **ExpressJet**	**32,956**	6 jetBlue	35,834
7 jetBlue	30,428	7 Alaska	26,132
8 SkyWest	**27,131**	**8 ExpressJet**	**16,852**
9 Alaska	19,700	**9 SkyWest**	**14,953**
10 Airtran	17,817	10 AirTran	14,172
Bolded airlines = ATA members.			
FREIGHT TON-MILES (MILLIONS)		**TOTAL OPERATING REVENUES ($MILLIONS)**	
1 FedEx	11,113	1 FedEx	44,287
2 UPS	7,458	2 United	38,287
3 Atlas	3,647	3 Delta	37,818
4 Delta	2,349	4 American	25,760
5 United	2,207	5 Southwest	17,699
6 American	1,836	6 US Airways	14,936
7 **Kalitta Air**	**1,366**	7 UPS Airlines	8,900
8 **Polar**	**1,182**	8 jetBlue	5,442
9 **Southern**	**1,023**	9 Alaska	5,150
10 ABX	551	10 **SkyWest**	**1,828**

Source: *Bureau of Transportation Statistics, 2014*. FedEx and UPS operating revenues sourced.

Private air transportation has been estimated to include approximately 60,000 company-owned planes, with over 500 U.S. corporations operating private air fleets. In addition, thousands of planes are used for personal, recreational, and instructional purposes.

Deregulation in 1978 was expected to result in a larger number of airlines competing for passengers and freight traffic. The number of major airlines did increase initially, but the number of airlines has remained steady over the last several years with several consolidations taking place. Available seat miles for 2013 increased by 1.7 percent from 2012 as some carriers are increasing the size of their aircraft.[4] The number of flights decreased from 9.3 million in 2012 to 9.1 million in 2013. However, the percent of on-time departures decreased to 79.19 percent in 2013 from 82.4 percent in 2012.[5]

Competition

Intermodal

Due to their unique service, air carriers face **limited competition** from other modes for both passengers and freight. Air carriers have an advantage in providing time-sensitive, long-distance movement of people or freight. Airlines compete to some extent with motor carriers for the movement of higher-valued manufactured goods; they face competition from automobiles for the movement of passengers and, to a limited extent, from trains and buses. For short distances (under 800 miles), the access time and terminal time offsets the speed of the airline for the line-haul.

Intramodal

Competition in rates and service among the air carriers is very intense, even though the number of carriers is small. As noted, passenger air carrier regulation was significantly reduced in 1978, and new carriers entered selected routes (markets), thereby increasing the amount of competition (see Chapter 4 for a discussion of the Theory of Contestable Markets). Also, existing carriers expanded their market coverage, which significantly increased intramodal competition in certain markets. Carriers may also have **excess capacity** (too many flights and seat miles on a route) and attempt to attract passengers by selectively lowering fares to fill the empty seats. Between the first quarter of 2013 and the first quarter of 2014, average passenger air fares decreased from $384.42 to $380.69.[6]

New entrants to the airline market initially caused overcapacity to exist on many routes. To counter this and add passengers to their aircraft, carriers reduced prices and fare wars began. This caused financially weaker carriers to exit the market. This was especially true of carriers with high operating costs (many times due to high-cost union labor contracts), high cost of debt, or high levels of fixed costs. (Many of these maintained high fixed investments in hub-and-spoke terminal operations.) The remaining carriers began to enjoy economies of density (discussed later in this chapter), and the cost per passenger mile decreased and margins increased, even in the existence of relatively low fares. So, even with the discounted prices in today's airline market, many carriers have been able to remain profitable.

Service Competition

Competition in airline service takes many forms, but the primary service competition is the **frequency and timing** of flights on a route. Carriers attempt to provide flights at the time of day when passengers want to fly. Flight departures are most frequent in the early morning (7:00 a.m. to 10:00 a.m.) and late afternoon (4:00 p.m. to 6:00 p.m.).

In addition to the frequency and timing of flights, air carriers attempt to differentiate their service through the **advertising** of passenger amenities. Carriers promote such things as on-time arrival and friendly employees to convince travelers that they have the desired quality of service. jetBlue Airways was the first airline in the world that offered live satellite television free of charge on every seat in its fleet.[7] Frequent flyer programs and special services for high-mileage customers are popular examples of other services to attract loyal customers.

A post-deregulation development in service competition was **no-frills service**. The no-frills air carrier (for example, Southwest Airlines) charges fares that are lower than that of a full-service air carrier. However, passengers receive limited snacks and drinks (coffee, tea, or soft drinks). Southwest offers passengers an opportunity to purchase a boxed meal at the gate before they enter the aircraft. Another hallmark of such carriers is that they only provide one class of service. Also, the passengers provide their own magazines or other reading materials. Overall, there are fewer airline employees involved in no-frills services operations, which contributes to lower costs. The no-frills carriers have had a significant impact on fares where their service is available.

Cargo Competition

For cargo service, competition has become intense. As a result of the complete deregulation of air cargo in 1977, air carriers have published competitive rates, but these rates are still higher than those available via surface carriers. Freight schedules have been published that emphasize low transit times between given points. To overcome accessibility problems, some carriers provide door-to-door service through contracts with motor carriers. Major airline freight companies (such as FedEx and UPS Airlines) have their own fleets of surface delivery vehicles to perform the ground portion of this door-to-door service.

Although the number of major and national carriers is small, the competition among carriers is great. An interesting development has been the number of surface carriers that have added air cargo service, such as UPS. Competition for nonpassenger business will become even greater as more carriers attempt to eliminate excess capacity resulting from currently reduced passenger travel patterns. Another interesting dimension has been the growth in volume of express carrier traffic, which is an important reason for the attraction of surface carriers into this segment of the business.

Operating and Service Characteristics

General

As indicated earlier, the major revenue source for air carriers is passenger transportation. From August 2013 to July 2014, approximately 99.2 percent of total operating revenue miles were derived from passenger transportation. This revenue was generated from about 758.5 million passenger enplanements during the same period.[8] Air transportation dominates the for-hire, long-distance passenger transportation market.

By the end of the third quarter of 2014, approximately 2.1 percent of the total operating **revenues** were generated from **freight** transportation.[9] The majority of freight using air service is high-value and/or emergency shipments. The high cost of air

GLOBAL **PERSPECTIVES**

U.S. Airports Ramp Up Competition for Cargo Dominance

With world trade growing faster than demand for air cargo, both airports and air carriers face a significant challenge—how can they attract air freight and fend off competition from other cheaper modes of transport such as intermodal and trucks?

According to Jones Lange LaSalle's (JLL) *Airport Outlook Report*, this environment now finds U.S. airports engaged in a fight for a larger share of the challenged U.S. air cargo market.

"Airport executives are increasingly focused on the bigger picture, specifically the role their airport and the supporting infrastructure play in making shippers' supply chains more efficient," says Rich Thompson, managing director of JLL's Ports Airports and Global Infrastructure (PAGI) group. "The market is not growing as a whole, so they must use every tool they have to stand out and attract shipping volume."

Instead of relying on airline revenues for driving growth, airports are focused on leveraging nearby commercial real estate assets and logistics corridors to position themselves as an essential link in the supply chain. In fact, some airports are now seeing more than 60 percent of their revenue derived from non-airline sources.

"There are two factors that could increase global air freight," says Thompson. "The rapid growth of e-commerce sales to consumers who demand rapid package arrival, and the demand for time-sensitive and high-value goods such as food, perishables, biologics, and pharmaceuticals."

Here's a quick overview of the top three "aerotropolis" districts—the areas surrounding these cargo-intense airports—that stand out in JLL's annual *Airport Outlook Report.*

1. Chicago O'Hare (ORD) moves to the top position, up from second in last year's index. Infrastructure is a priority, with new cargo facilities planned that offer both airside and landside access. For supply chain executives, the greater Chicago market offers six major railroad connections and is a one-day drive to nearly a third of North American consumers, positioning ORD as a gateway of choice.

2. Miami (MIA) scores second highest in the index, down from the top position in last year's report. The airport and surrounding businesses control the food and flower trade (moving 71.2 percent of all U.S. perishables), and a lack of a single dominant carrier makes room for enhanced competition and demand for real estate.

3. Los Angeles (LAX) moved up in the rankings from last year's report and now ranks third. Freight forwarders were especially active near the airport in 2013, and real estate demand from logistics providers, consumer nondurables, and food and beverage was notable throughout the surrounding market. China remains LAX's largest trading partner, followed by Japan, Hong Kong, Thailand, and South Korea.

Source: Patrick Burnson, *Logistics Management*, April 2014, p. 36. Reprinted with permission of Peerless Media, LLC.

transportation is usually prohibitive for shipping low-value routine commodities unless there is an emergency.

For **emergency shipments**, the cost of air transportation is often inconsequential compared to the cost of delaying the goods. For example, an urgently needed part for an assembly line might have a $20 value, but if the air-freighted part arrives on time to prevent the assembly line from stopping, the opportunity value of the part might become hundreds of thousands of dollars. Thus, the $20 part might have an emergency value of $200,000, and the air freight cost is a small portion of this emergency value.

Examples of **commodities** that move via air carriers include mail, clothing, communication products and parts, photography equipment, mushrooms, fresh flowers, industrial machines, high-priced livestock, racehorses, expensive automobiles, and jewelry. Normally, basic raw materials such as coal, lumber, iron ore, or steel are not moved by air carriage. The high value of the products that are shipped by air provides a cost-savings trade-off, usually but not always from inventory, that offsets the higher cost of air service. The old adage "Time is money" is quite appropriate here.

Speed of Service

Undoubtedly, the major service advantage of air transportation is speed. The terminal-to-terminal time for a given trip is lower via air transportation than via any of the other modes. Commercial jets are capable of routinely flying at speeds of 500 to 600 miles per hour, thus making a New York to California trip, approximately 3,000 miles, a mere six-hour journey.

This advantage of high terminal-to-terminal speed has been dampened somewhat by reduced frequency of flights and congestion at airports. As a result of deregulation, the air traffic controllers' strike of 1981, and lower carrier demand, the number of flights offered to and from low-density communities has been reduced to increase the utilization of a given plane. As previously noted, commuter airlines have been substituted on some routes where major and national lines find the traffic volume to be too low to justify using large planes. The use of commuters requires transfer and re-handling of freight or passengers because the commuter service does not cover long distances.

Air carriers have been concentrating their service on the **high-density routes** like New York to Chicago, for example. In addition, most carriers have adopted the hub-and-spoke terminal approach, in which most flights go through a hub terminal; Atlanta (Delta) and Chicago (United) are examples. These two factors have aggravated the air traffic congestion and ground congestion at major airports and have increased total transit time while decreasing its reliability. Also, some carriers have been unable to expand because of limited "slots" at major airports. At hub airports, these slots are controlled by the dominant carrier, making it difficult for new carriers to offer service at that hub.

The shippers who use air carriers to transport freight are primarily interested in the speed and reliability of the service and the resultant benefits, such as reduced inventory levels and inventory carrying costs. Acceptable or improved service levels can be achieved by using air carriers to deliver orders in short time periods. Stock-outs can be controlled, reduced, or eliminated by responding to shortages via air carriers.

Length of Haul and Capacity

For passenger travel, air carriers dominate the long-distance moves. In 2012 the average length of haul for passenger travel was 886 miles for U.S. air carriers.[10] The capacity of an airplane is dependent on its type. A wide-body, four-engine jet has a **seating capacity** of about 370 people and an all-cargo carrying capacity of 16.6 tons. Table 7-2 provides capacity and operating statistics for some of the more commonly used aircraft in both domestic and international markets. Comparable data to update this table is not available. But Table 7-2 provides a summary of the different operating characteristics of many aircraft still in service today.

TABLE 7-2 Aircraft Operating Characteristics—2007

MODEL	SEATS	CARGO PAYLOAD (TONS)	SPEED AIRBORNE (MPH)	FLIGHT LENGTH (MILES)	FUEL (GALLONS PER HOUR)	OPERATING COST $ PER HOUR	OPERATING COST $0.01 PER SEAT MILE
B747-200/300*	370	16.60	520	3,148	3,625	9,153	5.11
B747-400	367	8.06	534	3,960	3,411	8,443	4.6
B747-100*	–	46.34	503	2,022	1,762	3,852	–
B747-F*	–	72.58	506	2,512	3,593	7,138	–
L-1011	325	0.00	494	2,023	1,981	8,042	5067
DC-10*	286	24.87	497	1,637	2,405	7,374	5.11
B767-400	265	6.26	495	1,682	1,711	3,124	2.71
B-777	263	9.43	525	3,515	2,165	5,105	3.98
A330	261	11.12	509	3,559	1,407	3,076	2.51
MD-11*	261	45.07	515	2,485	2,473	7,695	4.75
A300-600*	235	19.12	460	947	1,638	6,518	5.93
B757-300	235	0.30	472	1,309	985	2,345	2.44
B767-300ER*	207	7.89	497	2,122	1,579	4,217	4.38
B757-200*	181	1.41	464	1,175	1,045	3,312	4.47
B767-300ER	175	3.72	487	1,987	1,404	3,873	5.08
A321	169	0.44	454	1,094	673	1,347	2.05
B737-800/900	151	0.37	454	1,035	770	2,248	3.88
MD-90	150	0.25	446	886	825	2,716	4.93
B727-200*	148	6.46	430	644	1,289	4,075	6.61
B727-100*	–	11.12	417	468	989	13,667	–
A320	146	0.31	454	1,065	767	2,359	4.14
B737-400	141	0.25	409	646	703	2,595	5.48
MD-80	134	0.19	432	791	953	2,718	5.72
B737-700LR	132	0.28	441	879	740	1,692	3.28
B737-300/700	132	0.22	403	542	723	2,388	5.49
A319	122	0.27	442	904	666	1,913	4.22
A310-200*	–	25.05	455	847	1,561	8,066	–
DC-8*	–	22.22	437	686	1,712	8,065	–
B737-100/200	119	0.11	396	465	824	2,377	6.08
B717-200	112	0.22	339	175	573	3,355	12.89
B737-500	110	0.19	407	576	756	2,347	6.49
DC-9	101	0.15	387	496	826	2,071	6.86
F-100	87	0.05	398	587	662	2,303	8.46
B737-200C	55	2.75	387	313	924	3,421	19.89
ERJ-145	50	0.00	360	343	280	1,142	8.63
CRJ-145	49	0.01	397	486	369	1,433	9.45
ERJ-135	37	0.00	357	382	267	969	9.83
SD 340B	33	0.00	230	202	84	644	11.6

*Data includes cargo operations.

Source: Air Transport Association, *2008 Annual Report.*

Normally, small shipments that are time-sensitive are moved by air carriers. Rates have been established for weights as low as 10 pounds, and rate discounts are available for shipments weighing a few hundred pounds. Adding freight to the baggage compartment on passenger flights necessitates rather small-size shipments and thus supports rate-making practices for these shipments.

In addition to small shipment sizes, the packaging required for freight shipped by air transportation is usually less than other modes. It is not uncommon in air transportation to find a palletized shipment that is shrink-wrapped instead of banded. The relatively smooth ride through the air and the automated ground-handling systems contribute to lower damage and thus reduce packaging needs.

Accessibility and Dependability

Except in adverse conditions such as fog or snow, air carriers are capable of providing **reliable** service. The carriers might not always be on time to the exact minute, but the variations in transit time are small. Sophisticated navigational instrumentation permits operation during most weather conditions. On-time departures and arrivals are within 15 minutes of scheduled times. Departure time is defined as the time the aircraft door is closed and, in the case of passenger aircraft, the vehicle is pushed away from the gate. Arrival time is defined as the time when the aircraft wheels touch down on the runway.

Poor **accessibility** is one disadvantage of air carriers. Passengers and freight must be transported to an airport for air service to be rendered. This accessibility problem is reduced when smaller planes and helicopters are used to transport freight to and from airports, and most passengers use automobiles. Limited accessibility adds time and cost to the air service provided. Even with the accessibility problem, air transportation remains a fast method of movement and the only logical mode when distance is great and time is restricted. The cost of this fast freight service is high, about three times greater than motor carrier and 10 times greater than rail. Nevertheless, the high speed and cost make air carriage a premium mode of transportation.

Equipment

Types of Vehicles

As previously mentioned, there are several different sizes of airplanes in use, from small commuter planes to huge, wide-body, four-engine planes used by the nationals. These various-sized planes all have different costs associated with using them; these costs will be addressed later in the section titled "Cost Structure." Table 7-2 compares some of the major aircraft types in terms of seats, cargo payload, speed, fuel consumption, and operating cost per hour. Airlines have many options to select from when purchasing equipment.

Terminals

The air carriers' **terminals** (airports) are financed by a government entity. The carriers pay for the use of the airport through landing fees, rent and lease payments for space, taxes on fuel, and aircraft registration taxes. In addition, users pay a tax on airline tickets and air freight charges. Terminal charges are becoming increasingly more commonplace for passenger traffic. Table 7-3 summarizes the various types of taxes paid by carriers, shippers, and passengers in the airline industry.

ON THE LINE

International Standards: IATA Launches "Secure Freight"

A supply chain security program recently initiated by the International Air Transport Association (IATA) promises to provide guidelines and tools for U.S. shippers operating overseas.

Titled "Secure Freight," it promotes government standards and principles in which cargo is secured upstream early on in the supply chain and then protected from unlawful interference until it reaches its destination.

"Secure Freight addresses deficiencies in existing cargo security regimes and brings countries up to the level of International Civil Aviation Organization (ICAO) compliance," says Tony Tyler, IATA's director general and CEO.

The Secure Freight tools include:

- The Secure Freight Standards Manual that defines how Secure Freight operators in that state comply with standards that allow shipments to be transported securely across supply chains.
- The Secure Freight operational procedures that provide practical guidance on how to move cargo and its associated information through the secure supply chain.
- Security programs template for Secure Freight operators.
- Validation and certification check lists for Secure Freight operators, among others.

Secure Freight pilot programs are currently running in a range of countries on different continents. "Following completion of a pilot, authorities are expected to implement quality assurance processes that ensure adherence to the standards outlined in the program as well as to undertake the necessary changes to national law for full implementation," says Tyler.

Source: Patrick Burnson, *Logistics Management*, July 2014, p. 54. Reprinted with permission of Peerless Media, LLC.

The growth and development of air transportation is dependent upon adequate airport facilities. Therefore, to ensure the viability of air transportation, the federal government has the responsibility of financially assisting the states in the construction of airport facilities. The various state and local governments assume the responsibility for operating and maintaining the airports.

At the airport, the carriers perform passenger, cargo, and aircraft servicing. Passengers are ticketed, loaded, and unloaded, and their luggage is collected and dispersed. Cargo is routed to specific planes for shipment to the destination airport or to delivery vehicles. Aircraft servicing includes refueling; loading of passengers, cargo, luggage, and supplies (food); and maintenance. Major aircraft maintenance is done at specific airports.

As carrier operations become more complex, certain airports in the carriers' scope of operation become **hubs**. Flights from outlying, less-populated areas are fed into the hub airport, where connecting flights are available to other areas of the region or country.

For example, Chicago, Denver, and Washington-Dulles are major hub airports for United Airlines. Flights from cities such as Toledo and Kansas City go to Chicago, where connecting flights are available to New York, Los Angeles, and Dallas. Delta Airlines uses the Atlanta and Cincinnati airports in the same way. By using the hub

TABLE 7-3 Federally Approved Taxes and Fees: 1992–2014

FEE	1992	2003	2014
	AIRPORT AND AIRWAY TRUST FUND (FAA)		
Passenger Ticket Tax[1a]	10.0%	7.5%	7.5%
Flight Segment Tax[1a]	–	$3.60	$4.00
Frequent Flyer Tax[2]	–	7.5%	7.5%
International Departure Tax[3]	$6.00	$16.10	$17.50
International Arrival Tax[3]	–	$16.10	$17.50
Cargo Waybill Tax[1b] (domestic)	6.25%	6.25%	6.25%
Commercial Jet Fuel Tax	–	$0.043	$0.043
Non-commercial Jet Fuel Tax	$0.175	$0.218	$0.218
Non-commercial AvGas Tax	$0.15	$0.193	$0.193
	ENVIRONMENTAL PROTECTION AGENCY (EPA)		
LUST Fuel Tax[4] (domestic)	$0.001	$0.001	$0.001
	LOCAL AIRPORT PROJECTS		
Passenger Facility Charge	–	up to $3	up to $4.50
	DEPARTMENT OF HOMELAND SECURITY (DHS)		
September 11th Fee[5]	–	$2.50	$5.60
Aviation Security Infrastructure Fee[6]	–	–	Varies
APHIS Passenger Fee[7]	$2.00	$5.00	$5.00
APHIS Aircraft Fee[7]	$76.75	$70.50	$70.50
Customs User Fee[8]	$5.00	$5.50	$5.50
Immigration User Fee[9]	$5.00	$7.00	$7.00

[1a]Applies only to domestic transport or to journeys to Canada or Mexico within 225 miles of the U.S. border.

[1b]Applies only to flights within the 50 states.

[2]Applies to the sale, to third parties, of the right to award frequent flyer miles.

[3]Does not apply to those transiting the United States between two foreign airports; $8.70 on flights between the mainland United States and Alaska/Hawaii.

[4]Congress created the Leaking Underground Storage Tank (LUST) trust fund in 1986.

[5]Funds TSA at up to $5.60 per one-way trip (from 2/1/02 through 6/30/14 was $2.50 per enplanement up to $5.00 per one-way trip); suspended 6/1/03–9/30/03.

[6]Funds TSA since 2/18/02; suspended 6/1/03–9/30/03.

[7]Since 5/13/91 (passenger fee) and 2/9/92 (aircraft fee), funds agricultural quarantine and inspection services conducted by CBP per 7 CFR 354.

[8]Since 7/7/86, funds inspections by U.S. Customs and Border Protection; passengers arriving from U.S. territories and possessions are exempt.

[9]Since 12/1/86, the majority of the collections fund inspections by U.S. Customs and Border Protection and a smaller portion of the collections fund certain activities performed by U.S. Immigration and Customs Enforcement that are related to air and sea passenger inspections.

Source: Air Transport Association, 2014.

airport approach, the carriers are able to assign aircraft to feed passengers into the hub over low-density routes and to assign larger planes to the higher-density routes between the hub and an airport serving a major metropolitan area. In essence, the hub airport is similar to the motor carrier's break-bulk terminal.

Airport terminals also provide services to passengers, such as restaurants, banking centers, souvenir and gift shops, and snack bars. The Denver airport also includes some major general purpose attractions similar to a shopping mall. The success of the Atlanta airport has resulted in other airports expanding restaurants to include many popular chains (McDonald's, TGI Friday's, Pizza Hut, and so forth) and popular shops for clothing, accessories, books, and other items.

Cost Structure

Fixed- Versus Variable-Cost Components

Like the motor carriers, the air carriers' cost structure consists of high variable and low fixed costs. Approximately 80 percent of total operating costs are variable and 20 percent are fixed. The relatively low fixed-cost structure is attributable to government (state and local) investment and operations of airports and airways. The carriers pay for the use of these facilities through landing fees, which are variable in nature.

By the end of the third quarter of 2014, 34 percent of airline operating costs were incurred for fuel and amounted to $36.7 billion; maintenance costs equaled 5 percent of total operating costs. Both of these expenses are variable costs. The next major category of expense is wages and benefits, which totaled $27 billion and about 25 percent of total operating costs. Depreciation accounted for about 6.8 percent of total operating expenses.[11]

Table 7-4 provides a comparison of airline cost indices for 2001, 2005, and 2009 (year 2000 = 100). Transportation related expenses increased from 2001 to 2009, as did

TABLE 7-4 Airline Cost Indexes

YEAR	2001	2005	2009
Compostite Index	108.5	177.9	197.3
Labor Costs	107.8	117.3	127.4
Fuel	98.6	206.6	234.9
Aircraft ownership	102.3	99.1	93
Nonaircraft ownership	139.4	106.1	114.8
Professional Services	102.8	105.5	118.5
Food and beverage	100.5	61.3	59.7
Landing fees	109.2	130.7	158.9
Maintenance material	96.3	59.1	83.3
Aircraft insurance	163.5	157.1	150.8
Nonaircraft insurance	171.3	319.9	184.4
Passenger commisions	86.4	31.6	26.7
Communication	109.6	73.3	77.1
Advertising and promotion	93	75.5	61.7
Utilities and office supplies	103.6	87.6	99.8
Transportation-related expenses	119.1	475	524.9
Other operating expenses	126.4	108.6	123.8
Interest	98.1	120.6	118.7

Source: U.S. Census Bureau, Statistical Abstract of the United States: 2012, Table 1074.

total fuel expense. From 2001 to 2009, labor, fuel, professional services, landing fees, non-aircraft insurance, transportation-related expenses, other operating expenses, and interest expense all increased.

The increased price competition in the airline industry has caused airlines to try to operate more efficiently by cutting costs where possible. There has been much effort put forth to decrease labor costs because the airline industry tends to be labor-intensive compared to other modes, such as railroads and pipelines. The airlines have negotiated significant labor cost reductions with many of the unions represented in the industry.

Fuel

Escalating **fuel costs** have caused problems in the past for the airlines. The average price per gallon of fuel for domestic operations was about 89 cents in 1983 compared to 57 cents in 1979 and 30 cents in 1978. It dropped to under 60 cents in 1986 but rose again in 1990 to above the 1983 level. It decreased again by 1998 to about 55 cents per gallon. By September 2014, the price per gallon of aviation fuel was $2.86 per gallon.[12]

The impact that such fuel increases have had can be shown by analyzing fuel consumption for certain aircraft that are commonly used today. The Air Transportation Association's annual report shows that the number of gallons of fuel consumed per hour for the following planes is as follows (see Table 7-2):

367-seat 747	3,411 gallons/hour
286-seat DC-10	2,405 gallons/hour
148-seat 727	1,289 gallons/hour
101-seat DC-9	826 gallons/hour

Using a cost of $2.86 per gallon, the fuel cost per hour is $9,755.46 for a 747, $6,878.30 for a DC-10, $3,686.54 for a 727, and $2,362.36 for DC-9. Consequently, rapidly escalating fuel costs in recent years have caused airlines to suffer financially in an already depressed pricing market.

When fuel costs rise, carriers scrutinize planes in the fleet as well as routes served. More **fuel-efficient** planes have been developed and added to carrier fleets. In the short run, carriers are substituting smaller planes on low-density (low demand) routes and eliminating service completely on other routes. Commuter lines have provided substitute service on the routes abandoned by major and national carriers. The average cost per gallon of fuel decreased from $3.17 to $3.03 from 2012 to 2013 and fuel consumption decreased by 60.7 million gallons (0.6 percent decrease) from 2012 to 2013, resulting in a reduced fuel expense of $1.57 billion.[13]

Labor

In 2013, average salaries and wages increased by 5.4 percent over 2012. In 2013 carriers employed 330,722 people at an average annual compensation of $72,634.[14]

Airlines employ people with a variety of different skills. To operate the planes, the carrier must employ pilots, copilots, and flight engineers. The plane crew also includes the flight attendants who serve the passengers. Communications personnel are required to tie together the different geographic locations. Mechanics and ground crews for aircraft and traffic service provide the necessary maintenance and servicing of the planes. The final component of airline employment consists of the office personnel and management. Overall employment has decreased as airlines have moved aggressively to reduce costs to improve their competitiveness and lower prices in selected markets.

Strict safety regulations are administered by the FAA. Acceptable flight operations, as well as hours of service, are specified for pilots. Both mechanics and pilots are subject to examinations on safety regulations and prescribed operations. FAA regulations also dictate appropriate procedures for flight attendants to follow during takeoff and landing.

The wages paid to a pilot usually vary according to the pilot's equipment rating. A pilot who is technically capable (has passed a flight examination for a given type of aircraft) of flying a jumbo jet will receive a higher compensation than one who flies a single-engine, six-passenger plane. Table 7-5 shows the average pilot compensation for the major airlines in the United States for narrowbody aircraft. Southwest averages the highest pilot wages, whereas Amerijet has the lowest. Pilot and copilot wages have increased by 11.9 percent from 2012 to 2013.[15]

Equipment

As mentioned earlier, the cost of operating airplanes varies. Larger planes are more costly to operate per hour than smaller planes, but the cost per seat mile is lower for larger planes. That is, the larger plane has the capacity to carry more passengers; thus, the higher cost is spread out over a large number of output units.

Table 7-2 shows the hourly operating costs for four aircraft used by major carriers in 2007. The cost per block hour was $8,443 for the 367-seat 747 and $2,071 for the 101-seat DC-9. However, the cost per seat mile was $0.0046 for the 747 and $0.00686 for the DC-9. This reduced operating cost per seat mile for the larger planes indicates that economies of scale exist in aircraft.

Economies of Scale/Economies of Density

Large-scale air carrier operations do have some **economies of scale**, which result from more extensive use of large-size planes or indivisible units. Of the small number of

TABLE 7-5 Average U.S. Airline Pilot Hourly Wages—2012

AIRLINE	5-YEAR FIRST OFFICER	10-YEAR CAPTAIN
Delta	$111.00	$179.00
FedEx Airlines	$128.00	$206.00
United	$82.00	$134.00
US Airways	$75.00	$122.00
Southwest	$130.00	$212.00
American	$97.00	$163.00
Amerijet	$50.00	$85.00

Source: Airline Pilot Central, *2012 Airline Pilot Pay Snapshot*.

major and national carriers, approximately 10 transport over 90 percent of the passengers, indicating that large-scale operations exist.

The information contained in Table 7-2 suggests the existence of economies of scale with large-size planes. Market conditions (sufficient demand) must exist to permit the efficient utilization of larger planes (that is, if the planes are flown near capacity, the seat mile costs will obviously decrease). Contributing to the existence of economies of scale for aircraft is the inability to inventory an unused seat. For example, a 367-seat 747 is about to close its doors with 10 seats empty. If the plane takes off with the empty seats, the seats are "lost" for that flight because the airline cannot inventory the excess capacity for another flight that might be overbooked. On the other hand, the marginal cost of filling those 10 empty seats right before the doors on the aircraft are closed are negligible. This is the same concept of economies of scale as found in the railroad industry. The marginal cost of adding one more rail car to a train right before departure is negligible.

Another factor indicating large-scale operations for air carriers is the integrated **communication network** required for activities such as operating controls and passenger reservations. Small local or regional carriers find the investment required for such a communication system rather staggering, but without the communication system, the emerging carrier cannot effectively operate (provide connecting service with other carriers and ticketing to passengers). Such carriers have purchased passenger reservation systems from large carriers to be competitive.

The air carrier industry overall has a cost structure that closely resembles that of motor carriers. Long-run economies of scale, as compared to short-run economies of plane size and utilization, are not significant in the air carrier industry. Industries characterized by high variable-cost ratios (airlines and motor carriers) can relatively easily add equipment to a given market. As such, the ability to decrease fully allocated cost per mile by adding aircraft does not exist. On the other hand, when high fixed-cost industries (pipe and rail) add fixed capacity, they can decrease fully allocated cost per mile by adding volume to the fixed capacity. In high fixed-cost industries, however, capacity is not easily added in small increments.

Economies of density exist when a carrier has significant volume between an origin–destination pair to fully utilize capacity on forward-haul movements as well as utilize significant capacity on back-haul movements. This concept can exist across all modes of transportation. Southwest Airlines uses this concept aggressively when deciding which markets to enter, choosing those city pairs that offer high volumes of potential passengers to fill outbound aircraft. Table 7-6 shows the top 25 passenger markets in the United States. Of these, 5 have New York City as the originating point. jetBlue, based out of JFK Airport in New York, currently serves Fort Lauderdale, Orlando, San Juan, Tampa, and West Palm Beach. Economies of density, then, are important for all airlines to achieve to fully utilize capacity in a given market. History has shown that this has been a successful strategy for new entrants to the airline passenger market.

Over the years the federal government has provided direct operating **subsidies** (that is, public service revenues) to air carriers. The subsidies have been provided to ensure air carrier service over particular routes where operating expenses exceed operating incomes. The subsidies enable regional carriers to provide service to less-populated areas that otherwise would probably not have air service.

TABLE 7-6 Top 25 Domestic Airline Markets—2010[1]

			PASSENGERS (DAILY AVERAGE)
1	Los Angeles	New York	4,376
2	Chicago	New York	4,288
3	Ft. Lauderdale	New York	4,144
4	New York	Orlando	3,824
5	New York	San Francisco	3,309
6	Atlanta	New York	2,910
7	Los Angeles	San Francisco	2,596
8	Miami	New York	2,405
9	Las Vegas	New York	2,115
10	New York	West Palm Beach	1,924
11	Honolulu	Maui	1,895
12	Dallas	New York	1,790
13	Chicago	Los Angeles	1,766
14	New York	Tampa	1,744
15	Chicago	Washington, D.C.	1,738
16	Boston	New York	1,698
17	Chicago	Orlando	1,695
18	Las Vegas	San Francisco	1,690
19	Dallas	Houston	1,622
20	Boston	Washington, D.C.	1,607
21	New York	San Juan	1,538
22	Orlando	Philadelphia	1,535
23	Chicago	Las Vegas	1,533
24	Los Angeles	Washington, D.C.	1,500
25	San Francisco	San Diego	1,496

[1]Includes all commercial airports in a metropolitan area.

Source: Airlines for America, *2011 Economic Report.*

Rates

Pricing

Airline pricing for passenger service is characterized by the **discounts** from full fare. Seats on the same plane can have substantially different prices depending on restrictions attached to the purchase, such as having to stay over a weekend or having to purchase the ticket in advance. Businesspeople generally pay more for their airline travel due to the more rigid schedules they are on and the fact that they usually depart and return during the high-demand times. jetBlue, Southwest, and AirTran have aggressively discounted prices in major passenger markets. However, inflation-adjusted airfares increased by 2.5 percent from 2013 to 2014 and declined by 15.6 percent between 2000 and 2014.[16] The price of seats on different flights and the price of the same seat on a particular flight can vary due to competition with other airlines, the time and day of departure and return, the level of service (first class versus coach or no-frills service), and advance ticket purchase. Discount pricing has continued throughout the 2000s as airlines have attempted to increase their "payload." Industry load factors in 2013 were 82.78 percent, up from 82.53 percent in 2012.[17] This is a result of aggressive pricing as well as more systematic allocation of capacity to markets.

Cargo pricing is dependent mainly on weight and/or cubic dimensions. Some shipments that have a very low density can be assessed an over-dimensional charge, usually based on 8 pounds per cubic foot. This over-dimensional charge is used to gain more appropriate revenue from shipments that take up a lot of space but do not weigh much. An exaggerated example of a shipment to which this rule would apply is a shipment of inflated beach balls. Other factors affecting the price paid to ship freight via air transportation include completeness of service and special services, such as providing armed guards.

Operating Efficiency

An important measure of operating efficiency used by air carriers is the **operating ratio**. The operating ratio measures the portion of operating revenue that goes to operating expenses:

$$\text{Operating Ratio} = (\text{Operating Expense}/\text{Operating Revenue}) \times 100$$

Only revenue and expenses generated from passenger and freight transportation are considered. Like the motor carrier industry, the air carrier industry's operating ratio was in the low to mid-90s between 1994 and 2000, ranging from 96.9 in 1994 to 94.7 in 2000. The operating ratio for the industry in 2013 was 93.0.[18] The overall profit margin is small, and a loss is incurred when the operating ratio exceeds 100.

Another widely used measure of operating efficiency is the load factor (previously discussed). The load factor measures the percentage of a plane's capacity that is utilized.

$$\text{Load Factor} = (\text{Number of Passengers}/\text{Total Number of Seats}) \times 100$$

Airlines have raised plane load factors to the low 80 percent range. The particular route and type of plane (capacity) directly affect the load factor, as does price, service level, and competition.

Again, referring to Table 7-2, the relationship among load factor, cost, plane size, and profitability can be seen. Assume that a route requires one hour to traverse and has a load factor of 65 percent; the average operating cost per passenger for a 747 is \$35.39 (\$8,443 per hour/367 [capacity] = 0.65 [load factor]). If the demand drops to 80 passengers on the route, the load factor for the 747 would be 21.8 percent (80/367), and the hourly operating cost per passenger would be \$105.54 (\$8,443/80). At this level of demand, the carrier would substitute a smaller capacity plane, such as a 727 or DC-9. With 80 passengers, the load factor for the DC-9 would be 79.2 percent (80/101) and the average operating cost would be \$25.89 (\$2,071/80). The small aircraft would be more economical to operate over this lower-density route, and the carrier would substitute this more efficient plane (DC-9) on this hypothetical route.

Equipment substitution, however, might not be possible, and substitution might result in excess capacity. The jumbo planes have large carrying capacities that might not be utilized in low-demand routes. Thus, large-capacity planes are used on high-demand routes such as New York–Chicago and New York–Los Angeles, and smaller capacity planes are used on low-demand routes such as Toledo–Chicago and Pittsburgh–Memphis.

Current Issues

Safety

The issue of **airline safety** is of great importance to the airline industry. Any incident involving airplanes receives a great deal of publicity from the media because of the large number of people affected at one time. (Accidents involving motor vehicles affect only a few people in each incident but affect a greater number of people than do airline accidents in the long run.)

Several factors affect airline safety. First, airport security has come under close scrutiny over the past several years. On September 11, 2001, four aircraft were hijacked and two were flown into the Twin Towers in New York City, killing and injuring thousands of people. As a result, airport security has reached an all-time high, causing more delays at airport terminals. The U.S. government created the Office of Homeland Security to be the agency that monitors and manages the security of the U.S. borders.

Air travel is more popular than ever, as indicated previously, but there is still great concern about safety. The 1990s had some significant air disasters among major carriers, including TWA, American, US Airways, Swissair, and the ValuJet crash in the Florida Everglades. In addition, the frequent reportings of near collisions, minor accidents, and airplane recalls have heightened public awareness of the air safety problem. However, air travel is still the safest way to travel. Table 7-7 shows the trend of aircraft accidents from 2000 through 2010. The spike in 2001 was caused by the incident in New York City on September 11. Table 7-8 shows that even though there is a significant loss of life in an airline tragedy, air travel is still the safest mode for passenger travel based on total miles travelled, with automobiles being the most dangerous.

Finally, as with other transportation modes, the issue of substance abuse concerning pilots and ground crews has become important. Strict drug-testing policies and alcohol consumption guidelines are in effect for pilots and other aircraft personnel. In spite of these concerns, airline travel is still a very safe form of transportation; however, these

TABLE 7-7 U.S. Air Carriers Operating Under 14 CFR 121—Scheduled Service

YEAR	DEPARTURES (MILLIONS)	TOTAL ACCIDENTS	FATAL ACCIDENTS	FATAL ACCIDENT RATES[1]	FATALITIES
2000	9.0	49	2	0.018	39
2001	8.9	41	6	0.019	531
2002	9.3	34	0	0	0
2003	10.9	51	2	0	22
2004	11.4	23	1	0.009	13
2005	11.6	34	3	0.028	22
2006	11.3	26	2	0.019	50
2007	11.4	26	0	0	0
2008	10.9	20	0	0	0
2009	10.1	26	1	0.011	50
2010	10.1	27	0	0	0

[1]Fatal accidents per 100,000 departures; excludes incidents resulting from illegal acts.

Source: Airlines for America, *2011 Economic Report.*

TABLE 7-8 U.S. Passenger Fatalities

YEAR	AUTOS	BUSES	RAILROADS	AIRLINES
2003	42,843	41	33	699
2004	42,794	42	48	637
2005	43,452	58	67	603
2006	42,681	27	23	774
2007	41,223	36	42	540
2008	37,356	67	57	567
2009	33,857	26	31	548
2010	32,955	44	34	476
2011	32,424	55	35	489
2012	33,522	39	34	447
10-Yr. Avg.	38,310.7	43.5	40.4	578

Source: Bureau of Transportation Statistics, 2014.

issues are currently being addressed by the airlines to ensure that airline transportation remains safe.

Security

The aftermath of the tragic air fatalities of 9/11 gave rise to the establishment of the Department of Homeland Security as well as the Transportation Security Administration (TSA). Both of these agencies are responsible for the safety of passengers while in airports and in flight. New screening procedures have been established at airports for passengers and new guidelines developed for carry-on luggage. Another area of security concern is for freight loaded onto passenger-carrying aircraft. This freight, most times arranged for movement by air freight forwarders, has not been subject to a high level of security screening in the past. However, new legislation passed in the United States is calling for 100 percent screening of all freight loaded onto passenger-carrying aircraft. The intent of this legislation is to prevent unnecessarily dangerous freight from threatening the lives of passengers in an aircraft. Aircraft security is, and will continue to be, an important issue in defending the United States from terrorist acts.

Technology

Because the airline industry must offer quick and efficient service to attract business, it constantly needs more sophisticated equipment. With other modes such as railroads and water carriers, travel times are measured in days; however, air carriers measure travel time in hours.

For this reason, the airline industry has developed automated information-processing programs like the Air Cargo Fast Flow Program, which was designed by the Port Authority of New York/New Jersey. The Fast Flow Program is a paperless system that speeds the processing of air freight cargo through customs processing, which was found to take 106 out of 126 hours of processing time for international shipments. The system allows the air freight community to tie into customs-clearing systems and thus reduce paperwork and time requirements dramatically. The system also will provide better tracking of shipments and better communication between connecting carriers. These improvements will allow customers to receive their inbound shipments faster than ever before.

The FAA and the federal government are proposing an entire overhaul to the current air traffic control system that would rely on the use of GPS navigational aids. This would increase the capacity for aircraft in operating space as well as reduce travel times between origin/destination pairs. However, this change would also require new technology on current and new aircraft. The plan will cost billions of dollars and take years to develop but will offer airlines an opportunity to reduce operating costs and increase service.

SUMMARY

- The airline industry began its development in the early part of the 20th century, and its growth was influenced to a great extent initially by government interest and policy.
- The airline industry is dominated by revenue from passenger service, but air freight revenue is growing in importance.
- Both private and for-hire carriers operate as part of the airline industry, but private carrier service is predominantly passenger movement.
- For-hire carriers can be classified based on service offered (all-cargo, air taxi, charter, and so on) or annual operating revenue (majors, nationals, or regionals).
- All-cargo carriers and commuter operators have grown in importance in recent years and play a more important role in the total airline industry.
- A relatively large number of airline companies exist, but a small number (10) account for more than 90 percent of the total revenue.
- Deregulation of airlines was rationalized to some extent with the argument that an increase in the number of carriers would increase competition. Initially, there was an increase followed by a decrease; today the number is lower.
- Airlines are unique in that they face limited intermodal competition, but intramodal competition is very keen in terms of pricing and service and has been exacerbated by unused capacity.
- Airline service competition is usually in terms of frequency and timing of flights, but special passenger services and programs are important.
- The express portion of air freight has grown dramatically. A growing number of commodities use air freight service, and increased growth is expected.
- Speed is the major advantage of airlines for both passengers and freight, but the airlines' speed of service has been offset recently by congestion and fewer flights.
- The higher cost of airline service can be a trade-off against lower inventory and warehousing costs, as well as other logistics-related savings.
- Airline carriers are essentially long-haul service providers for passengers and freight because the cost of takeoffs and landings makes short hauls relatively uneconomical.
- Airlines usually provide service for small shipments where value is high and/or the product may be perishable.
- Airlines offer a generally reliable and consistent service, but their accessibility is limited.
- Airlines use different types of equipment that limits their carrying capacity, but their overall equipment variety is also limited.
- Airlines use publicly provided airways and terminals, but pay user charges on both, which helps make their cost structure highly variable.
- Major and national airlines use a hub approach to their service, which contributes to operating efficiency but often adds travel time.
- Fuel and labor costs are important expense categories for airlines and have received much managerial attention. The low fuel cost of the late 1990s helped the airlines improve their profitability; today, however, rising fuel prices are having a negative impact on industry profits.

- Economies of scale and economies of density exist in the airline industry, making larger-scale carriers usually more efficient, based on equipment, markets, and communications.
- In the era of deregulation, discount pricing has become very popular, and it has made the rate schedules of airlines for passenger services complex.
- Airline safety is an important issue, but overall airlines have a very good record.
- Traditionally, airlines have capitalized on new equipment technology to improve their operating efficiency and to expand capacity. In recent years, technology improvements have come in a variety of other areas.

STUDY QUESTIONS

1. Discuss the ways in which air carriers compete with each other. How have regulatory changes affected this competition?
2. What is the major advantage of air carriers? How does this advantage impact the inventory levels of those firms using air transportation? Explain how this advantage relates to the choice of modes when choosing between air carriage and other modes of freight and passengers transport.
3. Discuss the length of haul and carrying capacity of the air carriers. Explain how they both favor and hinder air carriers from a competitive standpoint.
4. What is the role of government in air transportation? Include both economic and safety regulations in your answer.
5. How does fuel cost and efficiency affect both air carrier costs and pricing?
6. What is the current situation of labor within the air industry? Are unions a major factor? How does skill level vary within the industry? Do you think this situation is similar to other modes? If so, which one(s)? Explain why.
7. Do air carriers have economies of scale at any level? Economies of density? Discuss and support your answer with examples.
8. How do air carriers price their services? Is the weight or density of the shipment a factor? Explain this factor as part of your answer. How does air carrier pricing relate to the value of the goods being transported?
9. What are the current issues facing the air industry? Discuss how each impacts the industry, its customers and employees.
10. What is the cost structure of the air industry? How does it compare with other modes? How does this affect pricing, particularly for passengers? Be sure your answer includes examples from either advertising or the Internet.

NOTES

1. Bureau of Transportation Statistics, *U.S. Department of Transportation*, Washington, DC, 2014.
2. Ibid.
3. Ibid.
4. Ibid.
5. Ibid.
6. Ibid.

7. Hoover's Online, June 7, 2004, http://www.jetblue.com/learnmore/factsheet.html.

8. Bureau of Transportation Statistics, *U.S. Department of Transportation.*

9. Airlines for America, *2014 Economic Report.*

10. Bureau of Transportation Statistics, *U.S. Department of Transportation.*

11. Airlines for America, *2014 Economic Report.*

12. Bureau of Transportation Statistics, *U.S. Department of Transportation.*

13. Ibid.

14. MIT Global Airline Industry Program, *Airline Data Project*, MIT, 2014.

15. Ibid.

16. Bureau of Transportation Statistics, *U.S. Department of Transportation.*

17. Ibid.

18. MIT Global Airline Industry Project, *Airline Data Project.*

CASE 7-1

Airspace Airlines

Airspace Airlines is a regional passenger airline operating in the southeastern United States. It operates as an independent airline between certain origin/destination pairs but also operates as a contract carrier for Delta out of the Atlanta airport. Airspace currently has a fleet of aging turboprop aircraft with an average capacity of 35 passengers. The average trip length for Airspace is 250 miles. Airspace employs only Airline Pilot Association union pilots.

Jim Gray is the vice president of operations for Airspace and is faced with the challenge of minimizing the impacts of fuel and labor costs on Airspace operating profits. The operating cost per seat mile for his fleet of aircraft is approximately $0.12. Maintenance costs are 15 percent of operating costs and are higher than the industry average. Pilot wages average $45 per hour. Airspace averages 50 departures per day out of the Atlanta airport.

Delta has approached Airspace about increasing the number of departures it offers out of Atlanta. Delta is also asking for a lower fare structure to help boost its profits. Jim knows that his current fleet will not be able to meet an increased demand and is pessimistic that he can lower operating costs without significantly reducing fuel costs and increasing pilot productivity. However, he is certain that the future financial viability of Airspace relies on a continued relationship with Delta.

CASE QUESTIONS

1. What suggestions would you give Jim to help Airspace lower its operating costs?
2. How would you help Airspace implement those plans?
3. What constraints can you identify that would prevent Airspace from implementing your suggestions?
4. How would you suggest Jim respond to Delta's requests for more flights at a lower cost?

CASE 7-2

Airline Consolidations

According to Airlines for America, there have been approximately 51 airline mergers/acquisitions since 1930. Although this is not necessarily a verifiable number, it does show the magnitude of the consolidations that have taken place in the passenger airline industry. Probably the most significant combinations of carriers began in 2009 with Delta and Northwest, followed by United and Continental in 2010, Southwest and Airtran in 2011, and American and US Airways in 2013. These four "mega-carriers" account for approximately 80 percent of all domestic airline passengers today.

The Airline Deregulation Act of 1978 was intended to open the passenger market to new entrants to increase the level of competition. Since then, however, there have been no new entrants into the traditional hub-and-spoke airline market. While there have been a few successful entrants into the market (for example, Southwest), they were point-to-point airlines that did not compete against the legacy hub-and-spoke carriers (for example, United).

CASE QUESTIONS

1. Based on publicly available data, compare the four mega-carriers across the following characteristics:
   a. Number of aircraft by type;
   b. Number of employees;
   c. Departures;
   d. Revenue passengers;
   e. Revenue passenger miles;
   f. Available seat miles;
   g. Operating revenue (total);
   h. Operating revenue per seat mile;
   i. Operating profit.
2. Knowing the intent of the Airline Deregulation Act of 1978, explain why the number of passenger airlines in the industry has actually decreased. Be sure to include a discussion of barriers to entry in your explanation.
3. With the total U.S. market being oligopolistic in nature and at some hubs monopolistic, should the federal government takes steps to impose economic regulation on the passenger airlines again? Explain your opinion.
4. In your opinion, why did the Justice Department allow such consolidations to take place?

CHAPTER

8

WATER CARRIERS AND PIPELINES

Learning Objectives

After reading this chapter, you should be able to do the following:

- Understand the importance of domestic and global waterways to the development of the global economy as well as the economy of the United States
- Appreciate the role and significance of the water carrier industry to the global economy and to the United States, and how the water carrier industry complements the other basic modes of transportation
- Discuss the various types of water carriers and their roles in the overall water carrier system
- Understand the competitive environment for water carriers on an intramodal as well as an intermodal basis
- Discuss the service and operating characteristics of water carriers as well as their cost structure and equipment challenges
- Understand the challenges and issues faced by the water carrier industry in the 21st century
- Appreciate the development and current position of the pipeline industry globally as well as in the U.S. economy
- Discuss the various types of pipeline companies and their importance in the global transportation system
- Understand the nature of the operating and service characteristics of pipeline carriers and what makes them unique in the transportation system
- Discuss the cost structure and rates of pipelines and understand how it impacts their rates and services

TRANSPORTATION **PROFILE**

Bigger Ships for the Bigger Ditch

When the Panama Canal was being constructed across the Isthmus of Panama in the early part of the 20th century, it was referred to by some popular pundits as another Big Ditch. In spite of some early criticism and political negativity about cost and location, the Panama Canal was a success for global, waterway commerce. It allowed vessels to avoid traveling around South America. Among other advantages, it provided East and West Coast ports with improved access from Asian-Pacific locations and West Coast ports with improved access from European points. Also, East–West flows of domestic commerce in the United States were provided possible improved access. However, the Canal is slow by modern standards because of wait times and capacity constraints, and the tolls are considered prohibitive by some shippers. Nevertheless, it has remained important for commercial traffic.

The Canal is no longer owned and controlled by the United States, but the United States has a continued vested interest in making improvements. Consequently, in 2007, the United States announced a $5.2 billion expansion of the Canal that would allow container ships up to 13,200 TEUs (20-foot equivalent units or 20-foot-long cargo containers) in the wider, deeper canal. The expansion has also been called the Third Set of Locks Project because it will add two new locks and double the overall capacity of the Canal as well as widen and deepen current channels. It will also raise the maximum operating level of Lake Gatun.

When the expanded canal opens, it could be a "game changer" for global supply chains. Historically, many shipments from Asian-Pacific locations went through West Coast ports for shipment throughout the United States, but with the Panama Canal expansion such shipments could go directly to East Coast ports and/or European ports without unloading containers on the West Coast of North America. The potential change in flows has generated interest in Europe and the United States to expand their port infrastructure to accommodate the larger vessels.

The expanded canal is projected to open in 2016, but potential changes in traffic flows are not a "slam dunk" for shippers. There are important logistical issues to be resolved. There will be multiple supply chain routes available and shippers will have to carefully evaluate the total landed cost of each one. Depending on circumstances, flexibility may be limited once an alternative supply chain is selected. A wrong decision could have a negative impact on the "bottom line" of companies for an extended period. Consideration needs to be given not only to the actual transportation cost but also to time, cargo value, inventory carrying cost, and risk to develop an accurate landed cost. Said analysis can be complicated and tedious. Nevertheless, the "new" canal will impact global supply chains for years to come and influence many short- and long-term logistics and supply chain decisions.

Source: Adapted from "Navigating Impacts of an Expanded Panama Canal," *Inside Supply Management*, August 2013, pp. 18–21.

Introduction

Water carriers and pipelines are frequently overlooked by the general public. Most people are aware of trucks, planes, and trains, but they have limited appreciation of the role and contribution of water and pipeline carriers to businesses and our economy. These two modes of transportation are a very important part of the global transportation system and overall infrastructure, particularly for certain types of products. For example, it has been estimated that the cargo operations for the West Coast ports of Seattle and Tacoma supported more than 48,000 jobs in 2013 and generated about $4.3 billion in economic activity. The combination of the global activity and the port infrastructure were the basis of this good news and is indicative of the growing importance of appropriate transportation infrastructure to economic development and employment growth.

In this chapter, we will explore the growing role and importance of water carriers and pipelines to a modern transportation system to gain an understanding and appreciation of their significance and potential impact in the global economy. One would expect that the general public will become more interested in these two modes of transportation in the future as they become more appreciative of how they contribute to global economic development and employment opportunities.

Brief History of Water Transportation

The inland or domestic waterways (canals, rivers, lakes, and oceans) have provided an important link for freight and people movement for centuries. Waterways can be a natural highway and even provide some motive power (currents and wind). Water transportation has, of course, been improved by modern technology and federal investment to enhance motive power, vessel carrying capacity, and even the waterways by building dams, locks, and canals and dredging to increase the potential of water transportation for economic development. Today, there are over 40,000 navigable kilometers of waterways in the United States.

In Europe and other countries, rivers have also been important and efficient channels connecting cities and countries for commerce and passenger transportation. The Danube and the Rhine in Europe, the Amazon (longest river) in South America, the Nile in Egypt, the Yangtze in China, and the Ganges in India are additional examples of natural waterways that have helped to promote commerce and development in their respective regions or countries. Each has a story to tell of their historical importance for economic, political, and social impact that rivals that of the Mississippi River System in the United States.

Water transportation played an important role in the early development of the United States, providing the settlers with a link to markets in England and Europe. In addition, many of our major cities, Boston, New York City, Philadelphia, Baltimore, and so on, developed along the Atlantic coast and still thrive in those locations. As the internal sections of the country developed, water transportation along the rivers and the Great Lakes linked the settlements in the "wilderness" with the coastal cities and also gave rise to interior cities such as Pittsburgh, Cincinnati, and Memphis. Buffalo became a major entry way to the Great Lakes with the opening of the Erie Canal in 1825. New York City was a major beneficiary with their access to the Great Lakes via the Canal, and also the cities on the Lakes such as Toledo and Chicago. New Orleans on the Gulf Coast was the beneficiary of the traffic on the Mississippi River as were other cities along that waterway route. The subsequent economic growth of New York City spurred interest in other East Coast cities to establish an efficient link to the Great Lakes. For example, Pennsylvania developed a canal system (canal and tram) to connect Philadelphia to Pittsburgh and the Ohio River and the Great Lakes.

The waterways were the most important and efficient form of transportation available until the railroads were developed in the mid-18th century, especially for the United States, and were a prime determinant of population centers, as well as industrial and commercial concentration at port cities along the rivers and Great Lakes. Early private and public sector construction projects in transportation included the Erie, C&O, and other canals to provide inexpensive and efficient water transportation. On a global basis, the oceans of the world provided an economical avenue of commerce to connect continents and countries and their respective ports of entry.

The Panama and Suez canals have been the most important man-made waterways for global commerce, but both have challenges with the new, larger ships. As noted previously, the Panama Canal is being expanded for larger vessels and increased speed through the channel. In addition, the Saint Lawrence Seaway provides access from the Great Lakes to the Saint Lawrence River onto the Atlantic Ocean but has serious challenges because its locks limit the size of vessels and the ice in the winter months is another hindrance to efficient movement. One of the oldest, but perhaps the most spectacular, canals is the Corinth Canal in Greece. Because of its limitations, it is used mostly for local traffic and tourist vessels. There are additional potential sites for man-made waterways throughout the world that would connect and/or provide access for geographic areas. However, the cost along with military and political issues have been a deterrent to their construction in spite of the potential economic benefits.

This chapter focuses on the basic economic and operating characteristics of water and pipeline transportation. An overview of each mode is provided first, followed by a discussion and overview of the types of carriers, market structure, operating and service characteristics, equipment cost structure, and current issues for both modes. Given the global scope of this edition, the tables and figures will refer both domestic and foreign commerce.

Water Transport Industry Overview

Significance of Water Transport

In spite of some recent declines in domestic traffic, water transportation remains a very viable mode of transportation for the movement of products, especially for basic raw materials. Domestic water carriers compete with railroads for the movement of bulk commodities (such as grains, coal, ores, and chemicals) and with pipelines for the movement of bulk petroleum, petroleum products, natural gas, and chemicals. Globally, water carriers are usually the primary means of transportation between countries for a large variety of finished products especially for those moved in containers on large ships as well as bulk commodities that can be moved in the holds of large ships. Container movements are also quite common on some inland waterways such as the Great Lakes and for coastal shipments. The significance and importance of water transportation will be examined from the perspectives of ton-miles, market share, and shipper-freight expenditures.

In 2012, for-hire transportation accounted for $442.1 billion of U.S. gross domestic product (GDP), approximately 14 percent of the total, which was an increase from 2011 of $4.7 billion. Water carriers accounted for about 3.85 percent of the total expenditures of for-hire transportation included in GDP. Motor carrier expenditures dominated the market with 29.41 percent of the total for-hire expenditures included in GDP. However, the water carrier share increased from 3.22 percent in 2008 to 3.85 percent in 2012.

The distribution of domestic intercity freight as measured in ton-miles changed since the advent of transportation deregulation in 1980. Motor carriers were the biggest beneficiary, as noted previously, but water carriers have not fared as well. From 2010 to 2011, internal domestic water traffic increased by about 6 billion ton-miles, but coastal traffic declined by slightly over 12 billion. From 2008 to 2011, waterborne transportation had a total decline of almost 4 percent in ton-miles. In contrast to 1990, when water transportation accounted for almost 18 percent of ton-miles, there has been a decline to 8.5 percent of ton-miles for 2011. To give a broader sense of the trend over the last decade, from 2001 to 2011 water transportation ton-miles declined by 19 percent (see Table 8-1).

As of 2012, domestic waterborne transportation accounted for 905 million short tons, with inland transportation accounting for 62 percent of the tonnage. Water carriers collectively (coastwise, lakes, internal, intraport, and intraterritory) had an overall decrease in tonnage of 11 percent in 2012 compared to 2002 because tonnage shipped declined from 1,021 million to 905 million tons (see Table 8-1).

While the relative importance of water carriers' in the U.S. transportation system declined somewhat over the past decade, many manufacturers and suppliers would experience serious problems in maintaining their competitive position without the availability of low-cost water transportation. The decline in water transportation shipments is attributable in part to the shift of the U.S. economy from basic manufacturing to growing service and technology industries. The focus on logistics and supply chain management has also impacted water transportation because some companies have switched to carriers offering better service, for example motor carriers, to offset other costs such as inventory and warehousing.

An interesting dimension of the freight traffic carried by water carriers is the impact of global commerce. Table 8-2 shows foreign and domestic waterborne commerce from 1990 to 2012 as well as the total commerce for the years indicated. The table indicates that total commerce increased over the 15-year period from 1990 to 2005 and then declined slightly over the next seven years. The biggest decline was in the volume of domestic traffic between 1990 and 2012, which was the result of the changes noted earlier—less basic manufacturing and more effective intermodal competition. However, it is interesting to note that the volume of foreign commerce on the waterways has increased, which mitigated the overall decline in the total waterborne commerce. A similar pattern is seen in the data (see Table 8-3) for the river system of the United States. Domestic commerce has declined, and foreign commerce has increased. As one would expect, the inbound flow of foreign commerce has increased more than the outbound flow reflecting the level of imports versus exports on our balance of payments.

Another interesting comparison is the principal commodities moving in waterborne commerce. Table 8-3 lists the commerce for 2011 and 2012 indicating the totals, as well as the splits between foreign and domestic commerce. Examining the data for total commerce, there is a 2.6 percent decline between 2011 and 2012. The data for the split between foreign and domestic flows shows that foreign commerce had the largest decline between 2011 and 2012 (3.9 percent versus 0.3 percent), but that foreign commerce was still larger than domestic commerce by 537 million short tons, which is another indication of the importance of global trade for the United States. The largest declines among

TABLE 8-1 Freight Carried on Major U.S. Waterways 1980–2012

	2000	2005	2006	2007	2008	2009	2010	2011
Total U.S. Ton-Miles of Freight	5,501,444	5,659,393	5,699,463	5,739,534	5,998,009	5,468,001	5,689,672	5,899,165
Air	14,983	15,745	15,361	15,141	13,774	12,027	12,541	12,134
Truck	2,326,524	2,453,347	2,405,811	2,495,786	2,752,658	2,449,509	2,512,429	2,643,567
Railroad	1,546,319	1,733,324	1,855,897	1,819,626	1,729,734	1,582,092	1,706,505	1,725,634
Domestic Water Transportation	645,799	591,277	561,629	553,151	520,521	477,122	502,212	499,748
Coastwise	283,872	263,464	227,155	228,052	207,877	196,290	192,348	180,212
Lakewise	57,879	51,924	53,105	51,893	50,263	33,509	45,346	49,079
Internal	302,558	274,367	279,778	271,617	260,960	244,995	263,242	269,192
Intraport	1,490	1,521	1,591	1,589	1,421	2,327	1,277	1,265
Pipeline	967,819	865,700	860,766	855,831	981,323	947,252	955,986	1,018,082

Source: U.S. Department of Transportation, Bureau of Transportation Statistics, *National Transportation Statistics*, Washington, DC, 2013, Table 1-50.

TABLE 8-2 Total Waterborne Commerce of the United States

	1990	2000	2005	2010	2011	2012
Total	2,163,854,373	2,424,588,877	2,527,622,229	2,334,398,600	2,367,483,603	2,306,810,362
Foreign	1,041,555,740	1,354,790,984	1,498,711,806	1,440,937,396	1,479,553,348	1,421,894,930
Domestic	1,122,298,633	1,069,804,693	1,028,910,423	893,461,204	887,930,255	884,915,432

Source: U.S. Army Corps of Engineers, *Waterborne Commerce of the United States* (Washington, DC: Author, Annual Issues).

TABLE 8-3 Trade Within U.S. Waterways (Millions of Short Tons)

RIVER SYSTEM		1995	2000	2005	2010	2011	2012
Great Lakes	Foreign	52.4	66.8	61.6	40.9	37.8	34.6
	Domestic	125.3	120.7	107.8	88.6	96.9	91.4
	Total	177.7	187.5	169.4	129.5	134.7	126
Gulf Intracoastal	Foreign	-	-	-	-	-	-
	Domestic	118	113.8	116.1	116.2	112.5	113.8
	Total	118	113.8	116.1	116.2	112.5	113.8
Mississippi River System	Foreign	197.3	188.2	165.5	187.2	199.6	203.8
	Domestic	510	527.2	512.6	474.3	471.1	479.7
	Total	707.3	715.4	678.1	661.5	670.7	683.5
Columbia River	Foreign	39.5	33.2	33.9	41.5	31.2	43.3
	Domestic	17.6	22	17.5	13.3	13.1	13.5
	Total	57.1	55.2	51.4	54.8	44.3	56.8
Snake River	Total	6.8	6.7	5.2	3.3	2.7	3.2

Source: U.S. Army Corps of Engineers, *Waterborne Commerce of the United States* (Washington, DC: Author, Annual Issues).

the commodities moved were 12.2 percent for chemicals and related products and almost 10 percent for petroleum and related products—both changes were attributable to intermodal competition and structural changes in the industry.

It is interesting to note the importance of petroleum and chemicals for both foreign and domestic commerce (52 percent of the total for foreign commerce and 43 percent for domestic). It will be interesting to see the future impact of the new oil wells in the United States based upon fracking technology. The new oil fields will make the United States less dependent upon imports of crude oil and most likely will mean an increase in exports. The impact upon the waterways remains to be seen because of the location of the oil sources and the increase in rail and pipeline infrastructure.

Types of Carriers

Like motor carriers, the first major distinction for the domestic water carrier industry is classification of for-hire and private carriers. A private carrier transports freight for the company that owns or leases the vessel. Private water carriers are permitted to transport, for a fee, exempt commodities; when they are hauling such exempt goods, they are technically exempt for-hire carriers. Bona fide private water carriers (transporting company-owned freight and exempt commodities) are excluded from federal economic regulation, as are water carrier shipments of three or fewer commodities within the same barge unit. The water carrier industry, as previously noted, has less stringent requirements than the motor carrier industry to meet the exemption qualifications.

The for-hire water carriers consist of regulated and exempt carriers that charge a fee for their services. Exempt carriers, as indicated earlier, are excluded from the federal economic regulations administered by the Surface Transportation Board (STB). When authority was transferred to the STB under the ICC Termination Act of 1995, the STB's authority was expanded over domestic water traffic. In addition to inland river traffic, the STB has jurisdiction over port-to-port traffic when both ports are in the United States as well as transportation between the United States and its territories. Water carriers are exempt from economic regulation when transporting bulk commodities, both dry and liquid. Because the majority of freight transported by domestic water carriers consists of bulk commodities, exempt carriers dominate the for-hire segment of the industry.

Regulated water carriers are classified as either common or contract carriers. Economic regulation, similar to that controlling motor carriers, is administered by the STB. Although the majority of water traffic is exempt from regulation, a small number of regulated common and contract carriers do exist.

The domestic water carrier industry is most commonly classified by the waterway used. Carriers that operate over the inland navigable waterways are classified as internal water carriers. Internal water carriers use barges and towboats and operate over the principal U.S. rivers—the Mississippi, Ohio, Tennessee, Columbia, and Hudson—plus smaller arteries. Internal water carriers dominate the north-south traffic through the central portion of the United States via the Mississippi, Missouri, and Ohio rivers. The volume of freight moved on the major inland waterways is listed in Table 8-3 from 1995 to 2012. As indicated previously, the Mississippi River System is clearly the most important with over 683 million short tons in 2012.

The Great Lakes carriers operate along the northeastern portion of the United States and provide service between ports on the five Great Lakes that border the states of

TRANSPORTATION **TECHNOLOGY**

Here Come the Mega Ships: Big Changes Coming

Mega ships offer the potential for efficient service to lower costs for shippers because of their scale of operations. The previous discussion of the Suez Canal expansion indicated the importance of investing in the infrastructure for waterways, but the port facilities and related infrastructure are just as important for the efficient flow and transfer of traffic to other modes of transportation (usually motor or rail). In regard to the port facilities, there are already serious delays occurring from Southern California to New York. The lack of port efficiency for unloading freight in turn negatively impacts the number of turns or trips that trucking companies and logistics companies can make in a day, which obviously impacts their productivity and related operating cost. The rates that they should charge to customers will need to be adjusted accordingly.

The decline in productivity at the ports has become a disincentive for the drayage companies that move the freight in and out of the port areas because they have been challenged in making a suitable return on their invested capital and cover their operating costs. These circumstances have manifested into more and more operators "throwing in the towel" with declining replacements. The subsequent decline in available drayage capacity will lead to higher rates and higher costs for shippers and higher prices for consumers. So far, there has been more "heat than light" generated by the discussions to resolve the several factors contributing to port congestion and related delays. The following challenges need to be addressed:

- Developing Innovative Technology to Help Improve Port Efficiency
- Resolve the Issue of Chassis Availability When Containers Are Unloaded from the Ships
- Reduction of Wait Times at the Port Gates and Inside the Port Terminals
- Better Deployment of Labor in the Port Area to Improve Delivery Times to Customers

These are multifacet issues requiring input from all parties involved in the ports with some short-run improvement possible with collaboration and better management practices, but the long-run solution requires increased investment in the port infrastructures to effectively and efficiently accommodate the new mega ships. The West Coast ports that are so critical to the Asian Trade appear to be most directly impacted. There are frequent reports of the challenges and issues they face in various transportation and business periodicals.

Source: Adapted from "Big Ships, Bringing Big Changes," *Cargo Business News*, September 20, 2014.

New York, Pennsylvania, Ohio, Michigan, Indiana, Illinois, Wisconsin, and Minnesota. The lake ships normally remain on the lakes, but access to Atlantic and Gulf ports is possible via the Saint Lawrence Seaway. This Great Lakes-to-Atlantic traffic is classified as a coastal operation.

As indicated previously, coastal carriers operate along the coasts serving ports on the Atlantic or Pacific oceans or the Gulf of Mexico. Intercoastal carriers transport freight between East Coast and West Coast ports via the Panama Canal. Coastal and intercoastal carriers use oceangoing vessels, but some operators use oceangoing barges (18,000-ton capacity). Currently, large quantities of petroleum, crude and refined, are moved between points on the Atlantic and Gulf of Mexico. Likewise, oil from Alaska moves via coastal carriers to refineries along the Pacific coast.

Table 8-3 indicates foreign, domestic, and total short-ton movements on the important inland waterways. Some highlights to be noted are that the Mississippi River is the most important component of the inland waterway system with 683.5 million short tons in 2012, which is about 70 percent of the total tonnage moved that year and is a clear indication of the overall importance of the Mississippi and why the initial profile about the "Big Muddy" is of special interest. Domestic traffic was clearly more important than foreign on the inland river system by a ratio of 2.5 to 1. However, on the Columbia River, foreign commerce was three times that of domestic, which is indicative of Canadian movements into the United States. The peak year for the period 1995 to 2012 was 1995, which supports the observation made previously about the decrease in waterway traffic in recent years reflecting structural changes in the economy and intermodal competition.

Number and Categories of Carriers

The domestic for-hire water carrier industry consists of a limited number of relatively small firms. The latest numbers available from the Bureau of Transportation Statistics are for 2011, when it was reported that there were 584 vessel operators in service, and that number had decreased from 1,114 in 2000.

Excluding support activities such as port and harbor operations and navigation services, total employment for water transportation was 63,000 in 2010. In 2012, vessels on the Mississippi and Gulf intracoastal water accounted for 77.5 percent of U.S. vessels, and Great Lakes vessels represent 1.4 percent; the remainder of the vessels navigates the coastal areas, including the Atlantic, Pacific, and Gulf of Mexico. Based upon operating revenues for hauling domestic freight, the inland waterways (rivers and canals) were the most important, followed by the coastal waterways and then the Great Lakes carriers. Operating revenues on the inland waterways have remained relatively constant over the last decade, whereas revenue on the Great Lakes has increased about 23 percent because of an increase in higher-valued freight movements. Freight revenue on the coastal waterways declined about 40 percent during the 1990s as explained below. Water carriers have experienced increased competitive pressure, but the intensity has varied from segment to segment, with carriers operating along the coastal waterways experiencing the greatest impact of the competition, especially from railroads and pipeline carriers.

Competition

Water carriers vigorously compete for traffic with other modes and, to a limited degree, with other water carriers. The relatively small number of water carriers results in a limited degree of competition. Because the number of carriers on a given waterway is limited, there is little incentive for the water carriers to compete with one another by lowering rates because they realize that the rate decrease will most likely be matched.

The major water carrier competition is with two other modes, namely rail and pipelines. Water carriers compete with railroads for the movement of dry bulk commodities such as grain, coal, and ores. For example, the movement of grains from the Midwest to New Orleans (for export traffic) is possible by rail as well as by water carrier. The water carriers can use the Mississippi and Missouri river systems to connect the Plains States with New Orleans. Both modes move sizable amounts of grain along this traffic corridor.

Rail and water carriers compete heavily to move coal out of the coal-producing states of Pennsylvania, West Virginia, and Kentucky. The water carriers are capable of transporting coal via the Ohio and Mississippi rivers to Southern domestic consuming points (utilities), as well as to export markets.

On the Great Lakes, water carriers compete with railroads for the movement of coal, ores, and grain. Iron ore and grain originating in Minnesota, Michigan, and Wisconsin are moved across the Great Lakes to other Great Lakes ports, or out of the Great Lakes region via the Saint Lawrence Seaway to Atlantic and Gulf ports or to export markets. As will be explicated below, the development of the technology for fracking oil and gas from new geographic areas in the United States and Canada has resulted in renewed competition between railroads and pipelines for moving these products, particularly oil. It has also caused rail equipment shortages for shippers of grain in the upper Midwest of the United States. In fact fracking capability is causing transportation challenges in other areas discussed below. These "new" oil fields are in some ways a mixed blessing, at least in the short run, as adjustments are made for substantial flows of traffic in new directions. Our ability to develop the so-called shale fields has outpaced the development of additional transport equipment and infrastructure for domestic and global movements. The example of the Port of Toledo discussed below is another indication of the criticality of infrastructure.

The Port of Toledo became an important interchange point between rail and water carriers for the transport of coal. Railroads haul coal out of the coal-producing states to Toledo, where the coal is loaded onto lake ships for movement to northern Great Lakes ports. In essence, the railroads helped to overcome the water carrier accessibility problem by moving coal from the mines to Toledo, which suggests that the modes are partners rather than competitors. Because the cost of the water–rail combination is lower than the all-rail route, shippers continue to request the combined water–rail service. Again, the infrastructure of the port and its facilities is an important ingredient for the efficiency and effectiveness of the total movement.

Water carriers and pipelines are vigorous competitors for the movement of bulk liquids as indicated earlier. Bulk liquids (petroleum, petroleum products, and chemicals) account for about one-third of the total tonnage transported by domestic water carriers. Bulk liquids are important commodities to both modes, and vigorous competition exists for moving bulk liquids along the Gulf, Atlantic, and Pacific coasts, as well as the Mississippi River System.

To a very limited degree, water carriers compete with trucks. However, trucks are usually used to overcome the accessibility constraints of water carriers because trucks tie inland areas to the waterways for pickup and/or delivery. Shipment quantities are usually prohibitive for an all-motor carrier movement for long hauls because one barge can transport the equivalent of 58 tractor-trailers or more.

Operating and Service Characteristics

Commodities Hauled and Related Characteristics Figure 8-1 indicates the relative importance of the major commodities moved on the U.S. waterway system in terms of their annual volume. In 2012, water carriers hauled over 943 million short tons of petroleum, which represents 42 percent of the total short tons hauled that year.

Coal was the second most important commodity with about 329 million short tons or 14 percent of the total. Crude materials were a close third with over 323 million short tons.

FIGURE 8-1 National Internal Commodities Shipped by Waterborne Traffic of 2012 (Millions of Short Tons)

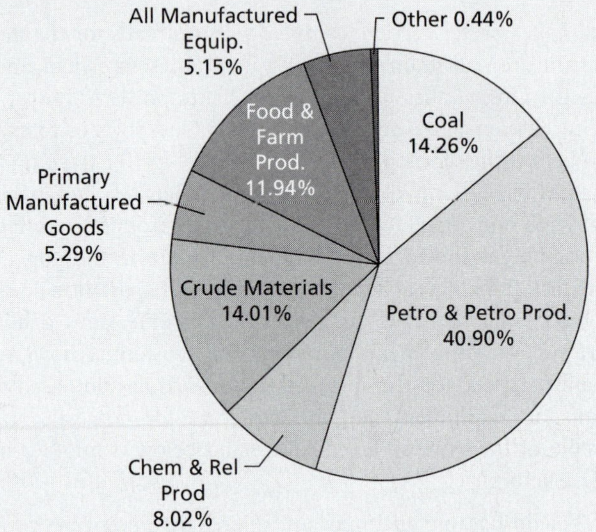

Source: U.S. Army Corps of Engineers, *Waterborne Commerce of the United States* (Washington, DC: Author, Annual Issues).

It is obvious that water carriers are important for low-value, bulk movements of liquid and dry materials. The low rates of water carriers are attractive to the shippers of such commodities, and the service requirements are not as stringent for these products.

Water carriers are considered to be medium-to-long-haul carriers. Their carrying capacity is relatively large, which makes short hauls with frequent stops uneconomical. However, the length of haul varies by segment from about 400 miles for inland water carriers to over 1,500 miles for coastal carriers. As noted, the carrying capacity is large. Barges are capable of carrying 1,500 to 3,000 tons, and lake carrier vessels can carry about 20,000 tons. A 1,500-ton load represents the typical carrying capacity of 15 railcars or about 50 trucks. The long hauls and the large carrying capacity combined with fuel efficiency allow water carriers to offer low-cost service—about 72 cents per ton-mile on average.

The low cost of the water carrier comes with some service disadvantages that need to be considered by shippers. Water carriers are relatively slow, with average speeds on inland rivers, for example, of 5.5 to 9 miles per hour. The limited accessibility of the water carrier usually necessitates pickup or delivery by another mode of transportation to bridge the accessibility gap. The transfer between modes will obviously add to the total cost.

Service can also be disrupted by weather. Rivers and lakes freeze during the winter months in the Northern states, which can interrupt service for several months. Drought conditions can lower water levels and restrict traffic flow. Conversely, heavy rains can cause flooding, which is also disruptive to service. The waterways are a natural highway, but Mother Nature can also constrain the flow of traffic.

Overall, water carriers are an attractive alternative for low-value traffic, where transportation rates are a significant part of the total delivered cost and price of the good. However, the poor service characteristics may add costs for the user, which have to be traded off against the low rate to calculate the true total cost.

Equipment

Types of Vehicles Because most domestic water carriers transport bulk materials, they use ships with very large hold capacity and openings to facilitate easy loading and unloading. Watertight walls dividing the holds allow a ship to carry more than one commodity at a time. However, most carriers will only carry a limited variety of products. The importance of the major types of equipment utilized on the inland waterways is indicated in Figure 8-2 in terms of their percentage of the total fleet.

The largest ship in the domestic water carriage industry is the tanker. A tanker can carry anywhere from 18,000 to 500,000 tons of liquid, generally petroleum or petroleum products. Due to oil spill problems, the use of double-hulled tankers has become preferable to the use of the more conventional single-hulled tankers. However, the building of these ships has diminished greatly since 1991.

Another type of vessel is the barge, a powerless vessel towed by a tugboat. Barges are most commonly used by internal waterway carriers. Additional barges can be added to a tow at very little additional cost. Consequently, barge transportation offers capacity flexibility comparable to railroads, at lower rates. Dry barge movements are the most popular.

Fuel As seen in Figure 8-3, the majority of fuel used by water transportation is residual fuel oil, also known as heavy fuel oil. This is the remainder, or residue, of fuel after crude oil is distilled. Diesel, also typically extracted from crude oil, makes up about a quarter of fuel consumption in water transportation.

Terminals Water carrier terminals are often provided by the public. Most ports are operated by local government agencies, and many ports have publicly operated storage facilities. It has been recognized for a long time that water transportation is a catalyst to economic activity in the community, and it is this belief that has spurred public investment in the operation of ports.

Some volume users of transportation invest in and operate port facilities or shipper terminals. Individual firms that handle such commodities as grain, coal, and oil commonly build docks, terminals, and commodity-handling facilities to meet their unique needs. The water carriers have the opportunity to use these private facilities owned by shippers.

Over the past few decades, major port improvements have centered on the mechanization of materials-handling systems, especially for internal waterway ports. Efficient handling of larger volumes of bulk commodities has been a prerequisite for ports that desire to remain economically competitive with other ports along the waterway and for water carriers that seek to be competitive with other modes.

The port facilitates ship loading and unloading, which means that the port must be equipped with cranes, forklifts, and other handling equipment. Certain commodities like oil, grain, and coal require more technically advanced loading equipment, such as pneumatic loaders and railcar dumping equipment. Such materials-handling equipment

FIGURE 8-2 U.S. Flag Vessels by Type

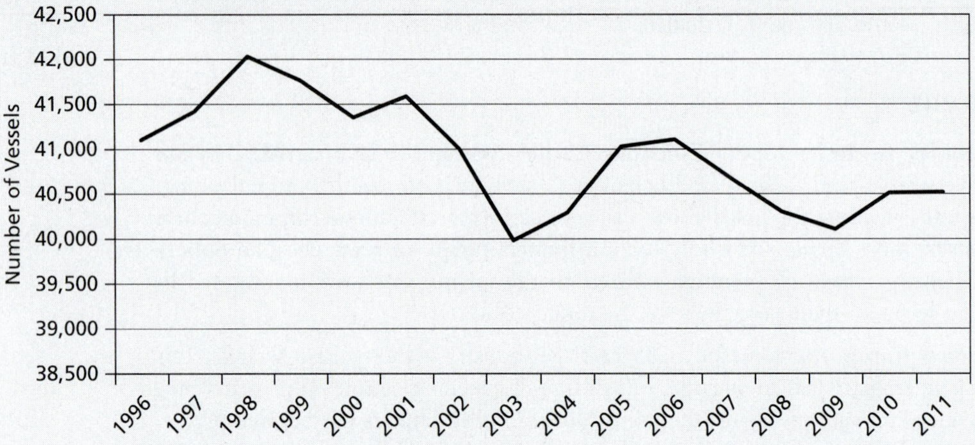

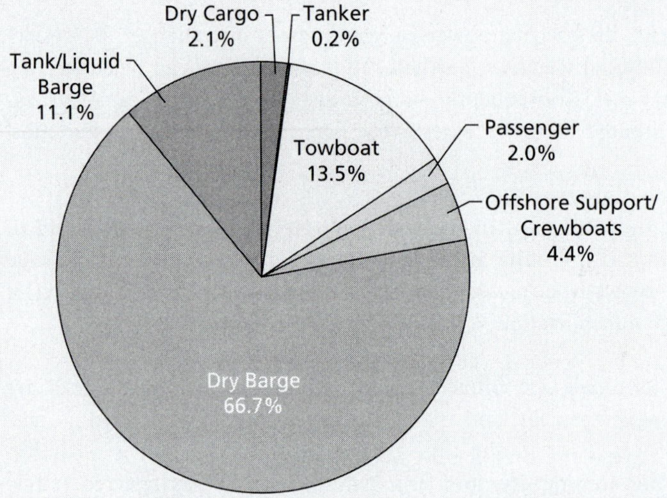

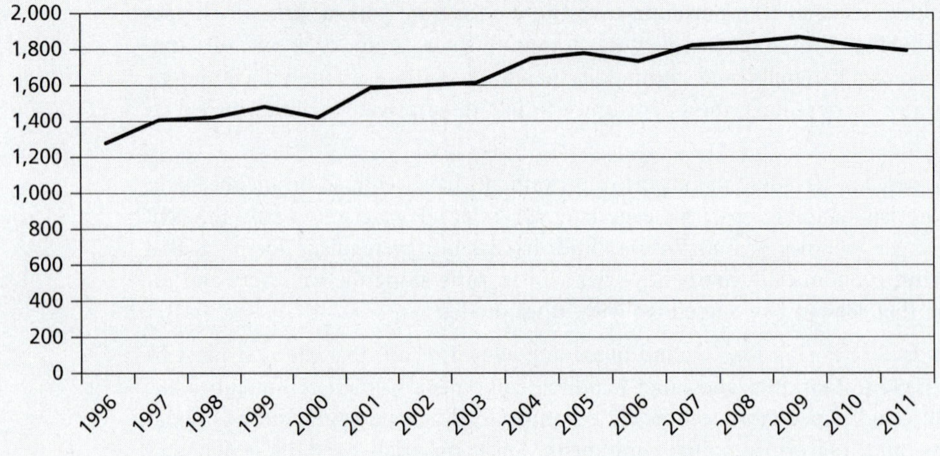

FIGURE 8-2 U.S. Flag Vessels by Type (*continued*)

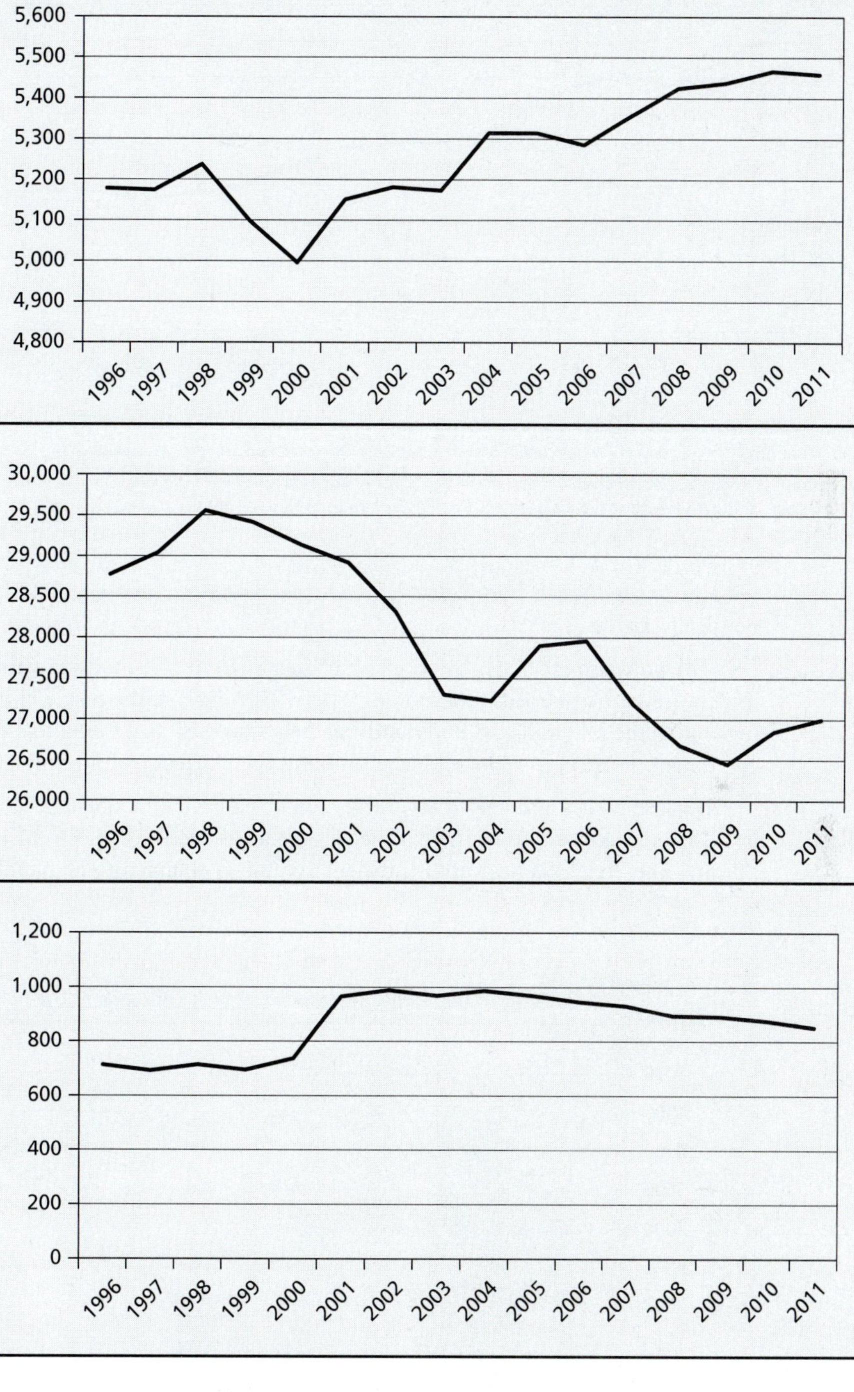

FIGURE 8-2 U.S. Flag Vessels by Type (*continued*)

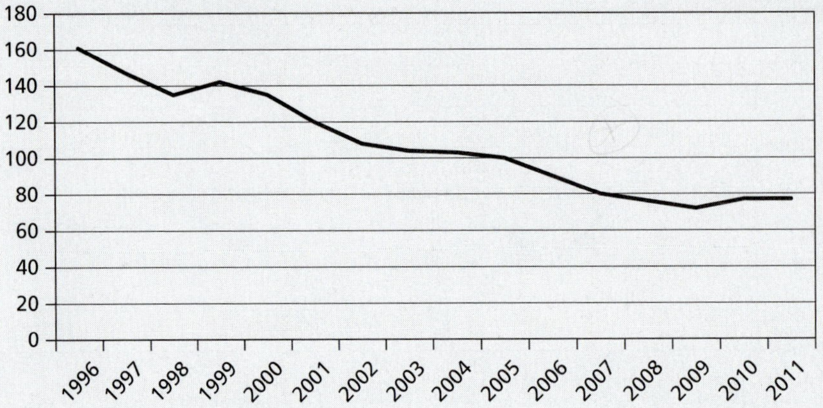

Source: U.S. Department of Transportation, Bureau of Transportation Statistics, *National Transportation Statistics*, Washington, DC, 2013, pp. 64–65.

Original Source: U.S. Army Corps of Engineers, *Waterborne Transportation Lines of the United States: Volume 1, National Summaries* (New Orleans, LA: Author, Annual Issues), Table 13, available at http://www.navigationdatacenter.us/wcsc/wcsc.htm as of Nov. 19, 2013.

reduces unproductive port delays and enables water carriers and ports to remain economically viable.

The port also facilitates the transfer of freight from one mode to another. The port is usually served by railroads and motor carriers. Terminals at the port will have railroad sidings to handle inbound and outbound rail freight as well as parking lots for motor carrier equipment. Ports play a key role in promoting the efficiency of intermodal transportation.

Because barges and ships carry larger loads than rail or motor carrier vehicles, storage facilities are necessary at the port. The storage areas receive cargo from many trucks and railcars. This freight is held until sufficient volume is obtained to be handled effectively by

FIGURE 8-3 Domestic Water Carrier Distribution of Fuel Consumption, 2012

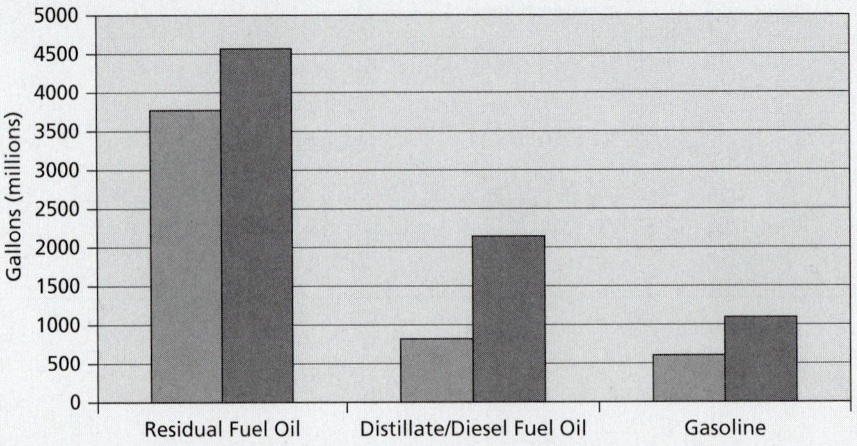

FIGURE 8-3 Domestic Water Carrier Distribution of Fuel Consumption, 2012 (*continued*)

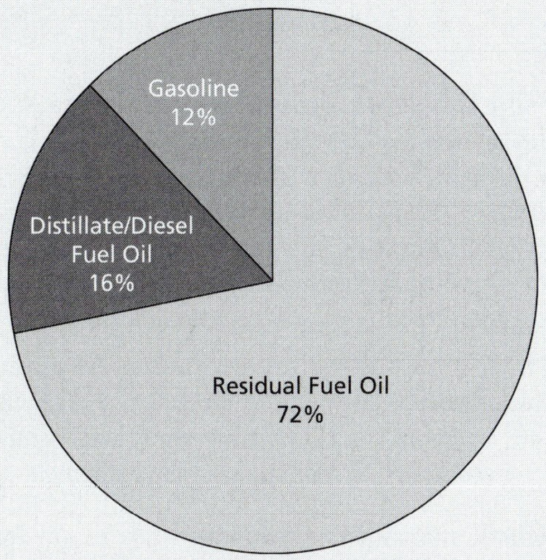

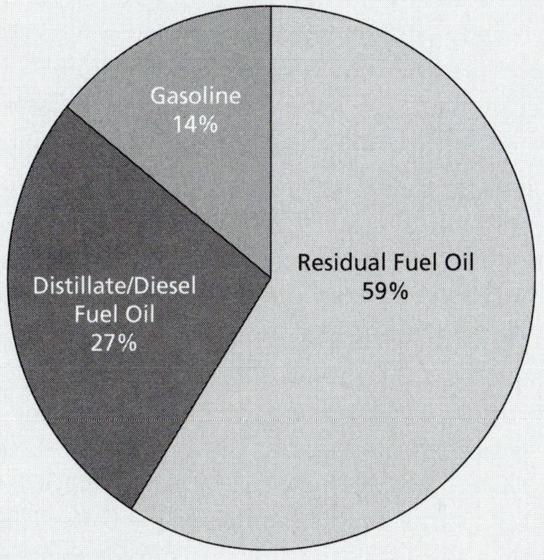

Source: U.S. Department of Transportation, Bureau of Transportation Statistics, *National Transportation Statistics*, Washington, DC, 2013, p. 247.

Original Source:

Residual and Distillate /Diesel Fuel Oil:

1960–80: American Petroleum Institute, *Basic Petroleum Data Book* (Washington, DC: Author, Annual Issues), Tables 10, 10a, 12, and 12a.

1985–2011: U.S. Department of Energy, *Energy Information Administration, Fuel Oil and Kerosene Sales* (Washington, DC: Author, Annual Issues), available at http://www.eia.doe.gov/oil_gas/petroleum/data_publications/fuel_oil_and_kerosene_sales/foks.html as of Mar. 9, 2012.

Gasoline:

1970–2011: U.S. Department of Transportation, *Federal Highway Administration, Highway Statistics*, Washington, DC, Table MF-24 and similar tables in earlier editions, available at http://www.fhwa.dot.gov/policy/ohpi/hss/hsspubs.cfm as of May 8, 2013.

barge or ship. Conversely, when a loaded vessel arrives at port, the freight is unloaded, stored, and then dispatched in hundreds of railcars or trucks at some later date.

Cost Structure

Fixed- Versus Variable-Cost Components The basic cost structure of water carriers consists of relatively high variable costs and low fixed costs. Like motor carriers and air carriers, water carriers do not provide their own highways (rights-of-way). The waterways are provided by nature (except canals) and are maintained, improved, and controlled by the government. The carriers pay user charges—lock fees, dock fees, and fuel taxes—for the use of government-provided facilities. These user charges are directly related to the volume of business and therefore are considered variable costs.

The operating costs for water carriers are approximately 85 percent variable and 15 percent fixed. Fixed costs include depreciation and amortization and general expenses. The major variable expenses are line-operating costs, operating rents, and maintenance. Line-operating costs are those expenses associated with renting operating equipment and facilities.

Infrastructure As indicated earlier, the domestic water carriers' low fixed costs can be attributed in part to public aid in the area of infrastructure. For water carriers, the major public aid is the construction and maintenance of waterways. The construction of canals with public fund opens new markets and sources of revenue for water carriers. The construction of locks and dams on rivers makes the waterways navigable for domestic water carriers. The dredging of the Mississippi River, for example, is performed by the Army Corps of Engineers to maintain channel depth and width. Port facilities are maintained by federal and local monies.

An example of a major public aid for domestic water carriers is the Tennessee Tombigbee (Tenn-Tom) project. Opened in 1985, the project connects the Tennessee River and the Warrior River via the Tombigbee River. Another example of public aid was when, in 1986, the federal government built two 1,200-foot locks and a new dam at Lock and Dam Number 26 on the Mississippi River System.

Critics of waterway projects like Tenn-Tom often refer to them as "pork barrel projects," suggesting that they are funded by government funds for the benefit of only a small number of the legislators' constituents. Critics question their value to society and maintain that these projects probably would not have been constructed if the actual users or local taxpayers had to assume the full burden of the costs. The U.S. Army Corps of Engineers has been responsible for conducting benefit/cost analysis to determine if such projects deserve to be funded by federal dollars, but critics question whether the Corps' analysis are realistic and whether the projects' expected benefits will ever be realized.

Labor Water transportation is not labor-intensive. In 2010, almost 8 million ton-miles of freight were transported for each water carrier employee. This compares to 7.9 million ton-miles for each rail employee, 2 million ton-miles for each motor carrier employee, and 22.7 million ton-miles for each pipeline employee.

Labor is required at the terminal to load and unload general commodities. The freight is moved from the dock onto the ship and into the appropriate hold for the voyage (and vice versa for unloading). In addition, labor is required to handle the loading of freight from connecting modes, such as truck and rail, and to store the freight waiting to be loaded onto the ship or connection carriers.

Domestic water carriers usually do not require much labor at the terminal, because the carriers primarily transport bulk commodities that can be loaded mechanically. Great

Lakes carrier companies have developed ships that are equipped with automatic unloading devices that reduce the amount of labor required to unload the ships. Even the container vessels operated on the Great Lakes are designed for expedited loading and unloading with appropriate cranes and other material handling equipment. Sometimes the biggest obstacle to efficiency is labor related.

Current Issues

Drug and Alcohol Abuse The grounding of the Exxon tanker *Valdez* off the shores of Alaska in March 1989 exemplifies the need for strong measures against drug and alcohol abuse in the water transportation industry. The captain of the *Valdez* was found to be intoxicated at the time the ship ran aground and spilled 10 million gallons of oil off Alaska's shores. The full impact of this disaster may not be known for many years to come; however, it is known that the environmental damage resulted in the deaths of hundreds of animals, including some endangered species, and the loss of income and jobs for many of Alaska's citizens (such as fishermen, for example).

In recognition of the problem of substance abuse, the U.S. Coast Guard now tests American seamen for drug abuse before they are issued a seamen's license and before they can be employed. Seamen are also tested randomly during their employment.

Port Development Because of today's environmental concerns, ports are having trouble keeping pace with the accelerated developments in global trade. They now have to balance competitive economic concerns with the concerns of the public, which, rightly or wrongly, often view ports as a main source of air, water, and noise pollution.

An example of the struggle would be the problems the Port of Oakland, California, faced in trying to get permission to dredge its harbors to a lower depth in order to berth new, larger vessels. Without the dredging, Oakland's competitiveness would decrease. But proposals for dumping the spoil from the dredging were denied at every turn. Soon another problem developed. The city's mayor decided to siphon port revenues into the city's coffers to alleviate budget problems. After local and international businesspeople united in support of the port's autonomy, the mayor backed down. Months later, thanks to the concerted efforts of two U.S. representatives and California's governor, the port got approval to dredge and dump the spoil in a cost-effective spot in the bay. Now, California is considering a bill that would allow the state to take revenue from the ports to replenish the state's depleted treasury.

Another current issue facing North American ports is the growth of multicarrier alliances, leading to the expansion of the already gargantuan ships. An increase from 6,000 to 10,000 TEUs has many ports worried for the future. The larger the ships are, the deeper they go, meaning that many of the smaller ports will need to begin the dredging process as soon as possible to be able to compete in the future. The dredging process would allow ports to make their waterways deeper and wider in order to accommodate these new, larger ships and allow them to stay competitive. However, as indicated earlier, the approval process for the dredging is sometimes problematic.

Brief History of Pipelines

Pipelines have played an important role in the transportation industry in the post–World War II era. Originally, pipelines were used to feed other modes of transportation, such as railroads or water carriers. The Pennsylvania Railroad initiated the development of pipelines in the oil fields of Pennsylvania in the 19th century and then sold out to the Standard Oil Company, establishing the precedent of pipelines being owned by the oil companies. Early in the 20th century, the oil companies operated the pipelines as integrated subsidiaries and often used them to control the oil industry by not providing needed transportation service to new producers. Consequently, after World War II, in a decision rendered by the U.S. Supreme Court, known as the Champlin Oil Case, pipelines were required to operate as common carriers if there was a demand by shippers of oil for their services. This decision was coupled with the growth in demand for gasoline after World War II and the need to move oil and oil products from the oil fields in Texas and Oklahoma to the markets in the northeastern states. The subsequent development of large-diameter pipelines, which were seamless for longer distance shipments, also spurred development and increased the efficiency of the pipeline industry.

Pipeline Industry Overview

The pipeline industry is unique in a number of important aspects, including the type of commodity hauled, ownership, and visibility. The industry is relatively unknown to the general public, which has little appreciation of the role and importance of pipelines. Pipelines are limited in the markets they serve and very limited in the commodities they can haul. Furthermore, pipelines are the only mode with no backhaul; that is, they are unidirectional with products that only move in one direction through the line.

Significance of Pipelines

As seen in Table 8-4, pipelines accounted for about 27 percent of total ton-miles in 1980, but their share of the total has declined in recent years and was 21 percent in 2009. However, their total ton-miles rose to a peak in 2008 of almost 954 billion ton-miles before declining in 2009 to about 910 billion ton-miles. Their share of total ton-miles moved in the United States is comparable to the share carried by water carriers. Few people in the United States would guess that pipelines are compared to other transport modes in terms of traffic volume. Pipelines are virtually unknown to the general public but represent a key component in our transportation system. Oil and oil products represent two-thirds of the ton-miles transported by pipeline, and natural gas makes up the other third.

TABLE 8-4 Pipeline Share of U.S. Ton-Miles of Freight

YEAR	TON MILES FROM PIPELINE (IN BILLIONS)	TOTAL U.S. TON-MILES (IN BILLIONS)	PERCENTAGE SHARE OF PIPELINE
1980	915.7	3402.9	27%
1990	864.8	3621.8	24%
2000	928.2	4328.8	21%
2005	938.7	4570.3	21%
2006	906.7	4630.8	20%
2007	904.1	4609.1	20%
2008	953.8	4647.6	21%
2009	909.7	4302.3	21%

Source: U.S. Department of Transportation, Research and Innovative Technology Administration (RITA), Bureau of Transportation Statistics (BTS), special tabulation.

TABLE 8-5 Pipeline Network (Thousands of Miles)

YEAR	OIL PIPELINE	NATURAL GAS PIPELINE
1960	191	631
1970	219	913
1980	218	1,052
1990	209	1,189
1995	182	1,278
2000	177	1,340
2005	131	1,489
2010	148	1,545
2011	150	1,564
2012	152	1,566

Sources:
2000 and before:
U.S. Department of Transportation, Bureau of Transportation Statistics, *National Transportation Statistics*, Washington, DC, 2008, p. 28.

After 2000:
U.S. Department of Transportation, Bureau of Transportation Statistics, *National Transportation Statistics*, Washington, DC, 2013, p. 34.

As shown in Table 8-5, the oil pipeline network grew steadily until about 1980, which allowed pipelines to move an increased amount of tonnage. However, does not adequately reflect the increase in total capacity because it does not show the diameter of pipelines. As we will discuss later, pipeline diameters have increased in recent years, and the larger diameters have increased capacity significantly because of the increased volume that can move through the pipeline. The larger diameter has also allowed the total oil network to decrease since the early 1980s to about 152,000 miles in 2012. Interestingly, natural gas pipelines (includes transmission and distribution lines) had more than 10 times the mileage of oil pipelines, 1,566,000 miles, in 2012. The distribution network of natural gas pipelines is the reason for the difference because it is the means of delivery to the ultimate user in most cases as opposed to truck deliveries for oil and oil products. The operating revenue of gas pipelines is more than six times greater than the operating revenue of oil.

The tonnage comparison shown in Table 8-4 is a sharp contrast to the IR revenue picture indicated in Table 8-6. Here the low rates of the pipeline, which are discussed later in this chapter, are reflected in the very low percentage of the total intercity revenue paid to oil pipeline carriers. The pipelines account for approximately 4 percent of the total transportation revenues, compared to motor carriers, for example, which account for more than 75 percent of the total revenue.

Types of Carriers

As noted earlier, due to the decision rendered by the U.S. Supreme Court in the Champlin Oil Case, many pipelines operate as common carriers. Hence, although some private carriers exist today, the for-hire carriers dominate the industry. Common carriers account for approximately 90 percent of all pipeline carriers.

TABLE 8-6 Total Operating Revenue of Pipelines ($ in Millions)

	OIL PIPELINE		GAS PIPELINE	
YEAR	OPERATING REVENUE	NET INCOME	OPERATING REVENUE	NET INCOME
2005	16,375	3,863	7,917	3,076
2006	17,122	4,015	8,516	3,743
2007	21,736	4,765	8,996	3,756
2008	19,797	5,104	9,243	3,931
2009	18,953	4,657	9,986	4,131
2010	29,790	5,210	11,219	4,582
2011	20,545	4,888	12,562	6,109
2012	20,969	4,764	14,007	6,423

Source: U.S. FERC Annual Reports (Forms 2, 2A, and 6) by Regulated Interstate Natural Gas and Oil Companies.

Ownership

With some exceptions, oil companies have been the owners of the oil pipelines—beginning with Standard Oil Company purchasing the pipelines operated by the Pennsylvania Railroad. Subsequently the oil companies developed pipelines more extensively to control the industry and enhance its market dominance. Oil companies became the principal owners of pipelines, but there has been some shift more recently with an increased number of pipeline companies operating as transport carriers.

The federal government entered the pipeline business briefly during World War II when it developed two pipelines to bring crude oil and oil products from the oil fields of the Southwest to the Northeast to ensure an uninterrupted flow of oil. These two pipelines, known as the Big Inch and the Little Inch, were sold to private companies after the war.

Some pipelines are joint ventures among two or more pipeline companies because of the high capital investment necessary for large-diameter pipelines. Individual, vertically integrated oil companies control the largest share of the pipeline revenues, followed by jointly owned pipeline companies. Railroads, independent oil companies, and other industrial companies control the remaining percentage.

Number of Carriers

Like the railroad industry, the pipeline industry has a small number of very large carriers that dominate the industry. In 2006 there were approximately 2,297 total pipeline operators. The oligopolistic nature of the industry is demonstrated by the fact that 20 major integrated oil companies control about two-thirds of the crude oil pipeline mileage.

There are a number of reasons for the limited number of pipeline companies. First, startup costs (capital costs) are high. Second, like railroads and public utilities, the economies of scale are such that duplication or parallel competing lines would be uneconomic. Large-size operations are more economical because capacity rises more than proportionately with increases in the diameter of the pipeline and investment per mile decreases, as do operating cost per barrel. For example, a 12-inch pipeline operating at capacity can transport three times as much oil as an 8-inch pipeline.

The procedural requirements for entry and the associated legal costs also contribute to the limited number of companies. An additional factor is the industry itself, which has been dominated by the large oil companies that joined together in the post–World War II era to develop pipelines from major fields and entry ports.

Oil Carriers The pipeline industry experienced rapid growth after World War II, but the rate of growth (percentage increase) has since decreased dramatically. Freight ton-miles increased to about 939 billion in 2005 but declined to about 910 in 2009. There were corresponding changes in other data, including the number of employees, which also decreased. Overall, however, oil pipelines play a major role in our transportation network because, as previously mentioned, they transport about 13 percent of the total freight ton-miles in the United States.

Natural Gas Carriers Another part of the pipeline industry is involved with the transportation of natural gas, which, like oil, is an important source of energy. The movement data for natural gas are recorded in cubic feet, rather than ton-miles. The industry is comparable in size to the oil pipeline industry in terms of the number of companies and, as in the oil pipeline industry, there has been a growth in the number of companies since 1975. It should be noted that there has been a reclassification of some companies since 1975, so the growth numbers are not exactly comparable. Natural gas pipelines represent about 7 percent of domestic ton-miles of freight. Finally, operating revenues have increased by about 41 percent between 2000 and 2005.

Operating and Service Characteristics

Commodities Hauled Pipelines are specialized carriers in that they transport a very limited variety of products. The four main commodities hauled by pipeline are oil and oil products, natural gas, coal, and chemicals.

Oil and Oil Products The majority of pipeline movements are crude oil and oil products. In 2007, pipelines moved about 66 percent of the total ton-miles of crude oil and petroleum products. Pipelines in total (including natural gas) experienced a 5.6 percent increase in freight ton-miles shipped from 1990 to 2006.

The total volume of petroleum transported domestically in the United States declined slightly during the 1990s. However, the split by modes between pipeline and water carrier has changed for several reasons. A pipeline was built across Panama during the 1980s, virtually eliminating long movements of Alaskan crude oil tankers around South America. The Alaskan crude oil is now transshipped via the pipeline to Atlanta tankers for Gulf and Atlantic Coast deliveries to refineries. Also, another large crude oil pipeline has been built, providing service from the West Coast to Midwest refineries and reducing the need for tanker movements even further.

The length of haul in the oil pipeline industry is medium in length compared to other modes. Crude oil movements average about 800 miles per shipment, and product lines average about 400 miles per movement. The average shipment size for these movements is very large. (This will be discussed later in the section titled "Equipment.")

Natural Gas Natural gas pipelines are an important part of our total pipeline network. They account for the second largest number of intercity miles of pipeline. (Figure 8-3 does not include all their transmission and distribution pipeline mileage, only intercity miles.) The natural gas pipeline companies produce about 10 percent of the gas they transport. Independent gas companies produce the remaining 90 percent and transport it via the pipelines. Similar to oil pipelines, the natural gas pipelines operate as public carriers.

Coal Coal pipelines are frequently called slurry lines because the coal is moved in a pulverized form in water (one-to-one ratio by weight). Once the coal has reached its destination, the water is removed and the coal is ready for use. Coal pipelines are primarily used for transporting coal to utility companies for generating electricity. The large slurry pipeline that operates between Arizona and Nevada covers 273 miles and moves 5 million tons of coal per year. Coal pipelines use enormous quantities of water, which causes concern in several Western states where their installation has been proposed, because there is a scarcity of water and the water is not reusable (as there is no backhaul).

Chemicals Chemical lines are another type of product line, although only a limited number of different types of chemicals are carried by pipelines. The three major chemicals are anhydrous ammonia, which is used in fertilizer; propylene, which is used for manufacturing detergents; and ethylene, which is used for making antifreeze.

Relative Advantages

A major advantage offered by the pipeline industry is low rates. Pipeline transportation can be extremely efficient with large-diameter pipelines operating near capacity. Average revenues for pipeline companies are below one-half of a cent per ton-mile, which is indicative of their low-cost service.

Two additional user cost advantages complement the low rates. First, pipelines have a very good loss and damage record (L and D). This record is attributed in part to the types of products transported, but it is also related to the nature of the pipeline service, which provides underground and completely encased movement.

The second important cost advantage is that pipelines can provide a warehousing function because their service is slow. In other words, if the product is not needed immediately, the slow pipeline service can be regarded as a form of free warehousing storage. (Products move through pipelines at an average of 3 to 5 miles per hour.)

Another positive service advantage of pipelines is their dependability. They are virtually unaffected by weather conditions, and they very rarely have mechanical failures. Although the service time is slow, scheduled deliveries can be forecasted very accurately, diminishing the need for safety stock. The risk of terrorism is reduced when the pipelines are buried in the ground.

Relative Disadvantages

Although the pipelines' slow speed can be considered an advantage due to its use as a free form of warehousing, in some instances the pipelines' slow speed can be considered a disadvantage. For example, if a company's demand is uncertain or erratic, it will have to hold higher levels of inventory to compensate for possible shortages because the pipeline will not be able to deliver an extra amount of the product in a short period of time.

Pipelines are also at a disadvantage when it comes to completeness of service because they offer a fixed route of service that cannot be easily extended to complete door-to-door service. That is, they have limited geographic flexibility or accessibility.

However, because the source of the pipelines and the location of the refineries are known and are fixed for a long period of time, the fixed-route service factor may not be a critical problem. Frequently, pipelines depend on railroads and motor carriers to complete delivery, which adds to user costs.

The use of pipelines is limited to a rather select number of products: crude oil, oil products, natural gas, coal, and a limited number of chemicals. There is interest in using pipelines for other products because of their cost advantage, but the technology for such use has not yet been fully developed. Capsule and pneumatic pipelines can carry and extend the low-cost, high-volume, reliable service to other bulk products. Frequency of service (the number of times a mode can pick up and deliver during a particular period) is a characteristic of interest to some users. On one hand, the large tenders (shipment size requirements) and slow speed of pipelines reduces the frequency. On the other hand, service is offered 24 hours a day, seven days a week.

Pipelines are generally regarded as somewhat inflexible because they serve limited geographic areas and limited points within that area. Also, they carry limited types of commodities and only offer one-way service. Finally, the operations technology precludes small shipment sizes.

In summary, pipelines offer a very good set of services for particular types of products, but they have some serious limitations for many other products.

Competition

Intramodal Intramodal competition in the pipeline industry is limited by a number of factors. First, there are a small number of companies—slightly more than 100. The industry, as noted previously, is oligopolistic in market structure, which generally leads to limited price competition. Second, the economies of scale and high fixed costs have led to joint ownership of large-diameter pipelines because the construction of smaller parallel lines is not very efficient. Finally, the high capital costs preclude duplication of facilities to a large extent.

Intermodal The serious threats to the pipeline industry are in terms of traffic diversion to other modes of transportation. Technically, pipelines compete with railroads, water carriers, and motor carriers for traffic. However, even with these forms of transportation, the level of competition is limited. The most serious competition is water tanker operations, because their rates are competitive with pipelines. However, the limited coverage of water carrier service also limits its effective competitiveness. Trucks have increased the number of products they carry that can also be carried by pipelines. However, truck service complements rather than competes with the pipeline because trucks often perform a distribution function (delivery) for pipelines.

Once a pipeline has been constructed between two points, it is difficult for other modes to compete. Pipeline costs are extremely low, dependability is quite high, and there is limited risk of damage to the product being transported. The major exception is coal slurry pipelines because the need to move the pulverized coal in water can make the costs comparable to rail movements. Water carriers come closest to matching pipeline costs and rates as indicated.

Equipment

The U.S. Department of Transportation estimates that the total pipeline investment is in excess of $21 billion, based on historical costs. Also, the department estimates it would cost about $70 billion to replace the system at today's costs. This great investment in the equipment is necessary to finance the complex operation of getting oil from the well to the market. From 1980 to 2006, oil pipeline infrastructure (in standard miles) dropped 22.5 percent, while the natural gas infrastructure rose 45.9 percent.

Pipelines can be grouped into other categories in addition to for-hire or private carriers. For instance, they are frequently classified as gathering lines or trunk lines, particularly in reference to the movement of oil. The trunk lines are further classified or subdivided into two types: crude and product lines. The gathering lines are used to bring the oil from the fields to storage areas before the oil is processed into refined products or transmitted as crude oil over the trunk lines to distant refineries. Trunk lines are used for long-distance movement of crude oil or other products, such as jet fuel, kerosene, chemicals, or coal.

Early in the history of the oil industry, the refineries were located primarily in the eastern part of the United States, and thus the long-distance movement of oil was basically the movement of crude oil. The state of technology in the industry also made it much easier to control leakage with crude oil than with refined oil products such as gasoline or kerosene. After World War II, however, refineries were developed at other locations, especially in the Southwest, when better technology (limited seams and welding techniques) made the long-distance movement of oil products easy to accomplish.

When comparing gathering lines and trunk lines, there are several important differences to note. First, gathering lines are smaller in diameter, usually not exceeding 8 inches, whereas trunk lines are usually 30 to 50 inches in diameter. Gathering lines are frequently laid on the surface of the ground to ensure ease of relocation when a well or field runs dry. Trunk lines, on the other hand, are usually seen as permanent and are laid underground.

The term *trunk line* is often used in conjunction with oil movements and can refer to crude oil trunk lines or oil product lines. Oil trunk lines move oil to tank farms or refineries in distant locations, whereas oil product lines move the gasoline, jet fuel, and home heating oil from refineries to market areas. Technically, however, any long-distance movement via a large-diameter, permanent pipeline implies a trunk-line movement. Therefore, when coal, natural gas, or chemicals move via pipelines, such movement is usually classified as trunk-line movement.

Commodity Movement

Gathering lines bring oil from the fields to a gathering station, where the oil is stored in sufficient quantity to ship by trunk line to a refinery. After the oil is refined, the various products are stored at a tank farm before they are shipped via product line to another tank farm with a market-oriented location. A motor carrier most frequently makes the last segment of the trip, from the market-oriented tank farm to the distributor or ultimate customer.

Trunk lines, as indicated previously, are usually more than 30 inches in diameter and are the major component of the pipeline system. Stations that provide the power to push the commodities through the pipeline are interspersed along the trunk line. For oil movements, pumps are located at the stations, which vary in distance from 20 to 100 miles, depending on the viscosity of the oil and the terrain. Figures 8-4 and 8-5 illustrate the major interstate and intrastate pipelines in the United States.

FIGURE 8-4 Crude Oil Tonnage Moved by Pipeline, 2007

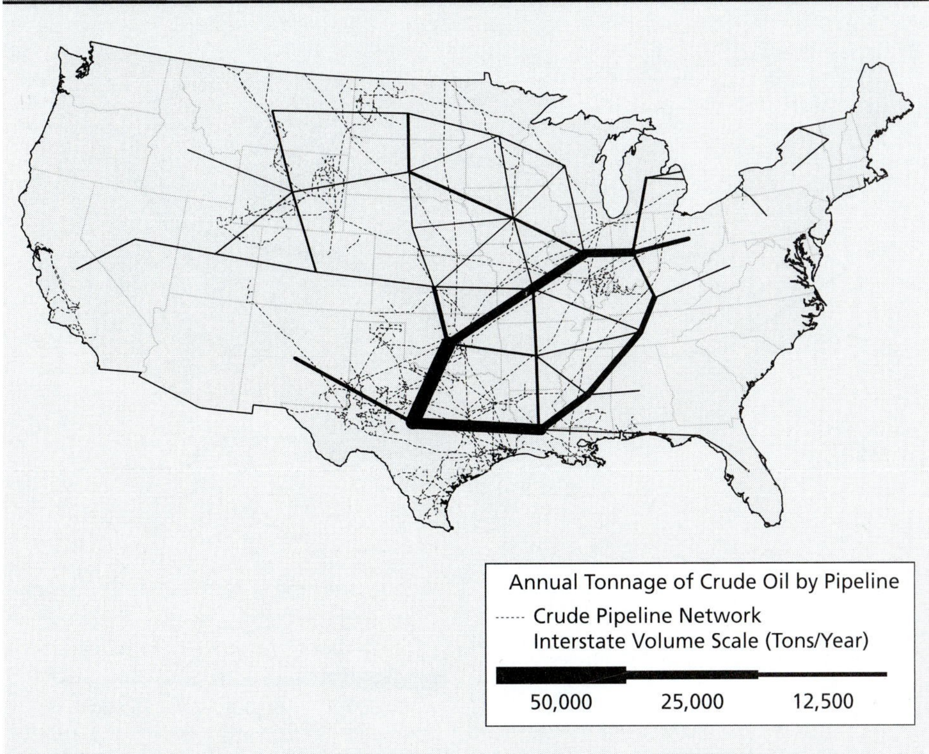

Source: U.S. Department of Transportation, *Federal Highway Administration*, Office of Freight Management and Operations, Freight Analysis Framework, version 3.4, 2012.

The pumping stations for large-diameter pipelines can provide 3,000 to 6,000 horsepower. Compressors are used for the movement of natural gas, and pumps are used for the liquid items that move through the pipelines.

Computers at the pumping stations continually monitor the flow and pressure of the oil system. Any change indicating a leak is easily detected. Routine visual checks and searches by airplane are sometimes used to locate leaks. Great care is rendered, not only because of the potential losses but also because of the lawsuits that could ensue as a result of damage to property and the environment.

In the oil segment of the pipeline industry, sophisticated operating and monitoring techniques are used because of the different petroleum products moving through the product lines and the different grades of crude oil moving through the crude oil lines. There are 15 grades of crude oil and a range of products including jet fuel, kerosene, and aviation fuel. When two or more grades of crude oil or two or more products move through a system at one time, the "batches" may need to be separated by a rubber ball called a batching pig. However, this is not always necessary because the different specific grades of the products helps to keep them separated. Any mixing (slop) that does occur is only minor amounts of high-grade products mixed into lower-grade items. Usually, products are scheduled one month in advance with kerosene moving first, then high-grade gasoline, then medium-grade gasoline, then various other products, with home heating oil last. Before the cycle starts again, the pipeline is usually scoured to prevent mixing problems.

FIGURE 8-5 Natural Gas Tonnage Moved by Pipeline, 2007

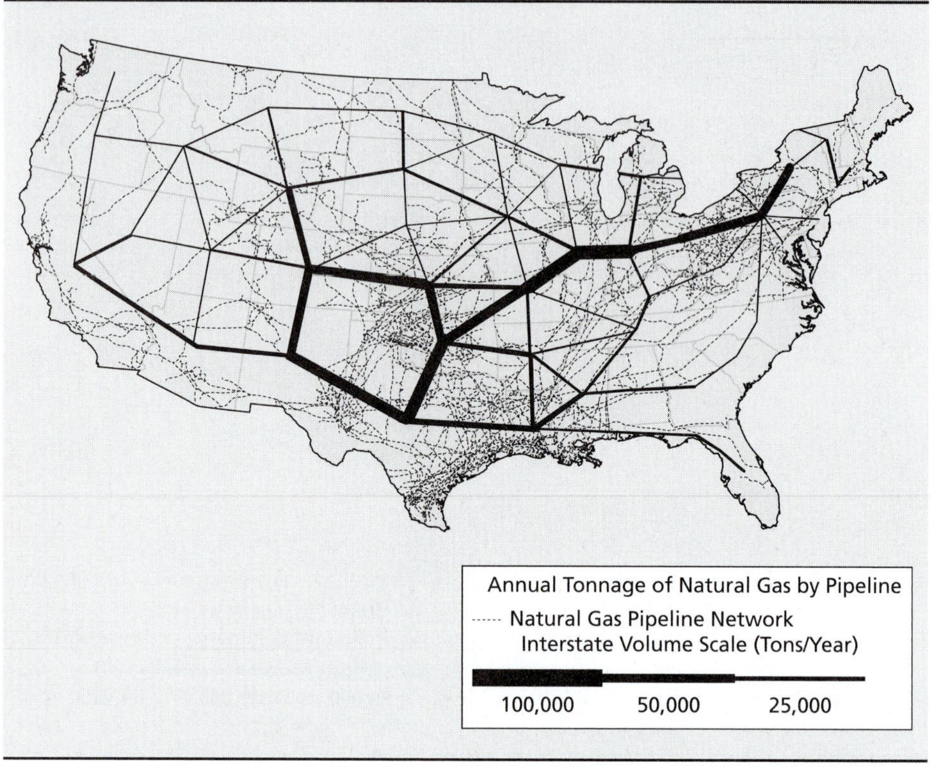

Source: U.S. Department of Transportation, *Federal Highway Administration*, Office of Freight Management and Operations, Freight Analysis Framework, version 3.4, 2012.

Cost Structure

Fixed- Versus Variable-Cost Components Like the railroad industry, the pipeline industry has a high proportion of fixed costs with low capital turnover. The pipeline owners have to provide their own right-of-way by purchasing or leasing land and constructing the pipeline and pumping stations along the right-of-way. The property taxes, amortizations of depreciation, return to investors, and preventative maintenance all contribute to the high ratio of fixed to variable expenses.

In addition to the right-of-way costs, the terminal facilities of pipelines contribute to the high level of fixed costs. The same types of expenses associated with the right-of-way, such as depreciation and property taxes, are incurred by the pipeline terminals.

As stated previously, the pipeline industry has significant economies of scale. The high fixed costs and the economies of scale help to explain the joint ownership and investment in large-diameter pipelines. Pipelines do not operate vehicles like other modes of transportation because the carrying capacity is the pipe itself, which is best regarded as part of the right-of-way. This unique element of the pipeline operation helps to explain the low variable costs because vehicles are frequently a major source of variable expense.

Labor costs are very low in the pipeline industry because of the high level of automation. One example is the Trans-Alaska Pipeline System, built at a cost of $9.2 billion and operated by 450 employees. The pipelines employ about 8,000 people compared to about 10 million in the motor carrier industry for comparable ton-miles on an intercity basis. Another variable cost is the cost of fuel for the power system.

Rates Pricing in the pipeline industry is unique compared to its major modal competitors. First of all, pipelines do not use the freight classification system that underlies the class rates of railroads and motor carriers. The limited number and specialization of commodities make such a practice unnecessary. A crude oil pipeline or natural gas pipeline has little need for an elaborate classification system.

Even though pipelines have high fixed costs, the differential pricing practices common in the railroad industry are virtually nonexistent among pipelines. The nature of operation (one-way movement, limited geographic coverage of points, limited products, and so forth) provides little opportunity to provide differential pricing practices.

ON THE **LINE**

The Politics of Global Pipelines

Similar to other modes of transportation, pipelines can provide the links for bringing nations together because they can establish political and economic alliances based upon convenience and/or necessity. In today's world, they can be viewed as one of the trade routes of the 21st century. Pipelines can be a vital delivery system for water, oil, oil products, and natural gas. They help sustain the economic and, perhaps, social wellbeing of some countries.

For countries that produce oil but do not have ports, pipelines carry material resources for hundreds, or even thousands, of miles. Pipelines, therefore, allow foreign revenue to flow into the producing country to support the local citizenry, and they can provide social capital to support economic improvements.

Pipelines can enable wealth, development, power, economic stability, global leverage, and so forth, but they also can lead to political tensions. It has been estimated by several sources that there are over a million miles of oil and natural gas pipelines crisscrossing the globe among independent nations. They are arteries of modern commerce in some parts of the world.

Pipelines crossing national boundaries create a need for interdependence and collaboration, which can give rise to national issues as well as international issues. Pipelines can be a major influence on political strategy and foreign policy. The United States, for example, consumes more oil than it produces and for political and security reasons purchases oil from a variety of sources. Some of those sources are landlocked, which necessitates pipeline transportation, usually to a port in another country where the oil can be transshipped to a tanker ship for movement to a designated refinery.

When new oil sources are discovered in a landlocked country, it usually necessitates the development of a pipeline to unlock the newly discovered resource. Russia is a good example of such a situation. Russia is one of the largest exporters of oil. The former Soviet Republics around the Caspian Sea also figure into this equation. Consequently, the United States is supporting development of pipelines designed to transport crude oil from the Caspian Port Baku, Azerbaijan, through Tbilisi, Georgia, to the port of Ceyhan in Turkey. This is only one example and there are others.

Pipelines have been described as an almost invisible part of the U.S. transportation infrastructure, but they are much more visible in global situations as described earlier. They connect nations and provide the basis for economic and political alliances, which, in turn, may promote stability in the geographic areas of the pipeline. Economic interdependence can help to stabilize alliances, as long as there are not any outside influences that disrupt or impede the flow of oil through the pipelines. In this age of terrorism and political unrest in the Middle East and South America, there is a continuing threat of disruption and permanent interruption.

Source: Adapted from Steve Goldstein, "Pipeline Diplomacy," *The Philadelphia Inquirer*, October 26, 2003, pp. C1 and C3.

Pipelines quote rates on a per-barrel basis (one barrel equals 42 gallons). Quotes for rates are typically point-to-point or zone-to-zone. Also, minimum shipment sizes, usually called tenders, are required; these range from 500 to 10,000 barrels.

Pipeline rates are very low, which is reflected in the fact that they carry about 20 percent of the total intercity ton-miles and receive only about 4 percent of the total revenues.

SUMMARY

- Water carriers played a key role in the development of many cities and regions both globally and domestically.
- The water carrier system is still a viable part of the total transportation system and competes with the railroad system and pipelines for the movement of bulk, low-value commodities.
- The domestic water carrier system can be classified in terms of inland carriers (rivers, canals, and Great Lakes) and coastal/intercoastal carriers. Both types are important components of the water carrier system.
- Intramodal competition among water carriers is not as important as intermodal competition with railroads and pipelines. All three of these modes compete for long-distance movements of bulk commodities.
- Water carriers offer low-cost services, but their transit time is slow and can be interrupted by weather conditions. Accessibility and potential product damage are also service disadvantages.
- Water carriers have relatively low fixed costs because they use a right-of-way provided by the government for which they pay user charges, like motor carriers and airlines.
- Water carriers are not labor-intensive for their movement operations but may require more labor in terminal areas for certain types of freight.
- The development of pipelines began in the 19th century in Pennsylvania by the Pennsylvania Railroad, but subsequently the ownership and development were taken over by the oil companies, who operated them as integrated subsidiaries.
- Ownership of pipelines by oil companies has continued to the present, but some oil pipelines are now owned by non-oil companies. Also, joint ownership by several companies has become common because of the large investment of capital necessary for construction.
- The pipeline industry is a large component of our transportation industry (more than 20 percent of intercity ton-miles), but it is largely invisible to many people.
- Because of market-control tactics used by some oil companies, an important U.S. Supreme Court ruling after World War II required pipelines to operate as common carriers even if owned by an oil company.
- Pipelines are very specialized in terms of the commodities that they carry. Most of the traffic is oil and oil products, but they also carry natural gas, chemicals, and coal.
- Only a small number of pipeline companies operate in the United States (about 100), and they have limited intramodal competition.
- Pipelines are low-cost carriers when operated near capacity, but they have high levels of fixed cost because of the heavy investment necessary in infrastructure. They need volume to lower unit costs.
- Pipeline service is relatively slow and has limited accessibility, but it is very reliable in terms of delivery with little or no loss and damage.
- Intercity pipeline service is provided by large-diameter (30–50 inches) pipelines called trunk lines. Small-diameter pipelines, called gathering lines, are used to bring the oil

from the producing area to the terminals for storage before processing and/or transporting.

- Pipelines are a highly automated, efficient form of transportation. Oil moves in one direction in large volumes at a steady, slow speed.
- Although there is always concern about safety and the environment, pipelines have been a relatively safe mode of transportation.

STUDY QUESTIONS

1. The integrated ownership of pipelines was initially used by some oil companies to gain control of oil-producing area. How did they use their transportation network to gain market control? What other reasons can be offered for integrated ownership? Are these reasons valid in today's business environment?
2. The pipeline industry has approximately 100 companies, as compared to the motor carrier industry with more than 50,000. What are the underlying economic causes for this difference, given the fact that they both carry approximately the same volume of intercity ton-miles?
3. The typical pipeline company has high fixed costs. What economic factors account for this situation? What advantages and disadvantages does their cost structure present?
4. Pipelines account for more than 20 percent of the intercity ton-miles but less than 5 percent of the revenue paid by shippers to transportation companies. What factors account for this contrast? Is this situation likely to change? Why or why not?
5. The economic and market position of the pipelines has been described as mature and stable with little likelihood of significant growth in the near future. Do you agree? Why or why not?
6. Water carriers played a dominant role in the transportation system of the United States in the 18th and 19th centuries. Why has their relative position declined during the 20th century? Are they still an important component of the total transportation system? Why or why not?
7. What would be the impact of higher fuel charges on the water carrier industry? Provide a rationale for raising their user charges.
8. Technology often offers the potential of improving efficiency and effectiveness of transportation companies, but water carrier do not appear to have applied much new technology to improve their service. What impediments slow technological progress in the water carrier industry?
9. Intermodal competition is more intense than intramodal competition for water carriers. Why?
10. Why are pipelines unknown to many individuals? Do you think the pipelines should advertise to change this?

CASE 8-1

Great Lakes Carriers: A Sequel

During the summer of 2014, Ben Heuer, president and chief operating officer of Great Lakes Carriers (GLC), and E. Kate Weber, vice president of business development, revisited the port directors of every major port on the Great Lakes. Their objective was to seek additional business for GLC's bulk cargo division with a related objective of exploring potential demand for increased container ship operations on the Great Lakes.

GLC was founded in 1940 by Ben's grandfather with one ship hauling coal and iron ore from the mines along the Great Lakes to the steel mills in Indiana, Ohio, and surrounding areas. Today the company has a fleet of 12 bulk vessels that move grain from the upper Great Lakes area to Chicago, Buffalo, and Erie. There is also some continued demand for bulk coal and iron ore movements. The demand for the movement of such commodities has decreased in the 21st century because of increased foreign steel production, and the railroads have increased their share of the grain movement with new larger hopper cars, which provide more dependable movement.

GLC has developed some container ship service on the Great Lakes, but the volume has been disappointing. Container traffic between the United States and the European Union can move via railroad to the port of Montreal, where it is transloaded to an oceangoing container ship. Substantial NAFTA container traffic (USA–Canada) moves via either railroad or truck to major cities adjacent to the Great Lakes. Lastly, the area surrounding the Great Lakes is a major manufacturing region with large volumes of traffic moving among the major port cities and to inland locations. Radio Frequency Identification (RFID) technology is providing GLC with some competitive advantage for higher-value container traffic where visibility could help improve supply chain efficiency and effectiveness. Kate also believed that they could charge higher rates with RFID tags and explore the possibility of diversifying even further into logistics-related services.

Ben and Kate discussed the type of vessel that would be needed to move containers and concluded that current GLC vessels could not be retrofitted for container operations. Furthermore, the new ship would have a maximum carrying capacity of about 1,000 containers because of the size limitations imposed by the locks on the Saint Lawrence Seaway. The typical oceangoing container ship has a minimum carrying capacity of 2,500 containers.

The proposed operation would consist of weekly sailing schedules beginning in Duluth and stopping at Chicago, Detroit, Toledo, Cleveland, Buffalo, and Montreal. Containers would be picked up and delivered at each port along the route. The transit time from Duluth to Montreal was estimated to be five to seven days, compared to four to five days by rail and two days by truck. For intermediate origin-destination pairs, such as Chicago to Cleveland, the transit time was estimated to be three days, which compared favorably with railroad service; however, the truck transit time was one day. The rate for the container service was estimated to be 40 percent of the current truck rate and 75 percent of the current rail rate, but the RFID program may allow higher rates because it would be a premium service and differentiate GLC from the rail and motor carriers.

The meetings with the port directors confirmed that the volume of grain and iron ore being handled by Great Lakes carriers was on the decline and the predictions for the next five years were for a continued decline. The lack of adequate container ship service on the Great Lakes was also confirmed and the port directors were enthusiastic about the possibility of GLC initiating such service. They were also interested in the advantages of the RFID technology even though it would require some additional investment for them. Ben and Kate decided to delay the decision to invest in the new equipment and technology because of the economic forecasts for the Great Lakes region and related potential cash flow problems. Also, the development of new oil fields more recently with the development of fracking technology in New York, Ohio, and Pennsylvania were changing the economic landscape of the Great Lakes region. Now they were reconsidering their alternatives before moving ahead, with their plans for investment in new technology and equipment.

CASE QUESTIONS

1. What is the overall impact of the new sources of energy in the Great Lakes area? What is the likely impact on commodity flows in that area? What will be the likely impact on GLC?
2. What are some of the logistics supply chain issues that GLC should consider?
3. What recommendation would you make to the GLC board of directors regarding a container ship operation and the possibility of new bulk shipments of oil and possibly chemicals?

CASE 8-2

CNG Pipeline Company

At the weekly brainstorming session, John Spychalski, president of CNG Pipeline Company (CNG), suggested that they build a new pipeline from Elizabeth, New Jersey, to the Midwest to move refined petroleum products, gasoline, and diesel fuel. Following some discussion, he asked the strategic planning group to consider the idea before the next brown-bag session.

Skip Grenoble, vice president for strategic planning, thought that John was not considering the cost and impact of this idea. How could CNG obtain land to build the pipeline, let alone obtain the necessary capital to finance the project? Then there was the question of the existing refineries located in Ohio, Indiana, and Illinois. Skip knew refined petroleum products were being transported from the Gulf of Mexico refineries via barge and pipeline to the Midwest market areas currently.

Skip turned over the project to Evelyn Thomchick, chief strategy analyst, to develop a preliminary analysis of the viability of building a new pipeline. In the span of six days Evelyn found the following strategic issues for the project:

- At least four Midwest refineries were being planned for closure within the next five years because of environmental and cost considerations.
- A number of major refineries were considering building new refineries offshore, closer to the sources of foreign oil. Both cost and environmental considerations suggested this consideration.
- The New Jersey–Midwest corridor was one of the most-developed land regions in the United States with the highest land values.
- The demand for refined petroleum products was expected to increase, but the keen interest in alternative sources of energy, new oil fields in several states, more fuel-efficient cars, and sustainability issues were matters of some concern.
- The project would require approximately 10 years to complete, including the time to obtain land via the eminent domain process.
- The capital requirements for the project were estimated at $800 billion.

CASE QUESTIONS

1. Do you feel the project has any merit for further investigation? Why or why not?
2. What likely impact will the new Shale oil fields in New York and Ohio have on the economic viability of this proposal?
3. What is your political assessment of building a pipeline that will traverse five states?

Suggested Readings

Chapter 5 Motor Carriers

Bernstein, Mark, "Wireless Takes to the Road," *World Trade* (April 2008): 26.

Burnson, Patrick, "Parcel Express Roundtable: Slugfest," *Logistics Management* (January 2009): 33–36.

Cantor, David E., Thomas M. Corsi, and Curtis M. Grimm, "Safety Technology Adoption Patterns in the U.S. Motor Carrier Industry," *Transportation Journal*, Vol. 45, No. 3 (Summer 2006): 20–45.

"Critical Issues in the Trucking Industry," *The American Transportation Research Institute* (October 2008).

Donath, Max, "Homeland Security and the Trucking Industry," *The American Transportation Research Institute* (July 2005).

Schulz, John D., "Only the Strong Will Survive," *Logistics Management* (April 2009): 46S–54S.

Schulz, John, "Cutting LTL Costs: Going to the Bench," *Logistics Management* (February 2009): 35.

Zuckerman, Amy, "Transportation Management Systems Give Shippers Power to Make Smarter Trucking Choices," *World Trade* (January 2008): 34.

Chapter 6 Railroads

Berman, Jeff, "Senate Committee Endorses Railroad Antitrust Legislation," *Logistics Management* (April 2009): 15–16.

Berman, Jeff, "2008 Annual Report—Railroads: Volume Is Down, but Business Is Up," *Logistics Management* (July 2008): 38.

Berman, Jeff, "Study Says Railroad Fuel Surcharges Exceeded $6.5 Billion," *Logistics Management* (October 2007): 19.

Boyd, John D., "Carloads in Reverse," *Traffic World* (January 5, 2009): 26.

McCue, Dan, "The Changing Landscape of U.S. Railroads," *World Trade* (January 2009): 30.

Sheys, Kevin, "Rail Safety Is No Paper Chase," *Traffic World* (January 5, 2009): 7.

Chapter 7 Airlines

Abeyratne, Ruwantissa, "Competition in Air Transport—The Need for a Shift in Focus," *Transportation Law Journal*, Vol. 33, No. 2 (2005–2006): 29.

Cheng, Yung-Hsiang, and Chian-Yu Yeh, "Core Competencies and Sustainable Competitive Advantage in Air Cargo Forwarding: Evidence from Taiwan," *Transportation Journal*, Vol. 46, No. 3 (Summer 2007): 5–21.

Sowinski, Lara, "Air Cargo Flies a New Heading," *World Trade* (August 2008): 34.

Theurmer, Karen E., "Air Cargo: Flying Low," *Logistics Management* (May 2009): 31.

Theurmer, Karen E., "2007 State of Logistics Report/Air Cargo: Nowhere to Go but Up," *Logistics Management* (July 2007): 42.

Wong, Jehn-Yih, and Pi-Heng Chung, "Retaining Passenger Loyalty Through Data Mining: A Case Study of Taiwanese Airlines," *Transportation Journal*, Vol. 47, No. 1 (Winter 2008): 17–29.

Chapter 8 Water Carriers and Pipelines

"Discussion of Effects of Long-Term Gas Commodity & Transportation Contracts on the Development of Natural Gas Infrastructure," *Interstate Natural Gas Association of America* (2005).

Farris, M. Theodore, "Are You Prepared for a Devastating Port Strike in 2008?" *Transportation Journal*, Vol. 47, No. 1 (Winter 2008): 43.

Higginson, James K., and Tudorita Dumitrascu, "Great Lakes Short Sea Shipping and the Domestic Cargo-Carrying Fleet," *Transportation Journal*, Vol. 46, No. 1 (Winter 2007): 38.

Ives, Buddy, "Pipeline Activity May Slow but Won't Be at Crawling," *Pipeline and Gas Journal*, Vol. 236 (March 2009): 64.

Jewell, Michael T., "The Evolving Pipeline Regulations: Historical Perspectives and a New Model for Pipeline Safety in the Arctic National Wildlife Refuge," *Transportation Law Journal*, Vol. 34 (2007): 173–189.

Shister, Neil, "Ocean Transport Adjusts to New Realities," *World Trade*, Vol. 21 (June 2008): 48.

Warner, Bruce E., and Mark S. Shaffer, "Carbon Capture and Sequestration (CSS): A Pipedream or a Real Business Opportunity for Gas Pipeline Developers?" *Pipeline and Gas Journal*, Vol. 236 (May 2009): 5.

PART III

The first eight chapters of the textbook provide a solid foundation of transportation knowledge. The topics have focused on key issues regarding the role of transportation and the modal options available to freight shippers. We now turn to the strategic activities and challenges involved in the flow of goods through complex, global supply chains. The six chapters in Part III focus on critical transportation management issues.

Chapter 9 examines the topic of transportation risk management. Companies must proactively work to understand and mitigate the potential freight flow disruptions that exist across the supply chain. Following a general overview of key concepts and the risk management process, the chapter focuses on transportation risk reduction strategies, methods, and outcomes. Special attention is given to the increasingly important topic of supply chain security.

The next two chapters address the ever-changing role of global transportation in the supply chain. **Chapter 10** focuses on the extensive set of planning activities related to the timely flow of freight between countries. Proper management of trade terms, insurance, and documentation set the stage for successful global flows. As companies shift their sourcing in the pursuit of lower landed cost and greater flexibility, they need to review and revise the mode, carrier, and route selection options that facilitate effective global freight flows.

The execution activities related to these flows are the focus of **Chapter 11**. International freight must be properly packed, transported, and cleared through Customs. This chapter discusses the key intermodal options for moving freight by appropriate combinations of land, sea, and air. Also highlighted are the key service providers who streamline the freight flows and minimize border crossing complications.

Chapter 12 explains the roles and industry composition of third party logistics (3PL) providers. Given the financial and service impact of transportation on supply chain success, many companies are turning to external experts to assist with their freight flows. This chapter discusses the structure of the 3PL industry and highlights the current perspectives of 3PL users. Specific issues related to establishing and managing 3PL relationships are addressed, along with a discussion of current and future 3PL industry issues.

While 3PLs and for-hire carriers are vital supply chain participants, private fleets are the hidden giant in freight transportation, generating over half of all trucking industry revenue in the United States. **Chapter 13** discusses the importance of private transportation and fleet management to companies of all sizes and geographic operations. Key highlights include discussions of the rational for using a private fleet, the types of private transportation, cost analysis, and current practices in fleet management.

Transportation is a dynamic field that must constantly adapt to the world it serves. As supply chain requirements expand, economic conditions change, and technological innovations emerge, transportation professionals must respond accordingly. **Chapter 14** tackles the major issues of environmental sustainability, congestion, labor availability, and infrastructure inadequacy, as well as other challenges. Emerging transportation strategies and technologies for improving transportation capabilities are also discussed in this forward-looking wrap up.

CHAPTER 9

TRANSPORTATION RISK MANAGEMENT

Learning Objectives

After reading this chapter, you should be able to do the following:

- Understand the nature of transportation risk and disruptions
- Explain the concept of risk management
- Describe the general process for managing transportation risk
- Identify the primary categories and types of transportation risk
- Understand the key factors in risk assessment
- Discuss the four techniques for managing transportation risks
- Appreciate the challenge of balancing transportation security and global trade efficiency
- Recognize key transportation security regulations and initiatives

TRANSPORTATION **PROFILE**

Battling the Global Piracy Challenge

Piracy against merchant ships is an ongoing risk for the global shipping industry. These attacks often result in cargo theft, hostage crises, ransom demands, and loss of life.

Piracy peaked in 2010 with 445 ships attacked worldwide. The numbers have declined each year, though there were still 264 attacks in 2013. The total cost in 2013 was estimated to be $3.2 billion to the shipping industry and governments battling the problem.

The shipping industry presents a desirable target for minimally equipped pirates. Large ships such as crude oil tankers travel slowly, hold large quantities of valuable cargo, and typically have small, unarmed crews. The pirates operate multiple, high-speed skiffs that quickly approach and attack the ship's bridge using automatic weapons. The goal is to slow the ship so that the pirates can board and hijack the ship. They demand a large ransom payment for the safe release of the crew, ship, and cargo.

Combatting the problem has not been easy. There are vast oceans and seas to patrol for suspicious activity and more than 50,000 merchant ships plying global seas. Also, the hijacking hot spots shift from year to year. In 2010 and 2011, the coastal waters near Somalia were the hotbed of activity. In 2013, piracy problems are rising along the coastal waters of western Africa and the Malaysian coastal waters of South China Sea. Finally, questions of jurisdictional authority and application of individual country's laws arise when pirates are detained in international waters.

Despite these challenges, the global shipping industry is taking steps to protect the freedom of the seas. Ship owners are adjusting routes to avoid piracy hotspots, placing armed security teams on ships, and traveling at best possible vessel speed to deter pirate encounters. Barriers such as razor wire, fencing, water cannons, and fire hoses can be used to ward off attempted boarding.

The governments of affected countries are collaborating to address the problem. Increased naval patrols in high-risk areas are used to deter potential pirates. Assisting ships under attack can result in the arrest and prosecution of criminals. Finally, effective government policies are being crafted to create a coherent national response to piracy that includes training and capacity building, maritime law enforcement, and judicial action to suppress piracy.

These efforts to mitigate piracy risks are having a positive impact on the problem but continued vigilance is needed. Countries and maritime companies will need to collaboratively develop new strategies, technologies, and knowledge to maintain momentum in this battle.

Sources: Cassie Werber, "Piracy Costs Fall, but Its Roots Remain, Says Report," *The Wall Street Journal,* May 7, 2014; "Piracy," World Shipping Council, retrieved August 20, 2014, from http://www.worldshipping.org/industry-issues/security/piracy; and James Kraska and Brian Wilson, "Combatting Piracy in International Waters," *World Policy Journal,* February 23, 2011, retrieved August 20, 2014, from http://www.worldpolicy.org/blog/2011/02/23/combatting-piracy-international-waters.

Introduction

Captain Phillips, the movie about the 2009 hijacking of the U.S.-flagged Maersk Alabama, reveals that piracy is more than an action movie genre. Bandits exist in the 21st century, and piracy is an ongoing problem for global trade and transportation. As the Transportation Profile highlights, companies are at risk of their freight being stolen or hijacked for ransom as it flows through dangerous trade lanes. In 2013, there were 264 reported attacks worldwide. Piracy hot spots include the Gulf of Aden, South China Sea, and the Atlantic coast of Africa, according to the International Maritime Bureau.[1]

Piracy is just one of the threats that organizations face when moving goods around the globe. Major incidents—hurricanes, pandemics, labor unrest, and terrorism—create societal problems and significant business challenges. From a transportation standpoint, they are disruptive events that result in supply chain disorder and discontinuity. The outcomes can vary dramatically from minor inconveniences and delivery delays to tremendous problems that threaten a company's image and financial outlook.

Companies cannot idly stand by and hope for the best when they move freight. They must actively work to limit exposure to legitimate hazards. This chapter focuses on the management of transportation risk and service disruptions. We will discuss the general concepts of disruption, risk, and business continuity, as well as the risk management process. Specific issues related to transportation risk management strategies will be addressed, followed by a discussion of expected outcomes. Throughout the chapter, you will gain an understanding of the true challenges involved in the global movement of goods as well as the methods available to mitigate transportation risk.

Risk Concepts

Risk is an everyday part of life. Whenever we get behind the wheel of our cars, the potential exists for us to be involved in an accident, to be delayed due to congestion, or to get lost. Although the likelihood of anything bad happening may be remote, each of these risks poses an unpleasant consequence for us—costs, missed appointments, stress, and so on.

The same issues arise when companies put freight in a container, railcar, or trailer. The freight can potentially be stolen, damaged, lost, or delayed while in motion or at rest in a port, trucking terminal, rail yard, or other intermediate facility. That is, freight is at risk of many disruptions from the time it leaves the origin location until it reaches its final destination.

So what exactly are disruptions and risks? A review of dictionary entries and magazine article descriptions would create a dizzying variety of definitions. For the purpose of this chapter, we will use the following characterizations as the foundation of our discussion:

Disruption—disturbance or problems that interrupt an event, activity, or process.[2]

Transportation Disruption—any significant delay, interruption, or stoppage in the flow of trade caused by a natural disaster, heightened threat level, an act of terrorism, or any transportation security incident.[3]

Risk—exposure to the chance of injury or loss.[4]

Transportation Risk—a future freight movement event with a probability of occurrence and the potential for impacting supply chain performance.

Problems arise when the threat of transportation disruptions and hazards become reality and the global supply chain is negatively affected. Unfortunately, these disruptions are common. In a 2013 APQC study, 83 percent of the participants had experienced at least one unexpected supply chain disruption in the last 24 months.[5]

At minimum, these disruptions are nuisances, creating extra work and delays. Recovery efforts hurt productivity, involve expensive expediting efforts, and require premium freight services. At worst, disruptions inflict long-term damage to a company's image, profitability, and stock price. A 2012 study by Accenture and the World Economic Forum indicates that significant supply chain disruptions reduce the share prices of affected companies by an average of seven percent.[6]

These eye-opening findings, along with high-profile events like the March 2011 earthquake and tsunami that caused the nuclear plant crisis in Japan,[7] have prompted supply chain managers to pay more attention to risk. These managers are actively engaged in efforts to reduce the probability of disruptions through a process called risk management:

> **Risk Management**—the identification, analysis, assessment, control, and avoidance, minimization, or elimination of unacceptable risks.[8]

How does risk management work? Going back to the driving example, it is possible for you to plan a car trip so that the likelihood of getting delayed or lost is minimized. By studying traffic patterns, mapping out a route, and printing step-by-step directions (or using a GPS navigation system), you can develop a plan to greatly reduce the risk of a trip disruption. This proactive planning initiative will minimize your potential for getting caught in rush hour traffic, being forced into construction detours, or becoming lost. Of course, your risk management plan isn't totally foolproof because unpredictable events such as accidents may still occur.

A key aspect of managing transportation risk is to prepare for the inevitable freight-related problems. Developing planned responses to deal with high-probability risks—like hazardous winter weather in Minnesota—is far more effective than waiting until problems occur to develop solutions. This process of proactive planning for fast recovery from disruptions is called business continuity planning:

> **Business Continuity Planning**—task of identifying, developing, acquiring, documenting, and testing procedures and resources that will ensure continuity of a firm's key operations in the event of an accident, disaster, emergency, and/or threat.[9]

Business continuity planning efforts focus on developing and testing your ability to deal with a crisis situation. In transportation management this involves having readiness plans to reestablish full functionality of delivery processes as swiftly and smoothly as possible when a disruption occurs. Poor advanced planning will produce ineffective, slow recovery and a protracted interruption of freight flows.

As you might expect, risk management and business continuity planning are not simple tasks. They demand significant time and expertise, involve financial investment, and require frequent revision. Hence, risk management activities must be driven by the top management of companies across a supply chain if global transportation disruption risks are to be minimized. They must view risk management as critical tool for protecting profitability and implement detailed, cyclical processes to control risk. A four-step risk management methodology is discussed in the next section.

Transportation Risk Management Process

Risk management is an integral part of effective transportation management. It is an iterative process that enables continual improvement in rational decision making. Risk management is the process of identifying risk, its causes and effects, and its ownership with a goal of increasing overall understanding in order to manage, reduce, transfer, or eliminate threats to supply chain success.

The objectives of **risk management** include the following:

- Develop a common understanding of risk across multiple functions and business units to manage risk cost-effectively on an enterprise-wide basis.
- Build and improve capabilities to respond effectively to low-probability, critical, catastrophic risks.
- Achieve a better understanding of risk for competitive advantage.
- Build safeguards against earnings-related surprises.
- Achieve cost savings through better management of internal resources.
- Allocate capital more efficiently.

It is important to align these risk management objectives with the organization's strategies and goals. These strategies and desired outcomes provide the context for risk management.[10]

Risk management objectives are addressed through implementation of the four-step process outlined in Figure 9-1. Step 1 involves identification of the potential threats and disruptions to which the organization is susceptible. Step 2 focuses on evaluation and prioritization of the risks. The more vulnerable the organization's transportation process is to a potential risk, the more attention it should receive. Step 3 requires the organization to develop proactive risk management and mitigation strategies. Structural and procedural changes may be required to execute the strategy. Step 4 prioritizes continuity, vigilance, and process improvement. Ongoing testing of strategies, evaluation of their success, and scanning for new risks are needed to achieve maximum protection. Each step is described in detail below.

FIGURE 9-1 Risk Management Process

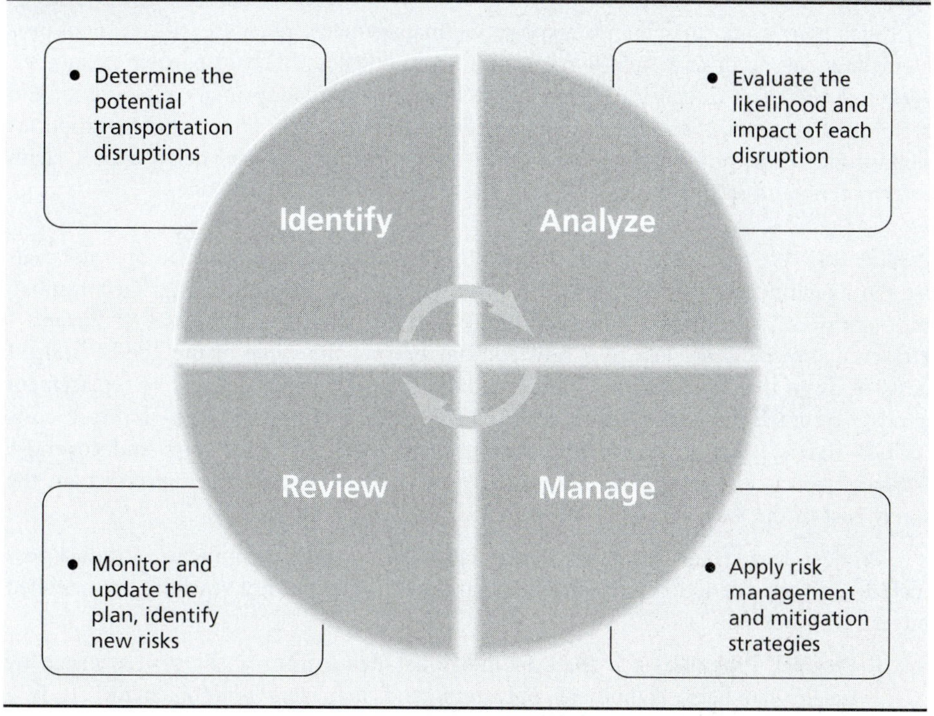
• Determine the potential transportation disruptions
• Evaluate the likelihood and impact of each disruption
Identify
Analyze
Review
Manage
• Monitor and update the plan, identify new risks
• Apply risk management and mitigation strategies

Step 1—Risk Identification

Accurate and detailed **risk identification** is vital for effective risk management. Thus, the first step in developing an effective transportation risk management program is to identify potential disruptions that can occur to freight that is moving through the supply chain. This involves a concerted effort to discover, define, describe, document, and communicate risks before they become problems and adversely affect freight flows.

The goal of risk identification is to capture as many transportation disruption risks as possible. During this process, all possible transportation risks that can occur along the global and domestic segments of the supply chain should be recorded. Both inbound and outbound transportation processes should be studied as well.

There are various techniques that can be used for risk identification. Useful techniques include:

- **Brainstorming** is common risk identification technique used to ascertain high-level risks. Knowledgeable participants engage in an open-ended dialogue to collaboratively develop a list of threats, concerns, and possible issues.
- Interviews and surveys can be used to capture transportation risk information from individuals. The goal is to quickly and efficiently capture their lessons learned from first-hand experience with disruptions.
- Analysis of transportation records for disruption information (frequency, service impact, and recovery costs) provides a data-driven risk knowledge base.

Regardless of the technique used, it is essential to include managers, supervisors, and hourly personnel in the initiative to ensure that no risks go undetected.

This process will produce a long list of potential disruptions. Rather than trying to assess each one independently, it is beneficial to organize the disruptions by similar characteristics. The process of categorizing the disruptions into broad risk categories will streamline the risk management process and limit duplication of efforts.

Such efforts are valuable in transportation management, given the wide array of problems that can occur as freight is transferred from one supply chain partner to another. Although the exact categorization may vary by company type, primary mode used, and region of the world, there are six common risk categories related to freight transportation: product loss, product damage, product contamination, delivery delay, supply chain interruption, and security breach.

Product Loss We have all seen news reports of cargo being stolen, but you may not realize the magnitude of this problem. BSI Group estimates that global cargo theft resulted in losses of $22.4 billion worldwide in 2013 with 32 percent of the losses in Europe.[11] However, the economic loss to a firm goes far beyond the value of the goods. Indirect costs of cargo theft include lost sales, expedite expenses for the delivery of replacement goods, disrupted customer service, and damaged brand value. Other indirect costs include claims processing and the potential impact on insurance rates and coverage. Security experts estimate these indirect costs to be three to five times greater than the direct cost of the loss.[12]

Product loss is not limited to criminals stealing entire shipments. Product loss includes any type of action or negligence that leads to product not reaching the intended buyer. This includes:

- **Product Pilferage**—the theft of individual items from a shipping package by freight handlers, equipment operators, and managers is problematic. It is a particular challenge with smart phones, pharmaceutical products, designer clothes and other high-value goods that can be easily concealed and later sold for cash.

- **Shipment Jettison**—in the movement of freight via water, it may be necessary to cast all or part of a ship's cargo overboard to save the ship, crew, and other cargo from perils such as catastrophic weather, running aground, or fire. The master of the ship has the absolute right to jettison cargo when he reasonably believes it to be necessary, and the owners of the ship incur no liability. If the ship is carrying goods of more than one shipper, the rule of **general average** provides for apportioning the loss among all the shippers because all have benefited by the master's action.
- **Piracy and Hijacking**—as discussed in the Transportation Profile, these product loss risks are a continuing challenge. Not only do these crimes create financial losses for companies but they often put ship crews and truck drivers at risk of being kidnapped, injured, or killed. There is also a strategic security concern issue because the money generated from these crimes may be used to fund, train, and assist terrorists.

Product Damage Though it would appear to be a relatively mundane risk, product damage is a potential peril that arises every time a shipment is handled. Employee inattention, negligence, and poor training all contribute to this very costly problem. Damaged product loses much, if not all, of its value. Repaired products can't be sold as new at full price. Otherwise, damaged product may need to be salvaged to recoup some value, or discarded, incurring a total loss. The cost of freight claims processing and product replacement add to the financial impact of damage incidents.

Product damage can result from a wide array of actions or inactions on the part of equipment operators and freight handlers. Damage risks include:

- **Equipment Accidents**—though the number of accidents involving U.S. commercial vehicles is declining, there were 282,000 property damage accidents involving large trucks and buses in 2012. The cost of such accidents is high, averaging $74,500 per incident for cargo damage, vehicle damage, loss of revenue, increased insurance rates, and other direct costs.[13] Accidents involving other modes also contribute to **freight damage**.
- **Poor Freight Handling**—a failure to use caution when moving product in/out of equipment can increase the risk of damage. Fragile goods require protection from impact, tilting, shaking, and rough handling. These hazards must be avoided to safeguard product integrity.
- **Improper Equipment Loading**—the long distance movement of freight may involve a rough ride, especially for rail and ocean transportation. Freight damage risks are high if the load is not properly secured and stacked. If too much space is left between freight, product may shift and fall. If product is improperly stacked (heavy product loaded on top of lightweight product), product may be crushed.

Product Contamination A particular risk to food, pharmaceutical goods, and other consumables is the possibility that product becomes contaminated while en route from origin to destination. Customers may reject a delivery of goods if there is evidence of possible adulteration. They do not want to assume the risk of product loss, customer liability, or the responsibility for disposal.

Product contamination risk increases along with trip distance and time in transit. The longer the goods are out of your control, the more opportunity exists for natural or man-made contamination issues to arise. Primary **freight contamination** risks include:

- **Climate Control Failure**—environmentally sensitive goods such as fruit, vegetables, electronics, biomedical samples, and chemicals often require transportation within a strict temperature or humidity range. Failure to provide a stable climate inside the container during transit will result in product degradation, spoilage, or contamination.
- **Product Tampering**—the deliberate contamination of goods after they have been manufactured is a risk that is remote but potentially devastating. Multiple individuals handle freight as it moves from the production facility to retail store shelves, making it difficult to fully safeguard product integrity. Given the threat of lawsuits and brand damage, the mere hint of tampering may require a costly effort to clear product from store shelves, restock the supply chain, and rebuild consumer confidence.
- **Exposure to Contaminants**—the risk of freight coming in contact with potentially undesirable substance (physical, chemical, or biological) occurs when different types of freight are commingled. Contamination issues also arise if transportation equipment is used to move different commodities on consecutive trips (for instance, filling a railroad tank car with food grade oil after it was used to transport an industrial solvent).

Delivery Delay There are few things more frustrating than late delivery of a time-sensitive shipment like concert tickets. If they arrive the day after the concert, the tickets are rendered worthless and you missed a great event. Companies who rely upon **just-in-time delivery** of inventory to keep their production lines running may experience the same frustration, only to a much higher level of financial pain. If a critical shipment is delayed a few hours, production lines will stop and the lost productivity cost may be tens of thousands of dollars. These companies are at huge risk if delivery commitments are not kept.

There are numerous **delivery delay** risks. Some transportation perils result from other supply chain strategies such as sourcing goods from low-cost manufacturers in the Far East. This strategy significantly increases supply chain complexity and distance, boosting the possibility of late deliveries. Other risks are out of the company's control, though it is important to recognize their potential impact. Common delivery schedule disruptors include:

- **Congestion**—overburdened roadways, railways, and port facilities impede product flows and create bottlenecks in the supply chain. As equipment sits idly in traffic and average speeds drop, slower-than-anticipated transit times are achieved and delivery windows are missed. Road congestion in the European Union (EU) costs nearly 100 billion Euro, or one percent of the EU's GDP, annually.[14] Global gateway ports are also struggling with congestion created by larger containerships, peak activity, and late ship arrivals.[15]
- **Poor Weather**—as environmental conditions deteriorate, it becomes more challenging to maintain an accurate delivery schedule. Companies located in or delivering to customers in areas of extreme climate conditions—frequent cold, snow and ice conditions, hurricane zones, and so on—must factor these uncontrollable issues into freight movement planning and delivery commitments.
- **Equipment Malfunction**—mechanical breakdowns of delivery vehicles can cause product to get stranded en route. Likewise, problems with freight handling equipment at ports (such as container cranes) and other freight transfer facilities can slow the flow of products moving in or out of the terminal. Both types of malfunctions delay shipments beyond their scheduled delivery times.

Supply Chain Interruption Many transportation risks are created by poor execution of day-to-day operations. Ineffective decision making, employee errors, and technology glitches cause temporary disruptions of freight flows. Such risks pale in comparison to the devastating effects of supply chain interruptions like border disputes and port strikes that bring transportation operations to a grinding halt. The cost of such disruptions is high and recovery time is prolonged.

Although they don't occur frequently, these problems often fall outside the control of the company. Recent examples of transportation-altering **supply chain interruptions** include:

- **Industry Consolidation**—in times of slack volume or high energy prices, financially unstable transportation companies are unable to compete. Such is the case in the global container shipping industry where carriers are merging or joining operations alliances to survive.[16] The changing market structure causes capacity and cost challenges for customers who end up with fewer options for freight movement.
- **Labor Disruptions**—many transportation companies and facilities rely upon unionized labor for freight handling and movement. When work-related disputes occur or labor contracts expire, a labor strike risk arises. Some strikes can be predicted in advance, though others are sudden "wild cat" strikes that occur with little warning and create havoc. The cost of these supply chain interruptions can be severe.
- **Capacity Shortages**—during peak economic growth, transportation capacity is stretched to the point that carriers are often unable to provide enough equipment and operators to service all demand. Transportation companies are able to increase rates or apply peak season surcharges to freight. At the same time, there is a risk of service quality failures due to facility congestion, equipment shortages, and operator inexperience.

Security Breach Terrorist attacks, organized crime activity, and illegal immigration have driven a worldwide effort to secure freight. Global transportation companies must refine their policies and procedures to protect in-transit freight. A failure to do so leaves the company, its customers, and the general public vulnerable to security threats. Repeated failures drive government demand for time-consuming freight inspections and costly countermeasures.

There is no shortage of security challenges facing organizations, especially with shrewd criminals scheming to exploit system flaws and security vulnerabilities. Common points of exposure are:

- **Lax Security Processes**—supply chain security and **resiliency** are not optional; they must be built into global transportation operations. Companies must think about their potential security vulnerabilities and develop appropriate defenses. A failure to establish strong security practices will make the company a prime target for intentional transportation disruptions.
- **Unprotected Transfer Facilities**—some transportation companies fail to do the simple things like lock doors, fence in facilities, and require security badges to limit access to freight and transportation equipment. Ease of facility entry and access will only promote product theft, deliberate contamination, or catastrophic disruptions (such as hiding a bomb in a freight container).
- **Shipment Control Failures**—freight **visibility** and access control are the keys to protecting in-transit goods from harm. When freight is not properly controlled,

security risks and disruption opportunities increase. For example, unsupervised or unlocked freight containers provide hiding spots for stowaways attempting to illegally enter a country. Often, the stowaways contaminate the container's contents and cause legal headaches for authorities.

Although we have identified six categories of risk and discussed 18 specific risks, the list is not by any means comprehensive. The perils of transportation are many and varied. Hazardous materials dangers, the corrosive nature of saltwater, border crossing issues, military conflicts, and a host of other global issues constantly threaten to disrupt transportation operations. Managers must remain vigilant to possible threats and constantly analyze transportation risk.

Step 2—Risk Assessment

Evaluating transportation risks is a challenging proposition because they do not affect organizations equally. Risks and their potential impact are influenced by supply chain strategy, modes used, and operational capabilities. For example, if a company focuses on just-in-time delivery of materials for their assembly plant, delivery delays from distant suppliers pose a high risk of shutting down the production line. In contrast, late deliveries are not a major issue for a company that stockpiles a month's worth of raw materials. Thus, managers must determine which risks are of direct relevance to their organization.

The objective of risk assessment is to evaluate the seriousness of each risk identified during Step 1 (Risk Identification). In making this determination, an organization should evaluate three parameters:

- **Probability**—the likelihood of the risk occurring
- **Impact**—the consequences if the risk does occur
- **Proximity**—the anticipated timing of the risk

Impact can be assessed in terms of the transportation risk's effect on time, cost, and/or quality. Proximity focuses on the temporal aspect of disruptive events, such as hurricanes or blizzards. Understanding their seasonality considerations and preparing appropriate strategies will help organization proactively manage these events.

Risk assessment can be qualitative or quantitative in nature. **Qualitative risk analysis** provides a baseline evaluation of risks in a rapid and cost-effective manner. Knowledgeable individuals classify each risk in terms of its probability and impact (see Figure 9-2). For example, a border crossing delay may be a medium-impact, medium-probability risk for freight moving from Mexico City to Dallas. In contrast, border crossing delays would be a low-impact, low-probability risk for freight moving between Paris and Amsterdam and other EU cities.

An issue landing in the "Major Risk" category is deemed unacceptable. The organization must actively seek to mitigate the probability and impact of these potential disruptions. The organization should also address issues in the "Moderate Risk" and "Minor Risk" categories through contingency planning. However, the required level of management attention is tempered by the reduced risk potential.

Quantitative risk analysis often builds upon the foundation created by qualitative analysis. Those risks falling into the "Major" risk level category may warrant detailed assessment of available data to evaluate their relative danger levels. Quantitative analysis incorporates numerical estimates of frequency or probability and consequence. This data can be expensive to acquire or may not be available.

FIGURE 9-2 Risk Assessment Matrix

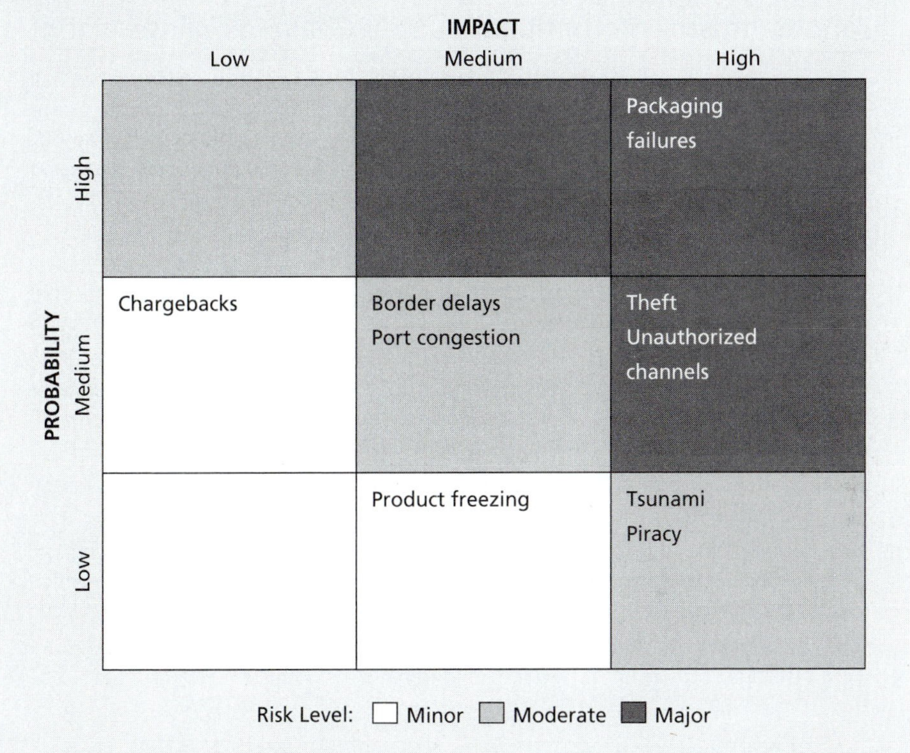

Risk assessment is a time-consuming task. To be of value, this activity needs to generate useful information for the organization. Based on the Risk Identification (Step 1) results, transportation managers should diagnose the risks to analyze what could happen if the hazard occurs.

Given the large variety of hazards inherent in global trade and transportation, the U.S. Customs and Border Protection (CBP) agency has developed a five-step risk assessment process. It is part of the Customs-Trade Partnership Against Terrorism (C-TPAT) security program. This assessment process is explained in the On the Line feature.

Risk assessment is an invaluable activity for identifying global transportation challenges and primary disruption concerns. This effort ensures that organizations focus their scarce resources on relevant risk management and mitigation strategies.

Step 3—Risk Management Strategy Development

Using the output from the risk assessment, the next step is to create a coherent strategy for managing and mitigating transportation risks in a cost-effective manner. The mitigation strategy identifies specific efforts, actions, and procedural changes that must be taken by management to reduce high priority risks. The goal is to lower the probability of risk occurrence and/or minimize the negative impact if the risk occurs. A risk can never be totally eliminated, but its frequency and effects can be reduced if properly addressed.

ON THE **LINE**

Conducting an International Supply Chain Risk Assessment

C-TPAT is a voluntary U.S. government industry initiative designed to strengthen overall supply chain and border security. It attempts to safeguard global trade from terrorism by extending the United States' zone of security to the point of origin rather than U.S. borders. C-TPAT emphasizes self-monitoring rather than government oversight starting at the foreign supplier and extending to the final destination to the United States.

Companies participating in C-TPAT must ensure the integrity of their organization's security practices. Each year, participants must analyze their security threats and vulnerabilities associated with the international supply chain from the point of origin until they reach their final destination in the United States. Foreign suppliers, transportation providers, and third party logistics companies must be evaluated.

This annual risk assessment requirement is a daunting task for inexperienced companies. Fortunately, CBP has developed a five-step risk assessment process for all C-TPAT participants to follow. The process steps include:

1. mapping cargo flow and identifying business partners (directly or indirectly contracted)
2. conducting a threat assessment focusing on terrorism, contraband smuggling, human smuggling, organized crime, and conditions in a country/region, which may foster such threats and rate threat—high, medium, low
3. conducting a vulnerability assessment in accordance with C-TPAT minimum security criteria and rate vulnerability—high, medium, low
4. preparing an action plan
5. documenting how risk assessments are conducted

This process will help a C-TPAT participant to effectively and efficiently evaluate its global trade and transportation risks. Additionally, the CBP has established mutual recognition agreements with foreign customs administrations to promote C-TPAT participation, create assessment efficiencies, and avoid audit redundancy. These agreements indicate that the security requirements or standards of the foreign industry partnership program, as well as its validation or audit procedures, are consistent with C-TPAT.

Based on these agreements, a U.S. company can rely upon the risk assessment process of its foreign business partners. This saves implementation time and cost, while reducing supply chain security risk.

Sources: U.S. Customs and Border Protection, "Customs-Trade Partnership Against Terrorism Mutual Recognition," retrieved August 29, 2014, from http://www.cbp.gov/border-security/ports-entry/cargo-security/c-tpat-customs-trade-partnership-against-terrorism/mutual-recognition; Karen King, "New CBP Guidance Can Help You Better Assess Risks to Your Global Supply Chain," *SupplyChainBrain*, October 7, 2010; and U.S. Customs and Border Protection, *C-TPAT 5 Step Risk Assessment Process Guide*, March 2010, retrieved August 29, 2014, from http://www.cbp.gov/sites/default/files/documents/supply_chain_assess_guide_3.pdf.

Mitigation strategies must not be haphazardly applied to disruption risks. First, the strategies must be in sync with the overall supply chain strategy and corporate strategy. Second, mitigation strategies and actions must focus on high priority issues. Third, the mitigation action must be reasonable in terms of cost and time to implement versus the likelihood of success. Otherwise, money and effort will be wasted on low priority risks or ineffective risk remedies. Finally, a standardized process should be used to mitigate disruptions.

Each **risk mitigation** strategy should produce an action plan that identifies:

- roles and responsibilities for developing, implementing, and monitoring the strategy
- resources required to carry out the planned actions
- timelines
- conditions present in order for risk level to be acceptable

A well-developed plan plays an important role in decreasing the risk of transportation disruptions as well as their effect on the supply chain and company performance. These plans typically focus on one of four techniques to manage and mitigate risk: avoidance, reduction, transfer, or retention.[17]

Risk Avoidance The simplest way to eliminate a risk is to not perform an activity that carries risk. For example, a company could avoid transportation hazards by refusing to accept a customer's order. No freight needs to be shipped, meaning that the risk of in-transit freight loss or damage is eliminated. However, the company also misses the revenue and profit opportunities related to accepting the order.

An alternative to this conservative pure avoidance strategy is to take steps to remove the risk. When possible, the ideal solution is to keep the risk from happening. Tools like root cause analysis can be used to pinpoint the reasons why a disruption occurs. Processes can be revised to eliminate the disruption's causes and greatly minimize the risk. For example, if an investigation revealed that all thefts occurred when a specific international port was used, the simple solution would be to never flow product through that port again. Hence, that particular theft risk would be removed.

Another avoidance strategy would be to sidestep the specific exposure. In the case of freight loss or damage risk, the seller could choose to work only on an Ex Works (EXW) basis. Under these International Commercial Terms—discussed in full detail in Chapter 10—the seller fulfills his obligations by having the goods available for the buyer to pick up at his premises or another named place such as the factory or warehouse. The buyer bears all risk, costs, and responsibilities after picking up the products at the seller's location. The seller evades the liabilities that come with owning in-transit freight without sacrificing the sale. In contrast, a buyer may want to minimize his risk by purchasing goods on a Delivered Duty Paid (DDP) basis. In that scenario the seller bears all transportation risk, cost, and responsibility.

Risk Reduction Given that many risks cannot be totally eliminated or avoided, it is important for companies to proactively mitigate or limit risk. This involves adopting risk management strategies that reduce the likelihood of a disruption and/or limit the severity of financial loss. For example, a company could attempt to reduce the risk of theft or hijacking by hiring armed guards to travel with high-value freight. This strategy could be effective at reducing risk to a more acceptable level, but it may be expensive and/or raise other risks.

There are numerous types of strategies to pursue the goal of risk reduction. Some companies will use a **hedging strategy** to offset or balance out the risks presented by a single option. This diversification avoids the inflated risk of having "all your eggs in one basket." In transportation, companies can disperse their freight among multiple carriers to reduce the financial risk of a sole sourced carrier bankruptcy or service interruption.

A **postponement strategy** seeks to limit risk by delaying a commitment of resources. Trucking companies could reduce the risk of productivity losses by delaying the dispatch of drivers until after a customer has loaded a trailer and submitted proper documentation. This will reduce driver wait time and maximize the use of available service hours for transporting freight.

A **buffering strategy** provides additional resources to reduce risks related to capacity shortages or performance problems. An air cargo company may have extra jets available to reduce the impact of equipment failures. They may also have a few pilots on call each day to be prepared for volume spikes. Both buffering actions will reduce the likelihood of freight delays.

Given the vast array of transportation risks, it is impossible to discuss in detail the reduction strategies that have been developed. Table 9-1 highlights a variety of risk reduction strategies that align well with the six risk categories and 18 specific risks discussed earlier.

Risk reduction requires that companies be proactive in establishing plans to deal with the high-probability/high-impact risks that emerge from the identification and analysis processes. The strategies discussed briefly below will help companies reduce a variety of common transportation risks that affect all modes around the world.

TABLE 9-1 Transportation Risk Reduction Strategies

RISK CATEGORY	SPECIFIC RISKS	REDUCTION STRATEGIES	ANTICIPATED OUTCOMES
Product Loss	Theft and pilferage Piracy and hijacking Cargo jettison	Use generic packaging & descriptions Avoid lawless hot spots Strategic routing	Mitigate risk of financial loss, reduce customer delivery delays, and avoid replacement shipment expenses.
Product Damage	Operator accident Poor freight handling methods Improper equipment loading	Use protective packaging Establish training programs Monitor carrier performance	Enhance freight safety, reduce freight claims administration, and profit margin protection.
Product Contamination	Temperature control failure Product tampering Exposure to hazardous materials	Secure freight/lock containers Isolate dangerous freight Leverage pervasive automation	Safeguard brand equity, decrease potential for product liability lawsuits, and trim product recalls and inventory replacement costs.
Delivery Delay	Congestion Poor weather Equipment malfunction	Use event management software Employ dynamic re-routing tools Avoid ill-equipped and congested ports	Proactive response to problems resulting in less wait time, greater delivery reliability, and improved customer satisfaction.
Supply Chain Interruption	Capacity shortage Carrier bankruptcy Labor disruptions and strikes	Contract with quality carriers Monitor carrier finances Secure backup capacity Identify alternate ports and service providers	Avoid major disruptions of product flows that can impact supply chain productivity, and product availability.
Security Breach	Shipment control breakdown Unprotected transfer facilities Lax security processes	Employ cargo tracking technology Screen & evaluate vulnerabilities Participate in C-TPAT and FAST	Greater protection against terrorist activity, fewer government inspections, and streamlined border clearance.

- Develop and maintain relationships with quality carriers—effective service providers are reliable, reasonably priced, and protect freight. Transportation buyers must make a concerted effort to balance service dependability, cost efficiency, and safety when selecting carriers. Hiring high quality carriers, actively monitoring their performance, and pursuing continuous improvement will reduce the risk of delays and damage.
- Use protective product packaging—freight is often handled by forklifts, conveyors, cranes, and multiple transportation vehicles on the way to its final destination. To minimize the risk of concealed product damage or contamination, protective materials like cardboard, bubble wrap, foam packing peanuts and forms, plastic bags, and other materials should be used inside shipping cartons. Insufficient packaging increases the risk of product damage and limits carrier liability in freight claim situations.
- Properly secure freight inside containers—assuming that the ride will be rough encourages companies to safeguard their in-transit inventory. Loads should be secured and protected as needed by using blocking and cleats nailed to the floor, braces, straps, load bars, or air bags and other void fill materials. In addition, the use of stretch wrap, shrink wrap, banding, and edge protectors will stabilize and protect unitized freight.
- Require the use of reliable equipment—allowing carriers to use defective or poorly maintained equipment to move your freight produces transportation risk. Poor vehicle maintenance raises the potential for delivery delays due to equipment breakdowns and inspection failures. Equipment malfunctions increase the likelihood of product damage due to accidents, poor ride quality, leaks, and other problems. To avoid these problems work only with carriers that perform preventative maintenance, regularly upgrade their fleets, and have a strong track record of equipment safety compliance.
- Leverage technology to maintain shipment control—monitoring in-transit freight not only provides peace of mind, it helps managers avoid potential problems and respond rapidly to disruptions. Visibility tools provide a seamless flow of timely information across the supply chain. Accurate knowledge of in-transit freight allows managers to be proactive in routing and scheduling to meet delivery windows. Exception management tools detect performance problems and alert the affected organization. Corrective action can be taken to resolve the situation before the supply chain is adversely impacted. The Transportation Technology box highlights the importance of these capabilities to the movement of temperature- and humidity-sensitive freight across the global cold chain.

Risk Transfer The risk analysis activity may identify potential problems that an organization deems too problematic to manage or mitigate on its own. In these situations, the organization may seek outside assistance in controlling those risks. This risk transfer strategy provides a means to place liability on a third party should the risk occur. Of course, the third party doesn't freely accept the risk. They are paid by the customer to assume or share the risk.

Insurance is a common method of risk transfer. Individuals can purchase medical, life, and property insurance. Transportation companies and their customers can also do the same to reduce their risks. For example, the financial risks stemming from commercial vehicle accidents and related lawsuits are very high. Rather than setting aside a large pool of money to self-insure against these possible problems, most transportation

TRANSPORTATION **TECHNOLOGY**

Protecting Product Along the Global Cold Chain

Risk is inherent in every supply chain, particularly the global cold chain for temperature-sensitive goods like food, vaccines, and chemicals. Long transit times, multiple product transfers, and slow border crossings are prime issues that can affect product quality. The result can be product contamination and loss.

In the fresh food cold chain, it is estimated that the waste factor approaches 25 percent due to spoilage. Much of this spoilage risk occurs during transportation when ingredients are moved from farms and suppliers to manufacturers and when finished goods move between manufacturers, distributors, retailers, and end consumers. Rapid product decay occurs when product is not transported at optimal temperature, humidity, and air quality.

To minimize these transportation risks, fresh food shippers must adopt a range of leading-edge tools and technology. Options include:

- Refrigerated shipping containers make it possible to transport cold chain products to virtually any global destination in a stable environment. State-of-the-art equipment options support temperature requirements from –25 to 25 degrees Celsius, provide fresh-air ventilation, and control moisture levels with dehumidifiers.
- Freight monitoring tools track temperature, atmospheric conditions, and delays of in-transit shipments. The latest technologies support the monitoring of real-time product conditions and GPS-based location tracking. It is anticipated that it will soon be possible to make remote adjustments to in-transit temperature and humidity conditions.
- Alerting systems provide real-time problem warnings to the transportation providers. Innovative systems use Internet-based interfaces to provide a gateway to critical visibility data that has been captured by automatic identification tags, GPS signals, and employee updates. These systems offer decision-making tools for rapid resolution of cold chain transportation issues.

Creating a stable, efficient cold chain requires much more than ice and insulated packaging materials. A strong, well-aligned infrastructure supported by specialized equipment and advanced technology is needed to protect in-transit food and other products as they traverse global cold chains.

Sources: Brian Gibson, *Essentials of Cold Chain Management* (Accenture Academy, 2013); Nick Pacitti, "Cold Chain Technology Is More Than Temperature Monitoring," *Food Logistics*, February 17, 2012; and Jim Tennerman, "Cold Chain for Beginners," *Pharmaceutical Processing*, June 20, 2012.

companies purchase coverage from insurance companies. They are using the strategy of risk transfer as the means to place financial liability on a third party (the insurance company) should the risk (a vehicle accident) occur.

Freight owners often purchase insurance as a means to transfer their risk of in-transit freight loss, damage, and delay. Most carriers assume very limited liability for these types of problems. For example, FedEx and UPS limit their risk to $100 per package. If they should lose or damage the contents of a package containing ten Apple iPads valued at $500 each, they will pay no more than $100. Hence, you can take a $4,900 gamble on their ability to deliver your package intact. Your alternative is to declare a higher value for the package and purchase commensurate insurance coverage to transfer the risk to the insurer. The same options are available to companies shipping freight worldwide. They can essentially self-insure (accepting the limited carrier liability amount) or purchase insurance through the transportation company, a cargo insurance broker, or an insurance underwriter.

It is also possible to transfer risk to **third party logistics** service providers (3PLs). These experts—discussed in more detail in Chapter 12—are external suppliers that perform all or part of an organization's logistics services. Companies contract with 3PLs because these service providers have the knowledge, capacity, technologies, and capability to mitigate some risk factors. 3PLs provide a diverse array of transportation services, administrative support, and strategic planning. Some 3PLs cover the full spectrum of global freight management issues while other companies assist with specific risks like asset protection, cargo loss control, or hazardous materials movement.

Regardless of a 3PL company's role and the risk transfer provisions in 3PL contracts and insurance policies, organizations are not absolved of their responsibilities. They must remain vigilant of potential risks and continually strive to reduce their exposures. After all, they own the freight and must protect it along with their customer relationships.

Risk Retention Risk is inevitable, but not all risk is created equal. Organizations must evaluate risk and make a judgment and determine what, if anything, they will do about it. Those issues falling in the minor risk categories of Figure 9-2, particularly the low-probability, low-impact issues, warrant little attention. These risks have limited potential to negatively affect the supply chain. They present an acceptable level and the organization will retain the risks.

In other situations, the cost of mitigating a risk may outweigh the benefits realized. For example, the potential savings from a low deductible insurance policy may not be enough to offset the additional policy cost. A transportation company may have a $2,500 or $5,000 deductible on their collision insurance. They will retain all financial risks related to small accidents and deductible portion of larger incidents.

Finally, some risks are so large or catastrophic that they either cannot be reasonably mitigated or insured against. Examples include war, terrorism, and natural perils like the 2010 Eyjafjallajökull volcano eruption in Iceland. The ash cloud rounded 107,000 flights over an eight-day period, affecting the movement of air cargo and 10 million passengers.[18]

Regardless of the reason for retaining a risk, it cannot be ignored. It is vital that all accepted risks have a viable fallback plan. Retained risks must be monitored to ensure that any escalation is captured and appropriate strategies are then implemented.

Collectively, these four types of risk management strategies help organizations adhere to the Boy Scout motto: "Be Prepared." When organizations conscientiously evaluate risks, determine the best course of action (avoid, reduce, transfer, or retain), and establish business continuity plans for major and moderate risks, the negative consequences and duration of incidents will be reduced. Furthermore, the organization will likely improve performance on all transportation fronts—cost, safety, product protection, and delivery reliability.

Step 4—Risk Review and Monitoring

Risk management planning is not a static, one-time process. Organizations cannot analyze risks, develop plans, and simply assume that the plans can be perfectly implemented as needed. Instead, a testing and review process must be instituted to ensure that existing risk mitigation efforts and disruption recovery processes work as intended. Thus, risk management requires ongoing effort by the organization. As Figure 9-1 suggests, it is a circular or continuous process.

Conducting tests of risk management action plans is the only way to know that they will actually work when a true disruption occurs. These testing initiatives should demonstrate and measure the effectiveness of risk mitigation activities. The central concern at this stage is to validate the process and its ability to reduce or eliminate unacceptable risks.

A thorough testing program simulates disruptions and defines benchmarks for recovery processes. Separate test plans should be developed by the organization for each disruption scenario. It is important to accurately simulate each disruption's impact on inventory, physical plant, people, and external parties. These stress tests help the organization understand its sources of disruptions, develop recovery responses, and evaluate how these responses affect cost efficiency.[19]

Organizations must also periodically review and update risk management plans. Risks are not static, making it imperative for organizations to regularly reassess the likelihood and expected impact of risks. This will help the organization evaluate whether their previously selected plans are still applicable and effective. Also, the organization must be cognizant of emerging challenges that change risk profiles and introduce new risks. As economic conditions change, competitive threats arise, new regulations are enacted, and customer expectations grow, the organization must respond to these new and diverse risks.

Realize that risk management and mitigation plans are not perfect. Testing, experience, and actual disruptions will necessitate action plan changes and improvements to better deal with the risks being faced. The goal of the risk review stage is to establish a repeatable, measurable, verifiable validation process that can be run from time to time to continually verify the organization's ability to manage risk.

In summary, the risk management process described in this section outlines the steps that organizations must take to identify, monitor, and control transportation risk. The purpose of the process is to effectively address, prevent, and reduce risks that prevent the organization from meeting its goals. It must always be remembered that the key to risk management is active engagement. The process will fail if organizational commitment and contribution are lacking and risks are not efficiently identified, assessed, and pursued to their conclusion.

Supply Chain Security

The terrorist attacks on September 11, 2001, brought global commerce between the United States and the rest of the world to a halt. International and domestic air transportation ceased within hours and flights were suspended for days. Ocean vessels loaded with containers and other freight were prevented from loading or unloading in major U.S. ports, forcing many ships to anchor off the coast and wait for days to be unloaded. Fresh produce rotted and materials needed to keep assembly lines running did not arrive on time. It was a frightening period of time, and the attacks showed just how vulnerable global supply chains were to intentional disruptions.

Prior to the events of September 11, 2001, shipments would frequently arrive in U.S. ports and clear U.S. Customs in a matter of hours. Since that fateful day, enhanced security measures have made the arrival and clearance process more complex. Increased **cargo inspection**, greater paperwork requirements (discussed in Chapter 10), and longer time to enter the country are now a reality. Some shipments are given very close scrutiny because of their country of origin.

This tightening of U.S. borders occurred during an era of unprecedented global trade growth. Given the importance of global trade to the U.S. economy, a delicate balance must be struck between security and the efficient flow of global commerce. If security is too tight it can impede the flow of goods, causing delays and decreased efficiency. If trade efficiency is overemphasized, security can be compromised.

Compounding the challenge of this dangerous environment is the variety of risks inherent in global trade. Some of the risks are purely physical in nature. Longer distances, greater product handling, multiple border crossings, and more intermediaries each make the supply chain more susceptible to loss, damage, and delay problems.

Other global trade challenges are man-made, motivated by political, ideological, or criminal intent. At minimum, they present theft risks; at worst they generate deliberate loss of life risk from nuclear, chemical, biological, radiological, and high explosive weapons. Illicit trade of drugs, currency laundering, and illegal entry of stowaways also present security challenges. These issues create an urgent safety dimension to transportation risk. A joint effort between government and industry is needed to limit the number and magnitude of security breaches.

Regarding this need for cooperation, President Barack Obama states in the *National Strategy for Global Supply Chain Security*: "In order to meet the challenge to strengthen the global supply chain we must promote integrated and collective action among all levels of government, the private sector, and other key stakeholders." The Strategy establishes two explicit goals: promoting the efficient and secure movement of legitimate goods and fostering a global supply chain system that is resilient to natural as well as man-made disruptions. The private sector and international stakeholders who have key supply chain roles play a critical collaborative role in guiding the implementation of the Strategy.[20]

Though the Strategy was published in 2012, a variety of proactive efforts have been under way since September 11, 2001, to improve security of the global supply chain. The Strategy incorporates and builds upon a number of legislative acts, including the Aviation and Transportation Security Act of 2001, the Maritime Security Act of 2002, and the Security and Accountability for Every Port Act. Voluntary government-industry transportation security initiatives such as C-TPAT and Free and Secure Trade (FAST) also serve to enhance transportation security while promoting international trade.

Aviation and Transportation Security Act of 2001

The Aviation and Transportation Security Act (ATSA) established the Transportation Security Administration (TSA) within the U.S. Department of Transportation (TSA would later be transferred to the Department of Homeland Security). One of TSA's primary roles is to screening of all passengers and property that will be carried aboard an aircraft. For flights and flight segments originating in the United States, the screening takes place before boarding and is carried out by uniformed federal TSA personnel.

Another important provision of the ATSA is the screening of cargo carried aboard passenger aircraft. The intention was to screen 100 percent of cargo transported on passenger aircraft beginning August 2010. To meet this requirement, TSA developed the certified cargo screening program, under which shippers tender cargo for transport on passenger aircraft via a cargo screening facility that use TSA-approved air cargo screening methods. Once screened, the cargo is forwarded to an air carrier for transport.

Each piece of cargo must be screened using one of the following methods:

- Explosive Trace Detection (ETD) is a device used to detect explosive particles. The ETD compares the chemical composition of the sample to the signature of known explosive materials. For cargo screening, the samples are usually taken from the outside of the box.
- X-ray is a device that captures computer images of the cargo content, which is displayed on a monitor for the screener to detect any anomalies that could be threat items.
- Physical search requires the screener to open the box or crate and examine the contents to prevent the introduction of any explosive, incendiary, or other destructive substance on to the aircraft. The contents are also matched to the description on the airway bill or manifest.[21]

According to the U.S. Department of Homeland Security, cargo screening is widely conducted. Similar to the screening of passengers' check baggage, 100 percent of all cargo transported on passenger aircraft departing U.S. airports is now screened. Also, international inbound air cargo is more secure than it has ever been, with 100 percent of identified high-risk cargo being screened.[22]

Maritime Transportation Security Act of 2002

The Maritime Transportation Security Act of 2002 (MTSA) seeks to protect U.S. ports and waterways from a terrorist attack. This is essential as approximately 90 percent of all global trade (weight basis) and over 25 percent of U.S. gross domestic product moves via the sea. A terrorist attack at our ports could severely disrupt the supply chain, which would be catastrophic to the U.S. economy.[23]

MTSA is the U.S. equivalent of the International Ship and Port Facility Security Code and was fully implemented on July 1, 2004. MTSA seeks to protect the nation's ports and waterways from terrorist attacks by requiring a wide range of security improvements. The key MTSA provisions include:

- conducting vulnerability assessments for port facilities and vessels
- developing security plans to mitigate identified risks for the national maritime system, ports, port facilities, and vessels
- developing the Transportation Worker Identification Credential (TWIC), a biometric identification card to help restrict access to secure areas to only authorized personnel
- establishing of a process to assess foreign ports, from which vessels depart on voyages to the United States

Under the MTSA, all tankers and other vessels considered at high risk of a security incident (such as barges, large passenger ships, and cargo vessels) entering U.S. waters must have certified security plans that address how they would respond to emergency incidents, identify the person authorized to implement security actions, and describe provisions for establishing and maintaining physical security, cargo security, and personnel security. High-risk vessels must also be equipped with automatic identification systems that will allow vessel tracking and monitoring while traveling on U.S. navigable waters. The U.S. Coast Guard can assign sea marshals to accompany tankers as they transit in and out of U.S. ports to ensure harbor safety and security.

The MTSA also specifies that all U.S. port facilities deemed at risk for a "transportation security incident," such as LNG marine terminals, fossil fuel processing and storage facilities, and cruise ship terminal facilities, must prepare and implement security plans for deterring such incidents to the "maximum extent practicable."[24]

Security and Accountability for Every Port Act

The Security and Accountability for Every Port Act (SAFE) is a comprehensive port security law designed to keep nuclear, chemical, and biological weapons out of freight containers traveling to U.S. ports. Enacted in 2006, it was an addition to the port security framework to create new programs, codify existing initiatives, and amend some of the original provisions of the MTSA. The SAFE Port Act included provisions that:

- codified the Container Security Initiative (CSI) and the C-TPAT, two programs administered by CBP to help reduce threats associated with cargo shipped in containers
- required interagency operational centers where agencies organize to fit the security needs of the port area at selected ports
- set an implementation schedule and fee restrictions for TWIC
- required that all containers entering high-volume U.S. ports be scanned for radiation sources by December 31, 2007
- required additional data be made available to CBP for targeting cargo containers for inspection

Some of the provisions have been delayed long beyond their original implementation dates. TWIC was fully implemented in 2009 but the 100 percent scanning rule has been postponed multiple times, most recently until 2016. Still, the SAFE Port Act has helped improve overall U.S. port security.

Container Security Initiative Initiated in 2002 by CBP, and codified in the SAFE Port Act, CSI addresses the threat to border security and global trade posed by terrorists using maritime containers to deliver and detonate explosives. The CSI program seeks to identify and inspect all containers that pose a potential risk for terrorism at foreign ports before they are placed on U.S. bound vessels.

CBP has stationed multi-disciplinary teams of U.S. officers from both CBP and Immigration and Customs Enforcement to work together with our host foreign government counterparts. Their mission is to target and prescreen containers and to develop additional investigative leads related to the terrorist threat to U.S. bound cargo.

The three core elements of CSI are:

- Identify high-risk containers. CBP uses automated targeting tools to identify containers that pose a potential risk for terrorism, based on advance information and strategic intelligence.
- Prescreen and evaluate containers before they are shipped. Containers are screened as early in the supply chain as possible, generally at the port of departure.
- Use nonintrusive inspection technology to prescreen high-risk containers to ensure that screening can be done rapidly without slowing down the movement of trade. This technology includes large-scale X-ray and gamma ray machines and radiation detection devices.

CSI is operational at 58 ports in North America, Europe, Asia, Africa, the Middle East, and Latin and Central America. These ports prescreen over 80 percent of all maritime containerized cargo imported into the United States.[25]

Customs-Trade Partnership Against Terrorism Another CBP-led program codified in the SAFE Port Act, C-TPAT is the voluntary government-business initiative discussed in the On the Line feature. Through this collaborative initiative, CBP encourages businesses to ensure the integrity of their security practices and verify the security guidelines of their business partners within the supply chain. This allows CBP to focus on high-risk shipments.

The partnership establishes clear supply chain security criteria for members to meet. When they join the anti-terror partnership, companies sign an agreement to work with CBP to protect the supply chain, identify security gaps, and implement specific security measures and best practices. Additionally, partners provide CBP with a security profile outlining the specific security measures the company has in place. Applicants must address a broad range of security topics and present security profiles that list action plans to align security throughout their supply chain.[26]

Certified C-TPAT members are considered low-risk based on their past compliance history, security profile, and the validation of a sample international supply chain. In return for achieving this designation, the companies experience fewer CBP inspections, shorter time and cost of getting cargo released by CBP, and reduced penalties. Ultimately, this means fewer disruptions and greater predictability of lead times.[27]

Aligned with C-TPAT, the FAST program is a commercial clearance program for known low-risk shipments entering the United States from Canada and Mexico. This innovative trusted traveler/trusted shipper program allows expedited processing for land based commercial carriers who have completed background checks and fulfill certain eligibility requirements. Participation in FAST requires that every link in the supply chain, from manufacturer to carrier to driver to importer, is certified under C-TPAT.

FAST is designed to enhance the security and safety of North America while also bolstering the economic prosperity of the United States, Canada, and Mexico by aligning, to the maximum extent possible, their commercial processing programs. The FAST program uses common risk-management principles, supply chain security, industry partnerships, and advanced technology to improve the efficiency of screening and clearing commercial traffic at ports of entry along the U.S./Canada and U.S./Mexico borders. Similar to C-TPAT, FAST participants gain access to dedicated border crossing lanes, experience fewer inspections, and receive front-of-the-line processing for CBP inspections.[28]

Transportation-based security programs aim to balance the protection of people and global trade from threats. Despite the advancements and program successes, security is an ongoing concern. Savvy criminals, terrorists, and others who seek to do harm to a country relentlessly pursue opportunities to exploit security weaknesses. Hence, security regulations and programs must constantly be scrutinized and improved. As the Global Perspective feature highlights, there must be greater collaboration between industry and governmental agencies to achieve success in this ongoing battle.

It is important to realize that mitigating security risks also benefits the participating companies. Some of these valuable outcomes are clear and tangible such as improved delivery times, decreased shrinkage, and improved responsiveness to disruptions. Other benefits—improved supply chain risk management culture, greater product integrity, and strengthened company reputation—are intangible but no less important.[29] A secure and resilient supply chain helps a company build significant competitive advantages over rival businesses.[30]

Clearly, supply chain security is more than a necessary evil. Companies should look at security as an opportunity to improve transportation service and enhance the bottom line.

GLOBAL **PERSPECTIVES**

Transportation Security—Global Collaboration Required

Achieving a more secure freight transportation system is neither the responsibility nor the forte of a single government. Security is enhanced only when governments, international organizations such as the World Customs Organization (WCO), and industry partners align to develop comprehensive and consistent strategies backed by investment and enforcement.

Many countries are working toward safer, incident-free flows of exports and imports. Japan established Advanced Cargo Information regulations to help its customs agency prescreen incoming freight information for high-risk cargo identification, inspection, and intervention. The China Customs-company classification program segments companies on the basis of pat security compliance so that inspections target risky or unknown organizations. And, the EU adopted the Authorized Economic Operator program in 2008 to ensure that parties involved in the international movement of goods comply with stated supply chain security standards.

Key organizations such as the International Air Transport Association are developing security programs for multicountry implementation. The Secure Freight program works across the whole air cargo supply chain, helping to secure shipments upstream by ensuring that cargo has come from either a known consignor or regulated agent. The United Kingdom, Malaysia, Kenya, Mexico, Chile, and the United Arab Emirates are among the participants.

Global transportation security is also promoted through mutual recognition arrangements (MRA). These formal bilateral agreements between Customs Administrations are adopted when the countries have compatible security standards, verification programs, and enforcement. For example, the United States uses MRAs to align the C-TPAT program with similar international industry partnership programs.

Collectively, these programs and initiatives create a unified and sustainable security posture that facilitates low-risk global trade.

Sources: International Air Transportation Association, "Secure Freight," retrieved September 5, 2014, from http://www.iata.org/whatwedo/cargo/security/Pages/secure-freight.aspx; U.S. Customs and Border Protection, "Unified Global Security: The Challenge Ahead," 2013, retrieved September 5, 2014, from http://www.cbp.gov/sites/default/files/documents/mutual_recognition_3.pdf; and Mitch Donner and Cornelis Kruk, *Supply Chain Security Guide* (New York: The World Bank, Washington DC, 2009).

SUMMARY

- Transportation risks are potentially disruptive events that produce supply chain disorder. Uncontrolled risk can produce negative outcomes ranging from minor delivery delays to major product losses that affect financial performance.
- Organizations can reduce threats to the continuing efficiency and effectiveness of their transportation operations through a process of risk management.
- Despite best efforts to reduce risks, most cannot be totally eliminated and disruptions may occur. Business continuity planning focuses on dealing with and recovering quickly from these disruption episodes.
- Risk management is the process of identifying risk, its causes and effects, and its ownership with a goal of increasing overall understanding in order to manage, reduce, transfer, or eliminate threats to supply chain success.
- The perils of transportation are many and varied. Managers must remain vigilant to all types of risk and work to discover, define, document, and communicate risks before they adversely affect freight flows. There are six common risk categories related to freight transportation: product loss, product damage, product contamination, delivery delay, supply chain interruption, and security breach.
- It is not enough to identify risks. Managers must work to understand how serious each risk is to the organization. They must assess both the likelihood of a disruption risk occurring and the consequences of a disruption incident.
- Transportation managers must be proactive in developing specific action plans and procedural changes to address supply chain risks. Risk mitigation options include risk avoidance, reduction, transfer, or retention.
- Risk is a never-ending challenge. Organizations must establish a repetitive, measurable, verifiable risk monitoring process to remain focused on existing and emerging transportation disruptions.
- Given their respective levels of importance to the U.S. economy and citizens, a delicate balance must be struck between transportation security and the efficient flow of global commerce.
- Security is not the responsibility or domain of a single group. Government and industry must collaborate on legislation, programs, and agreements to secure global supply chains. ATSA, MTSA, SAFE Port Act, CSI, C-TPAT, FAST, and other programs are solid success stories, though it is essential to remain vigilant and continuously improve security of the global supply chain.

STUDY QUESTIONS

1. Describe the concepts of disruptions and risks as they apply to transportation. Why are they important from financial and service standpoints?
2. Risk management consists of a series of steps that should be followed to reduce the consequences of disruptions. Briefly discuss these steps.
3. Six different categories of transportation risk were discussed in the chapter. Identify these categories, describe them, and give transportation examples for each risk categories.
4. Risk analysis is a critical component of risk management. When conducting this activity, what are the two components of risk that must be analyzed? Why are they important?

5. What are the key outputs of a risk assessment process? What should be done with these outputs?
6. What does it mean when a company tries to mitigate their transportation risk? How can they accomplish this?
7. What is the role of insurance in transportation risk management?
8. Why is risk management considered to be a continuous loop process?
9. Describe the challenges that governments and organizations face when addressing transportation security risks?
10. What are the key challenges of developing secure supply chain for global trade?
11. What programs, agencies, and legislation has the U.S. government created to reduce transportation security risks?
12. How can businesses collaborate with government agencies to create globally secure transportation networks?

NOTES

1. ICC Commercial Crime Service, "IMB Piracy & Armed Robbery Map 2014," retrieved August 20, 2014, from http://www.icc-ccs.org/piracy-reporting-centre/live-piracy-map.
2. Google Dictionary, retrieved August 20, 2014, from https://www.google.com/search?q=define+disruption&gws_rd=ssl.
3. http://USLegal.com, retrieved August 20, 2014, from http://definitions.uslegal.com/t/transportation-disruption/.
4. Dictionary.com, retrieved August 20, 2014, from http://dictionary.reference.com/browse/risk.
5. Becky Partida, "The Importance of a Thorough, Well-Managed Risk Strategy," *Supply Chain Management Review*, September/October 2013, pp. 70–72.
6. Steve Culp, "Supply Chain Disruption: A Major Threat to Business, *Forbes*, February 15, 2013, retrieved August 20, 2014, from http://www.forbes.com/sites/steveculp/2013/02/15/supply-chain-disruption-a-major-threat-to-business/.
7. CNN Library, "2011 Japan Earthquake—Tsunami Fast Facts," retrieved August 20, 2014, from http://www.cnn.com/2013/07/17/world/asia/japan-earthquake—tsunami-fast-facts/.
8. BusinessDictionary.com, retrieved August 28, 2014, from http://www.businessdictionary.com/definition/risk-management.html.
9. BusinessDictionary.com, retrieved August 28, 2014, from http://www.businessdictionary.com/definition/business-continuity-planning-BCP.html.
10. Protiviti KnowledgeLeader, "How to Define Risk Management Goals and Objectives in Your Organization," *KnowledgeLeader Blog*, November 14, 2012, retrieved August 28, 2014, from http://info.knowledgeleader.com/bid/164011/How-to-Define-Risk-Management-Goals-and-Objectives-in-Your-Organization.
11. Grace M. Lavigne, "Supply-Chain Interference: Cargo Theft, Piracy and Disruption in 2013," *JOC.com,* retrieved August 28, 2014, from http://www.joc.com/maritime-news/maritime-piracy/supply-chain-interference-cargo-theft-piracy-and-disruption-2013-infographic_20140502.html.
12. Michael Wolfe, "In This Case Bad News Is Good News," *Journal of Commerce,* July 26, 2004, p. 38.
13. U.S. Department of Transportation, *Pocket Guide to Large Truck and Bus Statistics*, 2014, retrieved August 28, 2014, from http://www.fmcsa.dot.gov/safety/data-and-statistics/commercial-motor-vehicle-facts.

14. Philip Blenkinsop, "Congestion Capital Brussels Looks to Unclog Traffic Arteries," *Reuters*, April 27, 2014, retrieved August 28, 2014, from http://www.reuters.com/article/2014/04/27/us-traffic-brussels-idUSBREA3Q03220140427.

15. Peter T. Leach, "Global Ports Grapple with Congestion Generated by Larger Ships and Alliances," *JOC.com*, August 25, 2014, retrieved August 28, 2014, from http://www.joc.com/global-ports-grapple-congestion-generated-larger-ships-and-alliances_20140825.html.

16. Alix Partners, "Change on the Horizon: 2014 Container Shipping Outlook," retrieved August 28, 2014, from http://www.alixpartners.com/en/Publications/AllArticles/tabid/635/articleType/ArticleView/articleId/1087/Change-on-the-Horizon.aspx#sthash.wJEFCwGr.dpbs.

17. Mark S. Dorfman and David Cather, *Introduction to Risk Management and Insurance 10th Edition* (Englewood Cliffs, NJ: Prentice Hall, 2012).

18. Gordon Rayner, "Holidaymakers Warned of Risk of 'Significant Disruption' If Icelandic Volcano Erupts," *The Telegraph*, August 19, 2014.

19. Sunil Chopra and ManMohan S. Sodhi, "Reducing the Risk of Supply Chain Disruptions," *MIT Sloan Management Review*, March 18, 2014, retrieved September 3, 2014, from http://sloanreview.mit.edu/article/reducing-the-risk-of-supply-chain-disruptions/.

20. *National Strategy for Global Supply Chain Security* (Washington, DC: Office of the President, January 2012), retrieved September 3, 2014, from http://www.whitehouse.gov/sites/default/files/national_strategy_for_global_supply_chain_security.pdf.

21. U.S. Department of Homeland Security, "Evaluation of Screening of Air Cargo Transported on Passenger Aircraft," September 2010, retrieved September 3, 2014, from http://www.oig.dhs.gov/assets/Mgmt/OIG_10-119_Sep10.pdf.

22. U.S. Department of Homeland Security, "Cargo Screening: A Multi-Layered Approach to Cargo Security," retrieved September 3, 2014, from http://www.dhs.gov/cargo-screening.

23. Frank A. LoBiondo, "Tenth Anniversary of the Maritime Transportation Security Act: Are We Safer?" *The Maritime Executive*, September 11, 2012.

24. U.S. Energy Information Administration, "The Maritime Transportation Security Act of 2002," retrieved September 3, 2014, from http://www.eia.gov/oil_gas/natural_gas/analysis_publications/ngmajorleg/mtransport.html.

25. U.S. Customs and Border Protection, "CSI: Container Security Initiative," retrieved September 3, 2014, from http://www.cbp.gov/border-security/ports-entry/cargo-security/csi/csi-brief.

26. U.S. Customs and Border Protection, "C-TPAT: Customs-Trade Partnership Against Terrorism," retrieved, September 3, 2014, from http://www.cbp.gov/border-security/ports-entry/cargo-security/c-tpat-customs-trade-partnership-against-terrorism.

27. U.S. Customs and Border Protection, "C-TPAT: A Guide to Program Benefits," retrieved, September 3, 2014, from http://www.cbp.gov/sites/default/files/documents/ctpat_prog_benefits_guide_3.pdf.

28. U.S. Customs and Border Protection, "FAST: Free and Secure Trade for Commercial Vehicles," retrieved, September 4, 2014, from http://www.cbp.gov/travel/trusted-traveler-programs/fast.

29. Scott Taylor, "Top 7 Tips to Tighten Your Supply Chain Security," *Security Solutions*, December 9, 2013.

30. Susan Avery, "Identifying Vulnerability in Step One to Mitigating Supply Chain Risk," *My Purchasing Center*, January 23, 2014, retrieved September 4, 2014, from http://www.mypurchasingcenter.com/logistics/articles/identifying-vulnerability-step-one-mitigating-supply-chain-risk/.

CASE 9-1

Young Again Pharmaceuticals

Joe Hannibal, senior director of transportation for Young Again Pharmaceuticals (YAP), is gearing up for his company's most critical product rollout in more than a decade. YAP has developed a breakthrough liquid suspension that reverses the aging process for anyone over 35 years of age. Available only by prescription, the new product has been dubbed "Twenty-something in a Bottle" by the media. Demand is expected to be very high despite the outlandish price tag of $395 for a month's supply.

The product is being manufactured in YAP's Dublin, Ireland, laboratory and will be distributed to major retail pharmacies in the United States and Canada. Hannibal is responsible for selecting the mode and contracting with carriers to deliver the product. He is concerned about the safe and timely delivery of the initial product shipments in April to the retailers' distribution centers. The product is high value, somewhat fragile, and susceptible to theft. Some product, stolen from the laboratory, has already appeared on auction websites.

In an effort to make effective transportation decisions and minimize YAP's risks, Hannibal decided to hold a brainstorming session with his logistics team before signing any carrier contracts. The discussion of key risks produced the following list of concerns:

- "If shipments are late or incomplete, retailers will penalize us with vendor chargebacks. You know they will hit us with small fines for delivery mistakes."
- "I'm worried about shipment delays or freight loss from hurricanes in the Atlantic Ocean."
- "You've got to consider temperature sensitivity issues. If the product freezes, we won't be able to sell it."
- "I've been reading about all the piracy problems experienced by ocean carriers. You know, a 20-foot container of our product has a retail value of nearly $875,000."
- "I worry about theft of individual cases at ports and while the product is on the road."
- "We're looking at border delays and Customs fines if we don't properly document and mark our freight."
- "Our brand image will take major damage if the product gets into unauthorized distribution channels due to theft or misdirected deliveries."
- "The company sustainability push has led to reduced packaging and biodegradable packing materials. If the cartons get wet or bounced around, we're going to end up with a lot of damaged, unsellable product."
- "The major U.S. East Coast ports can get very congested during peak shipping season. That will cause delays."

By the time the meeting was over, Hannibal realized that he needed to spend some time looking into these issues. While he was pretty sure that some problems were remote, Hannibal thought that it would be wise to evaluate each one. His new concern became how to conduct an effective risk assessment.

CASE QUESTIONS

1. Assess the risks identified in the brainstorming session. Create and populate a table similar to Figure 9-2.
2. Based on your answer to Question 1, what are the three primary risks that you believe YAP must address? Why?
3. What do you recommend that YAP do to mitigate each of the three risks identified in Question 2?
4. What should YAP focus on after attempting to mitigate these transportation risks?

CASE 9-2

Techno-Shades

Denny Butler, chief procurement officer for Techno-Shades International (TSI), is looking to hit a home run for his fledgling technology company. TSI is only six months away from a huge industry event, the Consumer Electronics Show. During this Las Vegas trade show, TSI will introduce a new line of wearable technology focused on athletes and sports fans. The stylish sunglasses contain a lightning-fast wireless computer that captures performance data, provides navigation, accesses live feeds from sporting events, and allows hands-free messaging, among other capabilities.

The company feels that the product is a higher quality, lower price alternative to Google Glass and has staked its future on this rollout. Demand is expected to be very high and profits will soar—if Butler can find a contract manufacturer to assemble Techno-Shades and fill the U.S. supply chain concurrently with the Consumer Electronics Show.

Butler has been traveling the globe in search of a high quality, low-cost assembler for Techno-Shades. He is also wary of product espionage that could lead to copycat products filling the market too quickly. After conducting a thorough analysis of twelve different manufacturers, Butler has narrowed his consideration to three potential suppliers:

- Supplier 1 is located in Ashkelon, Israel. The company has experience making technology products, boasts excess factory capacity, and has a strong stable of satisfied customers. Product prices are reasonable but the geographic location presents safety risks. The price is 1,700 ILS (Israeli Shekel) per pair, delivered to the Ben Gurion Airport in Tel Aviv.
- Supplier 2 is located in Wulumuqi, China. The company is a former state-owned maker of Red Army GPS devices. The far inland location creates a very low labor cost but increases the length of supply lines and the distribution channel. The factory-based price is $459 per pair.
- Supplier 3 is located in Salo, Finland. The company is a world-class manufacturer of mobile phones and is interested in co-developing products with TSI. They are somewhat constrained by factory capacity and road congestion to the airport can be troublesome, but promise to meet all deadlines. The cost of the product, cleared through U.S. Customs to a freight forwarder in Newark, New Jersey, is 385 Euros per pair.

As Butler considered his options, he consulted an online currency converter to evaluate the quotes. He found the following exchange rates: 1 USD = 3.935 ILS and 1 USD = .804 EUR.

Before making a final supplier selection, Butler thought that it would be wise to confer with Ricky Himmer, TGU's vice president of transportation. The executives met at company headquarters to compare the options. Himmer was impressed by the thoroughness of the supplier evaluation process and cost analysis. However, he complained about offshore sourcing risks and possible transportation disruptions. Himmer also kept talking in acronyms about security regulation compliance and paperwork requirements.

By the time the meeting was over, Butler was worried. Had he missed something in his analysis or was Himmer ranting aimlessly about nonissues? Butler decided that the analysis of the three potential suppliers should take on another dimension—supply chain risk and what could be done about it.

CASE QUESTIONS

1. What issues should Butler evaluate in his assessment of transportation risks?
2. Analyze each supplier option that Butler is considering. What specific risks does each supplier option present?
3. Which supplier would you recommend that Butler choose to best balance company goals with transportation and supply chain risks?
4. What types of transportation security issues and requirements will confront TGU if they off-shore manufacturing?

CHAPTER

10 GLOBAL TRANSPORTATION PLANNING

Learning Objectives

After reading this chapter, you should be able to do the following:

- Discuss the relationship between international trade and global transportation
- Identify the three critical flows in global supply chains
- Recognize the importance of proper global transportation planning
- Understand the role of Incoterms in determining transportation responsibilities, risks, and costs
- Describe the payment term options available to exporters and importers
- Appreciate the value of timely, accurate global freight documentation
- Analyze the key issues in effective international transportation mode and carrier selection
- Evaluate the critical factors in route design for international shipments

TRANSPORTATION **PROFILE**

Global Trade Expansion Drives Transportation Planning Challenges

Over the past 30 years, the ratio of world exports of merchandise and commercial services to global domestic product (GDP) has risen from 20 to 32 percent. This growth in global trade has driven a similar expansion of international freight transportation. During that span, spending on global freight transportation services has risen from $120 to $905 billion, according to the World Trade Organization.[1]

As the volume of freight and distance between exporters and importers increase, transportation complexity spikes. Moving freight across oceans and country borders is no simple task. Compared to domestic freight movement, global transportation of goods over long distances creates a variety of significant challenges: longer and more variable transit time, risk of in-transit product damage or loss, higher delivery and accessorial service expenses, and greater in-transit inventory carrying costs. These challenges must be accurately weighed against the benefits of sourcing goods globally or moving production offshore.

Transportation managers must also be cognizant of broader issues that impact the availability and cost of global transportation services. Proper long-range planning of the transportation function requires that managers take the time to monitor business trends, government intervention, and consumer demand. A failure to respond to changes in these macro-level issues creates unnecessary risk, capacity challenges, and potential competitive disadvantage.

While there is no shortage of external issues, the following challenges are worthy of extensive attention by global transportation managers:

- **Capacity Management**—overcapacity and thin profit margins have driven ocean carriers to mergers, acquisition, and the formation of operating consortia. The pooling of capacity and sailings seeks to generate greater control and pricing power. Freight shippers face fewer scheduling options and potential price increases.
- **Security Requirements**—as Chapter 9 highlighted, transportation plays a key role in mitigating terrorism. Detailed, timely freight documentation is required, inspection of goods will continue to increase, and border security will remain tight. Compliance with these requirements will enhance protection though at a financial cost.
- **Freight Protection**—product loss is an ongoing challenge in global transportation. Ship hijackings, freight theft, and damage from poor handling are costly issues. Estimates of the global financial impact of cargo losses range from $18 to $50 billion per year.
- **Freight Control**—in-transit visibility is difficult to maintain, given the long distances between far-flung origin and destination points for global freight. Add in the number of transfers between exporters, transportation service providers, and importers, and it becomes very difficult to know exactly where freight is and how long it will take to arrive at the final destination. An inability to monitor freight progress can impede efforts to mitigate delays and disruptions.
- **Peak Seasonal Availability**—in the months leading up to the holiday shopping season, equipment capacity shortages and port congestion issues often arise. Ill-prepared shippers face the prospects of freight delays and transportation surcharges.

These five issues are just the proverbial tip of the iceberg. Transportation managers must heed additional global challenges. Government regulation and intervention, fuel price volatility, labor disruptions, and sustainability initiatives create a complex operating environment. Global transportation managers must remain vigilant and develop appropriate transportation strategies to proactively control their freight flows and costs.

Sources: World Trade Organization, *Trade in Commercial Services*, retrieved September 9, 2014, from http://stat.wto.org/StatisticalProgram/WSDBViewData.aspx?Language=E; International Transport Forum, *ITF Transport Outlook 2013*, retrieved September 9, 2014, from http://www.keepeek.com/Digital-Asset-Management/oecd/transport/itf-transport-outlook-2013_9789282103937-en#page1; and Coyle et al., *Transportation: A Supply Chain Perspective* (Mason, OH: South-Western Cengage Learning, 2011) pp. 328–329.

Introduction

The global economy can go through extreme cycles. From 1990 to 2008, world trade average growth rate was 6 percent. Then, the worldwide financial crisis hit, leading to the 2008–09 "Great Recession." Figure 10-1 reveals that recovery has been slow, with the average rate of trade expansion at 3.4 percent from 2011 to 2013, far below the pre-crisis trend. The divergence between the pre-crisis trend and current levels of world trade continues to widen.[2]

These global economic conditions directly affect the market for global transportation services. During sustained growth periods, demand for transportation services is high and infrastructure capacities are tested. This is good news for carriers who can raise rates and expand fleets, but freight customers must scramble to secure containers and berths to move products to support customer demand.

During downturns, the opposite situation exists. Capacity is readily available causing freight rates to drop. This is good news for freight customers, but the transportation service providers must scramble to fill equipment with revenue-generating freight. They

FIGURE 10-1 Global Export Volume 1990–2015

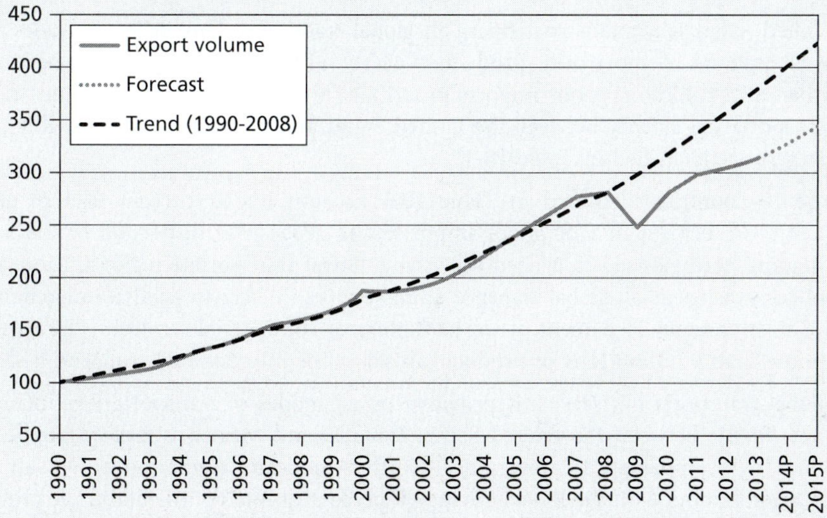

Source: World Trade Organization Secretariat. http://www.wto.org/english/news_e/pres14_e/pr721_e.htm

FIGURE 10-2 Global Transportation Planning

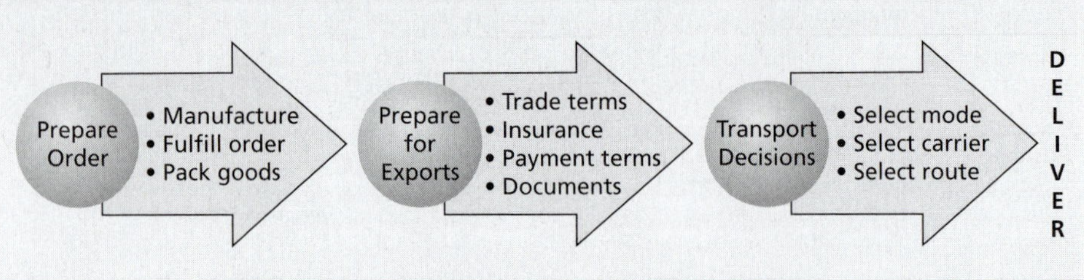

may also need to curb their fleet expansion activities to avoid spending money on unneeded equipment.

The challenge for both parties is to effectively manage current conditions while positioning themselves for the more robust growth predicted by the World Trade Organization. The dollar value of world merchandise exports in 2013 was $18.8 trillion. Forecasts for 2014 and 2015 are $19.6 trillion (4.5 percent expansion) and $20.7 trillion (5.3 percent expansion), respectively.[3] This level of trade drives an ongoing need for quality global transportation services.

Navigating the sometimes choppy waters of the global economy is no easy task for transportation managers as indicated by the Transportation Profile. However, they should not lose sight of the fundamental issues and practices that generate effective, efficient freight flows. This chapter focuses on the need for proper planning before freight begins its international journey. We will discuss global trade and transportation industry in terms of size, trade agreements, and channel issues. Specific planning issues related to trade terms and payment terms will be covered, followed by an overview of key transportation documents. The chapter wraps up with coverage of mode, carrier, and route selection. Throughout the chapter, you will gain a greater appreciation of the importance of the global transportation planning activities outlined in Figure 10-2.

Overview of Global Transportation

The United States is a major participant in global trade. The United States trades with nearly all nations of the world, producing nearly $1.6 trillion in goods exports and more than $2.3 trillion in goods imports in 2013.[4] This level of trade necessitates extensive transportation activity between the United States and its trading partners. Key trading partners are identified in Table 10-1.

The 10 countries identified in Table 10-1 account for 62 percent of U.S. goods exports and 68 percent of U.S. goods imports. The geographic dispersion of these primary trading partners creates a need for sizable global transportation flows. More than $905 billion was spent on global transportation services in 2013 to facilitate merchandise trade. This represents 20 percent of world exports of commercial services.[5] On a weight basis, more than 9 billion tons of product moved in the international seaborne trade.[6]

Global transportation service is provided by all modes of transportation, including pipelines. Traffic between the United States, Canada, and Mexico is largely handled by truck and rail companies. However, non-North American freight moves via air and water transportation, with the latter moving 90 percent of intercontinental trade (volume basis). Hence, the issues discussed in this chapter and next chapter will revolve around the movement of goods via these two modes.

TABLE 10-1 U.S. Trading Partners—2013

COUNTRY	GOODS EXPORTS ($ IN BILLIONS)	COUNTRY	GOODS IMPORTS ($ IN BILLIONS)
Canada	301.6	China	440.4
Mexico	226.1	Canada	332.6
China	121.7	Mexico	280.5
Japan	65.2	Japan	146.4
Germany	47.3	Germany	109.2
United Kingdom	47.3	Korea	62.4
Brazil	44.1	United Kingdom	52.8
Netherlands	42.6	Saudi Arabia	51.8
Hong Kong	42.3	France	45.7
Korea	41.7	India	41.8
Top Ten Total		Top Ten Total	
Grand Total	**1,592.7**	**Grand Total**	**2,294.4**

Source: U.S. Department of Commerce, Census Bureau, Foreign Trade Division.

Global Trade Agreements Stimulate Transportation Activity

The growth of global trade has been fueled by the establishment of **free trade agreements** (FTAs) around the world. This type of agreement is a pact between two or more countries or areas in which all participants agree to lift most or all tariffs, quotas, special fees and taxes, and other barriers to trade between the entities. The purpose of FTAs is to allow faster and more business between the countries or areas, which should benefit all participants. Expanded FTA trade between countries creates great demand for international freight transportation. The United States participates in both bilateral trade agreements and regional trade agreements. According to the Office of the U.S. Trade Representative, the United States pursues comprehensive free trade agreements to expand opportunities for American workers, farmers, manufacturers, and service providers. Currently, the United States has FTAs in effect with 20 countries: Australia, Bahrain, Canada, Chile, Colombia, Costa Rica, Dominican Republic, El Salvador, Guatemala, Honduras, Israel, Jordan, Korea, Mexico, Morocco, Nicaragua, Oman, Panama, Peru, and Singapore.[7]

Regional initiatives are also a key part of global trade strategy. A regional Asia-Pacific trade agreement between 11 countries, known as the Trans-Pacific Partnership Agreement, focuses increasing trade access to some of the fastest growing markets in the world.[8] Existing trade agreements include the Free Trade Area of the Americas, aimed at uniting the Western Hemisphere in a free trade zone; the Enterprise for ASEAN Initiative, designed to promote trade in Asian countries; the Middle East Free Trade Initiative; and the North American Free Trade Agreement (NAFTA), which links the United States, Mexico, and Canada in a free trade area of 450 million people. In 2013, the United States had $1.2 trillion in two-way trade of goods and services with Canada and Mexico.[9]

Signed by leaders of Canada, the United States, and Mexico on December 17, 1992, NAFTA establishes free trade between these three countries. The treaty states that the objectives of the three countries are based on the principles of an unimpeded flow of goods, most-favored-nation (MFN) status, and a commitment to enhance the cross-border movement of goods and services. MFN status provides the lowest duties or customs fees, if any, and simplifies the paperwork required to move goods between the partner countries.

An example of the trading arrangement between the United States and Mexico that is facilitated by NAFTA is a unique international operation known as a **maquiladora**. A maquiladora is a U.S. manufacturing or assembly operation located along the U.S.–Mexico border, or other locations specified by the Mexican government. U.S. raw materials and component parts are sent to the maquiladora, where the semifinished or finished product is manufactured or assembled. All or part of the maquiladora's output is subsequently returned to the United States without any Mexican import duties being paid. The U.S. companies with maquiladora operations are taking advantage of the lower labor rates in Mexico.

NAFTA also addresses transportation issues. It contains a U.S.–Mexico cross-border trucking provision that laid out a two-stage plan to open the border to motor carriers. By December 18, 1995, Mexican motor carriers would be allowed to serve California, Arizona, New Mexico, and Texas. U.S. carriers would be allowed to serve Mexico's six border states. By January 1, 2000, American and Mexican carriers would be able to travel freely in both countries. However, this provision has never been fully implemented as highlighted in the Global Perspectives feature.

In contrast, NAFTA does not address U.S.–Canada cross-border trucking. Canadian trucking companies operate in the United States under an agreement made prior to NAFTA. Canadian carriers are allowed to transport domestic U.S. traffic when such transportation is incidental to a return trip to Canada. For example, a Canadian trucker is allowed to deliver a cross-border load from Toronto to Chicago, move an incidental U.S. domestic load from Chicago to Detroit, and pick up a cross-border load in Detroit destined for Toronto.

GLOBAL **PERSPECTIVES**

NAFTA Cross-Border Transportation—an Unfulfilled Promise

More than 20 years after officials signed the North American Free Trade Agreement, transportation provisions remain unfulfilled. The lack of full-scale implementation by U.S. officials is largely due to political pressures from powerful lobbying groups. The Teamsters union and the Owner-Operator Independent Drivers Association fear job losses. Safety pundits decry the condition of Mexican trucks and qualifications of Mexican drivers. And, wary legislators raise concerns about illegal immigration and contraband smuggling. As a result, Mexican trucks have mostly been confined to a 25-mile commercial zone on the U.S. side of the border while Canadian trucks face no such restrictions or political controversy.

On December 17, 1995, the day before implementation of the initial NAFTA transportation rules, President Clinton issued an executive order to extend the moratorium on cross-border trucking with Mexico. The Mexican government filed a dispute in 2001 and an arbitration panel later concluded that the United States violated the NAFTA trucking provisions.

Subsequently, President Bush promised to comply with the trade agreement but only succeeded establishing a joint demonstration program to allow up to 100 trucking firms from Mexico to transport international cargo beyond the commercial zones along the U.S.–Mexico border and up to 100 U.S. trucking firms to transport international cargo into Mexico. The program ran from 2007 until 2009 when funding was not renewed by Congress.

The failure to extend the program led to rapid retaliation by Mexican officials who increased tariffs on 89 U.S. import products in March 2009. In response, the Obama administration crafted another pilot program to allow long-haul Mexican trucks into the United States in 2011. Under the three stage safety program that inspects equipment, audits safety, and evaluates performance of the Mexican carriers, the 14 carriers approved under the pilot program have made nearly 10,000 border crossings and deliveries, mostly to Texas and California. The pilot program was slated to conclude in late 2014.

Advocates of the NAFTA trucking provisions hope that permanent implementation will eventually occur, and they believe it creates a more globally competitive North American region. They further note that cross-border transportation costs can be reduced by 15 percent if long-haul carriage replaces inefficient cross-border drayage methods. Under this antiquated system, a Mexican trucker carries U.S.-bound freight to the border and unhooks his trailer; a drayage carrier moves the trailer across the border, where a U.S. trucker hooks up to the trailer and takes it to its final destination.

Will these advocates—the U.S. Chamber of Commerce, the Mexican government, and transportation companies from both countries—prevail in their quest to fully implement the NAFTA cross-border transportation provisions? Only time and politics will tell.

Sources: Sandra Dibble, "NAFTA Trucking Vision Unfulfilled," *San Diego Union-Tribune*, May 10, 2014; John Frittelli, *Status of Mexican Trucks in the United States: Frequently Asked Questions* (Washington, DC: Congressional Research Service, January 3, 2014); and Larry Copeland, "Mexican Truckers to Haul Freight on U.S. Roads," *USA Today*, August 8, 2011.

Logistics Channel Issues in Global Transportation

Global transportation involves more than the physical flow of goods via the modes mentioned above. As in any supply chain, the global flow of goods is supported by effective information flows between the **exporter** and **importer**. The flow of payments is also critical to timely completion of the transaction. Wood et al. (2002) used the concept of logistics channels or networks to describe the planning and execution of these key flows. These include the transaction channel, the communication channel, and the distribution channel.[10] Each is introduced below and addressed throughout the chapter.

Transaction Channel Activities When purchasing goods, paying for them, and preparing for their movement, the buyer (importer) must take steps to protect its financial interests and reduce risk. The importer must effectively negotiate details with the seller (exporter) that go beyond the basics of product quality, price, and quantity. In global transactions, it is also important to clarify the location and point in time at which legal title for the goods transfers from the exporter to the importer.

Why is this so important? **Transfer of ownership** is linked to responsibility for managing in-transit goods. This responsibility includes making key decisions regarding mode and carrier selection, **insurance** coverage, and **routing**. The transfer of ownership also determines who is responsible for payment of transportation services, insurance, and import duties. Finally, ownership determines responsibility for compliance with government regulations and financial **liability** in the event of freight damage, loss, or delay. **Terms of trade**, discussed later in this chapter, help to clarify the point of transfer and the responsibilities of each party to the transaction.

Another key transaction channel activity is payment for the goods. In a global transaction, both the exporter and importer are at greater risk than in a domestic transaction. The exporter is concerned about the risk of nonpayment by the importer. Payment in advance of shipment would be the ideal choice for the exporter. However, the importer may have some apprehensions about shipment delivery and product quality. Hence, the preferred option would be payment after delivery. There are other options to moderate the **terms of payment** risks faced by each party.

Communication Channel One of the major challenges in global transportation is maintaining visibility and control of freight as it move across borders and is handed off between carriers and intermediaries. Timely information sharing and the use of technology can vastly improve shipment visibility. Proper freight documentation ensures compliance with government regulations and facilitates the uninterrupted flow of goods through potential bottlenecks at border crossings and ports.

Documentation should be a simple issue in this era of information technology but communication channel challenges still exist. Far more documents are involved in a global transaction than in a purely domestic one. Different documents are required by the country of export, the country of import, transportation companies, banks, and the importer. Also, some documents are not yet in electronic format and copies must be physically distributed to each party involved in the transaction.

To combat the challenges and complexity of the communication channel, some global logistics service providers offer international trade document management assistance. These services focus on having the right trade documentation, authenticated by the right authorities, at the right time to keep international freight flowing smoothly.

Distribution Channel Managing an extended transportation network increases the potential for disruptions due to the extended travel distances, freight handling at multiple facilities, and involvement of numerous intermediaries. Also, transportation infrastructure, regulations, and service options vary from country to country, adding complexity to the situation. As a result, global freight is at greater risk of erratic and extended transit times, freight stoppages, visibility problems, and loss of control than domestic freight.

To overcome these challenges, global transportation managers must actively manage the distribution channel. They must recognize and act upon the need for effective transportation planning in terms of mode, carrier, and route selection. Properly matching freight to the most appropriate mode will facilitate safe and cost-efficient distribution of goods. Vigilant carrier selection processes will lead managers to reputable transportation service providers with significant experience in key markets, extensive capabilities, and a strong customer orientation. Optimal route selection from among the wide variety of options will provide for greater freight protection and more consistent service. Other important distribution channel issues include freight protection (proper packing and loading of goods) and process control (measuring and monitoring transportation performance).

Careful consideration of all three channels is essential to success. Managers must focus on the ownership transfer, freight control, and payment issues in the transaction channel. Also, managers must understand documentation requirements and the need to interact with multiple governments and stakeholders in the communication channel. Finally, managers must overcome the extended distance, time, and visibility challenges in the distribution channel. Coordinating decision across the three channels and making conscientious tradeoffs between them is critical to global transportation success.

Export Preparation Activities

Long before global freight is loaded and transported to its destination, key decisions must be made and requirements completed. Four primary export preparation activities are choosing the terms of trade, securing freight insurance, agreeing upon the terms of payment, and completing the required freight documentation. These pre-shipment steps help to clarify responsibilities of the exporter and importer, protect each party's financial interests, improve freight control and visibility, and facilitate problem-free transport.

Terms of Trade

When a company purchases goods from an international supplier, the buyer typically focuses on product price, quality, and quantity of goods. However, transportation issues must also be considered and a number of relevant activities must take place:

- clearing the goods for export
- organizing the transport of goods from origin to destination, often involving multiple moves and modes
- clearing customs in the country of import
- arranging payment for transportation, insurance, and duties

The terms of trade specified in the contract determine which of these responsibilities are handled by the exporter (the international supplier) and which are managed by the importer (the company making the purchase). Terms of trade are extremely important because they show precisely where the exporter's responsibilities end and where the importer's responsibilities begin. They govern decision making authority for movement of the product, establish when the ownership and title of the goods pass from the exporter to the importer, and clarify which organization incurs delivery-related costs. In short, the terms of trade facilitate international trade by streamlining the process for determining responsibilities and risks related to the international transport of goods.

A very challenging situation would arise for exporters and importers if each country established their own terms of trade. Inconsistencies, changes, and interpretation issues would hamper trade. Fortunately, a harmonized set of selling terms has been established by the **International Chamber of Commerce** (ICC) to reduce some of the confusion and complexity involving international shipments. Widely known as **Incoterms**, these *In*ternational *Co*mmercial *Terms* make international trade easier and facilitate the flow of goods between different countries. As described by the ICC, Incoterms are an internationally recognized standard and are used worldwide in international and domestic contracts for the sale of goods. First published in 1936, Incoterms rules provide internationally accepted definitions and rules of interpretation for most common commercial terms. They help traders avoid costly misunderstanding by clarifying the tasks, costs, and risks involved in the delivery of goods from sellers to buyers.[11]

Incoterms have been revised and refined six times since the original set was put into effect. The most recent set of trade rules, known as Incoterms 2010, simplify the 2000 rules by reducing the number of options from 13 to 11 and organizing the terms by mode. Additionally, Incoterms are now available to use for domestic contracts.[12]

Four of the Incoterms apply only to sea and inland waterway transport. The remaining seven Incoterms apply to any mode or intermodal transportation. Figure 10-3 indicates the proper usage of each Incoterm by mode. Also, Incoterms are typically expressed as three letter acronyms with a named location and the Incoterms version used to avoid any confusion. For example, a properly completed Incoterm description on a document would read: "DAP, Long

FIGURE 10-3 Incoterms Applicability by Mode

Mode	EXW	FCA	FAS	FOB	CFR	CIF	CPT	CIP	DAT	DAP	DDP
	✓	✓	✓	✓	✓	✓	✓	✓	✓	✓	✓
	✓	✓					✓	✓	✓	✓	✓
	✓	✓					✓	✓	✓	✓	✓
	✓	✓					✓	✓	✓	✓	✓

Beach, California, USA, Incoterms 2010" to indicate that the exporter is responsible for the goods from the point of origin until they are unloaded at the Port of Long Beach.

Incoterms can be divided into four primary groups. The E term is used when the importer takes full responsibility from the point of departure; F terms are used when the main carriage is not paid by the exporter; C terms are used when the main carrier is paid by the exporter; and D terms are employed when the exporter takes full responsibility to the point of arrival. Each group is discussed in more detail below.

E Terms There is only one Incoterm, **Ex Works (EXW)**. This is a departure contract that gives the importer total responsibility for the shipment. The exporter's responsibility is to make the shipment available at its facility. The importer agrees to take possession of the shipment at the point of origin and to bear all of the cost and risk of transporting the goods to the destination. Table 10-2 identifies additional responsibilities of the E term.

TABLE 10-2 Incoterms Importer/Exporter Responsibility

EVENT	EXW	FCA	FAS	FOB	CFR	CIF	CPT	CIP	DAT	DAP	DDP
Packaging	E	E	E	E	E	E	E	E	E	E	E
Loading Charges	I	E	E	E	E	E	E	E	E	E	E
Origin to Port Delivery	I	E	E	E	E	E	E	E	E	E	E
Export Duties and Taxes	I	E	E	E	E	E	E	E	E	E	E
Origin Terminal Charges	I	I	E	E	E	E	E	E	E	E	E
Loading	I	I	I	E	E	E	E	E	E	E	E
Port to Port Delivery	I	I	I	I	E	E	E	E	E	E	E
Insurance						E		E			
Destination Terminal Charges	I	I	I	I	I	I	E	E	E	E	E
Port to Destination Delivery	I	I	I	I	I	I	I	I	I	E	E
Import Duty and Taxes	I	I	I	I	I	I	I	I	I	I	E

F Terms The three F terms obligate the exporter to incur the cost of delivering the shipment cleared for export to the carrier designated by the importer. The importer selects and incurs the cost of main transportation, insurance, and customs clearance.

Free Carrier (FCA) can be used with any mode of transportation. Risk of damage is transferred to the importer when the exporter delivers the goods to the international carrier named by the importer.

Free Alongside Ship (FAS) is used for water transportation shipments only. The risk of damage is transferred to the importer when the goods are delivered alongside the ship. The importer must pay the cost of "lifting" the cargo or container on board the vessel.

Free On Board (FOB) is used for only water transportation shipments. The risk of damage is transferred to the importer when the shipment crosses the ship's rail (when the goods are actually loaded on the vessel). The exporter pays for loading. See Table 10-2 for additional responsibilities of the F Terms.

C Terms The four C terms are shipment contracts that obligate the exporter to obtain and pay for the main carriage and in some cases, cargo insurance.

Cost and Freight (CFR) is used for water transportation only. The exporter incurs all costs to the port of destination. The importer assumes all risks once the goods are onboard the vessel and is responsible for all activities and costs after the ship arrives at the destination port.

Cost, Insurance, Freight (CIF) is used for water transportation only. The exporter bears the cost of freight and insurance to the destination port. The importer is responsible for all activities and costs after the ship arrives at the destination port.

Carriage Paid To (CPT) can be used with any mode of transportation. The exporter incurs the cost of freight to a named place of destination but is not responsible for insurance. The importer assumes all risks during the delivery process and is responsible for all activities and costs after the goods arrive at the named place.

Carriage and Insurance Paid To (CIP) can be used with any mode of transportation. The exporter incurs the cost of freight to a named place of destination and is responsible for procuring insurance coverage to the named place. The importer is responsible for all activities and costs after the goods arrive at the named place. See Table 10-2 for additional responsibilities of the C Terms.

D Terms The D terms obligate the exporter to incur all costs related to delivery of the shipment to the foreign destination. There are three D terms and they can be applied to any mode of transportation. Each D term requires the exporter to incur all costs and the risk of damage up to a named delivery location.

Delivered At Terminal (DAT) means the exporter is responsible for transportation and incurs the risk of damage until goods are delivered to a named terminal in the destination country. The importer is responsible for import clearance and any further in-country carriage.

Delivered At Place (DAP) requires the exporter to pay for the main carriage and to deliver goods to the importer's facility or another named location (other than a terminal) in the destination country. The importer is responsible for import clearance and any further in-country carriage.

Delivered Duty Paid (DDP) requires the exporter to assume responsibility for all costs involved in delivering the goods to a named place of destination and for clearing

FIGURE 10-4 Role of Incoterms

INCOTERMS ARE USED TO DEFINE THE RELATIONSHIP BETWEEN EXPORTER AND IMPORTER REGARDING:	INCOTERMS WILL NOT:
• Mode of delivery • Arrangement of customs clearances and licenses • Passage of title • Transfer of risk and insurance responsibilities (i.e., who has to insure goods during transport) • What the delivery terms are • How transport costs are shared between the parties • When a delivery is completed	• Define contractual rights • Specify transport details regarding delivery of goods • Define liabilities and/or obligations between the parties • Dictate how the title of the goods will pass (although Incoterms dictate when they transfer) • Dictate obligations with regards to the goods prior to and after delivery • Protect a party from his/her own risk of loss

Source: Transportgistics, *Deciphering Incoterms.* Available from http://www.transportgistics.com/decipheringincoterms.htm.

customs in the country of import. The exporter provides door-to-door delivery, bearing the entire risk of loss until goods are delivered to the importer's premises. See Table 10-2 for additional responsibilities of the D Terms.

Proper choice of Incoterms will go a long way toward the effective balancing of responsibilities for international transportation between the exporter and the importer. Key determinants of Incoterm selection include the relative expertise of each firm as well as their willingness to perform the required tasks. Other relevant factors include the type of product being sold, the mode of transportation being used, and the level of trust between the firms.

Finally, it is important to realize that Incoterms do not cover every aspect of an international delivery. Incoterms do not constitute a contract between the exporter and importer. Figure 10-4 summarizes what responsibilities and obligations that Incoterms do and do not address.

Cargo Insurance

One of the issues addressed by Incoterms is responsibility for insuring the freight. The organization assuming this obligation faces one of the most complex issues in global transportation. Cargo insurance is challenging because of the unique terminology, centuries-old traditions, and confusing set of regulations that limit carrier liability.

Regardless of the challenges, cargo insurance is critical. Importers and exporters are exposed to countless perils and financial risks when their freight moves through the global supply chain. They must determine their insurable interests and how to most effectively manage risk. Each of these insurance-related issues are introduced below.

Financial Risks Trying to recover financial losses from international carriers for freight damage or loss is difficult and time consuming. Regulations like the Carriage of Goods by Sea Act limit an ocean carrier's liability to $500 U.S. per customary shipping unit. However, this liability is limited in 17 defensible situations. The regulation states that neither the carrier nor the ship shall be responsible for loss or damage arising or resulting from fire, perils of the sea, acts of God, acts of war, labor stoppage, and ten other circumstances.[13]

Similarly, an air carrier's liability is minimal versus the actual value of most air cargo. Again, liability is limited in special cases of inherent defect, cargo quality or vice, defective packaging, acts of war, or an act of public authority carried out in connection with the entry, exit, or transit of the cargo. In 2010, the International Air Transport Association helped standardize the cargo liability limits from the Montreal Protocol No. 4 to 19 Special Drawing Rights (SDR) per kilogram.[14] At a $1.50 U.S. rate per SDR, this is $28.50 per kilogram.[15] Often, this amount will not adequately offset the value of product loss or damage.

In both modes, the burden of proof is on the importer or exporter to prove that the carrier was at fault. With all the liability limitations provided in the regulations, substantiating carrier responsibility can be very difficult. If they cannot prove fault, importers and exporters have little legal recourse against international carriers.

Transportation Perils International cargo is subject to a wider array of loss and damage risks than domestic freight. This is due to the extended origin-to-destination distance, number of transfers between carriers, and varying climatic conditions. In particular, ocean freight faces considerable obstacles to loss- and damage-free delivery. In addition to the obvious issues of theft, hijacking, vessel sinking, or collision, risks include:

- **Cargo Movement**—ocean freight is subject to a harsh ride with the ship moving in six different directions (heave, pitch, roll, surge, sway, and yaw) during a voyage
- **Water Damage**—water from storms and waves can infiltrate cargo
- **Overboard Losses**—cargo containers can be lost overboard during storms
- **Jettison**—cargo may be purposely dumped overboard to save the ship or prevent further cargo losses
- **Fire**—most dangerous cargo (chemicals, ammunition, and so forth) moves via ocean transport, creating fire and explosion risk
- **Stranding**—mechanical breakdowns, storms, groundings, and other problems can lead to damaged or delayed freight
- **General Average**—loss or damage to another customer's freight is shared by all parties involved in the voyage
- **Other Risks**—freight contamination, government delays, and port strikes[16]

International freight moving via air also face perils, though they are minimal compared to ocean freight. Air cargo is a very safe mode with limited risk of loss due to crashes or accidents. Movement risk exists as cargo can shift during takeoff or landing and turbulence can occur during transit. Cold temperatures can also be a problem for sensitive freight. Finally, theft is an ongoing challenge, particularly when freight sits idle at air forwarder and freight terminal facilities.

Managing Risks Financial threats and transportation perils for international cargo must be actively managed. Chapter 9 provides a detailed discussion of risk management. This responsibility is shared by the owner of the goods in transit and anyone who anyone who would suffer a loss if the cargo were damaged or destroyed or who would benefit from the safe arrival of the cargo. This is known as an insurable interest. These interested parties have three options at their disposal: **risk retention**, **risk transfer**, or take a mixed approach.[17]

Retaining the risk is essentially a strategy of self-insurance. A company may determine that it is beneficial to forego cargo insurance for the anticipated risks. The company takes a calculated gamble that the potential loss or damage would be less expensive than the cost of insurance. The risk retention strategy can make sense for very large exporters and importers that can absorb occasional losses, ship low value goods or goods that are not susceptible to damage, or have extreme confidence in their carriers. Unfortunately, some companies retain risk through ignorance because they do not understand the scope of risks involved in international transportation or the limits of carrier liability.

Risk transfer means that a company shifts its potential problems to an insurance company through cargo insurance. There are a wide variety of policies available to the customer to cover both freight loss and general average liability in ocean shipping. Insurance can be obtained through carriers, freight forwarders, or directly from an insurance company. Insurance makes sense when a company's perceived risks are too high; the product is fragile or a theft risk, or operations would be severely disrupted.

A mixed approach combines self-insurance and risk transfer to a third party. Just as an individual may reduce their insurance policy costs through a higher deductible in the event of a loss, exporters and importers can use deductibles to reduce insurance costs. The company must negotiate a contract with an insurance provider for the amount above the maximum financial exposure that it is willing to risk.[18]

Terms of Payment

The financial transaction creates another set of risks. Exporters are concerned about nonpayment for goods that are sold internationally. They may not have personal experience with the importer, creditworthiness of the importer may be unknown, and there is limited legal recourse if the importer fails to pay for the goods. Also, the cost of litigation or mediation in the country of import is high. Hence, exporters must be cautious about extending credit to global customers.

Importers may also have concerns regarding payment timing and methods. When dealing with an unfamiliar supplier, an importer will not want to pay for goods before knowing that product quality, quantity, price, and delivery are consistent with the contract terms.

Balancing the parties' respective risks is challenging. Exporters would reduce their risk of nonpayment by demanding cash in advance. However, doing so creates a risk of losing business to a more aggressive competitor. Importers would reduce their risk of product problems by purchasing goods on **open account**. However, demanding this option may cause potentially excellent suppliers to walk away from the business. Between these two extremes are three payment term options that facilitate trade without placing all financial risk on one party. They are highlighted in Table 10-3.

A **letter of credit** (LC) is a financial instrument that ensures that the exporter gets paid and the importer receives the goods as expected. The importer's bank issues the LC to the exporter. The customer's bank charges a fee to the importer to issue a LC. The LC essentially guarantees that the bank will pay the seller's invoice (using the customer's money or line of credit) provided that the goods are delivered in accordance with the terms stipulated in the LC. These terms should reflect the contractual agreement between the seller and buyer.

Drafts, sometimes called bills of exchange, are similar to an importer's check. Like checks used in domestic commerce, drafts carry the risk that they will be dishonored. However, in international commerce, title does not transfer to the importer until the draft is paid, or at least engages a legal undertaking that the draft will be paid when due.

A **sight draft** is used when the exporter wishes to retain title to the shipment until it reaches its destination and payment is made. Before the shipment can be released to the importer, the original ocean bill of lading (the document that evidences title) must be properly endorsed by the importer and surrendered to the carrier.

A **time draft** is used when the exporter extends credit to the buyer. The draft states that payment is due by a specific time after the buyer accepts the time draft and receives

TABLE 10-3 International Terms of Payment

METHOD	USUAL TIME OF PAYMENT	GOODS AVAILABLE TO BUYER	RISK TO SELLER	RISK TO BUYER
Cash in Advance	Before shipment	After payment	None	All—relies on seller to ship goods exactly as quoted and ordered
Letter of Credit	After shipment is made, documents presented to the bank.	After payment	Gives the seller assurance of payments. Depends on the terms of the letter of credit.	Assures shipment is made but relies on exporter to ship goods as described in documents. Terms may be negotiated to alleviate buyer's degree of risk.
Sight Draft	On presentation of draft to buyer.	After payment to buyer's bank.	If draft not honored, goods must be returned or resold. Storage, handling, and return freight expenses may be incurred.	Assures shipment but not content, unless inspection or check-in is allowed before payment.
Time Draft	On maturity of the draft	Before payment, after acceptance	Relies on buyer to honor draft upon presentation.	Assures shipment but not content. Time of maturity allows for adjustments, if agreed to by seller.
Open Account	As agreed, usually by invoice	Before payment	All – relies on the buyer to pay account as agreed	None

Source: Adapted from Foreign Trade On-Line, *International Terms of Payment*. Available from http://www.foreign-trade.com/reference/payment.cfm.

the goods (for example, 30 days after acceptance). By signing and writing "accepted" on the draft, the buyer is formally obligated to pay within the stated time.[19]

Freight Documentation

Freight documents control the cargo on its journey from origin point in the country of export to its final destination in the country of import. Missing or incorrect paperwork can cause loading delays, Customs clearance delays, additional inspection, and improper application of duty rates. Hence, proper and accurate documentation is critical to the timely and cost-efficient flow of international cargo.

Documentation requirements are governed by the customs regulations of the exporting and importing nations. Because these regulations differ, the number and types of documents required may vary widely, depending on the origin and destination of the shipment. Experts suggest enlisting the assistance of specialists in this communication channel process like freight forwarders.

In general, international cargo travels with four types of documents: invoices, export documents, import documents, and transportation documents. Each is briefly discussed below, with an emphasis on the transportation paperwork category.

Invoices A critical document is the invoice for the goods. The exporter sends this document to the buyer requesting payment for the purchased goods. That sounds straightforward, but international invoice requirements are complex. Invoice types include the **commercial invoice**, **pro-forma invoice**, and **consular invoice**.

The most common type is the commercial invoice. This invoice accompanies the shipment unless the terms of payment dictate that the commercial invoice is sent directly to the importer or a bank involved in the transaction. Precision is critical as they are often used by governments to determine the true value of goods when assessing customs duties. Governments that use the commercial invoice to control imports will often specify its form, content, number of copies, language to be used, and other characteristics.

As the sample commercial invoice in Figure 10-5 indicates, a commercial invoice must contain a precise description of the product, quantities, and value, as well as the country of origin. These factors are critical as they may impact the duty rates applied to the shipment.

FIGURE 10-5 Sample Commercial Invoice

COMMERCIAL INVOICE

DATE OF EXPORT	TERMS OF SALE	REFERENCE	CURRENCY
11/21/2014	**FAS - Qingdao, China**	**LL-01-23-1962**	**US DOLLAR**

SHIPPER / EXPORTER	CONSIGNEE
Jinto Exports Intl. 2390 Xinhua East Hohhot, Niemongol, 00010 86-471-6607777	Moberg Enterprises 5549 Bobcat Ave. Athens, Ohio, US 45700 (740) 559-1000
COUNTRY OF ULTIMATE DESTINATION **UNITED STATES**	IMPORTER *(IF DIFFERENT THAN CONSIGNEE)*
COUNTRY OF MANUFACTURE **China**	
OCEAN BILL OF LADING NUMBER **95G630587-X1**	

FULL DESCRIPTION OF GOODS	WEIGHT (LBS.)	QUANTITY	UNIT VALUE	TOTAL VALUE
TC0085 TOOL CART	10230.00	220	58.00	12760.00
CJ01 ROLLING RACK	17500.00	500	35.00	17500.00
			0.00	0.00
SUB-TOTAL	27730.00	720		30260.00

TOTAL NO. OF PACKAGES			
720	Shipped via Maersk AVON From Quingdao, China to New York, USA Container No: CIU32587440	FREIGHT COSTS	3593.00
		INSURANCE COSTS	490.00
		ADDITIONAL COSTS	0.00
		TOTAL INVOICE VALUE	**$ 34,343.00**

I hearby certify that this invoice shows the actual price of goods described, that no other invoice has been issued, and that all particulars are true and correct.

SIGNATURE OF SHIPPER / EXPORTER

Sen Yiaboi

PRINT NAME HERE

Other important information includes the Incoterms used in the transaction, delivery-related charges paid by the exporter, and details regarding the companies engaged in the transaction (buyer, seller, shipping origin, and shipping destination). Payment terms and currency in which the payment is to be made should also be clearly stated.

Export Documents Many countries require exporters to report information on goods being sold internationally. This generates accurate trade statistics and helps to control the outflow of strategic materials (such as military items, telecommunications equipment, computer technology, and so forth) and national treasures. Sometimes, a government may prevent exporters from selling these products abroad or require authorization to export these goods. An **export license** is the government document that authorizes the export of specific goods in specific quantities to a particular destination.

The **Shipper's Export Declaration** (SED) is used to control exports and act as a source document for official U.S. export statistics. SEDs, or their electronic equivalent, are required for shipments of commodities whose value exceeds $2,500. SEDs must be prepared and submitted for all shipments, regardless of value, that require an export license or are destined for countries restricted by the Export Administration Regulations.[20]

A **Certificate of End Use** is a document intended to assure authorities in the exporting country that the product will be used for legitimate purposes. For example, enriched uranium will be used to operate a nuclear power plant rather than in nuclear weapons. End-use certificates are provided by the importing country's government. Other export documents facilitate government collection of export taxes and control of export quotas.

Import Documents Numerous documents are required by the governments of importing countries. The documents seek to protect its citizens from inferior quality products, properly classify products for collection of duties, and limit the importation of products that the government finds inappropriate. Some onerous import documents create artificial trade barriers to protect certain industries from foreign competition.

The **Certificate of Origin** is an international trade document attesting to the origin of specified goods. It is often required by the customs authorities of a country as part of the entry process. The document is completed by the exporter or its agent and certified by an organization in the country of the exporter, such as a chamber of commerce, trade organization, or consular office.

A **Certificate of Inspection** attests to the authenticity and accuracy of the goods. An independent company inspects the goods and confirms that they conform to the description contained in the commercial invoice. This document is used in situations where the payment terms involve a letter of credit or documentary collection.

The Importer Security Filing (ISF) applies to import cargo arriving to the United States by vessel. The information submitted in the ISF improves U.S. Customs and Border Protection's (CBP) ability to identify high-risk shipments in order to prevent smuggling and ensure cargo safety and security. Within the ISF, importers, or their agent, must provide eight data elements, no later than 24 hours before the cargo is laden aboard a vessel destined to the United States. Those data elements include:

- Seller
- Buyer
- Importer of record number / FTZ applicant identification number
- Consignee number(s)

- Manufacturer or supplier
- Ship to party
- Country of origin
- Commodity Harmonized Tariff Schedule of the United States number

Two additional data elements must be submitted as early as possible, but no later than 24 hours prior to the ship's arrival at a U.S. port. These data elements are:

- Container stuffing location
- Consolidator

Failure to comply with the ISF rule could ultimately result in monetary penalties, increased inspections, and delay of cargo.

Transportation Documents The disruption-free flow of goods also depends upon the availability of key transportation documents. Typically, freight carriers will not accept cargo unaccompanied by thorough and accurate paperwork. Otherwise, it will be difficult to create an accurate **manifest**. This internal carrier document lists the exact makeup of the cargo, its ownership, ports of origin and ports of destination, handling instructions, and other key information.

A distinction is made between a cargo manifest, a freight manifest, and a manifest of hazardous goods. The cargo manifest solely lists the details of the goods (nature, quantity, types and numbers, sender, destination, and so on) and service for customs declaration of the goods. In addition to that, the freight manifest lists details of the seaborne freight and serves to collect the sea freights payable at destination and as basis for certain commission calculations. A hazardous goods manifest solely lists hazardous goods onboard the vessel.[21]

For security purposes, many countries require that manifest information for import shipments be provided electronically to its customs agencies 24 hours prior to containerized freight being loaded onto an ocean vessel. The U.S. initiated their Advance Cargo Manifest Declaration Rule in 2002, followed by Canada and China. The European Union adopted a similar program called the Entry Summary Declaration for its 27 member counties, effective January 1, 2011. In comparison, road, rail, and air manifest information must be submitted between one and four hours prior to arrival.[22]

Another primary transportation document is the **bill of lading**. When signed, the carrier acknowledges that it has received the cargo in good condition in the right quantity. The bill of lading acts as a contract of carriage between the transportation company and the cargo owner—either the exporter or importer, depending on the Incoterm used. It specifies the price and instructions for moving the freight,

Various international bill of lading types exist. An **ocean bill of lading** is used for water transport and an **air waybill** is used for air carrier shipments. Figure 10-6 provides a sample ocean bill of lading. A **through bill of lading** allows the carrier to move cargo via several different modes of transportation and/or several different distribution centers. Each carrier has liability for its phase of the journey. In contrast, a **multimodal bill of lading** tasks the principal carrier or freight forwarder for liability across the entire journey.

Additional documents facilitate the transport of international cargo. A **packing list** is a detailed inventory of the contents of a shipment. It lists the seller, buyer, shipper, invoice number, date of shipment, mode of transport, carrier, and itemizes quantity, description, the type and quantity of packages, net and gross weight (in kilograms), package marks, and dimensions, if appropriate.[23] A **shipper's letter of instructions** is a

FIGURE 10-6 Sample Bill of Lading

MAPLE LEAF INTERNATIONAL
CONTAINER LINES

OCEAN BILL OF LADING

SHIPPER/EXPORTER		BOOKING NO.
		EXPORT REFERENCES
CONSIGNEE/IMPORTER		FORWARDING AGENT FMC NO.
		POINT AND COUNTRY OF ORIGIN OF GOODS
NOTIFY PARTY		ALSO NOTIFY - ROUTING AND INSTRUCTIONS
INITIAL CARRIAGE BY	PLACE OF INITIAL RECEIPT	
EXPORTING CARRIER	PORT OF LOADING	LOADING PIER TERMINAL
AIR/SEA PORT OF DISCHARGE	PLACE OF DELIVERY BY ON CARRIER	TYPE OF MOVE

PARTICULARS FURNISHED BY SHIPPER

MARKS AND NUMBERS	NO. OF PACKAGES	DESCRIPTION OF PACKAGES AND GOODS	GROSS WEIGHT	MEASUREMENTS

SHIPPERS DECLARED VALUE $__________ SUBJECT TO EXTRA FREIGHT | FREIGHT PAYABLE AT BY

CHARGES AS PER TARIFF AND CARRIERS LIMITS REFER TO CLAUSE 16 HEREOF

FREIGHT CHARGES	PREPAID	COLLECT	
			Received the goods, or packages said to contain goods herein mentioned, in apparent good order and condition unless otherwise indicated, to be transported and delivered as herein provided. The carriage is subject to the provisions of the U.S. Carriage of Goods by Sea Act of 1936. All the terms and conditions of the Carrier's regular form Bill of Lading, as filed with the Federal Maritime Commission available to any shipper or consignee upon request, are incorporated with due force and effect as if they were written at length herein, and all such terms and conditions so incorporated by reference are agreed by the Shipper to be binding and to govern the relations, whatever they may be between those included in the words "Shipper" and "Carrier" as defined in Carrier's regular form Bill of Lading. IN WITNESS WHEREOF the Carrier has signed and the Shipper has received THREE (3) original bills of lading, ONE of which being accompanied,the others to stand void. BY:__________ As agent for Maple Leaf International
TOTAL CHARGES			**BL. No.**

document that spells out the requirements for handling in-transit goods. It is an important document when the cargo is susceptible to damage or requires special attention (such as live animals and plants, temperature sensitive goods, and so forth). Special documentation is also required for dangerous or hazardous goods.

The transportation industry is slowly working toward a paperless environment with electronic documentation. The **International Air Transport Association** (IATA) estimates that the average airfreight shipment generates 20 different paper documents. These paper-based processes are inefficient, error-prone, and can cause unnecessary freight delays.[24] Similar challenges exist in the ocean transport industry.

The IATA began an industry-side initiative in 2006 called *e-freight* to replace the most widely used paper documents (packing lists, invoices, certificate of origin, and others) with electronic messages. After much foundation work, a plan was developed in 2012 around three pillars:

- Pillar I: Building a network of locations and airports where it is possible to remove paper from the transportation of air cargo with fully electronic customs procedures and where regulations support paperless shipments.
- Pillar II: Working collaboratively within the cargo supply chain to digitize the core industry transport documents, starting with the air waybill, the most important document in air cargo.
- Pillar III: Digitizing the key accompanying documents typically accompanying air cargo.

Achieving this paper-free air cargo supply chain is not easy. It requires engagement of multiple participants, creation of standardized business processes like an electronic customs environment, and compatible platforms for the exchange of electronic data. Hence, after eight years of work, the global penetration goal for electronic air waybill penetration was just 13 percent as of March 2014. The very aggressive IATA target is 80 percent by 2016.[25]

Government agencies are also developing technology-based systems to remedy the paper chase. Substantial improvements have been made to computerize various documents and processes, but these automation improvements have not been made in all countries. Canada has a computerized system called the Pre-Arrival Review System to speed the release or referral for examination of imports by the Border Service Agency. Taiwan uses a three stage automated customs system to clear cargo.

In the United States, an Automated Commercial Systems (ACS) is used by CBP to track, control, and process all imports. The Automated Brokers Interface System is a key component of the system that allows qualified participants to electronically file required import data with CBP. The systems facilitate trade efficiency while enhancing border security.[26] The Transportation Technology feature provides information on the next-generation information system that will replace the ACS.

Transportation Planning

With the key export preparation activities addressed, the next phase of global transportation planning focuses on the selection of the modes, carriers, and routes by which goods will be delivered. While trade terms and documentation issues are technical and rules-based, global transportation involves strategic and tactical decision making. These decisions must align with corporate strategies, control risk, and provide the required level of customer service. Also, transportation costs must not push the **total landed cost** for products beyond a competitive level in the marketplace.

Mode Selection

The fundamental decision in global transportation is mode selection—how will goods be transported from the origin to the destination? The exporter and/or the importer

TRANSPORTATION **TECHNOLOGY**

The Automated Commercial Environment: Nearing Completion

On February 19, 2014, President Obama signed an executive order called *Streamlining the Export/Import Process for America's Businesses.* It mandates a single, centralized access point to connect CBP, 47 federal agencies, and the trade community of importers and exporters. The goal is to create an electronic platform called the Automated Commercial Environment (ACE) to facilitate rapid flows of legitimate trade while targeting goods that present a security threat. ACE is the next-generation, Internet-based information system that will replace legacy systems by the end of 2016. To date, the U.S. government has spent more than $3.1 billion and a dozen years on ACE elements.

A three-step deployment schedule will create a "single window" for trade:

May 2015—electronic import and export manifest data must be transmitted via ACE to CPB for all modes.

November 2015—electronic cargo release data and documentation required by other government agencies must be submitted via ACE.

October 2016—all remaining cargo process transactions must be done through ACE.

With full implementation of ACE, the trade community will have the ability to effectively and efficiently comply with U.S. security requirements and trade regulations such as the 24-Hour Advanced Manifest rule. No longer will they need to manage the flow of 200 different import and export forms to 47 different government agencies. Instead, they will be able to focus on the flow of actual cargo.

Sources: U.S. Customs and Border Protection, *ACEopedia*, August 2014, retrieved September 14, 2014, from http://www.cbp.gov/sites/default/files/documents/ACEopedia%20August%202014.pdf; Toby Gooley, "ACE: The End Is Near—Really," *DC Velocity*, January 2, 2014; and Eric Kulisch, "ACE Nears Finish Line," *American Shipper*, November 2013, pp. 20–23.

will be involved in this decision, depending upon the Incoterm used for the transaction. Each party will choose the mode for the portion of the delivery for which they are responsible.

There are five traditional modes of transportation—truck, rail, water, air, and pipeline—available to the global transportation manager. Each mode has inherent service and cost advantages. While these relative advantages were covered in previous chapters, a summary is provided in Table 10-4. In an international situation, intermodal transportation (a combination of two or more transportation methods that will be discussed in Chapter 11) can be particularly useful.

Choosing among the modal options requires the consideration of multiple issues. According to numerous research studies, the key determinants in mode selection include accessibility, capacity, transit time, reliability, and product safety. Of course, cost is another critical modal selection factor. Each is discussed below.

Accessibility Freight buyers must considers a mode's ability to reach origin and destination facilities and provide service over the specified route. The geographic limits of a mode's infrastructure or network and the operating scope authorized by governmental regulatory agencies also affect accessibility. For example, moving cargo from Valparaiso,

TABLE 10-4 Comparison of Modal Capabilities

MODE	STRENGTHS	LIMITATIONS	PRIMARY ROLE	PRIMARY PRODUCT CHARACTERISTICS	EXAMPLE PRODUCTS
Truck	• Accessible • Fast & versatile • Customer service	• Limited capacity • High cost	Move smaller shipments in local, regional, and national markets	High value Finished goods Low volume	Food Clothing Electronics Furniture
Rail	• High capacity • Low cost	• Accessibility • Inconsistent service • Damage rates	Move large shipments of domestic freight long distances	Low value Raw materials High volume	Coal/coke Lumber/paper Grain Chemicals
Air	• Speed • Freight protection • Flexibility	• Accessibility • High cost • Low capacity	Move urgent shipments of domestic freight and smaller shipments of international freight	High value Finished goods Low volume Time sensitive	Computers Periodicals Pharmaceuticals B2C deliveries
Water	• High capacity • Low cost • International capabilities	• Slow • Accessibility	Move large domestic shipments via rivers and canals and large shipments of international freight	Low value Raw materials Bulk commodities Containerized finished goods	Crude oil Ores/minerals Farm products Clothing Electronics Toys
Pipeline	• In-transit storage • Efficiency • Low cost	• Slow • Limited network	Move large volumes of domestic freight long distances	Low value Liquid commodities Not time sensitive	Crude oil Petroleum Gasoline Natural gas

Chile to Brisbane, Australia is limited to air or ocean transport. Intermodal transportation can be used to overcome accessibility problems.

Capacity The amount of product being moved can render a mode infeasible or impractical. Transportation managers must match the capacity of a mode to the size and nature of the product being moved. Some modes are well-suited to handling a large volume of goods in an economical fashion while others are better suited to smaller shipments.

Transit Time Time is a key consideration in mode selection as transportation impacts inventory availability, stockout costs, and customer satisfaction. Transit time is the total elapsed time that it takes to move goods from the point of origin to its final destination. This includes the time required for pickup activities, terminal handling, line-haul movement, and customer delivery. Modal speed can greatly affect transit time.

Reliability The consistency of the transit time provided by a transportation mode is called reliability. It is easier to forecast inventory needs, schedule production, and determine safety stock levels if goods arrive with some certainty. Thus, many companies feel that transit time reliability is more important than speed in mode selection. Internationally, reliability is impacted by distance, port congestion issues, security requirements, and border crossings—especially when the two countries do not have a proactive trade agreement.

Safety Goods must arrive at the destination in the same conditions they were in when tendered for shipment at the origin. Precautions must be taken to choose a mode with the ability to protect freight from damage due to poor freight handling techniques, inferior ride quality, and accidents. Fragile products must be shipped via modes with the best ride quality. Temperature sensitive goods must move on modes with equipment that provides consistent atmospheric conditions. Perishable goods require modes with the fastest transit times.

Cost Transportation cost is an important consideration in mode selection. Expenses include the rate for moving freight from origin to destination plus any accessorial and terminal fees for additional services provided.

Product value must be factored into the cost analysis. If a company spends too much on transportation relative to the value of a product, the product cannot be sold at a competitive price. Thus, water, rail, and pipeline are suitable for low value commodities, while truck and air costs can be more readily absorbed by higher value finished goods.

Other factors impact mode selection. The nature of a product—size, durability, and value—may eliminate some modes from consideration as they cannot physically, legally, and/or safely handle the goods. Also, shipment characteristics—size, route, and required speed—are important considerations. Modal capacities must be matched to the total weight and dimensions of shipments, while modal capabilities must be matched to customer service requirements. Combined, these considerations tend to limit modal selection to two or three realistic options, one of which is intermodal transportation.

Mode selection strategy focuses on determining which mode or combination of modes best suits the requirements of the global transportation buyer. This long-range decision requires an analysis of the best fit and balance between modal capabilities, product characteristics, speed and service requirements, and transportation cost. This decision does not need to be revisited frequently unless there is a major price, infrastructure, service capability, or technological change in the modes.

Carrier Selection

After the modal decision has been made, attention turns to selecting individual service providers within the mode. Carrier selection is based on a variety of shipment criteria and carrier capabilities: geographic coverage, transit time average and reliability, equipment availability and capacity, product protection, and freight rates.

A major difference between modal and carrier selection is the number of options available to the transportation manager. Numerous trucking options exist for short distance cross-border transportation. Multiple ocean and air carriers serve major trade routes for intercontinental cargo movement. However, the number of carrier options is shrinking in all primary modes due to mergers, bankruptcies, and service area consolidation.

Another difference is the frequency of the decision. Carrier selection requires more active and frequent engagement than does the more long-range modal selection decision. This engagement does not focus on choosing a new carrier for each freight move; it focuses more on remaining vigilant and managing the performance of chosen carriers. It is critical to monitor each carrier's service level and freight rates on an ongoing basis. Should carrier performance deteriorate, it may be necessary to select new service providers.

The type of service provided within a mode impacts carrier selection. Most carriers have their roots in one of two types of service—direct service or indirect service. Direct service provides immediate point-to-point flows of goods. Chartering an entire ship for a voyage would be an example. Indirect service requires interim stops and/or transfer of freight between equipment. Using a portion of a regular-route containership is a common indirect option. Time and effort must be expended in evaluating service requirements and matching them to potential carrier capabilities, quality, and price.

Within a mode, most carriers have the capabilities to provide a similar level of service, but these service levels may vary greatly from one transportation company to another. Also, since the cost structures are essentially the same for carriers in a given mode, their rates tend to be aligned for a given movement. Given this similarity, transportation rates tend not to be the most important criterion in carrier selection. Service performance is the key determinant for this decision. Historically, carrier selection research indicates that transit time and service reliability, responsiveness to emergencies, freight protection, and financial stability, while more recent research adds supply chain security, integration, information technology, and energy use to the list of potential carrier selection criteria.[27]

Carrier selection strategy commonly focuses on concentrating the transportation buy with a limited number of carriers. This helps an organization leverage its purchasing dollars for lower overall rates, build synergistic carrier relationships, and effectively monitor carrier performance. A core carrier strategy narrows the carrier base to a select few service providers that have proven to be superior in terms of service quality and cost efficiency.

Even with these strong alliances, global transportation managers must remain vigilant, monitoring carrier performance, rates, and financial stability. Having a contingency plan with capable backup carriers provides protection against prolonged capacity loss or disruptions.

Route Planning

Routing planning and delivery scheduling activities are not trivial—they affect costs, impact customers, and can cause major headaches if not properly managed. Conceptually, they are not difficult problems to understand but they can be challenging to solve, particularly with the long distances and multiple route options involved in global transportation.

It would be easy to assume that route planning is the responsibility of the carrier. In general, that is true, but global transportation managers must not take a total hands-off approach to this topic. They should be involved because effective routing impacts customer satisfaction, supply chain performance, and organizational success. Transit time and on-time performance depend heavily on proper scheduling and sequencing of stops. Effective routing also helps avoid risky locations, poorly equipped ports, and congested border crossing points that may drastically delay cargo flows. The On the Line feature reveals how the Panama Canal is being upgraded to improve cargo flows and provide a viable routing option for mega-ships.

Efficiency is another major issue, given the sheer amount of money spent on transportation. Globally, over $1 trillion is spent on freight transportation services. Carriers must develop more efficient routes that maximize equipment capacity utilization. They also need to use routes that minimize tolls, port costs, and route-related surcharges.

Product safety is the third concern when developing routes, particularly for surface transportation. Major trouble spots for hijacking and product theft such as the Gulf of

ON THE LINE

Panama Canal Expansion to Double Capacity

The Panama Canal has played an integral role in global trade since 1914, providing a critical link between the Atlantic and Pacific Ocean. It reduces transit time and risk by eliminating the need for ships to sail around Cape Horn, the southernmost point of South America. This reduces the distance between major cities in the Far East and U.S. East Coast ports by approximately 8,000 miles.

An engineering marvel at the time of completion, the Canal relies upon a system of locks to lift a ship up 85 feet (26 metres) to the main elevation of the Panama Canal and down again. It has a total of six steps (three up, three down) for a ship's passage. Each lock has two independent transit lanes that are 110 feet wide by 1,050 feet long, allowing Panamax-sized ships (106 feet wide by 950 feet long × 39.5 feet draft) to move through the Canal. Modern containerships, passenger ships, and supertankers far exceed these dimensions, necessitating modernization of the Panama Canal.

According to the official website for the Panama Canal Expansion, construction began in September 2007 and is expected to be completed by 2016. The $5.25 billion project is the largest initiative in the canal's history. It is intended to double the Canal's capacity in anticipation of growing demand.

The project has several major elements. This includes construction of a new set of locks that are 180 feet wide by 1,400 feet long. A dredging program will deepen the navigation channel to 60 feet. As a result, traffic will move faster and containerships carrying up to 13,000 TEUs will be able to transit the Canal. A new Pacific Ocean access channel is being created and improvements are planned for the water supply that supports the locks.

The expansion project has the potential to alter the routes used by ocean carriers, allowing them to move Asian goods to the U.S. Eastern and Gulf coasts for less money on post-Panamax class ships. The project is also expected to boost Panama's strategic positions as a transshipment hub and business center for much of Central and South America.

Source: Canal De Panama, *Panama Canal Expansion*, retrieved September 14, 2014, from http://micanaldepanama.com/expansion/; JOC.com, *Panama Canal Expansion*, retrieved September 14, 2014, from http://www.joc.com/special-topics/panama-canal-expansion; and "Panama Canal Expansion, Changing the Channel," *Inbound Logistics*, December 2013.

Aden and the South China Sea should be factored into route planning. Land routes with poor quality roads and freight handling capabilities also pose problems. Sometimes a more expensive indirect or circuitous route is used to mitigate these safety risks.

It is important to note that routing decisions are not made independently of other global transportation processes. Routing decisions must be integrated into a larger transportation strategy that supports global supply chain excellence. Thus, global transportation managers must coordinate mode selection, carrier selection, route planning, and other transportation decisions. These decisions must also be properly aligned with global sourcing, inventory, and demand fulfillment strategies.

SUMMARY

- Moving goods globally adds layers of complexity to transportation decision making. Extensive planning efforts must be made to prepare for these extended cargo movements.
- The global flow of goods must be supported by effective information flows between the exporter and importer, as well as the timely flow of payments to complete the transaction.
- Global transportation creates a variety of significant cargo challenges: longer and more variable transit time, risk of in-transit product damage or loss, higher delivery expenses, and greater in-transit inventory carrying costs.
- Four primary export preparation activities must be addressed before moving cargo: choosing the terms of trade, securing freight insurance, agreeing upon the terms of payment, and completing the required freight documentation.
- Proper choice from among the 11 Incoterms should be based on the relative expertise of the exporter and importer to effectively balance international transportation responsibilities.
- Importers and exporters are exposed to unique financial risks and countless perils when their freight moves through the global supply chain. Hence, cargo insurance is an essential risk mitigation tool.
- Letters of credit and other payment tools can be used to balance the exporter's risk of nonpayment with the importer's risk of product problems and fraud.
- Four types of documentation are used to control global cargo and comply with government requirements: invoices, export documents, import documents, and transportation documents.
- Global mode selection involves the analysis of accessibility, capacity, transit time, reliability, safety, and cost. Often, only one or two of the five modes are realistic options, given the product and shipment characteristics.
- Carrier selection is based on a variety of shipment criteria and carrier capabilities: geographic coverage, transit time average and reliability, equipment availability and capacity, product protection, and freight rates.
- Route planning for global shipments is important as it affects transportation cost, product availability, and cargo security.

STUDY QUESTIONS

1. Why is global transportation such an important issue?
2. Why is transportation planning an important aspect of global freight movement? What types of planning must be done?
3. Identify and describe the three channels involved in global transportation.
4. What types of transportation challenges must organizations take into account when considering global sourcing?
5. What is the role of trade terms in global transportation? Briefly describe the four groups of Incoterms.
6. What risks and perils are present in global transportation? Discuss how exporters and importers can manage these risks.

7. What payment options are available for international transactions? How does each option protect the interests of the exporter and the importer?
8. Why is documentation important to global transportation? Briefly describe the primary documents used to facilitate global cargo flows.
9. How do governments use the information contained in global freight documents?
10. What factors impact mode selection for global transportation?
11. How does global carrier selection differ from mode selection?
12. When developing transportation routes for global freight, what considerations should influence the decision maker?

NOTES

1. World Trade Organization, *Trade in Commercial Services*, retrieved September 9, 2014, from http://stat.wto.org/StatisticalProgram/WSDBViewData.aspx?Language=E
2. World Trade Organization, "Modest Trade Growth Anticipated for 2014 and 2015 Following Two Year Slump," April 14, 2014, retrieved September 7, 2014, from http://www.wto.org/english/news_e/pres14_e/pr721_e.htm.
3. "WTO Predicts Steady Trade Growth through 2015," *Global Trade*, May 6, 2014.
4. U.S. Census Bureau, *FT900: U.S. International Trade in Goods and Services*, September 4, 2014, retrieved September 9, 2014, from https://www.census.gov/foreign-trade/Press-Release/2014pr/07/exh12.pdf.
5. World Trade Organization, *Trade in Commercial Services*, retrieved September 9, 2014, from http://stat.wto.org/StatisticalProgram/WSDBViewData.aspx?Language=E
6. United Nations Conference on Trade and Development, *Review of Maritime Transportation 2013*, retrieved September 9, 2014, from http://unctad.org/en/publicationslibrary/rmt2013_en.pdf
7. Office of the United States Trade Representative, *Free Trade Agreements*, retrieved September 9, 2014, from http://www.ustr.gov/trade-agreements/free-trade-agreements.
8. Ibid.
9. Office of the United States Trade Representative, *North American Free Trade Agreement*, retrieved September 9, 2014, from http://www.ustr.gov/trade-agreements/free-trade-agreements/north-american-free-trade-agreement-nafta.
10. Donald. F. Wood, Anthony Barone, Paul Murphy, and Daniel Wardlow, *International Logistics* 2nd ed. (New York, NY: AMACOM, 2002).
11. International Chamber of Commerce, *Incoterms—International Commercial Terms*, retrieved September 9, 2014, from http://www.iccwbo.org/products-and-services/trade-facilitation/incoterms-2010/.
12. Export.Gov, *Incoterms*, retrieved September 9, 2014, from http://www.export.gov/faq/eg_main_023922.asp.
13. Legal Information Institute, *Chapter 28-Carriage of Goods by Sea*, retrieved September 12, 2014, from http://www.law.cornell.edu/uscode/html/uscode46a/usc_sup_05_46_10_28.html.
14. International Air Transport Association, *News Brief: Cargo Liability Limited Standardized—Major Step Forward to Simplify Air Cargo*, retrieved September 12, 2014, from http://www.iata.org/pressroom/pr/pages/2010-07-14-01.aspx.

15. XE.com, *XDR—IMF Special Drawing Rights*, retrieved September 12, 2014, from http://www.xe.com/currency/xdr-imf-special-drawing-rights.

16. Pierre David, *International Logistics: The Management of International Trade* (Berea, OH: Cicero Books LLC, 2013) pp. 354–374.

17. John M. Sylvester, Michael T. Fitzgerald, and Thomas M. Exl, *Key Issues in Marine Insurance for Global Companies*, April 28, 2014, retrieved September 12, 2014, from www.rims.org/Session%20Handouts/.../GRM004KeyIssuesinMarine.ppt.

18. A detailed discussion of international freight insurance can be found in Pierre David, *International Logistics: The Management of International Trade* (Berea, OH: Cicero Books LLC, 2013) Chapter 10.

19. *A Basic Guide to Exporting: The Official Government Resource for Small and Medium-Sized Businesses*, 10th ed. (Washington DC: U.S. Department of Commerce, 2012) Chapter 14.

20. Ibid., Chapter 12.

21. Logistics Glossary, *Manifest*, retrieved September 12, 2014, from http://www.logisticsglossary.com/term/manifest/.

22. European Union, *The Entry Summary Declaration*, retrieved September 14, 2014, from http://ec.europa.eu/ecip/documents/procedures/entry_summary_declaration_en.pdf.

23. Export.gov, *Common Export Documents*, retrieved September 12, 2014, from http://www.export.gov/logistics/eg_main_018121.asp.

24. International Air Transport Association, e-freight Fundamentals, retrieved September 12, 2014 from http://www.iata.org/whatwedo/cargo/e/efreight/Documents/e-freight-fundamentals.pdf.

25. International Air Transport Association, *Fact Sheet: e-freight and e-Air Waybill*, retrieved September 12, 2014, from http://www.iata.org/pressroom/facts_figures/fact_sheets/pages/e-freight.aspx.

26. U.S. Customs and Border Protection, ACE and Automated Systems, retrieved September 12, 2014, from http://www.cbp.gov/trade/automated.

27. Mary J. Meixell and Mario Norbis, "A Review of the Transportation Mode Choice and Carrier Selection Literature," *International Journal of Logistics Management* Vol. 19, No. 2 (2008), pp. 183–211.

CASE 10-1

Music Explosion—Creating a "Sound" Global Transport Plan

Music Explosion (ME) produces those annoying car speakers that rattle your windows. A typical set of ME speakers retails for $350 and weighs 10 pounds. However, they are a bit bulky at 6 cubic feet per set (1.5 × 1.5 × 1). The speakers are not overly susceptible to damage, though moisture can be a problem.

The company manufactures "Blasters" speakers in San Diego for U.S. distribution. The company's growth is waning, so ME has decided to export product for the first time to Japan, Taiwan, and Australia. Nick Jagr, company president, has negotiated deals with automotive aftermarket retailers to sell the speakers. You have been hired to handle ME's transportation planning for this export initiative.

During your first day, Jagr holds a fast paced meeting that bounces across multiple topics. He occasionally mentions the global export project, making offhand comments that are relevant to your role. Since you want to be successful, you have written down some of Jagr's quotes. They read:

> *"The local market for our product is sad, sad, sad. We need to join the global marketplace but don't want to play with fire. Let's take a measured approach."*
>
> *"The retailers want to nail down trade terms with those three letter acronyms before signing on the dotted line. I tried to tell them that you can't always get what you want, but they were pretty insistent on establishing trade terms."*
>
> *"We have little experience with global freight. Still, we want to play some role in the transportation process or the retailers will ask for huge discounts. One buyer mentioned "Incoterms" and taking on responsibilities. We better get up to speed on that or they'll put us between a rock and a hard place."*
>
> *"Let's use those Incoterms to manage the transportation process up to a point and then let the retailers do the dirty work."*
>
> *"We have to tumble the dice and pick a mode of transport that balances service and cost. I like the idea of air freight."*
>
> *"Is it just my imagination, or are we still overlooking some transportation issues? One of the carriers mentioned documentation as being critical."*

After a few more comments, Jagr began to walk out of the meeting. Before leaving, he turned to you and said, "Welcome to the show. Get your initial thoughts for our global transportation strategy worked out and email it to me. Be quick, time is not on our side."

CASE QUESTIONS

1. Given the information in the case, which Incoterms group (E, F, C, or D) should ME pursue as the exporter? Why?
2. Based on your response to Question 1, what responsibilities and risks will ME assume?
3. Which mode of transportation should ME use to move Blasters to their new markets? What benefits does it bring?
4. Why should ME worry about something as mundane as paperwork? What documents must they prepare?
5. Identify and describe other global transportation issues that Jagr may be overlooking.

CASE 10-2

Tablets for the Masses

Jacob Kindl is trying to capture the attention of Black Friday shoppers for OptiShop, a discount chain with 1,500 stores in Canada and the United States. Jacob wants to offer a high power tablet computer at a price point of $249 that rivals much more expensive options from Samsung and Apple. He believes that it will be possible to sell 150,000 units during the holiday season and 15,000 units per month over the subsequent 12 months.

After much effort to ensure feasibility of the initiative, evaluate product quality, and compare supplier capabilities, Jacob has narrowed his focus to three options. Each supplier offers a reasonably priced, high quality tablet that meets OptiShop specifications. However, each supplier is in a different country, which gives Jacob some concerns about delivery costs, risks, and foreign exchange rate exposure. Highlights of each proposal are provided below.

Option 1—purchase tablets from Takena Electronics in Nagano, Japan, a longtime supplier of products to OptiShop. Takena works on an open account basis and promises to make shipments of 4,500 units in 40-foot containers under terms Incoterm DAP, Port of Long Beach. The price offered per unit is 20,000 JPY (Japanese Yen).

Option 2—purchase the tablets from RaoTex Industries, a Bhopal, India, based manufacturer. RaoTex has a solid reputation and Jacob nearly purchased smartphones from them last year. Their offer is based on OptiShop taking deliveries of 1,900 units in 20-foot containers under Incoterm FAS, Port of Mumbai. The price offered is 10,600 INR (Indian Rupees) using Letter of Credit payments.

Option 3—purchase the tablets from Luca Enterprises, an electronics distributor in Bucharest, Romania. Luca sources tablets from contract manufacturers in Eastern Europe. Their offer is based on OptiShop taking control of the product at the Luca distribution center under Incoterm EXW. The price offered is 555 RON (Romanian New Leu), cash in advance.

As Jacob considered his options, he consulted an online currency converter to evaluate the quotes. He found the following exchange rates:

1 USD = 107.2 JPY   1 USD = 61.1 INR   1 USD = 3.4 RON

CASE QUESTIONS

1. What is the price per tablet in USD for the Takena Electronics offer? What costs, responsibilities, and risks does OptiShop assume under DAP, Port of Long Beach?
2. What is the price per tablet in USD for the RaoTex Industries offer? What costs, responsibilities, and risks does OptiShop assume under FAS, Port of Mumbai?
3. What is the price per tablet in USD for the Luca Enterprises offer? What costs, responsibilities, and risks does OptiShop assume under EXW, Bucharest?
4. What other issues and transportation costs must Jacob consider to make an effective supplier selection?
5. Which of the three options would you recommend? Why?

CHAPTER

11 GLOBAL TRANSPORTATION EXECUTION

Learning Objectives

After reading this chapter, you should be able to do the following:

- Recognize the importance of intermodal service in global transportation execution
- Describe the intermodal options available to global transportation managers
- Recognize the importance of proper freight packing and preparation
- Understand the government's role in safe and secure global transportation
- Discuss ocean transportation services, equipment options, and rate structures
- Describe international air transportation services, equipment options, and rate structures
- Understand the role of ancillary service providers in facilitating global freight flows
- Appreciate the critical roles that seaports and airports play in the global supply chain
- Articulate the customs clearance process for import goods
- Analyze current issues impacting the execution of global transportation

TRANSPORTATION **PROFILE**

International Freight Challenges

Based on the widespread availability of imported products, retail shoppers may think that global supply chains are simple and direct. In the vast majority of cases, this isn't the case. Consumer demand is supported by a complex and lengthy international supply chain. Multiple transportation modes provide the key connections between global factories, wholesalers, retailers, and consumers. While they provide critical services, each mode also presents key challenges for freight customers.

The ocean shipping industry is going through major changes that affect freight buyers. Carriers are sharing vessels and merging operations, building larger containerships, and employing slow steaming (operating ships at speeds of 15 to 20 knots versus the typical 24 knots). This rationalizes capacity, improves operating efficiencies, and cuts fuel costs for carriers. However, these changes often lead to fewer options for customers, accompanied by higher rates and slower delivery speeds.

The trucking and rail industries provide the all-important inland intermodal connections for the ocean carriers. Each has invested in its intermodal capabilities, creating reliable and economical port-to-destination delivery services. However, they are struggling to keep up with the growing demand. A shortage of truck drivers, truck chassis, and drayage services is creating a capacity crunch and intermittent port congestion. The rail system capacity limitations, combined with a dearth of locomotives and crew resources, strain the industry's ability to digest the growth in intermodal traffic. Hence, customers may need to shift freight to less congested routes and monitor activity more closely to minimize freight delays and disruptions.

The air cargo industry faces a different set of challenges. Capacity is not an issue as the freighter fleet is stable and the wide-body passenger aircraft fleet has grown. The carrier problem is a decline in traffic due to freight being shifted to ocean transport and the trend toward on-shoring or near-shoring of production. Though this situation will reduce the likelihood of capacity shortages and delays, customers will need to reevaluate their options to ensure that they are achieving the best rates. They may be able to reduce costs by shifting freight to passenger carriers that are aggressively marketing their excess cargo capacity.

Without question, the international freight market will continue to evolve for all modes of transportation. Savvy freight customers regularly monitor the freight market for significant changes in carrier pricing, capacity, and service frequency. As needed, the customers will adjust strategies, reshape relationships, and revise networks to maintain smooth and cost-efficient global freight flows.

Sources: Merrill Douglas, "Intermodal: Too Much of a Good Thing?" *Inbound Logistics*, October 2014; John D. Schulz, "25th Annual State of Logistics: It's Complicated," *Logistics Management*, July 2014; and Adina Solomon, "IATA Economist Analyzes Recent Cargo Trends, *Air Cargo World*, May 6, 2014, retrieved December 9, 2014, from http://aircargoworld.com/Air-Cargo-World-News/2014/05/iata-economist-analyzes-recent-cargo-trends/6485.

Introduction

If you watch the occasional transportation company advertisement on television, the focus is on simplicity and ease. "One call does it all" and "bringing the world closer" are common themes. Oh, if it were only so easy!

While the preparation of global shipments is a fairly straightforward process, the real challenges begin when the freight starts to move from one country to another. The

FIGURE 11-1 Global Transportation Execution

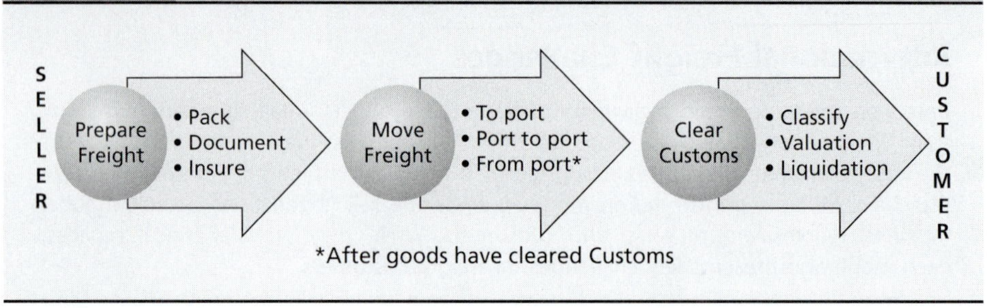

global journey often involves multiple carriers from different modes, numerous border crossings, and long distances. The risk of disruptions, delays, damage, and other problems make for an eventful time whether you are importing electronics or exporting fresh produce. Whether the issue is securing enough capacity, avoiding system bottlenecks, or keeping costs under control, the Transportation Profile reveals that global transportation execution is anything but a "set it and forget it" activity.

Overcoming these potential challenges to move products safely and quickly across borders requires great attention to detail and internal expertise. Flawless transportation execution also requires strong working relationships with capable transportation service providers. Following an overview of global freight flows, this chapter spotlights the key players in global transportation execution—transportation companies, party logistics firms, port operators, and ancillary service providers. Chapter 11 wraps up with a discussion of Customs clearance. Throughout the chapter, you will gain a greater awareness of the many options available to global transportation managers (and challenges faced) as they seek to move freight with minimal complication and maximum efficiency. These key execution activities are identified in Figure 11-1.

Overview of Global Freight Flows

The movement of goods internationally is a huge business, with trillions of dollars' worth of products moving around the world. For example, more than $1.1 trillion worth of goods moved between the United States and its North American Free Trade Agreement partners, Canada, and Mexico in 2013.[1] With all this freight flowing across borders, companies must proactively manage the process and make solid decisions regarding the type of service used, intermodal options, and freight preparation.

Global freight primarily moves via one of two service options—direct service or indirect service. Figure 11-2 provides a comparison of the two service types.

Direct service is commonly used in situations when international freight is moving relatively short distances between directly accessible origin and destination points. A single mode of transportation is used to move freight from the seller's location in one country to the customer's location in another country with no interim stop-offs or transfers to other modes or carriers. This on-demand type of service is effective for truckload moves across land borders. Examples would include freight flowing from Montreal, Quebec in Canada, to Boston, Massachusetts in the United States, or Berlin, Germany, to Prague, Czech Republic. Relatively few companies have the ability to leverage this type of service via other modes as their facilities are often not accessible by train, pipeline, airplane, or ship.

FIGURE 11-2 Global Transportation Service Types

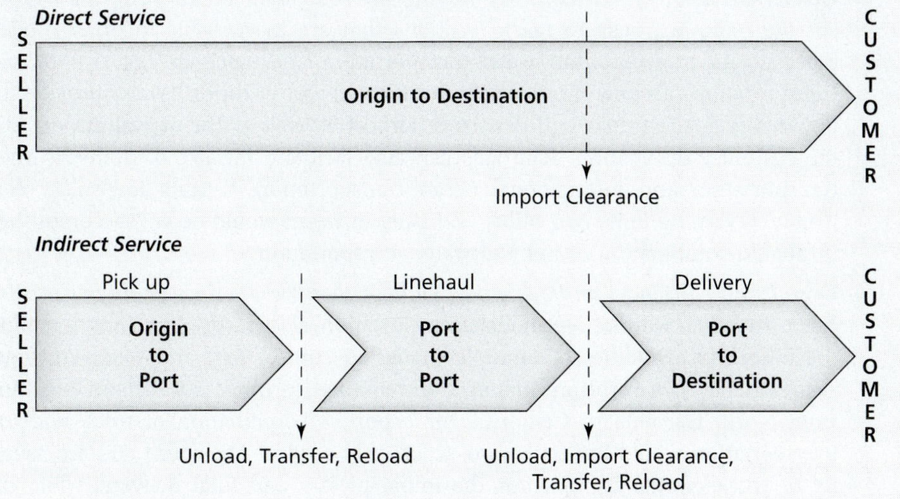

Indirect service is used in situations where freight is moving long distances between continents or facilities that are not directly accessible by the mode of choice. In this type of service, freight flows are slowed by interim stops and transfers of freight between carriers and modes. For example, freight moving from Paris, France, to São Paulo, Brazil, would involve three distinct moves—from the seller's location in Paris to the Port of Antwerp in Belgium via truck, from the Port of Antwerp to the Port of Santos in Brazil via ocean carrier, and onward to the customer in São Paulo on a truck. Similar combinations are required for international air transportation as few companies are located directly adjacent to an airport. Typically, indirect service is accomplished by combining the services of different modes—that is, intermodal transportation.

Intermodal Transportation

Intermodal transportation involves the use of two or more modes of transportation in moving a shipment from origin to destination. It is often said that international transportation is intermodal transportation because so many goods moving from one country to another involve the use of multiple modes and carriers. Virtually everything moving across an ocean will involve truck or rail carriers for product pickup and delivery and an air or ocean carrier for the linehaul portion of the trip.

Shifting freight between modes may seem inefficient and time consuming, but the improved reach and combined service advantages of intermodal transportation offsets these issues. The primary benefits of intermodalism include the following:

- *Intermodal transportation facilitates global trade.* The capacity and efficiency of ocean transportation allows large-volume shipments to be transported between continents at relatively low per unit costs. The rapid speed of air transportation allows perishable goods to flow quickly between countries. The final domestic leg of the delivery can take place via truck. The ocean-truck combination makes product competitive across global markets by keeping the landed cost in check.

The air-truck combination facilitates expedited flows of high-value goods and rapid replenishment of fast selling products like trendy clothing.

- *Greater accessibility is created by linking the individual modes.* The road infrastructure allows trucks to reach locations that are inaccessible to other modes, especially air transportation, water transportation, and pipelines. For example, air transportation can only move freight between airport facilities. Trucks provide the flow between the origin and departure airport as well as the arrival airport and the customer destination. Railroads can also facilitate the use of domestic river transportation and international ocean transportation. Getting low-sulfur coal from a Wyoming mine to a utility company in Japan would be best accomplished through a combination of rail and water transportation.
- *Overall cost efficiency can be achieved without sacrificing service quality or accessibility.* In other words, intermodal transportation allows supply chains to utilize the inherent capabilities of multiple modes to control cost and fulfill customer requirements. If a furniture manufacturer needed to move 20 loads of furniture from North Carolina to California for export, a combination of truck and rail transportation would improve upon truck-only service. The speed and accessibility of trucks would be used for the initial pickup and final delivery, while the cross-country transportation would be handled by the cost-efficient railroads.

Intermodal Transportation Options It can be argued that flexibility is another valuable trait of intermodal transportation. Companies can use any combination of the five transportation modes that best suits their freight. In a global scenario, this is essential because transportation options may be very limited at origin points and/or destination points. That is, the appropriate modal combination may be unavailable for another location. Figure 11-3 highlights the most prevalent options for intermodal transportation. The accessibility of truck transportation makes it ideally suited for short-distance

FIGURE 11-3 Common Intermodal Combinations

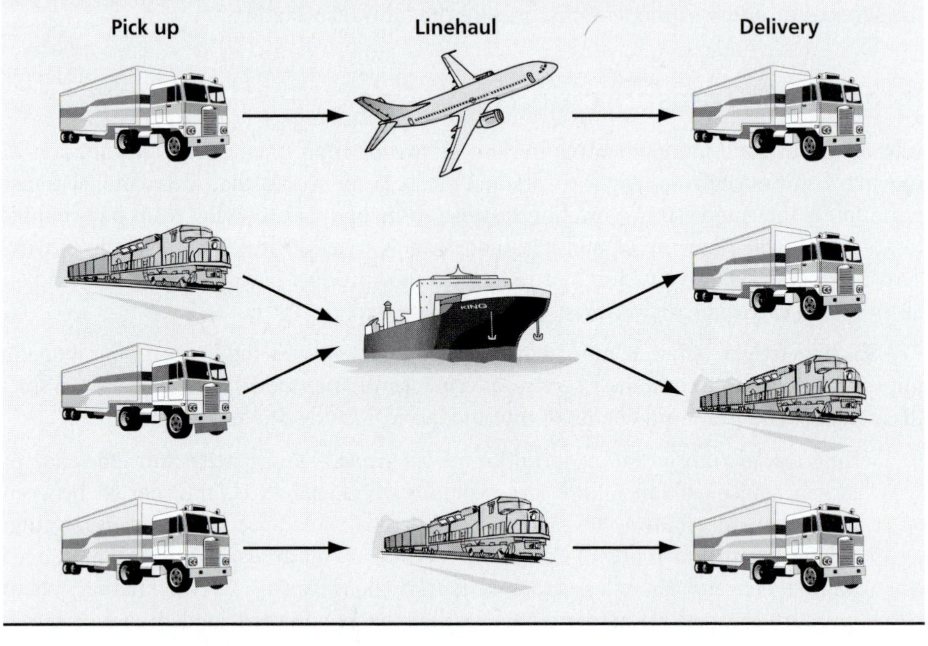

pickup and delivery of containerized international freight, while rail works well for long distance moves of containers to and from ports. Rail and barge transportation are suitable for moving export-bound raw materials and other bulk commodities to port facilities.

Large carriers, including Canadian National Railway, A.P. Moeller-Maersk, and DHL, offer multimodal capabilities. These allow them to utilize the most efficient and economical combination of intermodal transportation for their international customers. In the majority of cases, the carrier determines the modal combination to be used based on capacity, route, cost efficiency, and delivery deadline. After all, when customers drop overnight packages in an express delivery box, they are not concerned about the combination of modes used as long as their shipments arrive safely and on time!

Intermodal Freight Types Another valuable aspect of intermodalism is its ability to handle multiple types of freight. Whether the goods are commodities, component parts, or finished products, they can be transported by intermodal methods. The key is to have the right transportation equipment, freight handling capabilities, and transfer methods to effectively move goods between modes. The primary freight types are containerized freight and transload freight.

Containerized freight is loaded into or onto storage equipment (a container or pallet) at the origin and delivered to the destination in or on that same piece of equipment with no additional handling. For example, if a load of Blu-ray players needed to be shipped from the factory to the market, the players would be loaded into a 40-ft container at the factory in Taiwan, transferred to the port via truck, and loaded on a containership bound for Long Beach. Upon arrival, the container would be moved from the ship onto another truck and delivered to the retailer's distribution center.

The development of freight containers has made intermodal transportation of finished goods very economical. The widely used standard dry box container looks much like a truck trailer without the chassis. It can be lifted, stacked, and moved from one piece of equipment to another. Specialized freight containers are available for handling temperature-sensitive goods (refrigerated containers), liquids (tank containers), commodities (dry bulk cargo containers), and other unique cargoes.

A critical step in the growth of containerization and intermodalism was the development of container standards in the late 1960s. These standards defined sizes and fitting and reinforcement norms. Oceangoing containers are now built to consistent dimensional height and width specifications. This makes it possible to build transportation equipment to readily transport containers owned by any company and handling equipment to easily and safely transfer goods between modes. As a result, approximately 60 percent of world trade (in value) is containerized.[2]

There are five common standard lengths, 20 feet (6.1 m), 40 feet (12.2 m), 45 feet (13.7 m), 48 feet (14.6 m), and 53 feet (16.2 m). Container capacity is often expressed in **twenty-foot equivalent units (TEUs)**. An equivalent unit is a measure of containerized cargo capacity equal to one standard 20 feet (length) $\times$ 8 feet (width) container. For example, a 40-ft container is the equivalent of two TEUs. Figure 11-4 provides information regarding the capacity of widely available container sizes.

There is strong evidence that containerization is growing in importance and volume. Total world container traffic reached nearly 602 million TEUs, led by China and the United States. The ten-year growth rate was 201 percent; up from 299 million TEUs in 2003.[3] Figure 11-5 highlights this dramatic growth with a single dip during the global economic crisis in 2009.

FIGURE 11-4 Intermodal Container Dimensions

20′ Dry Standard	40′ Dry Standard	40′ Dry High-Cube
	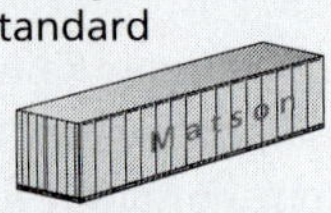	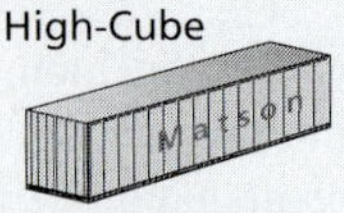
Outside Length: 20′	Outside Length: 40′	Outside Length: 40′
Outside Width: 8′	Outside Width: 8′	Outside Width: 8′
Outside Height: 8′6″	Outside Height: 8′6″	Outside Height: 9′6″
Inside Length: 19′4″	Inside Length: 39′6″	Inside Length: 39′6″
Inside Width: 7′6″	Inside Width: 7′9″	Inside Width: 7′9″
Inside Height: 7′8″	Inside Height: 7′10″	Inside Height: 8′10″
Door Opening: 7′6"W × 7′4"H	Door Opening: 7′8"W × 7′6"H	Door Opening: 7′8"W × 8′6"H
Tare Weight: 4,870 lbs	Tare Weight: 8,490lbs	Tare Weight: 9,612 lbs
Payload Weight: 48,000–62,000 lbs	Payload Weight: 58,000–63,000 lbs	Payload Weight: 58,000–63,000 lbs
Cubic Capacity: 1,172 ft	Cubic Capacity: 2,387 ft	Cubic Capacity: 2,686 ft

Source: Matson Navigation Company, Inc. Available from http://www.matson.com/china/equipment.html.

FIGURE 11-5 World Container Traffic

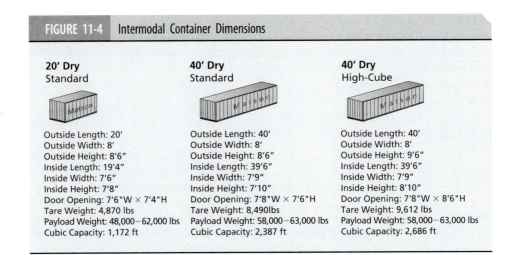

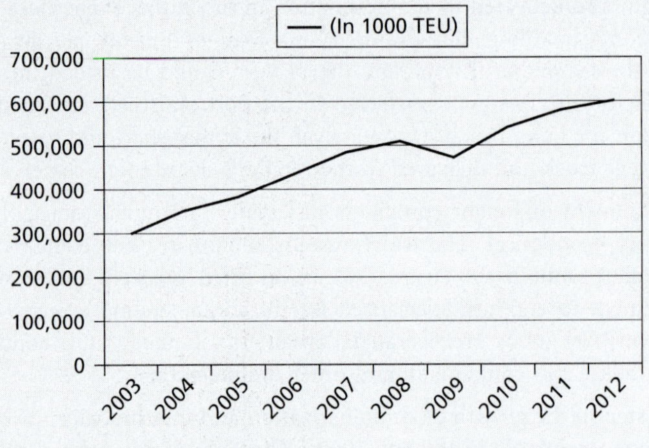

Source: International Association of Ports and Harbors, *World Container Traffic Data*, retrieved December 10, 2014, from http://www.iaphworldports.org/LinkClick.aspx?fileticket=PMewveDCUUg%3d&tabid=4879.

Other factors have contributed to the growth of containerized intermodal transportation. They include improvements in information systems to track containers as they move through the supply chain and the development of intermodal terminals to facilitate efficient container transfers between modes. In addition, new generations of ocean vessels, railcars, and truck trailers are being built specifically to handle intermodal containers in greater quantity and with greater ease, which contributes to better service performance.

Transload freight includes goods that must be handled individually and transferred between transportation equipment multiple times. Transload freight primarily consists of bulk-oriented raw materials that must be scooped, pumped, lifted, or conveyed from one container to another when transferred between modes. Given the massive weight and volume of these commodities requiring movement, water, rail, and pipeline are the primary modes employed. For example, orange juice concentrate may be picked up using a rail tank car, pumped into the hold of a cargo ship for the linehaul move, and then pumped into a tank truck for final delivery to the bottling facility.

Intermodal Routing The ability to use multiple modes of transportation opens up alternative route options to all-water service. The primary opportunity focuses on move international containers across a combination of water and land routes. Figure 11-6 highlights the three options:

- **Land Bridge**. This option involves a combination of ocean-rail-ocean intermodal transport. For example, a container travels from Tokyo to Seattle via ocean vessel, from Seattle to New York via train, and onward to Rotterdam via ocean vessel. This is an example of the Asia-America-Europe land bridge. The other primary route is the Asia-Europe land bridge.
- **Mini Land Bridge.** This option involves a combination of ocean and rail transport to a location across the destination country. For example, a container would move from Shanghai, China, to Los Angeles via ocean carrier with onward delivery to Savannah via rail.
- **Micro Land Bridge**. This option involves a combination of ocean and rail transport to an inland location. For example, a container would move from Shanghai, China, to Long Beach via ocean carrier with onward delivery to Denver via rail.

Land bridges serve as alternatives to long routes through the Panama Canal, the Magellan Straits, and other canals around the world, which reduces total transit time. Also, vessel size limitations are avoided, allowing the use of larger, more efficient ships.

Intermodal Challenges The growth of intermodal volume has created two ongoing problems—capacity shortages and transfer point congestion. The Transportation Profile

FIGURE 11-6 Alternative Intermodal Routing

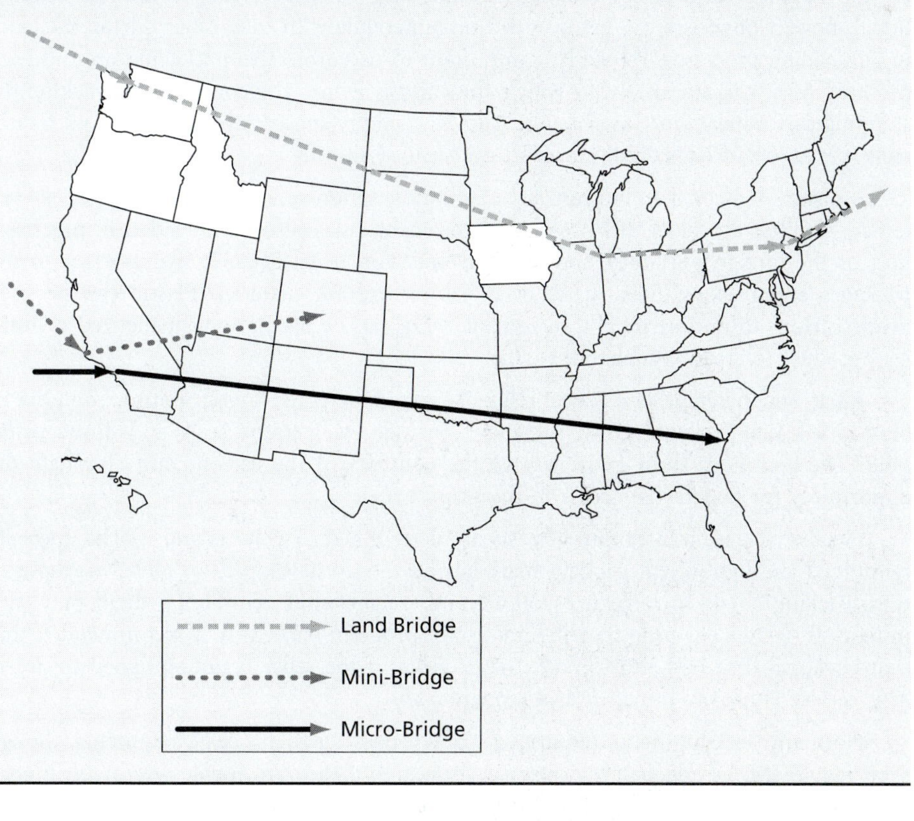

feature highlighted the landside capacity challenges of having enough truck and rail equipment, properly trained labor, and infrastructure to support intermodal traffic. Port congestion is a growing problem due to the increasing sizes of containership with much greater quantities of containers being off-loaded and loaded during each port call. During peak demand periods, U.S. seaport facilities along the Pacific coast have struggled to keep product flowing through their facilities in a timely fashion. Significant infrastructure investment, equipment purchases, and operator hiring will be needed to overcome these challenges to support the increasing demand for intermodal transportation.

Preparing Freight for Movement

Recall from Chapter 10 the amount of planning that goes into moving freight across oceans and country borders. The risk of in-transit product damage and delays cannot be ignored by transportation managers in the execution phase of global transportation. During preparation for release of the freight to the transportation company, key precautions must be taken. These include preventing freight damage through protective packaging and proper container packing, insuring the goods against key risks, and completing all necessary documentation.

Packing the Freight Exporters must pay attention to the stress that global transportation puts on packaged goods, particularly goods moving via ocean. Four potential in-transit problems should be kept in mind when choosing packaging materials: breakage, moisture, pilferage, and excess weight. While shipping containers provide some protection from these issues, it is critical to protect products as they are packed in shipping cartons and to protect the cartons when they are packed in the shipping container. To provide proper balance in the container, the weight must be evenly distributed.

There is a great deal of container handling and transfers during an indirect international move. Containers can get dropped or can collide with each other during the loading/unloading processes. Hence it is important to use protective packaging around each product. Also, it is important to secure the cartons within the container by packing the shipping cartons as tightly as possible. Gaps and empty spaces should be filled with dunnage, paper, or air bags to eliminate in-transit load shifting.

Moisture is a constant concern because condensation can accumulate inside the container. Another aspect of this problem is that cargo may also be unloaded in precipitation or the foreign port may not have covered storage facilities. It is important to use packages and packing filler made of moisture-resistant material. Plastic can be used inside cartons to protect freight and shrink wrap can be used around palletized or unitized product to create a moisture barrier.

Theft and pilferage are added risks. To avoid pilferage, avoid writing contents or brand names on packages. Other safeguards include using straps, seals, and shrink wrapping. The goal is to limit awareness of the contents of the cartons and eliminate the opportunity for undetected access to the shipment.

Finally, because transportation costs are determined by volume and weight, specially reinforced and lightweight packing materials have been developed for global transportation. Packing goods to minimize volume and weight while reinforcing them may save money, as well as ensuring that the goods are properly packed. It is recommended that a professional firm be hired to pack the products if the seller is not equipped to do so. This service is usually provided at a moderate cost.

Normally, air shipments require less heavy packing than ocean shipments, though they should still be adequately protected, especially if they are fragile and/or of interest to thieves. In many instances, standard domestic packing is acceptable, especially if the product is durable and there is no concern for display packaging. In other instances, high-test (at least 250 pounds per square inch) cardboard or tri-wall construction boxes are more than adequate.

While advertising and logos on cartons are not desirable, certain carton markings are essential. The information provided on the outside of the cartons must comply with customs regulations of the country of destination, enable freight handlers and receivers to correctly identify shipments, facilitate proper handling of shipments, and adhere to environmental and safety regulations for hazardous materials. At minimum, each carton should prominently display the following information:

- Customer and destination information—business name, ship-to address
- Seller and origin information—business name, ship-from address, and country of origin
- Cargo information—weight in pounds and kilograms, size in inches and centimeters, cautionary and handling markings using international pictorial symbols, handling instructions, and package number (for example, "2 of 14")
- Hazardous materials markings should also be used as needed. These markings should follow the United Nations harmonized standards and internationally recognized symbols.

Insuring the Goods International cargo is subject to a wider array of loss and damage risks than domestic freight. This is due to the extended origin-to-destination distance, number of transfers between carriers, and varying climatic conditions. In particular, ocean freight faces considerable obstacles to loss- and damage-free delivery. Because of these obstacles, sellers and customers are exposed to significant financial risks when their freight moves through the global supply chain.

Before tendering freight to the transportation company, the exporter and importer must determine their insurable interests and understand how to most effectively manage risk. For most organizations, the appropriate response is to transfer the risk of financial loss through the purchase of freight insurance. A detailed discussion of freight insurance is provided in Chapter 10.

Completing the Paperwork Freight documents control international cargo on its journey from origin point in the country of export to its final destination in the country of import. Missing or incorrect paperwork can cause delays and additional costs. In general, international cargo travels with four types of documents: invoices, export documents, import documents, and transportation documents. These documents must be completed fully and accurately prior to tendering freight to the transportation company. A detailed discussion of freight documentation and paperwork is provided in Chapter 10.

Policy and Regulatory Issues Impacting Global Flows

Given the strategic nature of transportation, governments around the world take an active interest in freight movement. Key roles include regulation of the transportation industry, investment in transportation infrastructure, and promotion of international trade. Government agencies may also control the import and export of strategic materials.

While many governments have taken a market-focused approach toward carrier competition, this does not mean that they have adopted a hands-off approach to transportation regulation. Oversight is growing in areas where the transportation industry has the potential to impact the quality of life, the safety of citizens, and the growth of commerce. For example, the United Kingdom's Department for Transport has adopted 11 policies to support the transportation networks that keep the United Kingdom on the move. One of these policies focuses on providing fair and effective regulation of the freight transportation industry. The goal is to move freight safely and securely by road, rail, and water across the United Kingdom.[4]

In the United States, the Department of Transportation's mission is to "Serve the United States by ensuring a fast, safe, efficient, accessible, and convenient transportation system that meets our vital national interests and enhances the quality of life of the American people, today and into the future."[5] U.S. transportation regulations and legislation focus on:

- Improving safety—protect the traveling public through regulations designed to limit the size of freight equipment, combined freight and equipment weight, and travel speed. Safety initiatives also focus on driver qualifications, equipment safety, random operator drug testing, and control of hazardous material transport.
- Reducing environmental impact—establish equipment emission standards to reduce air pollution and greenhouse gas emissions, expand transportation networks to reduce congestion, and mandate standards to abate transportation noise impact.
- Increasing security—tighten cargo clearance processes at U.S. borders to reduce the likelihood of terrorist acts. Chapter 9 discusses the regulations and policies used to provide the delicate balance between national security and efficient freight flows.

Effective management of freight flows requires that transportation managers take the time to understand and comply with government policies and regulations both at home and abroad. This includes both regulations that impact the flow of import goods as well as those that affect the flow of export goods. Failure to abide by these requirements will lead to delivery delays and potential penalties, including fines, freight confiscation, and/or denial of entry.

Global Transportation Providers

The global transportation market is served by carriers in all modes of transportation, including pipelines in North America and Eastern Europe. Intercontinental freight moves primarily via ocean and air freight. In contrast, intracontinental freight flows primarily via truck. Because intracontinental freight flows are similar to domestic moves, this section focuses on intercontinental ocean transportation and air transportation. Surface transportation and ancillary service providers are also briefly discussed.

Ocean Shipping

Ocean shipping is an essential resource in global supply chains; carrying more than 60 percent of goods on a value basis.[6] The vast majority of containerized finished goods, as well as bulk materials moving across oceans, travel via this mode. Ocean shipping is a very diverse industry with a variety of service options, equipment types, service providers, pricing alternatives, and key issues that must be addressed. Regardless of the commodity, freight volume, and geographic requirements involved, there is an ocean carrier with the capability and capacity to move the cargo.

Service Options Ocean transportation service providers can be segmented into three different categories—liner services, charter services, and private services.

Liner service is provided by ships that travel on regularly scheduled voyages, following fixed routes with predetermined ports of call. Typically, a liner ship will serve a particular trade area, such as the trans-Pacific lanes between Asia and North America, trans-Atlantic lanes between Europe and North America, or Asia-Europe lanes. Some liner ships travel the globe on "round the world" schedules, eastbound or westbound, passing through the Panama Canal and the Suez Canal.

There are different types and sizes of liner ships, many of which are assigned to specific routes based on their size, **draft**, and cargo handling capabilities. Liner ships may carry containers, break-bulk shipments, or a combination of freight types. Historically, liner freight rates were based on published company or liner conference tariffs. Currently, service providers have the flexibility to negotiate contract rates with individual customers.

Charter service is provided by ships that are hired for a specific voyage or amount of time. It is similar to hiring a limousine service or taxi for direct point-to-point service. The shipowner essentially leases the vessel to a **charterer** (the customer) who uses the ship to move its own cargo. Some charterers move cargo for other companies with the goal of making money on the difference between leasing costs and the price charged to other customers.

Charter ships operate in geographic regions defined by the individual customer according to the type of charter agreed to. Charter types include:

- A **voyage charter** is the hiring of a vessel and crew for a voyage between a load port and a discharge port. The charterer pays the vessel owner on a per-ton or lump-sum basis. The owner pays the port costs (excluding **stevedore services**), fuel costs, and crew costs.
- A **time charter** is the hiring of a vessel for a specific period of time. The owner manages the vessel but the charterer selects the ports and directs the vessel where to go. The charterer pays for all fuel the vessel consumes, port charges, and a daily charter rate to the owner of the vessel.
- A **demise charter** is a long lease of a vessel in which the charterer has total control of the vessel, manages the officers and crew, and pays all expenses for maintenance and operation. A **bareboat charter** is a demise charter in which the charterer places its own master and crew onboard the vessel.

Charter freight rates may be on a per-ton basis over a certain route (such as iron ore moving between Brazil and China) or alternatively may be expressed in terms of a total sum—normally in U.S. dollars—per day for the agreed duration of the charter. A standard contract form called a **charter party** is commonly used to document the agreed upon charter details.

Private service is similar to operating a private truck fleet. Private ships are owned or leased on a long-term basis by the company moving the goods. For example, Chiquita Brands International uses a private fleet of refrigerated ships to move bananas and other fruits from Central American plantations to the U.S. market. The return trip carries specialized shipping cartons and other supplies to the plantations. Oil and lumber products are also moved via private service. The economics of private shipping are similar to those of private trucking.

Equipment Types According to the 2013 Equasis database, there were 47,547 cargo ships in the world fleet.[7] Most ships fly a **flag of convenience**, with the owners registering their ships in countries that offer advantageous fees and regulations rather than in their home country. Popular countries for ship registration include Panama, Liberia, Malta,

Marshall Islands, and the Bahamas. These countries register ships of all types and sizes ranging from private yachts to oil **supertankers**.

Individual ships are designed differently and can be somewhat unique. However, there are five general groups of ship types relevant to international trade.

Containerships are built for the specific purpose of moving standardized 20-ft and 40-ft oceangoing containers. In general, these "box ships" hold containers under deck in specific slots created by vertical guides. After the hatch covers are put in place, the remaining containers are loaded above or on deck by stacking them on top of each other. These containers are secured via metal bars and twistlocks. Some newer ships have eliminated the hatch covers and decks and extended the vertical guides. This is done to increase the speed of loading and unloading at ports.

The number and size of containerships has flourished. There are over 5,000 containerships in operation, collectively capable of holding over 18 million containers. The largest of the containerships can carry over 18,000 TEUs. The Globe, owned by China Shipping Container Lines, sits 53 feet deep and can accommodate 19,100 TEUs. It was the largest containership at the time of its launch in 2014. It is highly fuel efficient, using 20 percent less fuel than a 10,000 TEU vessel.[8] Its initial operations focused on the Far East to Europe route. The top container lines in the world are presented in Table 11-1.

The combination of loading/unloading speed, intermodal transferability, and freight protection makes container shipping very popular. While a break-bulk ship might require many days to unload and load its cargo by small crane and manpower, a container ship can enter, unload, load, and clear a port in less than 12 hours using the huge portside container cranes. Such speed has brought about labor savings to both the shipper and the liner company, as well as increased ship (and capital) utilization. Because a ship is only earning revenue at sea, it is easy to see why containers have become a dominant form of packaged-goods international shipping.

Break-bulk ships are multipurpose vessels that are capable of transporting shipments of unusual sizes, unitized on pallets, in bags, or in crates. The ships tend to be smaller and have onboard cranes, giving them the flexibility to serve nearly any port.

TABLE 11-1 Top 10 Container Lines—2014

COMPANY	COUNTRY	TEUs	SHIPS OWNED	SHIPS ON ORDER
A.P. Moeller-Maersk	Denmark	2,916,607	615	13
Mediterranean Shipping Co.	Switzerland	2,550,637	502	48
CMA CGM Group	France	1,627,653	443	37
Hapag-Lloyd	Germany	950,876	182	6
Evergreen Line	Taiwan	948,220	197	14
COSCO Container Lines	China	819,429	162	10
China Shipping Container Lines	China	656,050	136	4
Hanjin Shipping Group	South Korea	608,459	98	6
MOL	Japan	604,720	113	6
APL	Singapore	568,017	96	0
Total of Top 10 Carriers		12,250,668		
Percent of World Fleet		65.2%		

Source: Adapted from Alphaliner, *Alphaliner–Top 100*, December 10, 2014, retrieved December 10, 2014, from http://www.alphaliner.com/top100/.

Many of these ships are engaged in specialized trades or specific trading lanes. The problem with break-bulk shipping is the labor-intensive loading, unloading, and load securing processes. Because each unitized piece of the shipment must be handled separately, port dwell times are longer, which is costly and time consuming. Hence, break-bulk shipping's share of international trade is decreasing.

Roll-on/roll-off (RORO) ships were created to move wheeled vehicles such as cars, trucks, farm equipment, and construction equipment that can be driven on and off the vessel. Since it would be costly and dangerous to use a crane to load this type of freight, the RORO ship has a ramp that drops down to the wharf, allowing vehicles to be quickly loaded or unloaded. The interior of the ship has many decks to store the cargo, similar to a parking garage. In some ships, the height of the decks can be adjusted to accommodate different sizes of rolling cargo.

Bulk carriers constitute a catch-all category for ships that are dedicated to the transport of a specific bulk commodity on a voyage basis. **Crude carriers** move petroleum products in massive quantities. The size and draft of these ships severely limits the routes available, as they need deep water ports. **Dry-bulk carriers** have several holds in their hulls in which loose cargo like grains, coal, ore, and other commodities are loaded. These ships are generally small enough to move through the Panama Canal and serve smaller ports. **Gas carriers** move compressed gasses like liquefied natural gas and liquefied petroleum gas in specialized tanks. These unique ships are employed on long-term time charters and travel a stable schedule similar to liner ships.

Combination ships are multipurpose vessels that can handle different types of commodities and load types. A typical ship design has under-deck holds for bulk or break-bulk cargoes, a tweendeck to hold vehicles or break-bulk cargo, and a main deck, which carries containers. These vessels are likely to have their own cranes and other equipment for loading and unloading cargo. The cargo flexibility, smaller size, and handling equipment help combination ships thrive in smaller markets and developing countries.

Rate Structure Ocean shipping rates are impacted by carrier cost structure, commodity, freight volume, origin and destination points, and ancillary services required. The type of service provided—liner or charter—has a major influence on rate structures. Our discussion of rates will be segmented by type of service.

The general cost structure of liner operations, as with most ship operations, is largely fixed and common in nature. Approximately 80 to 90 percent of total cost is fixed and 10 to 20 percent is variable. Liner companies tend to have large overhead costs for marketing, management, and business development.

A majority of the total costs of operating a ship is also fixed. Because cargo loading, unloading, and fuel are the only primary variable costs, the ship's operation cost is roughly the same regardless of the commodity or volume hauled. The problem of determining a cost per pound entails a difficult fixed-cost allocation process, which can be arbitrary at best. Ship operators will often determine unit costs in terms of cost per cubic foot of ship space used so as to better evaluate and price for the range of commodities handled.

Because the cost of owning and operating liner ships is relatively fixed, ship operators attempt to solicit and charge rates that will maximize the total revenue of the entire ship. This condition brings about the tendency to price according to the principles of value of service. That is, a floor of variable costs must be covered as a minimum; then the blend of high- and low-value-per-pound commodities, as well as the host of traffic elasticities, leads to pricing according to what the traffic will bear to maximize revenue.

Historically, the majority of liner rates were determined collectively by a group of carriers serving specific trade routes and ports. These shipping **conferences** are essentially legal cartels in which the carriers agree not to compete on price by publishing standardized rate **tariffs**. The conferences were allowed to exist with antitrust immunity by governments because of the high fixed-cost structure of the industry. Contract rates and independent rates were no widely available.

The 1999 implementation of the **Ocean Shipping Reform Act** (OSRA) altered the balance of ratemaking power in the liner industry. OSRA expanded the ability of shippers to negotiate private, confidential service contracts with liner companies. A service contract is an agreement in which the shipper commits to provide a certain minimum quantity of cargo over a fixed period of time and the ocean carrier commits to a certain rate or rate schedule and a defined level of service. Today, the vast majority of liner cargo moves under independently negotiated service contracts.

The total price for service under these service contracts will typically contain three components: a basic rate, mandatory surcharges, and extra services. The basic rate focuses on the cost of moving cargo. It is determined by cargo type, origin-destination route, and other factors. Mandatory surcharges are included to cover pass-through charges or charges beyond the ocean transport service. Frequently, these include a fuel surcharge called a bunker adjustment factor, terminal handling charges, and documentation charges. Special requests such as container cleaning or use of controlled atmosphere containers are additional costs.[9]

Charter shipowners also experience costs that are largely fixed in nature. Ownership costs present themselves in depreciation and interest costs. Fuel is not as greatly variable with the commodity weight load, as is ship speed or at sea versus port time. The key is that the shipowner minimizes empty nonrevenue miles and days.

Charter rates are individually negotiated based on the type of charter (voyage or time) and services required. The market for ship chartering is a fluid supply-and-demand situation. At any given time, the charter rate situation can be one of feast or famine for shipowners. This market can fluctuate over both the short and long term. In the short run, the demand for a ship and charter rates at a single port area will depend on shipper movement needs and available ship supply within a time span as short as a month. Over longer periods, a market can be considered glutted or tight, depending on the number of ships or types of ships that are available in the world during the span of a year.

The charter rate negotiation process involves the two primary parties involved in chartering: the shipowner and the charterer (customer). **Shipbrokers** are usually employed to investigate the market and conduct the negotiations. In most cases, both parties will have their own brokers and negotiate through these representatives, who should do their best to preserve their respective principal's interests and intentions.

A successful negotiation will result in a charter party, a contract in which the shipowner agrees to place their ship, or part of it, at the disposal of the charterer for the carriage of goods from one port to another port on being paid freight, or to lease the ship for a specified period, the payment being known as hire money. The charter party states in written form the agreement between a shipowner and a charterer, and factually records the agreement and the terms and conditions that have been negotiated.

Current Issues The ocean shipping industry is in the midst of significant change. One major shift is the introduction of larger, more efficient containerships. As stated previously, carriers like China Shipping Container Line are introducing ultra-large containerships (ULCS) that dwarf what were considered the 10,000 TEU megaships of a decade ago. Today, no less than 20 ships with capacities of 18,000 or more TEUs are in service. The Maersk ULCS fleet is featured in the On the Line feature.

ULCS offer unparalleled carrying capacity but they come with some challenges. First, only a few ports can handle ships of this length and draught, limiting the potential routes. Second, the added amount of time required to load/offload containers can create port congestion. Finally, success is dependent on high load factors. If China's export activity wanes, it will be difficult to profitably operate these ULCS.[10]

Another major change is the mechanism for ocean carrier alignment. As a result of the OSRA and other global reforms that rendered ocean conferences obsolete, large ocean carriers have formed alliances. An alliance seeks to pool and control freight capacity for a group of carriers serving common trade routes and ports. Originally conceived as a competitive tool to provide more frequent service and better reliability to customers, alliances are now a defensive response to prolonged overcapacity and faltering freight rates. These vessel sharing alliances seek to reduce excess capacity and prop up rates to

ON THE **LINE**

E × E × E = Mega Capacity

One of the biggest investors to date in ULCS has been Maersk Line. The ocean carrier has plans for 20 containerships each with a capacity of 18,000 TEUs. At 1,312 feet long and 194 feet wide, with a draft of 48 feet, the ships are powered by dual 32-megawatt diesel engines. Maersk has dubbed the fleet "Triple-E" class containerships based on three design principles: economy of scale, energy efficient, and environmentally improved.

Economy of scale is critical as each ship costs approximately $190 million to build. The 18,000 TEU capacity will allow Maersk to move massive quantities of product from Asia to Europe. For example, a single Triple-E containership could transport more than 182 million iPads or 111 million pairs of shoes from Shanghai to Rotterdam. The trip would take 25 days and burn 530,000 gallons of fuel. That comes to only 0.003 gallons per iPad. In contrast, the previous generation of Maersk E-class ships held 16 percent fewer containers.

Energy efficiency comes from a combination of design and slow steaming. To save fuel, a system captures heat from the massive engines and uses it to turn water into steam to drive a secondary turbine. The power generated by the waste heat recovery system is fed back to the propeller shaft. It also provides electricity for crew quarters and for refrigerated containers that hold perishable goods. Speeds of 19 to 20 knots will reduce fuel consumption by 37 percent versus the 23 to 26 knot speeds of smaller ships.

The third "E" of environmentally improved seeks to reduce emissions by 50 percent per container moved. This is accomplished by the greater carrying capacity and reduced fuel consumption. Given the ocean shipping industry's use of bunker fuels—which create far more carbon dioxide than jet fuel or diesel fuel—reducing emissions is essential. In addition, the ships were designed with end-of-life considerations to make disposal and scrapping easier.

In the long run, these Triple-E ships will be used by Maersk and its alliance partners in capacity sharing arrangements. Experts predict that this will gradually push competitors with smaller, less fuel-efficient ships out of the Asia-to-Europe routes.

Sources: *Triple-E: The World's Largest Ship*, retrieved December 11, 2014, from http://worldslargestship.com/the-ship/; Drake Bennett, "Risk Ahoy: Maersk, Daewoo Build the World's Biggest Boat," *Bloomberg Businessweek*, September 5, 2013, retrieved December 11, 2014, from http://www.businessweek.com/articles/2013-09-05/risk-ahoy-maersk-daewoo-build-the-worlds-biggest-boat#p1; and Costas Paris, "Maersk Line Considers Buying More Triple-E Megaships," *Wall Street Journal*, November 13, 2014, retrieved December 11, 2014, from http://www.wsj.com/articles/maersk-line-considers-buying-more-triple-e-megaships-1415892366.

secure future industry profitability.[11] Customers may have a tougher time negotiating contracts in trade lanes with strong ship alliances and controlled capacity.

A third change taking place is the shift away from inefficient, error-prone manual processes. Leaders are upending the status quo, becoming early adopters of process automation. Thanks to e-shipping-enabled processes, a customer booking a container shipment no longer needs to wait hours or days before receiving confirmation from a carrier that both equipment and space are available and booked. As carriers roll out e-invoicing and dispute resolution tools, they will drive down costs, reduce errors, and deliver the experiences their customers increasingly expect.[12]

International Air

Air cargo is a $70-billion business that transports 35 percent of the value of world trade by value of goods. While air cargo transportation is specialized mode in terms of tonnage, it is a critical part of the airline business and the supply chain. Air carriers transport small quantities of high-value, low-weight, semi-finished, and finished goods. Primary commodities moved globally as air cargo include technology products, precision instruments, electronics, pharmaceuticals, perishable foods, and apparel. In this section, international air transportation characteristics are discussed, including service options, equipment types, service providers, pricing alternatives, and key issues that must be addressed.

Service Options International air transportation is available in virtually every market of the world. Wherever passenger service is available, you can also find air cargo service. Two primary carrier types dominate this mode.

Combination carriers move freight and passengers, with cargo loaded in the belly of the aircraft. As demand has grown, some of the larger international carriers have created separate divisions or companies to focus on air cargo movement and provide scheduled service to meet the needs of global commerce. Eight of the top ten international air freight carriers (scheduled freight ton-kilometers), led by Emirates, Korean Air, and Cathay Pacific Airways, are combination carriers. Table 11-2 provides a list of the top international air cargo carriers.

TABLE 11-2 Top 10 Air Cargo Carriers—2013

COMPANY	COUNTRY	INTERNATIONAL FREIGHT-TONNES CARRIED
Emirates	United Arab Emirates	2,146,000
Federal Express	USA	1,970,000
UPS	USA	1,404,000
Korean Air	South Korea	1,365,000
Cathay Pacific Airways	Hong Kong	1,388,000
China Air	China	1,197,000
Singapore Airlines	Singapore	1,092,000
Qatar Airways	Qatar	1,002,000
Lufthansa	Germany	991,000
Asiana Airlines	South Korea	838,000

Source: Adapted from Adina Solomon, "The Top 50 Cargo Carriers: FedEx, UPS Top Rankings, but Middle East Grows at Fast Rate," *Air Cargo World*, August 27, 2014.

Air cargo carriers focus exclusively on the movement of freight, packages, letters, and envelopes. Like ocean carriers, customers have the option of using scheduled service or on-demand charter service. The majority of large air carriers provide regularly scheduled service through a highly coordinated network of operations and equipment.

Some air cargo carriers offer door-to-door service. **Integrated carriers** like FedEx and UPS have this capability because they own ground delivery equipment as well as aircraft. They can offer a consistent schedule of pickup and delivery windows and standard expedited service through their hub-and-spoke networks. Thanks to their well-controlled processes, they are key players in the global delivery of expedited movement of letters, packages, and small shipments.

In contrast, **nonintegrated carriers** like Cargolux and AirBridgeCargo Airlines provide transport service from airport to airport. They rely on air freight forwarders or the customer to provide delivery service to and from the airport. Some nonintegrated carriers provide on-demand (charter) service for customers whose requirements dictate rapid, direct movement of goods. Given the high cost of on-demand service from these carriers, it is reserved for emergency shipments, unique products, and unusual route requirements.

Equipment Types While there are many sizes of aircraft used for moving international cargo, the primary difference between equipment type focuses on the internal configuration of the plane. Some equipment is set up to carry freight only while others carry a combination of passengers and cargo. Each type is discussed below.

Air freighters are aircraft dedicated solely to the movement of freight. They range in size from the Cessna Caravan that FedEx uses for small market pickup and delivery (capacity of 4,000 pounds) to the Anatov AN-124, a huge plane capable of handling oversized payloads (capacity of nearly 265,000 pounds). The main deck of air freighters has no amenities and is set up to quickly move freight on and off the plane using a roller deck. A **roller deck** is a main deck equipped with rollers on the floor that allows palletized or containerized cargo to be pushed into position. In the air freight industry, these specially designed containers that fit properly inside the rounded fuselage are called **unit load devices** (ULDs). The pallets and ULDs are then secured to the aircraft floor using hooks and slings.

Cargo also travels on **passenger airplanes**. The passengers travel on the main deck or cabin of the plane while luggage and some cargo are loaded into the lower deck or belly of the aircraft. The cargo is commonly restricted to smaller individual shipments of cargo rather than full pallets or ULDs, due to the weight limitations of the aircraft, the capacity of the hold, and the exterior door size. Also, certain items considered hazardous or a fire threat (such as nonrechargeable lithium-ion batteries) are no longer allowed to be carried by passenger aircraft. A benefit of using passenger airplanes for cargo is the frequency of service and ability to move critical shipments on the next flight out.

A few airlines use hybrid **combi airplane**. The term *combi* refers to the flexibility to change the passenger/cargo mix on the main deck of the aircraft. A movable partition in the cabin separates the passengers from the cargo and allows flexibility to move more passengers or cargo based on demand. Combi aircraft typically feature an oversized cargo door, as well as tracks on the cabin floor to allow the seats to be added or removed quickly.

Whatever the international shipment requirement may be, an aircraft with an appropriate combination of payload, range, and speed is likely available.

Rate Structure The air carrier cost structure consists of high variable costs in proportion to fixed costs, somewhat akin to the motor carrier cost structure. Like motor and water carriers, air carriers do not invest heavily in facility infrastructure or byways. Governments around the world build airports and air cargo facilities terminals, as well as provide traffic control of the airways. Air carriers pay variable lease payments and landing fees for their use. Equipment costs, though quite high, are still a small part of the total cost.

Air cargo rates are based on the **value of service** or the **cost of service**. Value of service rates are demand based and consider the sensitivity of the cargo being shipped to freight rates. The less sensitive cargo is to rates, the higher the rate will be. On traffic lanes where demand is strong and plane capacity is limited, the air rates will be high and vice versa for traffic lanes where supply exceeds demand. Also, products with high prices or emergency conditions surrounding the move will be charged high rates because the freight rate is a small portion of the landed selling price.

Cost of service factors also enter into air carrier pricing of cargo. Given the limited cargo-carrying capacity of a plane, space is at a premium. The utilization of this space is related to the **density** of the cargo, with low-density cargo requiring more space per weight unit than high-density cargo.

Air carriers calculate the **dimensional weight** (dim weight) of a shipment to evaluate the weight versus space issue. Freight carriers use the greater of the actual weight or dimensional weight to calculate shipping charges. Carriers calculate international air shipments as (Length × Width × Height)/(Dimensional Factor). The common dimensional factor for international freight is 139 for shipments measured in inches and 5,000 for shipments measured in centimeters.

For example, an international shipment weighing 1,500 pounds with 100 cartons measuring 16 inches by 12 inches by 18 inches has a dim weight of 24.86 pounds per case (16 × 12 × 18/139) and a total dim weight of 2,486 pounds. Thus, the air carrier will charge the customer based on the higher dim weight of 2,486 pounds instead of the actual weight of 1,500 pounds.

Dimensional weight favors shippers of dense objects and penalizes those who ship lightweight cartons. For example, a carton of unpopped corn kernels will likely be charged by gross weight while a carton of popcorn will probably be charged by its dimensional weight. This is because the large box of popcorn takes up excess space but does not fill up a plane's capacity in terms of weight, making it an inefficient use of cubic capacity.

The pricing of international air freight is governed by the International Air Transport Association (IATA) via The Air Cargo Tariff (TACT). TACT is generally considered to be a set of guidelines that contains comprehensive information regarding air cargo rules, regulations, rates, and charges. TACT contains information regarding 4.5 million rates for 350,000 city pairs with information contributed by more than 100 airlines.[13] TACT includes three types of international air carrier rates: general cargo, class, and specific commodity rates. However, carriers are not required to use these rates and major carriers tend to develop their own rates based on the commodity and market competition.

Container rates are also available for cargo shipped in a container. The rate is cost based, rather than value of service or commodity based. The rate applies to a minimum weight in the container. Some carriers offer a container rate discount per container shipped over any route of the individual carrier. The discount is deducted from the tariff rate applicable to the commodity being moved in non-containerized form, and a charge is assessed for returning the empty container.

Current Issues After a number of years with flat or declining demand, the picture is looking brighter for the air cargo industry. Boeing forecasts that world air cargo traffic will grow an average 4.7 percent per year over the next 20 years. This total will more than double, increasing from 208 billion revenue tonne-kilometers (RTK) in 2013 to 522 billion RTK in 2033. Much of the growth will come from the intra-Asia markets while Asia-North America and Asia-Europe markets will grow slightly faster than the world average growth rate.[14]

To support this growth and to replace aging fleets, significant investment is taking place in the aircraft market. Higher capacity, fuel-efficient passenger jets and air cargo freights are being purchased in record numbers. Airbus predicts in its global market forecast that over 31,350 new passenger aircraft and freighters at a value of nearly $4.6 trillion will be required to handle the growth in traffic. The vast majority will be passenger aircraft delivered to the Asia Pacific and North American markets, while the largest proportion of freighters will be delivered to North American customers.[15]

There are three potential impediments to the air cargo industry's growth. The U.S. manufacturing trends of near-shoring and on-shoring moves production will reduce air cargo shipment distances and could result in modal shifts to water service. Second, protectionist trade activity by governments encourage a shift to domestic production, further eroding international air cargo activity. Third, changing economic conditions due to increases in fuel prices or interest rates could stall economic growth.[16]

Surface Transport

Moving goods across adjacent land borders is the primary domain of trucks, rail, and pipeline service. Trucking is clearly the major player for intracontinental freight flows in North America and Europe. Nearly 60 percent of the freight moving between the U.S. and its NAFTA trading partners is handled by trucks, as revealed by Figure 11-7. As issues related to U.S.-Mexico bilateral trucking service rules are resolved, this volume will also increase.

Despite the high volume of intracontinental truck traffic, the industry is hampered by a patchwork of domestic rules and regulations that impede international freight flows.

FIGURE 11-7 Intra continental Freight Flows

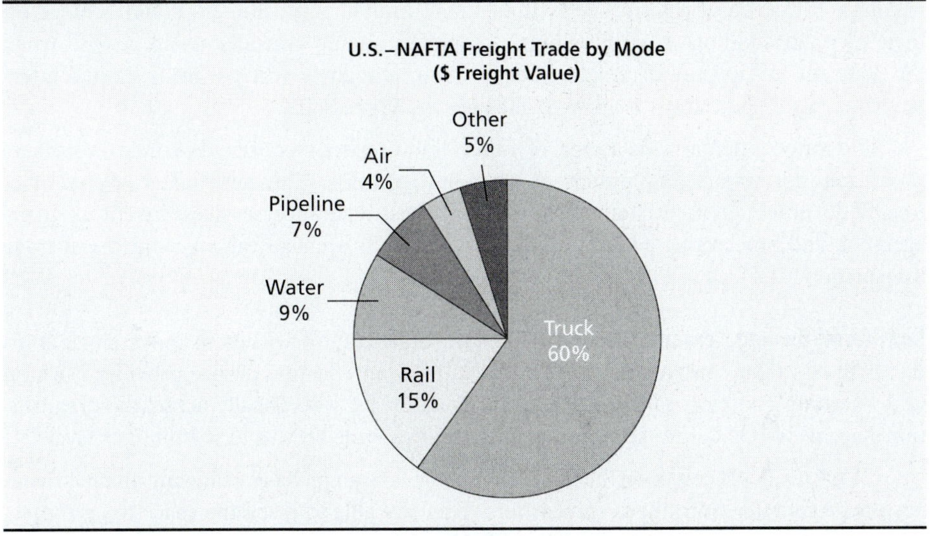

Source: Bureau of Transportation Statistics, TransBorder Freight Data, 2013, retrieved from http://www.rita.dot.gov/bts/press_releases/bts014_14.

There are few global standards for trucking or roadway infrastructure. Each country has its own regulations regarding equipment length, width, and carrying capacity. Safety regulations regarding driver hours of service, speed limits, and inspections are also inconsistent. Finally, some countries have mandated driving bans during certain times of the day and/or days of the week, making it difficult to plan delivery schedules. Motor carriers and their customers must understand the unique requirements of each country to ensure efficient and timely freight movement.

International rail service benefits from a standardized infrastructure and equipment. Still, North American rail traffic accounts for only 15 percent of the total regional freight volume. Rail activity mainly focuses on the movement of bulk raw materials and intermodal containers. Fuel price and tax issues, road congestion, and greenhouse gas emissions have created a push for more rail freight in Europe, though passenger trains have priority over all other traffic. In the North American market, significant investment in railroad infrastructure, deployment of fuel-efficient locomotives, and more effective track sharing will be needed to improve service and expand market share.[17]

Ancillary Services

The complexity of international transportation makes it difficult for importers and exporters to independently manage global freight flows. To overcome this challenge, they can leverage the expertise of third party logistics (3PL) companies. These service providers facilitate the movement of goods via ocean and air by developing exceptional capabilities in one or more steps in the global freight flow process.

International Freight Forwarders The primary role of an international freight forwarder (IFF) is to help importers and exporters transport their goods. Many IFFs specialize in particular service areas, modes of transport, or markets. IFFs are often seen as the travel agents of international freight transportation. These service providers identify and book the best routes, modes of transport, and specific carriers based on customer requirements at competitive rates.

IFFs can consolidate freight going to a single destination. This allows the IFF to negotiate lower transportation rates than many individual customers could achieve on their own. In addition to cost savings, companies should consider using an IFF when the scale and complexity of freight transportation is high or when there is limited internal time, experience, and expertise to manage the process.

IFFs often offer a wide range of other trade-related services that help customers avoid common errors and pitfalls of cross-border trade. These include completion of freight documentation, Customs clearance services, insurance services, inventory management, and other value added logistics services. IFFs are also valuable sources of trade information.

Non Vessel-Owning Common Carriers When an organization wishes to move small shipments in less than containterload (LCL) quantities, an effective service provider is a non vessel-owning common carrier (NVOCC). Unlike IFFs, who usually act as the organization's agent, NVOCCs are common carriers that provide service at a container level.

NVOCCs book container berths on ships on a regular basis, allowing them to gain advantageous rates from the ocean carriers. They are able to resell the space to customers in smaller increments at favorable rates. The NVOCC combines the goods from multiple customers into a single load to fill a container. The container is then given to an ocean carrier for movement to the destination port. Upon arrival, the NVOCC receives the container and delivers the contents to each final destination.

Export Packers Given the challenges of properly packing, marking, and loading shipments, many companies seek the assistance of export packing companies. These service providers work to ensure that products arrive safely. Export packers also help save money by using economical packing materials, improving space utilization inside cartons and containers, and taking steps to prevent theft. Finally, export packers also ensure that all packing regulations and marking requirements are met across the channel.

Port Operations and Customs Clearance

Most exporters and importers are not located directly on a waterway, rail line, or airport runway. Hence, they need freight handling and transfer services between carriers and modes at borders. Ports provide the infrastructure, equipment, and labor needed to load, unload, and transfer freight between carriers. Without efficient port operations, it would be extremely difficult to achieve the tremendous volume of global trade of the last decade.

Intercontinental trade moves primarily through airports and seaports, while intracontinental trade moves directly from origin to destination through international gateways or indirectly through intermodal transfer terminals and **inland ports**. Seaports and airports are discussed in detail below.

Port facilities can be privately owned, though the vast majority of major international seaports and airports are government owned. The facilities are managed by a **port authority**, a governmental or quasigovernmental public agency charged with creating and supporting economic development in the port area. At a landlord port, the port authority builds the wharves, which it then rents or leases to a terminal operator. When the port authority is an operating port, it owns the facilities, cranes, and cargo handling equipment, hires the labor, and manages most of the day-to-day operations.

Seaports

Given that the vast majority of intercontinental cargo moves via ocean carriers, seaports play a critical role in global trade. A seaport is an area of land and water with related equipment to permit the reception of ships, their loading and unloading, and the receipt, storage, and delivery of their goods. There are thousands of seaports around the world, though the vast majority of international trade flows through a small group of major, deep draft commercial seaports. Table 11-3 identifies the top global ports for various types of freight.

Infrastructure Before an exporter or importer determines which ports to use, they must consider infrastructure issues. These basic facilities, equipment, and services greatly impact the capabilities and capacity of a seaport. Some seaports have infrastructures that are tailored to containerized freight while others focus on bulk, break-bulk, or rolling freight. Hence, it is critical to match freight with the cargo handling capabilities of the port.

One important infrastructure issue is the depth of the water. Unobstructed deep water is needed in both the channel leading to the port and at the wharf to serve the growing population of post-Panamax ships. The turning radius of these large ships also

TABLE 11-3 Top Seaports—2012/2013

THOUSANDS OF TONS			MILLIONS OF TWENTY-FOOT EQUIVALENT UNITS		
RANK	**PORT**	**TONS**	**RANK**	**PORT**	**TEUS**
1	Ningbo-Zhoushan, China	744,000	1	Shanghai, China	33.62
2	Shanghai, China	644,659	2	Singapore, Singapore	32.60
3	Singapore, Singapore	538,012	3	Shenzhen, China	23.28
4	Tianjin, China	477,000	4	Hong Kong, China	22.35
5	Rotterdam, Netherlands	441,527	5	Busan, South Korea	17.69
6	Guangzhou Harbor, China	438,000	6	Ningbo-Zhoushan, China	17.33
7	Qingdao, China	407,340	7	Qingdao, China	15.52
8	Dalian, China	303,000	8	Guangzhou Harbor, China	15.31
9	Busan, South Korea	298,689	9	Jebel Ali, Dubai, U.A.E.	13.64
10	Port Hedland, Australia	288,443	10	Tianjin, China	13.01
11	Hong Kong, China	269,282	11	Rotterdam, Netherlands	11.62
12	Qinhuangdao, China	233,235	12	Dalian, China	10.86
13	South Louisiana, U.S.A.	228,677	13	Port Kelang, Malaysia	10.35
14	Houston, U.S.A.	216,082	14	Kaohsiung, Taiwan, China	9.94
15	Nagoya, Japan	202,556	15	Hamburg, Germany	9.30
16	Shenzhen, China	196,458	16	Antwerp, Belgium	8.59
17	Port Kelang, Malaysia	195,856	17	Keihin Ports, Japan	8.37
18	Antwerp, Belgium	184,136	18	Xiamen, China	8.01
19	Dampier, Australia	180,366	19	Los Angeles, U.S.A.	7.87
20	Ulsan, South Korea	174,117	20	Tanjung Pelepas, Malaysia	7.63

Source: Adapted from AAPA, *World Port Rankings 2012*, retrieved December 12, 2014, from http://aapa.files.cms-plus.com/Statistics/WORLD%20PORT%20RANKINGS%202012.pdf; and World Shipping Council, Top 50 Container Ports 2013, retrieved December 12, 2014, from http://www.worldshipping.org/about-the-industry/global-trade/top-50-world-container-ports.

requires the availability of a wide basin. Because most ports are not naturally deep, the waterway must be dredged regularly and occasionally deepened to handle large ships.

Wharfside freight handling capabilities are also critical. Seaports must offer an adequate number of ship berths to meet inbound and outbound demand. They also need the ability to quickly load and unload cargo. At a container port, gantry cranes wide enough to accommodate the loading and unloading of ULCS are needed. This will avoid the time-consuming task of turning the ship around. Bulk ports should have cranes, conveyors, elevators, and/or heavy lift equipment are needed to facilitate timely freight transfer. On-port freight handling equipment for moving cargo to and from the wharf is also needed.

Finally, ports must have adequate marshaling yards, warehouse facilities and transit sheds for storage, and interchange capabilities to move freight between modes. Ports must also have strong information technology and security systems to maintain visibility, control, and safety of the freight.

Operations Although there are many organizations involved in the day-to-day operation of an international port—the port authority, ocean carriers and their agents, pilots,

stevedores, **longshoremen**, **chandlers**, freight forwarders, **Customs brokers**, Customs agent, and landside carriers, to name the primary players—basic cargo flows are fairly straightforward.

On an export container move, a trucking company or railroad delivers the export freight to the port and checks in at the security gate. The container is then dropped at its assigned holding location. When the appropriate ship arrives, the container is retrieved and loaded on the ship.

At the point of import, the container is unloaded from the ship, after which it is moved to a storage area or loaded directly onto an outbound truck chassis or railcar. Prior to its release, the container will be scanned and possibly inspected by Customs for security purposes. The delivery carrier then moves the container to the final destination.

Current Issues To remain competitive, port authorities must remain vigilant of equipment innovations, operational congestion, and labor challenges. First, the size of containerships continues to increase because ocean carriers are motivated to achieve economies of scale. Waterways will need to be dredged, port authorities and terminal operators must invest in larger cranes, and sailing schedules will have to change to accommodate the longer unloading and processing times for these huge ships.

A related concern is congestion at major seaports. As freight volume and vessel sizes increase, substantially higher cargo volumes per ship call occurs. It is estimated that a port call from an 18,000 TEU ship could require 7,000 on/off container moves. This volume, combined with equipment shortages or poor landside operations, creates a high risk of port congestion and ships getting off schedule. During the first half of 2014, containership calling at the Port of Hamburg experienced delays averaging 70 hours.[18] The Transportation Technology feature reveals that port authorities are considering terminal automation technologies to combat delays and rising labor costs.

A third pressing issue is the periodic labor disputes and slowdowns that can result from protracted labor contract negotiations. For example, the 2014 negotiations between the International Longshore and Warehouse Union and the Pacific Maritime Association had the potential to disrupt 29 U.S. West Coast ports, including all the major West Coast container ports—Los Angeles, Long Beach, Oakland, Portland, Seattle and Tacoma.[19] Any work stoppages or slowdowns have the potential to send ripples across global supply chains.

TRANSPORTATION **TECHNOLOGY**

Port Automation Critical to Global Flows

Automation in the transportation industry is not new. Airport baggage handling systems, ship navigation systems, and automated dispatching software have long been used to facilitate rapid and efficient flows. Ports are picking up on the use of automation to improve their terminal operations. Driverless container transport vehicles, automated stacking cranes, and ship-to-shore cranes promise to increase container flow through, reduce manpower, and optimize space utilization.

Through their automation initiative, European ports are improving terminal capacity, equipment utilization, and overall container handling performance. Similarly, APM Terminals North America has benefitted from 30 remote-operated cranes at the Port of Virginia. TraPac Inc. at the Port of Los Angeles is installing equipment that moves containers from ships to shore cranes and trucks. When completed in 2016, it will be the first fully automated terminal on the West Coast and is expected to reduce labor requirements by 40 to 50 percent.

The decision to automate a terminal is an expensive proposition. Upgrading a facility that handles 2 million TEUs per year can cost $300 to $500 million. The Orient Overseas Container Line Asia Pacific Ltd. is adding robots as part of a $1.3 billion project to automate two container terminals in Long Beach, California. That's a major investment but a necessary one to stay competitive with other Pacific, Gulf Coast, and Atlantic ports. It also will handle millions of TEUs per year at a fraction of the cost for longshoremen labor.

Though traditional freight handling jobs will be eliminated, there will be a need for workers with specialized skills. Mechanics will be needed to maintain and repair the sophisticated equipment. Technology workers will be needed to aggregate, process, and manage data related to the control of containers, as well as integrate terminal operating systems with the equipment automation technologies. Their efforts will improve visibility of containers, automate information transfers, and increase terminal productivity.

Sources: James Nash, "U.S. Port Labor Talks Turn on Automation Cutting Workers," *Bloomberg*, September 18, 2014, retrieved December 14, 2014, from http://www.bloomberg.com/news/2014-09-19/port-labor-talks-turn-on-automation-cutting-dock-workers.html; Bill Mongelluzzo, "U.S. Ports Weigh Value of Terminal Automation Investment," JOC.com, October 2, 2014, retrieved December 14, 2014, from http://www.joc.com/port-news/port-productivity/us-ports-weigh-value-terminal-automation-investment_20141002.html; and Navis, *Automated Future for Ports*, October 2014, retrieved December 14, 2014, from http://navis.com/news/in-news/automated-future-ports.

Airports

International freight moves through thousands of cargo-friendly airports worldwide. A **commercial service airport** is broadly defined by the U.S. Federal Aviation Administration as a publicly owned airport that has scheduled passenger service with at least 2,500 passenger boardings each calendar year. **Cargo service airports** are airports that, in addition to any other air transportation services that may be available, are served by aircraft providing air transportation of cargo only, with a total annual landed weight of more than 100 million pounds.[20] Table 11-4 reveals that the twenty largest international airports are dual-purpose, handling both passenger and cargo traffic.

It is worth noting that air cargo companies are leveraging the capabilities of airports that focus on cargo. The purpose of Alliance Airport in Fort Worth, Texas, Montreal-Mirabel International Airport in Canada, and Paris-Vatry Airport in France is to provide alternative landing locations to congested international gateways and reduce operating costs.

Infrastructure Air cargo companies choose airport locations based on multiple factors. The first step is to create a short list of possible airports based on geographic access to key markets and minimal restrictions related to capacity caps or noise limits. Only when these hurdles have been cleared do air cargo companies consider landing fees, weather factors, and infrastructure issues such as runway length, terminal facilities, and ramp access for ease of freight transfer.[21]

The number and size of airport runways affect capacity and suitability for use. Multiple runways, as are found at most major international airports, support simultaneous takeoffs and landings. Single runway airports are severely capacity constrained and the slightest accident, malfunction, or weather issue immobilizes the entire operation. Longer

TABLE 11-4 Top Cargo Airports—2013

	METRIC TONS OF CARGO	
RANK	PORT	TONS
1	Hong Kong International, China	4,161,718
2	Memphis International Airport, U.S.A.	4,137,801
3	Shanghai Pudong International Airport, China	2,928,527
4	Incheon International Airport, South Korea	2,464,384
5	Dubai International Airport, U.A.E.	2,435,567
6	Ted Stevens Anchorage International Airport, U.S.A.	2,421,145
7	Louisville International Airport, U.S.A.	2,216079
8	Frankfurt Airport, Germany	2,094,453
9	Charles De Gaulle International Airport, France	2,069,200
10	Narita International Airport, Japan	2,019,844
11	Miami International Airport, U.S.A.	1,945,012
12	Singapore Changi Airport, Singapore	1,885,978
13	Beijing Capital International Airport, China	1,843,681
14	Los Angeles International Airport, U.S.A.	1,747,284
15	Taiwan Taoyuan International Airport, Taiwan	1,571,814
16	Amsterdam Airport Schiphol, Netherlands	1,565,961
17	London Heathrow Airport, United Kingdom	1,515,056
18	Guangzhou Baiyun International Airport, China	1,309,746
19	John F. Kennedy International Airport, U.S.A.	1,295,473
20	Suvarnabhumi Airport (Bangkok), Thailand	1,236,223

Source: Adapted from Airports Council International, *Preliminary World Airport Traffic and Rankings 2013*, March 31, 2014, retrieved December 12, 2014, from http://www.aci.aero/News/Releases/Most-Recent/2014/03/31/Preliminary-World-Airport-Traffic-and-Rankings-2013–High-Growth-Dubai-Moves-Up-to-7th-Busiest-Airport-.

runways are needed to support large aircraft and direct flights to and from faraway places. Runway and taxiway width has become another infrastructure issue due to the size and weight of the Airbus A380 and other large aircraft.

Airports must also have the necessary equipment to efficiently handle cargo. Terminals are needed to facilitate fast intermodal transfers of freight, while warehouses are needed to protect and store cargo. Finally, hours of operation impact airport selection. Since air freighters tend to fly at night and use airports during off-hours to avoid congestion with passenger flights, it is imperative that noise regulations not limit airport availability.

Operations Airport operations are less complex but more time sensitive than seaport operations. First, there are not as many organizations involved in air freight movement and transfers. Primary freight responsibilities for operations fall to the air cargo companies, cargo handling contractors, freight forwarders, trucking companies, and 3PL service providers.

Customs bureaus will also have an active role in clearing freight at international gateways. Export air cargo arrives at the international airport via truck or a domestic feeder flight from a smaller airport. In the United States, this outbound cargo is subject to the Transportation Security Administration's (TSA) **Known Shipper Program**, an initiative to positively identify valid businesses in the United States. Only shippers who apply for "known shipper" status can be approved through their cargo carrier to move cargo on passenger aircraft.

After screening and clearance, the cargo is loaded on the outbound international flight and flown to the destination airport. At the point of import, the cargo is unloaded from the aircraft, and moved to the terminal. Prior to its release from the airport, the cargo must be cleared by Customs or moved to a specialized warehouse. The freight forwarder or trucking company concludes the trip by moving the shipment from the airport to the importer's facility.

Current Issues Airports face a variety of challenges. They must flex capacity to deal with economic upturns and downturns and collaborate with airlines that are going through merger processes to maintain timely flows of cargoes and passengers through hub airports.

Achieving greater efficiency and timeliness can be a real challenge, given the interconnected nature of the international airways and the antiquated state of air traffic control systems. The U.S. Federal Aviation Administration is slowly rolling out its Next-Gen air traffic control system that relies on satellite-based navigation and digital communications. It will eventually replace the radar-based navigation and radio communications to accommodate high traffic levels, reduce fuel consumption, and improve safety.[22]

Another ongoing issue is the push for greater security in the transport of international cargo by air. Airports must work with airlines and freight forwarders to support the provision of the 9/11 Commission Act that requires all cargo transported on a passenger aircraft to be screened for explosives as of August 1, 2010. Security agencies and airports around the world must constantly work to improve passenger screening technologies, control access to at-risk areas, and update processes to stay ahead of evolving threats posed by skillful and adaptive enemies.[23]

Customs Clearance[24]

When cargo reaches its destination country, it must be cleared through Customs. Each country's regulations and process may be unique, so it is important to fully understand the process. Depending on the product, country of origin, and other relevant issues, theCustoms entry and clearance process can be complex. Many companies rely upon the expertise of Customs brokers to avoid the many pitfalls of Customs clearance. Figure 11-8 and the accompanying discussion provide a brief overview of the U.S. clearance process.

FIGURE 11-8 Customs Clearance Process

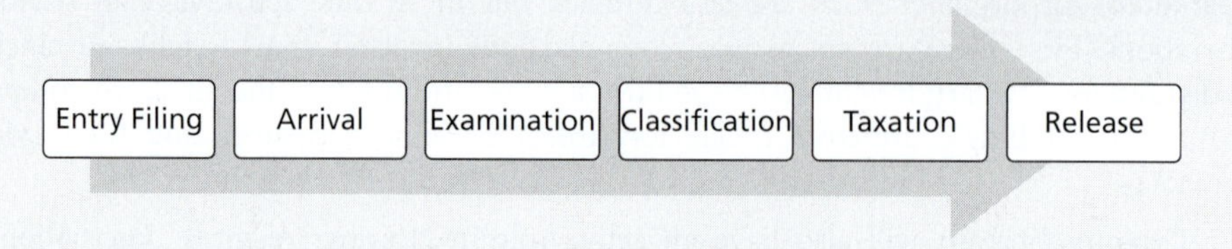

In the United States, the importer of record will file entry documents for the goods with the port director at the goods' port of entry. Imported goods do not legally enter the country until after the shipment has arrived within the port of entry, delivery of the merchandise has been authorized by U.S. Customs, and estimated duties have been paid. It is the importer of record's responsibility to arrange for examination and release of the goods.

Entry Filing Entering merchandise is a two-part process consisting of (1) filing the documents necessary to determine whether merchandise may be released from CBP custody, and (2) filing the documents that contain information for duty assessment and statistical purposes. To streamline the process, key documents should be filed 7 to 10 days prior to the physical arrival of the goods. These documents include the CBP entry summary, commercial invoice or pro forma invoice, packing lists, shipping documents, and related forms.

The entry must be accompanied by evidence that a bond has been posted with CBP. The customs bond is a form of insurance required by CBP to protect the Treasury in case an importer defaults on debts related to duties, taxes, and penalties that may accrue. Bonds may be posted in cash, secured through a surety company, or provided by a Customs broker.

Arrival As the goods arrive at the seaport or airport, CBP is notified of arrival and unloading. Carriers can apply for release of the goods upon arrival. If the application is approved, the shipment will be released expeditiously after it arrives at the port. This process is useful for time-sensitive products, perishable goods, and tariff quota merchandise.

Examination Following presentation of the entry documents and arrival of the shipment, it may be examined by CBP or the examination may be waived. Reasons for examining the goods and documents include determining: the value of the goods for Customs purposes and their dutiable status, whether the goods are properly labeled with their country of origin or other required markings, whether the shipment contains prohibited articles or illegal contraband, and whether the goods match the invoice. If no legal or regulatory violations have occurred, the clearance process continues. If problems are found, the shipment can be held pending correction, exported, or destroyed.

Classification All goods imported into the United States are subject to duty or duty-free entry in accordance with their classification in the Harmonized Tariff Schedule (HTS) of the United States. This classification is based on the name, use, and/or the material used in the construction of a good. Related duty rates are based on product classification, quantity, and country of origin. Access to the most current HTS is available from the U.S. International Trade Commission website (http://hts.usitc.gov/).

Taxation A **duty** is the tax that an importer must pay in order to bring goods into the country. When goods are dutiable, ad valorem, specific, or compound rates may be assessed. An ad valorem rate, the type of rate most often applied, is a percentage of the value of the merchandise. For example, a 5 percent ad valorem duty on a $50,000 shipment is $2,500.

Import duties vary by product and are driven by the commodity being imported, its declared value, its country of origin, and other factors like anti-dumping legislation and quota controls. Import duty values can be as low as zero for favored trading partner countries like Canada and Mexico or as high as 100 percent (or more) of the product's declared value.

Release After the clearance requirements are completed and CBP has accepted the rate and amount of duty ascertained, the entry is considered to be liquidated. The goods can be released to the importer for onward domestic delivery of the goods.

In some situations, the importer may wish to postpone release of the goods. The goods are placed in a CBP **bonded warehouse** under a warehouse entry. The goods may remain in the bonded warehouse up to five years from the date of importation. There, under CPB supervision, the goods may be cleaned, sorted, repacked, or improved (though no manufacturing can take place). At any time during this five-year period, warehoused goods may be re-exported without paying duty, or they may be withdrawn for consumption upon paying duty at the duty rate in effect on the date of withdrawal. Perishable goods, explosive substances, or prohibited importations may not be placed in a bonded warehouse.

Another option for postponing release of goods is through the use of a **Foreign Trade Zone** (FTZ). FTZs are sites within the United States (in or near a U.S. Customs port of entry) where foreign and domestic goods are held without time limit until they are ready to be released into international commerce. Merchandise may enter a FTZ without a formal CBP entry or the payment of Customs duties or government excise taxes. If the final product is imported, duties are not paid until the goods are released into the U.S. market. Items that are processed in FTZs and then re-exported are charged no duties. While in the FTZ, goods may be assembled, repaired, tested, repackaged, cleaned, or combined with other products.

Facilitating Role of Brokers Customs brokers are private individuals or firms licensed by the CBP to act as agents for importers. Brokers are experts at the entry process and, for a fee, help importers avoid Customs clearance pitfalls that delay shipments and increase costs. Brokers prepare and file the necessary Customs entry documents, arrange for the payment of duties, and speed the release of the goods in CBP custody. Other key duties include coordination of inland and ocean transportation, dockside inspection of cargo, and other roles requested by the importer.

SUMMARY

- Global transportation can be very challenging as it involves long distance flows of product across multiple borders using multiple modes and carriers. This creates disruption, delay, and damage risks.
- When moving cargo internationally, direct exporter to importer moves are used for short-distance, cross-border movements by truck or rail. Indirect moves via ocean or air are used for intercontinental cargo movements.
- Intermodal transportation—the use of two or more modes of transportation in moving a shipment from origin to destination—is widely used to improve accessibility and cost efficiency of global transport.
- Intermodal freight is either containerized or requires transloading. The vast majority of finished goods move in containers due to their enhanced safety, handling speed, and service availability.
- Global transportation may subject freight to a variety of damage risks. It is critical to protect products as they are packed in shipping cartons and to protect the cartons when they are packed in the shipping container.
- Exporters and importers must be prepared to comply with a wide variety of government regulations aimed at transportation safety, environmental impact reduction, and security.
- Ocean carriers have a huge role in global transport, moving 60 percent of trade value.
- Ocean transport customers can choose between liner service and charter service, based on their needs. A variety of vessel can carry an endless array of commodities.
- International air cargo transportation is a critical mode for time-sensitive, high-value freight. Over 35 percent of trade value moves via air.
- International air cargo moves on air freighters and passenger planes. The rates are based on weight or space utilization (dim weight), whichever is higher.
- A variety of 3PL service providers—international freight forwarders, customs brokers, NVOCCs, and export packers—help exporters and importers move international freight quickly and efficiently.
- Seaports and airports are critical links in the global supply chain, providing the infrastructure, equipment, and labor needed to efficiently load, unload, and transfer freight between carriers.
- When cargo reaches the destination country, it must receive government approval to enter the country and travel to the final destination. Customs clearance involves entry, arrival, examination, classification, taxation, and release.

STUDY QUESTIONS

1. How does direct service differ from indirect service in global transportation? When is it advantageous to use each type?
2. What are the benefits and drawbacks of intermodal transportation for international freight?
3. What combination of intermodal services would be most beneficial for the following products?
   a. Lumber moving from British Columbia, Canada to London, England

b. Seedless grapes moving from Valparaiso, Chile to Phoenix, Arizona

c. iPhones moving from Zhengzhou, China to Johannesburg, South Africa

4. If you need to move two TEUs of Adidas footwear from the factory in Vung Tau, Vietnam to the European distribution center in Antwerp, Belgium, what route options should be considered? Which would you choose?

5. If you are moving international cargo to the United States, what security issues and regulations would impact your operations? How will you comply with these requirements?

6. What are the major trends and issues in ocean transportation? How does this impact global supply chain operations?

7. How have the pricing activities of ocean carriers changed?

8. Given the high cost of international air freight service, why would companies choose this mode of transportation?

9. How are air cargo rates calculated? Calculate the cost of international air transportation for the following shipment: 200 cartons of fine jewelry weighing a total of 2,500 pounds. The carton dimensions are 18 inches by 12 inches by 12 inches (L × W × H). The freight rate is $10.25 per pound.

10. What value do third party logistics companies bring to global transportation execution? Discuss the roles of

    a. International freight forwarders

    b. NVOCCs

    c. Customs brokers

11. What roles do airports and seaports play in global transportation? How does cargo flow through these facilities?

12. Identify and briefly describe the six steps involved in the CBP Customs clearance process. What can individual companies do to streamline this process?

NOTES

1. Bureau of Transportation Statistics, *North American Transborder Freight Data*, retrieved December 9, 2014, from http://www.bts.gov/programs/international/transborder/TBDR_QA.html.

2. Pierre A. David, *International Logistics: The Management of International Trade Operations*, Berea, Ohio: Cicero Books, 2013, p. 423.

3. International Association of Ports and Harbors, *World Container Traffic Data*, retrieved December 10, 2014, from http://www.iaphworldports.org/LinkClick.aspx?fileticket=PMewveDCUUg%3d&tabid=4879.

4. Department for Transport, *Policy: Providing Effective Regulation of Freight Transportation*, retrieved December 10, 2014, from https://www.gov.uk/government/policies/providing-effective-regulation-of-freight-transport.

5. United State Department of Transportation, *About Us*, retrieved December 10, 2014, from http://www.dot.gov/mission/about-us.

6. United Nations Conference on Trade and Development, *Review of Maritime Transport 2013*, retrieved December 10, 2014, from http://unctad.org/en/pages/PublicationWebflyer.aspx?publicationid=753.

7. European Maritime Safety Agency, *The World Merchant Fleet—Statistics from Equasis*, retrieved December 9, 2014, from http://emsa.europa.eu/implementation-tasks/equasis-a-statistics/items.html?cid=95&id=472.

8. Alan Tovey, "A Quarter of a Mile Long and Heading for the UK—the World's Largest Ship," *The Telegraph*, December 9, 2014, retrieved December 10, 2014, from http://www.telegraph.co.uk/finance/newsbysector/transport/11281292/A-quarter-of-a-mile-long-and-heading-for-the-UK-the-worlds-largest-ship.html.

9. Maersk Line, "Freight Shipping Rates and Container Costs," retrieved December 10, 2014, from http://www.maerskline.com/en-ug/shipping-services/rates-and-pricing.

10. Noel Hacegaba, *Big Ships, Big Challenges: The Impact of Mega Container Vessels on U.S. Port Authorities*, June 30, 2014, retrieved December 11, 2014, from http://www.polb.com/civica/filebank/blobdload.asp?BlobID=12230.

11. MAREX, "Ocean Three vs. Other Mega-alliances," *The Maritime Executive*, September 14, 2014, retrieved December 10, 2014, from http://www.maritime-executive.com/article/Ocean-Three-vs-Other-Megaalliances-2014-09-15

12. Ivan Latanision, "The Ocean Shipping Evolution: Key Priorities for Ocean Transport Logistics," JOC.com, June 16, 2014, retrieved December 11, 2014, from http://www.joc.com/maritime-news/international-freight-shipping/ocean-shipping-evolution-key-priorities-ocean-transport-logistics_20140616.html.

13. International Air Transport Association, *The Air Cargo Tariff and Rules*, retrieved December 12, 2014, from http://www.iata.org/publications/Pages/air-cargo-tariff.aspx.

14. Boeing, *Air Cargo Long Term Forecast*, retrieved December 12, 2014, from http://www.boeing.com/boeing/commercial/cargo/01_03.page?.

15. Airbus, *Global Market Forecast: Flying on Demand 2014-2033*, retrieved December 12, 2014, from http://www.airbus.com/company/market/gmf2014/.

16. Adina Solomon, "IATA Economist Analyzes Recent Cargo Trends," *Air Cargo World*, May 6, 2014.

17. Zacks Equity Research, *Railroad Industry Poised for Improvement*, August 19, 2014, retrieved December 12, 2014, from http://www.zacks.com/commentary/33989/railroad-industry-poised-for-improvement.

18. Aidan Grange, "Port Congestion Looms Large Again," *Port Finance International*, September 1, 2014, retrieved December 12, 2014, from http://portfinanceinternational.com/features/item/1694-port-congestion-looms-large-again-by-aidan-grange.

19. JOC.com, *U.S. West Coast Labor Negotiations: Frequently Asked Questions*, retrieved December 12, 2014, from http://www.joc.com/port-news/longshoreman-labor/international-longshore-and-warehouse-union/us-west-coast-labor-negotiations-frequently-asked-questions.

20. Federal Aviation Administration, *Airport Categories*, retrieved December 12, 2014, from http://www.faa.gov/airports/planning_capacity/passenger_allcargo_stats/categories/.

21. John Gardiner, Ian Humphreys, and Stephen Ison, "Freight Operators Choice of Airports: A Three-Stage Process," *Transport Reviews*, Vol. 25, No. 1 (January, 2005), pp. 85–102.

22. Joan Lowy, "Air Traffic Control Modernization Hits Turbulence," Associated Press, October 31, 2013, retrieved December 13, 2014, from http://bigstory.ap.org/article/air-traffic-control-modernization-hits-turbulence-0.

23. House Committee on Homeland Security, *Passenger and Cargo Aviation Security*, retrieved December 13, 2014, from http://homeland.house.gov/issue/passenger-and-cargo-aviation-security.

24. This section is based upon materials from U.S. Customs and Border Protection. A detailed discussion of the process can be found at U.S. Customs and Border Protection, *Basic Importing and Exporting*, retrieved December 13, 2014, from http://www.cbp.gov/trade/basic-import-export.

CASE 11-1

As the Blade Turns

Revolving Wings (RW) is a Kalamazoo, Michigan, manufacturer of equipment for the renewable energy sector. The company has a strong domestic market for their fiber-glass composite wind turbine blades, thanks to federal tax breaks offered to power companies. RW has some excess plant capacity, thanks to a recent expansion and is investigating the opportunity to enter the export market. Demand for turbine blades is especially strong in India, where there is a strong commitment to renewable energy but a shortage of critical parts to meet the growing need for power generating capacity.

During its annual executive retreat, exporting is a major topic of discussion. After a presentation by the business development team and a similar evaluation by an industry analyst, RW's CEO sees the light. He quickly becomes a strong proponent of selling wind turbine blades to a power company near Bangalore, India. "Now all we have to do is figure out how to get the blades there quickly and without damage," says the CEO. "Darren, get your team on this one. I want some solid answers."

Darren Helm, RW's transportation director, knows this is a big opportunity for the company but it comes with tremendous challenges. Picking the right mode, finding ports that can handle the blades safely, and routing the freight are just a few of the issues that keep Helm awake the night after the CEO tagged him to lead the "export to India" project.

At his next staff meeting, Helm reminds his team: "These blades can be up to 148 feet long and weigh 12 tons. We have to first get them from the plant to the point of export. That's not easy, since we need to plan routes to avoid urban rush hours, sharp curves, narrow lanes, and weight-limited bridges."

"On top of those usual challenges, we have to find a high-quality international carrier to get the blades to India," Helm adds. "And don't forget the port challenges and final delivery to Bangalore."

Turning to you, Helm says: "Get me some answers fast! We need a plan of action for the CEO by Friday."

CASE QUESTIONS

1. What are the major problems and pitfalls that RW faces as it tries to go global with its product line?
2. What mode(s) of transportation would you recommend to Helm as most appropriate for moving the turbine blades domestically and internationally?
3. How would you route shipments of turbine blades from Kalamazoo to Bangalore? Why?
4. What role will ports play in the flow of turbine blades from the United States to India?

CASE 11-2

Get Me Those T-Shirts

With its conference championship win on November 15th, tiny Faber College in Cottage Grove, Oregon, has clinched its first ever berth in the collegiate lacrosse championship. Kent Dorfman, intern for the local bookstore, has been tasked with sourcing Faber College lacrosse t-shirts for the crazed fans before the big game on January 1st. His domestic search found only one supplier with t-shirts in the perfect shade of Faber blue. However, the delivered cost per t-shirt is $28, leaving no room for a markup by the bookstore.

Robert Hoover, the manager suggests that Dorfman look into international sources for the shirts. Hoover reminds Dorfman that the shirts must be on the shelf before the team leaves town on December 26th. So, Dorfman goes to work and identifies three sources.

Potential Suppliers

Source	T-Shirts Ilimitado	Sérgrein Shirts	Ropa Deportiva
Location	Nuevo Laredo, Mexico	Reykjavik, Iceland	Havana, Cuba
T-Shirt Materials	Polyester/Elastine	Polyester/Elastine	Cotton
T-Shirt Cost per dozen	2,500 MXN	16,300 ISK	87 CUC
Delivery Cost per dozen	180 MXN	2,200 ISK	9 CUC

Dorfman takes his work to Hoover who wants the information converted into U.S. dollars for comparison. A quick Internet search for exchange rates produces the following:

Exchange Rates

Country	Mexico	Iceland	Cuba
Exchange Rate	14.76 MXN = 1 USD	123.51 ISK = 1 USD	1 CUC = 1 USD

Hoover also asked about the issue of import duties, so Dorfman did some additional investigation. His Internet search revealed that there may be duties involved for these t-shirts. In the U.S. Harmonized Tariff Schedule there's a general rate of duty charged to goods coming from countries with normal U.S. trade relationship, a special rate of duty that gives preference to countries with special trade agreements, and a punitive rate of duty for a few countries that do not have normal U.S. trade relationships.

Harmonized Tariff Schedule

Heading/ Subheading	Stat. Suffix	Article Description	Unit of Quantity	Rates of Duty 1 General	Rates of Duty 1 Special	Rates of Duty 2
6109		T-shirts, singlets, tank tops, and similar garments....				
6109.10.00	07	Of cotton	Doz.	16.5%	Free (BH, CA, JO, MX)	90%
6109.90.10	07	Of man-made fibers	Doz.	32%	Free (BH, CA, JO, MX)	90%

With the additional information in hand, Dorfman feels that he can make an informed decision that may just help him land a full-time job at the bookstore after graduation.

CASE QUESTIONS

1. What are the individual costs per dozen for the Mexican supplier—t-shirts, delivery, and duties? What is the total cost per dozen?
2. What are the individual costs per dozen for the Icelandic supplier—t-shirts, delivery, and duties? What is the total cost per dozen?
3. What are the individual costs per dozen for the Cuban supplier—t-shirts, delivery, and duties? What is the total cost per dozen?
4. Which source should Dorfman use? Why?

CHAPTER

12 THIRD PARTY LOGISTICS

Learning Objectives

After reading this chapter, you should be able to do the following:

- Understand the concept of third party logistics and its role in the movement of goods
- Identify the different types of third party logistics service providers
- Describe the four types of transportation activities that are outsourced
- Discuss the reasons why companies seek integrated third party logistics services
- Understand the size and scope of the third party logistics market
- Evaluate the reasons for outsourcing and the results achieved
- Summarize the process for outsourcing transportation and logistics activities
- Appreciate the current challenges and competitive issues in the third party logistics industry
- Recognize the importance of information technology in managing outsourced activities

TRANSPORTATION PROFILE

Key Criteria for Evaluating Potential 3PL Providers

Selection of a third party logistics service provider (3PL) should not be a quick decision. You must take the time to evaluate and choose a partner that is capable of providing excellent service, driving innovation, and creating value for your supply chains. A weak selection process runs the risk of establishing a relationship with an ineffective, inconsistent 3PL service provider.

You must properly vet each potential service provider's cost, capacity, coverage, and capabilities to ensure that they can consistently meet your requirements. This vetting process includes a number of important considerations and related questions:

1. Expertise. Does the 3PL have a deep talent pool with industry-specific supply chain knowledge?
2. Integrated services. Does the provider offer multiple logistics capabilities–fulfillment, inventory management, multimodal delivery, and so on?
3. Global coverage. Does the 3PL conduct operations in your worldwide markets?
4. Performance excellence. Does the 3PL have an established and verifiable track record of highly effective and efficient service?
5. Scalability. Does the 3PL have the flexibility to handle your seasonal demand patterns, geographic expansion, and new fulfillment channels?
6. Technological innovation. Does the 3PL deploy integrated planning and execution tools that meet your needs for shipment visibility, process optimization, and remote data access?
7. Financial stability. Does the 3PL conduct its business in a profitable manner and maintain a reasonable debt load?

This level of due diligence in the 3PL evaluation and selection process is essential for achieving long-range success. A well-chosen 3PL service provider will provide tangible and readily measurable benefits of transportation cost reductions, inventory cost reductions, and logistics fixed asset reductions, as well as improvements in order fill rate, accuracy, and timeliness. Given these impacts you cannot afford to make poor 3PL selection decisions.

Sources: C. John Langley and Capgemini, *2015 Third Party Logistics Study: The State of Logistics Outsourcing*, retrieved November 24, 2014, from http://www.3plstudy.com/; and Jamie Wyatt, "Evaluating Potential 3PL Logistics Providers and What You Should Be Looking For," *Supply Chain 24/7*, May 19, 2013, retrieved November 24, 2014, from http://www.supplychain247.com/article/evaluating_potential_3pl_logistics_providers_and_what_you_should_be_looking.

Introduction

Outsourcing continues to grow in the second decade of the 21st century. Reliance on external experts for non-core services and capabilities is commonplace as few organizations can afford to manage all business activities in-house. Hence, it is common to shift information technology (IT) processes to an external service provider that manages the systems, software, and equipment. This allows the company to focus on using the technology to operate the business rather than having to manage all the technical issues and challenges. Similarly, external experts are frequently used for accounting, payroll and tax preparation, advertising, human resources benefits administration, and numerous other activities. Some companies outsource their production to contract manufacturers located around the world.

Transportation is another activity that is widely outsourced to external experts. Global companies like COSCO (China Ocean Shipping Company), Deutsche Post (owner of Exel and DHL), FedEx, Maersk Line, and UPS provide a wide variety of transportation and logistics services to individuals and companies around the world. These third party logistics service providers (3PLs) are experts in the management and flow of freight, allowing customers to focus their resources on other activities. Some of these larger organizations provide a one-stop shopping solution where customers can purchase all their transportation service needs, regardless of mode or geographic requirements.

Given the financial and service impact of transportation on a company's success, developing an effective transportation outsourcing strategy is critical. As the Transportation Profile suggests, you should not just hire the first 3PL that comes to the door. It is imperative to find a 3PL with a track record of providing quality transportation management and services that support execution excellence. How to accomplish this is the goal of this chapter. We will discuss the general structure of the 3PL industry, customer characteristics, and relationship options. Specific issues related to establishing and managing 3PL relationships will be addressed, followed by a discussion of current and future 3PL industry issues. Throughout the chapter, you will gain an understanding of the key benefits and challenges of outsourcing transportation requirements.

Industry Overview

If you were to conduct an Internet search for a definition of *third party logistics* or *3PL*, the responses would be numerous and varied. These explanations range from simple and arbitrary to extensive and specific. Here are a few examples:

EFT (eyefortransport): an organization that manages and executes a particular logistics function, using its own assets and resources, on behalf of another company.[1]

BusinessDictionary.com: arrangement in which a firm with long and varied supply chains outsources its logistical operations to one or more specialist firms, the third party logistics providers.[2]

Council of Supply Chain Management Professionals: outsourcing all or much of a company's logistics operations to a specialized company. The term *3PL* was first used in the early 1970s to identify **intermodal marketing companies** (IMCs) in transportation contracts. Up to that point, contracts for transportation had featured only two parties, the shipper and the carrier. When IMCs entered the picture—as **intermediaries** that accepted shipments from the shippers and tendered them to the rail carriers—they became the third party to the contract, the 3PL. Definitions have broadened to the point where these days, every company that offers some kind of logistics service for hire calls itself a 3PL. Preferably, these services are integrated, or "bundled," together by the provider. Services they provide are transportation, warehousing, cross-docking, inventory management, packaging, and freight forwarding. In 2008, legislation passed declaring that the legal definition of a 3PL is "A person who solely receives, holds, or otherwise transports a consumer product in the ordinary course of business but who does not take title to the product."[3]

Pulling the key points from these definitions, a 3PL firm may be defined as "an external supplier that performs or manages the performance of all or part of a company's logistics functions."[4] This definition is purposely broad and is intended to encompass

TABLE 12-1 Role of Outsourced Logistics Providers

ROLE	DESCRIPTION
1PL	Shipper or consignee
2PL	Individual, asset-based provider of logistics services
3PL	Firm that manages and/or provides multiple logistics services for use by customers
4PL	Firm that provides broader scope of services to help manage elements of supply chain
5PL	Broader range of companies that aggregate demands of 3PLs into bulk volumes to negotiate better rates with airlines and shipping companies
LSP	Logistics Service Provider—actually can refer to any or all of the above

Source: Based on C. John Langley Jr., Ph.D., Penn State University.

suppliers of services such as inventory management, warehousing, distribution, financial services, and transportation. This chapter will focus on the transportation aspects of the 3PL industry, though it is important to remember that transportation services provided by a 3PL must be well integrated with the customer's other logistical activities. The transportation focused 3PLs must also provide solutions to logistics challenges and supply chain problems.

Table 12-1 highlights the terminology related to the use and provision of logistics services. As you can see, while the term *1PL* relates to the shipper or consignee, *2PL* relates to the asset-based provider of logistics services. Then, 3PL includes those provider organizations that manages or provides multiple logistics services for use by customers. 4PL broadens the perspective to reflect the provision of a broader scope of services (for example, managing multiple 3PLs; advanced IT services; strategic consultancies; and "control tower"), and 5PL suggests the concept of further aggregating demand for logistics services in the interest of creating cost efficiencies. Your understanding of these concepts will improve as you become familiar with the content of this chapter.

Types of 3PL Providers

Just as there are many ways to define third party logistics, there are many ways to categorize the service providers. Figure 12-1 identifies the prominent types of logistics service providers and shows how they differ in terms of service offerings, asset intensity, and geographic diversity. For example, while asset-intensive ocean liners and railroads have more limited service offerings and geographic diversity, many 3PLs are significantly less asset intensive, more geographically diverse, and provide a broader range of service offerings. Also identified on the right side of this figure are several competitive threats that are faced to some extent by these various types of providers.

One very fundamental distinguishing feature of logistics service providers is the resources that they use to fulfill customer requirements. 3PLs with tangible equipment and facilities are called **asset-based providers**. In contrast, 3PLs that leverage the resources of other companies are called **non-asset based providers**. A few details on each of these types are included below.

Asset-Based Providers When a 3PL owns many or all of the assets necessary to run its customers' transportation and logistics activities, it is known as an asset-based provider.

FIGURE 12-1 Logistics Service Providers

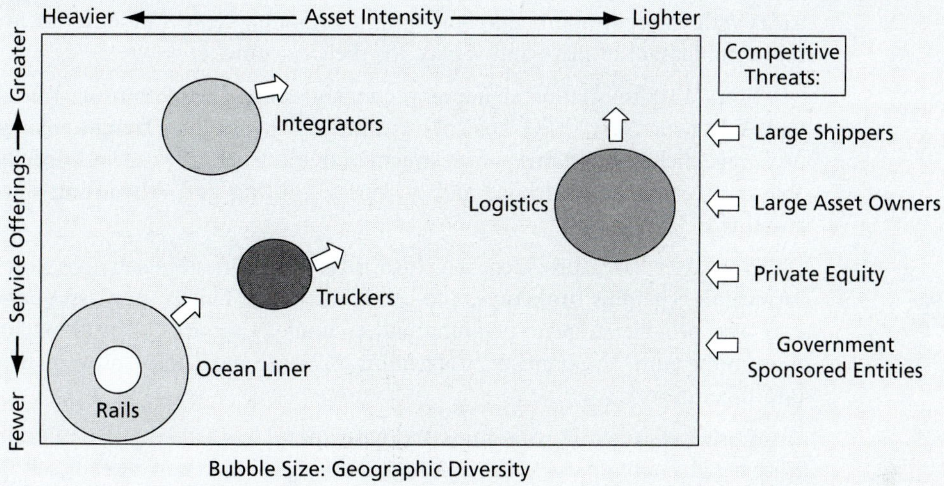

Sources: MergeGlobal, Containerization Internation, Company Data, Robert W. Baird & Co.estimates.

This category includes companies that own truck fleets, ocean vessels, aircraft, terminals and warehouses, material handling equipment, technology systems, and/or other resources. An asset-based provider typically has its own labor force to perform the customers' work and a management team to oversee the day-to-day operations. Having these internal resources allows the 3PL to leverage internal strengths and infrastructures to provide direct, immediate solutions.

This type of 3PL includes widely known companies such as UPS, J.B. Hunt, Exel, Ryder, and FedEx. We are familiar with them because we see their vehicles on the road and pass by their facilities. FedEx Corporation, for example, has a network of company-owned facilities that are linked by FedEx vehicles and aircraft. Their various operating divisions—FedEx Express, FedEx Freight, FedEx Custom Critical, and so forth—are capable of moving shipments ranging from single packages to full truckloads, as well as managing customers' inventory and order fulfillment needs from FedEx-owned distribution centers.

Many customers choose to work with asset-based providers because they have readily available **capacity**, permanent employees, and direct control of the customers' freight. They prefer to work with a single 3PL who will take total responsibility for the outsourced activity and assume accountability if problems occur. Customers can also maintain greater visibility of outsourced activities and inventory if they are handled by a technology savvy asset-based provider who performs all activities internally rather than handing them off to other companies.

The primary concern with asset-based providers is the potential for bias toward use of their internal resources. The argument is that these companies have made significant investments in physical assets and are tethered to those assets when developing solutions for customers. This internal focus may not always generate the most flexible solutions or produce the most cost-efficient transportation and logistics services for the customers.

Non-Asset Based Providers When a 3PL contracts with other firms to provide transportation and logistics services rather than owning the required equipment and facilities, it is called a non-asset based provider. This type of provider acts as a service integrator and is not restricted to using any particular warehouse or transportation company in providing services to its customers. Non-asset based providers offer expertise in negotiating contracts with transportation companies and distribution centers in an effort to achieve the best combination of price and service for their customers.

From a transportation standpoint, companies like C.H. Robinson, Kuehne + Nagel, CEVA Logistics, and XPO Logistics are heavily involved in **freight management** and brokerage, helping customers with freight activities such as securing capacity at reasonable costs, scheduling pickups and deliveries, **routing and scheduling** shipments, and auditing freight bills.

Non-asset based providers may also focus on international freight flows via freight forwarding, **customs brokerage**, and related activities. Finally, non-asset based providers may also provide strategic planning and technology services. Consulting firms such as Accenture, Bain & Company, Capgemini, KPMG, and some software firms may fall into this category.

Customers typically view non-asset based providers as being more flexible than their asset-based counterparts. The common thinking is that non-asset based 3PLs can be unbiased in their decision making as they are not limited to an internal infrastructure of assets. Because they are not restricted to using any particular transportation company or set of facilities to serve customers, they are free to objectively choose the best set of service providers and create innovative solutions for customers. This can lead to tailored services and lower overall costs for the customer.

There are also concerns with non-asset based providers. First, these companies do not have significant internal capability to handle customers' requirements. This can be a problem during times of economic expansion when there may be limited availability of purchased transportation alternatives. Also, there are more moving parts and relationships to manage when a non-asset based provider uses external service providers on behalf of their customers, and non-asset based providers need to make sure that their cost of purchased transportation services may align with how they price their services to their clients and customers. Last, it is imperative to have strong IT capabilities to maintain control and visibility of customers' freight that is dispersed among a variety of transportation and warehousing companies.

Another method for distinguishing 3PLs is by the primary services provided. While many 3PLs promote themselves as **integrated service providers** with a comprehensive range of logistical capabilities, most have their origins and greatest level of expertise in a specific logistics activity. Hence, the easiest way to categorize these service providers is on the basis of their foundation service offerings. 3PLs are typically categorized as being transportation-, distribution-, forwarder-, financial-, or information-based firms. Each of these is discussed briefly in the following paragraphs.

Transportation Based These 3PLs trace their origins to freight movement via truck, rail, air, or other modes of transportation. As customer requirements expanded, these transportation companies developed 3PL subsidiaries or major divisions to provide a broader set of capabilities to serve the marketplace. Not only do these organizations move freight, they may also manage transportation operations on behalf of customers, provide **dedicated contract carriage**, operate fulfillment centers, and develop logistics solutions, among other services.

Transportation company–based 3PL services include UPS Supply Chain Solutions, FedEx Trade Networks, Schneider Logistics Services, Damco (Maersk Group), and

BNSF Logistics. Some of the services provided by these 3PLs leverage the transportation assets of their parent companies, while others rely upon the assets of other companies. In all instances, these firms extend beyond the transportation activity to provide a more comprehensive set of logistics offerings.

Distribution Based These 3PL suppliers originated from the public or contract warehousing business and have expanded into a broader range of logistics services. Based on their traditional orientation, these types of organizations are heavily involved in logistics activities such as inventory management, warehousing, and order fulfillment. Some have added transportation services to assist customers with the coordination, optimization, and execution of shipments via all modes. The combination of distribution and transportation capabilities creates a one-stop integrated logistics service offering so that customers have the option of working with a single 3PL.

Distribution-based 3PLs range from single facility operators to global organizations with strategically located operations centers. Major players include Exel, DSC Logistics, Ozburn-Hessey Logistics, Saddle Creek, and UTi Worldwide. This category also includes a number of 3PL firms that have emerged from larger corporate logistics organizations. For example, Neovia Logistics Services was developed by Caterpillar Inc. and Intral Corporation was created when The Gillette Company spun off its in-house import/export logistics department in an effort to focus on core competencies, increase efficiencies and recognize bottom-line savings.

These providers have significant experience in managing the logistics operations of the parent firm and, as a result, prove to be very capable providers of such services to external customers. Though it has not technically spun off its logistics expertise into a standalone organization, Amazon.com is rapidly developing a variety of 3PL-like fulfillment and transportation services. The company's capabilities are reviewed in the On the Line feature.

Forwarder Based This group of 3PLs includes **freight forwarders**, brokers, and agents that primary facilitate the flow of goods on behalf of customers. Though these companies do not own equipment, they arrange transportation services for LTL (less-than-truckload) shipments, air cargo, and ocean freight, as well as providing other transportation related services. Many are engaged in the support of international freight movement, booking cargo space with carriers, arranging freight movement to and from carrier facilities, preparing and processing documentation, and performing related activities.

Some of these brokerage-based organizations, such as C.H. Robinson Worldwide Inc., Hub Group Inc., and Kuehne + Nagel Inc. have extended their primary roles into a broader range of 3PL services. Others are focusing on consolidating assets in the highly fragmented freight brokerage space. This merger and acquisition activity is driven by the goal of increasing profitability through economies of scale. For example, XPO Logistics made 13 acquisitions between 2011 and 2014. The company expects to spend $2.75 billion on acquisitions over the next several years.[5]

Financial Based This category of 3PL providers helps customers with monetary issues and financial flows in the supply chain. Their traditional roles include **freight rating**, freight payment, **freight bill auditing**, and accounting services. Some of the financial-based 3PLs have added information systems tools to provide freight visibility (such as **tracking and tracing** capabilities) and assist customers with electronic payment, carrier compliance reporting, and freight claims management.

ON THE LINE

Amazon.com: More than an Online Retailer?

When the vast majority of people think of Amazon.com, they focus on online shopping for books, technology products, and millions of other goods. They may also think of the Amazon Prime program that features two-day delivery service. Yet, few think twice about the scope of Amazon's fulfillment and delivery capabilities when in fact, some experts suggest that Amazon is morphing into a 3PL.

This is not as far-fetched as you might imagine. First and foremost, the company has a vast global distribution network with 145 distribution centers that not only fulfill Amazon orders but the orders of other companies as well. They have been doing this since 2006 through the Fulfillment by Amazon (FBA) program. According to the company's website, "Amazon has created one of the most advanced fulfillment networks in the world, and your business can benefit from our expertise. You store your products in Amazon's fulfillment centers, and we pick, pack, ship, and provide customer service for these products."

Additionally, Amazon has been developing transportation capabilities to support its various initiatives. In the race to provide same-day delivery, Amazon allows customers to choose from millions of items, order by noon and receive them by 9 p.m. in select cities. The service is offered seven days a week. The company is also establishing a delivery network in major cities to support the Amazon Fresh grocery business. Finally, the company made a major public relations splash with its announcement and demo of Amazon Prime Air, a delivery system that promises to get packages into customers' hands in 30 minutes or less using unmanned aerial vehicles (drones). It is conceivable that transportation services, when fully established, will be available to FBA clients.

A final example of Amazon's foray into the 3PL world is its Vendor Flex program that uses shared fulfillment facilities. By piggybacking on the warehouses and distribution networks of companies like Procter & Gamble and Kimberly Clark, Amazon is able to reduce its own costs of moving and storing goods, better compete on price with major retailers, and cut the time it takes to get items to doorsteps. This is a major opportunity for manufacturers who have limited online sales experience.

Fulfillment services plus transportation capabilities plus supply chain collaboration certainly looks like the hallmarks of a 3PL. Will Amazon eventually spin-off their capabilities into a standalone 3PL? Only Jeff Bezos knows for sure!

Sources: Robert C. Lieb and Kristen J. Lieb, "Is Amazon a 3PL?" *CSCMP's Supply Chain Quarterly*, Quarter 3, 2014; Sarah Perez, "With Newly Announced Expansions, Amazon's Same-Day Delivery Service Now Outpaces Competitors," *TechCrunch*, August 6, 2014, retrieved November 26, 2014, from http://techcrunch.com/2014/08/06/with-newly-announced-expansions-amazons-same-day-delivery-service-now-outpaces-competitors/; and Serena Ng, "Soap Opera: Amazon Moves in with P&G," *Wall Street Journal*, October 14, 2013.

Primary players among this category include Cass Information Systems, Inc., CT Logistics, U.S. Bank (Syncada), enVista, and TranzAct Technologies. In addition, companies like GE Capital (General Electric) and CIT Transportation Finance provide transportation equipment financing, leasing services, and asset tracking.

Information Based The Internet has provided an excellent platform for the growth of information-based 3PLs. These companies have digitized many activities that were previously performed manually or required the use of licensed software. Today, these information-based 3PLs provide online freight brokerage services as well as cargo planning, routing, and scheduling. They also offer companies access to **transportation management systems**, warehouse management systems, and performance management tools via the Internet on a per use basis. This software as a service capability allows customers to avoid the high cost of licensed software implementation, instead paying for access on a variable cost basis.

Though many information-based 3PLs have come and gone during the Internet era, a few strong players have emerged. Companies like Descartes Systems Group, Transplace, and MercuryGate are among the leaders in creating robust information tools and online capabilities for the coordination, optimization, and control of transportation and logistics activities. The emerging generation of transportation management systems from information-based 3PLs will empower shippers and 3PLs that want to better manage the transportation process—perhaps even blending their own private or dedicated fleets with third-party assets—to reduce costs and gain significantly greater supply chain visibility.[6]

3PL Services and Integration

As the preceding discussion indicates, there are many types of 3PL service providers offering a vast array of capabilities. Name any type of transportation or logistics requirement that a customer may have and there is a 3PL able to support it. These customer requirements range from strategic supply chain design to daily operations. Within the transportation function, 3PLs provide four primary types of services: freight movement, freight management, intermediary services, and specialty services. Figure 12-2 highlights key capabilities within each service type.

Most of the service offerings related to freight movement and freight management are discussed in detail by other chapters. However, you may not be familiar with some of the intermediary and special services offered by 3PLs to their customers. Each service option is briefly described below.

Surface Freight Forwarding Surface freight forwarders pick up, assemble, and consolidate shipments and then hire carriers to transport and deliver the consolidated shipments to the final destination. They match demand with capacity and help customers obtain economic rates for the consolidated shipments. From the perspective of the customer, freight forwarders act as the carrier, and, therefore, are liable to shippers for loss and damage to freight that occurs during transit.

FIGURE 12-2 3PL Primary Transportation Offerings

FREIGHT MOVEMENT	FREIGHT MANAGEMENT
• For hire carriage	• Carrier selection, routing, & scheduling
• Contract carriage	• Contract compliance
• Expedited service	• Performance analysis
• Time definite service	• Freight bill auditing and payment
• Intermodal service	• Transportation management systems
INTERMEDIARY SERVICES	**SPECIALTY SERVICES**
• Surface forwarding	• Dedicated contract carriage
• Air forwarding	• Drayage
• Freight brokerage	• Pool distribution
• Intermodal marketing	• Merge in transit
• Shippers associations	• Household good movement

Air Freight Forwarding Air freight forwarders consolidate small shipments for long-haul movement and distribution. They primarily use the services of major passenger and freight airlines for long-haul service. The air freight forwarder serves the shipping public with pickup service, a single bill of lading and freight bill, one-firm tracing, and delivery service.

Freight Brokerage Brokers function as middlemen between the shipper and the carrier much the same as a real estate broker does in the sale of property. A broker is an independent contractor paid to arrange transportation. The broker normally represents the carrier and seeks freight on their behalf to avoid moving empty equipment. They may also represent shippers seeking capacity on the spot market.

Intermodal Marketing Companies IMCs are intermediaries between shippers and railroads and are also known as consolidators or agents. They are facilitators or arrangers of rail transportation service. They assume little or no legal liability; the legal shipping arrangement is between the shipper and the railroad, not the agent. Freight charge payment usually is made to the IMC who, in turn, pays the long-haul carrier.

Shippers Associations These nonprofit transportation membership cooperatives arrange for the domestic or international shipment of members' cargo with motor carriers, railroads, ocean carriers, air carriers, and others. The association aggregates cargo and ships the collective membership cargo at favorable volume rates.[7]

Dedicated Contract Carriage 3PLs offering this hybrid private/for-hire arrangement serve as a customer's private fleet with a customized turnkey solution. Dedicated contract carriage includes the management of drivers, vehicles, maintenance services, route design, delivery, and administrative support for a fixed price. Companies gain the advantages of a private fleet without the direct responsibility of capitalizing and operating it.

Drayage These companies provide local transportation of containerized cargo. Drayage companies specialize in short-haul movement of intermodal containers from origin to ocean ports and rail yards and from these facilities to their ultimate destination. They are typically contracted by the rail or ocean carrier to provide these pickup and delivery services.

Pool Distribution As an alternative to direct LTL service, a 3PL may move a large quantity of product in bulk to a specific market or regional terminal. From there, the pooled freight is offloaded, sorted by customer, and then reloaded onto local delivery trucks for distribution to final destinations. Pool distribution can reduce transit times, maintain shipment integrity, reduce claim potential due to less handling, and generate cost discounts versus LTL rates.

Merge-In-transit A merge-in-transit system unites shipments from multiple suppliers at a specified merge point located close to the end customer. It avoids the need for traditional warehousing, in which orders are assembled from inventory in stock for shipment. Merge-in-transit provides a number of customer benefits, including the delivery of a single, consolidated shipment, reduced order cycle time, and lower transportation costs with less inventory in the system.

Last Mile Delivery The final leg of the transportation journey can be very expensive, accounting for up to 28 percent of total delivery costs.[8] It has become a significant challenge with the growth of e-commerce delivery of goods that consumers would normally purchase in-store and carry home. While UPS, FedEx, and postal services handle the bulk of these deliveries, they do not typically provide same-day delivery or handle large shipments like appliances and furniture. In response, a new breed of last mile service providers has emerged to cover the final dock-to-door or store-to-door delivery and provide value-added services such as inside delivery, product assembly, installation, and testing, and packaging removal. These last mile service providers represent the final opportunity to impress customers and provide a high quality delivery experience. Retailers like Macy's, eBay, and Amazon provide a wide array of last mile services including same-day delivery in an attempt to differentiate themselves from the competition.

While many 3PLs have expertise in different areas, leading 3PLs are pursuing two additional capabilities. First, they are developing integrated service offerings to accommodate customer desires for one-stop shopping with a single service provider. Second, they are expanding service territories to meet the requirements of increasingly global customers.

These two customer driven moves go hand in hand. As customers embrace global sourcing and distribution, their supply chains become more complex and challenging. In turn, they need the assistance of highly capable 3PLs to develop integrated, cross-functional global supply chains. Transportation expertise is not enough to capture the attention of these increasingly sophisticated customers. 3PLs must play an essential architect role in the design and execution of interconnected supply chain networks.[9] This requires strong IT tools, multimodal capabilities, and the ability to manage and streamline the flow of goods through the supply chain.

In response to the demand for integrated services, larger 3PLs (such as Deutsche Post, UPS, and FedEx) have embarked on an aggressive plan to expand and integrate their capabilities. Table 12-2 provides an example of this expansion, revealing how FedEx has acquired numerous companies since 1998. The company has leveraged the strength of its express delivery service to create a more diversified portfolio of global transportation, e-commerce, and business services. For example, FedEx SupplyChain executes solutions that leverage the FedEx shipping and information networks in commercial markets around the world. The division provides integrated services for customers with high-value products or complex supply chain requirements.

FedEx is not alone in the pursuit of integrated capabilities and global reach. Customers' increasing activity in global sourcing and distribution has driven 3PLs like Exel, CEVA Logistics, and Geodis Wilson to bolster their international resources through the creation of internal divisions, acquisition of smaller 3PLs, or the development of partner relationships with other 3PLs. They are building logistics expertise and well developed transportation networks to accommodate the growing volume of trade between key regions of the world.

Another option to address customers' global service requirements is to invest in strategically located transportation and distribution facilities. These assets can help an organization establish critical hubs, streamline flows, and support customer fulfillment needs. UPS has been very active in this regard, establishing a physical presence in Asia, Europe, and Latin America that allows the company to serve more than 200 countries and territories. The Global Perspective feature highlights the recently expanded UPS facility in Incheon, South Korea, that the company expects to facilitate trade growth between Korea and key markets around the world.

TABLE 12-2 FedEx Capability Expansion Timeline

YEAR	EVENT
1998	• Acquires Caliber System Inc. comprised of small-package carrier RPS, LTL carrier Viking Freight, Caliber Logistics, Caliber Technology, and Roberts Express.
1999	• Acquires air freight forwarder Caribbean Transportation Services.
2000	• Company is renamed FedEx Corporation. • Expanded service capabilities are divided into operating companies: FedEx Express, FedEx Ground, FedEx Global Logistics, FedEx Custom Critical, and FedEx Services. • FedEx Trade Networks is created with the acquisitions of Tower Group International and WorldTariff. • FedEx Supply Chain Services became part of FedEx Services.
2001	• Acquires LTL carrier American Freightways.
2002	• FedEx Freight is created with rebranding of Viking Freight and American Freightways.
2004	• Acquires Kinko's printing company.
2006	• Acquires LTL carrier Watkins Motor Lines.
2007	• Acquires international firms to enhance global capabilities: express company ANC (United Kingdom), Flying-Cargo Hungary Kft (Hungary), Prakash Air Freight Pvt. Ltd. (India), and DTW Group's fifty percent share of the FedEx-DTW International Priority express joint venture (China).
2011	• Acquires the logistics, distribution and express businesses of AFL Pvt. Ltd. and its affiliate, Unifreight India Pvt. Ltd to generate more robust domestic transportation and added capabilities in India. • Acquires the distribution, transportation, and retail operations of MultiPack (Mexico).
2012	• Acquires the Polish courier company Opek Sp.z o.o. • Acquires TATEX, a leading French business-to-business express transportation company. • Acquires Rapidão Cometa, one of the largest transportation and logistics companies in Brazil.

Source: FedEx Timeline, available at http://about.van.fedex.com/article/fedex-timeline. Used with permission.

GLOBAL PERSPECTIVES

UPS Expands Incheon Air Hub in Korea

UPS opened its newly expanded hub at Incheon International Airport in September 2014. Situated within the airport's Cargo Terminal Area, the newly expanded hub occupies over 9,000 square meters, more than 60 percent increase in size. The increased capacity allows UPS to increase import, export, and transshipment capability by around 50 percent. This is essential, given the growth of UPS cargo flights at Incheon Airport from 30 per week to 40 per week.

In December 2013, UPS began to pursue an expansion of its hub terminal in Incheon in an effort to strengthen its continent-to-continent and region-to-region logistics services using Incheon Airport as a base and connecting Asia, Europe, and the United States. The expanded terminal has state-of-the-art logistics systems including an automated incoming freight sorting system. By using the auto-sorting system and a new cargo X-ray system, the logistics company now has the ability to handle bulky or palletized shipments. As a result, UPS is putting forth its best effort to improve operational efficiencies and reduce shipment delays.

These efforts should increase Incheon Airport's logistics competitiveness as it will be able to respond to the needs of clients for faster, more accurate, and safer express shipping service. Businesses in Korea of all sizes will have access to greater supply chain reliability and numerous delivery options to 220 countries around the world. This will enable UPS customers to effectively compete in the global marketplace, according to J.K. Rah, managing director of UPS Korea.

UPS will also benefit from the hub expansion, moving closer toward its long-term strategy of building an extensive and integrated logistics network across Asia Pacific. The expanded facility will integrate well into UPS's industry leading capabilities in air freight, ocean freight, contract logistics, and innovative technology.

Sources: "Express Global Shipping Company UPS Expands Hub Center in Incheon Airport," *Incheon Airport News*, September 23, 2014, retrieved November 25, 2014, from http://www.airport.kr/notice/NoticeView.iia?functioncode=46&bulletinid=11582; "UPS Expands Incheon Air Hub in Korea," *UPS Pressroom*, September 23, 2014, retrieved November 25, 2014, from http://www.pressroom.ups.com/Press+Releases/Archive/2014/Q3/UPS+Expands+Incheon+Air+Hub+in+Korea, and "UPS Expands Hub Center in Incheon International Airport," *The Korea Bizwire*, September 25, 2014, retrieved November 25, 2014, from http://koreabizwire.com/ups-expands-hub-center-in-incheon-international-airport/20089.

3PL User Overview

In the previous section, you were introduced to different types of 3PLs and specific service providers, as well as brief references to 3PL customers. In this section, we dig into the customer aspects of 3PL. The key issues include who these customers are, why they outsource transportation and logistics activities to 3PLs, and what services they require. As you will learn, outsourcing has become a way of life for shippers, who rely heavily on 3PLs to help plan, execute, and control their supply chains.

Table 12-3 provides an overview of global logistics expenditures for 2013, as reported by Armstrong & Associates in their annual study of service trends, 3PL market segment sizes, and growth rates.[10] As you can see, the steady growth and expansion of

TABLE 12-3 Global Logistics Costs and Third-Party Logistics Revenues (US$ Billions)

REGION	2013 GDP	LOGISTICS (% of GDP)	2013 LOGISTIC COST	3PL REVENUE (%)	2013 3PL REVENUE
North America	18,970.1	8.8%	1665.2	10.5%	176.2
Europe	16,414.1	9.2%	1506.1	10.5%	158.1
Asia Pacific	22,921.4	12.8%	2964.7	8.6%	255.6
South America	4,409.2	12.3%	525.0	8.5%	44.9
Remaining Regions/ Countries	11,071.7	17.5%	1917.1	3.7%	69.0
Total	**73,786.5**	**11.6%**	**8578.1**	**8.2%**	**703.8**

Source: Armstrong & Associates, 2014.

FIGURE 12-3 U.S. Spending on 3PL Services ($ billions)

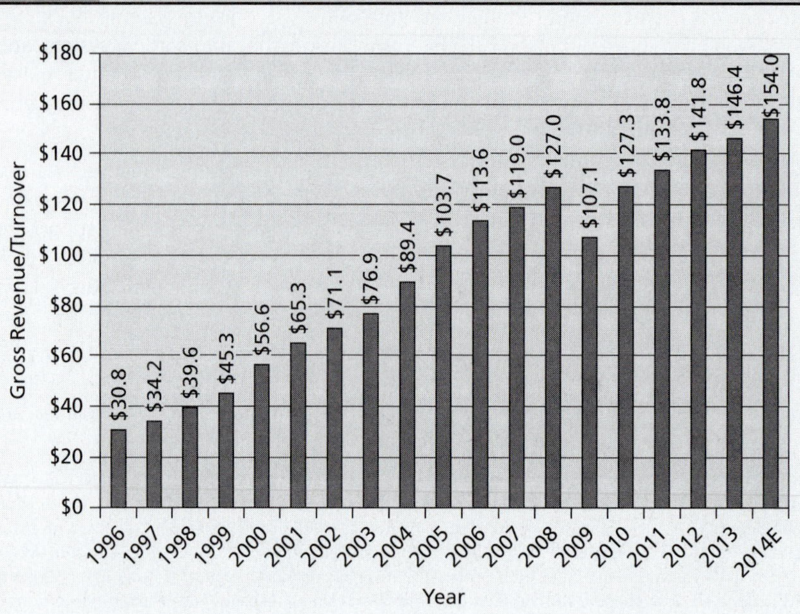

Source: Armstrong & Associates, 2014.

the global 3PL industry produced 3PL revenues in 2013 of $703.8 billion. Looking at this figure, the 3PL industry in the United States accounted for $176.2 billion, or 25 percent of the global total.

Looking more closely at the United States, Figure 12-3 provides annual data on 3PL revenues from 1996 to 2014 (estimated). Over this time frame, these revenues have increased from $30.8 billion in 1996 to $146.4 billion in 2013 and an estimated $154 billion in 2014. With the exception of the U.S. revenues in 2009 (global economic recession), there has been steady growth in these revenue figures for almost the past 20 years.[11]

This spending, in both the domestic and international markets, is driven by large companies. The 2013 Armstrong study found that 86 percent of the Fortune 500 companies outsourced some or all of their logistics and supply chain functions with technology, automotive, and retailing industries as leading users. Major 3PL users include companies such as General Motors, Procter & Gamble, and Walmart with each using 50 or more 3PLs to help manage and operate their extensive supply chains.[12] While many 3PLs rely upon these Fortune 500 clients for current revenues, future growth opportunities also lie also with small and midsize companies.

Reasons for Outsourcing

The most logical reason for using 3PL services is a lack of internal capabilities. Companies with little transportation and logistics expertise would be wise to outsource rather than attempting to build internal operations. Instead, they can leverage the knowledge, skills, networks, and resources of experienced 3PLs.

You may be surprised to find that Procter & Gamble and Walmart, companies with premier supply chain capabilities, make extensive use of 3PL services. They, like other companies, use 3PLs when it is appropriate to reduce costs, increase resource capacity,

TABLE 12-4 Reasons for and Against 3PL Use

REASONS FOR USING 3PL SERVICES	REASONS AGAINST USING 3PL SERVICES
Opportunity for cost reductions	Logistics is a core competency of company
Ability to focus on core competencies	Cost reductions would not be experienced
Opportunity to improve customer service	Control over outsourced function would diminish
Improve return on assets	Service level commitments would not be realized
Increase in inventory turns	Company has more expertise than 3PL providers
Productivity improvement opportunities	Logistics is too important to consider outsourcing
Generate logistics process flexibility	Outsourcing is not a corporate philosophy
Access to emerging technology	Global capabilities of 3PL need improvement
Expansion to unfamiliar markets	Inability of 3PLs to form meaningful relationships
Ability to divert capital investments	Issues related to security of shipments

Sources: B.S. Sahay and Ramneesh Mohan, "3PL practices: an Indian perspective, *International Journal of Physical Distribution & Logistics Management*, Vol. 36, No. 9, 2006; and, Georgia Tech and Capgemini LLC, *Eleventh Annual 3PL Study*, 2006.

and fill gaps in expertise. For example, Walmart contracts with Exel to handle distribution of automotive tires to its U.S. stores. Walmart avoids the cost of building a dedicated tire warehouse, leverages Exel's inventory management capabilities, and reduces the need to expend energy on a product line that is not sold in all stores.

Numerous studies have identified why companies outsource or do not outsource their transportation and logistics requirements. Table 12-4 provides lists from two studies that highlight these factors. Note that there is some conflict between the results as a reason for outsourcing may also be listed as a reason for not outsourcing. Clearly, outsourcing transportation and logistics is not for every organization. Before choosing to use 3PL services, an organization should spend time developing clear transportation objectives and then analyze if and how 3PLs can provide key support.

Primary Activities Outsourced

While the use of 3PLs has grown significantly, customer engagement patterns have not changed dramatically from year to year. Organizations predominantly use 3PL service providers for approximately three different services, led by transportation management as the most frequently used service, according to Armstrong and Associates. Their recent study of nearly 6,400 shipper-3PL relationships revealed that 81 percent remain "tactical" in nature, meaning 3PLs are mostly used for specific tasks such as transportation or warehousing. Only 19 percent of the relationships are classified as "strategic," where a 3PL manages a customer's entire logistics and supply chain operation on an integrated basis.[13]

Table 12-5 provides information pertaining to logistics activities outsourced from the annual Penn State–Capgemini, KornFerry International, and Penske study of 3PL customers and 3PLs (www.3plstudy.com).[14]

TABLE 12-5 Activities Outsourced to 3PLs

OUTSOURCED LOGISTICS SERVICES	PERCENTAGES OF 3PL USERS
Domestic transportation	80
International transportation	70
Warehousing	67
Customs brokerage	53
Freight forwarding	51
Reverse logistics (defective, repair, return)	36
Freight bill auditing and payment	33
Product labeling, packaging, assembly, kitting	30
Cross-docking	30
Transportation management and planning	25
Order management and fulfillment	18
Inventory management	18
Supply chain consultancy services provided by 3PLs	15
Service parts logistics	14
Information technology (IT) services	14
Fleet management	13
LLP (Lead Logistics Provider) / 4PL services	11
Customer service	5
Sustainability/green supply chain-related services	3

Source: 2015 19th Annual Third Party Logistics Study, C. John Langley Jr., Ph.D., Penn State University, and Capgemini LLC.

As you can see in Table 12-5, domestic and international transportation are the top two logistics activities outsourced, with 80 percent and 70 percent of global shippers, respectively, indicating they outsource at least some of these two activities. Also among the more widely outsourced activities are warehousing, customs brokerage, and freight forwarding.

The heavy use of tactical transportation activities does not mean that 3PLs should abandon their drive toward integrated global service capabilities. Over three-quarters of the participants in the Penn State–Capgemini study look to their 3PLs for needed integration, rather than trying to accomplish it internally. 3PL customers, particularly those with mature and complex supply chains, prefer to work with strategic services providers that can integrate processes, people, and services. It is not surprising that these customers view IT as exceptionally critical to this integration capability.[15]

Results Achieved

3PL users are satisfied with their outsourcing results, according to results of the Penn State–Capgemini annual studies. The 2014 study participants, from across industries and around the globe place a high value on their relationships with 3PL service providers. A distinct majority of users (90 percent) and 3PL service providers (97 percent) state that their relationships are successful. In addition, 55 percent of the users indicate that their use of 3PL services has led to year-over-year incremental benefits in order fill rates and accuracy.[16]

These positive evaluations are not surprising, given the financial results achieved on a year to year basis. For the most recent year of the Annual 3PL Study, study participants report logistics cost reductions of 11 percent, inventory cost reduction of 6 percent, and fixed logistics asset reductions of 23 percent.[17]

Establishing and Managing 3PL Relationships[18]

The development of a 3PL relationship should not happen by chance. A purchaser should carefully evaluate potential 3PL service providers and select the one whose capabilities, commitment level, and price match the buyer's requirements. This can be a time-consuming process but it will greatly increase the likelihood of a mutually beneficial relationship.

Figure 12-4 outlines the steps involved in establishing and sustaining 3PL relationships. For purposes of illustration, let us assume that the model is being applied from the perspective of a manufacturing firm, as it considers the possibility of forming a relationship with a 3PL service provider.

Step 1: Perform Strategic Assessment This first step focuses on the company becoming fully aware of its transportation and logistics needs and the overall strategies that will guide its operations. An audit provides a perspective on the firm's transportation and logistics activities, as well as generating useful information for assessing 3PL relationship options. Information derived from this audit includes:

- Overall role of transportation and logistics in supporting business goals and objectives

FIGURE 12-4 3PL Relationship Development Process

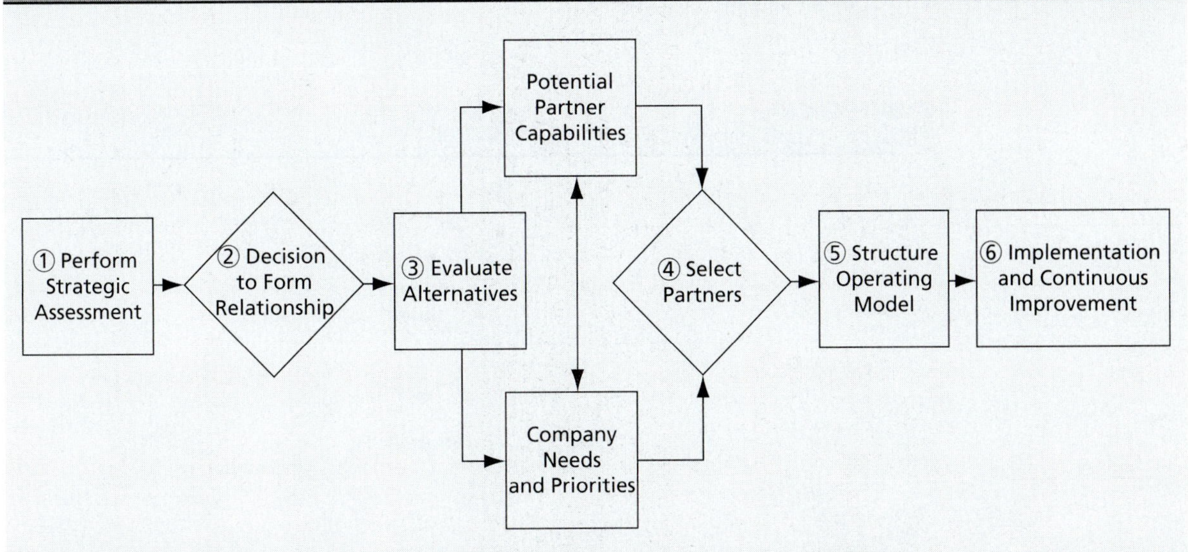

Source: C. John Langley Jr., Ph.D., Penn State University, and Capgemini LLC. Reprinted with permission.

- Needs assessment to include requirements of customers, suppliers, and key logistics providers
- Identification and analysis of strategic environmental factors and industry trends
- Profile of current logistics network and the firm's positioning in respective supply chains
- Benchmark, or target, values for logistics costs and key performance measurements
- Identification of gaps between current and desired measures of logistics performance (qualitative and quantitative)

Given the significance of most transportation and logistics relationship decisions, and the potential complexity of the overall process, time taken at the outset to gain an understanding of one's needs is well spent.

Step 2: Decision to Form Relationship When contemplating a 3PL relationship, it is necessary to identify needed capabilities. A suggested approach is to make a careful assessment of the areas in which the company appears to have **core competency**. As Figure 12-5 indicates, for a firm to have core competency in transportation and logistics, it is necessary to have expertise, strategic fit, and ability to invest. The absence of any one or more of these may suggest that the use of 3PL services is appropriate.

Determining whether a partnership is warranted and, if so, what kind of partnership should be considered has been the subject of much research. One such study created a partnership model that incorporates the identification of "drivers" and "facilitators" of a relationship; it indicates that for a relationship to have a high likelihood of success, the right drivers and facilitators should be present.[19]

Drivers are defined as "compelling reasons to partner." Drivers are strategic factors that may result in a competitive advantage and may help to determine the appropriate type of business relationship. The primary drivers include:

- Asset/Cost efficiency
- Customer service
- Marketing advantage
- Profit stability/Growth

FIGURE 12-5 3PL Core Competency Requirements

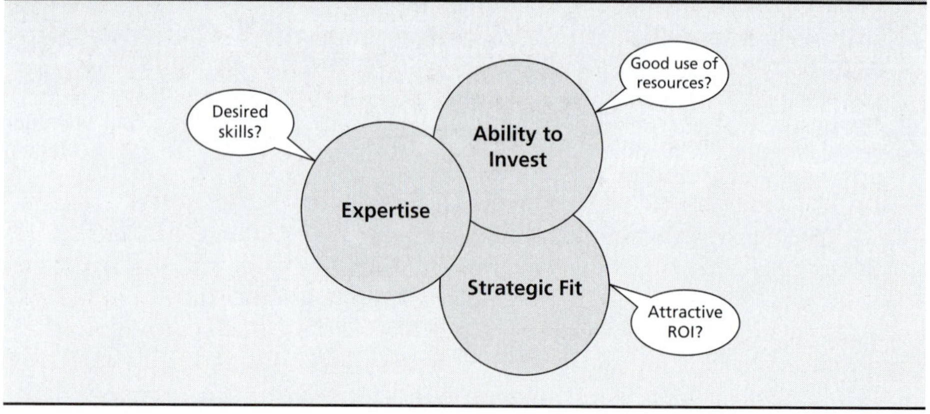

Source: C. John Langley Jr., Penn State University.

For a relationship to be successful, the participants must believe that they will receive significant benefits for one or more of these drivers and that these benefits would not be possible without a partnership. **Facilitators** are defined as "supportive corporate environmental factors that enhance partnership growth and development." When present, these factors promote success in the relationship. The main types of facilitators include:

- Corporate compatibility
- Management philosophy and techniques
- Mutuality of commitment to relationship formation
- Symmetry on key factors such as relative size, financial strength, and so on

A number of additional factors have been identified as keys to successful 3PL relationships. Included are factors such as: exclusivity, shared competitors, physical proximity, prior history of the potential partner, previous experience with the partner, and a shared high-value end user.

Step 3: Evaluate Alternatives These drivers and facilitators can be used to identify the most appropriate type of 3PL relationship. If neither the drivers nor the facilitators are present, then the relationship should be more transactional or "arm's length" in nature. Alternatively, when all parties to the relationship share common drivers, and when the facilitating factors are present, then a more structured, formal relationship is justified.

It is also important to conduct a thorough assessment of the company's needs and priorities in comparison with the capabilities of each potential partner. This task should include critical measurements of past performance, interviews of key personnel, and site visits.

Transportation and logistics executives have the primary roles in the decision to form 3PL relationships. However, it can be advantageous to bring managers from other functions such as finance and production into the evaluation process. Their valuable perspectives will contribute to the analysis and promote a strong decision. Thus, it is important to promote broad representation from across the company in this step of the partnership formation process.

Step 4: Select Partners While this stage is of critical concern to the customer, the selection of a transportation or logistics partner should be made only after very close consideration of the credentials of the top candidate 3PLs. Also, it is highly advisable to interact with the final candidates on a professionally intimate basis.

It is important to achieve consensus on the final selection from the executives involved in the evaluation process. This will create a significant degree of buy-in and agreement among those involved. Due to the strategic significance of a 3PL relationship, everyone must have a consistent understanding of the final selection and what is expected of the chosen service provider.

Step 5: Structure Operating Model The process does not end with the selection of a service provider. The companies must also develop working agreements and contracts that clarify the activities, processes, and priorities that will drive day-to-day operations. A well-designed operating model will clarify each party's responsibilities and will help to sustain the relationship. A suggested list of operating model elements includes:

- Planning
- Joint operating controls

- Communication
- Risk/Reward sharing
- Trust and commitment
- Contract style
- Scope of the relationship
- Financial investment[20]

Step 6: Implementation and Continuous Improvement With commencement of 3PL service operations, the most challenging step in the relationship process begins. Depending on the complexity of the new relationship, the overall implementation process may be relatively short or it may be extended over a longer period of time. If the situation involves significant restructuring of the company's transportation or logistics network, then full implementation may take longer to accomplish. In a situation where the degree of change is modest, the time needed for successful implementation may be abbreviated.

Finally, the future success of the relationship will be a direct function of the ability of the involved organizations to achieve both continuous and breakthrough improvement. As indicated in Figure 12-6, there are a number of steps that should be considered in the continuous improvement process. In addition, efforts should be made to create breakthrough improvements that drive the relationship to new levels of competitive advantage.

The ultimate goal of this six-step process is to develop productive relationships between companies and 3PL service providers that create outstanding customer service and cost-efficient operations. Like any relationship, both organizations must invest time and energy into its development and sustainment. Both parties must share information, trust their counterparts, and be open to new ideas and methods.

FIGURE 12-6 3PL Continuous Improvement Process

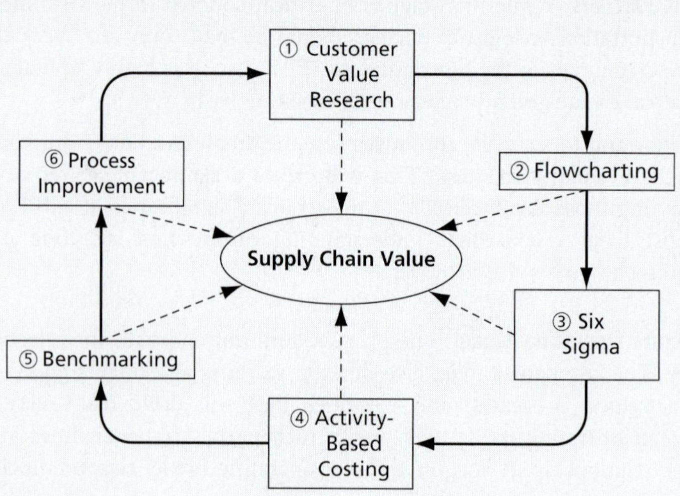

Source: Adapted from Ray A. Mundy, C. John Langley Jr., and Brian J. Gibson, Continuous Improvement in Third Party Logistics, 2001. Used with permission.

The most successful long-term 3PL relationships occur when the organizations collaborate on a regular basis, adopt a team approach to problem solving, and leverage each other's capabilities.

Strategic Needs of 3PL Users

As discussed earlier, results from the Penn State–Capgemini 19th annual study indicates that 3PL users are satisfied with their outsourcing activities. However, the continuous change taking place in supply chains and the ongoing need for improved service and relationships means that 3PLs cannot be complacent. Figure 12-7 highlights the capabilities needed by 3PLs to keep pace with the strategic needs of their customers.[21] Although the 3PLs bear primary responsibility for providing these capabilities, the customers must take an collaborative role in achieving maximum success. Among the most important needs of 3PL users are strategic innovation, technological strength, capacity access, talent availability, omni-channel agility, and sustainability expertise. Each issue is discussed briefly below.

Strategic Innovation The 3PL community has long been lauded for their execution prowess and performance consistency. They are viewed as fast and reliable but not particularly innovative. This is a problem for customers whose supply chains are changing quite rapidly due to the explosion in omni-channel activity, the growth of nearshoring initiatives, and the increasing level of transportation regulation. Traditional fulfillment channels and delivery methods may not effectively serve user requirements in these scenarios.

FIGURE 12-7 Capabilities & Services Users Need from 3PLs

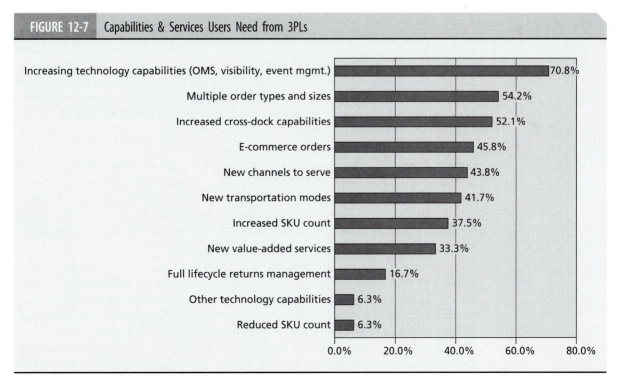

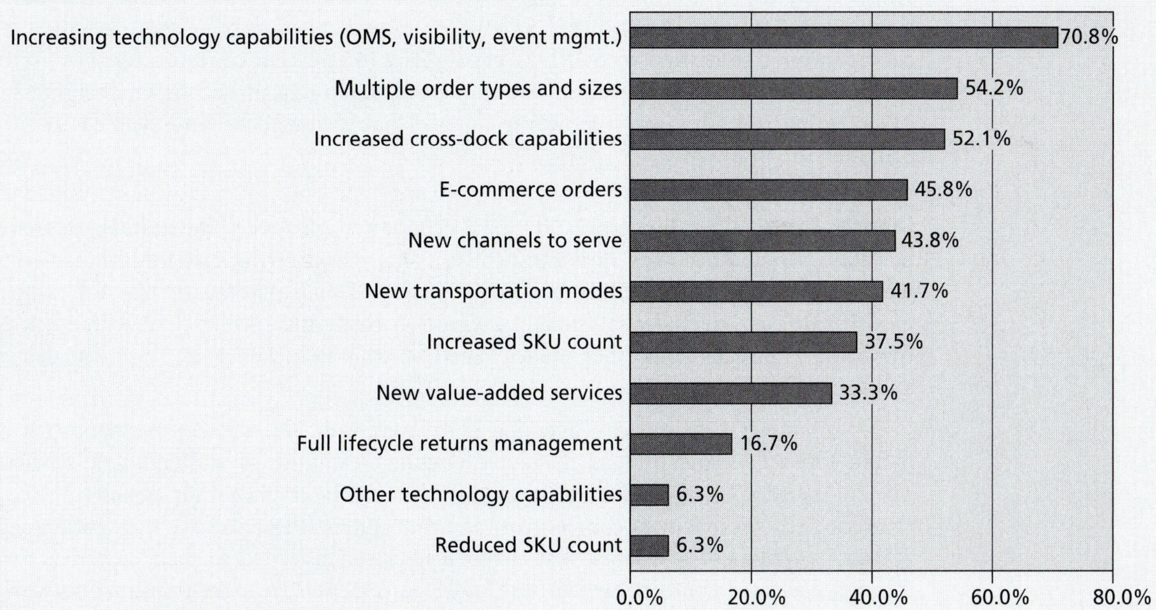

Source: 2014 Tompkins Supply Chain Consortium.

To provide maximum value to the customer base, 3PLs must be innovative and collaborative in solutions development. Information sharing on changing requirements is essential for the two parties to understand the dynamics of the situation at hand. Then, the 3PL must have the willingness and capability to develop novel solutions. They also need to be more proactive in suggesting strategic solutions.

To encourage innovation, the customer must be patient as breakthrough improvements are not developed overnight. They need to realize that a pure cost savings focus with related financial metrics do not encourage innovation. There is risk and cost involved in creating solutions. Thus, customers must collaborate with 3PLs on risk mitigation and create incentives to maximize innovative thinking.[22]

Technological Strength As Figure 12-7 indicates, a top need of 3PL users is upgraded technology capabilities. Customers view technology as a critical capability of 3PL service providers to improve order management, cross-chain communication, enhance shipment visibility and **event management**, and manage day-to-day transportation operations. This need for strong, integrated technology capabilities from their service providers is essential for proactive control of freight as it moves across global supply chains.

The good news is that most large 3PLs have integrated systems platforms to support global transportation and warehouse management operations. These platforms offer the much desired Internet-based shipment tracking and process visibility, exception resolution capability, and transportation management systems functionality. This allows customers to effectively manage orders, control inventory, and optimize thousands of shipments across large geographical areas.[23] Additional benefits of working with 3PLs these types of IT capabilities are highlighted in the Transportation Technology feature.

Of course, not every 3PL uses cutting-edge technology to manage customer activity. This is evidenced by the IT gap revealed in the Penn State–Capgemini annual study. It highlights a 36 percent gap between the users who indicate that IT capabilities are a necessary element of 3PL expertise (96 percent of respondents) and the percentage who are satisfied with 3PL IT capabilities (60 percent of respondents).[24] With technology rapidly evolving and customer needs changing, it will be challenging for 3PLs to narrow this gap. However, those that do will become valued service providers.

Capacity Access When domestic and global economies are strong; the market for transportation services becomes very competitive. This makes it difficult for companies to maintain access to adequate transportation capacity. This is particularly true for companies that do not have adequate freight volume to create purchasing clout with trucking companies, railroads, and other modes. This can lead to higher costs, shipment delays, and service inconsistency.

A solution to the capacity dilemma is to work with 3PL service providers such as freight forwarders and brokers that have ongoing relationships with multiple carriers. The combined volume of the 3PL's customer base can be leveraged for consistent access to much needed capacity at competitive rates. Integrated 3PLs also have their own transportation equipment and labor that can be exclusively assigned to their customer base through dedicated contract carriage and other agreements. To make the situation workable, 3PL users must accurately plan their capacity needs and effectively collaborate with

TRANSPORTATION **TECHNOLOGY**

The Payoffs of 3PL Investment in IT Capabilities

When a 3PL makes effective investments in integrated IT tools that contain both planning and execution capabilities, both the customers and the 3PL will reap valuable results.

Choosing a technology savvy 3PL will help a customer gain relatively rapid access to valuable resources without a significant out-of-pocket investment. This will generate the following benefits:

- **Lower IT costs**. The shipper can leverage the 3PL's software for its outsourced transportation and logistics activities. The key is to clarify the IT commitments in the contractual agreement.
- **Higher levels of service**. Use of transportation management systems (TMS) helps the 3PL better plan, execute, and manage product flows for customers. This will promote in-transit visibility and delivery optimization that improve customer satisfaction.
- **Stronger communication**. Deployment of event management tools generate early warning signals of delivery problems so that the 3PL can rapidly resolve the issue. This will avoid the surprises and long delays that dissatisfy customers.

Fortunately, IT benefits are not one-sided. The 3PL can also gain value from their technology spending. The service provider payoffs include:

- **Increased customer satisfaction.** Technology drives the dissemination of timely and accurate transportation information to customers. This supports operational control and informed decision making, both of which boost customer satisfaction.
- **Better data for planning.** Access to a data warehouse of customer transaction information (delivery lanes, volume, spending, and so forth), will help the 3PL better plan its operations. This will ensure capacity is available when and where it is needed at the right price.
- **Lower costs.** 3PLs can use technology to optimize performance across multiple customers' transportation activities. The 3PL can use TMS tools to create better routes and utilize capacity more effectively to reduce the cost of serving customers.

Given these dual benefits, IT capabilities have become an essential component of the 3PL-customer relationships. When the technology helps the 3PL improve its capabilities and performance, customer satisfaction will increase and future revenue growth will be achieved.

Sources: Adapted from Chris Norek and C. John Langley Jr., "IT in the 3PL Industry: Trends and Expectations," *Logistics Quarterly*, Fall/Winter 2013/14. Used with permission.

the service providers on their volume growth, geographic delivery patterns, and service requirements.

Talent Availability At a time when SCM is gaining stature as a strategic driver of success, many organizations face a critical supply chain talent void due to years of headcount reduction, training budget cuts, and the retirement of highly skilled individuals. Supply chain leaders must address this talent gap by assembling a team of talented professionals with skills that are core to the organization's SCM mission.[25]

One way to address the talent crisis is to hire a 3PL with strong and stable talent. Top 3PLs have the strategic foresight to invest in training, development, and retention programs that help them maintain a strong pipeline of leaders who can diagnose customer needs, develop effective solutions, and manage the implementation process. These people investments boost morale, increase productivity, and reduce turnover, which are essential for relationship continuity and customer satisfaction. In turn, strategic workforce spending translates to revenue and profitability growth for the 3PL.[26]

Omni-channel Agility The emergence of new distribution channels has created a much more complex working environment for transportation and logistics managers, particularly for retailers. No longer are they merely managing deliveries to the back door of retail outlets. Today, they are supporting home delivery, manufacturer direct delivery, alternate site delivery, and variations of buy online and pickup in stores. On top of this, companies like Amazon.com, eBay, and Macy's offer same-day delivery in some markets.

Collectively, this makes for huge omni-channel transportation and logistics challenges that many companies are not equipped to handle with their existing processes, talent, and IT resources. As highlighted in Figure 12-7, these customers desire to work with 3PLs that can effectively handle a growing inventory base and e-commerce orders that vary in type, size, and delivery location. These 3PLs must offer flexible solutions for rapidly moving inventory through these networks to customer and managing returns from customers.

Sustainability Expertise The execution of supply chain processes has a significant impact on the environment—delivery processes require heavy use refined oil products, generate carbon emissions, and contribute to congestion. Transportation managers are under increased pressure to deploy delivery methods that have lower environmental impacts—without raising the cost or reducing the quality of service. This is a difficult task, given the scope of global transportation networks and the growth of e-commerce home delivery, but one that has important societal and financial implications.

3PL users need to work with service providers that are committed to sustainable supply chain practices and have developed expertise over time. While many 3PLs have adopted TMS tools to help them minimize resource use through the optimization of routes and the reduction of empty miles, a much smaller group has invested in alternative fuel equipment and LEED-certified facilities. For example, Saddle Creek has established a 175-truck fleet that runs on compressed natural gas, one of the cleanest-burning alternative fuel options available with near-zero emissions. The equipment reduces carbon footprint and noise levels, leverages the domestic U.S. fuel supply, and minimizes fuel cost fluctuations.[27] This investment is a win for the company, its customers, and the environment.

Future Requirement 3PL industry revenues have increased from $30.8 billion in 1996 to $154 billion (estimated) in 2014. This is due to the 3PL service providers' collective ability to provide high quality, competitively prices services in increasingly complex supply chains. As customers shift their global activities, expand their omni-channel activities, and pursue new innovations, the level of supply chain complexity will also grow. In turn, their service requirements will evolve. 3PLs, especially those developing far reaching physical networks, integrated logistics capabilities, and effective IT tools, will be well positioned to serve the emerging transportation and logistics needs of their customers.

To maintain pace with customers' future requirements, 3PLs will need to effectively expand their capabilities through internal growth, mergers, and strategic acquisition of competitors. As customers shift production from far away locations to nearby emerging markets where the cost of labor, shipping, and land is less expensive, 3PLs will need to establish a presence in these new regions. 3PLs will also need to enhance their breadth of capabilities and strategic services to serve customer desires for one-stop shopping and lead logistics provider skills. Finally, 3PLs will need to be a driving force of transportation and logistics innovation to ensure that they can meet the cost-efficiency and service quality requirements of customers.

SUMMARY

- A third party logistics (3PL) service provider is defined as an "external supplier that performs all or part of a company's logistics functions." It is desirable that these suppliers provide multiple services and that these services are integrated in the way they are managed and delivered.
- The several types of 3PLs are transportation-based, distribution-based, forwarder-based, financial-based, and information-based suppliers.
- Asset-based providers serve customers with tangible equipment and facilities, while non-asset based providers leverage the resources of other companies.
- 3PLs provide a variety of transportation services, including freight movement, freight management, intermediary services, and specialty services.
- Customer demands for integration of 3PL services have led to significant expansion and acquisition activities among major service providers.
- The 3PL industry is a growing and substantial force in logistics, with more than $703 billion spent globally on 3PL services in 2013.
- When outsourcing labor-intensive logistics operations, companies seek cost reduction, the ability to focus on core competencies, and service improvement.
- According to an annual study of 3PL users, customers are satisfied with their 3PL relationships and credit 3PLs with helping them attain goals related to reduction of operating costs, fixed asset investment, and order cycle time.
- There are six steps involved in the development and implementation of a successful 3PL relationship. The ultimate goal of the process is to develop outstanding customer service capabilities and cost-efficient operations.
- Although the industry is poised for future growth, 3PLs must support customers' needs through strategic innovation, technological strength, capacity access, talent availability, omni-channel agility, and sustainability expertise.

STUDY QUESTIONS

1. Define the concepts of outsourcing and third party logistics. What role does transportation play in 3PL?
2. What are the basic types of 3PL firms? How do they facilitate the planning and execution of freight transportation?
3. Why would a company use an asset-based 3PL service provider versus a non-asset based provider?
4. Discuss the four primary types of transportation services offered by 3PL service providers.
5. Why is service integration an important issue to the 3PL industry? What companies are developing these capabilities?
6. What are some of the more frequently outsourced logistics activities? Less frequently outsourced?
7. To what extent are clients/customers satisfied with 3PL services? What can 3PLs do to improve customer satisfaction?
8. Describe the six steps involved in establishing and managing 3PL relationships. Which step(s) do you feel is (are) most critical?

9. If you were given the task of outsourcing your company's transportation operations, what types of capabilities and core competencies would you seek in a 3PL service provider?
10. After implementing a 3PL relationship, how should transportation managers promote continuous improvement of performance and achieve supply chain value?
11. Discuss the strategic needs and challenges that transportation managers face. How can 3PL service providers help them improve performance and reduce costs?
12. Why is information technology an important issue to customers when outsourcing transportation and logistics activities?

NOTES

1. "eyefortransport Transportation Glossary," retrieved November 24, 2014, from http://events.eyefortransport.com/glossary/ab.shtml
2. "Third party logistics (3PL) definition," retrieved November 24, 2014, from http://www.businessdictionary.com/definition/third-party-logistics-3PL.html.
3. Council of Supply Chain Management Professionals, *Supply Chain Management Terms and Glossary*, 2013, retrieved November 24, 2014, from http://cscmp.org/sites/default/files/user_uploads/resources/downloads/glossary-2013.pdf
4. John J. Coyle, C. John Langley, Jr., Robert A. Novack, and Brian J. Gibson, *Supply Chain Management: A Logistics Perspective* 9th ed., chap. 4, Mason, OH: Cengage Learning, 2013.
5. Gillian Tan, "XPO Logistics Gets $700 Million Investment to Fund Acquisition," *Wall Street Journal*, September 11, 2014.
6. Scott Vanselous, "The Next Generation of TMS Helping More Carriers Become Comprehensive Logistics Service Providers," *Logistics Viewpoints*, November 25, 2014, retrieved November 25, 2014, from http://logisticsviewpoints.com/2014/11/25/the-next-generation-of-tms-helping-more-carriers-become-comprehensive-logistics-service-providers/
7. Export.gov, "What Is a Shippers Association?" October 14, 2012, retrieved November 25, 2014, from http://www.export.gov/logistics/eg_main_023294.asp.
8. Jean-Paul Rodrigue, Claude Comtois, and Brian Slack, *The Geography of Transport System*, 2nd ed., New York: Routledge, 2009.
9. François Fulconis, Virginie Hiesse, and Gilles Paché, "Catalyst of Coopetitive Strategies—An Exploratory Study," *Supply Chain Forum An International Journal*, Vol. 12, No. 2 (2011).
10. Armstrong & Associates, Inc., *Trends in 3PL/Customer Relationships*, 2014.
11. Ibid.
12. Armstrong & Associates, Inc., "3PL Customers Report Identifies Service Trends, 3PL Market Segment Sizes," July 11, 2013, retrieved November 30, 2014, from http://www.3plogistics.com/PR_3PL_Customers-2013.htm.
13. Ibid.
14. Penn State and Capgemini, *The State of Logistics Outsourcing*, 19th Annual 3PL Study, 2015.
15. Ibid.
16. Ibid.
17. Ibid.

18. Unless otherwise noted, information in this section is adapted from John J. Coyle, C. John Langley, Jr., Robert A. Novack, and Brian J. Gibson, Supply Chain Management: A Logistics Perspective, 9th ed., chap. 4, (Mason, OH: Cengage Learning, 2013).

19. Douglas M. Lambert, Margaret A. Emmelhainz, and John T. Gardner, "Developing and Implementing Supply Chain Partnerships," *International Journal of Logistics Management*, Vol. 7, No. 2 (1996): 1–17.

20. Ibid.

21. Bruce Tompkins and Chris Ferrell, *Reinventing the 3PL Model: Trends, Challenges, and Opportunities*, September 2014, retrieved November 28, 2014, from http://www.tompkinsinc.com/reinventing-3pl-model-trends-challenges-opportunities-3/.

22. Patrick Burnson, "Optimizing 3PL Relationships: How to Avoid Commoditization," *Logistics Management*, October 2014.

23. Richard Armstrong, "Where the 3PL Action Is: A Scan of Logistics Providers & Services Worldwide," *SupplyChainBrain*, March/April 2014.

24. Penn State and Capgemini, *The State of Logistics Outsourcing*, 19th Annual 3PL Study, 2015.

25. Brian J. Gibson, Sean P. Goffnett, Zachary Williams, and Robert L. Cook, *SCM Talent Development Module 1: The Acquire Process*, Oak Brook, IL: Council of Supply Chain Management Professionals, 2013.

26. Penn State and Capgemini, *The State of Logistics Outsourcing*, 19th Annual 3PL Study, 2015.

27. "More Clean Energy CNG for Saddle Creek," *Fleets & Fuels*, July 11, 2014, retrieved November 30, 2014, from http://www.fleetsandfuels.com/fuels/cng/2014/07/more-clean-energy-cng-for-saddle-creek/.

CASE 12-1

Jetstream Aerospace

Jetstream Aerospace is a world leader in the design and manufacture of innovative aviation products and services for the regional, business, and amphibious aircraft markets. These product lines encompass such internationally known and respected names as Thrifty regional jets and Luxuria business aircrafts. Jetstream's global workforce of over 20,500 associates delivered 532 aircrafts in 2009, generating over $9 billion in sales and creating a remarkable $11.7 billion order backlog.

The company also provides aftermarket support for its aircraft. When an airplane breaks down or a critical part needs to be replaced, the clock begins ticking, eating valuable time and profits as the aircraft sits idle. Therefore, Jetstream's customers need fast response when an aftermarket service part is needed. Speed, in many cases, is more important than cost to the customers, who want their aircraft flying instead of sitting on the tarmac.

Unfortunately, Jetstream has struggled to provide the level of delivery service demanded by its customers. After a series of acquisitions, the company's service parts business was fragmented and disjointed, resulting in declining service quality and a threat to customer loyalty. Also, the customer base has become much more global, meaning that the company has to quickly deliver service parts to nearly every region of the world.

The topic of aftermarket service received great attention during the quarterly update meeting of senior management. Jetstream's CEO opened the discussion with, "Folks, I'm getting pretty tired of answering emails and calls from our major customers about planes being grounded because a $75 repair part wasn't in stock or couldn't be tracked during delivery. We need to figure out this problem and fix it fast. The goal is to regain our number one ranking in customer service by restoring market confidence in the Jetstream aftermarket support capabilities. Now get busy!"

The brainstorming session among the senior managers became very animated. They quickly outlined a set of goals: improved service quality, improved aftermarket parts velocity and responsiveness, and sustained sales growth and profitability through cost containment.

Next, a heated discussion ensued about how to accomplish the goals. A few managers advocated the idea of centralizing all customer service operations in Amsterdam at the company's distribution center near Schiphol International Airport. The rationale was greater inventory availability and better control of order fulfillment. Others wanted to set up a network of company-owned regional distribution facilities in Jetstream's major market areas. They felt that this arrangement would reduce distance to customers and improve order cycle times. A lone dissenter brought up the idea of hiring a 3PL to help manage the aftermarket business. Her justification was simple: "Jetstream is a great manufacturing company but is challenged in the service parts area. Why don't we bring in a company with logistics expertise to optimize our service parts business?"

The response was immediate and negative from the other managers. They felt that Jetstream was highly capable and didn't need outside help. "A few tweaks here and there are all we need," said the Director of Customer Relations.

His comment was gaining great support until the CEO cleared his throat and boldly stated: "Third party logistics? That sounds intriguing. Tell me more."

CASE QUESTIONS

1. Discuss the pros and cons of using third party logistics for Jetstream's aftermarket services.
2. What potential risks exist with outsourcing the aftermarket services to a 3PL?
3. What transportation and logistics activities should be considered for outsourcing in this situation? Should Jetstream obtain these services on a tactical or strategic basis?
4. What type of 3PL service provider is best suited to meet Jetstream's aftermarket service goals? How should they go about finding a capable 3PL service provider?

CASE 12-2

Closet Concepts Ltd

Closet Concepts Ltd. (CCL) is a rapidly growing provider of home storage and organization products. They manufacture a wide range products ranging from wire closet organizers to wood shelving systems. Basic CCL product lines are sold through home improvement retailers and the premier product line is sold through designers and custom homebuilders.

The CCL leadership team has been pondering an e-commerce strategy and worries that it may lose sales to competitors if a CCL.com online shopping option is not soon established. Fortunately, the CCL website is fairly robust and it would not be difficult to add shopping capabilities to it. All that was really needed was the approval to begin the project.

The approval came during a quarterly executive retreat. During her opening speech, the CEO stated: "Increasingly, do-it-yourself customers have expressed a desire to order product directly from CCL. The customers claim to have difficulty in getting unique items and parts from the CCL product line because the retailers don't carry them in stock. This can delay project completion and create customer dissatisfaction. By the end of this retreat, I want a high-level plan that establishes our e-commerce strategy and our plan for managing customer orders. I want us to have excellent omni-channel fulfillment and delivery capabilities, but we cannot compromise our service quality to existing retailers, designers, and builders. Now, break into teams and do some brainstorming."

A fulfillment analysis team was hastily assembled. It consisted of Riley Sheahan, the chief customer relations officer; Jim Howard, the vice president of logistics, and Tomas Tatar, the senior director of transportation. All agreed that it would be a challenge to quickly add omni-channel fulfillment capabilities and each had contrasting ideas about how to proceed.

Sheahan suggested that CCL handle all fulfillment activities in-house and to use its private fleet to move customer orders to major markets for pool distribution by local delivery firms. "This will give us the greatest control over our processes to ensure a superior customer experience," she explained.

"I'm not so sure about that strategy," replied Tatar. "Our fleet is small and we use it to deliver high margin custom orders to 30 key distributors. You're talking about a tenfold increase in the number of delivery points." He also noted that total demand for online orders was unknown and nobody had any idea about average order size.

Howard noted that CCL's distribution centers were geared toward massive orders from home improvement retailers that moved in cost-efficient truckload quantities "We already have difficulty handling the smaller orders from designers and builders. Besides, Tomas will tell you that our products can be odd-shaped and low density, attributes that lead to high less-than-truckload delivery rates."

Sheahan replied: "I don't want some second rate trucking company trying to fill our orders or damaging our product just because Tomas is looking to save a few transportation dollars. We must maintain exceptional control over these direct customer engagements. This e-commerce initiative is just too important for us to cut corners."

"I agree that we want it done correctly but we don't have the resources or expertise to do this in-house," stated Howard. "We need to find a high quality 3PL that knows how to handle Internet orders."

"Good point," noted Tatar. "Partnering with the right provider could be the ideal solution. They can serve CCL customers effectively without busting our budget."

"I need to know more about these so-called 3PL experts," replied Sheahan. "Gather some information and bring it to our late afternoon session." With that statement, she got up and left the meeting.

CASE QUESTIONS

1. What roles can third party logistics play in the CCL e-commerce initiative? Is it a viable alternative to Sheahan's private fleet/pool distribution strategy?
2. What type of 3PL service provider is best suited to serve the CCL e-commerce customers? Why?
3. Should Howard and Tatar consider the use of an integrated 3PL? Why or why not?
4. If CCL decided to add installation services to its e-commerce initiatives, what types of 3PL service provider should be used? Why?

CHAPTER

13

PRIVATE TRANSPORTATION AND FLEET MANAGEMENT

Learning Objectives

After reading this chapter, you should be able to do the following:

- Understand the legal basis for private transportation companies and the rationale for their place in the transportation system
- Discuss the role and importance of private transportation for various private and public organizations and the differences among the various modal types—rail, air, water, pipeline, and trucking
- Appreciate the advantages and disadvantages of private transportation service contrasted to for-hire carrier service
- Discuss the cost structure of private transportation services, especially trucking, and understand the various components of their fixed and variable (operating) cost structure
- Understand how driver and equipment costs can be calculated for private carriage
- Discuss the role of leasing for private transportation and how it impacts the cost structure and operating costs of private trucking
- Appreciate the challenges associated with the daily operation of a private fleet
- Discuss the importance of the overall managerial and financial control for a private fleet to improve efficiency and effectiveness
- Appreciate the challenges and issues associated with the administration of regulations pertaining to private trucking and the associated reporting to various regulatory agencies

TRANSPORTATION **PROFILE**

The Silent Partner: Private Fleets

Private carriage is an important part of the transportation system in the United States and in most other countries of the world. In fact, private transportation has a long history in the United States and was the primary component of the system until the development of the railroad and canal sectors in the 19th century. The large fixed cost and capital investment required for an effective rail system precluded individuals and the small companies that existed at that time from providing private rail service. Railroads were the first "big business" in the United States with absentee ownership, that is, shareholders. To the typical user at that time, not having an owner available locally was an important issue and a challenge when service and rates were not satisfactory to them. Subsequently, the other modes of transportation also developed larger companies that provided for-hire service to the general public with absentee ownership. This contributed to the demand for regulation of railroad transportation

While the motor carrier sector developed a large number of for-hire carriers, private carriage has always been a very important part of the motor carrier industry, as noted in Chapter 5. The development of public highways after World War I by the federal, state, and local governments provided an opportunity for small to large companies to purchase trucks. They provided private transportation on the publically provided infrastructure and paid user charges for that privilege. The list of private fleet operations reads like a *Who's Who of Corporate America*. Many of these companies found private motor carrier service to be an attractive and advantageous alternative to for-hire rail and water carriers.

The success of private trucking reflects the growth and development of the economy in the United States. Successful companies use technology and software to administer and manage their private fleets for service and profitability. America's private fleets include some of the largest names in U.S. business—Walmart stores, Verizon, Pepsi Bottling Group, and Safeway. Less well-known companies, like Sysco Food Corp, provide essential day-to-day deliveries and services to many other industries. These private fleets often contract out to for-hire carriers for additional services and income.

Not only do private fleets haul products, they also help to provide essential services for many smaller service businesses—plumbers, contractors, electricians, and so forth. Combined, these small businesses operate sizeable private fleets. Private trucking provides a large slice of service and revenue to U.S. industry.

Source: Adapted from *America's Private Fleets*, National Private Truck Council.

Private Transportation

Private transportation may be construed as "do-it-yourself" rather than "buy it" transportation services. It is very analogous to the so-called **make or buy decision** that manufacturers and other organizations have evaluated for many years. Currently, this option is frequently considered under the label of **outsourcing**. Organizations have the option of providing items or services themselves internally or buying them from another source. To be completely independent is almost impossible, particularly in today's complex, global economy. On some scale, large and small organizations have to make decisions as to what goods or services to provide internally or purchase externally. The decision is usually made based upon availability, total cost, and convenience. Sometimes the decision is fairly straight forward while in other cases, it can be much more complex and can sometimes be more subjective than objective. Transportation service is an area that has been and is still being examined and analyzed for possible benefits such as decreased cost and/or increased profitability. Companies sometimes change their position and move from private to public or vice versa. Also, circumstances can change over time making the alternative more attractive.

The firm engaged in private transportation is **vertically integrated** to perform the services that can be provided by for-hire carriers. The private transportation decision is a classic "**make versus buy**" decision, as indicated earlier, in which a company must determine if it is better to make (engage in private transportation) or buy transportation (use a for-hire carrier).

In this chapter, the private transportation issue is examined for all modes, but emphasis is given to private trucking, the most pervasive form of private transportation. Attention will be directed to the decision to enter into private trucking and the operation of a private truck fleet.

What Is Private Transportation?

Private transportation is not the opposite of public (government) transportation. Private transportation is a legal form of transportation that was defined in the Interstate Commerce Act as "any person who transports in interstate or foreign commerce property of which such person is the owner, lessee, or bailee when such transportation is for the purpose of sale, lease, rent or bailment, or in the furtherance of any commercial enterprise."

This legal definition may be interpreted as follows: Private transportation is the movement of goods owned by a firm that also owns or leases and operates the transportation equipment for the furtherance of its primary business.

A private carrier does not provide service to the general public. Rather, the private carrier serves itself by hauling its own raw materials and/or finished products. The private carrier was permitted to haul goods for others (the public) in the past but only if such service was provided free of charge. Notable exceptions to this general prohibition against the private carrier charging a fee included the movement of exempt commodities and freight of firms that were 100 percent owned subsidiaries.

In the past, the Interstate Commerce Commission (ICC) strictly enforced the prohibition of private carriers hauling public goods for a fee. This enforcement was an extension of the control over entry for common and contract carriers, who must prove public convenience and necessity. However, the 1980 Motor Carrier Act greatly reduced controls over entry into the common and contract carrier fields, and grants of authority became easier to obtain even for an existing private motor carrier. After the abolition of the ICC in 1995, the responsibilities of regulating private transportation were transferred to the Surface Transportation Board.

Although private trucking is the most prevalent, private transportation is found among other modes as well. A brief analysis of private transportation in rail, air, pipeline, and water follows.

Private Rail Transportation

Private transportation in the railroad industry usually takes the form of privately owned railcars of other businesses that are moved by a common carrier railroad. Private rail transportation does not exist in the form of a business operating a typical rail service to transport goods or personnel on an intercity basis.

Many businesses purchase or lease specialized rail equipment, such as hopper, temperature-controlled, and tank cars, to ensure an adequate supply of vehicles. It is common for agribusiness firms to own (or lease) a supply of hopper cars to haul grain from the farms to the grain elevators to end users during the harvest season. Railroads normally do not have a sufficient supply of hopper cars to meet these peak demands. Thus, many agribusiness firms have acquired a private fleet of rail equipment to ensure an adequate supply of railcars to meet their demand for adequate service.

As stated earlier, there are no businesses that own a private railroad to transport their freight on an intercity basis since the cost of the infrastructure is prohibitive. The private railcars are usually moved intercity by a for-hire railroad. The railroad grants the shipper permission to have the private car moved over its lines, and the railroad provides an allowance from the normal rate to the shipper for use of the private railcar. The car allowance takes the form of either a mileage allowance or a reduction from the published rate for the specific commodity movement. The car allowance recognizes that the user is incurring a portion of the transportation expense (the capital cost of the vehicle) that is normally incurred by the railroad.

Private rail transportation usually includes the cost of a private siding or spur track that connects the railroad's track with the user's plant or warehouse. The rail transportation user desiring service to its door must provide and maintain the rail track on its property. In the absence of a private siding or spur track, the shipper must use a public side track and incur an additional transportation (accessibility) cost to move the freight usually by truck between the public siding and the user's facility.

Some large manufacturing firms have built small railroads within the confines of their plants to shuttle railcars from building to building. Such private railroads may be construed as materials handling systems that move railcars loaded with goods such as raw materials. The switch engine performs the same function as the forklift; that is, the switch engine places the railcars in the proper location to permit loading and unloading. The switch engine of such private railroads does not operate outside the plant limits.

A number of large firms own for-hire railroads that primarily connect the owner's facilities with other for-hire railroads. These railroads are legally classified as for-hire common carriers, not private rail carriers. As an example, consider a large forest products company that owns and operates a short-line railroad in a rural community. The railroad is classified as a common carrier but provides service primarily to the area's major rail shipper, the forest products company.

Private rail transportation basically means that the user buys or leases railcars, provides rail tracks on its property and, in some limited cases, provides switching within the plant. The motive power and right-of-way infrastructure are usually provided by a railroad company.

Private Air Transportation

Private air transportation, unlike the other modal forms of private carriage, is used extensively, if not exclusively, to transport people. The private airplane fleets are purchased and operated to typically serve the travel needs of business executives. However, smaller companies may own or lease individual planes for their business-related travel. This can be an attractive alternative when one or more company employees have a pilot's license. Also, as the screening at airports has become more time-consuming, a growing number of companies have found the private air alternative attractive especially through a leasing arrangement, which can be shared by several companies or even individuals.

The private airplane fleet may also be used to transport freight in certain emergency situations. Documents that are needed to consummate an important sale or repair parts that will prevent an assembly line from closing are examples of emergency situations in which the corporate jet may be called upon for freight duty. The objective of the private air fleet is usually to serve the travel needs of management, not to make routine deliveries of freight.

The cost of flying via a company plane is expensive and, depending on the size and accommodation provided, can be three to four times greater than commercial flights. Thus, the value attached to managers using a private plane must be high enough to offset or justify the higher cost. Since the 9/11 incidents and the heightened security measures at public airports, many companies have increased their use of private or leased air service to save the time of their highly paid, valuable employees.

Another justification for private air service is to provide movement to certain smaller and perhaps more remote communities where access is difficult. This is especially true for small communities that have lost some or all of their scheduled commercial flights because of a decrease in demand. The cost of the time of an executive waiting for commercial flights can justify the expense of a private plane.

Private Water Transportation

The use of company-owned or leased ships and barges is common for the transportation of bulk, large-volume products such as coal, ore, and oil. Most private domestic water transportation utilizes barge operations. Firms can lease or buy barges and towboats to transport their own bulk products over the inland waterways in the United States as well as in other countries. Some firms operate ships that carry ore and coal over the Great Lakes and along the Atlantic, Gulf of Mexico, and Pacific coasts. The Great Lakes ships may also move through the St. Lawrence Seaway to and from the Atlantic Ocean ports.

Private water transportation can be advantageous for the movement of bulk, low-value products that move in large volume between limited origins and destinations. As indicated earlier, coal, ores, and petroleum products are typical commodities moved by private water carrier fleets. These products are usually moved regularly and in large volumes from places such as mines, grain silos, and ports of entry to steel mills, electrical generating plants, refineries, processing mills, or storage facilities.

A relatively large investment (capital) is required to begin private water carrier operations. This investment includes the capital required for the vehicles (barges, towboats, and ships) and for the dock facilities. It should be noted that the dock facility expenses would be incurred if either private or for-hire water transportation were used. The shipper (receiver) is responsible for providing docking facilities to load and unload cargo at the shipper's plant just as the side track is used for rail operations to a shipper's plant. Public ports are available, but the private water carrier would be required to use some form of land transportation (truck or rail) to move the cargo between the public port and the shipper's plant, and also there is usually a user fee at the public dock or port.

Private Oil Pipeline Transportation

Private oil pipeline transportation exists in a constrained form similar to that found with some smaller railroads. Although the vast majority of oil pipelines are regulated and required to operate as for-hire transportation companies, it is common for the major oil companies to own for-hire oil pipelines. Essentially, the owners of the oil pipeline have invested in a transportation company that provides service to them as well as to other shippers of petroleum products. The regulation of oil company–owned oil pipelines is meant to ensure that the independent, oil companies have access to pipeline transportation at reasonable rates as noted in Chapter 8.

The rationale for the shipper-owned oil pipelines was originally based upon market control as noted in Chapter 8, but there is an economic rationale also. A very large investment is required to develop a pipeline. The large fixed costs necessitate high traffic volume for the service to be economical. Like the railroads, duplicate or parallel oil pipelines can create excess capacity and economic waste. Thus, shipper ownership, especially multiple shipper ownership, mitigates the high start-up cost barrier to entry and provides a requisite economic volume of shipper-owner traffic to be moved through the oil pipeline. It should be noted again that there are independent oil pipelines not owned by oil companies, and the number of pipeline miles operated by such companies is increasing. It should be noted again that the discovery and more economical recovery of so-called shale oil in the United States, Canada, and other countries is reshaping the oil transportation systems, including pipeline movements.

Private Trucking

Private trucking is the most frequently used and most pervasive form of transportation in the United States and in some other countries. ACT, a trucking research firm, says that private fleets in the United States generate $217 billion in revenue.[1] Just over half of the tons of commodities shipped domestically are hauled by private carriers.[2] Private fleets also contribute to 2.5 percent of the gross domestic product.

Prior to the dissolution of the ICC, the exact number of private fleets in operation was difficult to determine because firms were not required to report private trucking operations. However, the Department of Transportation (DOT) now requires private trucking firms to register with the DOT which provides more accurate data. The U.S. Census Bureau estimates that there are 4 million private trucks on the road, as reported by the National Private Truck Council.

It is safe to state that private trucking is an integral segment of the transportation system employed by the shipping public in the United States and most other countries because of its relatively low start-up cost and flexibility of operations. At one time or another, almost every company will study or actually operate a private truck fleet, even if the fleet consists of only one truck. For this reason, an in-depth analysis of private trucking (from the reasons for private trucking to the operation of a fleet) is provided below.

Why Private Trucking? The primary reasons for a firm having a private truck fleet are improved service and/or lower costs. In either case, the private fleet operator is attempting to improve the marketability and profitability of its products. Through improved levels of service, the firm attempts to differentiate its product (lower transit time) and increase its sales and profits. Reduced costs permit the company to keep prices constant (a price reduction during inflationary times), to lower prices, or to increase profits directly. The advantages and disadvantages of private trucking are summarized in Table 13-1. This table provides a convenient reference for the discussion that follows about private truck transportation and can be a useful tool for the evaluation of the potential for private trucking in specific situations. Tables 13-2 and 13-3 provide insight into the types of costs for private trucking, and an example is provided to demonstrate how this information could be applied to determine whether private transportation was feasible.

TABLE 13-1 Advantages and Disadvantages of Private Trucking

ADVANTAGES	DISADVANTAGES
Improved Service Convenience, Flexible Operation, Greater Control, Lower Transit Times, Lower Inventory Levels, Reduced Damage, Driver/Salesperson, Last Resort (special needs) **Lower Cost** Reduced Transportation Costs (Eliminates Carrier Profit), Reduced Inventory Levels, Advertising, Bargaining Power With For-Hire Carriers, For-hire authority to backhaul, Lower Driver Turnover	**Higher Cost** Transportation Cost Higher Than For-Hire, Empty Backhaul, Lack of Managerial Talent, Added Overhead and Managerial Burden, Capital Requirements, Cargo Damage and Theft Responsibility, Liability for Accidents, Increased Paperwork, Breakdown on the Roads, Labor Union

TABLE 13-2 Private Truck Costs

FIXED COSTS	OPERATING COSTS
Depreciation (lease) Trucks, Trailers, Garage, Office	**Labor (drivers)** Wages, Fringe Benefits, FICA (Workers Compensation), Layover Allowances
Interest On Investment Vehicles, Garage, Office, Maintenance Equipment	**Vehicle Operating Costs** Fuel, Oil, Grease, Filters, Tires, Tubes, Maintenance (Labor and Parts), Road Service, Tolls
Management Costs Salaries, Fringe Benefits, Travel and Entertainment, FICA (Workers Compensation)	**Insurance** Liability, Collision and Comprehensive, Cargo
Office and Garage Costs Salaries, Utilities, Rent or Property Cost, Supplies, Communication	**License and Registration Fees** **Highway User Taxes** Fuel, Ton-Mile, Federal Use Tax

TABLE 13-3 Fixed Costs of Trucking*

COST ITEM	CENTS/MILE
Fixed Costs	
Depreciation on Vehicle	8.7
Interest on Vehicle	3.2
Depreciation and Interest on Other Items	1.6
Management and Overhead	13.6
Total Fixed	27.1

*Based on Long Distance Haulers of Refrigerated Fruit.
Source: U.S. Department of Agriculture.

Improved Service A private truck fleet permits a firm to have greater control and flexibility in its transportation system so it can respond to customer needs, both external (for finished goods) and internal (for raw materials). The increased responsiveness is derived from the direct control that the private carrier has over the dispatching, routing, and delivery schedules of the fleet. Such control means the private carrier can lower transit times to the customer, lower inventory levels, and possibly lower inventory stock-outs.

Because the driver is really an employee of the seller, improved relations may result from private trucking. The driver now has a vested interest in satisfying customer needs and in being courteous. In addition, the private carrier driver would probably exercise greater care in handling freight and would reduce the frequency of freight damage.

Private fleets usually have higher driver retention due to better pay, benefits, and human resource policies. While national truckload carriers often have driver turnover over 100 percent, private fleets on average have 16 percent turnover.[3]

Some firms use the private truck as a moving store, calling on many customers along a route to take orders and to deliver merchandise. (The delivery milk truck, now virtually extinct, is a good example of the moving store.) For such merchandising operations, a for-hire carrier does not allow the firm to exercise the necessary control and direction, and private trucking is the only viable alternative.

The last-resort advantage of private trucking emanates from a lack of capable for-hire carrier service. Firms that ship products requiring special equipment (for example, cryogenics [liquid gas] require a pressurized tank trailer) may have difficulty finding for-hire carriers with such special equipment and are virtually forced into private trucking to remain in business.

Capital availability can be a problem for some firms. The money invested in truck, trailers, and maintenance facilities is money that is not available for use in the company's primary business. This capital problem can be mitigated by leasing the equipment.

As a private carrier, the firm bears the risk of loss and damage to its freight. To hedge against possible loss, the private carrier can buy cargo insurance or act as a self-insured carrier (merely absorb all losses). Customers receiving damaged goods will contact the seller (private carrier) for reimbursement, and failure (or delay) of payment is a direct indictment against the seller. When a for-hire carrier is used, the seller can "wash its hands" of the claim because the dispute is between the buyer and the carrier, assuming FOB origin terms of sale.

The risk of public liability resulting from a vehicle accident is incurred by the private fleet. This risk can be mitigated by insurance, but the possibility of excessive court judgments is always present.

The cost of paperwork and maintenance for long-distance, multistate operations is greater than for short-distance or local operations. The clerical costs associated with accounting for mileage driven in various states, gallons of fuel purchased in different states, and vehicle licenses or permits required by different states escalate as the scope of the private carriage operation becomes multistate.

Breakdowns away from the home terminal or garage requiring emergency road service are more expensive than normal maintenance service. The possibility of such emergency service increases as the operating scope increases. Breakdowns also reduce the service levels and have an impact on customer service and eventually sales and profits.

As indicated earlier, there are disadvantages to private trucking, but the fact that there are so many private truck fleets suggests that the advantages can outweigh the disadvantages for many firms. The firm's analysis of costs and benefits of private trucking is critical at the evaluation stage as well as throughout the operation of the fleet.

Private Trucking Cost Analysis

Efficient and economical private truck operation requires a working knowledge of the actual cost of operating the fleet. The manager must know the facts affecting the individual cost elements of private trucking to make effective decisions that lower costs and improve service.

Fixed Costs Fixed costs are those that do not vary in the short run. For private trucking, these costs can be grouped into four areas: depreciation (lease payments), interest on investment, management, and office and garage. For example, the fixed costs are approximately 27.1 cents per mile for fleets of long-distance haulers of refrigerated products.

The fixed cost per mile varies inversely with the number of miles operated per year. The greater the number of miles driven, the lower the fixed cost per mile; that is, the total fixed cost is spread over a larger number of miles. Therefore, most private truck fleet managers who refer to the scale economies associated with increased vehicle utilization are concerned with spreading fixed costs over a larger number of miles.

For example, if annual use equals 140,000 miles, total fixed cost for the operation described in Table 13-3 is $37,940 (140,000 miles × $0.271). If the vehicle is operated over 200,000 miles, approximately 43 percent greater utilization than the 140,000 miles per year, the fixed cost per mile would decrease to 19.9 cents per mile ($39,740 ÷ 200,000).

Interest on vehicles (investment) accounts for 3.2 cents per mile or approximately 12 percent of total fixed cost per mile, as indicated in Table 13-3. Because of the relatively low cost of borrowing money, vehicle interest cost has dropped from 25 percent in 1989 to 12 percent or less of total fixed costs in recent years.

Management and overhead (office and garage) costs are approximately 13.6 cents per mile or about 50 percent of total fixed costs. It is quite common to find management costs being understated in a private trucking operation. Management time, and therefore costs, is siphoned from the primary business of the firm to assist in managing the fleet. Rarely is this "free" management talent accounted for in the private fleet cost analysis.

Vehicle depreciation can represent about 32.1 percent of total fixed costs or 8.7 cents per mile. The actual cost of a truck depends upon the size, carrying capacity, engine, and market conditions.

Operating Costs Operating costs are those costs that vary in the short run. Private trucking operating costs consist of fuel, driver wages, maintenance, insurance, license fees, tires, and user taxes. As indicated in Table 13-4, operating cost as reported by the American Transportation Research Institute (published 2008) was $1.73 per mile. Again, it is important to note that is a dynamic number that will change with economic circumstances.

The total operating cost varies directly with the number of miles operated per year. The greater the number of miles operated, the greater the total operating costs. The operating cost per mile will remain approximately the same in the short run.

For example, total operating cost for 140,000 miles per year is $242,200 (140,000 miles × $1.73). If the mileage per year is increased to 200,000 miles, total operating cost will increase to about $346,000. In reality, license, insurance, and certain miscellaneous costs

TABLE 13-4 Example of Operational Trucking Costs

MOTOR CARRIER MARGINAL EXPENSE	COSTS PER MILE	COSTS PER HOURS
Vehicle-based		
Fuel-oil Costs	.634	$33.00
Truck/Trailer Lease or Purchase Payments	.206	$10.72
Repair and Maintenance	.092	$4.79
Fuel Taxes	.062	$3.23
Truck Insurance Premiums	.060	$3.12
Tires	.030	$1.56
Licensing and Overweight-Oversize Permits	.024	$1.25
Tolls	.019	$0.99
Driver-Based		
Driver Pay	.441	$16.59
Driver Benefits	.126	$6.56
Driver Bonus Payments	.036	$1.87
Total Marginal Costs	**$1.73**	**$83.68**

Source: American Transportation Research Institute, 2008.

will remain constant per year and then decrease per mile; maintenance costs, however, will increase.

Fuel and oil costs represent 36 percent (63 cents per mile) of operating costs. After a spike in retail prices in late 2008, seen in Figure 13-1, diesel fuel prices have dropped off and have averaged about $2.20 per gallon over the first half of 2014. A diesel tractor averages about 4.5 to 5.5 miles per gallon, and a gasoline tractor averages a little less. For most transportation companies, fuel is usually the second highest operational expense, exceeded only by labor costs, and can be the foremost expenditure.[4]

FIGURE 13-1 U.S. On-Highway Diesel

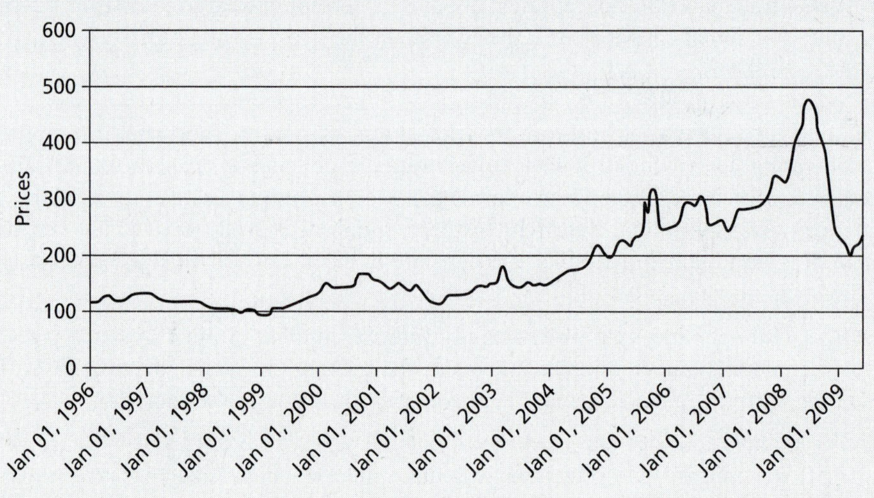

Table 13-4 indicates that maintenance, repair, and tire costs were 12 cents per mile or 7 percent of total operating costs. Maintenance cost includes the cost of normal preventative maintenance such as oil lubrication and new tires and major and minor repairs.

The remaining operating cost (insurance, license, and miscellaneous) account for about 10 cents per mile. Insurance cost includes the cost of vehicle collision and comprehensive protection, public and personal liability, and cargo insurance. The company's rate of accidents determines the insurance premium assessed.

The cost of licensing and registering the vehicle is determined by the size of the vehicle and by the individual state and the number of other states in which the vehicle operates. The license fee for a given truck is not uniform among the states. Most states require a registration fee to use state highways. Thus, the greater the geographic scope of the private truck operation, the greater the license and registration cost.

Miscellaneous costs include such operating items as tolls, overload fines, and driver road expenses (lodging and meals). A private truck fleet manager must scrutinize miscellaneous operating costs closely because miscellaneous costs can "hide" inefficient and uneconomical operations.

A fundamental requirement for an economical private truck fleet is knowing the costs. Once the costs are known and analyzed, effective decisions can be made. In the next section, attention is directed to the major operating decisions in private trucking.

ON THE **LINE**

Taking the Company Private

Following the passage of the Motor Carrier Act of 1980, the for-hire sector of the motor carrier industry became increasingly competitive. As noted in Chapter 3 and 5, the Act essentially deregulated the motor carrier sector by eliminating many of the restrictions on rates. Routes and commodities allowed carriers and shippers an opportunity to negotiate rates and service levels but more importantly increased the number of carriers available to provide service in the best traffic lanes. This increased competition served to reduce many of the prevailing rates on those traffic lanes, sometimes by a substantial amount, and many companies started to outsource their transportation requirements to reduce their overall costs and reduce their investment in fixed assets.

The 21st century has ushered in a renewed interest in private trucking. Increased carrier rates, capacity shortages in some areas, and concerns about delivery service have caused companies to reconsider the private trucking option. This is particularly true of companies with predictable routings, the potential for backhauls, and demanding customers who expect "perfect orders." Some companies are also seeing advertising value with their names, logos, and so forth on the sides of their trucks. Of course, there could be a negative aspect in the case of an accident or some driver transgression. Changes in regulations give private carriers new opportunities to sell their unused capacity.

Private fleets still face the same potential issues as for-hire carriers, such as higher fuel charges, driver shortages, and road and infrastructure conditions. Private fleets usually have much lower driver turnover rates than for-hire carrier fleets with consequent customer service benefits. Another alternative for shippers is to purchase dedicated service from larger carriers. Dedicated service is analogous to buying guaranteed carrying capacity for the future, as discussed in Chapter 5.

Source: Danielle Gallagher, Center for Supply Chain Research, The Pennsylvania State University, 2010.

Major Operating Decisions

Fleet operators try hard to improve fuel mileage because the savings potential is great. For example, assume the fleet depicted in Table 13-3 was able to increase vehicle mileage per gallon by 10 percent, from 5 miles per gallon to 5.5 miles per gallon. The total fuel cost savings for 140,000 miles per year would amount to $2,800 per truck or 9.1 percent. Such potential savings are usually sufficient justification for a $200 to E$400 expenditure for an air deflector or for radial tires.

Driver cost (non-union) was 60.3 cents per mile or 35 percent of total operating cost, as given in Table 13-3. Over-the-road drivers are usually paid on the basis of the miles driven. City drivers are paid on an hourly basis. Table 13-5 provides an example of a union contract covering drivers in the Midwest.

As indicated in Table 13-5, over-the-road drivers were paid 42.0 cents per mile; this rate of pay was the same whether the tractor-trailer was loaded or empty. The rate was 43.0 cents per mile for driving a tractor pulling double trailers or twins. However, the over-the-road driver was paid $17.10 per hour for delays such as breakdowns. If we assume an over-the-road driver drives 125,000 miles per year (2,500 miles per week × 50 weeks), the fringe benefit cost equals 15.0 cents per mile ($18,803.70/125,000).

The city (pickup and delivery) driver was paid $17.36 per hour. To this hourly rate for city drivers (and over-the-road drivers) must be added the cost of fringe benefits, which amounted to $9.79 per hour. The 1993 total driver costs, then, were $27.15 per hour ($17.36 hourly rate plus $9.79 fringe benefits per hour) Fringe benefits represented 36.1 percent of the total city driver cost.

TABLE 13-5 Example of Driver Costs

	Driver Wages	
Over-the-Road		**City**
.42 cents/mile (5 axle combination) .43 cents/mile (double trailer) $17.10/hour (waiting)		$17.36/hour
	Fringe Benefits	
Benefit	**Total Cost**	**Cost/Hour (1920 hrs/yr)***
Hospitalization ($112.70/week)	$5,860.40	$3.05
Pension ($88.00/week)	4,576.00	2.38
Holidays (10 days @ $138.88/day)	1,388.80	.72
Vacation (2.0 weeks @ $781.20/week)**	1,562.40	.81
FICA (7.65%)	2,775.60	1.45
Federal Unemployment	64.00	.03
State Unemployment***	762.38	.40
Worker's Compensation***	1,814.12	.95
Total Fringe Costs	$18,803.70	$9.79

*Total hours possible = 52 weeks × 40 hours/week
Less: Vacation (80 hours), Holidays (80 hours) Hours worked/year 2,080 hours − 160 = 1,920

**Vacation is an average; Actual is based on years of service

***Varies by state (5% rate used)

Equipment The private trucking manager is concerned with two basic equipment questions: What type of equipment should be selected, and should this equipment be purchased or leased? Each of these questions is discussed below.

Choosing the type, size, make, model, type of engine, and so on of the vehicle used in private trucking seems to be an overwhelming challenge. However, the equipment used is determined by the firm's transportation requirements. The size of the shipment, product density, length of haul, terrain, city versus intercity operation, and special equipment needs are the equipment determinants to be examined. Table 13-6 provides a summary of the equipment selection factors and implications.

The size of the shipment and product density determine the carrying capacity desired in the vehicle. Shipments averaging 45,000 pounds will require five-axle tractor-trailer combinations. However, a low-density commodity such as fiberglass insulation requires a large carrying capacity, even though the weight of the shipment is low (10,000 pounds of fiberglass insulation can be carried in a trailer 40 feet long).

Long-distance operations, 300 miles or more one way and 75,000 or more miles per year, usually indicate the use of diesel-powered equipment. Diesel engines have a longer life and get better mileage than gasoline engines, but diesel engines have a higher initial cost. Some recent developments in diesel engine design have produced an economical, short-range, city diesel engine.

The terrain over which the vehicle travels affects the selection of certain equipment component parts such as the engine and drive train. For mountainous operations, the truck will require a high-powered engine and a low-geared drive train. For level, interstate highway operations, a lower-powered engine with a high-geared drive train is in order. Vehicles

TABLE 13-6 Equipment Selection Factors and Implications

SELECTION FACTOR/CHARACTERISTICS	EQUIPMENT IMPLICATION
Shipment Size	
• Large Size Shipment (> 35,000 lbs)	Vehicles That Can Haul 80,000 lbs
• Small Size Shipment (< 10,000 lbs)	Vehicles That Can Haul 30,000 lbs
Product Density	
• Low Density (< 15 lbs/feet cubed)	High Cube Capacity Vehicles (Trailers That Are 110 Inches High, 102 Inches Wide, and 57 Feet Long)
• High Density (> 15 lbs/feet cubed)	Normal Cube Capacity
Length of Haul	
• < 75,000 Miles Annually	Gasoline Powered
• > 75,000 Miles Annually	Diesel Powered
• Trips > 1,000 One-Way Miles	Diesel Powered with Sleep Cells
City Operations	Gasoline Powered
Intercity Operations	Diesel Powered
Terrain	
• Mountainous	Higher-Powered Engines
• Level	Lower-Powered Engines
Special Needs	
• Controlled Temperature	Refrigerated Trailers
• Customer Required Unloading	Power Tailgate

designed for mountainous operations usually are restricted to the mountainous regions because it makes sense to use different powered units in different regions.

Another transportation factor to be considered is the need for special equipment—refrigeration, power tailgates, high cube capacity, and so on. The nature of the product and customer requirements will dictate the type of special equipment to be considered.

A final consideration is the use of sleeper cabs for tractors. The sleeper cab adds several thousand dollars ($2,000–$4,000) to the initial price of the vehicle and is usually only considered when the trips are more than 1,000 miles one way. The sleeper permits the use of two drivers: One can accumulate the required off-duty time in the sleeper bed while the other driver continues to drive. The two-driver team produces lower transit time and better service. However, lower transit time also can be accomplished by substituting drivers at appropriate intervals.

The sleeper cab also can eliminate the cost of lodging for a one-driver operation. Instead of paying for a room, the driver accumulates the required eight hours off duty in the sleeping bed. However, there is a fuel cost to run the engine to produce heat or cooling for the driver in the sleeper. This fuel cost for a large diesel engine is typically 2 to 4 gallons of fuel per hour or $4.40 to $8.80 per hour (at $2.20 per gallon). The sleeper cost per eight-hour rest could be $35.20 to $70.40, which is comparable to current daily lodging costs. An increased focus on reducing idling time, reducing both fuel costs and emissions, is a trend that many firms are embracing. Using auxiliary power units (APUs) to provide secondary power to sleeper cabs can reduce fuel costs during non-driving hours.

Leasing One of the disadvantages of private trucking, identified in Table 13-1, is the capital requirement for the equipment. Many firms are finding it difficult to buy money to use in the primary business; they cannot afford to buy a fleet of trucks as well. Leasing the equipment for a private truck operation reduces demands on company funds and enables existing capital to be used in the primary business of the company.

There are two basic types of lease arrangements available: the full-service lease and the finance lease. Both types are available with a lease-buy option that gives the lessee the option to buy the equipment, at book value, at the end of the lease.

The full-service lease includes the leased vehicle plus a variety of operating support services. The more services requested by the lessee, the greater the lease fee. The full-service leasing fee consists of a weekly or monthly fixed fee per vehicle, plus a mileage fee.

In addition, the cost of fuel purchased from the lessor will be charged to the lessee. The full-service lease is a popular method of leasing trucks and tractors that require maintenance and other services.

The finance lease is only a means of financing equipment. Under the finance lease, the lessee pays a monthly fee that covers the purchase cost of the equipment and the lessor's finance charge. No services are provided by the lessor: All maintenance is the responsibility of the lessee. The finance lease is a common method of leasing trailers that require little maintenance.

The economic test of buying versus leasing is a comparison of the net present cost of buying versus leasing. The net present cost is a flow discounted cash approach that considers the cost and savings of both buying and leasing as well as the tax adjustments.

Fleet Operation and Control The daily operation of a private fleet is a complex undertaking, and the discussion of daily operations is beyond the scope of this text. However, attention will be given to the operational areas of organization, regulation, driver utilization, the empty backhaul, and control mechanisms.

Organizing the Private Fleet Once the fleet is in operation, intra-organizational conflicts may arise. These conflicts center on the incompatibility of departmental (user) demands and the private fleet goals.

To avoid this conflict, the goal of the fleet is normally a cost-constrained service goal. That is, the goal is to provide good service at a given level of cost. The fleet manager can then provide the best service that a given level of cost will permit.

Another organizational problem is the user's concept that private trucking is free transportation.

One organizational approach to eliminate the idea of free transportation is to establish the private fleet as a profit center. The income generated by the fleet is a paper or internal budget fee assessed to the using departments. The real costs are subtracted from the paper income to generate a paper profit. The manager's performance is evaluated on this paper profit. To guard against the idea that the private fleet must make a profit at any cost to the user, the departments must be given the option of using the private fleet or for-hire carriers (competition).

By establishing the fleet as a profit center, the fleet is operated as a separate business entity with management responsible for profitability and asset utilization. The establishment of a separate corporate entity for the fleet that has secured operating authority permits the fleet to solicit business from other shippers, thereby increasing the fleet utilization, eliminating the empty backhaul, and possibly generating a profit for the parent firm.

The question of where to position the fleet in the organization (in which department) is another important question. Usually a profit-center fleet is set up as a separate department reporting to the chief executive officer of the parent company.

Many private fleets are centrally organized because that permits the fleet manager to provide service to different departments and divisions in the organization, thus increasing fleet utilization. A decentralized operation usually is found where separate divisions have different operating and vehicle requirements and have sufficient volume to make the separation economical.

Controlling the Private Fleet A key element to an effective and efficient private truck fleet is control over cost and performances. Table 13-7 is a list of cost and performance criteria for effective private truck fleet control.

Costs by function must be collected at the source. Fuel costs (and gallons) should be noted for each vehicle. This notation of functional costs at the cost source permits analysis of individual cost centers for the actual costs incurred. It is very difficult to analyze the fuel efficiency of individual vehicles in a fleet when fuel costs are aggregated for the entire fleet.

Further, the collection of functional costs by driver, vehicle, plant, and so on will permit analysis of problem areas within the fleet. The use of fleet averages only may conceal inefficient operations at particular markets or plants. However, functional costs by vehicle, plant, and driver can be compared to fleet-wide averages, and a management-by-exception approach can be practiced. That is, if the specific costs (fuel cost/given driver) are within acceptable limits, nothing is done. Management action is taken when the specific costs are out of line with the desired level.

TABLE 13-7 Private Cost and Performance Control Criteria

COST	PERFORMANCE
By function Fuel (and gallons), Driver, Maintenance, Interest, Depreciation, Tires, Parts, Management, Overhead, License and Registration	Miles Operated By Vehicle, By Driver Empty Miles Total, By Location Human Resource Hours Total, Driving, Loading and Unloading, Breakdown
Functional Cost By Vehicle, Driver, Plant, Market, Warehouse, Customer	Vehicle Operating Hours By Vehicle Number of Trips By Vehicle/Time Period Tonnage By Vehicle Number of Stops (Deliveries) By Driver

The performance criteria to be considered are miles operated (loaded and empty), human resource hours expended, vehicle operating hours, number of trips made, tonnage hauled, and the number of stops made. By collecting the above performance data, the fleet manager is able to measure the fleet's utilization and the drivers' productivity. Control measures such as overall cost per mile, per hour, and per trip can be computed and used in determining unacceptable performance areas in the fleet. Such information also is valuable to marketing and purchasing departments that determine the landed cost of goods sold or purchased.

Likewise, performance measures must be collected and identified at the source. Total fleet mileage and total fleet fuel consumption (gallons) will permit determination of overall fleet fuel efficiency. However, collection of fuel consumption and mileage per individual vehicle will provide the information necessary for purchasing fuel-efficient vehicles as replacements or additions to the fleet.

The performance criteria enable the fleet manager to analyze the productivity of drivers. The number of miles driven per day, the number of stops (deliveries) made per day, or the number of hours per run or trip are driver productivity measures that can be collected for each driver. From this productivity data, individual drivers who drive fewer miles per day, make fewer stops per day, or take a longer time to make a run than the standards (fleet average, for example) are singled out for further investigation and corrective action.

Regulations As stated earlier, bona fide private trucking is exempt from federal economic regulations in the United States. The private carrier need not secure authorization (certificate of public convenience and necessity) to transport the firm's products. Because private coverage is not for-hire service, no tariffs are published.

A common problem many private fleets face is how to eliminate the empty backhaul. Miles traveled without a load add cost to the company, including the time consumed. In Figure 13-2, the cost of filling that backhaul can be calculated in comparison to leaving those miles empty.

FIGURE 13-2 Backhaul Cost Analysis Form

Total trip miles including backhaul	=	______	miles (A)
Normal deliver round-trip miles	=	______	miles (B)
Difference (excess miles)	=	______	miles (C)
Multiplied by cost per mile	=	$ ______	(D)
Additional labor expended			
___ (hr) × $___ (avg wage + benefits)	=	$ ______	(E)
Total cost (D + E)	=	$ ______	(F)
Gross backhaul revenue	=	$ ______	
Less total cost (Line F)	=	$ ______	
Profit (or loss)	=	$ ______	

Source: National Private Truck Council, "Filling Backhaul Miles for Private Fleets," 2006.

Fleets with for-hire authority must publish rates and charges with the government, which is a shift from the lack of reporting requirements under exclusive private transportation.[6]

One option that eliminates the requirement for for-hire authority is trip leasing. The lease agreement is between a private carrier and another firm, for a single trip, and cannot last more than 30 days. The private carrier is responsible for licensing and recordkeeping, and a copy of the trip lease agreement must be carried in the vehicle during the trip.[7] The private carrier also may trip lease to another private carrier and charge a fee for the service provided.

Another solution to eliminating empty backhaul is the transportation of exempt commodities. Exempt commodities may be hauled without ICC authority or other economic regulations. Some examples of exempt commodities are ordinary livestock, agricultural products (grain, fruits, vegetables), horticultural goods (Christmas trees), newspapers, freight incidental air transportation (to and from airports), used shipping containers, and fish.

Private trucking is subjected to all federal safety requirements in the areas of:

- driver qualifications
- driving practices
- vehicle parts and accessories
- accident reporting
- driver hours of service
- vehicle inspection and maintenance
- hazardous materials transportation
- vehicle weight and dimensions

These safety regulations are enforced by the U.S. Department of Transportation (DOT), Bureau of Motor Carrier Safety, and the private carrier must register with the U.S. DOT.

In addition, the private fleet must comply with the state safety regulations governing speed, weight, and vehicle length, height, and width. Such state regulations fall within the

FIGURE 13-3 Driver's Log

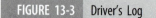

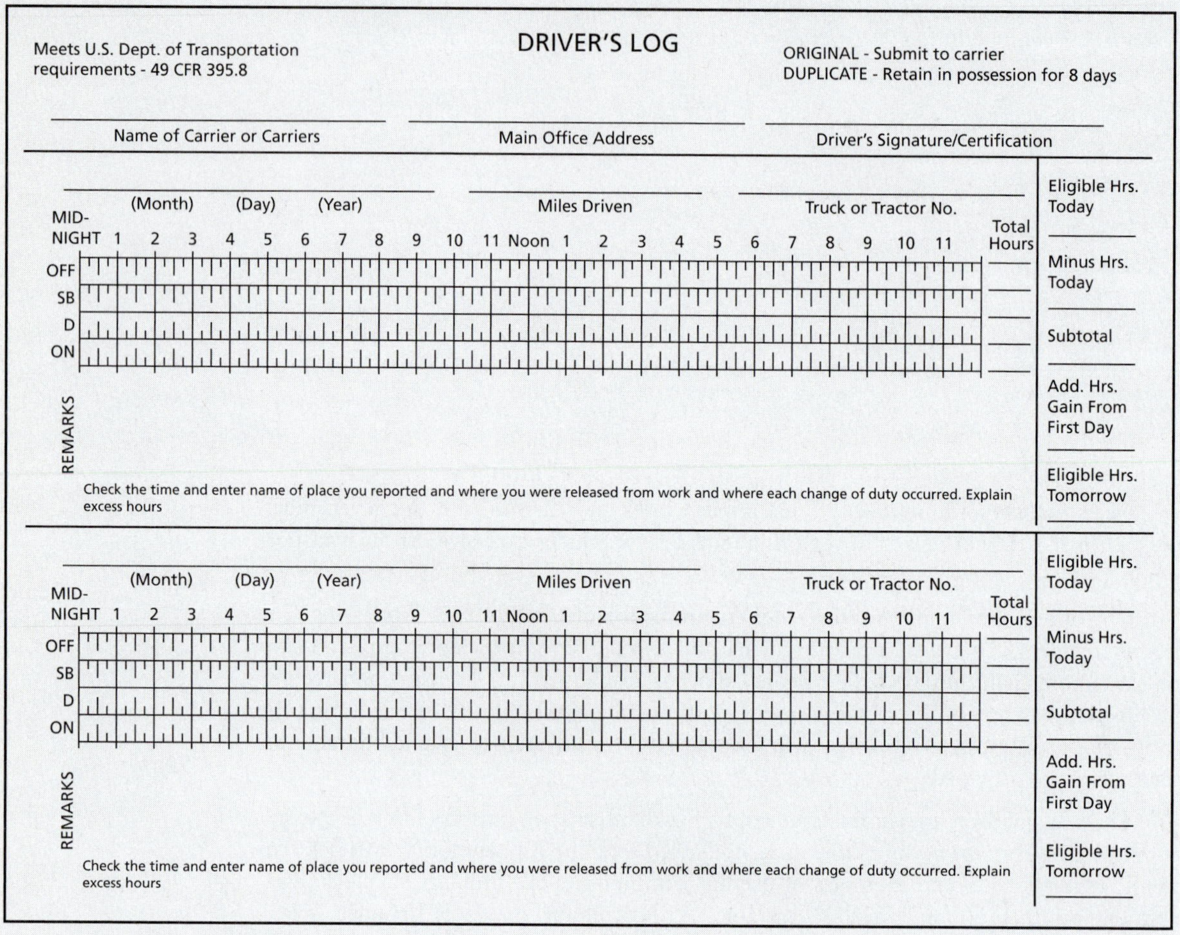

Source: U.S. Dept. of Transportation requirements - 49 CFR 395.8

purview of the constitutionally granted police powers that permit states to enact laws to protect the health and welfare of their citizens. Because the safety regulations are not uniform among the states, the fleet management must be aware of specific regulations in each of the states in which the fleet operates.

Driver hours-of-service regulations establish the maximum number of hours (minimum safety level) a driver may operate a vehicle in interstate commerce, and consequently they affect the utilization of drivers.

SUMMARY

- Private transportation is an important component of the transportation system in most countries of the world, including the United States where it plays a significant and complimentary role to the for-hire sector of the total transportation system for all five modes of transportation.
- Private transportation was defined in the Interstate Commerce Act, and it essentially involves the movement of goods owned by a firm that also owns or leases and operates the equipment for the furtherance of its primary business.
- While private transportation is most prevalent in the trucking sector of the transportation system, it is also important in the rail, air, water and pipeline sectors. Private transportation in each of these five modes has some unique characteristics.
- Private rail transportation is special in that it usually takes the form of privately owned or leased rail cars of other businesses that are moved by a for-hire railroad company over their tracks. There are, however, some large manufacturing companies that operate on their own lines within the limits of their plant properties.
- Private air transportation, unlike the other modes of transportation, is used primarily for the movement of passengers. While usually more expensive than commercial airline service, private air service is usually rationalized on the basis of the time saved for valuable employees, especially currently with all the security controls at airports. Also, such service may be justified as the only alternative for getting to remote points by air.
- Private water transportation is very common in the movement of bulk, large-volume, low-value products such as coal, ore, mining products, oil, and agricultural products. Most private, domestic water service is provided by barge movements on the inland waterways, the Great Lakes or coastal waterway systems.
- Private pipeline service has been a major part of the oil industry since the 19th century where it was initially implemented for industry control purposes. However, the oil company pipelines were subsequently required by federal law to also operate as common carriers to ensure that other oil companies had adequate service at a reasonable cost.
- Private trucking is the most frequently used and most pervasive form of private transportation. About half of the ton-miles of commodities shipped domestically by trucks are moved by private truck transportation.
- Private trucking is typically justified on the basis of cost (efficiency) or service (effectiveness). Some private fleet operators maintain that both objectives are achieved, which obviously enhances overall profitability of the company.
- The decision to provide private transportation service requires careful analysis of all the costs involved as well as the value of the benefits. The cost analysis requires estimating both fixed and variable/operating costs and is frequently very challenging to ensure accuracy.
- Leasing of equipment is an attractive alternative to outright ownership for a growing number of companies that do not want to make the capital outlay for some reason. Leasing companies provide a variety of leasing arrangements that may benefit private fleet operations.
- Private truck transportation for some companies can be a complex undertaking because of the daily operation of a fleet of equipment, which requires knowledge of

state and federal regulations about equipment and service; different taxes; driver management and utilization; equipment control and maintenance; and controlling empty back hauls.

STUDY QUESTIONS

1. Provide a legal and working definition of private transportation? Discuss the legal constraints imposed on the operation of a private carrier.
2. The nature of private transportation varies among the modes. Compare and contrast the nature of private transportation among the modes.
3. Private trucking is the most pervasive form of private carriage. Discuss the reasons why private trucking is such a popular alternative in the United States and in other countries.
4. Service and cost are the two areas most often cited as reasons for establishing a private trucking operation. Discuss the service and cost advantages afforded by private trucking.
5. What are the disadvantages of private trucking?
6. Using the data in Table 17-3, determine the managerial impact of (a) an increase in the annual miles operated per tractor/trailer from 100,000 to 125,000; (b) a decrease in the average load per trip from 40,000 pounds to 34,000 pounds; and (c) a 20 percent increase in the price of fuel from $1.10 to $1.32 per gallon.
7. If you were going to select trucks to operate over-the-road from Denver to Los Angeles, what type of equipment would you specify? Why? Would you specify the same type of equipment for a delivery operation within the county of Los Angeles? Why?
8. Why would a private fleet be organized on the basis of a cost center? A profit center?
9. Describe the methods available to a private carrier to operate as a for-hire carrier.
10. Discuss the economic and safety regulations imposed on private trucking by the federal government.

NOTES

1. John D. Schulz, "Transportation Best Practices/Trends: Private Fleets Master Their Destiny," *Logistics Management*, April 2013.
2. National Private Truck Council, "Industry Profile," 2014.
3. M. Theodore Farris, "Evaluating the Private Fleet," *Transportation Journal* (Fall 2008).
4. Ibid.
5. National Private Truck Council, "Filling Backhaul Miles for Private Fleets," 2006, p. 1.
6. Ibid.
7. Ibid.
8. Farris, "Evaluating the Private Fleet."
9. David Cantor, Thomas M. Corsi, and Curtis M. Grimm, "Do Electronic Log Book Contribute to Motor Carrier Safety Performance?" *Journal of Business Logistics*, Vol. 30, No. 1 (2009): 203.

CASE 13-1

Nittany Products: A Sequel

Nittany Products produces a variety of outdoor grills for private households as well as for commercial use. The business was started by Nick Shannon as a hobby. Nick Shannon liked to cook and particularly, liked to do outdoor cooking on a grill. The size of the groups that he entertained kept growing as his barbeques became almost legendary. During this period, Nick became very dissatisfied with his standard size grill that had been purchased at the Pleasant Gap Hardware Store. Being a metal fabricator by trade, he decided to build his own larger grill in his garage shop. Like most prototypes, it did not meet all of Nick's expectations, and he built additional versions until he was satisfied. His guests and neighbors were intrigued with his grill and asked him to build them similar grills. The number of requests were small enough that he could produce them in his garage. Nick estimated that he might receive 20 requests per year, which was manageable. When the requests reached 50 per year, he realize that he could not satisfy the demand using his garage shop. It was too small and precluded options to operate more efficiently So, Nick borrowed money from the local bank using his home for collateral and rented a nearby abandoned service station. He also purchased new tools and equipment and hired students from the local vocational school to work part-time during the school year and full-time in the summer to meet peak demand. His decisions resulted in much more business and lower production costs.

The success lead them to consider expanding their market area in central Pennsylvania. The population of the area had expanded significantly over the last 10 years since Nick initially began to build and sell grills because of the improved highway system and the growth of the nearby University. Nittany Products, to this point in time, had built the grills to customer needs, and shipped them assembled to customer locations when requested in 15–20-foot vans that they leased. Customers also had the option of picking up the grills themselves to eliminate the delivery charge. Nick needed to rethink the approach to production, marketing and logistics with an expanded market area, a much larger potential volume of sales, and an expanded product line.

Nick felt that it was more economical to ship the grills unassembled and have them assembled at the delivery point. He also recognized that home owners and restaurant owners could be challenged to assemble the grills especially since these were larger grills available with a variety of fuel options. He assumed that they would need to make deliveries in trucks with a driver who could efficiently assemble the grills for customers on-site. Such a strategy would require premium pricing and specially trained drivers. Nick and his daughter, Tracie, who joined her father in the business to manage the delivery service, felt that the delivery option offered a value added service that could enhance sales especially for their commercial customers who purchased larger, more expensive grills usually for their restaurant operations. They believed that they could sustain a private fleet with the expanded sales and market area.

CASE QUESTION

1. You have been hired by Nittany Products to develop a report presenting them with the advantages and disadvantages of offering customers delivery service as well as the special issues and challenges that their type of business would face with private transportation service. Based upon your discussion would you recommend private transportation service or some other option for delivery?

CASE 13-2

Naperville Hardware Distribution

Matt Weber and Quinn Domyancic, CEO and COO respectively of Naperville Hardware Distributors (NHD), were frustrated with their fourth quarter financial results. At the beginning of the quarter they had been enthusiastic about the profit picture for the company. The economy had been in an economic slump for several years, but the first quarter results of this year had shown a positive upturn in sales. The second and third quarter results were even better. Matt and Quinn had been almost exuberant even though profits had not shown much improvement. They both felt the profits in the fourth quarter would improve significantly because they had carryover expenses from the previous period, which they covered with revenue generated during the second and third quarters. While their net profits had again improved in the fourth quarter, the results were not what they expected.

NHD purchased the various hardware and plumbing products that they distributed from several manufactures located in Indiana, Illinois, and Wisconsin. They purchased in truckload quantities and had the items moved to a warehouse facility that they maintained in Naperville. They also operated a store that was contiguous to the warehouse plumbing contractors as well as some retail customers who did their own remodeling and repairs. NHD would make deliveries to customers in the greater Chicago area, especially builders and plumbing contractors.

Matt and Quinn asked their CFO, Carl Weber, do a "deep dive" on their costs for the last three years. Carl also did some benchmarking for them. Carl came to the conclusion that NHD was spending too much money on transportation and related distribution service. NHD was currently utilizing a third party logistics services company, LMZ for transportation (inbound and outbound). Carl recommended that they "in-source" all the transportation services.

Matt and Zach were surprised by Carl's conclusion about the outsourcing of their transportation services because they had been dealing with LMZ for about 10 years. Private transportation service and order fulfillment were not among their core competencies. They had some reservations. Carl pointed out that they had options that they could consider including leasing equipment and drivers.

CASE QUESTION

1. Matt and Quinn have hired you as a summer intern to evaluate their options and requested you to write a short report presenting the opportunities and challenges they would face in pursing Carl's recommendation. They also asked you to make your own recommendation based upon your analysis.

CHAPTER

14

ISSUES AND CHALLENGES FOR GLOBAL SUPPLY CHAINS

Learning Objectives

After reading this chapter, you should be able to do the following:

- Appreciate the serious challenges and major issues faced by the current transportation system for continued domestic and global economic growth
- Understand why and what factors contributed to the growth and prosperity that was experienced in recent years
- Discuss the economic and competitive challenges being caused by the decaying U.S. infrastructure and the threat to the economic viability of the major modes of transportation in the United States
- Gain a perspective on the critical role of government leadership and policy to resolve the crisis that exists for our global economy without capital funding for the U.S. transportation system
- Understand why sustainability has become a major objective for businesses and especially for transportation and the potential positive benefits of proactive sustainability strategies
- Appreciate the impact of new energy sources for the global economy
- Discuss the role and objectives of the SmartWay Transport Program sponsored by the U.S. Environmental Protection Agency
- Develop insights into the special challenges that transport companies will face in the 21st century with increased competition and changes in energy sources

- Understand the opportunities that transportation carriers will have to improve overall supply chain performance through proactive collaboration and appropriate use of new technology
- Discuss how supply chain technology can help transport carriers to improve efficiency and effectiveness for their operations and for their customer's costs and service

TRANSPORTATION PROFILE

Dark Clouds on the Horizon

Logistics and transportation professionals have been warning business and government organizations of the decaying transportation infrastructure throughout the United States. They have pointed to the deterioration of the roads and bridges both on the Interstate System and on state and local highway systems. Not only are funds for maintenance and repairs deficient, but new investment has not increased in relationship with the growth in the economy and the demands of global trade.

The rapid growth in global trade is also placing great pressure on U.S. ports, particularly coastal gateways through which nearly 80 percent of U.S. global freight by weight is moved to and from the ports by inland transportation. Congestion has been an issue, particularly at West Coast ports, due to growth in trade between the United States and the Asian-Pacific countries. The luxury of inland transport excess capacity, primarily truck and rail transport, of the 1980s and 1990s is nonexistent now. Congestion is also an issue on the nation's highways and at major freight rail gateways and corridors, most of which are critically important for traffic between West Coast port gateways and inland locations. While this issue was abated somewhat with the cyclical/short-run downturn in the global economy during the 2008–2009 time period, the problem is now more urgent than ever with the growth in the global economy that has occurred since that time.

Carrier capability to invest in the transportation infrastructure is also limited. The railroads' budget shortfall for expansion needed over the next 20 years is estimated to be over $50 billion. Similarly, the end-of-year balance of the Highway Trust Fund (HTF), which indicates whether the expected revenues will be sufficient to cover the anticipated spending, is declining. The HTF is largely financed by the federal fuel tax, which is 18.4 cents per gallon for gasoline and 24.4 cents for diesel; the rates have not changed since 1993. There is great reluctance to increase these taxes because of the burden on the general public and the potential impact on the prices of consumer goods.

When fuel prices were rising, vehicle miles traveled in the United States was declining, reducing funding for highways and transportation infrastructure initiatives even further. More fuel-efficient vehicles also contributed to the decline. The HTF is currently projected to be facing a major deficit of growing proportions, according to the White House. Driver shortages add further to the trucking service capacity concerns, especially in the long-haul truckload sector. In fact, with a high number of drivers near retirement age and higher levels of driver turnover, the long-haul truck driver shortage probably will reach 111,000 by 2015. The driver shortage was also mitigated during the 2008–2009 downturns in the global economy, but the resurging economy has exacerbated the problem again. Unfortunately, the driver shortage is a long-run/secular problem because of the average age of the long-haul drivers and the higher turnover rate. Consequently, it is not an issue that is going to go away and will need to be addressed more aggressively. It should be noted that some trucking companies have been proactive in working with their long-haul drivers to mitigate the problems associated with their home life. Some authors propose a simplistic solution, that is, raising driver wages. This tactic may be successful when there are limited employment opportunities, but it is not a long-run solution. Also, the consequent impact on rates will most likely raise the cost of goods to the consumer.

The transportation infrastructure problem has reached the crisis stage at the ports and in states like Pennsylvania. The federal government has to take the lead and stop ignoring the problem and encourage the states to follow their lead.

Source: Kusumal Ruamsook and Dawn Russell, White Paper, *Center for Supply Chain Research*, Penn State University, January 2011.

Introduction

Chapters 1 and 2 discussed the role and importance of transportation in the firm and in the economy. The economic, political, and social contributions and significance of transportation were examined. Transportation was described as the "glue" that holds supply chains together and the "life blood" of economies, regions, and cities. Our modern civilization and the developments, which have occurred in many countries, would not have been possible without an efficient and effective transportation system. It was also noted that transportation has been a critical part of economic, political, and social development for hundreds of years. In fact, transportation may be the most important business for a developed economy.

During the 1980s, 1990s, and the early part of the 21st century, transportation became relatively less expensive for a given level of service, which contributed significantly to enhanced productivity and economic growth. This phenomenon was attributable to two major factors, namely, relatively inexpensive fuel and competition, particularly in the motor carrier sector of the transportation industry. In fact, one could argue that we were "spoiled" by these two conditions that fostered economic prosperity. However, times have changed, with increased fuel prices and a reduction in available capacity in the motor carrier sector, due to driver hour restrictions and other factors discussed in Chapter 5. The other modes of transportation, especially air carriers, have faced similar challenges. This change has occurred at a crucial time in global development. The concern is that fuel charges, competitive market forces, and other factors could cause the cost of moving goods to increase in the years ahead. There are a number of factors, including congestion, the environment, and the transport infrastructure, that may affect the long global, and frequently, vulnerable supply chains with their movements of high-value, time-sensitive commodities. If these challenges are not mitigated, the cost of moving freight will thwart economic progress in developed as well as underdeveloped economies. Figure 14-1 clearly indicates the long-run potential for the U.S. transportation system when all three flows for the system are considered. The flows associated with imports into the country are particularly noteworthy. It is imperative to the economic health of the United States and its citizens that the challenges indicated above and discussed in this chapter be addressed in an objective manner.

FIGURE 14-1 Total Value of Shipments in the United States

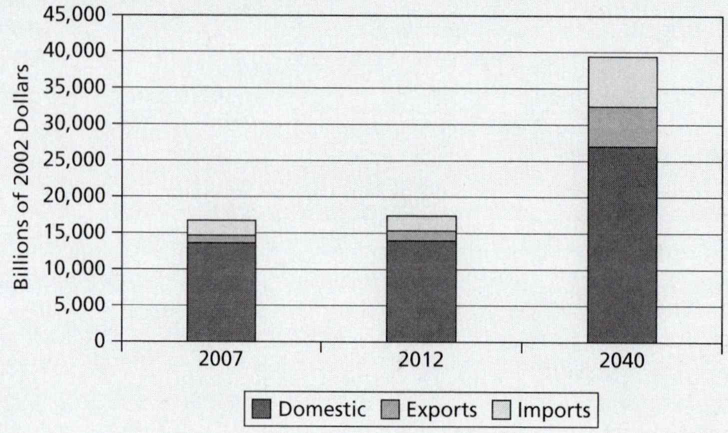

Source: Federal Highway Administration, U.S. Department of Transportation, Freight Facts and Figures 2013, Table 2-2: Value of Shipments by Transportation Mode: 2007, 2012, and 2040.

Since the transportation industry will have to address these challenges and issues in the future, we will discuss major issues in detail and examine their impact on the important sectors of the transportation industry. The initial issue will be the transportation infrastructure, followed by energy, technology, and sustainability.

Transportation Infrastructure

Everyone has probably experienced the frustration associated with congestion, usually when riding in an automobile on the highway; or perhaps it was on an airplane trying to takeoff or land at an airport. Some individuals experience congestion on a regular, daily basis if they live in or near a city and have to commute to and from work. However, we seldom consider the total or real cost of congestion. For individuals, the cost of extra fuel is the most obvious cost of congestion, but there is also the cost of the personal time lost, which could reduce personal earnings. If the congestion does not cause an obvious economic loss, it usually has an impact in the area of what an economist would call a social cost—reduced opportunity for leisure, reduced time with family, inconvenience for friends and family, and so on. The social cost is difficult to calibrate, but nevertheless, it is a societal cost that needs to be included in the analytical equation for congestion.

For many businesses, however, the cost of congestion is real and important. Consider the fact that Nike estimates that they have to spend an additional $4 million per week to carry an extra 7 to 14 days of inventory to compensate for congestion delays. One day of delay requires American President Lines' eastbound trans-Pacific services to increase its use of containers and chassis by 1,300 units, which adds $4 million of additional cost per year. The bottleneck delays of trucks on U.S. highways cause over 250 million hours of delay to truckers throughout the United States. A conservative estimate of the cost of these delays is about $7 billion per year. When fuel costs and/or labor costs increase, the costs are compounded.[1]

Increased costs to carriers are eventually reflected in higher transportation rates for shippers. Between 2003 and 2006, rates increased 13 percent for truck transportation,

25 percent for rail transportation, 11 percent for scheduled air freight, 11 percent for water transportation, 9 percent for port and harbor operations, 5 percent for marine cargo handling, 22 percent for pipeline transportation of crude oil, and 8 percent for refined oil products.[2] Obviously, these increases reflect a combination of cost and demand factors, but the cost factors are the most important.

Highway Traffic and Infrastructure

It is estimated that congestion on highways will spread from large urban areas and some intercity routes to large stretches of intercity highways in both urban and rural areas. Without operational improvements, it is estimated that by 2035 recurring peak-period congestion will slow traffic on 20,000 miles of the National Highway System and create stop-and-go conditions on an additional 45,000 miles. The top 10 highway interchange bottlenecks cause an average of 1.5 million annual truck hours of delay. The (conservative) estimated delay costs are about $30/hour to the trucking companies, but the cost to the shippers would usually be higher.[3]

Figure 14-2 indicates the funding challenges faced by our highway system. The revenue inflow is below the "need to maintain" level required to keep the current highway system operating effectively. The delay costs indicated above will also need funds to improve the current system. The graph shows the projections for the 50 states and federal-level needs for what are considered to be required improvements. The combined total shows a staggering gap for the future. Revenues will have to be increased or the demand for highway usage decreased. Evidence of the problem is evident in almost every state and certainly on most parts of the Interstate System. While national defense and societal needs are important, the highway infrastructure is the life blood of the

FIGURE 14-2 Status of Highway Trust Fund

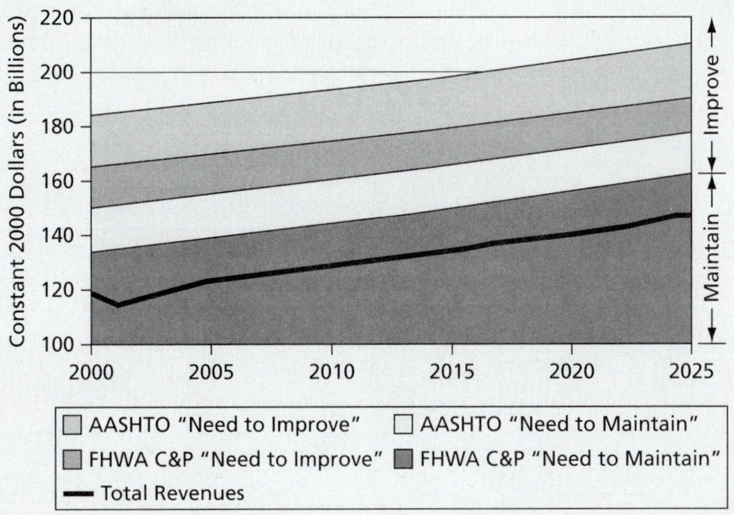

Source: An Initial Assessment of Freight Bottlenecks on Highways, white paper, October 2005. Prepared for Federal Highway Administration, Office of Transportation Policy Studies. Prepared by Cambridge Systematics, Inc. in association with Battelle Memorial Institute. Accessible online at http://www.fhwa.dot.gov/policy/otps/bottlenecks/index.htm.

economy's engine. The lack of federal and state investment is a very shortsighted for the U.S. economy's future staying power.

Railroad Traffic and Infrastructure

The large interregional freight railroads have experienced a significant increase in demand, especially for trailer-on-flatcar (TOFC) and container-on-flatcar (COFC) movements. TOFC and COFC, once a relatively small market segment, is now a major source of revenue and traffic. These relatively high-speed intermodal trains compete for network space with the bulk traffic trains. The congestion is frequently exacerbated by seasonal surges in freight demand and disruptions that add to the congestion as volumes reach capacity on the reduced mainline rail network (reduced 50 percent between 1960 and 1980).

Congestion on the mainline railroad network is forecast to spread significantly by 2035. The American Association of Railroads reports that congestion will increase to almost 16,000 miles on the main lines of the railroads (30 percent of the network) if current capacity is not increased. Rail routes that have moderate to very limited capacity to accommodate maintenance without servicing delays and disruption will almost double by 2035, which will affect about 25 percent of the network. A potential solution to the rail congestion problem is the construction and return of double tracks to accommodate two-way traffic simultaneously, which was common on the main lines of most large railroads prior to World War II. The Union Pacific Railroad has already initiated a double-track program in some areas. The addition of another track can be accomplished more quickly and usually at less cost than adding lanes to an Interstate highway, but there is still a major investment cost that railroads are reluctant to accommodate on a private basis; that is, they want a government subsidy to underwrite the cost in whole or in part, similar to the other modes of transportation. Figure 14-3 clearly indicates the magnitude of the budget funding gap.[4]

The challenge for the railroads since 2010 has been the increased volumes of additional traffic associated with the development of fracking technology for exploiting gas and oil in the new reserves in various areas of the United States especially in the Upper Midwest, the Great Lakes Region, and eastern states like Pennsylvania and New York. There were no pipelines in place, as previously noted, which placed the burden on motor carriers and railroads to transport these products that has caused a critical

FIGURE 14-3 Cost Breakdown to Grow and Modernize the Railroads

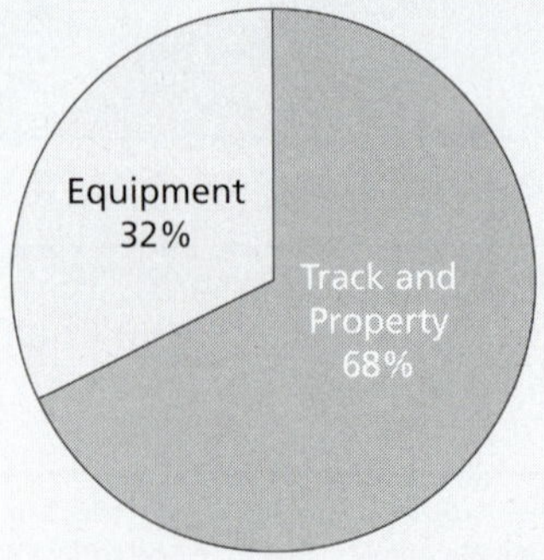

shortage of capacity for other products, such as grain, and safety issues because of the hazardous nature of the petroleum products from the Upper Midwest.

A bumper harvest of grain in 2014 contributed to an increase in demand for grain transportation by rail of 15 percent. There was also an increase in demand for transportation of oil/petroleum products of over 13 percent. Figure 14-4 shows the increased demand for a number of other basic products. The demand for coal is relatively flat for 2014 but that is likely to change. There is tremendous pressure building on railroads like the BSNF Railway to speed delivery on its congested tracks of critical products for the winter like coal. The BSNF Railway organization has invested $5.5 billion in its infrastructure to fix the problem and had added 500 locomotives and 5,000 railcars and hired 6,000 new employees to solve their delivery challenges. If the problem is not fixed, the utility customers will have to pay much higher rates for electricity and other energy-related products. This situation illustrates again the critical and important role of transportation for the economic viability of the U.S. and other economies of the world.[5]

Waterway Traffic and Infrastructure

On inland waterways, aging infrastructure and locks frequently cause bottlenecks. For example, of the 510,000 commercial vessel passages through federal and state locks, 31 percent experienced delays. Average delays for barge tows were one hour and 32 minutes. The average processing time was about 30 minutes. The challenge is that inland waterways are especially susceptible to weather delays, including problems caused by flooding, draughts, ice- and other storm-related disruptions.

Deep-draft ports on the three major coastlines have capacity challenges, which will be explored in the next section. The inland ports have capacity issues also, but most of them are not as problematic as the ocean ports. As indicated previously, the congestion problem at the ports is a significant challenge, especially since these ports are the gateways for imports and exports, and the long-run projection for growth in global trade (imports and exports based upon weight) in the United States is 77 percent. The West Coast ports are particularly vulnerable because of the growth in trade with Asian countries and the new mega container ships.[6]

The concentration of vessels bringing freight through the West Coast ports is evident in Figure 14-4A. To what extent the expansion of the Suez Canal will shift some of the traffic to East Coast ports remains to be seen. However, it is quite evident that even with a shift to some East Coast ports the port infrastructure on both the West Coast and East Coast is insufficient to support the needs of the global flows of traffic for global economic progress. Houston had the most activity, but the majority of the vessels are non-container ships that are usually smaller vessels moving oil and oil products that do not cause the same level of activity in the port area, which means less congestion. It is also interesting to note in Figure 14-4B the top global ports of call. China is clearly number one with container ships accounting for more than half of the total. The United States is second on the list, but non-container ships account for twice as many calls as container ships. China is unique compared to all of the other counties listed in terms of container versus non-container ships. This phenomenon is due to the export of finished products noted in Chapter 1.

The port congestion problems are manifested in several areas. A growing share of waterborne commerce, especially imports, moves in very large container ships, the largest of which can carry more than 8,000 containers. These large ships can take five

FIGURE 14-4A Top Vessel Calls by U.S. Port, 2011

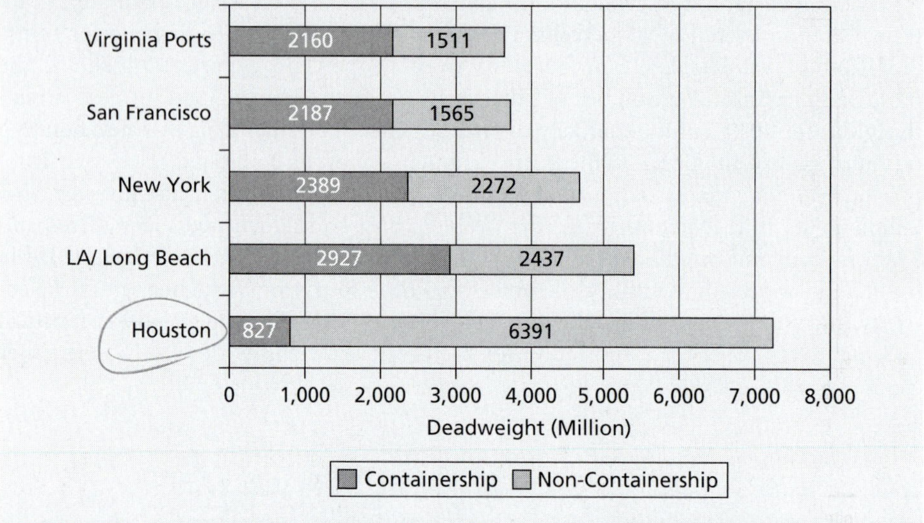

Source: Vessel Calls Snapshot, 2011, U.S. Department of Transportation Maritime Administration.

FIGURE 14-4B Top Vessel Calls by Country, 2011

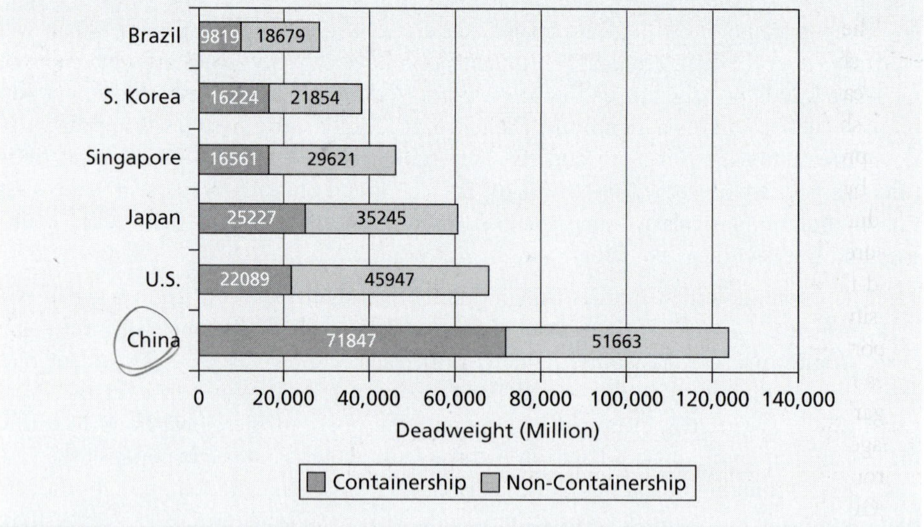

Source: Vessel Calls Snapshot, 2011, U.S. Department of Transportation Maritime Administration.

to seven days to unload, compared to two to three days for most container ships. Only a few ports can accommodate these ships because of the draft requirements in the channels leading into the port areas. They also require more berths for unloading, special cranes for unloading and loading, and more dock space and transportation-related equipment for moving the containers from the dock area to local terminals or distribution centers. In addition, the congestion problem is exacerbated by the fact that transloading of the containers is frequently required since domestic containers can usually

FIGURE 14-5 Deadweight Capacity Growth

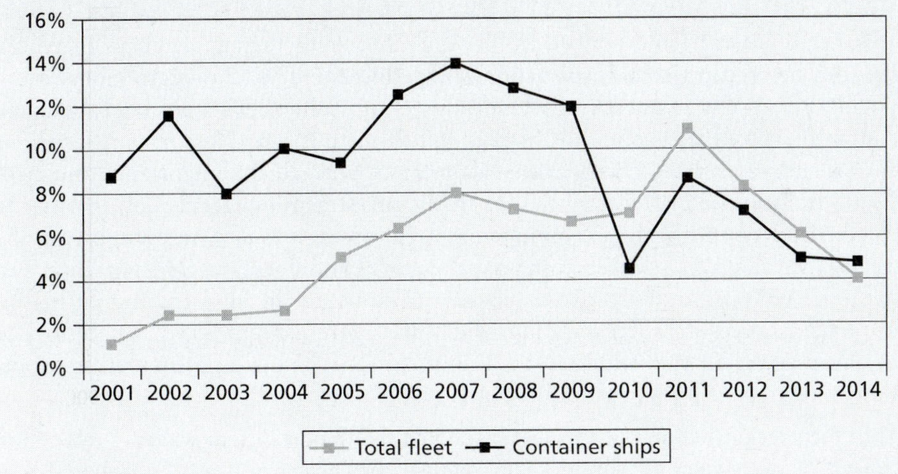

Source: United Nations Conference on Trade and Development, Mechant Fleet by flag of registration and by type of ship, annual, 1980–2014.

hold 50 to 60 percent more freight than the ISO international containers. In fact, this has caused an imbalance and shortage of the international ISO containers. Another related problem is that many port areas are constrained by the scarcity of land nearby and/or the high cost of such land for the development of marine terminals and related facilities.

The growth in Container Ships relative regular vessels is clearly indicated in Figure 14-5, which shows percentage growth in Deadweight Capacity from 2001 to 2014. There are only four years (2010 to 2013) where the percentage gfrowth of Deadweight Capacity for container ships is lower. Currently, the port congestion challenges are being partially addressed by improved port access (for example, with dredging); investment in technology and equipment by carriers and port operators; and longer operating hours. These strategies are aimed at reducing the dwell time of ships and containers in port areas and relieving some of the pressure for expansion. The trade-off costs associated with improving access routes and round-the-clock operations, which often include overtime payments, need to be evaluated. The situation is also exacerbated by the public's hue and cry about the disruption around the port areas when vessels are loading and unloading. There are also environmental challenges in the port area with the discharge of various fluids (intentionally or unintentionally); the garbage, trash, and other debris that may be thrown overboard; and other ecological damage. Some port areas are notorious for their insensitivity to the ecology of the marine environment. Major efforts are underway to improve the environmental impact of port area.[7]

On a related note, the larger container ships have also caused some capacity and congestion problems on certain key waterways. A case in point is the Panama Canal, with locks that were built almost a hundred years ago when ships were much smaller. Most of these larger ships have had to take the longer route around South America, which adds about 9,000 miles to the journey. Cognizant of this problem, the Panama Canal authority has undertaken a $5.25 billion construction project to add a third lane to the ocean-linking canal waterway, add two new locks (one on the east side of the canal and the other on the west side), and to dredge the existing waterway, which will double the canal's capacity and allow the canal to accommodate the super-size container ships. The third lane is scheduled to open in 2015 or 2016 and should have a major impact on global trade routes as the large container ships begin to use the canal.

Technology and Transportation: A Necessary Marriage

Transportation has been described as the "glue that holds the supply chain together," but it can be argued that transportation is the "life blood" of a modern global economy and is probably its most important industry or business. This is a bold statement about an industry that is often overlooked unless there is a problem or is regarded by some executives as a "necessary evil." Adam Smith realized the importance and criticality of transportation and the need for public investment (social capital) in order to advance the economy and its economic base. That said, it is also very important and perhaps critical at this point in time that the global and domestic transportation systems be as efficient and effective as possible. Investment in infrastructure by public and private sources is a necessary ingredient, but more is required. It is necessary to take advantage of all opportunities to advance efficiency and effectiveness in transportation systems.

In the previous edition of this text, we noted the importance of what we referred to as the art or soft side of the supply chain, namely, the "power of people" collaborating as team members in an organization to make improvements and/or between and among organizations in a supply chain to make advances in performance. Collaboration is a powerful tactic or strategy that has led to many improvements in supply chain performance, and should be continued because there are still opportunities for collaboration internally or externally to lower costs and/or improve customer service and execution. The latter is particularly true since most supply chains operate in dynamic environments where change is the only constant.

There are many initiatives underway in the area of tactical or operational collaboration, including cooperative efforts to reduce loading and unloading times at consignor and consignee shipping and receiving facilities; increase hours of operation for drop yards and warehouse facilities; allow faster payment for carriers; reduce driver-assist times; and share capacity forecasts with carriers. "This type of collaboration has had direct benefits for supply chains in the form of lower costs for shippers and carriers and improved customer service."

The most important potential of collaboration is at the strategic level, and it involves the sharing of information to improve results for all members of the supply chain. For example, some consumer product companies offer **vendor-managed-inventory (VMI)** programs for their largest customers. Under this program, they manage or co-manage their customer's DC inventory replenishment. Information is shared with logistics service providers for improved scheduling of pickups and deliveries, consolidated shipment dispatches, and reduction of empty trailer miles. This is a win-win-win scenario for the buyer, seller, and logistics service provider. It is an example of collaboration at its best—organizations working together and sharing information to improve the efficiency, effectiveness, and execution of supply chains.[8]

The example discussed above to illustrate the benefits of collaboration also has elements of visibility built in via an old technology, namely, **Electronic Data Interchange (EDI)**. Visibility has become a popular buzzword in transportation, logistics, and supply chain circles. Benefits and advantages are touted by an increasing number of individuals. Interestingly, there is no universal definition of visibility. Initially, visibility was used mostly in conjunction with assets, for example, the level of inventory in a warehouse by SKU on a daily basis, the number and location of equipment, and the level of chemicals or other liquids in a storage tank.

The visibility applications introduced during the last decade expanded to include insight into the status of orders, inventory turns, and shipments across the supply chain, as indicated in the previous example of the VMI programs of consumer products companies. In other words, they became more practical tools to capture and analyze supply chain data for decision making, risk mitigation, and process improvement. Also, visibility applications could be used to alert analysts of supply chain disruptions such as shipment delays, unusual stockouts, and so on.

A good example of the benefits and opportunities associated with a comprehensive visibility program is the fully automated track-and-trace program of Dole, Inc. Faced with the many challenges associated with producing and distributing fresh produce and with increased government regulations, Dole created full visibility of its supply chain by leveraging technology to develop a fully automated track-and-trace process. The process uses **Radio Frequency Identification (RFID), Global Positioning System (GPS)**, and cell phone technologies, starting at the harvest field and running throughout their supply chains. Included are stops through cooling center warehouses, carrier terminals, and sorting plants. Dole is tracking time and quantities and will add temperature to the mix soon. The key to the Dole example is tagging products as they leave the field. This visibility has allowed Dole to understand how product moved through the system and to be alerted to possible time and temperature abuse.

The Dole company changes provide some insight into the power of technology for improving the effectiveness and efficiency of supply chains and transportation in the future. Globalization has been a powerful external or exogenous force for change and improvement of supply chains for almost 25 years. Technology has also a related and significant force, but globalization was the major driver. In the last several years, technology has become the major force for change if on views it more broadly than the information technology providing the visibility in the Dole case. In fact, the visibility aspect is only a part of the information technology domain.[9]

If we examine technology broadly, there are five major categories of technology that may drive and change not only transportation but also the entire supply chain, namely, mobile communication, cloud computing, deep learning, intelligent robotics, and manufacturing digitalization. These types of technologies can be game changers in helping organizations improve their competitiveness, align their supply chains, reduce complexity, and provide mobility.[10]

Mobile communication technologies, which include mobile phones and related devices, mobile platforms, and applications have advanced significantly in recent years allowing improved connectivity at a lower cost and have revolutionized the capabilities of mobile phones and devices, For transportation, the new technology and applications have led to: (1) better freight and carrier management (rate quotes tracking shipments, shipment status, shipment notifications, and load sharing); (2) improved transportation operations (real-time routing directions, traffic reports, dynamic driver dispatching, hours of service reports); (3) better asset management (real, vehicle time equipment location); (4) improved customer service (order and delivery status).

Intelligent Robotics are another type of technology that will influence and improve transportation operations in the future. Robotics have a relatively long history in manufacturing, and their use has increased dramatically in recent years to not only reduce cost but also to improve the quality of manufacturing. Amazon is now using robots in order fulfillment centers and will include loading and unloading transportation equipment in the future. The robots of the future will work alongside of humans with the opportunity to make software adjustments as needed for improved efficiency. The other technologies mentioned earlier also have potential for use in transportation and supply chains, but these technologies have not been fully developed and exploited at this point. The important point is that technological development will improve and help shape transportation services and systems in the future to improve efficiency, effectiveness, and execution.[11]

Sustainability: Going Green with Transportation

Going green is a slogan that was given lip service for many years by individuals and organizations. Advocates were often labeled as "tree huggers" and ridiculed in private. There was an assumption that going green would mean increased cost to the enterprise, which was viewed as unacceptable. Pressure began to build in a number of quarters for green supply chains, which meant that both shippers and carriers would have to initiate efforts to eliminate pollutants, reduce carbon footprints, and so forth. The local, state, and federal governments also began to exert pressure on carriers and shippers to improve. Interestingly enough, some organizations found that they could actually reduce their carbon footprint and still lower their costs, along with their initiatives to lower the negative impact on the environment.

Some discussion of the term ***carbon footprint*** is appropriate at this point. It is widely used by the various media (print, radio, and TV), academics, politicians, and others and has become a part of our vernacular. However, in spite of its ubiquitous use, definitions vary and are frequently not very specific. The common interpretation is that a carbon footprint is equated with a certain amount of gaseous emissions that are relevant to climate change and are associated with human production and consumption activities. However, there does not appear to be any consensus on how to measure or quantify the carbon footprint. The spectrum of definitions range from direct CO_2 definitions to full-lifecycle greenhouse gas emissions. There is an emphasis, however, on measuring CO_2 emissions directly and indirectly caused by an activity, which is the preference of the authors.

There is no doubt that the higher fuel prices in 2008 helped spur interest among carriers and shippers to reduce fuel consumption. This effort to improve fuel efficiency also reduced the carbon footprint of commercial transportation, but it is only one of six reasons that is motivating business to drive their sustainability agenda. In fact, it has been documented that the rising energy costs was number five on the list of six market pressures. The others included corporate responsibility, a desire to increase or maintain brand reputation, competitive pressures, and internal and external stakeholder pressure, or expectations as well as potential regulatory action by the federal and state regulatory agencies.

The unexpected happened in the second decade of the 21st century with developments discussed above, namely, new technology (fracking), that made the drilling and production of oil economically feasible in additional areas in the United States and other countries such as Canada. The impact began to be felt in 2014 with significant reductions in gasoline prices at the retail level below $3.00 per gallon. These price levels were much lower than what experts deemed possible again. The lower cost of so-called fossil fuels made some alternate energy sources economically impractical and provided an economic growth engine for parts of the United States and Canada. There is some concern that these lower prices will lessen the impetus for sustainability initiatives of the previous decade. However, it is important to note that the green supply chain initiatives had important economic benefits that will likely continue and will be supported by government pressure.

It should also be noted that in addition to fuel efficiency, there are a number of other sustainability issues that are impacted by supply chains. These areas include packaging, facilities, and waste disposal. The important point is that there are many opportunities for transportation and logistics service companies to improve in areas related to sustainability and to reduce their negative impact on the environment. The internal and external stakeholder pressures have provided impetus for such change, but in the long run, the recognition that going green has economic advantages impacting profitability will be the most important driving force.

It is important to understand that there is an interrelationship or systems impact in play among logistics-related factors impacting the green supply chain. There are several time-proven axioms from transportation economics that are important to consider, such as "don't ship air" and "don't ship water." The first one recognizes that empty space in a motor carrier trailer or railcar from empty backhauls or less-than-capacity dispatches is wasted and never recovered. Transportation companies do not have the luxury of accumulating inventory. As noted in Chapters 1 and 2, they provide capacity to transport between two or more points, which is instantly perishable if not used.

Transportation companies and shippers put an emphasis on consolidation to fill equipment to capacity or near capacity. Such a strategy has the potential to significantly reduce network miles, especially in the motor carrier sector. The reduction in network miles will improve fuel efficiency and reduce the carbon footprint. During the era of low-cost fuel and with pressure to have lean, demand-driven supply chains, transportation equipment was frequently dispatched without enough consideration for capacity utilization in an effort to improve customer service and lower inventory costs. Higher fuel charges along with sustainability-related costs have changed the system dynamics and more emphasis is being given to "don't ship air," for the reasons cited above. While consolidation efforts may have an impact on shipment time, the reductions in fuel and carbon levels mitigate it. Also, when necessary, shipments can be expedited.

It should be noted that in addition to consolidation, packaging has an impact on wasted transportation capacity. Marketers have often followed one of their axioms from the theory of consumer behavior, namely, "perception is reality." Consequently, if consumers perceive that they are getting more for their money, it is "reality." One approach to influencing value perception is through packaging—using larger packages. For example, the paper-based rolls inside plastic wrap and aluminum foil were larger than they needed to be, but it resulted in an overall larger package. The larger package filled transportation equipment, warehouse space, and retailer shelves more quickly than necessary. The net result was a lot of "air" and wasted space. The trade-off was more sales revenue (hopefully). The current economic and social environment has led companies like Walmart to request change, and it has happened. The smaller rolls have led to smaller packages and improved capacity utilization in transport equipment, warehouses, and retail stores. This is only one example of many possibilities. Hopefully, the impetus for improving sustainability will lead to other packaging changes. Excess packaging is prevalent in our economy, and it usually ends up in landfills and, of course, increases logistics cost. The caveat on packaging is that it is also used to reduce damage, which can be a big issue for carriers. Obviously, this issue requires consideration, but there are many instances of too much packaging and wasted space inside packages—there is room for improvement.

The other old axiom noted above was "don't ship water," and it has a relationship to the "don't ship air" axiom. This maxim is based upon the premise that water is ubiquitous; that is, it is found almost everywhere. Early location theory and transport economics concluded that water should be added as close as possible to the point of consumption to reduce cost and especially to reduce transportation cost. The classic examples are beer and soda, which are about 90 percent water in terms of finished product weight. The conventional wisdom was that breweries and soda bottling plants should have market-oriented locations, where the water was added, to reduce total transportation costs by moving the water relatively short distances. The growing popularity of so-called "craft beers" from smaller, more localized breweries is a positive impact for sustainability.

Over the course of the last several decades, an increasing number of consumer products that were sold in a liquid form had water added, which gave the appearance of "getting more for your money." This was especially true of liquid detergents. Walmart and other retailers put pressure upon their suppliers, to eliminate about half the water. The result was a smaller plastic bottle that had the same washing power. However, the total supply chain (manufacturer, warehouse, transporter, and retailer) benefited because the final product weighed less and occupied about 50 percent of the original space. It was an important outcome for sustainability. The cost of transportation and warehousing was significantly reduced while improving the shelf space challenge of retailers—a classic win-win-win! It also reduced the cost of packaging and improved capacity utilization. It was clearly a "home run" in spite of some initial resistance by consumers. There are many other possibilities for removing water and/or reducing the size of consumer packages. Consider, for example, the possibility of manufacturing a detergent tablet, and all the water being added in the washing machine (this concept is not new, but it received consumer resistance when previously tried).

The examples of green initiatives discussed are cascading through supply chains and encouraging initiatives by other suppliers and transportation companies. The transport sector is being pushed in this direction by customers, the government, and increased operating costs. As indicated above, most of the steps taken by the trucking industry to become greener are focused upon cost reductions related to fuel efficiency. However, fleet managers are investigating "clean" fuels and hybrid tractors and joining with shippers to examine reducing network miles, consolidating loads, and even changing the type of light bulbs used in terminals. Some of these changes, such as load consolidation and network mileage optimization, can be made in the short run for immediate impact, while others, such as alternative fuels and hybrid tractors, are longer-run changes that need evaluation. Again, the reduction in fuel prices has raised a red flag and concern that companies will lack the impetus to continue their sustainability efforts.

The sustainability initiatives were frequently enhanced by government programs such as the Smart-Way Transport Partnership. This is a federal program initiated by the Environmental Protection Agency (EPA) in 2004 to target selected carriers to reach out to shippers. The goals of the program are a cleaner environment, more efficiency, and less costly transportation options through collaborative efforts. The program has doubled in size each year since 2004 and topped 1,100 members in 2008. The EPA expects the program to double again in a year or two. The members include motor carriers, railroads, ocean carriers, logistics service providers, and large shippers including Best Buy, Target, Coca Cola, Johnson & Johnson, Procter and Gamble, and WalMart. Even nonprofit groups such as the American Trucking Association are participating in these programs. SmartWay offers several tools and recommends several fuel-saving strategies. According to the EPA, carriers can save an average of $4,000 per truck per year by implementing some or all of the recommended measures. Collectively, SmartWay participants are saving close to 620 million gallons of diesel fuel per year and lowering fuel costs by about $2.5 billion. Furthermore, they are reducing carbon dioxide emissions by 6.8 million tons.

Sustainability and an emphasis on "green supply chains" have gained momentum among major shippers and the various transportation modes. The recognition of the environmental and economic benefits for carriers and shippers along with government policy and public pressure has given these efforts much momentum. However, transportation companies still have many opportunities to improve. For example, have any trucks passed you lately on the highway when you were driving at the maximum posted speed (hopefully)?

TRANSPORTATION **TECHNOLOGY**

Truck Navigation

Navigational devices in personal automobiles have become very popular with many drivers. They are relatively inexpensive and very convenient for navigating in new locations and sometimes in familiar ones too. This technology has replaced maps for many individuals, particularly for short hauls. If you want to get specific directions, the technology has the capacity to provide voice directions that can be less distracting while driving for some drivers.

Rand McNally, which is probably best known for its printed road maps and truck navigation software, has joined with a digital map company to create new software that can literally provide dock-to-dock directional information to motor carrier drivers. The software is designed to use GPS-accurate data developed specifically for trucking, including highway and street restrictions on truck driving, to help carriers and shippers navigate more efficiently. This is especially helpful for drivers who are unfamiliar with a particular geographic area.

The software allows class 8 and longer combination vehicles to route from origin to destination. It can provide comprehensive coverage for almost 7.0 million miles of road used by trucks in the United States, with more than 23 million links that contain unique truck attributes. The map data, combined with the truck attributes, will provide a level of routing accuracy and quality unparalled by other systems. The complete identification of truck attributes for height and weight restrictions will also offer more complete and complex truck combinations for driers and trucking companies. The program will also be able to integrate other logistics software packages that can be utilized for loading and other vehicle utilization efficiency.

This dock-to-dock software program can fill an important need for carriers, enabling them to route and deliver effectively as well as efficiently from the first to the last mile. Given the growing concern over driver shortages and sustainability, the ability to manage the truck to save miles can cut time and reduce the carbon footprint. Furthermore, the program can minimize road delay, reduce the risk of accidents, and mitigate the probability of fines. The reduction in the level of uncertainty related to road conditions and restrictions can be an important benefit to the drivers. Customers will also benefit because of on-time deliveries. Equipment utilization should also improve dramatically.

Source: Adapted from SCMR reports, *Reed Business Information*, May 22, 2009, p. 1.

Fuel Cost and Consumption

Fuel price volatility, including frequent price changes, has been an issue for transportation carriers and shippers since the mid-1970s. Overall, it can be argued that this is the result of changes in the global demand and the supply of crude oil. The demand for oil as a source of energy to power transport equipment and for private use has been growing steady. The new technology discussed above and the opportunity to recover oil and natural gas from important new sources in the United States and elsewhere has alleviated the situation and resulted in lower fuel costs. However, the historic volatility of energy prices, particularly oil and natural gas, requires caution and careful management by individuals and organizations as well as effective government policies. The reduction in price also has important economic implications for counties and regions that have been supplying oil for many developed counties. In other words, it is good news and bad news, depending on whether the country is a net importer or exporter of oil.

As illustrated in Figure 14-6, the pattern of price changes and volatility have been a special challenge and issue in the first decade of the 21st century. World crude oil prices increased 113 percent between 2005 and mid-2008, when they reached a peak of $137.11 per barrel in July of 2008. The prices abated significantly in 2009 because of the economic recession that triggered a global decrease in demand for oil and other energy related minerals. The price of a barrel of oil dipped to $75 per barrel in 2009 but rose again in 2010 with the economic recovery in major countries like the United States. The economic recovery resulted in increased demand, but the impact has been mitigated by the exploitation of new sources of fossil fuels mentioned above. The price of oil slipped to $65 per barrel in December of 2014 and was expected to be reduced further. Gasoline was reported to be selling at about $2.00 a gallon in Texas and some other states which was about 50 percent of the previous high for gasoline at retail pumps.

The challenge, then, for carriers and shippers will be to deal with the uncertainty and volatility of fuel prices, and the expectation that the price will be increasing over

FIGURE 14-6 WTI Crude Oil Prices

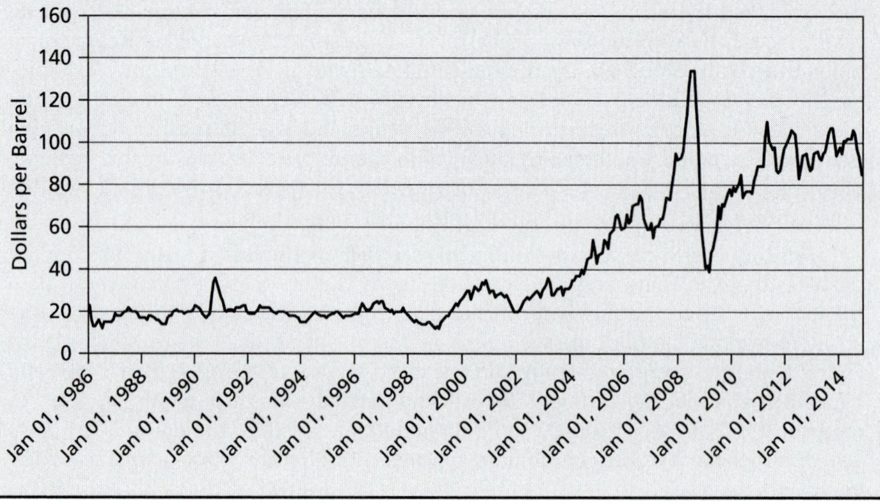

Sources: FRED Graph Observations, Federal Reserve Economic Data, Economic Research Division and Federal Reserve Bank of St. Louis.

time. The impact of lower prices will vary among the modes of transportation because some are more fuel efficient than others, as noted in Chapters 5 through 8. Also, there is interest in low-sulfur diesel fuel, which is cleaner for the environment.

Some discussion of the future impact of fuel prices on the various modes of transportation is appropriate at this point. As one would expect, the impact of fuel price will differ among the modes because of their different operating and market conditions.

Motor Carriers

As previously noted, the motor carrier industry is highly fuel intensive and therefore very sensitive to price increases and associated volatility. Motor carriers consume over 54 billion gallons of fuel per year. The annual cost for fuel escalated over 70 percent over the course of 2004–2008. To put this in perspective, the 2008 diesel expenses for the motor carrier industry were more than three times higher than the annual fuel bill for airlines, which is the most fuel-intensive mode of transportation. Fuel approached the annual labor cost in 2008, which is usually the largest expense for the motor carrier industry. Fuel surcharges helped the industry cope during that period, but it was still challenging and some companies did not survive. In fact, almost 3,000 motor carrier companies went bankrupt in 2008, reducing truck capacity by about 130,000 trucks. This was the largest number of carrier failures since 2001. The truckload carriers had the biggest challenges in passing off the increased fuel charges.

The lower fuel prices reached in late 2014 helped the motor carriers to be more competitive with the railroads in certain market situations, particularly for long-haul truckload traffic. When oil prices are in the $50 to $60 per barrel range, over the road motor carriers can be more competitive with TOFC movements. However, infrastructure-related congestion can mitigate the impact of lower fuel charges.

Air Carriers

As indicated previously, airlines are the most intensive users of fuel. Similar to motor carriers, fuel costs have grown to be the largest expense for airlines. Fuel was normally 12 to 15 percent of the operating costs of airlines, but it grew to over 30 percent by 2008. The airlines have also used fuel surcharges for freight movements, but with limited success, and the surcharges inhibited air cargo growth because their rates were already relatively high. The increased gap between air cargo rates and ground transportation rates has shifted traffic away from airlines for distances up to 1,500 miles. The new, lower fuel costs could decrease the aforementioned gap and bring more freight traffic back to the airlines.

The high fuel charges were also challenging for passenger movements. Competition among the airlines is a deterrent to significant price increases between major hubs. They have responded instead by decreasing aircraft size and seat size as well as eliminating some flights to improve passenger revenue miles, which had a negative impact on air freight volume. Bankruptcy filings among some of the largest airlines have been an outcome of the higher fuel prices. The fuel price reductions of 2009 provided some relief, and more is anticipated with the lower prices in 2014. The airlines are the most sensitive mode to increased fuel charges. Like motor carriers, oil prices in the $50 to $60 per barrel range would have a positive impact on airline efficiency and the expected lowering of air fares could generate more traffic as long as capacity increased.

Water Carriers

While water carriers are very fuel efficient, they are not insensitive to fuel price increases. This is particularly true for the global container shipping lines. Annual marine bunker fuel costs nearly doubled between 2005 and mid-2008. Fuel cost became the biggest challenge, reaching 50 to 60 percent of ship operating costs, depending on the type of ship. In addition, the marine carriers pay surcharges to the motor carriers and railroads that provide their intermodal moves for through service to and from inland points. To the extent that these surcharges cannot be passed on to shippers, they are additional cost pressures on the carriers. Consequently, the shipping lines became more aggressive about collecting bunker fuel surcharges, but they were not as successful as trucking companies in implementing an explicit set of charges related to the price of bunker fuel. Lower fuel costs would be expected to have a positive impact on global traffic flows.

Rail Carriers

With the advantages of fuel efficiency and constrained capacity, the railroad sector has not experienced the same level of cost pressure as the other modes of transportation. In fact, railroad profits increased by double digits in 2008 even with some decrease in traffic levels. The improved profit levels were attributable to a number of factors, including rate increases, fuel surcharges, and added efficiency. The latter was the result of faster line-haul time, faster terminal turnarounds, and some workforce ration allegation.

Domestic rail service benefited from the higher fuel costs, since more shippers were interested in switching to rail intermodal service for long-haul freight. This is true for both trailers (TOFC) and containers (COFC) moving on an intermodal basis. Even with the decline in fuel prices in 2009, the demand for rail intermodal service remained high. The later phenomenon is probably attributable to a belief that the fuel price reduction will be a short-run event; that even with lower fuel prices, rail intermodal service is more economical; and to the improved service times of the rail carriers. A sustained lowering of fuel costs would not be as beneficial to the railroads as it would be to motor and air carriers since it makes the latter carriers more competitive for certain types of traffic.

Pipeline Carriers

As indicated previously in this chapter, during the period 2003–2006, pipeline rates for moving crude oil increased 22 percent, and for refined oil products, they increased 8 percent, which is an indication of higher operating costs. Some of this cost increase was attributable to the increase in pipelines' energy cost, but it is also a reflection of other cost increases related to security along the pipelines. As noted, pipelines operate very efficiently compared to other modes, which allowed them to price their services competitively as fuel prices escalated between 2006 and 2008. Also, some shippers are "tied" to the pipelines because of their location and limited alternatives for service. The net result was that pipeline traffic did not vary much in volume with the changes in fuel costs. The new oil fields have resulted in pipeline investment in infrastructure, but they have not been able to keep up with demand, especially for natural gas movements, leading some to conclude that they have become victims of their own success.

Carriers' Responses

Fuel surcharges have become the major component of the strategy of carriers to increase revenues for fuel cost recovery measures. Carrier contracts have become more sophisticated, with new surcharge formulas and new contract clauses to be more transparent and to correlate more closely with the fuel fluctuations. Surcharges have become a common practice for all modes in recent years and have become a centerpiece for carrier-shipper negotiations. However, there is no standard surcharge policy or formula for the transportation industry. The biggest challenge appears to be in the ocean shipping area because of the multiplicity of fuels, indexes, and carriers.

A second response, suggested above, has been service capacity and network rationalization. Some TL carriers have focused upon shorter routes or traffic lanes. One relatively simple response that impacts service capacity is to reduce cruise speed. Both the trucking companies and the ocean liners have implemented this approach with mixed results. There are definite fuel savings, but the reduced speed impacts customer service, which has been a contentious point with some shippers. Network rationalization usually means cutting or reducing service on unprofitable routes.

The important point for the future is that fuel prices will continue to have a major impact on transport carriers in terms of cost and service, which in turn will impact shippers. Some shippers are responding by implementing regionalized distribution centers with the expectation that with fuel price volatility and price increases, change will continue.

A third response to the fuel issues is to improve the operational efficiency of carriers. This can be done through fleet replacement and equipment modernization in terminal areas. As part of the fleet replacement program, carriers—especially motor carrier companies—can consider the option to buy equipment that utilizes alternate fuels.

The future will bring technology improvements that hopefully will make feasible alternatives available, such as electric hybrids. Also, lighter-weight equipment can be utilized. Again, there will be continuing pressure, because of fuel costs and the environment, to investigate opportunities to improve operating efficiency through equipment and network change.

A fourth response both to the fuel issue and sustainability is the use of technology to manage and control equipment effectively. With large and/or widely dispersed fleets, this usually requires technology to provide visibility of the assets and related information to improve operations. Large motor carrier companies in particular are investing in relatively expensive technology that allows them to track-and-trace equipment on a real-time basis. It is useful for security purposes but is also enabling them to reduce their fleet size, because it does not get "lost." Also, the improved visibility can provide exception reporting when there is a problem, such as a breakdown, and corrective action can be taken.[12]

The visibility feature can also allow carriers to share information with their shippers/customers. This can lead to shared information about shipment needs to help carriers plan in advance to meet demand. Such collaborative efforts offer much promise for a win-win environment for improving equipment efficiency.

SUMMARY

- Demand for transportation service has increased significantly during the last 10 years with the expansion of global trade, but the investment in transportation-related infrastructure has not kept pace with the growth in traffic on a domestic basis or on a global basis. The declining fuel costs will present an opportunity for the state and federal governments to increase fuel taxes to alleviate the infrastructure problem.
- Congestion has become a major issue for the U.S. transportation system, causing delays and inconvenience to ordinary citizens and increased cost in operations for carriers and shippers. Shippers have also experienced increased inventory carrying cost and stockouts because of the delays.
- Highway congestion has some significant costs associated with it for carriers. It is estimated that the top interchange bottlenecks cause an average of 1.5 million annual truck hours of delay.
- Rail and water carriers also are challenged by congestion and infrastructure problems. The projected growth in demand by 2035 will strain an already busy system of highways, railways, and waterways unless improvements are made.
- Sustainability will become even more important in the future, and transportation and related supply chain services will continue to be a focus for reducing carbon footprints to improve the environment, but there are opportunities to also reduce cost.
- The green supply chain focus of many companies has led them back to some old axioms for transportation efficiency, namely, "don't ship air" and "don't ship water." The former refers to unused space or capacity in transportation equipment. The latter refers to the extra weight of water in products, which could be added in near the point of sale. Both axioms have an impact on sustainability and also on cost.
- The federal government's SmartWay Transport Partnership, initiated by the EPA, has solicited carriers to reach out to their customers in an effort to collaborate and to develop less costly transport options that are more environmentally friendly. SmartWay offers strategies to save fuel and help reduce carbon footprints.
- The volatility in fuel prices has been a challenge for carriers in terms of their costs and profits. This situation has led carriers to insert fuel surcharges into their price structure to protect their financial viability when fuel prices increase. The recent decreases in oil prices have dramatically changed the transportation market dynamics.
- Fuel cost was the first or second highest cost for motor carriers, airlines, and even some water carriers but the declining prices beginning in 2014 will change the competitive ratemaking in various market areas and will result in traffic shifts among modes of transportation during a shakeout period.
- Rail carriers fared well during the era of higher fuel changes since they are very fuel efficient; their intermodal service has become more attractive to shippers and other carriers, especially motor carriers. The lower fuel prices will change some of these patterns in the future.
- Transportation and logistics organizations have an opportunity to provide leadership and promote more efficient and effective supply chains through collaborative strategies and technology applications.

STUDY QUESTIONS

1. There have been an increasing number of editorials in newspapers and magazines about concerns over transport capacity and infrastructure. What is the nature of this issue? Why is it such a problem? How can it be resolved?
2. While we have concerns about transportation service currently, there did not appear to be any special challenges or big problems during the 1980s and 1990s. Why were these two decades so different as far as transportation is concerned?
3. We have all experienced highway congestion and "bumper-to-bumper" traffic, but congestion is a bigger issue for supply chains and transport service providers. Why?
4. Sustainability and the environment have captured the attention of ordinary citizens and also of shippers and carriers. What is the nature of the concern? How can shippers and carriers mitigate their impact on the environment?
5. "Don't ship air" and "don't ship water" are the bases of some important supply chain strategies. What do these statements really mean? What are the related strategies? How do these strategies help?
6. The U.S. Environmental Protection Agency has implemented the SmartWay Transport Partnership. Discuss the nature and role of the program. Do you think it will be effective? Why or why not?
7. Fuel prices have been very volatile during the last five years. What factors have contributed to this volatility? What impact will lower fuel prices have on transportation?
8. What is collaboration? How can transportation companies and shippers use collaboration to their advantage?
9. What is your view of the use of technology in transportation systems in the future?
10. Are you optimistic or pessimistic about transportation services for shippers in the 21st century? Why?

NOTES

1. "An Economic Analysis of Transportation Infrastructure Investment," National Economic Council and the President's Council of Economic Advisors, The White House, July 2014, pp. 3–6.
2. FHWA, "The Economic Cost of Freight Transportation," Freight Management and Operations, U.S. Department of Transportation, Washington, DC, May 2009, pp. 1–5.
3. Ibid.
4. "Rail," *CSCMP's Supply Chain Quarterly*, Vol. 8, Special Issue, 2014, pp. 21–22.
5. "Surge in Rail Shipments of Oil Side Tracks Other Industries," *Wall Street Journal*, March 13, 2014.
6. "Rail," pp. 25–26.
7. Ibid.
8. Mary Sigfried, "Collaborating with the Competition," *Inside Supply Management*, Vol. 23, No. 2, March 2012, pp. 20–27.
9. Ibid.
10. John J. Coyle and Kusumal Ruamsook, "Game Changing Trends and Supply Chain's New Normal," *Supply Chain Quarterly*, Vol. 4, No. 8, 2014, pp. 22–28.
11. Ibid.
12. "Sustainability: The 'Embracers' Sieze the Advantage," *Sloan Management Review*, Research Report, Winter 2011.

CASE 14-1

Green and Lean

George Harry and Jeff Pilof, friends and former classmates in college, had not seen each other face-to-face for about 15 years when they had one of these chance meetings in the Atlanta Airport. They both just received the news that their flights to their respective destinations, Philadelphia and Boston, had been canceled. As they walked into an airport restaurant to get a sandwich and wait for their new flights, they spotted and immediately recognized each other. After the customary greetings and questions about family and mutual friends, they started discussing their current jobs and responsibilities. George had spent the last 20 years with two pharmaceutical companies, while Jeff had worked for a chemical company and a large retailer and had established his own package-delivery company. They were both now vice presidents of transportation for their latest companies—a very large retailer and a large consumer products company.

Surprisingly, George and Jeff found that they were both concerned about the same general area in their respective companies. Now that fuel cost has decreased dramatically for transportation services, they did not want to lose their focus on sustainability.

CASE QUESTIONS

1. Why would declining fuel prices lead to less emphasis on sustainability?
2. What advice would you give George and Jeff?

CASE 14-2

Bald Eagle Valley Trucking

SCOR is a local nonprofit organization that provides advice and direction to new and/or small companies. The volunteers for the SCOR organization are all retired executives and/or entrepreneurs. At their weekly meeting, Herb Graves and Ned Book were discussing a proposal that they had received from a local trucking company that had been founded about two years ago. The company, Bald Eagle Valley Trucking (BEV), had enjoyed some success and had been able to secure a loan enabling them to expand to 10 tractor and trailer units. Their success had been based largely upon a water bottling plant, owned by the Coca Cola company that had been increasing the volume they shipped. BEV felt that there was an opportunity to expand their business with Coca Cola into the Philadelphia, New York, and Washington, DC areas, but they needed additional capital to buy more equipment. BEV had requested help from SCOR to assist them with developing a strategic plan and supporting their request for a loan from a Pittsburgh-based bank.

Herb and Ned were very experienced executives but they had no direct experience in the transportation and supply chain business. So they contacted a nearby state university with a large and well-known Supply Chain and Logistics department. The department had a program whereby their students could be assigned a business-related project for course credit, and it would be supervised by a faculty member.

CASE QUESTIONS

1. You have been chosen to work on the BEV project, which will require you to answer the following questions:
   a. What are the major opportunities and issues trucking companies face presently?
   b. What insights can you provide to help BEV mitigate some or all of the issues?
2. Herb and Ned both feel that BEV can be a successful company with appropriate planning and direction. What major points do you think that they should consider in their strategic plan for the future? Indicate at least five such points of emphasis and why you think that they are important.

Suggested Readings

Chapter 9 Transportation Risk Management

Manuj, Ila, and John T. Mentzer, "Global Supply Chain Risk Management," *Journal of Business Logistics*, Vol. 29, No. 1 (2008): 133–156.

Murphy, Sean, "Stepping Up Security: An Interview with James Williams," *Supply Chain Management Review*, Vol. 12 (November 2008): 40.

"Ocean Supply Chain Security," United States Government Accountability Office (April 2008): GAO-08-240.

Sarathy, Ravi, "Security and the Global Supply Chain," *Transportation Journal*, Vol. 45, No. 4 (Fall 2006): 28–51.

Voss, M. Douglas, Judith M. Whipple, and David J. Closs, "The Role of Strategic Security: Internal and External Security Measures with Security Performance Implications," *Transportation Journal*, Vol. 48, No. 2 (Spring 2009): 5–23.

Chapter 10 Global Transportation Planning

Bichou, Khalid, Kee-Hung Lai, Y. H. Venus Lun, and T. C. E. Cheng, "A Quality Management Framework for Liner Shipping Companies to Implement the 24-Hour Advance Vessel Manifest Rule," *Transportation Journal*, Vol 46, No. 1 (Winter 2007): 5–21.

Burnson, Patrick, "Ocean Shipping Strategies: Risk Versus Reward," *Logistics Management* (September 2007): 35.

Miller, Tan, and Renato de Matta, "A Global Supply Chain Profit Maximization and Transfer Pricing Model," *Journal of Business Logistics*, Vol. 29, No. 1 (2008): 175–200.

Schulz, John D., "Global Transportation: The Big Picture," *Supply Chain Management Review*, Vol. 11 (March 2007): 20.

Wagner, Stephan M., "Innovation Management in the German Transportation Industry," *Journal of Business Logistics*, Vol. 29, No. 2 (2008): 215–232.

Chapter 11 Global Transportation Execution

"America's Container Ports: Delivering the Goods," *Bureau of Transportation Statistics* (2007).

Burson, Patrick, "Ocean Shipping Strategies," *Logistics Management* (November 2008): 33–36.

Burson, Patrick, "U.S. Seaport Update: Location Matters," *Logistics Management* (September 2008).

Burson, Patrick, "Top U.S. Seaports: Slower Trade Means Time to Rebuild," *Logistics Management* (February 2009).

Carmichael, Gil, "Intermodal a 'No Brainer' for Energy Efficiency," *Logistics Management* (May 2007): 16.

Paul Bergant, Interview, "Soaring Fuel Prices Are Driving Shippers to Embrace the Intermodal Option," *Global Logistics & Supply Chain Strategies* (August 2008).

Quinn, John Paul, "U.S. Ports Expand Keeping Pace with Import Growth," *Supply Chain Management Review*, Vol. 11 (April 2007): 57.

Theurmer, Karen E., "Intermodal Grows Up," *World Trade* (January 2009): 36.

Chapter 12 Third Party Logistics

Bolumole, Yemisi A., Robert Frankel, and Dag Naslund, "Developing a Theoretical Model for Logistics Outsourcing," *Transportation Journal*, Vol. 46, No. 2 (Spring 2007): 35–54.

Burnson, Patrick, "Improving 3PL Management: Parting Is Such Sweet Sorrow," *Logistics Management* (April 2009): 29–32.

Kerr, John, "Burton Catches Air in New Markets," *Logistics Management* (January 2009): 37–41.

Lieb, Robert, and Karen Butner, "The North American Third-Party Logistics Industry in 2006: The Provider CEO Perspective," *Transportation Journal*, Vol. 46, No. 3 (Summer 2007): 40–52.

Maloni, Michael J., and Craig R. Carter, "Opportunities for Research in Third-Party Logistics," *Transportation Journal*, Vol. 45, No. 2 (Spring 2006): 23–38.

Terreri, April, "Creating a Winning Team," *Food Logistics* (May 2009): 18–23.

Chapter 13 Private Transportation and Fleet Management

"America's Private Fleets," *National Private Truck Council* (2008).

Burnson, Patrick, "Green Transportation Planning: Private Fleets Lead the Way," *Logistics Management* (August 2008): 52.

Dutton, Gail, "A Common Sense Approach to Transportation Fleet Management," *World Trade* (March 2009): 32.

Dutton, Gail, "Managing Fleets in Turbulent Times," *World trade* (February 2009): 28.

Hunter, Olen, "Full-Service Leasing Often Costs Less than Ownership," *Food Logistics* (May 2009): 34.

"Legislative and Policy Positions," National Private Truck Council (2009).

Petty, Gary, "The Evolution of the Private Fleet," *Fleet Owner* (June 2008): 38.

Schulz, John D., "Private Fleet Management: Silent Success," *Logistics Management* (April 2008): 28.

Chapter 14 Issues and Challenges for Global Supply Chains

Berman, Jeff, "Shippers Say Wall Street Crisis to Hinder Transportation Operations," *Logistics Management* (November 2008): 21.

Bowen, Douglas John, "Pacific Harbor Line Goes Green," *Railway Age* (April 2009): 23.

Bowman, Robert J., "Ships and Ports Find Many Ways to Go Green," *Global Logistics & Supply Chain Strategies* (September 2008).

Burnson, Patrick, and Jeff Berman, "Panama Canal Development Project on Pace for Completion," *Logistics Management* (January 2009): 20–21.

Burnson, Patrick, "Update on Vietnam and India Logistics: Strained," *Logistics Management* (May 2009): 36–38.

Hong, Junjie, and Binglian Liu, "Logistics Development in China: A Provider Perspective," *Transportation Journal*, Vol. 46, No. 2 (Spring 2007): 55–65.

Lu, Chin-Shan, and Ching-Chiao Yang, "Comparison of Investment Preferences for International Logistics Zones in Kaohsiung, Hong Kong, and Shanghai Ports from a Taiwanese Manufacturer's Perspective," *Transportation Journal*, Vol. 45, No. 1 (Winter 2006): 30–51.

Quinn, Paul John, "The Greening of America's Ports," *Logistics Management* (September 2007): 62S.

Glossary

A

accessibility The ability of the carrier to provide service between the origin and destination. It also refers to the carrier's ability to serve the shipper or consignee's place of business. For example, in order to ship and receive a railcar, both the origin and destination must have a side track.

advanced shipment notices (ASNs) Electronic notification of pending deliveries; an electronic packing list.

advertising The public promotion of some product or service.

air cargo carriers Carriers that focus exclusively on the movement of freight, packages, letters, and envelopes.

air carriers A transportation firm that operates aircraft for the transportation of passengers or freight as a "common carrier."

air freighters Aircraft dedicated solely to the movement of freight.

air traffic control system The method by which aircraft traffic is controlled in the air so that planes are separated by altitude and distance for safety. This system is administered by the Federal Aviation Administration.

air waybill A contract for transportation between a shipper and an air carrier, which also evidences receipt of the cargo by the carrier.

airline safety The theory, investigation, and categorization of flight failures and the prevention of such failures through regulation, education, and training.

Airport and Airway Trust Fund A federal fund that collects passenger ticket taxes and disburses those funds for airport facilities.

all-cargo carrier An air carrier that transports cargo only.

Amtrak A quasi-governmental agency that provides interstate rail passenger service.

Army Corps of Engineers A federal agency and major military command whose mission is to provide military and public works services to the United States by providing vital engineering services and capabilities, as a public service, across the full spectrum of operations—from peace to war—in support of national interests.

asset-based providers 3PLs that fulfill customer requirements via tangible equipment and facilities they own.

average cost Production cost per unit of output, computed by dividing the total of fixed costs and variable costs by the number of total units produced (total output); also known as "unit cost."

B

backhaul The return trip made, as by a truck or cargo ship, after delivering a load to a specified destination.

bareboat charter A long-term lease or charter where the lessee provides the crew, fuel, and supplies and operates the ship. The lessor provides only the ship.

benefit/cost ratio An analysis of the cost effectiveness of different alternatives in order to see whether the benefits outweigh the costs.

bill of lading A transportation document that is the contract of carriage between the shipper and the carrier; it provides a receipt for the goods tendered to the carrier, the "terms and conditions of sale" between the carrier and shipper, and the evidence of who has title to the goods while in transit.

bonded warehouse Building in which goods, on which the duties are unpaid, are stored under bond and in the joint custody of the importer or his agent and the customs officers.

brainstorming An informal group problem solving technique in which members spontaneously share ideas and solutions.

break-bulk Ocean cargo that is not containerized but must be handled manually into and out of a ship.

break-bulk ships They are multipurpose vessels that are capable of transporting shipments of unusual sizes, unitized on pallets, in bags, or in crates.

buffering strategy Method of reducing risk related to capacity shortages or performance problems by providing additional resources.

bulk carriers Catch-all category for ships that are dedicated to the transport of a specific bulk commodity on a voyage basis.

bull whip effect Businesses that must forecast demand to properly position inventory will often carry an inventory buffer to anticipate spikes in demand, which varies in size depending on the participant's place in the supply chain. It has been observed that variations are amplified as one moves upstream in the supply chain, not unlike the cracking of a whip.

business logistics The process of planning, implementing, and controlling the efficient, effective flow and storage of goods, services, and related information from the point of origin to the point of consumption for the purpose of conforming to customer requirements. Note that this definition includes inbound, outbound, internal, and external movements.

C

capability The ability of a carrier to provide service or multiple services to the shipper to meet the specific requirements of that customer.

capacity The ability to bear people or things.

carbon footprint The total set of greenhouse gas emissions caused by an organization, event, or product, often expressed as an amount of carbon dioxide.

cargo inspection Critical appraisal involving examination, measurement, testing, gauging, and comparison of materials or items to determine if the material or item is in proper quantity and condition.

cargo preference A federal law requiring that at least 50 percent of certain U.S. government owned or –sponsored cargo move on U.S. flag–registered vessels.

cargo service airports Airports that, in addition to any other air transportation services that may be available, are served by aircraft providing air transportation of cargo only, with a total annual landed weight of more than 100 million pounds.

carload A full weight or size shipment placed into or on a railcar. This term also refers to rates that apply to a specific minimum weight for railcar shipments.

carrying capacity The capability of a transport vehicle to carry or transport shipments of a particular weight or size in relation to the shipper's requirements. As an example, a 53-foot trailer could carry 48,000 pounds or a shipment of 3,392 cubic feet.

car-supply charge In a rail contract rate, a fee imposed that depends on the specific type of car supplied for loading and shipment.

Certificate of End Use Document that attests that the product will be used for legitimate or approved purposes.

Certificate of Inspection A legal document that attests to the authenticity and accuracy of the goods.

Certificate of Origin A legal document that verifies the country where a particular product originated. This certificate must often accompany the shipment so the importing country can determine if it complies with that country's laws.

chandlers Dealers in sails and ropes and other supplies for sailing ships; retail dealers in provisions and supplies.

channel members Other parts of a transportation system delivering similar services or utilizing similar or different modes.

"charging what the traffic will bear" Setting the highest price you can sell your goods at in the market you are in.

charter carriers An exempt for-hire air carrier that will fly anywhere on demand; air taxis are restricted to a maximum payload and passenger capacity per plane.

charter party Standard charter contract used to record the exact rate, duration, and terms agreed between the ship owner and the charterer.

charter service In ocean shipping, ships that are hired for a specific voyage or amount of time.

charterer The customer who hires a ship for charter service.

Civil Aeronautics Board Federal agency, created in 1940, that focused on safety rulemaking, accident investigation, and economic regulation of the airlines.

class rate A rate constructed from a classification and a uniform distance system. A class rate is available for any product between any two points.

Clayton Act A law that strengthened the Sherman Anti-Trust Act and specifically described some business practices as violations of the law. This was done to counter some practices that were used to avoid the Sherman Anti-Trust Act.

Coast Guard A military unit attached to the Department of Transportation. The Coast Guard is charged with certain law enforcement tasks related to protecting the shores of the United States and the usage of waters both domestically and along the coasts. The Coast Guard is also tasked with safety standards for commercial users, search and rescue missions on inland and coastal waters, and small boat safety programs.

combi airplane Hybrid type of aircraft with the flexibility to move passengers and/or cargo on the main deck of the aircraft, depending on temporary configuration via movable partitions.

combination carriers They are carriers that move freight and passengers, with cargo loaded in the belly of the aircraft.

combination ships Multipurpose vessels that can handle different types of commodities and load types.

commercial invoice A specifically prepared invoice for the merchandise contained in a shipment. The document is often required for international shipments.

commercial service airport A publicly owned airport that has scheduled passenger service with at least 2,500 passenger boardings each calendar year.

commodities Some good for which there is demand but which is supplied without qualitative differentiation across a market; that is, it is the same no matter who produces it.

commodity rates A rate for a specific commodity and its origin–destination.

common carrier A transportation company that provides freight and/or passenger service to any who seek its services.

common costs A cost that a company cannot directly assign to particular segments of the business; a cost that the company incurs for the business as a whole.

common law A legal system based on court decisions and precedents that recognizes past decisions when deciding current legal questions. The legal system of the United States is based on common law along with civil or statuary law.

communication network Infrastructure and devices linked together so that messages may be passed from one part of the network to another over multiple links and through various nodes.

commuter air carriers An exempt for-hire air carrier that publishes a time schedule on specific routes; a special type of air taxi.

"Compliance, Safety, and Accountability Act of 2010 (CSA 2010)" The act initiated by the federal government in 2010 with a goal of reducing accidents by identifying and addressing areas of concern.

conferences Groups of carriers that serve specific trade routes and ports and cooperate as legal cartels when setting prices for certain routes, agreeing not to compete on price and publishing standardized rate tariffs.

consular invoice A specifically prepared invoice that is prescribed by the importing country for the merchandise contained in a shipment. The invoice will be written in the language of the importing country and may be required to be signed by an employee of the government of the nation to which the shipment is destined.

container rates A rate that applies only when the shipment is placed into a container prior to tendering the shipment to the carrier. This rate recognizes that the shipment is much more easily handled by the carrier.

containerized freight Freight that is loaded into or onto storage equipment (a container or pallet) at the origin and delivered to the destination in or on that same piece of equipment without additional handling.

container-on-flatcar (COFC) A type of rail shipment where only the container or "box" is loaded on the flatcar. The chassis with the wheels and landing gear is only used to carry the container to and from the railroad.

containerships Ships built for the specific purpose of moving standardized 20-foot and 40-foot oceangoing containers.

core competency The set of skills, technologies, and processes that provide the basics for what a company does well.

cost of service A method used by carriers when they seek to only cover the actual expense of providing that specific service. Such pricing does not usually cover shared or overhead costs.

cost-of-service pricing A method used by carriers when seek to only cover the actual expense of providing that specific service. Such pricing does not usually cover shared or overhead costs.

crude carriers Ships that move petroleum products (crude oil, gasoline, diesel fuel, and so forth) in massive quantities.

customs brokerage Company that clears goods through customs barriers for importers and exporters (usually businesses).

customs brokers A firm that represents importers/exporters in dealings with customs. Normally responsible for obtaining and submitting all documents for clearing merchandise through customs, arranging inland transport, and paying all charges related to these functions.

D

decreasing cost industries The relation between market price and the quantity supplied by all firms in a perfectly competitive industry after the industry has completed its long-run adjustment; an increase in the quantity produced leads to a decrease in the price per unit.

dedicated contract carriage A third-party service that dictates equipment (vehicles) and drivers to a single customer for its exclusive use on a contractual basis.

delivery delay Failure to make a scheduled delivery.

demand elasticity The amount that the demand for a product or service will change by the changes in price and the availability of substitutes.

demise charter The hiring of a ship and crew that shifts the control and possession of the vessel; the charterer takes full control of the vessel along with the legal and financial responsibility for it.

density A physical characteristic measuring a commodity's mass per unit volume or pounds per cubic foot; it is an important factor in rate making because density affects the utilization of a carrier's vehicle.

derived demand The demand for a product's transportation is derived from the product's demand at some location.

differential A distinction between individuals or classes.

dimensional weight Unit of measurement used by air carriers to calculate rates for carrying cargo, based on measuring volume taken as well as cargo weight.

direct service Movement of a shipment straight from its origin to its destination without transshipment.

discounts Reductions made from the gross amount or value of something.

draft A type of bank transaction that insures payment for goods. It is a written order for a sum of money to be paid by the buyer to the seller upon presentation of the document to the buyer's bank.

drivers In the context of forming a partnership, compelling reasons to partner.

driving time regulations U.S. Department of Transportation rules that limit the maximum time a driver may drive in interstate commerce; the rules prescribe both daily and weekly maximums.

dry-bulk carriers Ships with several holds in their hulls in which loose cargo such as grains, coal, ore, and other commodities are loaded.

duty A tax on imports.

E

economic deregulation The removal of governmentally enforced price and entry controls in the transportation industry. The "free market" will provide the necessary competition to ensure competitive prices and services.

economies of density Savings realized wherein unit costs are lower in relation to population density. The higher the population density, the lower the likely costs of infrastructure required to provide a service.

economies of scale As production of a good increases, the cost of producing each additional unit falls.

emergency shipments Expedited, as-soon-as possible delivery of items.

employee assistance programs (EAPs) Employer-sponsored programs provided to their employees suffering from substance-abuse problems.

end-of-the-line (EOL) terminal Terminal that serves a local area, providing direct contact with both shippers and receivers; The basic transportation service provided at this terminal is the pickup and/or delivery of freight.

end-to-end mergers Type of railroad company merger that aims to result in more effective intermodal and intramodal competition, usually by combining firms from different but complementary territories.

equipment substitution Advantageous replacement of a carrier's mode of transportation in order to maximize return; for example, changing a flight to a smaller plane in response to a shortfall in reservations.

Erie Canal Man-made waterway extending 363 miles from Albany to Buffalo, New York linking the Atlantic seacoast to the Great Lakes; in the years after its completion in 1825, the cost of transporting goods between the Midwest and New York City fell precipitously, in some cases by 95 percent.

event management An aspect of shipment visibility that incorporates when things happen into its reporting system.

Ex Works (EXW) The price that the seller quotes applies only at the point of origin. The buyer takes possession of the shipment at the point of origin and bears all costs and risks associated with transporting the goods to the final destination.

exception rates A deviation from the class rate; changes (exceptions) made to the classification.

excess capacity Underused or unused facilities and/or infrastructure; for example, an empty seat on an air carrier's flight.

exempt carriers A for-hire carrier that is exempt from economic regulations.

existence charge A shipping charge related to the existence of some tangible item that is made against the person or unit regardless of the extent of use made of the services.

export license A document indicating that a government has granted a licensee the right to export specified goods to specified countries.

exporter One who sells to merchants or industrial consumers in foreign countries.

extended enterprise A way of looking at a process that extends beyond the bounds of a single firm to span the related activities of several participating or affected firms; a supply chain is an example of an extended enterprise that crosses the boundaries of the individual firms.

F

facilitators In the context of forming a partnership, supportive corporate environmental factors that enhance partnership growth and development.

fair wage A wage fairly and reasonably commensurate with the value of a particular service or class of service rendered.

FAK rates They are rates expressed in cents per hundredweight or total cost per shipment

Federal Aviation Administration The federal agency within the Department of Transportation that is responsible for regulating air safety, promoting development of air commerce, and controlling navigable air space.

Federal Energy Regulatory Commission The federal agency that oversees rates and practices of pipeline operators and is part of the Department of Energy.

Federal Highway Trust Fund A fund that receives federally collected fuel taxes used for highway construction and upkeep.

Federal Maritime Commission The federal agency that regulates international rates, practices, agreements, and services of common carrier water carriers.

Federal Motor Carrier Safety Administration Federal agency, created in 2000, whose primary mission is to reduce crashes, injuries, fatalities, and property loss involving large trucks and buses by regulating the workers involved.

Federal Railroad Administration The federal agency that oversees railroad safety by establishing and enforcing rules and regulations. This agency is part of the Department of Transportation.

Federal Trade Commission The federal agency that administers the Sherman Anti-Trust Act and the Clayton Act. This agency does not have direct control over transportation.

flag of convenience A ship registered in a foreign country for purposes of reducing operating costs or avoiding government regulations or taxes.

Foreign Trade Zone (FTZ) An area or zone set aside at or near a port or airport, under the control of the U.S. Customs Service, for the holding of goods duty-free, pending customs clearance.

for-hire A carrier that provides transportation service to the public on a fee basis.

free cash flow In corporate finance, describes the fiscal condition of companies with negative working capital who must collect from their customers before they can pay their vendors or suppliers.

free trade agreements Treaties between nations that agree to eliminate tariffs, quotas, and preferences on many goods and services traded between them.

freight Goods to be shipped; cargo.

freight bill auditing A thorough examination of carrier's invoice for a freight shipment's transportation charges.

freight contamination To make goods unfit for use by the introduction of unwholesome or undesirable elements.

freight damage Injury or destruction of cargo.

freight forwarders A carrier that collects small shipments from shippers, consolidates the small shipments, and uses a basic mode to transport these consolidated shipments to a consignee destination.

freight management A strategic system to optimize the efficiency of freight and commercial transport.

freight rating Performing the calculations appropriate to calculate freight costs based on contract and tariff terms.

frequency and timing How often and at what time a group of scheduled events occurs.

fuel costs Amounts paid for materials used to power the engines driving a carrier's machines.

fuel-efficient Operable using comparatively less fuel.

G

gas carriers Ships that transport compressed gases such as liquefied natural gas and liquefied petroleum gas in specialized tanks.

general average The legal principle of maritime law according to which all parties in a sea venture proportionally share any losses resulting from a voluntary sacrifice of part of the ship or cargo to save the whole in an emergency.

Global Positioning System (GPS) Signals that enable companies to accurately pinpoint the exact location of equipment and materials.

granger laws A series of laws passed in the western United States after the Civil War to regulate grain elevator and railroad freight rates and rebates and to address long- and short-haul discrimination and other railroad abuses against farmers.

green supply chains Supply chain management with an emphasis on energy efficiency and environmental friendliness.

H

hazardous materials Materials that the Department of Transportation has determined to be a risk to health, safety, and property; includes items such as explosives, flammable liquids, poisons, corrosive liquids, and radioactive material.

headhaul The first half of a round-trip move from origin to destination. The opposite is "backhaul," which is the return of the equipment to its origin point.

hedging strategy Method of reducing risk by diversifying the risks presented by a single option.

high-density routes Transportation route with the greatest number of users or carrying the highest amount of cargo.

highway development Planning and construction of high-speed roadways.

home-flag airline An airline owned or sponsored by the government of the country in which the carrier is based. Typically, only home-flag airlines are allowed to operate between airports within that country. This prevents foreign carriers from serving domestic locations.

Hours of Service (HOS) A piece of legislation under Compliance, Safety, and Accountability Act with a new requirement of stricter rules effective from 2013 on a driver's restart options with the intent to improve safety.

hubs A central location to which traffic from many cities is directed and from which traffic is fed to other areas.

I

ICC Termination Act of 1995 Federal statute that eliminated the Interstate Commerce Commission and transferred economic rail regulation to the Surface Transportation Board.

importer One who brings goods or merchandise from other countries into this one.

incentive rates A rate that induces the shipper to ship heavier volumes per shipment.

Incoterms International terms of sale developed by the International Chamber of Commerce to define sellers' and buyers' responsibilities.

indirect forms of promotion Subsidies and incentives intended to preserve the domestic shipbuilding industry.

indirect service Movement of a shipment from its origin to its destination, making interim stops and/or transfer of freight between equipment.

inelastic In the context of economic supply and demand, elasticity refers to the sensitivity of customers to changes in price; if customers are not sensitive to price, then demand is considered inelastic.

information flow The flow or movement of information or data between trading partners or companies that facilitates commerce or business.

inland ports A specialized facility that executes some functions traditionally carried out at a seaport, made possible by the use of container shipping.

insurance Coverage by contract whereby one party promises to guarantee another against loss by a specified contingency or peril.

integrated carriers Air carrier companies that have the capability to provide door-to-door service because they own ground delivery equipment as well as aircraft.

integrated logistics management The management of all activities involved in physically acquiring, moving and storing raw materials,
in-process inventory, and finished goods inventory from the point of origin to the point of consumption.

integrated service providers For-hire firms that perform a variety of logistics service activities such as warehousing, transportation, and other functional activities as a package service.

intermediaries Those being or occurring at the middle place or stage, such as brokers between ocean shippers and rail carriers.

intermodal marketing companies Intermediary that sells intermodal services to shippers.

International Air Transport Association (IATA) An international industry trade group of airlines that represents the airline industry.

International Chamber of Commerce (ICC) An international organization established to reduce some of the confusion and complexity involving international shipments.

Interstate Commerce Commission (ICC) A former independent federal agency that supervised and set rates for carriers that transported goods and people between states.

intrastate commerce The transportation of persons or property between points within a state. A shipment between two points within a state may be interstate if the shipment had a prior or subsequent move outside of the state and the shipper intended an interstate shipment at the time of shipment.

J

just-in-time delivery Component of an inventory strategy that strives to improve a business's return on investment by reducing in-process inventory and associated carrying costs.

K

Known Shipper Program A security system put in place following the attacks of 9/11 that essentially eliminates the anonymous shipment of all documents, parcels, counter-to-counter packages, and freight on both passenger and cargo-only flights originating within the United States.

L

landed cost The cost of the product at the source combined with the cost of transportation to the destination.

Lardner's Law A finding by transportation economist Dionysius Lardner that when transportation cost is reduced, the area where the producer can compete is increased in a directly proportional basis.

Law of Squares An increase in the distance over which a given amount will cover the transport of goods will increase the market area of the product in an even greater ratio; also known as Lardner's Law.

less-than-truckload A less-than-truckload shipment, one weighing less than the minimum weight a company needs to use the lower truckload rate.

letter of credit (LC) A document issued by the buyer's bank that guarantees payment to the seller if certain terms and conditions are met.

liability Any legal responsibility, duty, or obligation.

limited competition A condition in which the competition is limited among the sellers.

line-haul A part of the trip where the shipments are loaded into 28-foot, 48-foot, or
53-foot trailers depending on the state's
trailer configuration permitted over the route of travel.

liner service International water carriers that ply fixed routes on published schedules.

longshoremen Persons employed loading or unloading cargo from ships.

M

major carriers For-hire air carriers with annual revenues of more than $1 billion.

make or buy decision A situation in which organizations have the option of providing items or services themselves internally or buying them from another source.

manifest A list of all cargoes that pertain to a specific shipment, grouping of shipments, or piece of equipment. Ocean carriers will prepare a manifest for each container.

maquiladora The name for a manufacturing facility established inside Mexico within close distance of the U.S. border. Materials are shipped from the United States, processed in the maquiladora plant, and returned to the United States. No customs duties or fees are accessed.

marginal cost The cost to produce one additional unit of output; the change in total variable cost resulting from a one-unit change in output.

Maritime Administration (MARAD) A U.S. Department of Transportation agency that aids and advances the use of water transportation.

market share pricing In an industry whose revenues are stagnant or declining, a firm will try to take market share from competitors through the use of lower prices.

marketing mix This consists of the four basic elements of marketing: product, price, place, and promotion. This is also known as the "four P's" of marketing.

mileage rate A rate or price based on the total mileage between the origin and destination including stop-offs, if any.

minimum level of safety A base requirement for all aspects of safe operation by a transportation firm, as prescribed by a government agency.

modal split The relative use that companies make of transportation modes; the statistics include ton-miles, passenger-miles, and revenue.

monopolistic The ability of very few suppliers to set a price well above cost by restricting supply or by limiting competition.

monopolistic competition A condition in which there are many small sellers but there is some differentiation of products.

monopoly A market segment where there is only one supplier, such as public utilities.

Motor Carrier Act of 1980 An act by the federal agency which defines a zone of rate freedom for motor or railroad carrier policies in which a rate change of 10 percent either up or down in one year is presumed to be reasonable.

multimodal bill of lading A transportation document that tasks the principal carrier or freight forwarder for liability across the entire journey.

N

national carriers A for-hire certificated air carrier that has annual operating revenues of $75 million to $1 billion; the carrier usually operates between major population centers and areas of lesser population.

national defense A primary function of a sovereign state is its ability to defend its territory, national waters, and air space against internal and external threats.

"National Transportation Safety Board" This agency is responsible for investigating transportation-related accidents, regardless of whether or not the incident involved the private sector or a public carrier. They are responsible for recommending preventative measures to avoid future accidents.

"National Highway Traffic Safety Administration (NHTSA)" This branch of the U.S. Department of Transportation is responsible for motor vehicle safety. In this role, NHTSA oversees design features, sets performance-related safety standards, and oversees governmental fuel economy standards.

nationalization Public ownership, financing, and operation of a business entity.

no-frills service Any service or product for which the non-essential features have been removed to keep the price low.

non-asset based providers 3PLs that fulfill customer requirements via the resources of other companies.

nonintegrated carriers Air carrier companies that only provide service from airport to airport.

O

ocean bill of lading A contract for transportation between a shipper and an ocean carrier, which also evidences receipt of the cargo by the carrier.

Ocean Shipping Reform Act Federal law passed in 1998 that effected significant deregulation of the ocean carrier industry.

oligopoly A shared monopoly where there are few suppliers and, in the case of transportation, entry barriers and cost are significant. Examples would be railroads and airlines.

open account A credit account extended by a business to a customer or another business.

operating ratio A measure of operating efficiency defined as operating expenses/operating revenues x 100.

outsourcing Purchasing a logistics service from an outside firm, as opposed to performing it in-house.

P

packing list A detailed inventory of the contents of a shipment.

passenger airplanes Aircraft designed to carry people.

passenger revenues Fares paid by passengers for traveling on transportation routes.

passenger transportation The means and equipment necessary for the movement of persons, as opposed to freight.

passenger-mile A measure of output for passenger transportation that reflects the number of passengers transported and the distance traveled; a multiplication of passengers hauled and distance traveled.

peddle run A truck operation where many pickups or deliveries are made while the vehicle travels over a preset route.

penetration price A pricing strategy that sets a price designed to allow the supplier to enter a market where there is already established competition by slightly underpricing the existing firms.

per se violation A violation of the law that is, on its own, deemed to be harmful, regardless of its effect on the market or competitors.

physical distribution management The management and control of the activities involved in the storage, handling, and movement of goods within an organization and in their shipment to customers.

pickup and delivery (PUD) The act of collecting freight from shippers or delivering freight to consignees.

Pipeline and Hazardous Material Safety Administration Federal agency, created in 2004, whose primary focus is pipeline safety and hazardous materials transportation safety operations.

place utility The usefulness or value of a good or service as a function of the location at which it is made available; For example, snow shovels have greater place utility in Boston than in El Paso.

place value The usefulness or value of a good or service as a function of the location at which it is made available; For example, snow shovels have greater place utility in Boston than in El Paso.

police powers The United States constitutionally granted right for the states to establish regulations to protect their citizens' health and welfare; truck weight and speed, length, and height laws are examples.

port authority A state or local government that owns, operates, or otherwise provides wharf, dock, and other terminal investments at ports.

postponement strategy Method of reducing risk by delaying a commitment of resources.

private air carrier Air carrier that only transports company personnel or freight for the company that owns or leases the planes in support of the company's primary business.

private carrier A carrier that provides transportation service to the firm that owns or leases the vehicles and does not charge a fee. Private motor carriers may haul at a fee for wholly owned subsidiaries.

private service Charter service where the ships are owned or leased on a long-term basis by the company moving the goods.

product density The mass of a product that directly impacts the use of the carrier's vehicle and the cost per hundredweight.

profit maximization The process by which a firm determines the price and output level that returns the greatest profit.

pro-forma invoice A document issued by the seller to acquaint the importer/buyer and the importing country's government authorities with the details of the shipment.

pure competition A condition in which there is a large number of sellers, the product or service is standardized and interchangeable, and no one seller can control the price or output. An example would be the LTL sector.

Q

qualitative risk analysis A baseline evaluation of risks.

quantity utility The usefulness or value of a good or service as a function of timely delivery and undamaged condition.

R

Radio Frequency Identification (RFID) Signal that can tag a container, trailer, or car to track the progress of the shipment.

Railroad Revitalization and Regulatory Reform Act of 1976 (4R Act) Federal statute that provided federal funding for the startup of Conrail.

rate base point The major shipping point in a local area; carriers consider all points in the local area to be the rate basis point.

rate basis number This number is an expression of the relative distance between an origin and destination. The number may be given in miles or another factor and will form one of the required inputs to develop a rate between the two points.

Reed-Bulwinkle Act of 1948 Federal law permitting motor carriers to fix rates in concert with each other, thus exempting such carriers from antitrust laws.

regional carriers A for-hire air carrier, usually certificated, that has annual operating revenues of less than $75 million;

the carrier usually operates within a particular region of the country.

Regional Rail Reorganization Act of 1973 (3R Act) A law passed by Congress in response to the bankruptcies of the Penn Central and other railroads. Conrail, which has since been purchased by the Norfolk Southern Railroad and CSX, was created from this law to operate the lines of six northeastern U.S. railroads.

relative use A fee placed on the users of a service or facility to cover the cost of providing that service or facility.

relay terminals A motor carrier terminal that facilitates the substitution of one driver for another who has driven the maximum hours permitted.

reliability A carrier selection criterion that considers the carrier transit time variation; the consistency of the transit time the carrier provides.

reliable Suitable or fit to be relied upon; dependable.

resiliency The ability to recover from or adjust easily to misfortune or change.

return on investment (ROI) The amount of money realized or generated on an investment that flows back to the lenders. This is often used to gauge the worthiness of an investment by measuring the potential profits and the source of the capital.

reverse flow logistics Logistical systems for the return of products that were unacceptable to the buyer for some reason (damage, maintenance, obsolescence, etc.); employed by an increasing number of organizations.

rights-of-way The privilege of someone to pass over land belonging to someone else; the right of one vehicle or vessel to take precedence over another; the passage consisting of a path or strip of land over which someone has the legal right to pass.

risk identification The effort to discover, define, describe, document, and communicate hazards before they become realized.

risk management Systematic approach to identifying risk, its causes and effects, and its ownership with a goal of reducing or eliminating hazards.

risk mitigation Reduction of the chance of a hazard occurring.

risk retention Self-insurance; a company may determine that it is more economical to forego cargo insurance for the anticipated risks and bear the loss itself.

risk transfer Purchasing insurance to cover anticipated risks.

Robinson-Patman Act of 1936 Federal law that prohibits sales that discriminate in price on the sale of goods to equally situated distributors when the effect of such sales is to reduce competition.

roller deck The main deck of an air freighter equipped with rollers on the floor, which allows palletized or containerized cargo to be pushed into position.

roll-on/roll-off A type of vessel that has ramps upon which vehicles can be driven directly into the hold of the ship. This type of vessel is often used to transport buses, trucks, construction machinery on wheels, and other types of wheeled shipments.

routing Directing to a specific direction or destination.

routing and scheduling Directing to a specific direction or destination by a predetermined time.

Rule of reason An alleged violation of an anti-trust law where economic harm to competitors must be proved.

S

seating capacity The maximum number of passengers that can be accommodated.

security The actions of a carrier to protect the goods entrusted to their care from loss or damage.

"Sherman Antitrust Act" A body of law that restricts businesses' ability to dominate a market by engaging in certain practices. This includes price fixing and other free-market–constricting activities.

shipbrokers A firm that serves as a go-between for the tramp ship owner and the chartering consignor or consignee.

Shipper's Export Declaration A document filed by the shipper/exporter or its agent with the government of the country in which the shipper/ exporter resides. This form supplies the government with information about the shipment for statistical and control purposes.

shipper's letter of instructions Document that spells out the requirements for handling in transit goods; important when the cargo is susceptible to damage or requires special attention, such as live animals and plants.

Shipping Act of 1984 A body of law that governs the pricing and services of ocean carriers operating between the United States and foreign countries.

side-by-side A merger of railroads whose lines operate in proximity of each other, rather than end to end.

sight draft A customer's order to a financial institution holding the customer's funds to pay all or part of them to another institution in which the customer has another account.

skimming price A price set by a provider who seeks to attract a market that is more interested in quality, uniqueness, or status and is relatively unconcerned with price.

slip seat operation A motor carrier relay terminal operation in which a carrier substitutes one driver for another who has accumulated the maximum driving time hours.

social responsibility pricing Lowering prices in pursuit of advancing ethical or social values apart from maximizing profitability.

Staggers Act of 1980 Federal statute that provided major deregulation of the railroad industry.

Staggers Rail Act of 1980 Federal statute that provided major deregulation of the railroad industry.

standards Accepted or approved examples of something against which others are judged or measured.

state regulation Laws passed on the state and federal level that restrict a company's freedom of action.

statutory law This is based on the Roman legal system and refers to a body of law passed by legislative bodies.

stem time The time consumed by a truck to reach its first delivery after leaving the terminal and the time consumed by the truck to return to the terminal after making its last pickup.

stevedore services Services provided by persons employed loading or unloading cargo from ships.

stevedores Persons employed loading or unloading cargo from ships.

stowability and handling The ease or difficulty experienced in loading, handling, and unloading freight. This factor influences the carrier's cost of providing a service and will be reflected in the price charged for the shipment. This is also two of the four factors considered when classifying freight.

subsidies Grants by a government to a private person or company to assist an enterprise or industry deemed advantageous to the public.

supertankers The largest of the ships designed for the bulk transport of oil.

supply chain interruptions Problems with a transportation channel that fall outside the control of the company.

supply chain management The integration of the flows of products, information, and financials through the entire supply pipeline from the supplier's supplier to the customer's customer.

Surface Transportation Board The agency created under the Interstate Commerce Commission Termination (ICC) to replace the ICC and exercise economic jurisdiction of the modes of transportation.

survival-based pricing The use of low prices to increase cash flow and volume and to encourage the higher utilization of equipment.

sustainability The skill or potential of a process or a thing to retain itself without interference.

T

tariffs A publication that contains a carrier's rates, accessorial charges, and rules.

terminals Either end of a carrier line having facilities for the handling of freight and passengers.

terms of payment Contractual terms governing what will be given in exchange for the object of the transaction and the method of its delivery.

terms of trade In an international transaction, terms specified in the contract that determine which shipping responsibilities are handled by the exporter (the international supplier) and which are managed by the importer (the company making the purchase).

third party logistics An external supplier that performs all or part of a company's logistics functions.

third-degree price discrimination A situation where a seller sets two or more different prices for separate groups of buyers of essentially the same commodity.

through bill of lading A single bill of lading covering receipt of the cargo at the point of origin for delivery to the ultimate consignee, using two or more modes of transportation both domestically and internationally.

time charter A rental or long-term lease that includes both the vessel and crew and is for a specific length of time.

time draft A customer's order to a financial institution holding the customer's funds that is payable at a specified point in the future or under certain circumstances.

time utility The usefulness or value of a good or service as a function of its timeliness in meeting seasonal demand; the demand for a particular commodity may exist only during certain periods of time.

time value of funds This relates to the value of money over the lifetime of a project. As inflation reduces the value or purchasing capability of a dollar over the life of a project, this must be taken into consideration when establishing an interest or discount rate for the borrowed funds.

TL (truckload) A shipment weighing the minimum weight or more. Carriers give a rate reduction for shipping a TL-size shipment.

ton-mile A unit of measurement utilizing the distance that freight is hauled, measured in miles, and the weight of the cargo being hauled, measured in tons, expressed as a product (that is, multiplied by each other); thus moving one ton for one mile generates one ton-mile.

total landed cost Total cost of a product once it has arrived at the buyer's door, including the original cost of the item, all brokerage and logistics fees, complete shipping costs, customs duties, tariffs, taxes, insurance, currency conversion, crating costs, and handling fees.

tracing Determining a shipment's location during the course of a move.

tracking Observing, plotting, and reporting the location of cargo or a cargo item throughout the transportation channel.

traileron-flatcar (TOFC) A method where a highway trailer complete with wheels and chassis is loaded on a flatcar.

transfer of ownership Act of conveying possession along with its benefits and responsibilities.

transit time The total time that elapses between a shipment's pickup and its delivery.

transload freight Freight that must be handled individually and transferred between transportation equipment multiple times.

transportation management systems (TMS) Logistics tool used to improve management of a firm's transportation processes, both inbound and outbound. A TMS can help optimize the movements of freight into multiple facilities, assist in tracking the freight through the supply chain, and then manage the freight payment process to the user's carrier base.

twenty-foot equivalent units (TEUs Twenty-foot equivalent unit, a standardize intermodal container.

U

U.S. Coast Guard A branch of the U.S. military (but operating under the Department of Homeland Security during peacetime) whose mission is maritime law enforcement.

U.S. Department of Transportation A federal Cabinet department of the U.S. government, established in 1966, that is concerned with transportation.

U.S. Post Office Federal agency responsible for the posting, receipt, sorting, handling, transmission, or delivery of mail.

unit charge A shipping charge assessed for use of a facility or resource; variable according to use, but does not distinguish between passengers or freight within each unit.

unit load devices Specialized containers used in air freighters that fit properly within the rounded fuselage of an aircraft.

unit train An entire, uninterrupted locomotive, car, and caboose movement between an origin and destination.

unit volume pricing This is a technique whereby the carrier sets its prices to utilize its capacity to the fullest. Multiple pickup discounts in the LTL area and multiple car rates in the railroad sector would be two examples.

user charges Costs or fees that the user of a service or facility must pay to the party furnishing this service or facility. An example would be the landing fee an airline pays to an airport when one of its aircraft lands or takes off.

V

value of service The rates charged for a transportation service or a particular level of service influence the demand for the product and thus the demand to transport the product; this impact on demand can be assessed as the value of service provided to the user of the product.

Value-of-service pricing Pricing according to the value of the product the company is transporting; third-degree price discrimination; demand-oriented pricing; charging what the traffic will bear.

vertically integrated It is a process in which the supply chain of the firm is self-owned.

visibility In the context of cargo shipping, the capability to track the whereabouts of items throughout their journey through the channel.

voyage charter A rental or term lease that includes both the vessel and crew and is for a specific trip.

W

working conditions The physical environment in which an employee works, including the actual space, the quality of ventilation, heat, and light, and the degree of safety.

Z

zone pricing The constant pricing of a product at all geographic locations within a zone.

Name Index

Subject Index

B

I

Q

R

S

Y

Z